The Creative World of South Vietnam

1954 – 1975 To The Present

Volume I

The Creative World of South Vietnam
1954-1975 To The Present
First Edition - Volume 1

Author Ngô Thế Vinh
Translator Eric Henry

Copy Editor Trần Thị Nguyệt Mai
Jacket Painting by Tạ Tỵ
Cover Design by Uyên Nguyên

Publishing Group:
Việt Ecology Press & Văn Học Press

ISBN: 9781088177860

NGÔ THẾ VINH
Translator ERIC HENRY

THE CREATIVE WORLD OF SOUTH VIETNAM 1954-1975 TO THE PRESENT

VOLUME 1

Việt Ecology Press
Văn Học Press
2025

AUTHOR & WORKS

Ngô Thế Vinh, born in 1941, graduated from Saigon University's Faculty of Medicine in 1968, was a former editor-in-chief of Tình Thương Magazine [1963-1967], a former ARVN Airborne Ranger who served as a Green Beret M.D. during the Vietnam War. A widely renowned writer, winner of the 1971 National Prize for Literature for his novel *The Green Belt.* Ironically he was also penalized for his writing, when he was summoned to the court of law because of the title story of this collection: *The Battle of Saigon.* This short story records the spiritual journey of a soldier who accepts sacrifice and hardship in the struggle for freedom of South Vietnam, a soldier who at the same time longs for a better society in the future.

After 1975, he was imprisoned in different communist re-education camps for three years. In 1983, he arrived in the US, succeeded in becoming an intern, then resident physician in SUNY Downstate New York. Ngô Thế Vinh currently resides in Southern California, is an internist and staff physician at a Long Beach Medical Center.

In Vietnamese:

- *Mây Bão* [Sông Mã, Sài Gòn 1963, Văn Nghệ, California 1993]
- *Bóng Đêm* [Khai Trí, Sài Gòn 1964]

- *Gió Mùa* [Sông Mã, Sài Gòn 1965]
- *Vòng Đai Xanh* [Thái Độ; Sài Gòn 1970; Văn Nghệ, California 1987; Văn Học Press, California 2018]
- *Mặt Trận Ở Sài Gòn* [Văn Nghệ, California 1996]
- *Cửu Long Cạn Dòng Biển Đông Dậy Sóng* [Văn Nghệ, California 2000, tái bản 2001; Nxb Giấy Vụn Việt Nam 2014]
- *Mekong – Dòng Sông Nghẽn Mạch* [Văn Nghệ, California 3/2007, Văn Nghệ Mới 12/2007, Nxb Giấy Vụn, Việt Nam 2012]
- *Audiobook Mekong – Dòng Sông Nghẽn Mạch* [Văn Nghệ Mới, California 2007; Việt Ecology Press & Nhân Ảnh 2017]
- *Chân Dung Văn Học Nghệ Thuật và Văn Hóa 1 & 2* [Việt Ecology Press 2017 & 2022]
- *Y Sĩ Tiền Tuyến Nghiêm Sỹ Tuấn, Người Đi Tìm Mùa Xuân* [Tập San Y Sĩ Việt Nam Canada, Việt Ecology Press 2019]

In English:

- *The Green Belt* [Ivy House 2004]
- *The Battle of Saigon* [Xlibris 2005]
- *Mekong – The Occluding River* [Universe 2010]
- *The Nine Dragons Drained Dry, The East Sea in Turmoil* [Việt Ecology Press & Nxb Giấy Vụn, Vietnam 2016]
- *The Creative World of South Vietnam 1954 – 1975 To the Present, Vol. 1 & 2* [Việt Ecology Press & Văn Học Press 2025]

In Vietnamese - English Bilingual Form:

- *Mặt Trận Ở Sài Gòn / The Battle of Saigon* [Văn Học Press & Việt Ecology Press 2020]
- *Vòng Đai Xanh / The Green Belt* [Văn Học Press & Việt Ecology Press 2020]
- *Mekong Dòng Sông Nghẽn Mạch / Mekong The Occluding River* [Văn Học Press & Việt Ecology Press 2021]

CONTENTS

My written words – ordained by fate
to be reduced by fire to ash

Văn chương vô mệnh lụy phần dư

Nguyễn Du

The fires of violent Qín are there – but how
can verse and prose be lost in flame?

Thi thư dù lửa bạo Tần có thiêu?

Vũ Hoàng Chương

THE CREATIVE WORLD OF SOUTH VIETNAM 1954-1975 TO THE PRESENT

Translator's Introduction

This book is a translation of a collection of personal, literary, and journalistic vignettes of Vietnamese individuals who have made notable contributions to literature, art, and science. It is a rich source of information on the social, cultural, and political history of South Vietnam, as well as the individual careers of its human subjects.

The people described for the most part came into prominence in the period 1954 – 1975. After the fall of the South to North Vietnamese forces in 1975, most of them were imprisoned for some number of years in communist reeducation camps after 1975. Later, in the 1980s, some of them made their way to the U.S., and most continued to be creatively active.

Võ Phiến, essayist, novelist, and literary historian, characterized the literature that arose under the southern Vietnamese republic as follows:

> *"In the Vietnam of 1954 to 1975, a totally different type of literature arose. Gay and sharp laughter spread freely over books and journals, laughter that attacked mistaken deeds*

and perverse policies, and made fun of elements guilty of unworthy behavior... The objects of attack were provincial or national leaders and power brokers. The sound of laughter ran freely and noisily across all books and journals. At the same time, every view of human life, every faith, both fine and deluded, both noble and crazed, existed as well; one could seek to understand, expound, and promulgate these beliefs, just as one pleased. At no time before or after 1954 – 1975 in the South can one find any literary tradition in our country that developed in such a free and open manner."

The regime that took over in 1975 sought to eradicate this legacy by criminalizing it and by physically destroying all remnants of it that could be collected. As a result, the most complete collections of the literature of Vietnam from this period are to be found, not in Vietnam, but in certain academic libraries in the U.S., such as those of Cornell University, Yale University and the University of Hawaii.

The author of this book, Dr. Ngô Thế Vinh, is himself one of the leading figures in the literary life that emerged in South Vietnam during the time of the Southern Republic, and was personally acquainted with all the figures he discusses. Dr. Vinh is a full-time internist and staff physician at Long Beach Medical Center in California, but he is also a tireless author, whose work includes novels, books of cultural commentary (such as this one), and investigative reporting. In particular, he has personally explored the entire length of the 4,800 km long Mekong River and has written two books that deal with the survival of the Mekong as a great river of the world, and with the livelihood of more than 70 million people living along the river and in the Mekong Delta. These and other books of his have been awarded many prizes and have attracted many appreciative reviews. He remains a committed and unrelenting environmentalist. In addition, I have found Mr. Vinh to be a supremely gifted journalist with a quasi-magical ability to track down obscure documents and facts.

The author had close friendships with all the individuals he discusses in this book, so his portraits often include excerpts from their correspondence. As a doctor, he was also naturally interested in their medical situations, so this too forms part of many of these portraits. The individuals he portrays in this volume are the following:

• Mặc Đỗ (1917 – 2015)

A journalist, novelist, short story writer, and translator, he was born in Hanoi to a family steeped in Confucian ways, but also amenable to western cultural influences. He emigrated to the South in 1954 and helped establish a literary group called Quan Điểm ("Viewpoint") and the newspaper Tự Do ("Freedom"). In addition to his own novels and short stories, he translated works by Hemingway, Fitzgerald, Mauriac, Tolstoy, Pasternak, and others.

• Như Phong (1923 – 2001)

Characterized by the author as "a journalist's journalist," Như Phong was a novelist, an expert on communist affairs in North Vietnam, and a strategist who often worked behind the scenes as a political advisor to people in public life. In the U.S., he made many young friends to whom he expounded grand schemes concerning the role that journalism would play in the future of Vietnam.

• Võ Phiến (1925 – 2015),

An essayist, story writer, literary historian, and editor, he was one of the principal authors associated with Cyclopedia (Bách Khoa) magazine in Saigon. After 1975 his home in Los Angeles became a center of expatriate literary culture. He wrote several deeply researched books about the literary history of South Vietnam. He is also the subject of a study by John Schafer: *The Sadness of Exile.*

• Linh Bảo (1926 – 2024)

One of the earlier woman writers of Vietnam, Linh Bảo spent much of her life in other countries, including a number of years in Guangzhou and Hong Kong. A novelist, gifted story writer, freelance journalist, feminist activist, her books use ridicule to expose the negative aspects of life. Her style, the author says, was merciless, contrary, demonic, and devil-may-care, but at the same time full of pain.

• Mai Thảo (1927 – 1998)

He was a novelist, short story writer, poet, and the founder-editor of the avant-garde magazine *Creation* (*Sáng Tạo*). After emigration to the U.S, he lived a monastically simple existence in a single-room apartment, which was also his office–the place where he prepared each issue of the expatriate journal *Literature* (*Văn*). He is one of the few figures treated in this book who was not imprisoned in a reeducation camp. He instead spent two desperate years living in hiding in Saigon before escaping as a boat person to Malaysia and then to the U.S.

• Dương Nghiễm Mậu (1936 – 2016)

A novelist, short story writer, essayist, he was born in Hanoi and emigrated with his family to the south in 1954. His first novel, *Mother's Legacy*, won the National Prize for Literature in 1966. He entered the army in that year and worked as a war correspondent. After imprisonment in a reeducation camp from 1975 to 1977, he did lacquer work for a living. He is one of the few authors discussed in this book who chose to remain in Vietnam rather than emigrate.

• Nhật Tiến (1936 – 2020)

A prolific and varied novelist, short story writer, playwright, Nhật Tiến identified strongly as a Rover Scout with the Vietnamese scouting movement, and remained loyal to its traditions throughout his life. With more than twenty books to his name, his creations are particularly associated with childhood, and often deal with the suffering of children.

• Nguyễn Đình Toàn (1936 – 2023)

He was a poet, novelist, short story writer, songwriter, and host of an influential radio program called "Themes in Music – Nhạc Chủ Đề." Most of his novels appeared in parts in various journals before appearing as books, and devote more attention to atmosphere than to plot. He wrote the lyrics, obscure but suggestive, of "First Love Song" by the musician Vũ Thành An: "Joy chases the drifting, windblown clouds, / Gloom rains heavily into life."

• Thanh Tâm Tuyền (1936 – 2006)

He was born in the city of Vinh in Nghệ An, went first to Hanoi, but then emigrated to Saigon in 1954. He was one of the principal contributors to the magazine *Creation* (*Sáng Tạo*). He gained early notoriety with his obscure and starkly original *poésie libre*, but later in life took up more traditional forms. From 1975 to 1982 he was imprisoned in very harshly-run reeducation camps in North Vietnam. He was a novelist, fiction writer, and playwright, as well as a poet.

• Nguyễn-Xuân Hoàng (1937 – 2014)

He was a novelist, short story writer, essayist, and editor. He was active in Saigon before 1975, and emigrated to the U.S. after years in reeducation camps and served as the editor of a number of Expatriate Vietnamese literary periodicals.

• Hoàng Ngọc Biên (1938 – 2019)

An artist, painter, poet, novelist, Proust scholar, translator, and musician, he is one of the most versatile and enterprising people discussed in this volume His works in many media are wide-ranging and highly experimental.

• Đinh Cường (1939 – 2016)

An artist, painter, poet, and art instructor. By 2005 he had had more than twenty-four solo exhibitions and twenty-one exhibitions with other artists. He is also the author of three books, one consisting of essays on art, and two consisting of poems.

• Nghiêu Đề (1939 – 1998)

An artist, painter, poet, originally from Quảng Ngãi Province. An old associate of the author's, he was much in demand as a cover designer for literary works. Of a capricious and eccentric disposition, he never troubled to make a careful record of his activities. He moved with his family to the U.S. and died in 1998 before attaining his sixtieth birthday.

• Nguyên Khai (1940 –)

An artist most of whose work consists of oil paintings. His nature was reserved and contemplative. He once said in an interview, "Art does not turn its back on reality, but also does not illustrate reality. Art gives us another means of viewing things; a means of viewing things that are not realistic, so that the true nature of goodness and beauty can be expressed."

• Cao Xuân Huy (1947 – 2010)

A combat marine and writer, best known for his war memoir: *My Gun Broke in March*, a uniquely passionate, vivid, and expressive book. The author has much to say concerning this figure's spirited battle against eye melanoma during his last years.

• Phùng Nguyễn (1950 – 2015)

An IT expert who was also a short story writer, essayist, and blogger. The author devotes much attention to a phase of his life that he never talked about but which nevertheless exerted a strong influence on his later activities: his prolonged recovery from a severe leg wound that he suffered in the course of a military operation. In addition to authoring a Blog entitled "Forest and Trees," he published two collections of short stories: *Tower of Memory* (1988) and *Oakland Night and Other Stories* (2001)

• Phạm Duy (1921 – 2013)

A songwriter, lyricist, musicologist, and memoirist, he was the most prolific and distinguished of all the Vietnamese songwriters of the last century, of whom there have been a great many. The portrait in this volume examines his activities in several phases of his career and examines the evolving nature of his relations with his numerous friends and associates.

• Eric Henry (1943 –)

Henry is an American scholar in Chinese and Vietnamese culture, and is the translator of the present volume. The author devotes much attention to Henry's early experiences in Vietnam and to his recent efforts to overcome the refusal of Phạm Duy's family to grant permission for the publication of his translation of Phạm Duy's four volumes of memoirs.

• Phạm Biểu Tâm (1913 – 1999)

He was a doctor, surgeon, eminent medical professor, and university rector. The author's portrait deals with this figure's enormous contributions to the establishment of a modern medical system in Vietnam, paying particular attention to his activities as an educator and to his personal selflessness and generosity.

• Phạm Hoàng Hộ (1929 – 2017)

Dr. Hộ was a scientist-botanist, the founder-rector of Cần Thơ University, and the author of the multi-volume, exhaustively complete *Illustrated Flora of Vietnam*. His portrait in this volume examines his gradual evolution as a scientist, together with his unceasing activities as an educator and university rector and his efforts to overcome the limitations imposed on him by the current government of Vietnam.

Dr. Vinh is the author of a second book of cultural portraits dealing with eighteen additional figures (Nguyễn Tường Bách, Hứa Bảo Liên, Hoàng Tiến Bảo, Tạ Tỵ, Trần Ngọc Ninh, Lê Ngộ Châu, Nguyễn Văn Trung, Dohamide, Lê Ngọc Huệ, Nghiêm Sỹ Tuấn, Đoàn Văn Bá, Mai Chửng, Trần Hoài Thư, Phan Nhật Nam, Võ Tòng Xuân, Vũ Xuân Thông, Trần Mộng Tú, and John Steinbeck). This volume concludes with a cultural portrait, not of a person, but of a uniquely organized bookselling district next to the central post office in Saigon. I hope to translate and publish this volume soon as "The Creative World of South Vietnam, Volume 2."

Together, these two volumes of portraits amount to a vibrant portrait of a culture with much to offer to the world and at the same time offers a strong correction and refutation of the communist government of Vietnam's attempts to deny the significance of this culture.

ERIC HENRY

Chapel Hill, North Carolina
April 30, 2025

MẶC ĐỖ'S JOURNEY FROM SAIGON TO *NOON OVER CORAL REEF* THE SPIRITUAL DISCIPLINE OF STILLNESS

Portrait of Mặc Đỗ
Photo by Trần Cao Lĩnh

Mặc Đỗ, literary man, journalist, translator, was a prominent figure in the literary world of the South before 1975. After '75, he came to the U.S. as a refugee at the age of 58, still brimming with creative ability, but he nevertheless chose to live a "secluded life" (quy ẩn) as Mai Thảo put it. Mặc Đỗ refrained almost totally from appearing or participating in the literary activities of the overseas expatriate community (or, as he said, the "biển ngoài"–"community beyond the sea,"), and this deliberate choice caused his name to sink into relative obscurity.

MẶC ĐỖ, BIOGRAPHICAL DATA:

Real name: Đỗ Quang Bình; born 1917 in Hanoi to a family steeped in Confucian study, but also amenable to western cultural ways. He studied law but didn't enter legal practice, choosing instead to be a writer. The name "Mặc Đỗ" was bestowed on him by his father; it means "a silent fellow surnamed Đỗ. He began quite early with short stories, plays, and translations. After the 1954 Geneva Accords he emigrated to the South, and together with Nghiêm Xuân Hồng and Vũ Khắc Khoan established the Viewpoint Group (Quan Điểm), the main purpose of which was to publish books by the group's members. On the journalistic side Mặc Đỗ, along with the writers Vũ Khắc Khoan and Tam Lang (Vũ Đình Chí) and the poets Đinh Hùng, Như Phong (Lê Văn Tiến) and Mặc Thu (Lưu Đức Sinh) founded the first Tự Do ("Freedom") newspaper in the South. After 1975 he emigrated to the U.S.

WORKS:

Bốn Mươi ("Forty"; 1956), Siu Cô Nương ("Sister Siu": 1958), Tân Truyện I ("New Stories" I; 1967), Tân Truyện II ("New Stories" II; 1973), Trưa Trên Đảo San Hô ("Noon Over Coral Reef," 2011), Truyện Ngắn ("Short Stories" excludes only the stories in the 1973 collection Tân Truyện II; published by Mặc Đỗ) self-published under the name "Quan Điểm Publishing House"

Translations:

Lão Ngư Ông và Biển Cả (The Old Man and the Sea, Ernest Hemingway; Quan Điểm, 1956), Con Người Hào Hoa (The Great Gatsby, F. Scott Fitzgerald; Quan Điểm, 1956), Một Giấc Mơ (Grand Hotel (Menschen Im Hotel), Vicki Baum; Cảo Thơm, 1956), Người Vợ Cô Đơn ("The Lonely Wife," François Mauriac; Cảo Thơm, 1966), Thời Nhỏ Trong Gia Đình Luvers (Essay in Autobiography),

The front and back cover of *Forty* by Mặc Đỗ, Quan Điểm Pub. House, 1957

Boris Pasternak; Văn (Literature), 1967), Tâm Cảnh ("Mood," André Maurois; Văn (Literature), 1967); Anh MÔN (Le Grand Meaulnes, Alain-Fournier, Cảo Thơm, 1968), Vùng Đất Hoang Vu ("Wilderness," Leo Tolstoy; Đất Sống, 1973), Giờ Thứ 25 (The Twenty-fifth Hour, Virgil Gheorghiu; Đất Sống, 1973)

In "Dream of a Lifetime," ("Mộng Một Đời"; see below) we can see that from a very early age Đỗ Quang Bình – who had not yet adopted the pen name Mặc Đỗ – cherished the dream of becoming a writer. As he recounts: To develop a style, the best choice for a young man is to translate foreign works into Vietnamese. The literary techniques of the foreign writers one translates will help quite a bit in one's efforts to improve the structure of the long narratives one wishes to create." This choice of Mặc Đỗ's allowed him to "kill two birds with one stone" – it enabled him to develop a style that was inimitably his own under the influence of western literature, and a second consequence was that his very beautiful and correct translations from French and English became a second aspect of his career, standing alongside his purely creative work. These translations of his were continuously republished in subsequent years.

MORE THAN HALF A CENTURY:

With regard to age, Mặc Đỗ is a generation older than me. I started reading his things very early in my life, beginning with the novels *Forty* (*Bốn Mươi*), 1957, *Sister Siu* (*Siu Cô Nương*), 1959 and then the volume *New Stories* (*Tân Truyện*), 1967. I was friends with him from the 1960s on – more than half a century by now. I felt when I first met him that he had all the traits of a literary man.

When I chose to study medicine, I was also a journalism student with the periodical *Medicine and Compassion* (*Sinh Viên Y Khoa Tình Thương*) and had started to produce journalism and other writing. Issues of *Sinh Viên Tình Thương* were sent gratis to Mặc Đỗ.

In 1962, having completed a draft of my novel, Mây Bão ("Storm Clouds) I sent copies of it to Mai Xuyên (Đỗ Thúc Vịnh) and Mặc Đỗ for them to give it a preliminary reading. They both responded with direct and unstinting criticism.

Mr. Đỗ Thúc Vịnh laid great stress on purity and correctness of language, and was also very concerned with *"The Coming Generation" ("Những Người Đang Tới")* – which was to be the title of a book he produced later on. Đỗ Thúc Vịnh is no longer alive – his dates are 1920 to 1996 – so his death occurred only a little less than twenty years ago.

Mặc Đỗ held the view that a young person just starting to write should practice at first by writing short stories, and he held that, in writing, technique was the essential element. My first literary effort was a novel rather than a group of short stories, so my "first step" was not in accord with his advice. *Mây Bão* was published in 1963 with all of its original content and with a front cover designed by my close friend, the artist Nghiêu Đề.

Due to the secluded existence that he led after his 1975 emigration – which amounted to almost half his life – it is difficult to create a portrait that shows all facets of the man. I will choose some excerpts from his letters to me, while removing portions that deal only with personal trivia – this will help the reader know about Mặc Đỗ in his "secluded" period.

Moving into the 21st century – the age of the computer – Mai Thảo, for one, persisted in patiently writing his manuscripts by hand – he did this even when addressing the mailers he used to send copies of his journal *Văn* ("Literature") to individual subscribers, but as for Mặc Đỗ, he remained loyal to the portable typewriter he had always used. All the letters he sent to me were typewritten letters. I have only one rare specimen of a letter from him written entirely by hand, and that letter was the result of an accident – the cherished typewriter that had accompanied Mặc Đỗ wherever he went fell and broke. Shortly after that, a friend of the writer in France gave him another typewriter as a Christmas gift, and from that time on his letters to me were all entirely typed except for his signatures, which were handwritten.

HIS HANDWRITTEN LETTER:

Cher Vinh,

I clumsily dropped and broke my beloved typewriter, and "hospitals" for those devices in the U.S. would rather change parts than fix ailing machines – so while I wait for an Asian hand, I have no choice but to trace letters – which requires that I pour all my attention into a few of my fingers, which is unutterably wearisome for the brain, so I can only write a brief, concise note. A single page letter run through a printer would lack all personality.

Thanks, Vinh, for letting me see you more clearly still. The fire within me existed before the day that I listened to a friend's advice and buried the draft of *"Perpetual Unease" ("Đứng Ngồi Không Yên")* under three layers of paper and shelved it in a cabinet – I saw bits of that fire here and there in your conversations with me. After that day, my pen has not known AN ["stillness"] any more, the AN of Buddhism. I'm glad to see that your pen is still "AN."

In conclusion, let me say that I feel you are a bit optimistic. Look again at that "half empty" when you look at humanity in general. Loving one's native land is a sort of greed."

Yours,
[Mặc Đỗ, Feb. 5, 1996]

The cover of *Văn*, Issue 1, Aug. 1982. Literary Portrait in each issue: Mặc Đỗ Quy Ẩn

The front cover of *Sister Siu* by Mặc Đỗ; Quan Điểm Pub. House, 1959

FROM BỐN MƯƠI ("FORTY") AND SIU CÔ NƯƠNG ("SISTER SIU") TO TÂN TRUYỆN ("NEW STORIES")

Bốn Mươi ("Forty"; 1957), is a novel. In it, Mặc Đỗ wrote about a class of petty bourgeois intellectuals (giai cấp trí thức tiểu tư sản) who were of an age when, according to Confucius, one is "free of doubts" [i.e. forty; cf. *sì shí ér búhuò* 四十而不惑]. They came from wealthy families, studied abroad, graduated, and then returned to their homelands to lead lives of ease in the upper reaches of society. They were all, in the most fashionable sense "luminaries of the salon" who mingled naturally with the class of scholar bureaucrats from a former era – very removed from ordinary conditions of life, but with much political influence – they believed in the leadership role of the petty bourgeois intellectuals in the war between the nationalists and the communists.

Sister Siu (*Siu Cô Nương*) was Mặc Đỗ's second novel. It was about three men and two women set against the background of the North in 1954 after the Geneva Accords when Vietnam was about to be cut in two. The three young men also belonged to the class of idealistic forty-year-olds who believed in the role of middle-class intellectuals and who advocated the creation of a western-style democracy, and who were unwilling to accept communism. So, they bid farewell to Hanoi and emigrated to the South, or as Mặc Đỗ puts it, they "fled to escape from Qin ["tỵTần"; an allusion to the tyrannical role of the founder of the Qin dynasty in China]. He wrote the two syllables as one word and used them from that point on to refer to the actions of all who strove to escape from the threat of communism. The characters in *Sister Siu* have a wider scope of activity than those in *Bốn Mươi*, but they still belong to the society of the high-ranking in which impetuous love affairs occur – all of which provides an occasion for historical occasions that the author regards with the eye of a prophet.

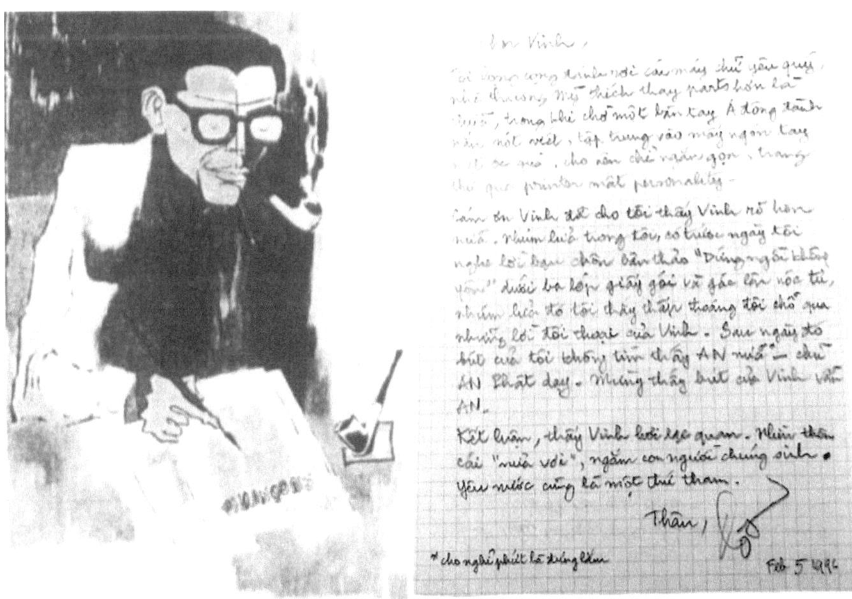

Em Vinh,

Thân,

Feb 5 1996

Left: Mặc Đỗ as drawn by Tạ Ty; source: *Gió O*; right: the handwritten letter of Mặc Đỗ sent to the author in 1996.

We should also note that the principal theme of *Bốn Mươi* and *Sister Siu* is the struggle between classes, which led to the twenty-year period of civil war that followed. And the ultimate consequence of all this was the second "flight from Qin" that occurred after 1975 in which millions of Vietnamese spread to all corners of the earth.

Let us see what Mặc Đỗ himself says about *Sister Siu*: "I remember in the concluding portion of *Sister Siu* a character on a train gazing out on green fields on either side of the tracks with hard-at-work farmers, worrying whether in days to come those people would all turn into enemies? This worry pervades all the five hundred pages that came after *Sister Siu*. (Mặc Đỗ, correspondence, 1994).

Tân Truyện I ("New Stories," *Quan Điểm*, 1967) and *Tân Truyện II* (*Văn*, 1973) were two collections of short narratives that Mặc Đỗ called "nouvelles" or "new stories." Each one is like a jade bead on a string of beads with a point of view based on the conventions of short fiction to which are added technical devices of the author. The tales are conveyed in language full of images, but at the same time spare and refined. Each of these "nouvelles" by Mặc Đỗ leaves the reader with a special, highly memorable, impression.

It seems that here too we should set forth one of Mặc Đỗ's written observations: "From the time I first began to write I have chosen a particular path: I have never put anyone else's personal life, whether of a person known or unknown to me, into a story. The people I create are all made from details, images, and bits of language that I have recorded on innumerable occasions through observation and definition. Each character is an amalgam of many chosen details. (Appendix: "Stories that Cannot be Written," *Noon Over Coral Reef*, Quan Điểm Publishing House, 2011).

A number of short stories in *Tân Truyện I* and *II* were chosen by Mặc Đỗ for inclusion in the two collections *Noon Over Coral Reef* (2011, 13 stories) and *Truyện Ngắn* (2014), amounting to thirty stories in all, including the thirteen stories in *Noon Over Coral Reef*. None of these stories have any indication of their date of composition.

To say that Mặc Đỗ wrote nothing after going abroad would be incorrect. He wrote some, but one must say that he wrote very little. He contributed a piece to the first issue of *Lửa Việt* ("Vietnamese Fire") with the story *"The Sweater With the Color of Moss"* ("Cái Áo Len Màu Rêu"). He also contributed some pieces to the *Literature and Art Journal* (Tạp Chí Văn Học Nghệ Thuật) of Võ Phiến. These consisted of several essays and stories in the first issues of the journal: in Issue 1: "A Programme for Opposing Women" ("Kế Hoạch Chống Đàn Bà"); in Issue 2: "The Pursuit of Literature and Art While Living the Life of a Refugee" (Làm Văn Học Nghệ Thuật Trong Hoàn Cảnh Tỵ Nạn"); Issue 4: "The Vietnamese Arts Abroad" ("Văn Nghệ Việt Nam ở Hải Ngoại"); Issue 7: "The Russian Human Being in the Communist Mold" ("Con Người Nga trong khuôn đúc cộng sản") (VHNT, old series, 1978; http: //tapchivanhoc.org)

In a personal letter he wrote: "In the first one or two years after I came here, I wrote pieces for various journals to help out some friends when there was a shortage of writers, but later on our ranks swelled and I took to sitting still without making a sound, except on a few occasions when I had incurred obligations on account of having received many issues of journals for free.

And one year later, in a letter marked "Year 17 since the flight from Qin" he wrote: "Yesterday I started receiving the lunar new year's issues of various journals. The first was *Văn / Literature* [directed by Mai Thảo; author's note]. I was pleased to see that my friends were remembering to send me their journals on a regular basis, but when I read them I was not particularly pleased. Only rarely did I see any articles written with artistic care and cultivation. What I saw instead was much evidence of hurried writing and hasty editorial acceptance… I was overly familiar with life beyond the ocean, and there were few things for me to savor, so I wasn't pleased at all. (Mặc Đỗ, Jan. 11, 1992)

When it came to literary creation, Mặc Đỗ held rather strict views that he applied to himself as well as others. He always said that technique was the most important factor in writing fiction.

And he recounted the following: "I have lost quite a few young friends who had me read their draft manuscripts or published books, because I expressed my views very frankly after reading them. I complained about this with a few elderly friends (not writers) and got the reply that people must guard against touching on the weak points of others. But I went on ignoring that advice because I felt that I had to be frank and open with anyone inclined to trust me – and to myself as well. (Mặc Đỗ, Feb. 5, 1994)

On the subject of his own existence, he wrote: "As for my personal prospects, after trying out various things and evaluating the abilities that remain to me, I see that I am still quite clear-headed, but also pessimistic and unambitious. I have held this attitude since I consigned the manuscript of *'The Bubbles Fly' ('Bong Bóng Bay')*, the result of ten year's hard work, to the flames." (Mặc Đỗ, Nov. 1, 1995) This "book-burning" that took place on American soil was a thing he did himself – it was not due to some Qin-like tyrant of the 21st century.

Then at the age of 90, he decided to publish the short story collection *Noon Over Coral Reef* (2011), which he called his "concluding work," with a front cover completely empty, except for a few lines of untrammeled, spiritually exalted verse:

Mountains loom all by themselves,
The earth grows cold and one day breaks away,
And drifts into a realm of nothingness.

Noon Over Coral Reef consists of thirteen short stories arranged in reverse chronological order. The first seven stories he wrote as a refugee (or to use his expression, in the period of "flight from Qin"); the three following stories were written in Saigon before 1975, and the three last stories were written in Hanoi in the period 1946-52. Mặc Đỗ wrote: "The three last stories are the first three that I wrote, when I felt ready to begin after many years of study and practice." Though only a book of short stories it nevertheless stands as testimony to three segments of the author's journey, as well as three phases of his creative life: Hanoi, Saigon, and the United States.

In his "Concluding Words" he says: "I feel that the future lying ahead of me is quite short, (as well as my prospects for writing stories, whether short or long), so I am self-publishing this group of tales after a period of absence from the overseas literary community; and I offer it as a sort of farewell."

But following this, three years after *"Perpetual Unease"* (the name of a lost work by the author), he published the collection Truyện Ngắn ("Short Stories"; 2014), which included all his new stories written before and after 1975. Both this work and the previous were self published under the name "Tủ Sách Quan Điểm" ("Viewpoint Library").

LOST WORKS

The house belonging to Mặc Đỗ's family in Saigon was not the sort of luxurious villa typical of the scenes described in the novel "Forty," but a modest two-story home on Trần Hưng Đạo Boulevard, a cozy domicile through many years. I visited it once after April 30, 1975 (the day that Saigon fell to the Communists). It looked utterly abandoned, with empty folding chairs scattered around. The beautiful cubist paintings of Tạ Tỵ that had once adorned the living room no longer hung on the walls. Only then did I realize that Mặc Đỗ's whole family had quietly retreated from Saigon on the night of April 29, only one day before my visit. Of course, like everyone else, he had been able to carry nothing away but a small valise.

In a later letter he explained to me more clearly the fate that had befallen the draft manuscript of *"Perpetual Unease," ("Đứng Ngồi Không Yên")* and then how it had turned into a pile of ashes."

"After completing *"Perpetual Unease",* I took the manuscript to several people I respected [among them he mentioned the name of Nguyễn Đức Quỳnh[1]] and for many reasons asked them to read it. As

1 Nguyễn Đức Quỳnh (1909 – 1974), pen name: Hà Việt Phương. Writer, journalist, and political commentator. Born in Hưng Yên, North Vietnam. In Saigon, managed the newspaper *Đời Mới (New Life)* and organized the famous intellectual discussion group with vision "Đàm Trường Viễn Kiến." He was a mentor to the songwriter Phạm Duy. Like the latter, he fought with the Việt Minh against the French, but returned to the French-controlled cities in 1952.

it happened they all made one and the same observation: 'This is full of things that will offend people!' This reaction made me reconsider, and I wrapped the whole draft and its accompanying documents in a box, tied it securely with string, and glued a notice to the outside that said: '*Reserve for the next generation.*' After I left in 1975, a young fellow came to rummage around in what I had left. He took the wrapped manuscript along with many other things, imagining that they were very valuable. When he got home and opened the box, he was both angry and scared, so he threw it all into an iron bin, poured gasoline on it, and burned it to cinders. How many thoughts of mine turned into ashes! Later on, when relating these details, I could only chuckle – it was what should have happened! The draft should have been burnt!

"The above words are from a conversation I had with Dr. Ngô Thế Vinh of the Special Paratroopers. This is saying to the writer NTV… It was early fall, and I was getting ready for a flu shot, and I remembered a group of young high school students during the French era around the time of World War II who referred to old men and women as *PPH – Passera Pas cet Hiver* – "elders who cannot survive the winter – could we be the same?"

Large Works that Could Not be Written

Following the section "Concluding Words" in the short story collection *Noon Over Coral Reef*, there is an additional appendix entitled: "Tales that Cannot Be Written." Here, Mặc Đỗ confides the following: "For a writer, nothing is sadder than to be forced to admit to oneself that one cannot write something that one longs to write. As I look at the history of our country, I can see no period that can be compared with the century immediately preceding. In the most recent century, three mighty upheavals followed one upon the other, with a thousand scenes brimming with the most vivid possible details. The misery of separation was made concrete by the division of the North and the South. "Independence," as experienced by the Vietnamese in the two regions, was a phenomenon that collected with dizzying force, amid tears. And how immense the next upheaval was! But it was not

Left: sketch portrait of Mặc Đỗ; right: the front and back covers of *Noon Over Coral Reef*, Mặc Đỗ's farewell work.

long afterward that it came into being, and it has lasted more than thirty years by now! [note: these lines were probably written around 2005.] Those two upheavals led to yet another, the strangest of all, when nearly two million Vietnamese made their way to strange shores, and began to put down roots there. An image arose from this scene: a girl of mixed Vietnamese and American blood, and a story grew in my head that would embrace the three upheavals enumerated above. For many months afterward I was enamored with the theme of that story and worked on building an armature for it upon which episodes could be hung… But who would write it? The observations, impressions, and emotions that filled my head, could be used for the first part of the story… but from April 29, 1975 on, I was not in the country anymore to observe, record, and feel... I could not write it... I hope for myself, and I hope for the multitudes of Vietnamese readers, for such a story, because no work has yet appeared that provides a continuous record of that unique stretch of history, at once tragic and worthy of tear-provoking laughter… That treasure must await the appearance of Vietnamese who will dare to accept the honor and responsibility of being writers." (from the postscript to *Noon Over Coral Reef*, pp. 219-30)

That is the sadness–and also the very heavy price he must pay – of a writer in exile, unable to write. A Dream of a great work–cherished

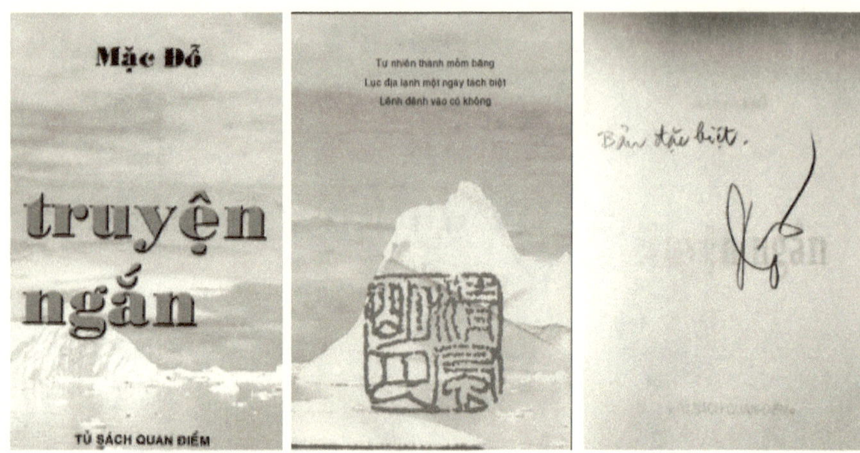

The cover pages of *Short Stories* (2014), the second farewell work of Mặc Đỗ.

for ever so many years – kept lingering like a huge obsession that refused to depart from the writer Mặc Đỗ.

I enter life, ablaze with eager passion,
And then am sunk in heavy sorrow;
I close my eyes and still feel sorrow.

SEEKING STILLNESS ["AN" ~ "PEACE"] IN BUDDHISM

"From the time that I read *"The Occluding River"* [a work by Ngô Thế Vinh on the damming of the Mekong River] I have been overcome with sorrow at the prospect that sooner or later become a reality, and at the irresistible shallowness of the tendencies that are now overtaking today's world. You and your friends, Vinh, are engaged in this praiseworthy effort, and many other people in various countries are also engaged in different attempts with the common aim of saving life on earth. It pains me that human beings these days are far too eager to trample on every decent principle. When she was alive, my wife and I would often gaze at each other, absorbed in a shared sorrow: 'Alas for our children, our grandchildren, and great grandchildren… and those born later on!' Just like me, anyone who reads *"The Occluding River"* can have no means to avoid being moved by the facts that have emerged even earlier than the future prospect that we fear." (Mặc Đỗ, April 6, 2007)

At the bottom of the above typewritten letter Mặc Đỗ added a handwritten postscript: "Vinh, do you think about the great war that may break out, and that Vietnam will have to suffer?" With the ominous troubles now arising in the East Sea, it appears that these prophetic words of his may be realized. Mặc Đỗ always spoke of STILLNESS ("AN," capitalized) in a Buddhist sense. The word appears, for example in a letter that he wrote from Austin:

"Cher Vinh, This year the return of Spring in the Mekong River Delta brings me no gift of STILLNESS. After reading "Seeking to Return"[2] before Tết, the aftertaste it left me with extended without a break till past Tết. I still remember when I was little at home, whenever there were death anniversaries or meetings of relations, I understood nothing of my connection with those who came before me, but I got to hear accounts of their warlike deeds and their accomplishments during the southward advance of our people, with all of the details… And on every such occasion my mother would weep and ask when the wrongs we had suffered would ever be wiped clean. Now, in the midst of this year's Tết, I continue to be obsessed by that mournful observation of hers… Now the time is about to come when the dust can no longer be hidden under the rug, I feel sadder still. Repressing this feeling, I still cherish a dream: 'The Vietnamese people will wake up and see that they must join hands to deal with their problems, and see that they must talk to each other.'" (Mặc Đỗ, Feb.18, 2000)

Three of the principal writers whom I have known in the Quan Điểm group all turned to Buddhism in their final years. Tuyết Ngưu (Vũ Khắc Khoan; 1917 – 1986), author of the play *Genghis Khan* (*Thành Cát Tư Hãn*) in the "land of ten thousand lakes" (Vạn Hồ) in Minnesota took to reading and listening to the sutras so as to "float in the mist at the threshold of the dharma assembly, alone." Tịnh Liên (Nghiêm Xuân Hồng; 1920 – 2000), author of *Revolution and Behavior* (*Cách Mạng và Hành Động*), took up meditation after 1975, absorbed the thought of the Surangama Sutra (Kinh Lăng Nghiêm)

---

2 This refers to the chapter "Seeking to Return to the East," (Tìm Về Phương Đông) in The Nine Dragons Drained Dry, The East Sea in Turmoil [*Cửu Long Cạn Dòng, Biển Đông Dậy Sóng*], by Ngô Thế Vinh, Văn Nghệ Publisher, 2000)

and began to write and lecture about Buddhism. Vũ Khắc Khoan and Nghiêm Xuân Hồng slipped quietly away, one after the other, amid the sounds of chanted sutras. And for years on end Mặc Đỗ lived a secluded life like a pilgrim on an endless quest for STILLNESS.

Verse Capping and Spring Festival Verses

"One day at the end of the year, an elderly friend, anh Đoàn Thêm [a member of the Bách Khoa group, author of *Những Ngày Tháng Không Quên ("Unforgotten Days and Months");* author's note] sent a poem "Complaining of Age," ("Than Già") to me, another old friend. The poem had five rhyme words: "rồi-trôi-nòi-thôi-hồi." Another old friend made an answering verse, and then many others, at irregular intervals, began to do the same. Seeing that this put them in a good mood, I decided to jump in, though this was only the second time in my life that I participated in a word game that I thought suitable only for classical Chinese scholars. On jumping in, I found that it gave me pleasure, like doing a crossword puzzle, for example. I'll copy out two of the poems I wrote for you to amuse yourself with as an end-of-the-year gift. Only when you play at verse-capping can you see the real pleasure of maneuvering with Vietnamese words – one rhyme word can be used to convey many different meanings. Another pleasure is to do more capping at random, so as to place them in journals and get a name for oneself. (Mặc Đỗ, Jan. 11, 1992)

Left-over Life

The precious words of ancient times have all been taught,
But still our days pass languidly, like floating clouds.
Our urges still persist; we dare not let them drop,
A thousand vivid lives are but a single stream.
Our debt to country, love of family, our careers–
Once snow and frost descend, it all comes down to one.
To live without an aim is aimlessness indeed,
Old gentlemen collide at random seeking spots to sit.
Mặc Đỗ

New Year

The moment having come, just stop and count your years.
Just sit beside the grassy bank and let things drift.
You bend your head to learn; stupidity remains.
You crane your neck to seek enlightenment–no use.
You leaf through records of your days; most marks are red.
Your losses–turn them over, let them be erased.
I smile to see how destiny out-schemed Bùi Tín,
Few get to go back home in handsome, festive clothes.
Mặc Đỗ

I must say I was surprised and delighted to see a person steeped in western studies like Mặc Đỗ step boldly into the school of verse-capping with its rules of rhyme and prosody. I was particularly impressed by the poem "Left-over Life" *(Dư Sinh)* with its near-perfection of form.

"Reflecting as I lay awake on the night preceding the first day of Tết. 2003, my thoughts turned to the many Vietnamese lost and scattered over the earth." With these words, Mặc Đỗ sent me a poem he had just composed:

Spring Festival Verses for the New Year

(Composed at 2:00 or 3:00 a.m. on the eve of Lunar New Year:)

My joints know that life in me is growing dim,
But still my heart is warmed just as it was in days of yore.
I speed you on and welcome you with strong tea in my cup,
The love bestowed by sky and earth lasts long, goes on and on.
My two hands joined, I pray for the fulfillment of your aims,
As threads of incense smoke twist up till high above they soar.
Each love I've cherished, still as fresh as ever in the past,
Alone amid the circle of my friends, with neither moon nor star,
On all sides silence; not a single sound of crashing surf,
And time itself sits down at ease, no reason now to wait.
My sadness and my joy aren't old and neither are they new.
Mặc Đỗ

PREPARING FOR A WEIGHTLESS JOURNEY

The loss of his wife was a heavy blow to Mặc Đỗ; it affected both his spirit and his life. His chief concern after that event was to prepare for his own departure; he wanted it to be light and effortless. "I have a French friend," he said, "who cared for his wife through fourteen years of living death."

In 2006 he wrote a living will in his own hand: "Advance Medical Directives of Binh DoQuang." He shared it with me, regarding me as a witness from afar, perhaps because of our friendship, and perhaps because of my career as a doctor. "I wrote the directive out in French so that the meaning would be completely correct before translating it into English legalese."

What he wrote shows his understanding of the illness known as "Alzheimer's," together with the effects of this illness on the patient, his family, and on society in general as it progresses. The writing is that of an "old gentleman" (lão giả – his expression) who with absolute objectivity and clarity of thought puts his choices on paper:

"Si jamais j'attraperais ce mal Alzheimer, situation bien établie par mon docteur et d'autres spécialistes consultés, je demande que toute nourriture solide et liquide soit interrompue, nourriture ou d'autre substance donnée par quel moyen que ce soit. J'implore tous les membres de ma famille, toutes les autorités judiciaires, administratives, religieuses, politiques, et autres, à ne pas s'opposer à ma décision et me laisser périr comme un vieil arbre paisiblement."

("If I should ever contract Alzheimer's disease, and the situation is firmly established by my doctor and other medical consultants, I request that all solid and liquid nourishment be interrupted–nourishment of whatever sort, delivered by whatever means. I implore all the members of my family, all judiciary, administrative, religious, and political authorities, and others, to refrain from opposing my decision and to let me perish peacefully like an old tree.")

His choice could serve as an example to many people; he knew enough to accept the cycle of birth and destruction as a natural feature of heaven and earth. It also could provide a corrective to the bankrupt

American medical system, which strives to preserve the lives of people who have sunk into a vegetative state (here I quote expressions used by Mặc Đỗ).

One morning in the year 2015, nine years after he wrote his living will, when I was in the hospital where I ordinarily work, I was very pleased to have a fairly long telephone conversation with him – this was on June 14 of that year – and to see that he was still the writer Mặc Đỗ and that his speech was clear and his thought processes were sharp as ever. It could be that due in part to his genes, and due also to a disciplined style of life (from his early youth he had risen early, taken cold baths, and lived in measured fashion in all his later years, even choosing while in Saigon to follow a diet based on brown rice with salt and sesame), it was easy for him to approach a hundred years of age while living independently and with all the ordinary attributes of life. One day, still far off, one hoped, he would pass away in a manner that medicine would call a natural death – like an old tree grown dry and withered – the words also of Mặc Đỗ.

A MANUSCRIPT BEQUEATHED TO ME BY MẶC ĐỖ: A LIFETIME DREAM

"My dear Ngô Thế Vinh:

"I'm sending you a piece of writing for you alone to read, so that you can save it somewhere until my body has turned to dust and then give it to whatever journal you choose so that it may be printed. If it should happen that some journal has an issue with some articles concerning my life as a writer, printing this piece together with the others would be the most fitting arrangement.

"I've wanted to write it for so many years, but felt too sad to do so. Last month I finally decided that I should write it while my head was still sharp. Then, having written it, it occurred to me that since you, Vinh, are true to me, and conversant with journals and those who work as journalists, I should turn it over to you. Please accept it and use it to send me on my way when my life is over.

Mặc Đỗ"

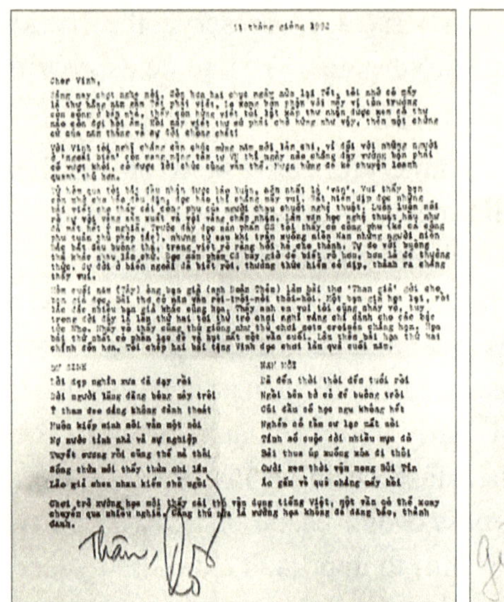

[illegible]

Tôi đẹp nghìn xưa đã đẹp rồi
Đời người lăng đăng bóng mây trôi
[illegible] tham đeo đẳng không đành thoát
Muôn kiếp sinh sôi vẫn một nòi
Nợ nước tình nhà và sự nghiệp
Tuyết sương rồi cũng thế mà thôi
Sống thừa mới thấy thừa chi lắm
Lão già chen nhau kiếm chỗ ngồi

Đã đến thời thôi đến tuổi rồi
Ngồi bên bờ cỏ để buông trôi
Cúi đầu cố học ngu không hết
Nghển cổ tầm sư lạc mất nòi
Tính số cuộc đời nhiều mục đỏ
Bài thua úp xuống xóa đi thôi
Cười xem thời vận nong Bùi Tín
Áo gấm về quê chẳng mấy hồi

Chơi trò xướng họa mới thấy cái thú vận dụng tiếng Việt, một vần có thể xoay chuyển qua nhiều nghĩa. Cũng thú nữa là xướng họa không dễ dàng bảo, thành danh.

Thân,

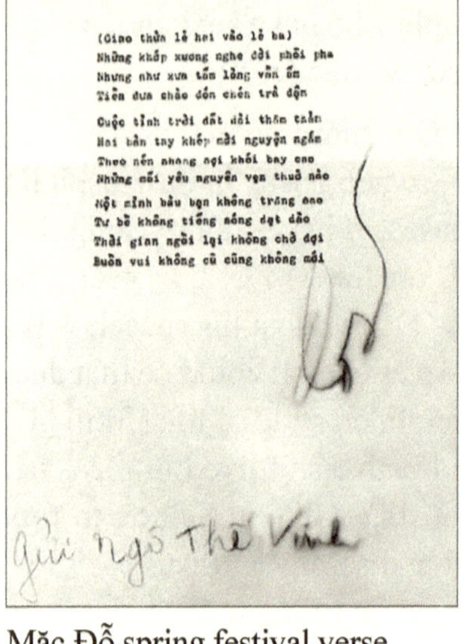

KHAI BÚT

(Giao thừa lẻ hai vào lẻ ba)
Những khớp xương nghe đời phôi pha
Nhưng như xưa tấm lòng vẫn ấm
Tiễn đưa chào đón chén trà đậm

Cuộc tình trời đất dỗi thăm thẳm
Hai bàn tay khép mời nguyện ngắm
Theo nến nhang ngọi khói bay cao
Những mối yêu nguyên vẹn thuở nào

Một mình bầu bạn không trăng sao
Tư bề không tiếng sóng dạt dào
Thời gian ngồi lại không chờ đợi
Buồn vui không cũ cũng không mới

Gửi Ngô Thế Vinh

Mặc Đỗ's capping verses
(Ngô Thế Vinh, archives)

Mặc Đỗ spring festival verse
(Ngô Thế Vinh, archives)

There was once a child who grew up bearing two languages on his shoulders–the natural language of his mother and a foreign language with which he chanced to become acquainted quite early. And also, from an early time, many stories dropped into his ears–episodes from Chinese tales, native tales, French tales, and things that happened in his own life that bit deeply and flavorfully into his soul. Because he loved to read stories even before he knew how to read, he was eager to study from his earliest days at school, so that he could read to his heart's content. And, as he became more accustomed to reading, the thought naturally grew in him, as he matured, that one day he would write stories as well.

There were two things that happened during the summer when he was preparing to go to high school. They were ordinary, easy-to-forget things, but they just about determined what the future course of his life would be like. A companion of his, the son of a nearby French family, went on vacation to escape the heat. Without his companion, the child wandered about his home with no idea what to do, when he saw a little book lying on the surface of a chest. He picked it up, went out to the garden with it, and went by a tree to read it. Looking at the title on the cover, he thought he would return the book to its place on the chest but, feeling curious, he read a few pages and then, captivated, read all of its twenty-odd pages-worth of fine print. The book told of the sorrows of a young woman, who, bewildered and alone, goes to her husband's home and endures endless fault-finding from the mother and two elder sisters of her husband. He had to wait a day before he had a chance to ask his mother about this situation and was informed by her that it was fairly common in the society of that time, both in the countryside and in county seats, for daughters-in-law to meet with such circumstances. The mother could not say everything she knew all at once–on many subsequent occasions they sat by a tree and the mother continued to talk, the son paying close attention.

The writer Mặc Đỗ's at the age of 95
in a photo taken in October, 2012
(Trần Huy Bích, archives)

The second event occurred subsequent to the day when the child, being companionless, had chanced upon an unfamiliar book. The companion came back home, and the two children resumed meeting frequently. One day at noon, as they were playing chess on the balcony at his friend's house, the child heard a Huế river-call drifting up from somewhere beyond the rear yard. The child strained his ears to hear it, and made out a line that went: "Each dusk I go and stand alone upon the lane / And gaze with twisted entrails at the homeland of my mother."

This painfully mournful river-call reawakened in the child's heart all the aspects of a daughter-in-law's bereft existence that his mother had recounted for him. The river-call, then and afterwards, seemed like the very personification of words coming from the mouth of the daughter-in-law cut off from her mother's family.

Immediately upon returning from the home of his companion, the child sought out his mother and, drawing close to her, said, "When I grow up, I will write stories. I will write about the lives of daughters-in-law. In response, his mother reminded him that he must satisfactorily complete the studies proper to a scholar before choosing a profession. The child promised that he would attend conscientiously to his studies so as to have a solid foundation before beginning. Never-theless, the river-call that he had heard at noon that day caused the language of the folk-verse to remain transcendent in his memory, and it continued to obsess him even as he strove to master his lessons at school.

While conscientiously absorbing knowledge from books, the child also sought to read stories, so as to increase his understanding of the technique of writing through the art of the authors. Along with the instruction of his teachers and the assigned reading at school, he engaged in much extracurricular study due to his eager fascination with the many French stories and French translations on bookshelves in his home. At the same time, the child was an eager reader of Vietnamese journals and newspapers, and remembered many details concerning the life of the day that he saw in such publications. When he was just entering high school, the newspaper at home was *Trung-Bắc Tân-Văn* ("New Literature from the Central Area and the North"). Chance happened to deliver to his eyes an opportunity to study that continued to influence him throughout the literary career that he took up later. For a long period lasting about a year, he would open up that four-page publication to the middle and would see on page two a square with an advertisement for a book entitled: "*The Mask of Communism." ("Mặt nạ Cộng sản").* He asked his elder brother about the meaning of the word "cộng-sản." His brother said that the word was a translation of the French word " communisme," and that he would understand it better when he got older. Having asked the question out of curiosity, the child grew even more curious and at the first opportunity asked his teacher at school about it.

Luckily for the child, the teacher he asked had devoted much attention to communism. He went to the teacher's house on a Thursday and spent almost the entire morning there to continue his questioning. The teacher took a book from his shelves and placed it in the child's hands. The book cover announced that it was a Vietnamese translation of a French translation of a German work, but the author was a Belgian. The teacher gave a careful, detailed exposition of the principles – principles that had been set forth for ages, but which had only been applied, in a much altered and distorted form, at the beginning of the twentieth century. The teacher had the child take the book home and promise to talk with him some more when he returned it, after having read it. The child took the book back with him and read it carefully. On Thursday morning of the following week, he returned to the teacher's house to return the book and posed a question: The title on the French book was different from the one on the Vietnamese book; it said Le Masque du Communisme – were the two books different from each other? The teacher took the book and opened it to the title page, revealing a line of small print. The title of the original German work was Moskau Ohne Maske, which the French edition changed to Moscou Sans Voiles, just changing Maske to Voiles, which was more literary and more in accord with French usage. The Vietnamese edition made the biggest change, replacing "Moscow" with "Cộng-sản" (Communism) to make the title easier for Vietnamese readers to understand.

Continuing with his explanation, the teacher allowed the student to understand what the intent of the author was. While plotting to overthrow the czarist imperial government, the Russian Soviets had an underground newspaper that bore the name Pravda ("Truth") that was devoted to exposing the wicked deeds of the government. After the imperial Russian government was overthrown, Pravda became the official propaganda organ of the new government. The author stripped away the mask hiding the truth of the matter: that the Soviet regime was full of faults similar to those that had characterized the Russian

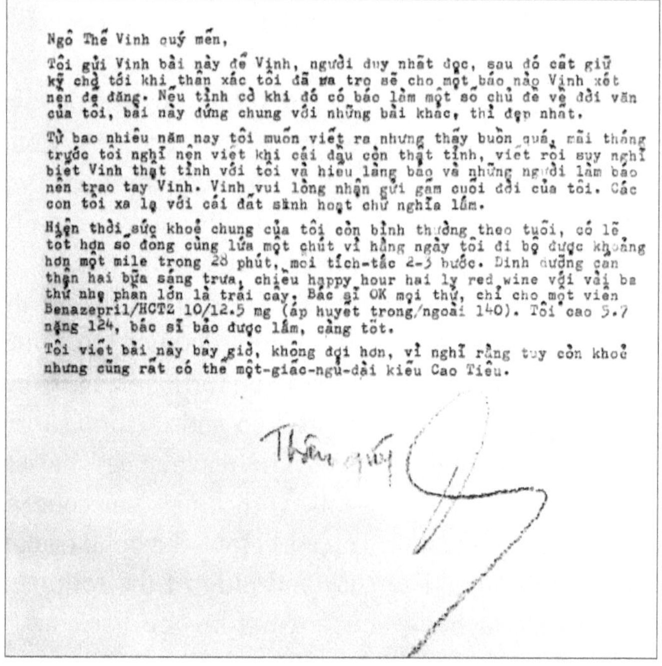

Ngô Thế Vinh quý mến,

Tôi gửi Vinh bài này để Vịnh, người duy nhất đọc, sau đó cất giữ kỹ chờ tới khi thân xác tôi đã ra tro sẽ cho một báo nào Vịnh xét nên để đăng. Nếu tình cờ khi đó có báo làm một số chủ đề về đời văn của tôi, bài này đứng chung với những bài khác, thì đẹp nhất.

Từ bao nhiêu năm nay tôi muốn viết ra nhưng thấy buồn quá, mãi tháng trước tôi nghĩ nên viết khi cái đầu còn thật tỉnh, viết rồi suy nghĩ biết Vinh thật tình với tôi và hiểu làng báo và những người làm báo nên trao tay Vinh. Vinh vui lòng nhận gửi gắm cuối đời của tôi. Các con tôi xa lạ với cái đất sinh hoạt chữ nghĩa lắm.

Hiện thời sức khoẻ chung của tôi còn bình thường theo tuổi, có lẽ tốt hơn số đông cùng lứa một chút vì hằng ngày tôi đi bộ được khoảng hơn một mile trong 28 phút, mỗi tích-tắc 2-3 bước. Dinh dưỡng cẩn thận hai bữa sáng trưa, chiều happy hour hai ly red wine với vài ba thứ nhẹ phần lớn là trái cây. Bác sĩ OK mọi thứ, chỉ cho một viên Benazepril/HCTZ 10/12.5 mg (áp huyết trong/ngoài 140). Tôi cao 5.7 nặng 124, bác sĩ bảo được lắm, càng tốt.

Tôi viết bài này bây giờ, không đợi hơn, vì nghĩ rằng tuy còn khoẻ nhưng cũng rất có thể một-giấc-ngủ-dài kiểu Cao Tiêu.

Thân quý

Manuscript of the letter Mặc Đỗ sent to Ngô Thế Vinh with his testament *"A lifetime Dream."* After receiving it, I learned that Mặc Đỗ had made the story publically available at an earlier time. *(Ngô Thế Vinh, personal archives)*

imperial regime. The truths of former times that Pravda had attacked and the truths of the soviet era were both truths. The child returned, silently repeating the words of his teacher and kept murmuring the words "truth is true." The meaning of those three words continued to follow him throughout the stages he passed through in his effort to become a writer; they remained in his memory from youth to adulthood. "A truth of any sort is still the truth–when I write I shall always treat what my eyes have seen and what my ears have heard; I shall clearly depict the truth."

His resolve to go in search of the truth to be put into his stories impelled the child, until he attained adulthood, to devote all his time outside of school to going here and there to observe life and to see all the scenes in a great part of the northern region. He pedaled to nearby places on a light bicycle; and for places further off, he would put the bicycle on trucks and trains and pedaled around in the areas where the truck or train stopped, meeting people and taking note of situations. He travelled here and there in the delta region, going as far at times as the piedmont areas, sometimes managing to remain for extended periods, and even at times got up to points in the Northeast such as Móng Cái and Lạng Sơn, and in the Northwest, such as Lào Cai deep in the Chapa area. A thing worthy of note in these travels was that he often got to see people he was acquainted with, or to whom he had letters of introduction, who knew a great deal and brought him into contact with people directly involved with different situations. The young man did not rely solely on his eyes and ears to record these experiences, but developed a system for writing everything out in those student notebooks known as "Cent Pages" which were to be found everywhere in those days, reserving the ones with blue covers for what he observed in the countryside and small towns, and the ones with red covers for what his curious eyes and attentive ears had perceived in the cities. He recorded all the details, reserving, for example, a particular notebook for all the formal and casual names for the places he passed through. During one summer vacation when he spent many days in Đồng Đăng, a town near Lạng Sơn right on the Chinese border by the Nam Quan Pass, where he became well acquainted with a girl of the Thổ ethnicity. One day, standing by a plum tree full of fruit, the girl picked two ripe plums, bit one of them in half, and delivered half of it to the lips of her friend, singing a bit of folk-verse: "This plum's taste surpasses that of apricots."

Naturally, her friend ate the plum-half, and remembered the rural flavor of the line of verse, along with all the other details collected for writing on his excursions. For more than ten years, from his high school days to the end of college, the young man amassed a great store of written notes and kept them as he did his books and journals, packing them away tightly beneath his tall-legged bed every night when preparing to retire.

Upon finishing college, the young man found a suitable position in the South. The position allowed him to have a place of his own to live, a little rent-free villa, and to enjoy, month by month, a fairly sufficient monetary account at the Bank of Indochina. He had in addition a sufficiency of time after work in which to cultivate his literary skills– the chief aim of his life. To be able to write, the young man had to work to develop a distinctive style and a rich store of Vietnamese words. He just about memorized the 605-page Chinese-Vietnamese dictionary of Đào Duy Anh. To develop his style the young man chose the method of translating short paragraphs, which then became entire stories. After several years of this training he had produced piles of translations of French novels or French translations of novels. What the young man produced in this way was perceived by everyone as a notable literary accomplishment. Immersed as he was in his studies and exercises, the young man did not forget his intention of using his store of collected material. The writing techniques of the authors he had translated helped him quite a bit to organize in his head the structures of the stories he wished to write.

Before leaving Hanoi to take up his new position in the south, he had to face the problem of collecting and putting away the stacks of materials stored beneath his bed at home. The young man went to "Wooden Case Lane" (Phố Hàng Hòm)[3] in the center city with the idea of purchasing a large wooden chest. What he came across there were two chests which, though old in appearance, were very secure and came with two keys for each chest. The people at the store let him know those chests were of the sort used as carrying-cases for French regimental soldiers. Though old, they were fairly cheap, so the young man bought the chests and brought them home. They were of just the right capacity for his materials. He left the two chests

---

3 The old capital Hanoi has 36 streets described in a classic book entitled "The Thirty-six Guild-streets of Hanoi (*"Hà Nội 36 Phố Phường"*) by the celebrated novelist Thạch Lam. These streets, which in the old days had homes as well as stores, were named after the goods sold there, e.g. Phố Hàng Đường – "Sugar Goods Street," but now those goods are almost gone, except in some old quarters still selling some items reflecting their names.

in his parents' home. His parents had long been aware of the great efforts their cherished son was making to pursue a literary career, so his mother took charge of the chests' safekeeping.

How many were the upheavals that took place in the nation after the day of the son's departure from Hanoi! When the young man returned for a visit, he saw that the appearance of his beloved city hadn't changed much, except that there were now quite a few African faces in front of the base camp of the French army.

When he returned to his home, his mother was already waiting for him. Before he could greet her, and without a word from her, the two of them embraced. The mother burst into tears, and four salty streams of tears flowed down, because the son had already known for some time that half the house had been burned to the ground on purpose. The consuming flames had raged for several days, and had burned to cinders the two chests of materials along with many other precious family items. The mother had through countless years placed the utmost value on the labors of her son, while the son saw clearly that he now had no means of writing a thing about all that he cherished, not only about the things suffered by his mother, but about the miseries of his sisters, which had always had priority in his plans. Through the rich experience he had gained through study and through reading the work of others, the young man needed to lay before readers, with all the details he had gathered, expansive depictions of life in which images of women stirred about. But in the heads of mother and son at that moment, there existed only a borderless emptiness before which one could only weep till tears were gone. A lifetime dream had flown away in the smoke of the cruel fire.

After that, the young man found means to earn a living to the best of his ability, but did not cast aside the fascination that had possessed him even before he had learned to read and had passed through so many years of study and practice. Every time he published a book, he would bring a copy to offer to his mother. His mother would look at the front cover, then turn the book to gaze at the back, and he would hear, indistinctly, the same sad, loving words from his mother: "Well, this too will do."

...

"At the end of 2011, the year Tân Mão, the third collection of short stories, my final work, was all printed, and a package of twenty new copies was sent by Viên Linh from California. I picked up one of the volumes turned it this way and that in my hand, looking at the front and back covers and dreamily imagined the sad, loving words my mother had uttered so many times: 'Well, this too will do.'"

Mặc Đỗ
(Testament sent by Mặc Đỗ to Ngô Thế Vinh)

The Final Haiku Verse

The above study – under the title "Mặc Đỗ's Journey from Hanoi – Saigon to *Noon Over Coral Reef*" – was completed on June 20, 2015. Since I knew that the writer Mặc Đỗ did not use the internet, I sent a printed copy of it to him the next day by Priority Mail. I think he received and read it. I occasionally had occasions to chat with him on the phone–his voice and manner were still the same: clear and with thought processes that were still absolutely sharp.

Only Mặc Đỗ's sons and elder daughters read the article on the internet and in the email messages I sent them.

Here for example is a response I received from his daughter Thúy-Nhi via the site "http://www. diendantheky.net/2015/06." She sent it to a site of mine: "ngo-vinh-con-uong-mac-o-tu-ha-noi-sai.html#more":

Anh Vinh:
Because I've been excessively busy, it is only today that I have time to respond to your message. I have read a number of articles among those you sent me. Now that I have a set of printed hard copies, I am very pleased; thank you very much.

Thúy-Nhi

P.S. I have forwarded your email to all my sisters.

Ms. Thúy-Nhi, the youngest daughter of the writer Mặc Đỗ, was the child of his who remained closest to him and cared for him in his last months and years.

On September 20 of that year (2015), I received the news that Mặc Đỗ had passed away. Having passed the age of 98, he was like a sturdy old tree that had gradually grown dry and sapless. From the standpoint of traditional medicine, he could be regarded as having died a natural death. But the American medical system requires that an illness-related "cause" be put on the death certificate of the deceased, no matter what age he attains.

I conveyed my condolences to Thúy-Nhi and the whole family over the telephone. In doing so, I learned from her that, according to the old writer's wishes, the memorial would be organized very simply within the circle of the family, without visitors and funeral elegies. I also learned from her that my old friend had departed from life very peacefully, amid the gathered members of his family, including his children and very numerous grandchildren, some of whom had come from France. She also told me that he had read out a haiku verse for his children to record only a few hours before he passed away. Soon afterward, I received an email message from the family:

Anh Vinh,

I would like to send you the last haiku verse that father composed at 4:30 a.m. on September 19, 2015:

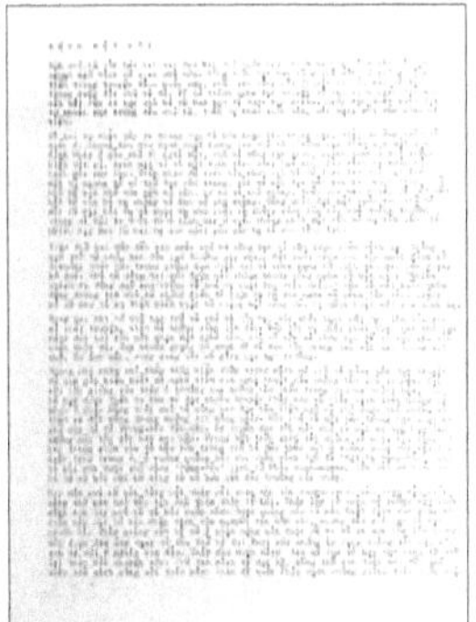
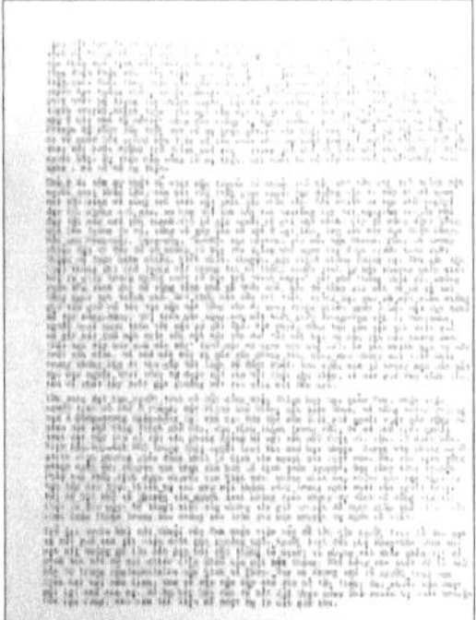
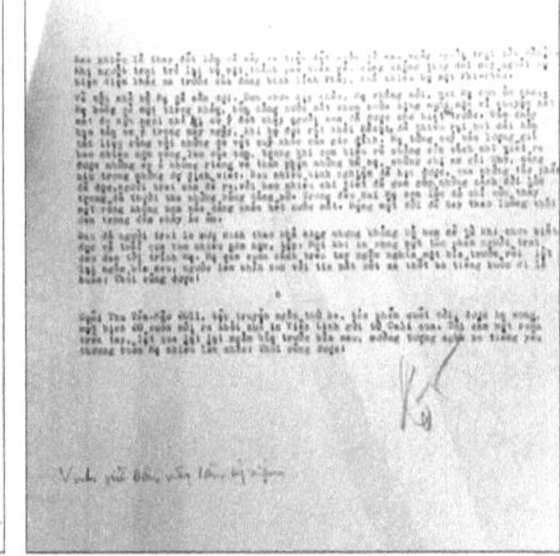

Manuscript of "A Lifetime Dream": three typewritten pages with the author's handwritten signature at the end, with the notation "Vinh, keep this as a souvenir." *(Ngô Thế Vinh, archives)*

"Nhớ sống muốn tìm thơ
Khi nào thơ đến bắt đầu sống
Sống cuộc đời như xưa."

His grandchildren from two continents translated the poem in English and French versions as follows:

"Longing for life I seek poetry
With poetry life begins anew
Back to the life I knew."

"Nostalgie de vie recherche de poésie
Avec la poésie recommence la vie
La vie tout comme avant."

The memorial service was carried out.

Thúy-Nhi D. Morel
Attorney-at-Law
Austin, Texas 78731

This verse in the Japanese Haiku [pái jù 俳句] form was calmly read by Mặc Đỗ for his children to record only a few hours before he closed his eyes forever – it was very moving, very transcendent. It had a total of seventeen syllables, arranged simply in three sentences, with five syllables apiece in the first and last lines, and seven in the middle one. With nothing superfluous and nothing lacking, the "old gentleman – lão giả" Mặc Đỗ described his feelings before what was at once his end point and precisely his starting point, or more correctly his feeling of the absence of a beginning and an end in the continuous flow of life. The pilgrim Mặc Đỗ didn't die but instead stepped into a new living realm. Mặc Đỗ had lived a hidden, secluded life for many years, like a pilgrim ceaselessly seeking STILLNESS as taught by Buddhism, and now this distinguished old gentleman had found this STILLNESS as he crossed the threshold between life and death.

A very little-known and precious photograph taken 36 years (April 10, 1980) in Houston, Texas. From the right: Mặc Đỗ, Dr. Trần Văn Tính, Hoàng Ngọc Ẩn, Võ Phiến, Trần Ngọc Bích, and Huy Lực.

In the afternoon of the same day, I phoned Ms. Thúy-Nhi and suggested to her that I would like to make that poem known to the public. One day later I received the following email message from Ms. Thúy-Nhi.

Anh Vinh,

This is the last part of my email message. The cremation ceremony will be carried out at 1:00 today. I have discussed your suggestion on writing an article with the family, and they all gave their approval. I think my father would be pleased to know that you gave his final haiku verse to the public.

Goodbye, Dear Vinh

Thúy-Nhi

SAD NEWS FOR THE MEDIA AND THE LITERARY WORLD (LÀNG BÁO LÀNG VĂN)

"The writer, journalist, and translator Mặc Đỗ (Đỗ Quang Bình) peacefully rejoined his forebears on September 20, 2015 in Austin, Texas (USA) having attained the great age of 98. In accordance with his wishes, the memorial took place within the circle of the family only, without visitors and funeral elegies."

This is a belated article a year later, as an aromatic incense stick in memory of the writer Mặc Đỗ on the first anniversary of his death (Sept. 20, 2015 – Sept. 20, 2016).

Long Beach 2015 – 2017

A LITERARY PORTRAIT OF NHƯ PHONG (LÊ VĂN TIẾN) FROM *FREEDOM* (*TỰ DO*) TO *SMOKE AND WAVES* (*KHÓI SÓNG*)

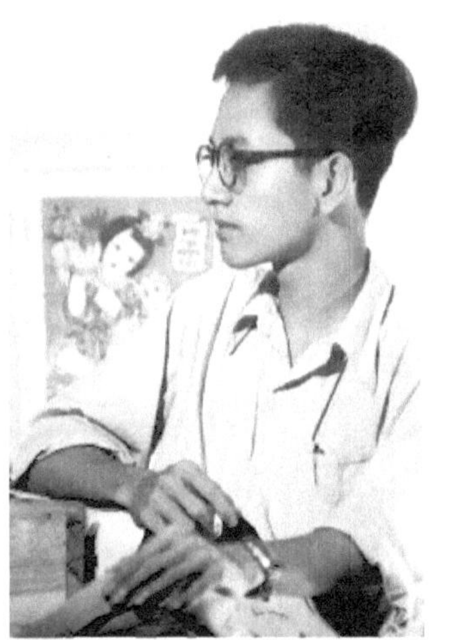

Như Phong in His Youth
(Đinh Quang Anh Thái, personal archives)

I, Ngô Thế Vinh, knew Như Phong from before 1963, and grew closer to him when I became a student journalist with Y khoa Tình Thương ("Medicine and Compassion") and maintained my relationship with him both inside the country and abroad until the day he died.

This "Portrait of Như Phong" speaks a good deal about this close relationship.

Như Phong in 1990 in front of the well-known painting "Spring Garden of the Three Regions" (Vườn Xuân Trung Nam Bắc) by the artist Nguyễn Gia Trí. *(Nguyễn Tường Giang, personal archives)*

BIOGRAPHICAL DATA:

It is not clear what the actual birth date of Như Phong (Lê Văn Tiến) was, but his identification certificate records the date as Feb. 1, 1923, in North Vietnam. His real name is little known; it was Nguyễn Tân Tiến. Later, due to his needs when was seeking to become active in the Revolution, he changed it to Lê Văn Tiến. Starting in 1945, Như Phong worked with the weekly magazine *Ngày Nay, Bộ Mới* ("These Days; New Series") in Hanoi, and after that worked as an editor in the offices of Thông Tin Bắc Việt ("Information Office, North Vietnam"). In 1954 he emigrated to South Vietnam, working at first for Việt Tấn Xã (Vietnam News Agency), and later for the newspaper Tự Do ("Freedom daily") which he served throughout two periods until it had to close its doors in 1963. Aside from working for Vietnamese-language journals, Như Phong was also a correspondent for the *China Quarterly*, based in London, from 1964 to 1972. The articles he wrote about members of the intelligentsia in North Vietnam and about the

Nhân Văn Giai Phẩm ("Humanities" and "Belles Lettres" - the names of two journals) movement established his reputation as a figure in the international news media. Professor Patrick J. Honey, director of the Vietnamese division of the BBC, was the friend and colleague of Như Phong through many decades, and was also the person who made English translations of Như Phong's many articles.

After the fall of the Southern Republic, Như Phong suffered imprisonment for many years, but managed to emigrate to the U.S. in 1994.

After relocating to the U.S., Như Phong wrote articles for the *Asian Wall Street Journal* in Hong Kong (1994 – 1996).

Starting in 1997, Như Phong served as an editorial advisor for Radio Free Asia. He died on Dec. 12, 2001 in Virginia at the age of 78.

NHƯ PHONG AND THE *TỰ DO ("FREEDOM") DAILY*

Immediately after the promulgation of the Geneva Accords in 1954, when Vietnam was divided at the 17th parallel, one of the consequences was a historic emigration to the South of more than a million people from North Vietnam who were fleeing communism. Western journals called this emigration the *"Journey to Freedom."*

Joining in the peaceful and prosperous life in the South at that time, what can be called a transposed journalistic culture in which "a hundred voices contended to bloom" came into existence in a "friendly land with perching birds," and a flood of journalistic activity with a northern tradition began to flourish concurrently with established southern periodicals such as the dailies *Thần Chung* [1] ("Morning Bell") run by Nam Đình, *Đuốc Nhà Nam* ("The Southern Torch"), under Trần Tấn Quốc, and *Sài Gòn Mới* ("New Saigon"), under "Bà Bút Trà" ("Mrs. Tea-time Pen" – Nguyễn Đức Nhuận).

---

1 Thần Chung (Chinese: thần = morning; chung = bell). The newspaper is also known in French as La Cloche du Matin = Morning Bell) is a daily newspaper published every morning except Sunday.

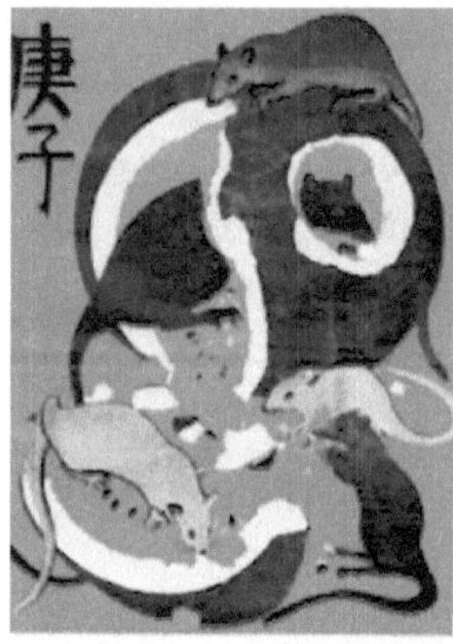

Left: cover designed by the artist Nguyễn Gia Trí for the spring issue of *Tự Do* in 1960, the year Canh Tý, a "year of the rat"; Right: The artist Nguyễn Gia Trí sitting with Như Phong after 1975. *(Phạm Phú Minh, personal archives)*

In 1955, one year after the Geneva Accords, the daily journal *Tự Do* came into existence in Saigon with a board of editors that included all the northern writers who had emigrated to the South. These people had all had experience with the communists in the North. At the start of the journal, the editorial offices included Tam Lang (Vũ Đình Chí), Mặc Đỗ (Đỗ Quang Bình), Đinh Hùng (pen name Thần Đăng), Như Phong (Lê Văn Tiến), and Mặc Thu (Lưu Đức Sinh). Tam Lang fulfilled the role of editor-in-chief. Mặc Thu acted as the manager, and Như Phong, the youngest of the group, acted as the editorial secretary. Vũ Khắc Khoan wrote for *Tự Do* but was not was not formally associated with the editorial board. Later on *Tự Do* grew larger and took on three new members: Nguyễn Hoạt (pen name Hiếu Chân),[2] Hi Di (Bùi Xuân Uyên), and the artist Phạm Tăng.

---

2 Nguyễn Hoạt, pen name Hiếu Chân. Born 1919, Hà Nội. A refugee to the South in 1954, member of editorial board of Tự Do Daily, author of a delightful column consisting conversation-like essays: "Should It Be Said or Not?" ("Nói hay Đừng"). After May 1975 he was put in prison by the communist authorities where he died in March 1986. Author of Trăng Nước Đồng Nai ("The Moon Over Đồng Nai River", 1958)

According to Như Phong, the first phase of the daily *Tự Do* was rather brief. It was shut down, not because of internal problems, but for political reasons. The office of the Vice President (Văn phòng Phủ Tổng Thống) saw that it was very influential and that it enjoyed the fervent support of northerners who had emigrated to the South, but it had articles that criticised the government, and no one working for it was Roman Catholic, which was a more sensitive matter still, and it lacked people who were from Central Vietnam.

A short time later, the daily *Tự Do* resumed publication, but with a new chief of staff, Phạm Việt Tuyền, and a new manager, Kiều Văn Lân. Both had worked in the Presidential Palace, and both were Roman Catholics. Before that, beginning in 1955, Phạm Việt Tuyền had been editor-in-chief of the weekly *Tân Kỷ Nguyên* ("New Age") with an editorial board that included Lê Xuân Khoa, Lê Thành Trí, Trần Việt Châu, and Hồ Nam.

As the daily *Tự Do* entered its new phase, Như Phong continued to act as the editorial board's secretary. Hiếu Chân (Nguyễn Hoạt) continued to be in charge of the column "Everyday Affairs" (Chuyện Hằng Ngày), which later changed its name to "Should It Be Said or Not?" (Nói hay Đừng) and was very popular due to its sharply satirical writing. Two other figures took turns writing this column: Mai Nguyệt (that is, the writer Tchya Đái Đức Tuấn) and Phạm Xuân Ninh (pen name Hà Thượng Nhân or Tiểu Nhã). Mention should also be made of the participation of the political commentator Mai Xuyên (Đỗ Thúc Vịnh), Trần Việt Sơn, and the artist Nguyễn Gia Trí.

There was an event that occurred in the time of the First Republic that affected the journal *Tự Do* – it is by now just a historical datum, but it seems proper to mention it here. The matter concerned the cover of the spring issue in 1960, a Canh Tý year. Because the word "Tý" indicated that it was the year of the rat, the cover naturally featured that animal, as had been the case for untold numbers of years. The cover artist created an image of five rats munching on fragments of a large watermelon. Some people conjectured that the image was intended to suggest that the five brothers and sisters of the ruling Ngô family were greedily engaged in "hollowing out" the nation of Vietnam. Though without foundation, the rumor spread, and as a result the issue was confiscated and almost all the members of the editorial board were arrested, except for Như Phong and Phạm Việt Tuyền. Then Phạm Việt Tuyền lost his position as editor-in-chief and the journal was shut down in August of 1963, only three months before the military upheaval of November 1, 1963 and the tragic assassinations of Ngô Đình Diệm and his brother brought an end to the First Republic, which had lasted for nine years.

When speaking of *Tự Do* in its first two phases, lasting from 1955 to 1963, we cannot forget to mention the strong impression made by Như Phong (Lê Văn Tiến). As secretary for the editorial board, he devoted himself totally to the journal, and in addition wrote a daily feuilleton under the pen name Lý Thắng. *Smoke and Waves* (*Khói Sóng*) is a long and very attractive novel that he wrote as a young man following in the artistic footsteps of Hoàng Đạo (Nguyễn Tường Long) and Nhất Linh (Nguyễn Tường Tam), who rebelled against the communists in the war zones of Vĩnh Yên and Việt Trì. Until the last days of his life, Như Phong often referred to *Smoke and Waves*, expressing the hope that he could recover a copy. But I know that Như Phong himself had destroyed the manuscript in 1975 prior to his arrest.

It is possible that the libraries of Cornell and Hawaii Universities have complete sets of *Tự Do*, which would include *Smoke and Waves*. It has been fourteen years since Như Phong's death. When I met his adopted daughter Ánh Chân, she referred again to that wish of her father.

After the book *Thoughts of Như Phong, Journalist* (*Tưởng Niệm Nhà Báo Như Phong*) was published in 2016, I learned from Phạm Lệ Hương, a Senior Librarian currently residing in the U.S., that a set of all the issues of *Tự Do* is preserved in the Library of Saigon (formerly called *"Thư viện Quốc Gia"* - the National Library), that the novel *Smoke and Waves* appears in its issues over a period of five years (from 1955 to 1963), and that a group of her friends had, with a great deal of patience and effort, typed out all its sections – so that by now the work can be regarded as restored, though still not in complete form – a very welcome piece of news. Phase two will occur when the work *Smoke and Waves* is published in book form overseas, an event that I hope will occur in the near future.

NHƯ PHONG THE STRATEGIST:

Như Phong's profession was journalism, and Đỗ Quý Toàn refers to him respectfully as "a journalist's journalist" ("nhà báo của các nhà báo"). But Như Phong can also be termed a strategist, and even as a "coup broker." An American journalist of former days, Sol Sanders of the U.S. News and World Report, a friend of Như Phong's for more than half a century, from 1951 to 2001, referred to Như Phong as "My Coup-Broker Friend" when, on leaving Hanoi for Saigon, he wrote an article concerning Như Phong.

Như Phong was very close to Dr. Phan Huy Quát, but didn't accept any official position when the latter became prime minister. Như Phong was acquainted with a great many political figures, including opposition figures, generals and members of religious parties, such as the Cao Đài and the Hòa Hảo.

There are anecdotes about how Như Phong engaged in behind-the-scenes recruitment for General Nguyễn Cao Kỳ's "War Cabinet" (Nội các Chiến tranh), but later stood aside from his government, not accepting any appointment as a minister under Kỳ. Then in 1966, in order to support General Kỳ, Như Phong took on the role of his campaign manager, uniting the three wings of his "coconut party" with other groups of special interests, regions and political parties, but all three wings lost in the elections.

He was at all times a strategist, a "person on the sidelines," and never directly entered the world of government. One cannot speak of his political successes or failures, because he never became a true "homo politicus."

THE DAYS IN THE MONTH OF MAY 1975:

Of all the people who have attempted to understand the Vietnamese communists, Như Phong was second only to Hoàng Văn Chí, author of the two classic works *From Colonialism to Communism* (*Từ Thực Dân tới Cộng Sản*, 1964) and *Hundreds of Flowers Competing to Bloom in the North* (*Trăm Hoa Đua Nở Trên Đất Bắc*, 1959), continuously republished in subsequent years. Another pen name used by Như Phong was "Cô Thần" ("Lone Wolf"). This name appeared in a series or articles about the communists in the north that he wrote for *Tự Do*.

Foreign correspondents all placed a high value on Như Phong's understanding of the communist world. Whenever asked, he was able to respond at once and in full detail to any question concerning individuals in the communist system. Thus, Sol Sanders, an American journalist who had spent many years in Vietnam working for the U.S. News and World Report, exclaimed, *"Tiến was a walking biographical dictionary!"*

With his thorough knowledge of the communists, and with clear foreknowledge of the endless days and months in imprisonment camps that awaited him, Như Phong still chose to remain in the country. Foreign correspondents who had known him for years were eager to help Như Phong escape from Saigon before April 30, 1975; The Navy and the Airforce both had places reserved for his escape, but he stubbornly chose to stay.

His moving farewell to the family of Đỗ Thúc Vịnh on Tự Đức Street has been described by Vịnh's wife:

> *"Toward the end of April, starting perhaps around the 24th or 25th, Như Phong would come to our house and say, "You must find a way to leave right away! It doesn't matter where you go, as long as you get out of this country. They are now about to arrive here." My husband would take his hand and ask, "What about you, Tiến? Are you going to leave?" "No," he would say. "The two of you must leave for the sake of your children's future. As for me, I'll head for the western region [the Mekong Delta] and look for a way to resist them. Then*

Như Phong with a number of friends who are now also deceased. Như Phong and Võ Phiến; below from the left: Như Phong and Đỗ Thúc Vịnh, Lê Ngộ Châu and Như Phong *(Ngô Thế Vinh, personal archives)*

we'll meet again later on. Having said this, he would race out and leave rapidly on his motorbike. The two of us would gaze at each other, stupefied at the boldness of his decision. Just when everyone, including even the most dignified of our generals, were feeling helpless and seeking ways to escape, Tiến, full of courage and dauntless determination, was determined to follow in the footsteps of his ancestors, and refuse to bow before the enemy. He was determined to remain in a place of mortal danger in order to seek a path to survival."

(from Lòng Thành Tưởng Niệm)

When noon arrived on April 30, right after the order to surrender had been issued, he very likely observed rains of uniformly white confetti descending from the upper stories of many buildings–the shredded remains of military and official documents that had to be destroyed before communist troops conducted searches through the whole city of Saigon. Who knows how many military shoes and hats were hastily scattered on the city streets!

And then the noise of metal treads resounded as T54 tanks carrying liberation flags rolled down Trần Hưng Đạo Boulevard toward the center of Saigon.

A few days later I met Như Phong at the house of the lawyer Mai Văn Lễ across from the Sùng Chính Hospital on Trần Hưng Đạo Boulevard. Mai Văn Lễ was for a time the chair of the Law School at Huế University during the time of the Buddhist struggles. Now, he was alone. His wife and two children had left Saigon a week before.

Always a person in advance of current events, Như Phong foresaw correctly everything that was about to transpire: the campaigns against capitalism, the policy of changing the currency used by each household, after which the old bills would turn to waste paper–and then the appearance of a Gulag Archipelago. Everybody strove to use what money remained to them to purchase gold, or black-market dollars, but such things were not easy to obtain at that time. Như Phong just suggested to people that they purchase rolls of high-quality linen and stuff them in their sofa mattresses–later, when they needed to, they could bring them out gradually and sell them one by one in order to live. But this was just a mode of talking; everybody maintained a "wait and see" attitude.

Later on, Như Phong was arrested twice by the communists and in all spent fourteen years in captivity. The first time lasted from 1976 to 1988, and the second from 1990 to 1992. Như Phong's quasi-military sense of honor remained hard as steel throughout his imprisonment, which included years of mistreatment, periods of solitary confinement, lack of sustenance, and periods when he went on hunger strike for many days, not to protest anything, but to *"Pray for The Nation's Prosperity and the People's Security,"* with the result that he grew physically weak, though he always remained sharp of intellect. Như Phong made not only his fellow prisoners, but his jailors as well, regard him with respect. In the article "Remembering Cậu Tiến" the young prisoner Đinh Quang Anh Thái, wrote quite fully about his respect for the dauntlessly spirited prisoner Như Phong when the two of them were both in the Chí Hòa Prison. That Như Phong survived was astonishing to many people who knew he had suffered from tuberculosis some years before that time.

After his release from imprisonment, Như Phong chose to live inconspicuously. Through his acquaintance with the writer Doãn Quốc Sỹ, he was able to obtain a plot of earth from a seven-hectare farm owned by a married couple who were friends with Sỹ. There, Như Phong built a house with a brick foundation and a roof topped with coconut leaves. He grew rose bushes around the house. But the main object of his attention were potted orchid plants of all types. Như Phong adored orchids, just as the writer Nhất Linh did when he lived next to the Đa Mê Stream in Đà Lạt.

Phan Nhật Nam also suffered fourteen years of imprisonment, including periods of solitary confinement. After his release from imprisonment, Nam took up residence in a house on the opposite side of the river, which he crossed regularly to visit Như Phong. On a couple of occasions when Doãn Quốc Sỹ came to visit the farm, he also dropped in to visit Như Phong. During this period also, literary friends and acquaintances from his time of imprisonment, such as Đằng Giao and his wife, and even Tô Thùy Yên, the author of *Journey to the Spratly Islands* (*Trường Sa Hành*) were also frequent guests at his dwelling. One memorable event recounted by Phan Nhật Nam was that he once accidentally destroyed Như Phong's whole orchid garden when, in an effort to help his friend to water the garden, he used brackish water obtained from a nearby creek. Phan Nhật Nam at length emigrated to the U.S. in 1993, one year earlier than Như Phong.

NHƯ PHONG JOINS THE "FRIENDS OF THE MEKONG"

In 1993, when Như Phong was still in Vietnam, the organization Human Rights Watch / Asia issued an announcement saying that Như Phong had been awarded the Free Expression Award, an honor bestowed on journalists, and he was praised on that occasion as a man who had used his pen to defend Human Rights. The truth is that the choice of a man with a reputation like Như Phong did more honor to the granting organization than to the recipient.

In spite of efforts from many directions to secure Như Phong's release, it was not until 1994 when, after much calculation, the communists gave permission to the man they had imprisoned for fourteen years to leave the country. But he came to the U.S., not as a former political prisoner, but according to a family resettlement policy, known as ODP (Orderly Departure Program) thanks to the sponsorship of a younger brother with the same father but a different mother: Nguyễn Ngọc Ấn was a TV cameraman in Sacramento. Ấn also, like his elder brother, was in the media business. Như Phong was also sponsored by the family of his friend Đường Thiện Đồng. They were then living in Irvine.

When Như Phong was released from imprisonment, he lived in seclusion in a house roofed with coconut leaves in Hóc Môn. *(Đinh Quang Anh Thái, personal archives)*

Như Phong watering his pots of orchids. *(Đinh Quang Anh Thái, personal archives)*

Như Phong had numberless friends in his active, eventful life, but he acquired many new friends as well on American soil. A distinguishing feature of these new friends was that they were very young, younger than Như Phong by two or three generations. They valued him and quickly drew close to him. Như Phong planted dreams in their minds – he was always a "dream-sower." Unlike them, I had known Như Phong through many phases of activity prior to 1975.

On meeting him again in California, I saw that he was the same Như Phong, sharp and full of ideas, as always. At the age of 71, after almost fourteen years of imprisonment. He was still hard and healthy, but had not been able to give up smoking. This worried me, and I spoke to him about it some. Như Phong was like a "*Pine Tree in a Thunderstorm*," (Cây Tùng Trước Bão) to borrow the title of a book by Hoàng Khởi Phong. Like a true intellectual, he had the virtue of open-mindedness, and was always willing and ready to take on any new study, such as computer use, email, and fax machines. When a group of his young friends gave him a laptop, he began using it to write newspaper pieces and to send articles as attachments, and his laptop became one of his inseparable tools from then on.

Friends welcoming Như Phong to the U.S. From the right: Như Phong, Đường Thiện Đồng, Trần Huy Bích, Võ Phiến, and Ngô Thế Vinh. *(photo taken in the home of Ngô Thế Vinh)*

I have an unforgettable memory of an event involving Như Phong that took place in the refugee capital called "Little Saigon." It was a fine, sunny Saturday morning in southern California. Như Phong invited me that day to meet several young friends of his who belonged to a group that I had not heard of previously: the "Friends of the Mekong." They were having their first public discussion in the Activity Room in the offices of the newspaper *Người Việt* ("The Vietnamese People"). The discussion panel that day included the engineer Phạm Phan Long, the PhD Phạm Văn Hải, and the journalist Đỗ Quý Toàn. The engineer Phạm Phan Long was the first person to raise an alarm concerning the danger to the Mekong posed by the plan of China to build dams all along its course, beginning with the initial Manwan Dam in Yunnan Province. At that time (1993), only the first of those dams had been built: the 1,500 megawatt dam on the Lancang-Mekong river, referred to as the Manwan Dam.

That was truly a fateful day for me, because it was my first encounter with a new problem facing the country: the steps being taken to bring about the unsustainable development of the Mekong River. On that day also, I made the acquaintance of a group of new friends, such as the engineers Phạm Phan Long, Ngô Minh Triết,

Nguyễn Hữu Chung, and other people who belonged to the Mekong Forum, which later was to become the Việt Ecology Foundation.

I must mention as well an article printed in *Tuổi Trẻ Chủ Nhật* ("Sunday Youth," Nov. 3, 1996): "Exploiting the Mekong River: a Vietnamese Perspective" ("Khai thác Sông Mekong: Nhìn từ góc độ Việt Nam"). Though the author's name was given as Phạm Phan Long, it was actually the work of four people, all of them specialists who lived abroad. The others were Phạm Văn Hải (a PhD living in the U.S.), the engineer Nguyễn Hữu Chung (Canada) and Bình An Sơn (a PhD living in Australia.) The content of the article is just as timely now as it was then.

In 1999, a Mekong Conference was organized jointly by the Mekong Forum and the Vietnamese American Science and Technology Society in southern California under the title "The Crisis Facing the Mekong River: the Influence of Development on the river current, farmlands and inhabitants along the Mekong," with the participation of groups from the provinces of Tiền Giang and Hậu Giang, the doctorate holder Sin Meng Srun, a Cambodian based in the U.S., and Aviva Imhof of the International Rivers Network. At the conclusion of the conference, a formal announcement was issued, entitled "The 1999 Mekong River Declaration," which was sent to the MRC (Mekong River Commission) and many related organizations.

I should also mention here that Như Phong himself was the person who took up a pen and helped the Mekong Forum by making a Vietnamese translation of this document. The engineer Phạm Phan Long was moved to remark that "His Vietnamese translation differed entirely from the dry, lifeless translations that we had made. He infused what he wrote with the spirit of our people so as to give voice to the misery of our brethren in the delta area in the face of the huge problem that is about to descend on them."

Until the day he died, Như Phong continued to participate in the activities of the Friends of the Mekong with a geopolitical awareness of the connectedness of the Mekong's problems with the fate of the nation.

And in the 21 years that have flowed by since then (1995 – 2016), I have remained a faithful member of the "Friends of the Mekong," and have continued to act as a "storm-foretelling bird," chirping in response to the black, poisonous clouds growing denser by the day, that threaten us from the north.

THE GREAT DREAM OF NHƯ PHONG

Như Phong arrived in the U.S. with his head full of projects that he perhaps had sketched out during his many years of imprisonment. Among those schemes was one for a Vietnamese Journalism Network of global scope. Như Phong not only talked about this, but wrote about it with burning enthusiasm. His view was that we had to prepare now for a "post-communist Vietnam." He dreamed of becoming a power-wielding mogul within this journalistic system, holding in his hands journals, broadcasts, and television programs extending throughout the territory of Vietnam.

He would say that if the ship called "Hope," with its floating hospital, had been able to moor in the Saigon harbor before 1975, then why couldn't a ship called "Communications" belonging to

Khai thac song Mekong : nhin tu goc do Viet Nam

Khai thác sông Mekông...

Thị trường...

"Exploiting the Mekong River: a Vietnamese Perspective," the article printed in Tuổi Trẻ Chủ Nhật, Nov. 3, 1996

From left: Bùi Diễm, Trương Trọng Trác, Đỗ Văn, Như Phong, Nguyễn Tường Giang, Phạm Dương Hiển. *(Nguyễn Tường Giang, personal archives)*

the overseas Vietnamese community be gotten ready drop anchor somewhere in the Saigon harbor like a floating newspaper, complete with a broadcasting station and a TV station? In his entire career as a journalist, he had never seen the appearance of anything like such a grand prospect – according to him, his plan for the ship "Communications" would be a timely solution for Vietnam renewing itself after the dissolution of communism. A printing press capable of producing newspapers could be established on that ship, and it would have systems of floating broadcasting and television stations, the programs of which would cover the entire territory of the nation, and which would be the basis for a local-global network connecting the people within the country to all the Vietnamese communities distributed over the earth.

This great dream of Như Phong's was an utterly lonely one, grown on foreign soil with no financial support, and necessarily limited in time, because Như Phong had stepped across the threshold of age and frailty. His young friends all honored and loved him, but they regarded him as a person "walking on clouds," as the writer Nguyễn-

Xuân Hoàng put it. He had the romantic idealism of a modern-day Don Quixote, and one may suppose that it was due to this that he always had the air of a young man. And now I'm moved to remember a line full of fervant idealism by Dương Nghiễm Mậu, brought to me by the artist Nguyên Khai: *"The horse is exhausted, and the way to travel long–how can we predict what will happen?"*

And seven years after setting foot on U.S. soil, Như Phong, prostrate before this great dream, died of lung cancer at the age of seventy-eight.

A LITERARY PORTRAIT OF NHƯ PHONG

In my own writing, I made Như Phong into a fictional character, a journalist named Khắc in the documentary novel *The Nine Dragons Drained Dry, The East Sea in Turmoil (Cửu Long Cạn Dòng, Biển Đông Dậy Sóng)*, published in 2000, a year before Như Phong's death. An excerpt:

"A man with white-flecked hair wearing a pair of extremely thick glasses to correct nearsightedness was stepping lightly and rapidly along a line of jacaranda trees full of purple blossoms, a sign of truly hot days to come in southern California. He gave one the impression of a pine tree in a storm, who had weathered untold upheavals brought on by the times, though he had no lack of illnesses due to many months and years of imprisonment. Because of the lung disease for which he was undergoing treatment, the weather here was one reason that made him decide against the eastern U.S., with its Big Apple, as a propitious place to live. To him, as to many exiled artists choosing to travel to America, New York City had the attractive power of a metal-smelting factory that could turn one either into a heap of ashes or into pure steel. For a long time extending over years, he had gone down to subway trains, running noisily along as if carrying loads of wood beneath the earth and even beneath rivers, like a city underneath a different city. How could people have the power to create such wonders before having stepped into a world of advanced technology? For him, New York at that time was the only true America – the only place where one could take innovative steps with the pioneering generation. But then he would have to live in New York – a narrow, crowded place bustling with competitive strife–and he had to ask himself if he still belonged to the generation of those numberless refugees who had braved the waves and winds of the ocean to alight upon a new continent.

"On the day that he flew from New York to California, Mr. Khắc stopped in Washington just when the cherry trees there were flowering. Before he could be affected by the happy sight of the flowering trees, he came to a halt before the Wall of Sorrow. Gazing across to the other side of the park, he saw the White House where President Clinton had just completed two terms. Clinton, as everyone knew, had avoided military service in his youth. Equally well-known was the fact that he had smoked, but not inhaled, marijuana, on the campus of Oxford University at the height of the Vietnam war, when Hanoi was doing all it could to increase the number of naïve, innocent American youths who were going to their graves. At that time Mr. Khắc had been a war correspondent mingling with soldiers of the South who were advancing miserably over muddy fields or highland plateaus. Now, twenty-five years later, he had returned a second time to the U.S., and was standing before the wall of black marble, and in his mind were not only sixty thousand dead American youths, but piled above that were ranks and ranks and layers and layers of the millions of nameless Vietnamese who had had to die useless deaths due to the mistaken ideas of human beings…

"It was always the same when he came here–he could not repress his feelings. An American journalist, a friend of his, expressed the feeling that, regardless whether he had in the past chosen to resist communism on the muddy fields of Vietnam, or had resisted that very war on the city streets of the U.S., the existence of this wall always gave him pain. Not to mention the fact that he himself had had many friends among the sixty thousand on the wall who before their deaths had wrestled with the meaning of this war, and had never found an answer that gave them peace. Mr. Khắc suddenly had

Visiting the Vietnam Veterans Memorial.
From left: Nguyễn Tường Giang, Như Phong, Ngô Thế Vinh.
(photo by Phạm Bội Hoàn, former CBS cameraman)

the feeling that he was lost in a reality that seemed like a fantasy, or virtual reality – though the past was indeed a historical truth. When would he come to realize that that very past was in fact a fantasy – actually, he should have seen this early, so as to withdraw himself from the situation and discard its heavy burdens, and walk with lighter steps later on…

"After some long, lonely months working in a library in the south of France, Mr. Khắc had occasion to return to Little Saigon on none other than the 30th of April – but it was a quarter of a century later. Amid a forest of flags, one could still hear slogans enjoining young men to serve. As always, victory had countless "parents," while defeats were always "sons of bà Phước"–meaning "orphans." But Mr. Khắc had to ask himself whether the Vietnamese on this side or the other side had gained anything from this fratricidal war. Could there still be "historic dignity" belonging to the losers? Why not?" (Chapter 27, *The Nine Dragons Drained Dry, The East Sea in Turmoil*, Văn Nghệ Publishers, 2000)

Như Phong read that book also and wrote a review of it, but I have never been able to locate it. In the English translation of *The Nine Dragons Drained Dry, The East Sea in Turmoil* (Việt Ecology Press, 2016), the name of the character "Mr. Khắc" is changed to "Như Phong, journalist."

THE FINAL FAREWELL TO NHƯ PHONG

The journalist Như Phong died at the age of 78 on December 12, 2001 at 9:40 p.m. in the city of Fairfax, Virginia. The funeral was a simple one, and his wish was that someday his ashes would be scattered over a stretch of earth in his homeland.

This wish fulfilled, a number of young "second-generation" friends chose Như Phong as the subject of their doctoral dissertations–for these were in fact dissertations on the history of Vietnamese journalism in the latter half of the 20th century in which the activities of Như Phong provided a unifying thread joining many phases of the stormiest period in Vietnamese history.

Finally, let me express here the hope that after the book *Thoughts of Như Phong, Journalist* (*Tưởng Niệm Nhà Báo Như Phong*) is brought out on the occasion of his fifteenth death anniversary, his friends will form a plan to recover and publish his long novel *Smoke and Waves* (*Khói Sóng*) in accordance with Như Phong's final wishes.

Littlle Saigon, 10/07/2016

VÕ PHIẾN A WRITER IN EXILE FOR FORTY YEARS

Portrait of Võ Phiến in 2015
(Viễn Phố, personal archives)

"Before and after the period 1954 – 1975 in the South, I never saw any other place in our country where literature was able to develop in such an atmosphere of freedom and openness." (Võ Phiến in a conversation with Đặng Tiến. Oct. 28, 1995)

One can say that Võ Phiến is among the most written about and discussed of our authors. Before I became personally acquainted with Võ Phiến, I was thoroughly familiar with the characters in his novels, such as anh Ba Thê đồng thời ("Three-Wives-at-once"), anh Bốn thôi ("No More than Four"), ông Năm tản ("Five-Times-a-Refugee"), ông tú Từ Lâm ("Licentiate Từ Lâm"), and sister Bốn chìa vôi ("Four-

Days in Saigon in the 70's; from the right: Bình Nguyên Lộc, Võ Phiến, Lê Tất Điều. *(Viễn Phố, personal archives)*

wagtails") from his fictional pieces *Farewell* (*Giã Từ*), *Again, a Letter From Home* (*Lại Thư Nhà*), and *Alone* (*Một Mình*)...

Then, through my close friend Nghiêu Đề, who took me to the office of *Bách Khoa*, I got to know him some years before 1960, a connection that continued when he went abroad later on.

VÕ PHIẾN'S *CATCHING CHILDREN AMID GREEN FIELDS:*

Võ Phiến wrote *Catching Children Amid Green Fields* (*Bắt Trẻ Đồng Xanh*) and published it in *Bách Khoa* in October 1968. Its title was borrowed from the translation by Phùng Khánh and Phùng Thăng of *The Catcher in the Rye* by the American writer J.D. Salinger, but its content had to do with the communist practice in the North of kidnapping children in the South and bringing them to the North for training, so as to reintroduce them to the South later on. The Communists started doing this as soon as the Geneva Accords were signed in 1954. Võ Phiến wrote:

"In the final cruel phase of fighting in the South, the party and the communist nation would never undergo the heavy toil of collecting youths here and taking them to the North if there were not a serious reason to do so. They are exposing themselves to so much difficulty and exhausting labor… They are striving to implement a plan to kidnap children on a large scale and over the widest possible area. Our people have discovered that children are being kidnapped everywhere from Quảng Trị, Thừa Thiên, Pleiku, Kontum in the central area to Mỹ Tho and Cà Mau in the south; and people have even encountered children being moved to North Vietnam by airplane from Cambodia or being led north in small groups along the Hồ Chí Minh trail.

"Oh, children of the verdant delta of South Vietnam forced to travel in your ranks and squads, one after the other, to the mountains of North Vietnam! Your personal destinies have been cut off from this moment on, and the country will be plunged by your departure into a state of endless misery! The disaster now befalling you will be a disaster for your entire land! (Võ Phiến, *Catching Children Amid Green Fields*, *Bách Khoa*, October, 1968)

Catching Children was not at all an occasional essay or a short story; it was rather a political essay, a white paper denouncing the barbarism of the Vietnamese communists, who never harbored a sincere desire for peace – if there was to be a conference, it was merely an expedient they used to delay hostilities and prepare for the next phase of fighting. The article had the force of prophesy – an alarm signal that raised an upheaval in public opinion both within the country and among interational communities – and the price that Võ Phiến had to pay for this was that the Việt Cộng accused him of crimes and threatened his life – this was right after the killing of the journalist Từ Chung, the general secretary of the newspaper Political Discourse (*Chính Luận*), by a communist assassination squad. According to Lê Tất Điều, there was a period when Võ Phiến entertained the thought of going down to the Hòa Hảo area for refuge – it was a region regarded as being immune to every sort of communist infiltration. That was the reason why Võ Phiến taught literature for a time in the Hòa Hảo University in Long Xuyên. Adversity sometimes brings good fortune – it was there that Võ Phiến made the acquaintance of Đỗ Văn Gia, a young colleague who was then teaching Eastern Philosophy at the

Lê Ngộ Châu, the editor-in-chief of Bách Khoa; meeting again with Võ Phiến in the U.S. *(Viễn Phố, personal archives)*

same university. Later, after they went abroad, it was Đỗ Văn Gia, when he was a lecturer in Vietnamese language and literature at Cornell starting in 1982, that he assisted Võ Phiến by providing him with large quantities of material for his set of books on the literature of South Vietnam.

VIETNAMESE RICE-PAPER TRANSPLANTED TO THE U.S.

From 1980 on, Mr. and Mrs. Võ Phiến served as public functionaries in Los Angeles District, and have thus far lived in their home at 5621 Baltimore Street for twenty-three years. The house has a spacious garden with all sorts of fruit trees – lime, orange, grapefruit, and persimmon. Most plentiful of all are the rose bushes heavy with blossoms, with a bronze bust of Võ Phiến carved by Ưu Đàm, son of the artist Rừng. Inside the house, aside from bookshelves, there are statues of the Buddha, and of Christ, with only a small altar for family ancestors. In this house also, Võ Phiến wrote a number of his overseas works: the series *Literature of the South* (bộ *Văn Học Miền Nam*), *Letters Sent to a Friend* (*Thư Gửi Bạn*), *Intact* (*Nguyên Vẹn*), *Stories Truly Short* (*Truyện Thật Ngắn*), and *Dialogues* (*Đối Thoại*)...

My visits to Võ Phiến usually occurred at the end of the week, on Saturdays, because he and his guests were still of an age that required

From the left: Huỳnh Sanh Thông (1926 – 2008), Đỗ Văn Gia (1946 – 1992), Từ Mai Trần Huy Bích (1936 –) *(Võ Phiến, personal archives)*

them to hold down jobs. Those who visited generally belonged to distinct groups. Sometimes it would be Nguyễn Mộng Giác with Từ Mẫn (Võ Thắng Tiết), sometimes Tạ Chí Đại Trường with Thạch Hãn (Lê Thọ Giáo), and sometimes Mr. and Mrs. Trần Huy Bích – Bích's wife was an especially close friend of Mrs. Võ Phiến.

Trùng Dương at times referred to Mrs. Võ Phiến as "the woman behind the multi-volume *Literature of the South 1954 – 1975*." But it seems that I should also record here that a number of other friends contributed many sets of books from that period that they procured from libraries in French and American Universities to help Võ Phiến with materials necessary to complete his project. These people included Đặng Tiến in Europe, Trần Huy Bích on the interlibrary loan staff at UCLA, Đỗ Văn Gia at Cornell, and the artist Võ Đình. And before that, Huỳnh Sanh Thông at Yale University (translator of the *Tale of Kiều*) was the person whose introduction enabled Võ Phiến to secure a grant for his work from the Indochina Studies Program of the Social Science Research Council.

The guests usually stayed to eat lunch with Mr. and Mrs. Võ Phiến. The meals that Mrs. Võ Phiến prepared sometimes included a few dishes brought by the guests. To this day, there is one dish prepared by Mrs. Võ Phiến that I cannot forget – it was a kind of rice-paper (bánh tráng) dipped in water absolutely unique to Bình Định Province, flavored to taste with fish sauce with bits of lime and red pepper. The lime grew on the trees in the garden, and the red peppers grew there as well. Everyone thought that this simple dish with an exotic flavor was delicious, and the guests would find it still more delicious when the host would recount witty anecdotes linking rice-paper to the victory of Emperor Quang Trung – the rice paper had been used as dry rations for his troops during his lightning-swift march from Nghệ An to Thăng Long, where he vanquished 200,000 Qing-dynasty troops.

A CONVERSATION WITH ĐẶNG TIẾN IN 1998:

On November 4, 1998, Võ Phiến sent me photocopies of a three-page handwritten transcript of a conversation he had had with Đặng Tiến. It was accompanied by a few lines, as follows:

My dear friend: This is an edited version, not a literal transcription of what we said. When we were actually speaking, there were a few spots where Đặng Tiến interjected a few words. It seems that the broadcast in all likelihood occurred on Oct. 28, 1998. I don't know if this is correct or not. Yours, Võ Phiến.

Đặng Tiến (pen name Nam Chi), active as a literary critic starting from the end of the 1950s, was a "friend of old times" (bạn cựu, an expression applied by Võ Phiến to all acquaintances of longstanding). Đặng Tiến and Võ Phiến were like Bóyá and Zhōng Zǐqí[1]. Đặng Tiến followed all the literary accomplishments of Võ Phiến with avid appreciation from their first appearances in 1954 and through all the years that followed, and produced many critical articles and book reviews concerning his works.

As for me, I didn't get to hear that broadcast, but if I had, I would most likely have found that the content did not differ from the written transcript made by Võ Phiến. Through Phạm Phú Minh, I was able to communicate via email with Đặng Tiến, who was then in France, and

---

1 This refers to two figures in Chinese historical legend. Bóyá was the greatest zither player in the realm, and Zhōng Zǐqí was the only man in the realm who could listen to Bóyá's playing with complete understanding. The use of this allusion suggests that Võ Phiến and Đặng Tiến were complete soul-mates (EH).

asked him about the matter. He replied that he had no memory of the occasion. I wasn't surprised– fourteen years had passed since then. After that I sent him photocopies of the three pages that Võ Phiến had sent me, hoping that this would jog his memory and enable him to send me more details. But three days later, I received a reply in the same vein: "To NTV: I don't recall this. I'll search my memory and answer later. Stay in touch. ĐT.

As for Võ Phiến, there was no hope that he would recall things that occurred seventeen years earlier, but I shall nevertheless record the content of those three handwritten pages (only 938 words in total) as a datum that has some value as an overview of literature in the South in the period 1954 – 1975.

"My dear friend (Đặng Tiến)

"At the end of the pre-war period [c. 1946] Mr. Vũ Ngọc Phan made a critical study of literature in Vietnam over the preceding thirty years. Among all the prose writers of that period, he could distinguish only three writers of the south and central regions (Võ Phiến noted in the margin that they were Hồ Biểu Chánh, Thanh Tịnh, and Nguyễn Vỹ). All three were story-writers. As for plays, memoirs, and essays – there was nothing.

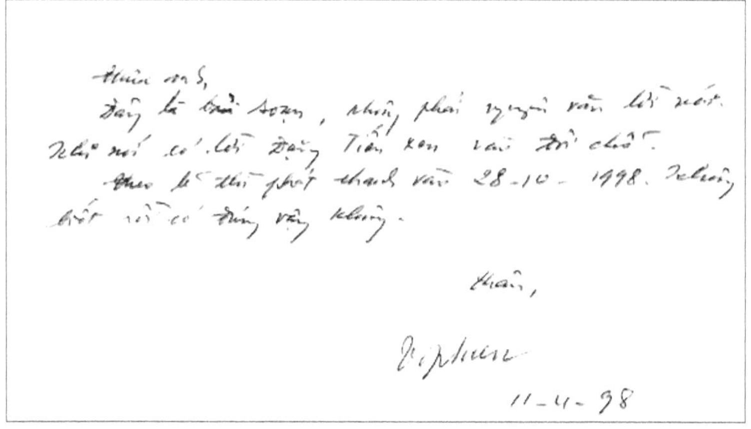

The handwritten note from Võ Phiến to Ngô Thế Vinh, November 4, 1998. *(Ngô Thế Vinh, personal archives)*

From left: Võ Phiến at the age of 70 (photo by Nguyễn Bá Khanh) and Đặng Tiến *(Viễn Phố, personal archives)*

"Toward the end of the period 1954 – 1975, Mr. Cao Huy Khanh made a critical study that included only novels written over a twenty-year period in South Vietnam. He stated that close to 200 people produced novels during this period, and of those writers, approximately 60 figures produced work of value. If anyone should suspect that Cao Huy Khanh was influenced by partiality to his friends and reduce his estimate by half – that is, thirty novelists of value – then those twenty years still produced more than ten times as many significant novelists than the thirty years that came before. And that is to pay no attention to the essayists and dramatists of the later period.

As for the pre-war period in the central area – from Phú Yên to Bình Thuận – no writer in that region became well-known – except for the married couple of Đông Hồ,[2] one could not find a single individual whose reputation had spread in the literary world. This view is based on the work of Vũ Ngọc Phan and Hoài Thanh.

But then in the twenty years beginning in 1954, one writer after another appeared in Phú Yên (Võ Hồng), in Ninh Thuận and Bình

---

2 This refers to the poet Lâm Tấn Phác (1906 - 1969) and his wife Mộng Tuyết (1914 - 2007), also a poet. They came from Hà Tiên in Kiên Giang Province in the extreme southwest of Vietnam. He used Đông Hồ ("East Lake") as a pseudonym, borrowing the name of a local geographical feature (EH).

Thuận (Nguyễn Bắc Sơn and Nguyễn Đức Sơn), in Cà Mau (Sơn Nam), Long Xuyên (Nguyễn Hiến Lê), Gia Định (Tô Thùy Yên), Vĩnh Long (Nguyễn Thị Thụy Vũ), Sóc Trăng (Vương Hồng Sển) [the names of writers in the preceding parentheses were all added by Võ Phiến]... The numbers of writers and poets were so great, and the literary world became so much broader, that this can only be regarded as a significant contribution.

Another contribution was the spirit of freedom, of expansive liberation in this literary period. Everyone spoke of the spirit of oppression that had prevailed in all the periods of domination by a foreign power – whether by China or by France. Actually, it was not just in such periods that this oppression existed – even in periods of independence, both the feudal warlord regimes and the democratic republics in our land failed to tolerate criticism of those who held power. Even when independence and democracy was established, only one kind of freedom was promulgated: the freedom to praise those in high positions.

In the Vietnam of 1954 to 1975, though in the midst of war, a totally different type of literature arose. Gay and sharp laughter spread freely over books and journals, laughter that attacked mistaken deeds and perverse policies, and made fun of elements guilty of unworthy behavior. These elements were not of the Lý Toét Xã Xệ sort [refers to comic, rural cartoon characters who were a staple of the northern periodical *Ngày Nay (These Days)* from 1930 to 1942 – no such "little people" were objects of ridicule in this period – the objects of attack were provincial or national leaders and power brokers. The sound of laughter ran freely and noisily across all books and journals...

At the same time, every view of human life, every faith, both fine and deluded, both noble and crazed, existed as well; one could seek to understand, expound, and promulgate these beliefs, just as one pleased.

At no time before or after 1954 – 1975 in the South can one find any literary tradition in our country that developed in such a free and open manner.

Aside from this freedom and openness, we may note a further contribution of this period: the phenomenon of philosophical thought in the South. Toward the end of the pre-war period, our novels were of about ten different types, including psychological and ethical novels, but novels of a philosophical bent had not yet appeared. In 1954 – 1975 philosophical concerns began to appear in many branches of literature: in novels, in songs and poems, in plays, and in essays. Philosophy sometimes spread through society as if it were a fad, and became the subject of ridicule.

Nevertheless, this new preoccupation had arrived at the right time, and in a suitable environment. The people were dying in their millions because of differences in ideology, differences in attitudes toward life. At such a time, how could one not think of the purpose of life; how could one calmly resign such concerns to the leadership? At the same time, that was also a period when many new schools of thought were creating upheavals in the West; our reaction in the South to these developments showed that we had a class of sensitive intellectuals, that we had a lively spiritual life.

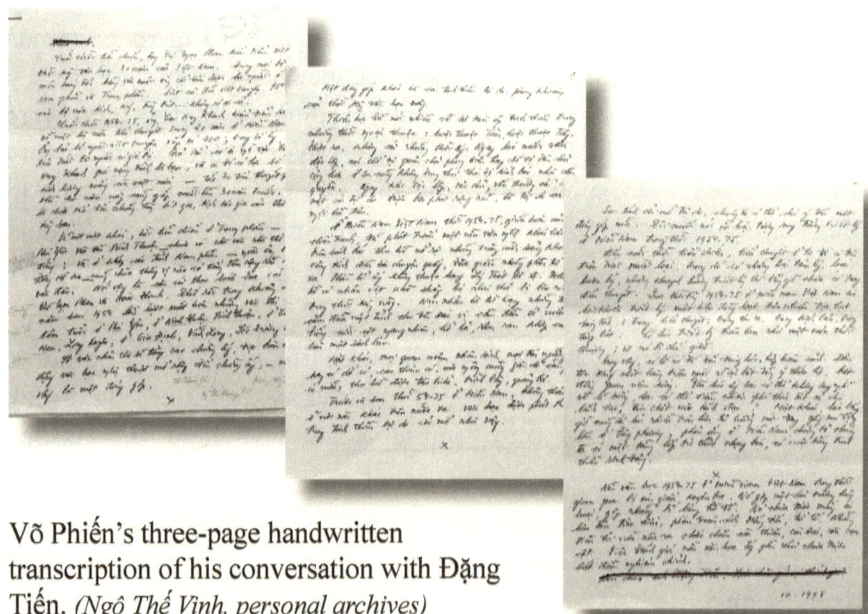

Võ Phiến's three-page handwritten transcription of his conversation with Đặng Tiến. *(Ngô Thế Vinh, personal archives)*

From the left: Trần Dạ Từ, Phạm Duy, and Mr. and Mrs. Võ Phiến at their home in Los Angeles

(Viễn Phố, personal archives)

The literature of South Vietnam in the period 1954 to 1975 has in the past been hidden away and distorted. It has met with proposals that it be destroyed, and met with stupid slanders. It has not yet met with anyone who sought to understand it, to make a correct and full estimate of its value. The observations I have made here are very likely inadequate, incorrect, and shallow. The assessment of this body of literature can scarcely be said to have seriously begun.

(My greetings to Đặng Tiến, and my greetings to the listeners.) Võ Phiến, October 1998.

THE SERIES "LITERATURE OF THE SOUTH, 1954 – 1975"

Võ Phiến's conversation with Đặng Tiến took place in October 1998, just one year before the completion of his series "The Literature of the South (Vol 1 was *A General View of the Literature in the South Vietnam 1954-1975*,[3] published in 1986, and the last was *Essays about Plays of the South [Bút Ký Kịch Miền Nam]*, published in 1999). It appears that we must pay particular attention to his concluding words

3 *Văn Học Miền Nam Tổng Quan*, Vol. 1 (*A General View of the Literature in the South Vietnam 1954-1975) translated by Võ Đình Mai (pen name Võ Đình), published by Vietnamese Language & Culture Publications, Melbourne, Australia; 1992

in the Conversation recorded above: "The assessment of this body of literature can scarcely be said to have seriously begun."

Thus, one can say that even though Võ Phiến had to toil with untiring patience for fifteen years (1984 – 1999) to complete his series of books on the literature of the South, he himself never regarded this as a perfectly realized project, and still felt that the evaluation of this literature in the period 1954 – 1975 still needed to be seriously undertaken.

Nevertheless, this set of books had certain limitations that led to heated disputes. People took him severely to task for certain omissions, such as his decision to exclude some well-known writers of the period 1954 – 1975 from *A General View of the Literature of the South*, and even the style he used to criticize writers and poets was borrowed from the manner he used in his occasional essays – this style, while effective in the essays, proved to be a liability in a work of historical criticism – it seemed to many that it was too ironic and satirical and at times too personal and too prone to odd and flighty judgements.

The writer Mặc Đỗ of the Quan Điểm (Viewpoint) group was quite indignant about it. Mai Thảo of the Sáng Tạo (Creation) group in his last conversation with Thụy Khuê in July 1997 was unable to repress his feelings about what he called the "Emperor Lê and Lord Trịnh gang" and didn't scruple to say, "Võ Phiến is satisfactory in some places, but unsatisfactory in others. In general he isn't satisfactory to me as a critic of literature. His *General View of the Literature of the South* isn't satisfactory. His writing about poetry is bad. What he writes about short theoretical essays is good.

But, speaking objectively, the written style of Võ Phiến did not lack self-deprecation, and he was capable of directing satire against himself. In the responses he gave in an interview conducted by Lê Quỳnh Mai on October 29, 2000 in Montreal on the TNVN Program "Literature and Art," he did not hesitate to compare himself to Xuân Tóc Đỏ ("Red-haired Xuân, a comically lucky nincompoop) in a work by Vũ Trọng Phụng: "If you wish to speak of luck, we probably must recall *Dumb Luck (Số Đỏ)* by Vũ Trọng Phụng – if some number of readers have paid attention to me, then the case is merely comparable to that of Xuân Tóc Đỏ in that book."

Võ Phiến himself knew quite clearly what the reaction of the literary community to this series of books was. In a letter sending to Lê Thị Huệ Gió-O on Dec. 16, 2001, he wrote:

"Among those who worked as writers in the South during the period 1954 – 1975, quite a few are highly critical of this set of books. I'll just have to put up with it. What sort of results can you obtain if you write solely to please everybody?!"

If the reader will calmly reread the introduction to A *General View of the Literature of the South*, he will see that Võ Phiến discusses his reasons for writing "this book full of digressions and lacunae."

He explains himself very clearly:

"First of all, I am not a critic or a scholar; to set myself up as such would be unjustifiable. Furthermore, the circumstances in which I write are very difficult; no materials lie around me, and I have no means of going in search of them; What can I use to pursue this investigation?"

He also foresaw the troublesome consequences that would ensue: "If you write anything that touches on others, and if you praise and blame them without reserve, then it is a certainty that you will arouse a storm of objections."

Having these reflections, he went on to write: "Though troubled to distraction by all this, I nevertheless decided to go ahead and write this book. The chief reason was my deep attachment to an era in our literary history that suffered misfortune. Yes indeed, the period from 1954 to 1975 was unfortunate to a degree seldom seen, one reason being that in this entire twenty-year period, no professional critic appeared on the scene. But before achieving a just and intelligent assessment, we may still hope for a bit of attentive concern.

Of this period, he wrote: "No one is unaware of the destruction of cultural artefacts of the South after 1975. We were unable to prevent this destruction, unable to preserve the literary accomplishments of this

From the right: Ngô Thế Vinh, Trúc Chi (Tôn Thất Kỳ), Mrs. and Mr. Võ Phiến, and Đỗ Anh Tài. *(Viễn Phố, personal archives)*

The campaign to collect and destroy the left-over literature of the "American Puppet Era" led to public book-burning in the South after 1975.

Left: Cover of *A General View of the Literature of the South*, by Võ Phiến, Văn Nghệ publishing house, California: 1986; Right: *Võ Phiến's Selected Items*, including occasional essays, stories, poems, opinion pieces, and criticism, Văn Mới publishers, Los Angeles: 2001; 2nd edition, 2006, Người Việt, California; supplemented with further stories and dialogues.

period; therefore, it behooves us now to make an overall assessment, a cursory examination, so that anyone who at a later time concerns himself with this, will have a little something to serve as a basis for further inquiry. How can we resign ourselves to omitting this step?"

Because of his "deep attachment to an era of literary history that was unfortunate… he was in the end forced, against all inclination, to write this book under conditions that should have discouraged him from writing it. He wrote it as a preliminary draft, an outline, a suggestion, a reminder, a way of introducing the problem, so that later on people with the necessary qualifications and means could write a book worthy of the subject." (Introduction, *General View...*)

Knowing that it would be inadequate, and knowing he would suffer limitations, Võ Phiến acted in a way contrary to his innate reserve and sense of responsibility and plunged into this risky venture–a task that would require much arduous and hidden labor and which would subject him to unpleasant consequences as well. We should also note in this place that through most of the fifteen years he devoted to this work of more than three thousand pages, he was a full-time employee of the Retirement Pension Office of Los Angeles District. This meant that he had to write this work during after-hours and on weekends. After retiring in July, 1994, he continued writing it for five more years in order to complete the Literature of the South in 1999. Without immense ambition and effort on the part of the author, this could not have been achieved.

In spite of all this, when he completed writing the work, Võ Phiến himself could not escape a crowd of self-doubts: "What have I written? Is it a study and assessment of the literature of the South? It is clear that three-quarters of it is not worthy to be called history or criticism at all. It lacks unity and breadth; in dealing with all types and tendencies of literature, it lacks persistence and precision of thought and analysis; it is nothing but a collection of very general observations on the works and writers of a particular period." (Introduction, *General View...*)

Actually, none of the faultfinding from within and without the Vietnamese literary community with regard to Võ Phiến's *General View of the Literature of the South, 1954 – 1975* was as severe as the criticism to which he subjected himself in his Introduction to that work.

This research project of Võ Phiến must be evaluated in the context of the decade that immediately followed 1975 and in light of the circumstances that prevailed when it was published: a time when, within the country, there was a deliberate policy of destroying that literature in toto, of erasing the twenty-year history of the culture of the South. In that context, Võ Phiến's project was one of salvation and rescue, and deserves to be recognized as a preliminary effort deserving the highest respect.

Everyone can grasp the fact that Võ Phiến's "unprofessional" set of books on the Literature of the South will never be the last word on that period, but it is still a first step, an initial facilitation, a roadmap that will conduct us to a substantial body of material that we may consult later; it is a "launchpad" for projects that will follow. This is indeed the responsibility and the professional duty of those who specialize as critics; they must have the boldness to make a serious beginning at the job of assigning value to the work of 1954 to 1975 by creating studies worthy of the subject, rather than obsessing about the "half-empty glass" of Võ Phiến's work.

So, I here propose a question: who among us can make a "serious beginning at pursuing this research project? And this leads to a further question: who will inherit the huge mass of material that Võ Phiến dealt with before it is all lost and forgotten?

LÊ NGỘ CHÂU THE PEACE BROKER

In 1994, Lê Ngộ Châu and his daughter came to the U.S. After eighteen years of directing the *Cyclopedia* (*Bách Khoa*) magazine, he had many close friends and, of these, Võ Phiến was perhaps the closest of all. Due to this personal relationship, he knew that there was a "problem" between Võ Phiến and Nguyễn Mộng Giác in the transition from the magazine *Văn Học Nghệ Thuật* (*Literature and Art*) to its successor *Văn Học* (*Literary Studies*).

Nguyễn Mộng Giác and Võ Phiến were compatriots–they came from the same province. In an interview, Võ Phiến once expressed himself as follows: "Meeting a writer from one's own province is a joy, and when one discovers that some special regional qualities lie at the basis of the beauty of his work, what else could be so pleasurable? How can one repress one's feelings? One must speak of Bình Định, what else, my friend!" (Interview of Lê Quỳnh Mai with Võ Phiến, Montreal, 2004).

But this feeling of shared provincial origin was not sufficient to prevent obstacles from arising in the management of *Văn Học* (*Literary Studies*) and in the selection of contributions to the magazine when Võ

The meeting organized to welcome Lê Ngộ Châu (October 30, 1994) at the clubhouse on Bellflower Road, Long Beach; from the left: Nghiêu Đề, Võ Phiến, Bùi Vĩnh Phúc, Hoàng Khởi Phong, Hà Thúc Sinh, Nguyễn Mộng Giác, Trúc Chi (Tôn Thất Kỳ), Như Phong (Lê Văn Tiến), Lê Ngộ Châu, Lưu Trung Khảo, and Từ Mai (Trần Huy Bích) *(photo by Ngô Thế Vinh)*

Lê Ngộ Châu during his 1994 visit to California; from the left: Đỗ Hải Minh / Dohamide, Lê Ngộ Châu, Ngô Thế Vinh, and Võ Phiến.

(Ngô Thế Vinh, personal archives)

From the right: Từ Mẫn (Võ Thắng Tiết), Lê Ngộ Châu, Võ Phiến, Nguyễn Mộng Giác, and Lê Tất Điều.
(Ngô Thế Vinh, personal archives, California, 1994)

Phiến's name still appeared as the director and when Nguyễn Mộng Giác was its editor-in-chief. A man of sensitive perception, Lê Ngộ Châu saw at once that an obstruction existed between the two, and set about immediately, and with a sense of urgency, to serve as a "peace broker" (*hòa giải*) - a word used by Lê Ngộ Châu himself.

As if to provide a pretext for this to occur, I arranged a meeting to welcome Lê Ngộ Châu at a clubhouse on Bellflower Road, Long Beach, near my home. Naturally Võ Phiến and Nguyễn Mộng Giác were there. Only Lê Tất Điều wasn't there; he took Võ Phiến to the clubhouse but didn't participate, but about twenty close friends and associates of Lê Ngộ Châu and *Văn Học* (*Literary Studies*) were there, including Từ Mẫn (Võ Thắng Tiết), Từ Mai (Trần Huy Bích), Trúc Chi (Tôn Thất Kỳ), Thạch Hãn (Lê Thọ Giáo), Khánh Trường, Hoàng Khởi Phong, and Cao Xuân Huy… The joyous feeling of "old friends meeting in a far-away place" prevailed in everyone's interactions and, as always, the lively, gay, and witty conversation of Lê Ngộ Châu served as a sort of "cement" uniting everyone who was there. One could see how Lê Ngộ Châu had kept a lively and complicated enterprise like *Cyclopedia (Bách Khoa)* running harmoniously for eighteen years prior to 1975.

That visit of 1994 was the only time that Lê Ngộ Châu came to the U.S. Like the director of the Khai Trí Bookstore, Nguyễn Hùng Trương, he chose to return to Saigon to live. In 2006, when I was attending a meeting of the Friends of the Mekong, I met Lê Ngộ Châu again in the editorial office of *Cyclopedia* (*Bách Khoa*) magazine at 160 Phan Đình Phùng. He still remembered our former meeting. When I asked him if he had thought of writing a memoir of his eighteen years with *Bách Khoa*, he laughed and delivered the following witty reply:

"Anh Vinh, you ask Võ Phiến if he would let me do it, okay?" He was referring to the various extra-literary things that occurred in the office of *Bách Khoa* throughout that period. I learned only a short time after my return to the U.S., that Lê Ngộ Châu had passed away on September 24, 2006. He was 84 years old.

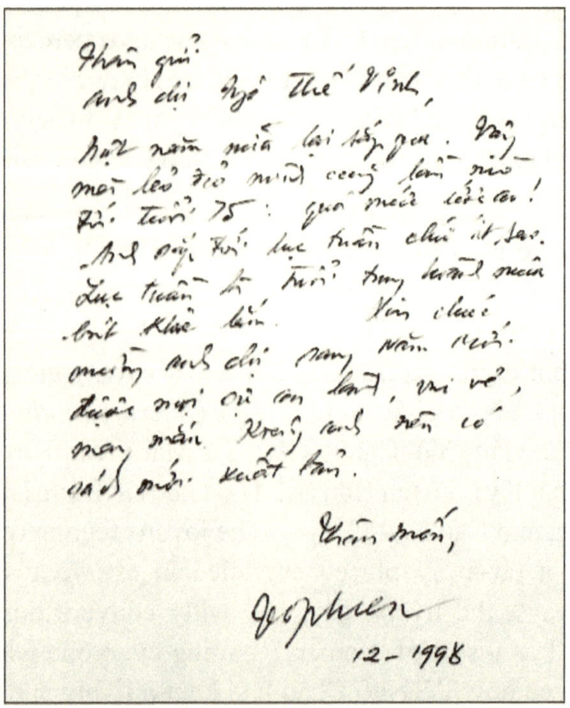

Thân gửi
anh chị Ngô Thế Vinh,

Thân mến,
Võ Phiến
12-1998

Handwritten note from Võ Phiến to Ngô Thế Vinh, December 1998) *(Ngô Thế Vinh, personal archives)*

VÕ PHIẾN AT AGE 75, "OLDER THAN HE HAD WISHED FOR"

At the end of 1998, in December, I received a spring festival card from Võ Phiến in which he wrote:

"Another year has slipped by, and I have staggered into my 75th year – more than I ever wished for! You are about to reach sixty yourself – not exactly young! But sixty is an age when you can let your pen dance along as it pleases. I wish you all good things in the coming year–and in particular you should be publishing a new book! Yours, Võ Phiến."

Actually, Võ Phiến had only attained the age of 73 that year; he was born in 1925, an "Ất Sửu" ["ox"] year. No less than three of his literary friends, the writer Doãn Quốc Sỹ, the journalist Như Phong, and the chief editor Lê Ngộ Châu were all born in the year "Quý Hợi" (1923, a "pig" year), and thus were two years older than Võ Phiến. Doãn Quốc Sỹ had the humorous habit of calling Lê Ngộ Châu "Lê Quý Hợi," and Châu in return called him "Doãn Quý Hợi." Of these three "Quý Hợi" gentleman, only Doãn Quốc Sỹ remains: the journalist Như Phong died in Virginia in 2001, and Chief Editor Lê Ngộ Châu died in Saigon in 2006.

In a letter to Lê Ngộ Châu dated August 29, 1996, Doãn Quốc Sỹ maintained the joking tone, referring to Võ Phiến as "Elder Warrior Bình Định" (Cụ Võ Bình Định), after his home province: "I saw a photo of Elder Võ Bình Định wearing a very young-looking shirt. Looking at his mirthful face in the photo, I imagined I was hearing the amused laughter that accompanied all my exchanges with him over the years in the office of *Bách Khoa* years ago."

Before passing the threshold into his 70s, Võ Phiến had undergone two major open-heart surgeries–coronary artery bypass procedures – the first was in 1960 when Võ Phiến had just turned 60. He began at that time to be obsessed with death:

"Having reached an even fifty years,
Where will another fifty take me?
A thousand years of trailing wispy clouds."

Seven years later, at the age of 67, Võ Phiến underwent his second heart operation, which was more difficult and complicated than the first. He was pessimistic about it and thought even more about death.

In *This Indifferent Life* (*Cái Sống Hững Hờ*), he made the following observations: "I myself once had to enter a hospital to undergo surgery. Plunged in sadness, I wrote a few letters to friends and entrusted a literary friend with the job of sending them to the recipients after… my final departure. It turned out that after the operation I continued, feebly, to live. I lived on, embarrassed and aimless.

The work *Cuối Cùng* (At the End) by Võ Phiến, published in 2009 by 21st Century (Thế Kỷ 21) in California. This copy bears an inscription inside, made with great difficulty and with the assistance of his wife Viễn Phố on Oct. 5, 2015.

(Ngô Thế Vinh, personal archives)

Handwritten note from Võ Phiến to Ngô Thế Vinh in May 2000: "Sent with affection to Ngô Thế Vinh. Thanks for your appreciation of this article. When it is printed in a book, I'll dedicate it to you. Whenever you have a convenient day, please come pay us a visit during these sunny summer days."

(Ngô Thế Vinh, personal archives)

"The years and months kept flowing on. As I entered my eighties, I began, furtively, to direct my thoughts to the conclusion of my life. It was surely, in any case, drawing near. What harm could there be in taking a peek at it? Peeking, and then peeking again, I was surprised to note that I was not overcome by any unusual feeling. Life kept going on, going on with utter regularity.

"The Creator has a tender heart; his fingers lightly direct our feelings; the older a person gets, the more his emotions cease to be turbulent, cease to be passionately committed. What finally remains is a feeling of indifference: 'Death? Who can avoid it? Why fear it?' Reflecting quietly on this, I begin to suspect that the benevolence of the Creator is revealed in this. We should not subject him to nagging demands, but should whistle tunes as we die. I just hope that the steps that I myself take toward my grave will be leisurely, indifferent steps. That, in sum, is all."

Though Võ Phiến and his wife had purchased grave sites years before so that their last rites could be carried out, Võ Phiến's steps did not lead him to the place he had reserved. His remains were instead cremated, and afterward the ashes were taken to Điều Ngự Temple, a place presided over by an abbot who, like Võ Phiến, was from Bình Định and who had always held him in the highest esteem. (author's note)

After Võ Phiến's wife retired, the two of them no longer needed to live close to the place where they had worked, so in 2003 they moved to a spot close to Little Saigon. Their new house was a pert and attractive two-story dwelling in a quiet residential district at the end of Fifth Street (no. 5) in the town of Santa Anna. This house also had a garden; it was very small, surrounded by rose bushes, and had a few fruit trees. It suited the strength of the elderly couple, who having entered their seventies, could enjoy adding to it and tending it. Aside from various reprinted books, such as *The Collected Works of Võ Phiến* (*Võ Phiến Toàn Tập*), *At the End* (*Cuối Cùng*) was Võ Phiến's last work. He completed it in his new home in 2007, and it was published in 2009 by 21st Century (Thế Kỷ 21).

In the house of Mr. and Mrs. Võ Phiến on Baltimore Street, Los Angeles, in April 1992. From the left: Professor Trần Ngọc Ninh, the writer Võ Phiến, and Ngô Thế Vinh.

(Ngô Thế Vinh, personal archives)

The autumn sun in the garden next to the house of Mr. and Mrs. Võ Phiến on Baltimore Street, Los Angeles, in September 2001.

From right to left: Mr. and Mrs. Võ Phiến, Tạ Chí Đại Trường, Nguyễn Huệ Chi, and Nguyễn Mộng Giác. In the background is the sculptural bust of Võ Phiến made by Ưu Đàm. This photo was taken in Võ Phiến's rear garden twenty years after his second heart operation, with a nurse – his wife – standing behind him.

(Viễn Phố, personal archives, with her annotation)

VÕ PHIẾN AT 90

Having been born on Oct. 20, 1925, Võ Phiến was exactly 90 in 2015. He was perhaps among the three writers of the South who lived to the greatest ages. In this regard he was behind only Mặc Đỗ in Austin, Texas who lived to be 98 (he was born in 1917) and Doãn Quốc Sỹ who is currently 92 in southern California (he was born in 1923).

When Võ Phiến sent me a spring festival card that year, he reused a sentence he had written on a card seventeen years earlier: "Another year has slipped by, and so I have staggered into my 90th year–more than I ever wished for!"

And so Võ Phiến's life kept going on, with utter regularity. His wife Viễn Phố made sure that he went for a walk each day with his walker, which was equipped with wheels. At the age of 90, his physical strength could be assessed as not too bad, though in terms of intellect, he was often afflicted with forgetfulness–the

VÕ PHIẾN

CUỐI CÙNG

forgetfulness of senile dementia. He didn't remember the faces of everyone close to him, but with a few "bạn cựu," "friends of old times" – his expression – people he had been intimate with for many years, like Hoàng Ngọc Biên, Đặng Tiến, and Lê Tất Điều–he still retained his longer-term memory through telephone conversations and face-to-face meetings.

Yet it's been forty years, twice Võ Phiến wept when he was about to depart from Vietnam, first in the office of *Bách Khoa*, and the second time on the ship Challenger, when he left Phú Quốc Island. (Ngô Thế Vinh, "Bốn Mươi Năm Dương Nghiễm Mậu và Tự Truyện Nguyễn Du" http://damau.org/rchives/35745). Throughout those twenty years, water flowed ceaselessly beneath the bridge, and Võ Phiến lived the life of a writer in exile, working sadly and in loneliness. (John Schafer, *Võ Phiến and the Sadness of Exile,* Southeast Asia Publications, Center for Southeast Asian Studies, Northern Illinois University, Mar. 1, 2006)

I sent the above article, finished in April, to Võ Phiến as he was entering his nineties, an age rarely attained by anyone. I also sent to Võ Phiến and Viễn Phố the wish that their "tree of life would remain always green and fresh." (Johann Wolfgang von Goethe: "All theory, dear friend, is gray, but the tree of life springs evergreen.")

A POEM BY VÕ PHIẾN IN THE YEAR 2000

After his death, I found a poem that Võ Phiến had written and bestowed on me as a gift in the year 2000.

Twenty Years In A House

Affectionately presented to:
Mr. and Mrs. Ngô Thế Vinh

I wonder all at once whose house this is–
In any case, I've been here twenty years–

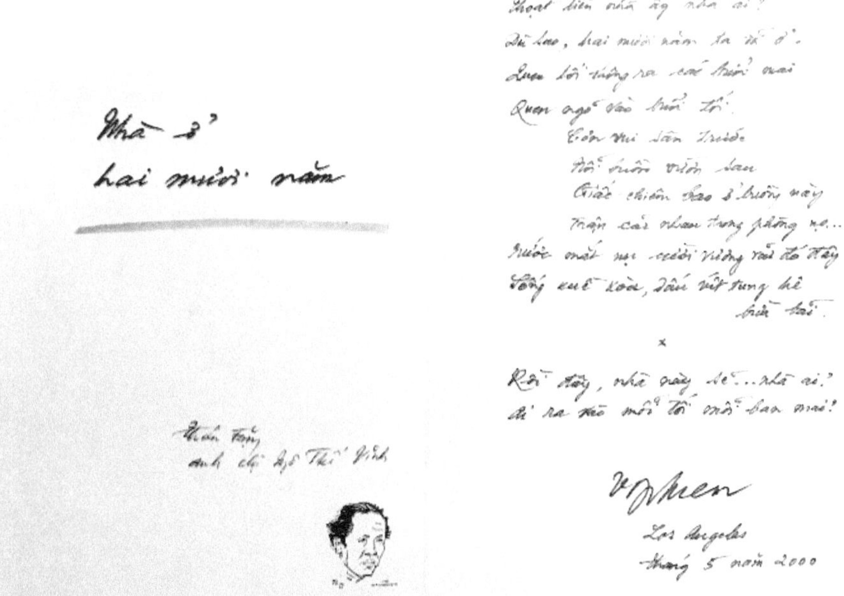

The poem "Twenty Years in a House," a copy handwritten by Võ Phiến.
(Ngô Thế Vinh, personal archives)

I know the pines I walked by of a morning,
The paths I entered in the evening–
The gaiety I felt before the house,
The sadness of the garden in the back,
The dream that overcame me in a room,
The tension that erupted in another,
The tears and smiles adhering here and there.
We lived at ease, the marks are strewn about,
And now the house will be … whose house?
Who'll go out, go in, each night, each morn?

Long Beach 04/2015

A VISIT WITH LINH BẢO
FROM *NORTH WIND* TO THE *CLOUDS OF QIN*

The writer Linh Bảo when she was living in Hong Kong.
(Linh Bảo, personal archives)

The homeward-coursing soul
pursues the far-away clouds of Qin
~*The Tale of Kiều*, Nguyễn Du

After the women writers of the prewar period, such as Thụy An and Mộng Sơn of the 1940s, Linh Bảo and Nguyễn Thị Vinh were the first to appear in the crowd of women writers who would later on populate the 1960s, like Nhã Ca, Nguyễn Thị Hoàng, Túy Hồng, Nguyễn Thị Thụy Vũ, Trùng Dương, and Trần Thị NgH.

Linh Bảo's presence in the literary scene of the South dates from the 1950s. Her books were published, one after another, in the South from 1953 to 1975. Only the *Clouds of Qin* (*Mây Tần*), a collection of short stories, was published abroad (1981). No book of hers was published within Vietnam after 1975. [1]

BIOGRAPHICAL DATA:

The writer Linh Bảo, real name Võ Thị Diệu Viên, was born into a family of officials in the imperial court of Huế on April 14, 1926. Her father, Võ Chuẩn, was the governor of Quảng Nam Province, and her mother, Tôn Nữ Thị Lịch, belonged to the imperial family. From early childhood, Linh Bảo nourished a desire to study abroad, so she left her family at an early age and wandered about in many countries outside of Vietnam: China (Nanjing and Guangzhou), Hong Kong, England, France, and the United States. Linh Bảo also had two other names: Lại Cẩm Hoa was the name on the ticket of the boat that took her across the sea to Hong Kong and Vũ Trung Thư (Cantonese: Mo Chung Shu) was the name she signed to go to school in Nanjing and Guangzhou. The letters that the writer Nhất Linh sent to Linh Bảo when she was in Hong Kong were all addressed to Lại Cẩm Hoa.

She had just completed two years at Sun Zhongshan (that is, Sun Yat-sen) University when the Red Army of Mao Zedong occupied the whole of mainland China, and Linh Bảo relocated again, fleeing as a refugee from Guangzhou to Hong Kong. There she worked at a variety of jobs in order to subsist: from working as a dentist's assistant to making Vietnamese voice-overs for the Chinese films that were then enjoying great popularity.

In 1951, Linh Bảo established a family with a Chinese man who had English citizenship, and as a result of that marriage became

---

1 In 2019, about two years after I wrote this, the Vietnam Writers' Association (Hà Nội) published a book entitled *Lời Thì Thầm của Ba Người Con Gái Huế Xưa* (The Whispers of Three Sisters from the Ancient Imperial City of Huế), a mixed collection of novels (*Những Đêm Mưa* / Rainy Nights) by Linh Bảo and 2 memoirs by Băng Thanh and Minh Đức Hoài Trinh.

The coed Vũ Trung Thư (Linh Bảo) at Sun Zhongshan University in Guangzhou, China.

(Linh Bảo, personal archives)

an English citizen. The origin of her pen name Linh Bảo was very simple; it was simply the name of her husband Trần Linh Bảo 陳靈寶 (Chén Língbǎo), and that name remained her pseudonym throughout her career as a Vietnamese writer.

In 1954, when a consulate for the Republic of Vietnam was first established in Hong Kong, Linh Bảo was one of the very few Vietnamese at that time who knew Cantonese, Mandarin, English, and of course Vietnamese, so she was chosen to be a staff member of the Hong Kong consulate, a position in which she remained until she returned to her country in 1957. Only two years later, however, in 1959, she again chose to live far from her home.

Residing by turns in Hong Kong, France, and England, Linh Bảo at length decided to emigrate to the United States after she was selected to teach Vietnamese language at the army language school known as the Defense Language Institute in Monterey, California. She worked there from 1962 until the school was disbanded after the Vietnam War in 1976. Linh Bảo now lives in southern California.

WORKS:

- *Gió Bấc* ("North Wind"), a novel, Phượng Giang publishers, 1953
- *Tàu Ngựa Cũ* ("The Old Stable"), short stories, Đời Nay, 1961
- *Những Đêm Mưa* ("Rainy Nights"), a novel, Đời Nay, 1961
- *Những Cánh Diều* ("Kites' Wings"), short stories, Trí Đăng, 1971
- *Mây Tần* ("Clouds of Qin"), novellas, Việt Nam Hải Ngoại, 1981

PHIM TÀU TIẾNG VIỆT

Trích Nhật ký Hong Kong của LINH BẢO

Viết nhật ký là thú vui duy nhất của cô Linh Bảo. Trong thời gian ở Hong Kong mặc dầu công việc mệt nhọc ban ngày, tối nào cô cũng dành thời giờ để ghi lại vài dòng cảm tưởng về cuộc sống linh động ở đông đất nước người.

A page from a Saigon newspaper in the 50s with an article by Linh Bảo on Chinese films. Though she worked at tiring jobs throughout the day during her sojourn in Hong Kong, she reserved time in the evenings to write commentaries on the bustling life going around her in that foreign setting. *(Linh Bảo, personal archives)*

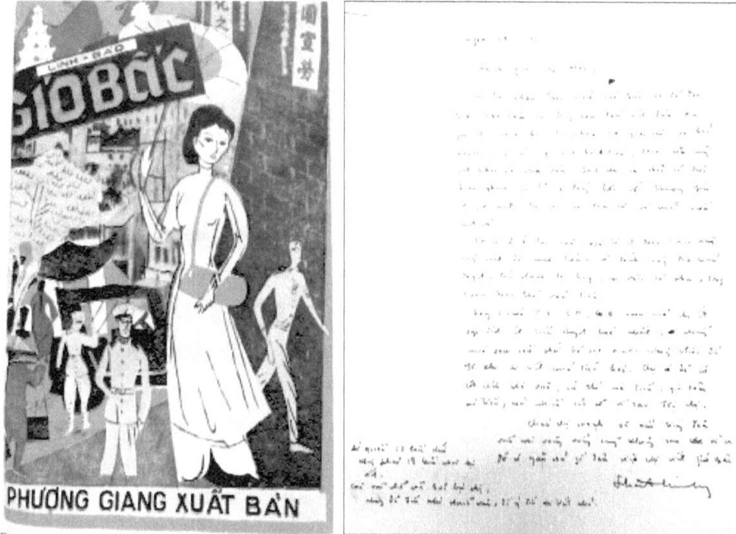

Left: The cover of *North Wind* (*Gió Bấc*) as published by Phượng Giang in 1953. Right: The letter sent by the writer Nhất Linh to Linh Bảo. *(Linh Bảo, personal archives)*

For Children:

- *Chiếc Áo Nhung Lam* ("The Blue Velvet Robe"), Sách Hồng, Đời Nay, 1953
- *Con Chồn Tinh Quái* ("The Fox Demon"), Ngày Mới, 1967

The Old Stable won the National Literary Prize for 1961. Except for the novel *North Wind* and the children's story *The Blue Velvet Robe*, both of which appeared in 1953, the chief works of Linh Bảo were all published in the period 1954-1975.

From "Northern Wind" (Gió Bắc) to "North Wind" (Gió Bấc)

In Hong Kong, Linh Bảo had the opportunity to become acquainted with two writers, Nguyễn Thị Vinh[2] and Trương Bảo Sơn.[3] The draft

2 Nguyễn Thị Vinh (1924-2020): a woman novelist and memoirist associated with the Self-Reliance Literary Group headed by Nhất Linh.

3 Trương Bảo Sơn (1916-2010): a writer and translator, married for a time to Nguyễn Thị Vinh (above)

manuscript of *Northern Wind* (Gió Bắc; it was not yet entitled North Wind or Gió Bấc)" was written in the first person, as if it were a memoir, and related the experiences of a young female student named Linh Bảo living an unsettled, wandering existence. This draft was given to Miss Nguyễn Thị Vinh and then passed into the hands of the writer Nhất Linh.

After reading the draft manuscript "Northern Wind," and feeling that the author had "what it takes" to be a writer, Nhất Linh wrote a letter to Linh Bảo containing two suggestions. The first was to rewrite the novel using the third person, and the second was to change the title from "Northern Wind" (Gió Bắc) to "North Wind" (Gió Bấc). Linh Bảo followed these two suggestions.

On May 29, 1953, Nhất Linh wrote a letter to Linh Bảo, who was still living in Hong Kong, addressing it to "Lại Cẩm Hoa":

"My respectful greetings to Miss Hoa:

"I have received your "North Wind," and have read it all. It is quite strong, and more effectively written than your first version–so I would like to take this occasion to praise you. Both the native and foreign characters are clearly more full of life, and the conclusion is very skillful and very suitable. Your book will surely be welcomed when it comes out. It will perhaps appear around the same time as *Love* (*Thương Yêu*) and *Cool Wind* (*Gió Mát*) [by Nguyễn Thị Vinh and Tường Hùng; author's note]. The three books will each have their own story to tell, and each will have its own quality.

"I will correct the text and delete a few passages (this will take about ten days), then type it up and send it to the censors. The main content is excellent, the style not quite as good, but still decidedly better than the first time.

"Of the three books, *Love*, *Cool Wind*, and *North Wind*, yours is the least shaped, the least "novelized." In your subsequent books, you must have more regard to structure… but enough of that–let's wait till you write your second book. You have what it takes to be a writer; if you go calmly forward in this manner, many accolades will await you.

"I wish you strength, and if the string instrument still echoes here and there [a reference to Linh Bảo's asthma, Nhất Linh refers to it as "the sound of your violin"; author's note] it matters not a whit, because it hindered you not at all in writing *North Wind*.

"Nhất Linh"

Who could have known that ten years after writing this letter, the writer Nhất Linh would sacrifice his own life at the age of 57. He lived from 1906 to 1963.

North Wind was the first work of Linh Bảo to be published by Phượng Giang in 1953. It may be regarded as the first secure step in Linh Bảo's career as a writer. After having established her name with this work, she wished for personal reasons to change her pen name, but Nhất Linh advised her not to, and she took his advice.

From *North Wind* to *Rainy Nights*

North Wind is the story of a young woman named Trang who was born and grew up in Huế. She was physically weak due to chronic asthma that began in early childhood and which varied with the seasons. Every time the north wind started to blow, the asthma worsened and subjected her to torments; nevertheless, the girl's spirit was strong. Her mother, due to old-fashioned beliefs, didn't encourage her daughter to engage in academic pursuits, but Trang still cherished the dream of going abroad to study. Due to dispersal arising from war, Trang went far away from her family at an early age, and wound up in Saigon, where she was arrested and thrown into prison. Then an opportunity appeared: she obtained a ticket that would allow her to board a boat with a Chinese name. The boat took her to Hong Kong, and then Nanjing, Shanghai, and Guangzhou. The frail girl lived through many historic upheavals: the revolution in Vietnam, and then the one in China, and had to pass through months and years of warfare and chaotic displacement. Wherever she went, she had to perform exhausting tasks in order to survive. Then she was able to enter Sun Zhongshan University in Guangzhou, but soon afterward the forces of Mao Zedong occupied the Chinese mainland, and she again became a refugee, this time going to Hong Kong. Here she had to work at many jobs to survive, until she met a Chinese man in Hong Kong named Bình, who was not greedy and had a kind nature. He sought Trang out and asked to share his life with her.

The last page of *North Wind* includes the following: "And Bình suddenly seized Trang's hand... 'Trang, will you give me permission... to care for you... throughout life, will that be all right?' She put up no resistance and accepted." *North Wind* was finished in Hong Kong when Linh Bảo had just turned 26.

Rainy Nights can be regarded as the continuation of *North Wind*. The protagonist, a woman, is still named "Trang." After Trang and Bình married each other, their life as a couple had not turned out to be dreamy and happy as Trang had hoped; instead, many sharp conflicts arose, especially when she gave birth to her first child, a daughter, in a household so lacking in necessities as to be at a dead end. Unable to continue living with a man whom she regarded as contemptibly ordinary, Trang packed her belongings and took her little daughter and her own swelling belly back to Huế in order to live for an indefinite period with her parents.

Disappointed as she was with her own marriage on returning to her parents' home, Trang had to be a witness to a further tragedy that unfolded in that setting: her father had abandoned her mother to a life of shame and sadness because of his infatuation with a series of younger mistresses. Even Trang was subject to unwelcome attention from her father. Then her father fell ill and died, and her mother, disillusioned with life, sought to join a Buddhist retreat. In consequence, Trang felt lonely and abandoned; looking where she would, she had no one around her to rely on. And so, once again, she took her departure, not knowing where she would go, but with no intention of returning to her former husband in Hong Kong.

On the last page of *Rainy Nights*, we find: "Trang had no need to read further in the letter to see what it would contain (she is looking at a letter from Bình, her former husband). In the years and months of their separation, Bình had regularly written two letters of this sort every week–though the content of his letters was sufficiently urbane, he never had sufficient spirit to recount anything, whether long or short, in its entirety. Trang looked after her child as if seeking the courage to do battle, to withstand the challenges of the adventure that was about to begin."

Rainy Nights was also completed in Hong Kong; the year was 1957, five years after *North Wind*. Linh Bảo was then 31 years old.

Both novels are full of things that Linh Bảo experienced in her own life. The unique value of the creations of Linh Bảo is due, however, not to their content, but to their literary artistry. She wrote with a sharp and intelligent pen, that uses ridicule to expose the negative aspects of existence. The style is merciless and the mode of expression is contrary, demonic, and devil-may-care, but at the same time full of pain. The women in the works of Linh Bảo are strong and hardy, able to endure anything, but they are nevertheless always the victims of the circumstances in which they live.

Looking further into the matter, one can say that the works of Linh Bảo were among the first that entered the battle for women's rights.

LINH BẢO'S DAYS IN SAIGON

Whether living in Vietnam or living abroad, Linh Bảo wrote with considerable regularity in the two decades stretching from the 1950s to the 1970s. Together with Nguyễn Thị Vinh, Linh Bảo was one of the two strongest women writers who appeared in the journal *Culture in the Present Era* (*Văn Hóa Ngày Nay*) of Nhất Linh, the journal *New Wind* (*Tân Phong*) of Nguyễn Thị Vinh and Trương Bảo Sơn, and the magazine *Cyclopedia* (*Bách Khoa*) of Lê Ngộ Châu, as well as a number of other periodicals.

After *North Wind*, Linh Bảo's fame grew bright with the long and short stories that appeared thereafter. *Rainy Nights* and *The Old Stable* were both works of hers remarkable for their high artistic value.

[It seems desirable to record here a few observations concerning Linh Bảo that appeared in a personal letter of Bình Nguyên Lộc, a writer whose entire production is full of the character of the South:

Tòa soạn **VĂN HÓA NGÀY NAY** 1958 *(từ trái qua)*:

The editorial board of *Culture in the Present Era* (*Văn Hóa Ngày Nay*) Sitting, from left: Linh Bảo, Quỳ Hương, Nguyễn Thị Vinh; standing in back, from left: Bình Nguyên Lộc, Duy Lam, Đỗ Đức Thu, Nhất Linh, Tường Hùng, Nguyễn Thành Vinh, Trương Bảo Sơn.

"Saigon, Sept. 21, 1958

"Dear Linh Bảo,

"I went to pay you a visit the other day, but you had gone out…

"I want to tell you of something I have learned–if I tell you, I'm afraid you will not believe me, but I cannot refrain from speaking of it: many literary friends of mine, on the non-communist side, are saying to me that, of all the fiction being published *Culture in the Present Era*, only the pieces by Linh Bảo are good. They don't use the expression "best." This means they are giving you a degree of praise higher than what "best of all" would express.

"As for me, I want to say that [what you are now doing] is very much better than *North Wind* (Bình Nguyên Lộc is here referring to *Rainy Nights*, which was then being serialized in *Culture in the Present Era*; author's note) and that your literary voice is now very clear, and it is by no means certain that anyone will appear in the next thirty years who will be able to equal it.

"This utterly astonishes me. On the outside, you are very much a woman, so how is it that your writing is that of a man? Having read the first four installments of *Rainy Nights*, I am terrified of you; terrified of your ability to observe both the internal and external aspects of your characters, and endlessly terrified of your calm, cool laugh. This terror is not the same as admiration. Of course, there is admiration, that goes without saying, but I fear being observed and laughed at by you, even if the laugh is only under your breath.

"Bình Nguyên Lộc

"P.S.: If you should go out somewhere, allow me to invite you to stop by my house–I live on Võ Tánh Street, near Thái Bình market. I'm always at home in the afternoon, except for Saturdays and Sundays.

The writer Bình Nguyên Lộc died at the age of 73 (1914 – 1987).

After writing about Nhất Linh and Bình Nguyên Lộc, Võ Phiến wrote also about Linh Bảo in the journal *Cyclopedia* (*Bách Khoa*) (no. 161, 1962) as follows: "Among the various women writers now

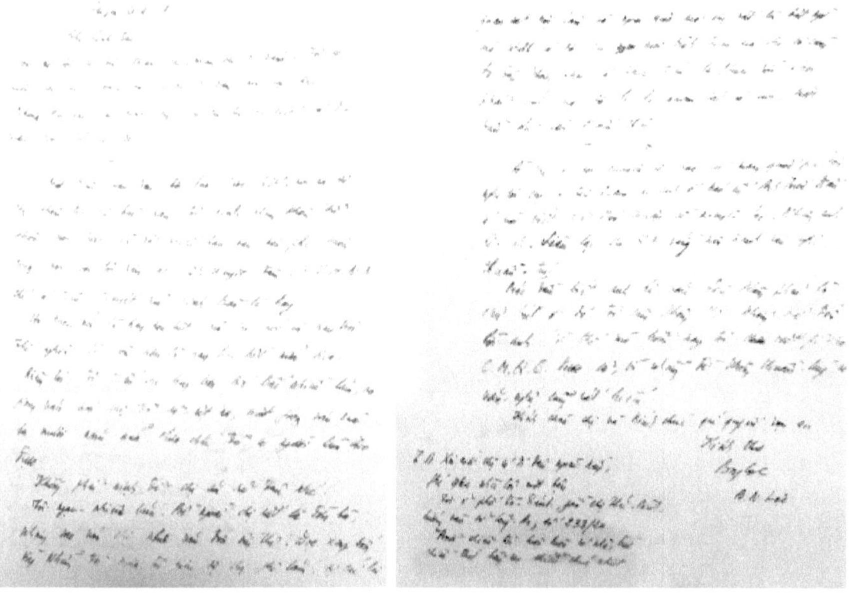

The letter sent to Linh Bảo by Bình Nguyên Lộc.

active, Linh Bảo is perhaps the most gifted. She is good at observation, and good at discussing what she observes with intelligence. Through observation and psychological analysis, Linh Bảo is able to present each of her characters with a distinct appearance and personality and with modes of life and behavior peculiar to themselves… Linh Bảo often seeks opportunities to make the reader smile, though in some passages the circumstances may be sad or tragic, as when a house is swept away in a flood, or when a married couple are enraged at each other. Her ability to retain her freshness even in the midst of sadness is a special skill native to women, and particularly to "courteous" women, that endows what she writes with beauty. Thus even though the laughter of Linh Bảo is often mournful, the reader remains attached to her literary voice.

As if by coincidence, the writers of all three regions – northern, central, and southern – all came to the same conclusion: Linh Bảo was a writer of genius. Though she did not write much, each work of hers had a special character. One can only regret that in the more than forty years that have passed since, Linh Bảo has shown almost no further interest in literary creation.

The Old Stable and the Literature Prize

The Old Stable (*Tàu Ngựa Cũ*) won the national literature prize in 1961. There were three literature prizes that year; two of the winning works were published by Ngày Nay: *Abandoned Porch* (*Thềm Hoang*) by Nhật Tiến for best novel, and *The Old Stable* (*Tàu Ngựa Cũ*) by Linh Bảo for the best short story collection. The third, *Preserve the Gold, Preserve the Jade* (*Gìn Vàng, Giữ Ngọc*), by Doãn Quốc Sỹ, was published by Sáng Tạo.

The Old Stable was a collection of nine short stories that had appeared in the journals *Culture in the Present Era* (*Văn Hóa Ngày Nay*) edited by Nhất Linh and *New Wind* (Tân Phong) edited by Nguyễn Thị Vinh and Trương Bảo Sơn. *The Old Stable* won its prize in 1961. The scholar Nghiêm Xuân Việt of the Vietnam PEN Club (Văn Bút Việt Nam), in a "friendly cultural exchange with other countries, chose two stories in *The Old Stable*, "Người Quân Tử" and

The cover of *Rainy Nights* (Những Đêm Mưa).
(Linh Bảo, personal archives)

The cover of *The Old Stable* (Tàu Ngựa Cũ).
(Linh Bảo, personal archives)

"Áo Mới" to be put into English under the titles "The Noble Man," and "Our Brand New Robes" and sent them to a short story contest organized by International PEN in 1961. The panel of judges included such famous figures as Storm Jameson (England), André Maurois (France), and Whit Burnett (U.S.).

The upshot was that both of these stories were chosen to be included in an international collection of the best short stories of that year. Linh Bảo was living in London at that time. At some later point, the two stories were put into French: "L'Homme Noble" and "Robes Nouvelles," so as to be put into a collection of stories by Vietnamese authors.

"The Old Stable" was the short story from which the whole collection took its name. It is a light but moving love story. In a train trip covering the whole distance from Huế to Saigon, Kỳ yearned to have a traveling partner so he could have someone to talk to. By pure coincidence a young woman boards the train at a halting place and sits next to Kỳ. A red mole on her wrist made Kỳ realize that she

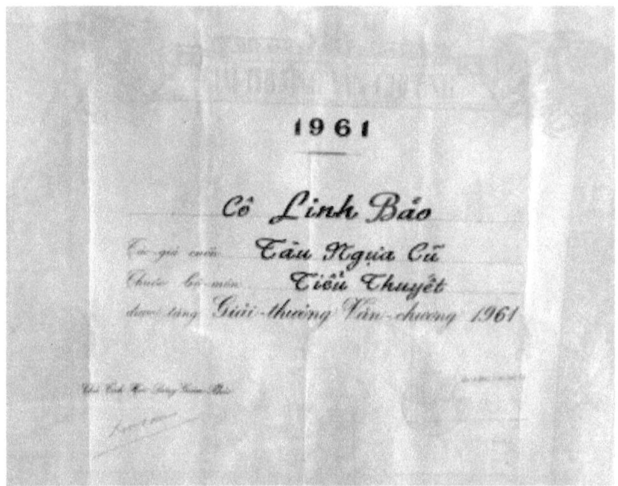

1961

Cô Linh Bảo

Tàu Ngựa Cũ

Tiểu Thuyết

Giải-thưởng Văn-chương 1961

The literature prize of 1961. *(Linh Bảo, personal archives)*

was a girlfriend from a time and place deep in the past–they had been deeply in love with each other at the time. They recognized each other and felt blessed as they sat together recalling former times. But when the train reached Nha Trang, Kỳ's wife appeared. The young woman stepped silently off the train without a word of farewell. Everything had passed like a dream. Kỳ returned to real life with a woman at his side who happened to be his wife. He felt like a horse that had been tamed, and who must go back on the road leading to his old stable.

"The Noble Man" ("Người Quân tử") is the story of a young beautiful woman named Dung who works for an airline and leads an independent life, but suddenly falls into adverse circumstances. She finds herself in the clutches of a man who has a wife, but who, through many perverse and even violent schemes, converts her into a "secretary of all work" and at the same time acts in many roles as a lover. She is an "unmarried wife," but still must bear his children and take their mother's name. Dung must serve this man like a female servant, but he nevertheless brainwashes her into believing that he is bestowing favors on her and protecting her, and that he is a man of high principles. This is so effective that Dung submits to it and is resigned to her circumstances.

"Our Brand-New Robes" has as its background a distant time of splendor in old Huế ruled by a declining imperial dynasty. It tells the tale of a robe purchased from the emperor's mother and brought back by another mother for her children. Because of its exalted imperial origin, the robe is carefully preserved and passed from the older to the younger children as an item to be worn only on special occasions such as Tết–the spring festival. But when it comes down to Hoa, the youngest child, it has become so tattered through age, that she can no longer array herself in the attire she dreamed of. Later, upon growing up, getting a job, and earning money to buy new clothes, she has lost her mother, so she derives no solace from her newly acquired outfits.

North Wind was Linh Bảo's first novel, but *Rainy Nights* and *The Old Stable* were the two works in which she revealed her full powers.

Linh Bảo was blessed with both talent and with opportunity. She later confided to me that if she had never met the writer Nguyễn Thị Vinh, the draft copy of *North Wind* would never have reached the hands of Nhất Linh; and in that case it is by no means certain that she would later have emerged as a writer. It was Nhất Linh who discovered the talent of the author of *North Wind* and at the same time created an opportunity for her to take a series of well-planned steps on the road leading to authorship.

THE DAYS IN MONTEREY

In 1972, I went for professional training in the field of Rehabilitation Medicine at Letterman General Hospital in Presidio, San Francisco. Before I went, Lê Ngộ Châu gave me some advice: "When you go, you must pay a visit to our sister Linh Bảo." And at the same time he gave me a handwritten letter to present to her, for the purpose, it seemed, of giving me the duty of visiting her.

One weekend, on a Saturday morning, having arranged matters with me by phone, Linh Bảo drove to a Greyhound station to pick me up. I had met her already in Saigon, so I was not the least bit taken aback when I met her–but this time we were in the U.S. Linh Bảo was

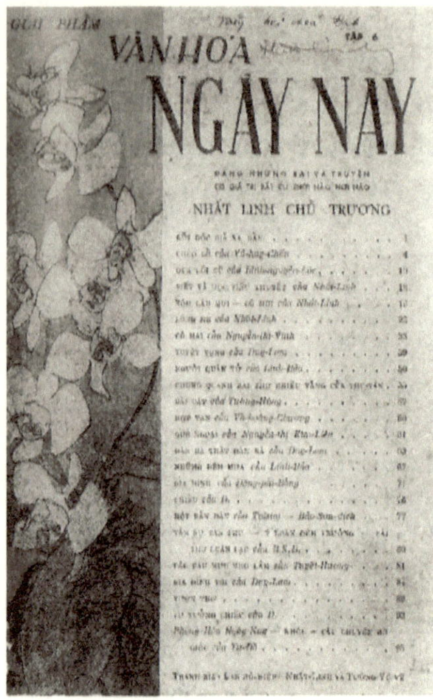

The cover of the belles lettres journal *Culture in the Present Era* (*Văn Hóa Ngày Nay*), no. 6, the issue containing Linh Bảo's "Noble Man," one of her two stories selected by PEN International as a finalist among 26 best international short stories in 1961.

(Linh Bảo, personal archives)

then 46 years old–perhaps her period of maximum beauty. She had the strong, healthy features of a western woman, but still retained the gentle, refined manners of the East. That morning I went with her to visit Monterey Bay. It was a fine, sunny day, the sky was clear and blue, and the seashore was carpeted with red flowers, with here and there the steeples of a few Spanish-style churches. Only when noon came did we reach her house, which was situated on the crest of a hill, and I got to meet "Mr. Linh Bảo," a professor at the university in Berkeley whose field was ecology, a field that I too was concerned with. I learned that the two of them had just returned from the east, where they had attended a conference of the American Institute of Biological Sciences at the College of Vermont. He had a deep love for the natural world and was concerned with the preservation of all the ecological systems on our planet. He had impossible dreams–dreams that could not be realized – and was called the "mad scientist" by Linh Bảo, but for me he had all the beautiful qualities of an intellectual at an American college. He often referred to the Tibetan Plateau, and was preparing to go there on a field trip to do research (that was the snowy Tibet of 1972, forty-three years ago, before the country had been semi-destroyed by China; author's note).

When she returned with me to her home, Ms. Linh Bảo at once put on an apron and went into the kitchen to prepare a lunch for three people. Though busy, she didn't appear hurried, and was fresh and smiling as she went back and forth. The meal she prepared was a sort of "fusion-cuisine," half Vietnamese and half American. It included meat, but didn't lack vegetables. It was very tasty and an atmosphere of easy intimacy between guest and hosts arose at once.

The two men plunged into a discussion of environmental issues in which Linh Bảo did not participate much. After the meal, as we were sipping coffee, "Mr. Linh Bảo," thinking no doubt that we had grown sufficiently close so that he could share a few personal, semi-humorous reflections, turned to a different subject: the experience of marrying an Asian wife. His initial impression was that Asian women were mild and obedient, but then, in a witty manner, made the following observation: "Only after having married Linh Bảo did I realize that they actually conceal iron hands beneath velvet gloves." The three of us all burst into laughter, but the impression of the visitor was that "Mr. Linh Bảo" was leading a happy life in the grip of those "iron hands."

In the afternoon, the three of us went to visit the school where Linh Bảo taught: the Defense Language Institute in Monterey, California. It was very large; more than three dozen languages were taught there to Americans before they were sent forth to different countries all over the world. I also visited a facility that provided care for handicapped children where Linh Bảo did volunteer work on weekends. After that I went to look at the center of Monterey, and it wasn't until late afternoon when they took me back to the Greyhound Station so that I could return to San Francisco.

Not long after my return to Vietnam, I received a letter from Linh Bảo dated Jan. 23, 1973 sent to me through the editorial office of *Cyclopedia* (*Bách Khoa*). She wrote: "I was delighted to get your letter and the book that came with it, because I was under the

Ngô Thế Vinh visiting Linh Bảo in Monterey, California, 1972. *(photos by L. Adams)*

impression that someone had used a spell to induce you to disappear into Canada. Do you know of a way I can buy a number of your books so that my students can read them? I was very pleased by your *Green Belt* (*Vòng Đai Xanh*) because it is just the sort of book that I want to read so that I can improve my understanding of things. Why don't you discuss your Miss Như Nguyện so I can hear your views? She surely must have practiced self-cultivation through many previous existences, right? (Như Nguyện is a character in *Green Belt*; author's note). I want to go and pay a visit to my home – Monterey just now has snow, a thing that hasn't happened for several dozen years. Linh Bảo"

LINH BẢO IN LITTLE SAIGON, 1991

I had no opportunity to visit Linh Bảo again until, after my years of "voluntary reeducation", I returned to California from New York. This time, thanks to a mutual friend, Ms. Công Huyền Tôn Nữ Nha Trang, a PhD at UC-Berkeley, she worked together with Linh Bảo for a time to complete the book *Women Writers of South Vietnam, 1954 – 1975*. Ms. Nha Trang and her husband William L. Pensinger later became the translators of my book *Vòng Đai Xanh* (*The Green Belt*, Ivy House, 2004).

[After 1975, she abandoned writing almost entirely and paid little attention to the works by means of which she had established her literary career. She was always like a "kite's wing." living abroad in exile but still turning in her spirit to Vietnam.

Linh Bảo compared the fate of Vietnamese to that of kites arbitrarily swept to the four corners of the earth by the storm of modern events:

The Clouds of Qin (Mây Tần), a short story collection by Linh Bảo, published by Việt Nam Hải Ngoại, California, 1981. *(Ngô Thế Vinh, personal archives)*

From the left: Linh Bảo and Võ Phiến's wife Viễn Phố in the days when they both lived with their families in the Los Angeles area. *(Viễn Phố, personal archives)*

"The sky was deep blue, with a few snow-white wisps of cloud drifting here and there on gusts of wind, making acquaintance with a crowd of flying kites, when all of a sudden a whirling windstorm approached. The kites, as if with one will, flew high above the clouds. A great number were cut off from the flock, and some plummeted to the earth. The formation of flying kites was no longer under control; the multicolored kites flew rapidly and freely. They were like little dots imprinted on the deep blue background of the sky. The wind blew them to the tops of mountains, to the sea, to the cities, to the countryside; they were blown with violence to all locations.

"Those kites were people far from home. Some were cut off from their kindred, became orphans cut off from their homelands, and had no one left with whom to be close… Some, having no other choice, or due to their own volition, became people with no roots. Among these people with no roots, some were miserable but bore up under their condition, some recreated themselves, and some were proud of their rootlessness and strove to erase all vestiges of their past that still clung to them. Some still communicated with their families, or with their homelands but it was a moot question whether their love of family and homeland was stronger than their greedy desire to enjoy the material happiness and peace of their strange countries.

"I implore heaven that a kind wind will arise that will conduct all the kites back to their motherland! (*Kites' Wings* [*Những Cánh Diều*, p. 5-7, Trí Đăng publishers, Saigon, 1971]

The writer Linh Bảo was molding a sculptural portrait of her mother in a sculpture studio at a college in south California.
(Linh Bảo, personal archives)

But as long as the Motherland remains governed by a regime that "imprisons the wind" (*Nhốt Gió*, the title of a work by Bình Nguyên Lộc), barring the friendly winds of democracy blowing back from overseas, there will still be more than three million kites living abroad still yearning for "The soul of the homeland follows the distant Qin clouds" as in the poem of the great writer Nguyễn Du from more than 200 years ago.

IN SEARCH OF LOST TIME, 2015

With no urge remaining to write, Linh Bảo found further activities that gave her pleasure: she took courses in painting and sculpture; she learned how to imprint images on plates; she gardened, did yoga, and even studied martial arts. A thing that few people knew was that she had a black belt in the martial arts school of Bảo Truyền.

Linh Bảo now lives in a small house in Midway city that has a garden with trees in back and a pond with Koi fish. Living in the same

Lê Ngộ Châu visiting Linh Bảo in 1995 from the right: Ngô Thế Vinh, Linh Bảo, Lê Ngộ Châu, and Võ Phiến.
(Ngô Thế Vinh, personal archives)

house are three generations, which at the same time are three different worlds: Linh Bảo, her daughter, and her daughter's daughter, who herself has reached the mature age of 30.

The writer Linh Bảo is about to enter her 90s (she was born two years later than Nguyễn Thị Vinh, but only six months later than Võ Phiến: Oct. 20, 1925). She is still clear headed, still sounds like she always did when she speaks, reads books without glasses, has a straight back, walks around with assurance, and lives independently.

I'm sending this article, adorned as it is with bits of my personal reminiscences, as an early birthday gift to Linh Bảo before she enters the rarely attained age of 90.

California, 4th of July 2015 – 2017

JOURNEY TO FREEDOM
THE WRITER BOAT-PERSON MAI THẢO

Mai Thảo in front of a signed painting by Tạ Tỵ. *(Source: E. E. Emprunt Empreinte)*

"Perhaps some day Vietnam will be free and I will be able to return. I lead a fortunate life here, but inside I feel very sad–sad for my people. I don't know if there will be a future for our people. Far from our homeland, it is truly hard to maintain our traditions. We feel as if we have lost a part of our soul."
Mai Thảo

It has been 36 years since the day Mai Thảo gave this reply to his interviewer Jane Katz on July 10, 1980, two years after he had set foot on U.S. soil, and it has been 18 years since the day he passed away – and Vietnam still lacks freedom – and his body lies buried on a continent very distant from his homeland.

MAI THẢO'S DESK-IN-EXILE:

It is hard to picture the desolation of Mai Thảo's life in America. His existence consisted merely of a small room, no. 209, on the second floor of an apartment complex reserved for the elderly directly behind the restaurant Song Long ("The Paired Dragons"). It had only a desk and a narrow, single-person bed, a cracked lamp at the head of the bed, and some bottles of strong spirits beneath the bed. On the wall there were some photos of Mai Thảo, and in particular one that showed him, tall and thin, looking frail in a beige-colored long jacket, sitting on a porch next to the poet Vũ Hoàng Chương, looking frail in a black silken gown (*áo dài*). Beneath this photo was a shelf of books. Mai Thảo had many friends, but among the many photos that show him sitting next to them, this was perhaps the one he particularly liked. With regard to age, Vũ Hoàng Chương was a dozen years older than Mai Thảo, so Nguyễn-Xuân Hoàng was astonished, on one occasion, to hear Mai Thảo addressing him with the intimate pronoun "mày."

Nguyễn Hưng Quốc reported that he heard Mai Thảo make the following remarks about his friend Vũ Hoàng Chương: "He's a strange fellow, an authentic poet. The expression on his face always has traces of child-like bewilderment. But his remarks about poetry are beyond splendid. He refers to everyone as "fellow (*thằng*)." Li Bo is a "fellow." Nguyễn Du is a "fellow." He's a person who loves poetry, and has an endless knowledge of poetry."

Nguyễn Đình Toàn, having been born in 1936, was nine years younger than Mai Thảo, but he and Mai Thảo still used the intimate pronouns "mày" and "tao" with each other–which shows that in their literary life, they were two hapless companions beneath heaven–and that literary friends know no distinctions of age.

Mai Thảo and Vũ Hoàng Chương. *(Source: Literature (Văn), special issue commemorating Mai Thảo, Feb. 1998)*

That cramped room, hot by day and cold by night, was both Mai Thảo's living space and also the editorial office of his overseas journal *Literature* (*Văn*). Every time I went to visit him, I would observe his little portable desk shoved tight against the frame of a low window, through which one could catch a glimpse of the prospect outside. While drawing near the bookshelf, I saw a few books that bore the name "Mai Thảo"; instead there were a few books in French, a few issues of *Literature* and a few new books that friends had given him as gifts. Mai Thảo was good at French, and read many books in that language. He also kept close to U.S. Literature and was fond of such authors as Henry Miller, Hemingway, and John Steinbeck, but he read those authors too in French.

I paid particular attention to a book on his shelves with an eye-catching red cover: *Artists in Exile, American Odyssey*, by Jane Katz. In that book, Katz, a journalist, interviewed writers and artists from all over the world who had come to the U.S. as refugees. They were from diverse locales such as Russia, China, Afghanistan, South Africa, Argentina, and Vietnam... Katz interviewed and introduced Mai Thảo as a "boat person," the author of forty-two books in Vietnamese, all of which were kept in the library of Cornell University. The interview with Mai Thảo took place on July 10, 1980, two years after he first stepped onto American soil, with translation provided by Nguyễn Thanh Trang, a friend of Mai Thảo's, who had arrived from San Diego. Though it was an interview, the questions of the interviewer are omitted, so in content it has the character of a personal reminiscence.

Jane Katz recorded her feelings after the interview as follows: "He speaks with quiet dignity, and with the restraint which years of privation have taught him."

I took the book, which had Katz's handwritten inscription, from the shelves and asked to borrow it. I made a cursory translation of the interview and published it in literary magazines, including, eventually, the special issue of *Literary Studies (Văn Học)* devoted to Mai Thảo, giving the name of the translator as "Tâm Bình."[1] Then I returned the book to his shelves.

The interview with Jane Katz will be included in this essay as a commemoration of Mai Thảo on his eighteenth death anniversary.

When he turned the journal *Literature (Văn)* over to Nguyễn-Xuân Hoàng in 1996, Mai Thảo's health had begun to take a decisive turn for the worse; he moved about with difficulty. It got so bad, according to an account by Khánh Trường, that once, on returning home late at night, he lacked the strength to climb the single flight of stairs that led up to his accustomed room where he had dwelt for years. After that, he had to move to a different room on the ground floor. Right above that room was the room of the artist Khánh Trường. Khánh Trường's health was not all that good either, but he was strong enough to assist Mai Thảo when it was necessary. The means Mai Thảo used to signal Khánh Trường was not the telephone, but usually a cane that he used to knock on the ceiling.

---

1 Nguyễn-Xuân Hoàng, "Remembering Mai Thảo" ("Nhớ Mai Thảo"), *Literature* (*Văn*), special issue on Mai Thảo, Feb. 1998.

Front cover of *Artists in Exile* by Jane Katz, jacket design by Ted Berstein, Stein and Day Publishers, New York: 1983.

A portrait of Mai Thảo, photo by Kathryn Oneita, with the inscription "The sea was calm, and the people began to sing".

To Mai Thao,
With gratitude for your
beautiful interview.
Jane

The handwritten inscription by Jane Katz in a special printed edition of her book that she presented to Mai Thảo.

Khánh Trường was a dashing habitué of the *Confluence* (*Hợp Lưu*) group[2] and Mai Thảo was at the center of the *Literature* (*Văn*) group – they differed greatly in age and mode of life, but they were nevertheless loyal to each other as friends. "The Street Artist of New York" was the name Mai Thảo used to refer to Khánh Trường. It was like the case of Cao Xuân Huy, a bold soldier who at first kept his distance from

2 *Confluence* (*Hợp Lưu*) was a Vietnamese-language journal devoted to literature and art founded by the artist Khánh Trường and published in California from 1990 to 2003.

Mai Thảo and the "Street Artist of New York," a sobriquet he bestowed on Khánh Trường. *(Khánh Trường, personal archives)*

Mai Thảo, but after that drew near to him and developed an intense regard for him. In the book *Portraits of Fifteen Writers and Poets of Vietnam* (*Chân Dung 15 Nhà Văn Nhà Thơ Việt Nam*), published in the U.S. by Văn Khoa in 1985, Mai Thảo has incisive descriptions of his literary friends: "A Nhật Tiến Still Standing Out in the Sun" ("Một Nhật Tiến vẫn đứng ở ngoài nắng), "A Mode of Being: Bình Nguyên Lộc" ("Một nhân cách Bình Nguyên Lộc"), "A Mặc Đỗ Living in Seclusion" ("một Mặc Đỗ quy ẩn"), "The Road of Dương Nghiễm Mậu" ("Con Đường Dương Nghiễm Mậu), "The Sword of Lê Tất Điều" ("Đường gươm Lê Tất Điều") "Nhã Ca in the Deluge" ("Nhã Ca Giữa Hồng Thủy")...

THE JOURNAL *LITERATURE (VĂN)* ON AMERICAN SOIL:

Mai Thảo's reputation is closely connected with the journal *Creation* (*Sáng Tạo*), though that journal's period of existence was relatively short. The journal *Literature* (*Văn*), however, carried his writings for a longer period, from the period before 1975, when it was in-country, to the period abroad, when it lasted until 1996. *Literature* began in 1964 with Trần Phong Giao as the secretary of the editorial board, and lasted for eight years. In 1972, *Literature* passed into the hands of Nguyễn-Xuân Hoàng, who took over his predecessor's role. In 1973, Mai Thảo joined with Nguyễn-Xuân Hoàng in the direction of *Literature*. In 1974, Nguyễn-Xuân Hoàng withdrew from the journal, and Mai Thảo continued managing it until April 30, 1975.

In 1982, two years after arriving in the U.S., Mai Thảo resumed publishing *Literature*, and kept it going for fourteen years. It is hard to imagine how he managed it – he did not drive, and belonged to the school of those who "write by hand," using a pen only, never resorting to a typewriter or computer. Bent over his desk, he even wrote out the addresses of the subscribers, who numbered in the hundreds, on the mailers before sending out the issues. He had young friends who wanted to save him some time by using a computer to print out mailing

The wayfarer Mai Thảo in January 1996, a photo taken two years before he died. *(photo by Nguyễn Bá Khanh)*

labels, but he refused. Mai Thảo laid stress on feeling; he wanted to have a personal relationship with each of the journal's readers through the presence of his own handwriting on each issue. Throughout the fourteen years in which he lived with, and by means of, the journal, he was always elated whenever he discovered some new writer endowed with talent. *Literature* also served as a collecting place for all the writers of the South living abroad in exile. An example is Thảo Trường, a one-time writer for *Creation*. On coming to the U.S. after seventeen years in communist prisons, he sent his first new articles to Mai Thảo for publication in *Literature*.

In speaking of the journal *Writing*, Mai Thảo once offered these reflections: "Since restarting the journal *Literature* in the U.S. a few years ago, I have felt that my daily existence as a wanderer has been a little less forlorn, because the work has allowed me to drift back to the atmosphere of an editing office, an atmosphere of governance – though different, it has some vague resemblance to the past – I work at a desk beneath a bright light, a life I led for years in the homeland, and this provides my mind with occasions to wander back in memory to my office of former days on 38 Phạm Ngũ Lão Street in Saigon.

By the year 1996, after the publication of issues 158 &159, due to poor health, Mai Thảo had to relinquish his editorship of the journal, turning it over to Du Tử Lê. After issue 160, the journal was officially turned over to the direction of Nguyễn-Xuân Hoàng, and the next three issues, 161 to 163, were produced under him.

At the beginning of 1997, Nguyễn-Xuân Hoàng published the first issue of *Literature, New Series*, and continued to publish it for twelve years. In 2008, the final issues, nos. 125-129, devoted to the artist Thái Tuấn, with all the articles laid out, were delivered to the printer, but then, for financial reasons, Nguyễn-Xuân Hoàng had to discontinue publication. *Literature* could still be sold, but the profits were not great enough to pay a debt (to Kim Select Graphics and Printing on Euclid Street) that later Nguyễn-Xuân Hoàng and his wife would try their best to gradually repay.

From the left: Mai Thảo, Kiều Loan (the daughter of Hoàng Cầm), and Nguyễn-Xuân Hoàng in 1996, the year Mai Thảo turned the journal *Literature* over to Nguyễn-Xuân Hoàng. *(photo by Nguyễn Bá Khanh)*

A further, deadlier reason that no one wanted to discuss was that when *Literature* under Nguyễn Xuân Hoàng ceased publication, the case was similar to that of *The Arts* (Văn Nghệ) under Từ Mẫn (Võ Thắng Tiết). Both publications had to cease activity because, though they could still be sold, the bookstores did not promptly pay the publishers what was owing to them.

MAI THẢO'S COMPASSION:

Mai Thảo was known to everybody as a writer, a well-known author of occasional essays, and later on as a poet. On making his acquaintance, people came to revere him even more. His feelings with regard to others were truly beautiful. He was kind to everyone and also very direct. He would speak frankly to people who held views opposite to his own, sometimes even becoming angry, but would later forget it all, never dwelling on such disagreements. Throughout his career as a writer, he never used his pen to speak ill of anyone, though there was no lack of articles that subjected him to heavy criticism. Perhaps he never read them; at any rate, he never responded.

His younger brother Nguyễn Đăng Khánh wrote about him as follows: "Many times when I read articles in journals that cast severe aspersions on him, I would be upset and go to him, asking, 'Why don't you protest when you see people criticizing you so severely?' He would reply, 'When you live with others, and live with life, you have to have heart. "Heart, in this matter, is the same as *bonté* [goodness]. A person devoid of *bonté* is to be cast aside. One must live sincerely with others, and with life. That is why I never use my pen to raise a protest or to criticise or speak ill of anyone, or to respond to attacks made on me. If people wish to criticise me or speak ill of me, let them do so. You see, Khánh, people criticize me in journals only because they wish readers to see their names on the same page as the name Mai Thảo. If they like to do so, let them go ahead–I will never write a reply.'"

On another, earlier occasion in 1989, Mai Thảo expressed similar views to Nguyễn Hưng Quốc in Paris: "I have a principle in this life: don't ever use literature to do anything ugly. It is not at all the case that I am unaware that some people are kind, and some ugly, in their dealings with me. But whichever it is, I ignore it. If people are kind, I draw near and share a glass with them; if they are ugly, I just keep my distance. I have not the slightest desire to get involved. But one should never drag such things onto paper and engage in dirty disputes. Literature is beauty; it is the realm of beauty, and that realm has its own currency. One must use that currency. One must be honest; one must have principles. The currency to be used may be termed "beauty."

An article by Thái Tú Hạp, "A Few Memories of the writer Mai Thảo" ("Một Vài Kỷ Niệm với nhà văn Mai Thảo") appeared in the *Saigon Times* toward the end of 1997. It tells how the author visited Mai Thảo when he was in the hospital in Fountain Valley. Thái Tú Hạp remembers with emotion something that Mai Thảo confided in him when he was still strong. He often went to the restaurant Doanh Doanh at the end of Sunset Boulevard in Los Angeles – it was a family run place, very cultured, run by Thái Tú Hạp and his wife Ái Cầm, with classical music and even a large oil painting by Nguyên Khai. Mai Thảo said, "I will tell you something Hạp – in this life it's possible that one won't like this person, feel antipathy for some other person, and trade curses and insults with them for a while... cast it all aside! Don't drag the fight into some journal – that's no way to behave! Let the realm of literature remain clear and bright. Use your pen in a principled way, so as to fulfill your obligations to every person..."

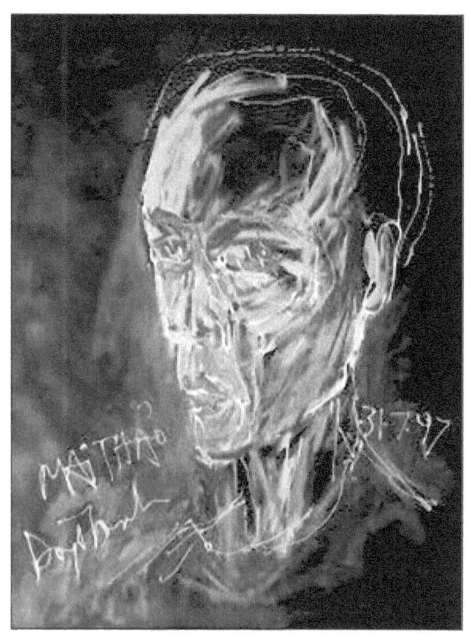

Mai Thảo, as represented in a drawing by Duy Thanh (July 31, 1997) collected by Lê Thiệp.

(source: Literature, special issue to a commemoration of Mai Thảo, Feb. 1998)

In an interview that took place on June 5, 2008, ten years after Mai Thảo's death, the last question addressed by Thụy Khuê to Trần Vũ was: "What more do you wish to say about Mai Thảo?" Trần Vũ replied, "When he was still alive, Mai Thảo would often stress the following: 'I never use words for non-literary purposes. I never curse anyone. Literature is not a place for me to cast dirt. I don't have the right to.' When his temper was aroused, he would get grumpy. Not just once, but many times he would offer advice, or give orders. Now he is dead, and I too am no longer young, but whenever I think of him, I always think of those words of his. Yesterday, and today, I still keep the promise I made to the person who was my highest authority."

Throughout his life as a user of the written word, he continued, with utter consistency, to be the same Mai Thảo, always protecting the purity and elevation of the realm of literature. Though not a practicing monk, he nevertheless had the heart of a Buddha.

And now I suddenly recall two lines from the poem "She's Been Living a Fantasy Since Ancient Times" ("Em đã hoang đường từ cổ đại") in his verse collection *We See Our Images: So many Shrines* (*Ta thấy hình ta những miếu đền*):

My heart, a Buddha, yours, a Buddha too;
On each heart there rests a stick of incense.

HIS DAYS AND MONTHS IN THE HOSPITAL:

Not long after Mai Thảo turned his journal over to Nguyễn-Xuân Hoàng, his health began to decline rapidly; sometimes he had insufficient strength to leave his room, even though he had moved to the ground floor. His sense of loneliness, and the signs of his illness had already caused him, a few years earlier, to make the poem "Beckoning to Illness" ("Dỗ Bệnh):

Each time my body causes trouble,
I engage it in a conversation;
I urge it not to bring things to extremes
It seems to think this over and permits
The illness in me to become a friend

From left: Mai Thảo, Kiều Chinh, and Võ Phiến at a gathering.
(Viễn Phố, personal archives)

His first poetry collection: *We See Our Images: So Many Shrines* (*Ta Thấy Hình Ta Những Miếu Đền*); cover photo designed by Trần Cao Lĩnh; inscribed autograph by Mai Thảo. *(Ngô Thế Vinh, personal archives)*

Lingering long, it grows a cozy partner,
And the two of us grow firm as gold and stone.[3]

When he could "beckon illness" no longer, the time came when he had to forsake his desk-in-exile (bàn viết lữ thứ), depart from his room behind the "Paired Dragons" restaurant and take turns living in the hospitals of Fountain Valley in Orange County, Good Samaritan Los Angeles and then Barlow County Hospital. He never afterward had a chance to return to his former surroundings.

Good Samaritan was the hospital where I went to visit him. There I met Nguyễn Phúc Vĩnh Khiêm, a young doctor specializing in cardiovascular medicine, who was providing his immediate care. Khiêm had studied in French schools from early childhood and on attaining adulthood had studied medicine in the U.S., so he knew nothing about the literary work of Mai Thảo, but thanks to his father, he knew that he was caring for a person named Nguyễn Đăng Quý, a famous Vietnamese writer with the pen name Mai Thảo.

3 The expression "gold and stone" (đá vàng) is used in Vietnamese to refer to unshakeable friendship. (EH)

Khiêm was also the doctor in the Good Samaritan Hospital who had operated on Abbot Thích Mãn Giác (that is, the poet Huyền Không) and was a member of the team that had carried out Võ Phiến's second heart operation. Due to our respective medical specialties, I had many opportunities to discuss Mai Thảo's medical status with Khiêm. He needed an oxygen tube in order to breathe, and for nourishment needed a G-tube that fed food into his stomach. In this period his life depended totally on machinery and on special care. After hospital treatment, Mai Thảo's health stabilized, but his recovery was very slow due to his general weakness, and due to many years of drinking alcohol, eating little, and smoking cigarettes. He was seriously undernourished and had difficulty even in breathing.

When Nguyễn Mộng Giác went with his wife Nguyễn Khoa Diệu Chi and two other women (Bùi Bích Hà and Trần Thị Lai Hồng, the wife of the artist Võ Đình) to visit Mai Thảo in Barlow Hospital in Los Angeles, his writer's instinct suggested to him that "though we had no knowledge of medicine, we all felt that Mai Thảo was on a one-way street, and that there was no chance that he could return to a normal existence."

After he was freed from the breathing tube, it was no longer necessary for him to stay in acute care, so Mai Thảo was transferred

Left: the Bolsa apartment complex for the elderly behind the Paired Dragons restaurant; right: room 209, the address of *Literature* and of Mai Thảo's desk-in-exile *(photos by Ngô Thế Vinh)*

to a rehabilitation facility in Orange County. He didn't have any terminal disease. Though he had been a drinker for so many years, he still had a "liver of iron" – but he continued to decline like a tree deprived of sap until the day of his death on Jan. 10, 1998.

I recall that when Mai Thảo had just died, Đỗ Ngọc Yến had the idea of establishing a literary prize in his name. I said to Yến that, before establishing such a prize, the thing to be done right away was to preserve his desk-in-exile, as a memento of the cultural life of Little Saigon.

After his death, all the objects in Mai Thảo's living space were collected by his younger brother Nguyễn Đăng Khánh – they filled only a few cardboard boxes. And there was no longer the slightest trace of the desk-in-exile of the "boat person" named Mai Thảo.

When the Vietnamese, driven all across five continents, make pilgrimages to the refugee capital, they surely deserve to see more than the commercial Phước Lộc Thọ shopping center, with Văn Khoa, its lone bookstore, now also gone. A young family friend came with his group of second-generation children from the snowy land of Toronto and observed that Little Saigon should surely offer an opportunity for

A gathering in the home of Nguyễn-Xuân Hoàng, July 1994. From left: Nguyên Sa, Thụy Khuê, Mai Thảo, Nguyễn Mộng Giác, Đỗ Ngọc Yến, Võ Phiến, and Hoàng Khởi Phong. *(Viễn Phố, personal archives)*

them to see more than just some "phở" shops and some signs posted in front of doctors' and lawyers' offices. He wanted to suggest the idea of *a Vietnamese Cultural Park.*

THE INTERVIEW OF JANE KATZ WITH MAI THẢO

And here is the introduction of Jane Katz, the interviewer of Mai Thảo, July 10,1980:

"Since the fall of Saigon to the Communists in 1975, the South China Sea is strewn with refugees, people from all segments of Vietnamese society who are willing to risk their lives in small boats on the high seas, rather than endure food shortages, force resettlements, and political repression in their native land. One of these "boat people" is Mai Thảo, a journalist and a popular novelist in Vietnam, author of 42 books in the Vietnamese language before he was forced underground by the Communist takeover. Mai Thảo escaped by boat to Malaysia in 1977, and from there came to Seattle, where he is editor of Đất Mới (New Earth)*, a Vietnamese language newspaper, and is president of the Washington-based Vietnamese Cultural Association. All of his books can be found in the Cornell University collection. He speaks with quiet dignity, and with restraint which years of privation have taught him. His friend Tony Nguyễn, an earlier emigré from Vietnam, serves as translator."*

[Artists in Exile, American Odyssey, page 74 by Jane Katz]

...

And here is this author's cursory translation of the interview with Mai Thảo, which appears in English in the book *Artists in Exile, American Odyssey*, by Jane Katz, Stein and Day Publishers, 1983.

"I was born in 1930[4] in Nam Định Province, North Vietnam. My father was a landlord, a man of substance who was much respected by the people of our village. He was our head of household. My mother stayed at home with those who helped her. I and my brothers and sisters obeyed our father in everything.

---

4 Author's note: Mai Thảo was born on June 8, 1927. The detail in Katz's interview that he was born in 1930 is perhaps not accurate.

After the people of the West invaded our land, conflicts arose between the younger and older generations. But the foreigners were unable to damage the foundations of the family in our country. That was a system that had existed for ages, and no one had the ability to destroy it.

My father managed farms. He was wealthy, so he didn't have us work in the fields. I had to go to school and study, but after school I was able to run about in the fields and amuse myself. I mingled with the water buffalo that pulled ploughs in the Red River delta area. The grassy fields were green and fertile. Some people in the village worked for my father, and others had fields of their own.

My people love their fields, and they believe that the souls of their ancestors are alive in them. Every family worked in the fields and no one had to suffer hunger.

When I turned ten years old, my father lost all his fields. My family had to withdraw to Hanoi. It was terribly difficult for my father to be forced to forsake his fields, which belonged to our ancestors and to the village. He knew everyone in the village. He had a secure basis there that he could not find in the city.

In Hanoi, I got to see the city walls, and ancient temples dating from the eighth to the tenth centuries. One temple was called Ngọc Sơn, and a different structure, a shrine, was called Quan Thánh. In the middle of the city was a large lake, a place where people met after putting in long days of work. In the summer, we went out to the sea.

Though we lived in the city, we still preserved our ancient traditions, such as respecting the old and reverently observing rites proper to particular occasions.

A spirit of loyalty to the nation was part of Vietnamese tradition. For a thousand years the Vietnamese people were ruled by the Chineses. This influenced our educational system and our thought, but the Vietnamese never entirely submitted to this influence. Then in the nineteenth century, when the French attacked and occupied many provinces in Vietnam, they established an administrative system, created a government to rule the country, and set up regional civic organizations.

When I was sixteen, I joined the anti-French resistance movement. We organized musical and dramatic programs in all the villages in order to stimulate patriotic feelings. We wrote many essays concerning history and yearned for freedom. Four years later I abandoned the resistance when I learned that the communists had exploited the movement to destroy our traditional social order and stir up class conflict.

The Franco-Vietnamese war ended in 1954 and the country was divided in two. I emigrated with my family to Saigon. That was a way of resisting the communists. My father didn't trust them, and they didn't trust him. Under communist domination the people ceased to pay attention to art. How can you create paintings when every day you have to worry about every bite of food? Intellectuals lost their freedom and were often forced to join the army.

Beginning in 1958, an open struggle began between two regions of the country: the North, ruled by the communists, were supported by the communist Chinese and the noncommunist South was supported by the United States and the various allied countries.

A constant war of propaganda was maintained on both sides. The North proclaimed everywhere that it was necessary to liberate the South from imperialist America, while the government of the South maintained that we must resist being governed by Communist China and the Soviet Union. The armed forces of the communists hid in the deep forests and used guerrilla tactics. American aircraft scattered poisonous substances everywhere to force those forces to reveal themselves. In doing this, they also poisoned the forests and mountains, the vegetation, the animals, and food sources in general.

My memories of the war are very vivid. I can still see the houses hit by bombs, the trees deprived by fire of foliage with bare limbs sticking out, a shrine consumed in fire, children with distended bellies, with missing eyes or legs, and old ladies with no homes, wandering about as if they had lost their souls…

I started writing in 1950. Writers are highly respected in my land. My books were published by many small private companies in South Vietnam and were widely distributed. Some became "best-sellers," but to live by one's pen is very difficult. I wrote many stories and novels. We didn't have many translators, and my books were not put into foreign languages. I also was the editor-in-chief of a few journals and literary magazines.

I have read some American authors whom I like very much, such as: Henry Miller, Hemingway, and John Steinbeck – in French translations. These authors had no influence on my own writing. Our own literature is very different. We have our own thousand-year-old literary tradition. Our literature is very formal; and it has the goal of advancing society.

I wrote a short story that I like very much with the title "The Testament on the Highest Peak" ("Bản Chúc Thư Trên Ngọn Đỉnh Trời"). A man and a woman lived together next to a stream in a forest. For a reason the woman could not understand the man left one day. The man's journey led him to the highest point at the top of a mountain to the east. He wanted to know how high the mountain was. He wanted to find absolute truth and happiness. When he reached the highest point on the mountain, he fell into despair because he perceived that absolute truth can never be obtained. The woman went to look for him and found the man's body lying by the stream. No one knew how the man had died. The woman took the man's body into the village and asked herself why the man had died. And, finally, the woman came to the realization that while on his journey to seek the truth, the man had chosen death.

As a writer, I touch on the problem of human life: it is not my purpose to find a solution. Most of my books and stories are based on my own experience, or on that of people I have known. Things that I remember are mixed with things that I make up. Style – that's the important element.

The Americans left Vietnam in 1975. Because of my previous anti-communist writings, my name was on a blacklist of authors who had done harm to the regime. Almost all the authors whose names were on that list were arrested and put in prison, and many of them died in prison because they lacked food and medicine.

I was relatively lucky – I was cared for and shielded by the people. If it had not been for their love, I could not have survived in Vietnam.

The communists announced that anyone who offered support to writers on the blacklist would be arrested. Their security system was very thorough. They directed everyone in a neighborhood to keep an eye on each other and make reports to the regional authority. But there will still be people who took risks in order to shield me. They hid me in eight different houses for two years. I lived in dark tunnels, because any light or activity discovered in the neighborhood would pose a danger to my hosts. The places where I stayed had to be houses without children, because families all taught their children that they must not tell lies. The communists conducted searches in several houses, but achieved nothing, because they failed to find me.

I was in hiding for two long years, living like an animal in the darkness. There were nights when I went without sleep, and my days were dispiritingly the same. A friend brought me a mahjong set, and I would play both sides at once. A few times when my despair grew too great, I had to find some way of going out while maintaining secrecy in the darkness. At times I was unable to imagine that I had to live in these conditions. Sometimes I gave way to despair and imagined that I was in the midst of a long sleep from which I would never awaken. But Vietnamese people are accustomed to putting up with harsh conditions and finally escaping from them. I deeply felt that writers belong to society and to the people with whom they live. And thinking of the people who had joined together to preserve my life, I felt that I had to be courageous in order to be worthy of the help that I had received.

I am not a Buddhist, though my family are followers of that faith. But I am a writer and a person who thinks, so I must look at my life and try to find meaning in it. For many hours every day I had stilled my heart and meditated. In such circumstances especially, people must seek truth, and seek meaning in their life. I had that opportunity. I believe that each one of us is home to a supreme being. A person can save himself from the turmoil of his life through his own actions and thoughts. This realization remains within me always.

Toward the end of 1977, private organizations appeared that helped people to cross the ocean. They made contact with me and told me to wait in my current shelter. I understood that an escape of this nature was an expensive undertaking, and I did not have a penny. I had no way of communicating with my family that would not expose them to danger. I waited. One dark night, a person wearing a black shirt came on a Honda, stopped beneath a tree behind the house, directed me to mount the motorcycle, and furtively drove toward the bank of the Saigon river where a small fishing boat was waiting. I was told to pole a raft, pretending that I was a fisherman. After two or three hours, I was transferred to a motorboat on the ocean. Then the lady in charge of the boat told me that I could smoke a cigarette. I looked for the last time at the city of Saigon and burst into tears, because I realized that I would never again see it. The people of the south are very tightly bound to the city they call Saigon. I have the feeling that I have forsaken my own inheritance.

Once I was on the open ocean, I had the feeling that I had been released from confinement. I was now a free person. It was a dark night with no moon. We reached the open ocean, but then a storm blew us from the Philippines. Tossing about in a small boat, we had no choice but to return to shore. I resumed hiding. A few days later, I received word that my father had died at the age of 92. According to Asian custom, a son must return to take part in the mourning for his parents or be considered an unfilial child. But my elder brothers all urged me not to return, because I was being followed and might be seized. Fortunately, I was able to go secretly at night to my father's grave and utter prayers to express my feelings of remembrance, and that lessened my distress.

Then a different motorcycle came in the dark night. The second escape was riskier than the first. A small fishing boat delivered me to a hut. I had to hide there for two days in a place full of sticky mud covered with foliage. Finally, a raft arrived and carried me to the open sea in the middle of the night. There I was transferred to a larger fishing boat. Suddenly and noiselessly a signal light flashed.

The writer / boat person Mai Thảo in Dec. 1977, after reaching the shores of Pulau-Besar, Malaysia.

(internet photo)

It took careful calculation and a great deal of luck. I stepped onto a boat capable of carrying twenty people, but it had been boarded by fifty-eight. We had to be very sparing in our use of water and rice because there was no storage space. Everyone drank and ate little, and no one died.

The people on the boat consisted of political refugees, students, schoolchildren, and families with toddlers. We were on the boat for six days and nights. Everyone was hungry and thirsty, and some fell sick. As we approached Malaysia, the sea was calm and the night was clear, and everyone began to sing. They asked me to intone a poem. I read a poem by a friend that spoke of a man having to leave his home with no one to bid him farewell.

We got to Malaysia, but they didn't want to receive us. The officials were unfriendly because too many refugees had already come. Malaysia was a poor country; they could not rescue everybody. Each time we tried to approach a pier they would push us out again. Finally, a Malaysian fisherman signaled us – he said that we should drive our boat directly onto the shore; if our boat broke and could no longer be used, they would have to accept us. We did as he advised, and it was effective. The boat that carried us broke. We helped the little children, the old, and the sick to reach land. United Nations officials came and met us and gave us money to buy food with. The first thing I bought was a pack of cigarettes. They conducted us to a refugee camp. The camp was very crowded, but there was enough food, and there were tents to stay in. And, as for us, we were free. We were not kept pent up in the camp. I began to love the people of Malaysia. There was a broadcasting station in the camp, and I was asked to write articles and read them on its program. I also acted as a chairperson of the camp.

I came to the U.S. because I had two younger siblings who lived here. Also, I was acquainted with a few writers who had preceded me to the U.S. What I write is based on my own experience. I hope that my novels will be translated into English. I am also active in seeking ways to restore freedom to writers imprisoned in Vietnam. I'm afraid that our literature and art will be annihilated.

I send money back to my mother. I hope she will join us in the U.S., but she doesn't want to be a burden to her children who are over here. She also doesn't want to die in a place far from her homeland.

I want to say to the world that twenty years of war have destroyed my country. The homes and roads can be rebuilt, but not the beauty of the land, nor the spirit of the people. At the very time we sit conversing with each other over here, the destruction continues under the communist regime.

Perhaps one day Vietnam will be free, and I will be able to return. I lead a fortunate life over here, but in my heart I'm sad. Sad for my people. I have no way of predicting if we have a future. Living so far from our homeland, it is hard to preserve our traditions. We feel that half our souls have been taken away. *(Artists in Exile: American Odyssey, Jane Katz)*

THREE POEMS WRITTEN IN CONFINEMENT

After April 30, 1975, Mai Thảo, like most of the South's writers and artists, was trapped. He was among those that the communist regime particularly wished to capture. Since he had for a time been part of the Resistance movement, he understood the communists, and was determined not to announce himself to the new regime, because he knew that if he did so, he would be tortured, imprisoned, and would very likely meet with death.

Mai Thảo lived in hiding for almost two years, from '75 to the end of '77 under the protection of family and friends, among whom one must note that Nhã Ca was particularly courageous. She had a flock of children and a husband in prison, and lived under constant surveillance, but, disregarding danger, she concealed Mai Thảo in a house on Tự Do street until he was able to escape to Malaysia as a boat person. During his time as a fugitive, at times sunk in despair, Mai Thảo made some poems that reflect his feelings when he was in confinement, stripped of freedom.

Four people who have now entered the eternal past: from the right: Thanh Tâm Tuyền (died 2006), Đinh Cường (d. 2016), Mai Thảo (d. 1998), and Ngọc Dũng (d. 2000).*(Đinh Cường, personal archives)*

Here are three poems of uncertain date written by Mai Thảo in the period '75-'77 in Vietnam (source: Phan Nguyên, E. E. Emprunt Empreinte):

Crystal

I toss and turn amid immense bed sheets
My cramped dreams still caught in toils of life
My dream cannot erase the person who
In night's deep pit is stirred by crystal laughter

Metal

A piece of leather binds my eyes, night comes
A metal spike, my mouth is like the grave;
Arms and legs, securely bound by rope
That leather, spike, and rope is now precisely me.

Image

Immured inside, I peer out through the door
Near me, leaves; far off, the sea and sky
The leaves astir: a thousand lives away
The sea is still; the image of a realm not mine

BIOGRAPHICAL DATA

Mai Thảo's real name was Nguyễn Đăng Quý. Aside from "Mai Thảo," he also used the pen name Nguyễn Đăng. He was born on June 8, 1927 in Cồn Market, Hải Hậu District, Nam Định Province. When little, he studied in his village school. He went to middle school in Nam Định and later went to Hanoi, where he was a student at the Đỗ Hữu Vị and Chu Văn An schools. In 1945, he retreated with his school to Hưng Yên. When war broke out in 1946, he went with his family into a rural retreat in Cồn Market, after which he went to Thanh Hóa to join the Resistance. There, he wrote articles for journals and took part in performance troupes that toured all around Interzones III and IV (Liên khu III & IV) and in the Việt Bắc military zone. In 1951, Mai Thảo left the Resistance and returned to the city. In 1954 he emigrated to the South, where he wrote short stories for the journals *Democracy* (*Dân Chủ*), *Vietnamese Fire* (*Lửa Việt*), and *The Vietnamese People* (*Người Việt*). He helped found the journals *Creation* (*Sáng Tạo*; 1956), *The Arts* (*Nghệ Thuật*; 1965), and looked after *Literature* (*Văn*) starting in 1974. On Dec. 8, 1977 he crossed the sea to Pulau-Besar, Malaysia. Early in 1978, he emigrated to the U.S. At first he worked with *New Earth* (*Đất Mới*), run by Thanh Nam in Seattle and a number of other expatriate journals. In July, 1982, he reestablished the journal *Literature*, and was its editor-in-chief until 1996, when, for reasons of health, he turned the publication over to Nguyễn-Xuân Hoàng. He died two years later on Oct. 1, 1998 at the age of seventy-one.

WORKS

The researcher and scholar of library science Phạm Trọng Lệ in the February 1998 issue of *Literature* put together a Remembrance of Mai Thảo (*Tưởng Mộ Mai Thảo*) that included the call numbers of all the works by him held in American libraries. This study was later supplemented and subdivided by Thụy Khuê.

Short Story Collections

The Night I Bade Farewell to Hanoi (*Đêm Giã Từ Hà Nội*, Người Việt, 1955), *Young Grass in the First Month* (*Tháng Giêng Cỏ Non*, 1956), *The Testament on the Highest Peak* (*Bản Chúc Thư Trên Ngọn Đỉnh Trời*, Sáng Tạo, 1963), *A Pack of Rabbits on Your Birthday* (*Bầy Thỏ Ngày Sinh Nhật*, Nguyễn Đình Vượng, 1965), *A House in a Saltwater District* (*Căn Nhà Vùng Nước Mặn*, An Tiêm, 1966), *The Night I Lost My Way* (*Đêm Lạc Đường*, Khai Trí, 1967), *The Splendid River Current* (*Dòng Sông Rực Rỡ*, Văn Uyển, 1968), *My Old Teacher* (*Người Thầy Học Cũ*, Văn Uyển, 1969), *A Boat Trip on the Red River* (*Chuyến Tàu Trên Sông Hồng*, Tuổi Ngọc, 1969), *Occasional Essays* (*Tùy Bút*, 1970), *Rain in the Mountains* (*Mưa Núi*; stories from two previous collections: *The Night I Bade*

Farewell to Hanoi and *Young Grass in the First Month*); Tân Văn, 1970), *The Blind Lighthouse* (*Ngọn Hải Đăng Mù*, Làng Văn, Toronto, 1987), *One Saturday Night* (*Một Đêm Thứ Bảy*, Tổ hợp xuất bản miền Đông Hoa Kỳ, 1988), *Hong Kong Underfoot* (*Hồng Kông Ở Dưới Chân*, Xuân Thu, 1989), *The Fifth Card Player* (*Chân Bài Thứ Năm*, Nam Á, Paris, 1990), *A Metro Trip From Belleville* (*Chuyến Métro Đi Từ Belleville*, Nam Á, 1990)

Novels

A Head of Hair from the Past (*Mái Tóc Dĩ Vãng*, Tiểu thuyết tuần san, 1963). *Do You Like Brahms?* [essays] (*Cô Thích Nhạc Brahms?* [adaptation of the French novel Aimez-Vous Brahms? by Françoise Sagan]), *When Autumn Comes* (*Khi Mùa Thu Tới*, Thái Lai, 1964), *An Engraved Bronze Bullet* (*Viên Đạn Đồng Chữ Nổi*, Văn, 1966), *One Transcendent Night, We Went on the Same Path* (*Đêm Kỳ Diệu, Cùng Đi Một Đường*, 1967), *After the Storm Came* (*Sau Khi Bão Tới*, Màn Ảnh, 1968), *Arriving at Some Age* (*Tới Một Tuổi Nào*, Miền Nam, 1968), *Enough to Make You Forget About Life* (*Cũng Đủ Lãng Quên Đời*, Hồng Đức, 1969), *The Path Beneath the Leaves* (*Lối Đi Dưới Lá*, 1969), *Ten Nights of Ivory and Jade* (*Mười Đêm Ngà Ngọc*, Hoàng Đông Phương, 1969), *High Fashion* (*Thời Thượng*, Côi Sơn, 1970), *You Only Live Once* (*Sống Chỉ Một Lần*, Nguyễn Đình Vượng, 1970), *The End of a Full Moon* (*Hết Một Tuần Trăng*, Tủ Sách Văn Nghệ Khai Phóng, 1970), *After the Curfew Hour* (*Sau Giờ Giới Nghiêm*, Tủ Sách Văn Nghệ Khai Phóng, 1970), *Clear as a Lake in Autumn* (*Trong Như Hồ Thu*, Tủ Sách Văn Nghệ Hiện Đại, 1971), *Taking It down to the Underworld, (Mang Xuống Tuyền Đài*, Tủ Sách Văn Nghệ Khai Phóng, 1971), *A Day of Nhã* (*Một Ngày Của Nhã*, 1971), *So as to Recall the Fragrance* (*Để Tưởng Nhớ Mùi Hương*, Nguyễn Đình Vượng, 1971), *Submerged Wave* (*Sóng Ngầm*, Hoa Biển, 1971), *Living Like a Reflection* (*Sống Như Hình Bóng*, Tiếng Phương Đông, 1972), *Happiness Comes at Night* (*Hạnh Phúc Đến Về Đêm*, Nguyễn Đình Vượng, 1972), *A Life I Still Remember (Một Đời Còn Tưởng Nhớ,* Hải Vân, 1972), *Close to Seventeen* (*Gần Mười Bảy Tuổi*, Nguyễn Đình Vượng,

1972), *It's Only an Illusion* (*Chỉ là Ảo Tưởng*, Sống Mới, 1972), *Poison Spring* (*Suối Độc*, Nguyễn Đình Vượng, 1973), *Love the Color of Pale Gray Smoke* (*Tình Yêu Màu Khói Nhạt*, Nguyễn Đình Vượng, 1973), *Side By Side With a Dream* (*Bên Lề Giấc Mộng*, Ngày Mới, 1973), *Sinking Gradually Into Forgetfulness* (*Chìm Dần Vào Quên Lãng*, Tiếng Phương Đông, 1973), *Outside School Door* (*Cửa Trường Phía Bên Ngoài*, Đồng Nai, 1973), *The Flame at the End of the Tunnel* (*Ánh Lửa Cuối Đường Hầm*, Anh Lộc, 1974), *Hugging the Guitar To The Midst Of Life* (*Ôm Đàn Tới Giữa Đời*, Gìn Vàng Giữ Ngọc, 1974), *Lovers Born Under the Sign of Pisces* (*Những Người Tình Tuổi Song Ngư*, Xuân Thu, 1992)

Comments and Recollections

Portraits of Fifteen Writers and Poets of Vietnam (*Chân Dung Mười Lăm Nhà Văn, Nhà Thơ Việt Nam*, Văn Khoa 1985)

Poetry

We See Our Images: So Many Shrines (*Ta Thấy Hình Ta Những Miếu Đền*, Văn Khoa, California, 1989)

GOING TO VISIT MAI THẢO

The first day of winter in southern California is still sunny and beautiful, though slightly chilly. A group of us, including Từ Mẫn (Võ Thắng Tiết), originally the director of Lá Bối Publishers, and then of *The Arts* (*Văn Nghệ*), and Phạm Phú Minh, originally the editor-in-chief of Thế kỷ 21 and then of Diễn Đàn Thế Kỷ, agreed to pay a visit to the grave of Mai Thảo. Only the poet Thành Tôn, the person with the most complete collection of materials on Mai Thảo, found at the last minute that he was too busy to go.

Mai Thảo's grave lies in the Eternal Garden (Vườn Vĩnh Cửu) near the Thủy Tạ House. The Peek Family waitress working there recognized the name of the writer Mai Thảo at once and let us know that visitors from afar often came to visit him. Mai Thảo's grave is surrounded by fresh green grass, and in the middle rests his memorial plaque made of black stone, which remains intact after weathering the eighteen years that have passed since it was placed there. It has a portrait of Mai Thảo beneath which are inscribed four lines from his verse collection *We See Our Images: So Many Shrines*:

> *The world has a million things I fail to grasp,*
> *And fail still more as I approach the end of life.*
> *No matter; after I am safely in the ground*
> *Read in the stars, you will understand.*

The grave of Mai Thảo is inscribed with four lines drawn from his verse collection *We See Our Images: So Many Shrines*. Resting on the grave is the special issue of *Literature* devoted to a Remembrance of Mai Thảo. *(Thành Tôn, personal archives)*

From the right: Từ Mẫn (Võ Thắng Tiết) and Phạm Phú Minh visiting the grave of Mai Thảo on Dec. 4, 2016. *(photo by Ngô Thế Vinh)*

We placed some incense sticks on Mai Thảo's memorial plaque, upon which rested the special issue of *Literature*, and lit the incense, so that smoke billowed over it. Thus, we paid him a visit, and remembered him with a line from Nguyễn Du: "The body falls away; the essence brightly stays" ("Thác là thể phách còn là tinh anh").

California 12/2016

FORTY YEARS OF DƯƠNG NGHIỄM MẬU AND THE "AUTOBIOGRAPHY OF NGUYỄN DU"

Dương Nghiễm Mậu closes his eyes and smiles before a clock with drooping hands.
(photo by Trần Cao Lĩnh)

...People who harbor dissatisfactions usually resort to writing memorials to the throne. These scattered, pitiful memorials are usually ignored. There are some fellows who, having written a lot of them with no response, cast aside their robes and headdresses and return home to be civilian deputies, but are still content because they are receiving stipends from the imperial court. A few writers with a bit of self-respect choose the path of withdrawal and obscurity. Because they don't choose the path of banditry, their names are not to be found in Accounts of Marauders.

("An Unofficial Account of Từ Hải," Dương Nghiễm Mậu, 2005)

BÙI GIÁNG AND THE PATH OF DƯƠNG NGHIỄM MẬU

After April 30, 1975, writers who neither escaped nor, like Dương Nghiễm Mậu, chose to remain, and who were not among the secret northern agents residing in the South, all awaited the day when they would enter captivity in the communists' labor reform camps. During that tense and gloomy period, there was one person who with the utmost indifference went about seeking to visit his old friends in the arts. That person was none other than the poet Bùi Giáng of *Conifer Leaves* (*Lá Hoa Cồn*). This middle-aged poet was always thin and looked older than his age, his beard and hair unkempt as always. A startling apparition in the middle of Saigon, he had picked up from somewhere in the streets the uniform of a "puppet" soldier with the insignia of a full bird colonel Bùi Giáng dared fate to swoop down on him directly, and went strutting wildly through the streets as if on military parade. This was perhaps the last beautiful image of the Vietnamese war: a new recruit volunteering to enter an army now utterly disbanded. And in his wanderings Bùi Giáng came also to the Ba Chuông ["three bells"] Church area, the section where Dương Nghiễm Mậu lived. Bùi Giáng walked obliviously into the narrow alley, festooned here and there with red flags, that led there. Alert

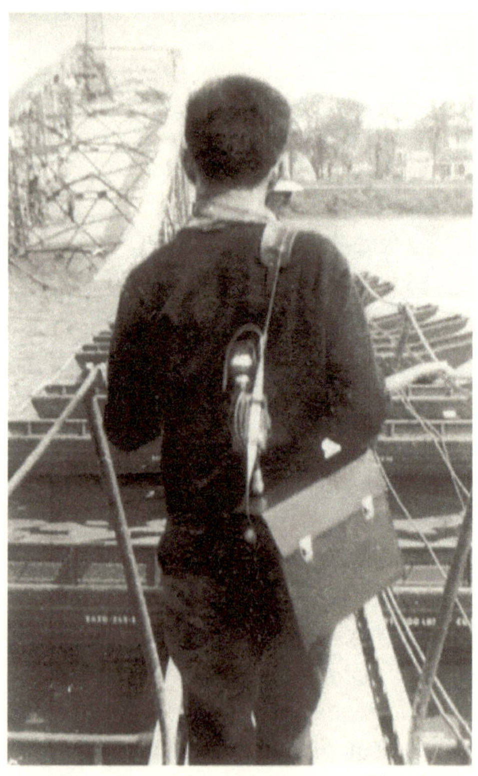

War correspondent Dương Nghiễm Mậu crossing the Tràng Tiền Bridge, destroyed in the Tết 1968 battle. Huế, 1968.
(photo by Đinh Cường)

The editorial board of *Bách Khoa* before 1975 at 160 Phan Đình Phùng: from the right: board chief Lê Ngộ Châu (d. 2006), Vũ Hạnh, Nguyễn Hiến Lê (d. 1984), Vi Huyền Đắc (d. 1976), Lê Phương Chi, and Võ Phiến.
(source: Lê Ngộ Châu, personal archives)

and clear-headed, he remembered the precise place, knocked loudly on the door, and demanded to enter and see his old acquaintance. Faced with this situation, the quiet and retiring Dương Nghiễm Mậu was like a girl who finds herself on a pole. At that time, his neighbors were all still close associates. The nets cast by public security agents weren't yet sufficient to cause trouble. After leaving Dương Nghiễm Mậu's house, I don't know if Bùi Giáng went to knock on other peoples' doors, or if he went to the head of the Trương Minh Giảng Bridge and stood like a policeman directing traffic in the chaotic current of history and afterwards was struck by the "Revolutionaries of April 30" or was beaten by the security police till his face was puffy – but surely in the end he sought to return the "queen mother" Kim Cương[1] and sat before her door so he could wield his pen and write a poem to present to her.

During the week preceding April 30, 1975 members of the Mẹ Việt Nam ("Mothers of Vietnam") Broadcasting Station and the writers who worked with them were offered a plan by the Americans to depart

1 Kim Cương was a famous stage actress.

from Vietnam so as to avoid becoming objects of revenge. Before the day when they were to board a boat going to Phú Quốc Island, the writer Võ Phiến came and paid a visit to the editorial offices of Bách Khoa, the "rice-pot" where he wrote *Catching Children Amid Green Fields*, as he sat with Vũ Hạnh of *Blood Pen* (*Bút Máu*) – it was also the place to which he had been attached for eighteen years – as many years as that of the journal itself. As Lê Ngộ Châu, the editor-in-chief of Bách Khoa later related, Võ Phiến, knowing that he had to depart and, sensing that the future held no day of return, was plunged in deep sadness. He sat there weeping silently and finally left the editorial office without a word of farewell.

One day before the fall of Saigon, nearly the entire staff of the station Mothers of Vietnam, which included the families of Võ Phiến, author of *Farewell* (*Giã Từ*), Lê Tất Điều, author of *Destroying the Mountains* (*Phá Núi*), Viên Linh, author of *Metamorphosis* (*Hóa Thân*), Túy Hồng, author of *Face to Face With Myself on the Walls* (*Tôi Nhìn Tôi Trên Vách*), Thanh Nam, author of *Small Shadow Long Road* (*Bóng Nhỏ Đường Dài*) were conducted from Phú Quốc Island to the large ship Challenger, which lay ready in the ocean beyond. When Phú Quốc had faded into the distance on that occasion, Lê Tất Điều saw Võ Phiến weeping. Together with other ships of the Seventh Fleet, they floated on the eastern sea for several days in order to reach Guam. Guam had been the base for the squadrons of B52s that had gone on carpet bombing missions in the Vietnam war, which had the destructive impact of earthquakes The island of Guam had an area of only 552 square kilometers. After April 1975, it became a stopping point for hundreds of thousands of Vietnamese refugees before they came to the U.S. Vũ Khắc Khoan of *The Spirit of Turtle Tower* (*Thần Tháp Rùa*), Nghiêm Xuân Hồng of *The Tenth Stranger From Afar* (*Người Viễn Khách Thứ 10*), and Mặc Đỗ of *Sister Siu* (*Siu Cô Nương*) of the Viewpoint (Quan Điểm) group all passed through there at various times before setting foot in various American internment camps.

Before a week had passed, on the fifth of May 1975, Phạm Việt Châu, one of the long established authors of Bách Khoa and author of *The Hundred Vietic States in the Land of Fate* (*Trăm Việt Trên Vùng

Định Mệnh) ended his existence in his own home when the communists had occupied all of the South. The sudden and very early death of a writer with a comprehensive vision of the history of his people and boundless creative ability at the age of forty-three was like a death knell foretelling many other tragedies that would occur subsequently.

THE BOOK-BURNING CAMPAIGN

In the days that followed April 30, 1975, two of Vũ Hạnh's children, wearing black peasant "bà ba" outfits and with red bands around their arms came to the office of Bách Khoa, which was also where Lê Ngộ Châu and his wife lived. In front of people who were strangers to them, one of them, a girl, said with a proud air, "We've returned from Hóc Môn; all last night we sprang ambushes until dawn." Unlucky villagers who happened to be on paths going through their fields that night were perhaps regarded by those youngsters as allies of the "puppet" government. The secret agents of the communists and the members of "Revolutionaries of April 30" were like copies of Mao's red guards, but they appeared a decade later. These elements were the principal activists in the movement to trace down and destroy all remnants of American cultural influence. They kicked and trampled on books, burned them in heaps, and even visited destruction on whole personal libraries. The books were ones that most of them had never read, including a whole cabinet-full of books devoted to moral instruction. Books by members of "cultural commando squads / biệt kích văn nghệ" were displayed in galleries devoted to "crimes of the American puppets" along with weapons and tiger cages. Naturally these books included works by Dương Nghiễm Mậu and even this author's *Green Belt*.

I am moved by the line in Nguyễn Du's poem "Reading Xiao Qing's Story" that goes "My written words-ordained by fate to be reduced by fire to ash" (Văn chương vô mệnh lụy phần dư 文章無命累焚餘). More than two thousand years after the event, no one has forgotten the burning of books and burial of scholars (phần thư khanh nho 焚書坑儒) of Qín Shǐ Huáng. But who knows if, after a hundred years, anyone in future generations will retain a memory of "There Was a Time of

That Sort" ("Đã Có Một Thời Như Thế") – the name of an article by Nhật Tiến about that stage in Vietnamese communist history when the regime burned books and imprisoned a whole generation of writers in the South?

1975: PHẠM XUÂN ẨN AND THE GIVRAL RESTAURANT

Before 1975, La Pagode, Brodard, and Givral, were all places where I, Phạm Đình Vy (the publisher of the periodical *Medicine and Compassion* [*Tình Thương*]) and my medical friends had occasion now and then to frequent even after we had graduated from school. Givral was also a meeting place for journalists, such as Phạm Xuân Ẩn, Cao Giao, Nguyễn Tú, and Như Phong (Lê Văn Tiến)... Phạm Xuân Ẩn was a former classmate of the writer Sơn Nam – they had been in middle school together in Cần Thơ. He was a southerner whose manner appeared rustic and simple. Throughout the Vietnam War Phạm Xuân Ẩn was known only as a correspondent for Reuters, after which he crossed over to *The Times*, which was in the Continental on the other side of the road. One also cannot neglect to mention the Caravelle Hotel, near the old parliament building, a gathering place for many foreign correspondents, and the location also of the offices of many news agencies and American broadcasting stations, such as ABC, NBC, and CBS... It was Morley Safer during a CBS Evening News Broadcast on August 5, 1965 who showed a film of U.S. marines who, as part of a broader operation, drove a group of people out of their village and then used Zippo lighters to burn down their homes, scenes that shook the White House and all of the U.S, like a deep scar in a war that had begun to be devoid of human principles. Seven years later, Nick Ut, an AP war correspondent, took the photo "Napalm Girl," in a skirmish that occurred in Trảng Bàng near Tây Ninh, on June 8, 1972. That was when the U.S. Congress cut off all further aid to South Vietnam.

Throughout the Vietnam war, this team of hardy journalists had the ability to determine the direction of public opinion through their reports of ugly events in particular places. This was sufficient to

From left: Cao Giao of *Newsweek*, Phạm Xuân Ẩn of the *Times*, Robert Shaplen of The *NewYorker*, Nguyễn Hữu Vượng of *Newsweek*, and Nguyễn Tú of *Chính Luận.*
(Photo by Richard Avedon, Continental Hotel Saigon, April 17, 1971; The Spy Who Loved Us, Thomas A Bass)

dampen the spirits of the American people, along with all the marines who came carrying weapons from halfway around the world. The traditions of the U.S. were a cause, not slight, though indirect, of the loss of the Free South, which was also the first lost war in American military history. And then that entire flock of journalists were able to escape scott free before Saigon changed masters.

And then in the first days of May, Givral came to be a meeting ground for friends who were stuck behind; they came there to learn who had remained and who had left and were agog to hear other news. Looking across the tables in the large, clear mirrors on the wall, I happened to see, and then meet with, Phạm Xuân Ẩn. Ẩn had previously come to pay a visit to the editorial office of *Medicine and Compassion / Y Khoa Tình Thương* on Nguyễn Bỉnh Khiêm Street. The wife and children of Phạm Xuân Ẩn had been provided by *The Times* with means to evacuate the country several days before that, but Ẩn had remained. Looking a bit surprised and concerned, he said to me, "Vinh, why haven't you left?" At the time this seemed merely a social pleasantry. It was only some time after that, when living within the barbed wire realm of reeducation camps, that I penetrated the meaning of Ẩn's question. It was a warning to be on my guard against the passage of years and months in confinement, a policy that Ẩn was quite clear about. On the surface he was a journalist working for *The Times*, an American newspaper, whereas he had actually been working for many years as a military espionage agent for the Hanoi communists. Later on, Phạm Xuân Ẩn himself confessed to Morley Safer on the CBS program 60 Minutes that when Saigon fell, that it was not at all easy to persuade soldiers armed with AK 47s that he was a colonel in their army, and not a member of the CIA. "They could have killed me," he said, "and barbecued my dog." (*Flashback, Vietnam Revisited 1989, The Spy in Winter*)

1975: THE FALL OF SAIGON

On April 30, communist troops entered the city. At noon the government of the Southern Republic, issued an order to surrender. Showers of white confetti rained down from the upper stories of many city buildings – they were the shredded remains of military and official documents that had to be destroyed.

And then, not long afterward, the noise of metal treads resounded as T54 tanks carrying liberation flags rolled down Trần Hưng Đạo Boulevard toward the center of Saigon.

1980: BETTER NOT COME FOR A VISIT

Three years after getting out of prison, I returned to a Saigon that had changed. If there was anything that still seemed familiar, it was a few friends, but few of them remained. The subject of this episode was one of the old acquaintances whom I first thought of visiting. He was a college professor who had graduated from a school in the U.S. and then returned to Vietnam at the end of the 1960s. He was full of ideals, and had big dreams about a social revolution. According to him, social justice would be the ultimate solution to a horrible war in which both sides, North and South, were stymied. I had met him in the United States and also, in subsequent years, in Vietnam. The quick collapse of the South was to him like "a shattered dream." Though he had not been forced to endure years and months of imprisonment, his family's circumstances, like those of the south in general, were clearly difficult. Bit by bit, he had sold his precious dictionaries, at that time high-priced items, to students from the north hungry for books. After that came paintings and pieces of sculpture, and finally there remained a large cabinet full of social science books that he had brought back from the U.S. Those books were now without monetary value. He could do nothing with them but have them weighed and sold as pulp. And his wife, too, who was a teacher, had to sit in the marketplace trying to eke out a living. It was hard for him to endure the pain and shame this caused him.

When I met him, he has face still bore the traits of an intellectual, and he welcomed me as he had always done, but there were clearly signs of anxiety in his eyes. His air was cordial, but he did not let this cordiality get out of hand, and looked apprehensively at the door as he spoke: "I'm glad to learn that you got out of prison, but I must also ask you not to come visiting. The frank directness with which he spoke was like a bucket of cold water, but I understood his situation and was very sorry for him. His wife's family in the U.S. were going through procedures that would allow them to sponsor him as an immigrant, and they thought that having a connection with a soldier of the "puppet" government and an internee in a labor reeducation camp might hinder the hoped-for journey of my friend to the shores of freedom. He was acting according to circumstances; I had no inclination to judge him and still regarded him with respect, and if I should at some point meet him again, it will surely be on a different continent. Quite soon in the South a network of eyes and ears had grown up among the people and among the public security agents, a network comprehensive enough to create suspicion and fear.

After I left his house, I felt a rush of joy when I ran into my close friend Nghiêu Đề. Nghiêu Đề informed me that he had just met Star-Over-Jungle (*Sao Trên Rừng*: Nguyễn Đức Sơn, an eccentric poet) coming down on a motorcycle from Đà Lạt, and was astonished to see him for the first time wearing a business suit with a tie. When Nghiêu

Đề asked him the reason for this, Sơn laughed scornfully and said, "This is the only way I can avoid being confused with those people." (Sơn uses "those people" to imply newcomers from the winning side – *bên thắng cuộc*)

1980: TRẦN PHONG GIAO SITTING OUT IN THE MARKET

Trần Phong Giao was muscular in appearance, and had the dark skin of someone who worked outside under the sun, rather than with words in an office. He was well known as the secretary of the editorial board of the journal *Literature (Văn)* during the eight years from 1963 to 1971, a publication that enjoyed a special position in the literary life of the south due to its discoveries of new writers who went on to develop commanding reputations. After *Literature*, he tried his hand at many other jobs, all within the domain of journalism and publishing, and then became a librarian, but didn't leave as many marks of his activities as he had in *Literature*. Not long after April 30, both he and his wife had to seek their living in the marketplace with a three-wheeled vehicle parked on Lê Thánh Tôn Street, where they stood selling bundles of firewood and clumps of bananas or bunches of fresh vegetables in order to feed their children. I went to visit him as soon as I got out of prison. He was still living in an alley near Kiệu Bridge, next to Tân Định district. He had become much thinner and his legs were very weak and his gait unsteady. His only possession that had any value was a cabinet full of books in which the most treasured item was a complete set of *Literature* bound in leather – something he had created himself – but he wasn't able to keep it. In order to have money for rice and medicine, he had to sell it to a Vietnamese from overseas (Việt Kiều) to bring back to the U.S. Trần Phong Giao died in poverty and illness (2005), though he did manage to live to a great age.

1981: AND FAMILY MEALS

Nghiễm's house was in an alley; it was narrow in front but went back fairly far. He was wearing shorts and a white T-shirt. His eyes were lively; he seemed always to be smiling at something, and gave the impression of being younger than someone born in 1936.

Though I lived close to *Chợ Cũ* (Old Market), a place full of sidewalk stalls and restaurants, very convenient for casual snacking, I would often stop by his house after my day's work rather than returning home, and let Trang, Nghiễm's wife, add a pair of chopsticks to the table so I could partake of dishes which, though plain, were delicious, because they were imbued with the happiness of their home. During our imprisonment, Nghiễm and I had grown accustomed to meals that left you hungry day and night. After getting out, meals were enough to take the edge off one's hunger even if they consisted only of vegetables and beans. For adults, such inadequacies didn't matter, but for young children still in the phase of "rapid eating and rapid growing," such meals had to be regarded as nutritionally inadequate. If it was not a day when I had to go out late, I would always stop by the market and purchase something to eat and bring it to Nghiễm's to add to the platter. With an added meat dish and a bit of something salty, those days, with their two children at the table, were like parties. When we met, Nghiễm and I didn't talk much. It seemed that the things Nghiễm was writing here and there, didn't have to be brought into conversation for us to understand each other. Only Trang, Nghiễm's wife, after an exhausting day of teaching, would enliven us with amusing accounts of things that happened in her day. The South was still rich in natural resources–the only hindrance to ordinary living was the regime's policy of imposing poverty and controlling each stomach through the imposition of food rationing

1982: DƯƠNG NGHIỄM MẬU AND A DIFFERENT THANH TÂM TUYỀN

I met Thanh Tâm Tuyền at the time of Saigon's downfall (April 30, 1975) in a small house in Gia Định. His wife had just given birth to their youngest child in the chaotic circumstances that prevailed in the Nguyễn Văn Học Hospital. *A Different Sunday* (*Một Chủ Nhật Khác*), his last novel from "a time to love and a time to die" had just then been printed but had not yet been distributed. When he left prison in 1982, I met the Thanh Tâm Tuyền of *Fire in the Kitchen* (*Bếp Lửa*). He was the same age as Dương Nghiễm Mậu, but he seemed much older. He had the blackened complexion of a man who had suffered chronic malaria (sốt rét kinh niên). It was hard to imagine how such a thin, frail man had survived seven years of imprisonment in which he suffered hunger and cold every day in the mountain camps of the North. Throughout seven years of cutting bamboo and chipping wood in the mountains, his legs were stabbed by bamboo, and with no surgery or medicines, he still survived. To resist the cold in prison he took up the habit of smoking water pipes (hút thuốc lào). Though without pen or paper, he still made poems, depending on his memory alone, but returned to traditional verse forms when he did so. *Poems Somewhere Far Away* (*Thơ ở Đâu Xa*) was his last collection of poems made in prison. He published them in the U.S. in 1990.

In 1993, in a rare interview, Thanh Tâm Tuyền explained the evolution of style that had taken place in his writing: *"Faire de la poésie dans un camp de redressement, c'est aussi retourner à la poésie de tradition populaire"*. (Making poetry in a labor reform camp was also a return to the traditional verse forms of our people.) (Lê Hữu Khóa, "Thanh Tâm Tuyền: La poésie entre la guerre et le camp," Publications de l'Université de Provence, France)

In a very private setting he recalled that Thái Thanh, with whom he was friends, had ceased completely to perform as a singer after 1975. Hearing that Thanh Tâm Tuyền had just gotten out of prison, she paid him a visit, taking a guitar with her, and sang the poems of his that had been turned into song lyrics: "Pink Night" ("Đêm Màu Hồng"), "Half My Soul in Pain," ("Nửa Hồn Thương Đau") "Tears from the Green Stone" (Lệ Đá Xanh)… though his heart was warmed by this meeting with an old friend, his sensibilities were not sufficiently intact to be receptive to those sounds of former times. He said "no" to many people who wanted to meet him and maintained the same attitude after emigrating to the U.S. That reserve of his stirred Mai Thảo once or twice to anger.

Then there was another meeting between us at the end of 1982. Dương Nghiễm Mậu, Doãn Quốc Sỹ, Thanh Tâm Tuyền and I walked from Nghiễm's house to a little sidewalk bar on Trương Minh Giảng Street near the railroad. What Nghiễm wanted to drink was always a bottle of beer. One of us happened to mention Tô Thùy Yên, author of *A Journey to the Spratly Islands* (*Trường Sa Hành*) – he was still in prison. Nobody dwelt on Yên's current miseries, instead the conversation turned to luckier friends in distant regions. We recalled a few people who had gotten away before 1975: Thanh Nam – Túy Hồng, Vũ Khắc Khoan, Mặc Đỗ, Võ Phiến, Lê Tất Điều, and Viên Linh… and then the name of Mai Thảo, author of "The Testament on the Highest Peak" ("Bản Chúc Thư Trên Ngọn Đỉnh Trời) came up like a point where all these matters converged. He was the unique example of a writer who eluded the efforts of the communists to hunt him down during his two years of hiding in Saigon. Even so, many people had taken risks to shield him. Trần Dạ Từ, author of *Confiding My Love in the Night* (*Tỏ Tình Trong Đêm*), together with many other writers and journalists, was in prison. Nhã Ca, author of *A Mourning Headband for Huế* (*Giải Khăn Sô cho Huế*) got out of prison early, and had to care for a swarm of little children – but she and they had to keep "uncle" Mai Thảo hidden in their house, a multi-story structure

Doãn Quốc Sỹ and Thanh Tâm Tuyền in front of Saigon's Notre-Dame Cathedral, 1985.

on a corner of Tự Do Street. This was the last hiding place of Mai Thảo until he managed to escape, relatively early, on a boat that took him across the ocean to Pulau Besar in Malaysia.

In 1979, two years after Mai Thảo's escape, one must speak of another mortally risky ocean journey of eighty-one boat people that included Nhật Tiến, author of *The Curtain Puller* (*Người Kéo Màn*) and Từ Mẫn (Võ Thắng Tiết), publisher of *Palm Leaves* (*Lá Bối*) and the married journalist-pair Dương Phục – Vũ Thanh Thủy… This group met with disaster when they were attacked by Thái sea pirates on Koh Kra Island, an event that became known to the public quite early through the testimony of Nhật Tiến and which began to disturb the conscience of the world. This was the starting point of the later Movement to Rescue the Boat People.

After our meeting at Nghiễm's house, Thanh Tâm Tuyền began preparing to emigrate to the U.S. in accordance with the provisions of the "Humanitarian Operation," though his heart's inclination [*tâm thái* – his own expression] lay entirely with his homeland, which he didn't wish to leave for a distant place. As for Doãn Quốc Sỹ, author of *Three Lives of Fire and Incense* (*Ba Sinh Hương Lửa*), he would be imprisoned for a total of fourteen years before he emigrated in 1995 and met Mai Thảo in Orange County.

1982: DƯƠNG NGHIỄM MẬU (1936 - 2016); BIOGRAPHICAL DATA

Dương Nghiễm Mậu's real name was Phí Ích Nghiễm. He was born in 1936, the same year as Thanh Tâm Tuyền and Thảo Trường.[2] He attended the Hàng Than school as an elementary student, and then went to the Chu Văn An middle school in Hanoi. I also attended those two schools, but Nghiễm was five years older than I was. Probably it was because he was several grades ahead of me that we did not meet. He emigrated to the South in 1954, and from 1957 on wrote many occasional essays, articles, short stories, and novels for *Creation*

---

2 Thảo Trường (1936 - 2010); real name Trần Duy Hinh; born in Nam Định. He was imprisoned in labor reform camps for 17 years after 1975 and emigrated to the U.S. in 1993.

(*Sáng Tạo*), *Twentieth Century* (*Thế kỷ 20*), *Cyclopedia* (*Bách Khoa*), *Intersection (Giao Điểm*), and *Writings on Politics* (*Chính Văn*). For a short time he was active in the group Discussion of Future Possibilities (Đàm Trường Viễn Kiến) of Nguyễn Đức Quỳnh, author of *Who Has Crossed the Bridge* (*Ai Có Qua Cầu*). Starting in 1962, he worked for the journal *The Arts* (*Văn Nghệ*) with Lý Hoàng Phong, the elder brother of the poet Quách Thoại. His first short story collection was *I Must Be Resigned* (*Cũng Đành*), published by *The Arts* in 1963. His first novel, *A Mother's Legacy* (*Gia Tài Người Mẹ*) won the National Prize for Literature in 1966.

He entered the armed services in 1966 with the rank of "Assimilation Corporal" (*hạ sĩ đồng hóa*) and worked from then until 1975 as a war

A number of the published works of Dương Nghiễm Mậu.
(Phan Nguyên, personal archives)

Dương Nghiễm Mậu in Saigon in 1997, a photo given to Võ Phiến by Thế Uyên. *(Viễn Phố, personal archives)*

correspondent. He was arrested after 1975 and released from prison in 1977, after which he did domestic lacquer work for a living.

Dương Nghiễm Mậu died suddenly of a heart attack on Aug. 2, 2016, at the age of 80.

2006: RAINSTORMS IN SAIGON

If one wants to reach the Ba Chuông Church area from a small hotel near Tự Do Street, going on foot is too long a hike, and taxis get caught in traffic, so I chose a Honda motorcycle taxi, but could not avoid seizures of panic, because its operator was too reckless; he snaked along at high speed, went against the direction of traffic, and even leapt on to a sidewalk full of pedestrians because he thought it was safer than following the rules of the road. I had no scrap of paper with the address written on it, but I have a nearly photographic memory, so I thought I would be able to find my way to Dương Nghiễm Mậu's house, which still lay in the same narrow alley, though we had not met for many years. The house had been rebuilt and was taller by another story. Nghiễm was now a lacquer artist, and his wife Trang still taught English at Marie Curie. His two sons had graduated from college and gone to work. The whole family had worked with all their might to be able to live as they now did.

WHEN A WRITER IS A PATIENT

After many years I met Nghiễm again in September 2006, when he had attained a great age. Thanh Tâm Tuyền had just died six months earlier (March 2006). Như Phong, author of *Smoke and Waves*, had been dead for five years, since December, 2001. Mai Thảo, the poet of *We See Our Images: So Many Shrines*, had died eight years earlier (January, 1998) in the same year as Nghiêu Đề, author of *The Hundred-Year Hairdo* (*Ngọn Tóc Trăm Năm*). They were all Vietnamese artists who had chosen freedom and thus had to live in exile buried far from their homeland.

Nghiễm had just suffered an accident at the age of seventy. While walking on the sidewalk he had been hit by a motorcycle, no doubt a motorcycle taxi, that surged up and hit him, breaking his ankle bone. It had to be operated on, and he wore a cast for two weeks, after which, since his ankle was still swollen and painful, he had to go about on crutches. Nghiễm was good at putting up with such things, and never complained about the pain, but his symptoms worried me. I felt he needed to be examined again, so as to obtain a second opinion. I thought of a medical colleague of mine, a specialist in orthopeadics, who taught medicine. His friends called him "the man with gold hands", due to his success in operating on people with musculoskeletal injuries. He had an office where he worked after hours, and I suggested to Nghiễm that he should go there for a consultation. Nghiễm was a bit reluctant, but finally went because he felt he couldn't refuse a friend.

I had no address, but I knew that the office of Doctor Võ Thành Phụng was on Lê Văn Duyệt Street, opposite from the former headquarters of the General Labor Confederation. With a broken ankle that was still swollen and painful, getting in and out of a taxi wasn't easy for Nghiễm. A tropical rainstorm continued to pelt down on us from the time we left his house to the time when he was able to step into the Doctor's office. On meeting Võ Thành Phụng's wife, and finding that she knew that the patient was Dương Nghiễm Mậu, I found that I had little further role to play. She had been a reader for many years and was very familiar with the writings of Dương Nghiễm Mậu from the pages of such journals as *Literature*, *The Arts*, and *Creation* that she had read years ago, not to mention Nghiễm's many books. The office was filled with clients, due to the arrangements she had made. Nghiễm was the first patient to receive the special favor of an early consultation. Dr. Phụng and I studied some X-ray films clearly showing that the break had not yet healed, but that the bones were not much displaced, so a second operation would not be necessary; we would need only to protect the ankle. Busy as he was with professional matters, Dr. Phụng was perhaps not a reader of Dương Nghiễm Mậu the way his wife was, but Nghiễm naturally became a special patient there that day. It had not yet stopped raining as we returned home in the taxi. I joked with Nghiễm that in my life as a writer, I had never had the good fortune to meet a female reader so in love with literature and so pleased with my work. Never a demonstrative man, Nghiễm responded only with a gentle smile.

AN UNOFFICIAL ACCOUNT OF TỪ HẢI - Từ Hải Ngoại Truyện

Before 1975, on reading "Jīng Kē with the Dagger on the Treacherous Soil of Qín" *(Kinh Kha với con chủy thủ trên đất Tần bất trắc)*, I saw that the stories of Nghiễm Mậu involved carefully selected situations that were highly symbolic and filled with hidden meanings. In writing about ancient events, he was speaking of the present day. After crossing the River Yì, Jīng Kē was able to make his way into the ruler's court. When he placed his dagger on the neck of the Qín king, the king, instead of trembling, raised his face and laughed, upon which Jīng Kē suddenly saw everything clearly: if he killed the tyrant, then another would take his place… and the image of Jīng Kē creeping back out of the palace was an image of unlimited pain – like a harbinger of injustice in the present day.

Nghiễm's "Unofficial Account of Từ Hải" was written about ten years after 1975 (Gia Định, 2005). Từ Hải was a character whom Nghiễm was much inclined to cherish. Phí Ích Bành, Nghiễm's younger brother gave me a sealed envelope with sixteen pages that bore words and lines in his handwriting. I read those pages at once, and saw, in that "Unofficial Account of Từ Hải," that this man, who

Dương Nghiễm Mậu with a broken ankle, sitting and smiling in front of his bookshelves, his arms resting on a walker.
(photo by Ngô Thế Vinh, Sept. 2006)

was half a hero and half a bandit, was quite different from the character in the "official" account who chose the path of official stipends and immurement in a court.

Here is an excerpt from "An Unofficial Account of Từ Hải" that deals with social issues: "One day, Master Kǒng was riding along a road in a carriage when he saw an old man who approached and greeted him. Kǒngzǐ had the driver halt the carriage, upon which it was immediately surrounded by a crowd of thin, ragged children. The old man said, "I've heard that you know a lot of words, so I've come to beg you for a few. Kǒngzǐ at once opened a wooden chest, took out a book, and handed it to the man. The old man grasped the book, gazed at it a bit, then turned over some pages, looking up and down at them. Then he closed the book and returned it to Kǒngzǐ, saying, 'I don't know how to use this for anything.' There was a volley of crude laughter from a man who was naked except for a codpiece, who said, 'These books have no value for people with no food to eat and don't know how to read. Go down into the rice fields, sir, plough the soil, and take some rice to give them – that would be more useful.' The story went only that far – so I don't know what Kǒngzǐ did."

In "An Unofficial Account of Từ Hải," Dương Nghiễm Mậu also wrote about the world of literary officials: "In *Accounts of Marauders (Sưu Tặc Ký)*, people who rise up and turn into bandits are usually boatmen, farmers, herdsmen, or woodsmen; one never encounters anyone who gained the highest prize in the examinations. Not a single bandit writes prose poems or has been any sort of government official or teacher before becoming a bandit. In other books, one reads that people who harbor dissatisfactions usually resort to writing memorials to the throne. Sometimes they demand that corrupt officials be executed, sometimes they denounce high taxes that lead to the starvation of poor farmers, and sometimes they protest the executions of honest people… but these scattered, pitiful memorials are usually ignored. There are some fellows who, having written a lot with no response, cast aside their robes and headdresses and return home to be civilian deputies, but are still content because they are receiving stipends from the imperial court. A few writers with a bit of self respect choose the path of withdrawal and obscurity. Because they don't choose the path of banditry, their names are not to be found in *Accounts of Marauders*.

TỪ HẢI NGOẠI TRUYỆN

DƯƠNG NGHIỄM MẬU

Từ lâu người dân Hàng Châu đã được nghe nói về một đám giặc nổi lên ở vùng Sơn Đông, đa phần là dân chài lưới nghèo khó, dần dần đám giặc mỗi lúc một đông, nhiều nơi dân chúng nổi lên giết quan quân mà theo giặc, thanh thế của chúng làm triều đình lo ngại và danh tiếng tên đầu đảng Từ Hải được nhiềungười nhắcđến. Vì xuất thân làm nghề chài lưới, quen với sông nước biển

28/09/2012

"An Unofficial Account of Từ Hải with a handwritten inscription by Dương Nghiễm Mậu.*(Ngô Thế Vinh, personal archives)*

Dương Nghiễm Mậu adds a few concluding words: "The pages that have been written about these figures by the ancients sometimes give rise to doubts… many books record that Từ Hải died on the battlefield amid a hail of arrows–a hero must have a heroic death. In "An Unofficial Account of Từ Hải, he dies at the end, but not die standing in the midst of a battle; he dies a different sort of death."

Then, passing from the ancient story to modern times, he writes: "Many books create heroes, such as people who turn themselves into living torches, or stuff themselves into the muzzles of cannons, or embrace bombs and hurl themselves into an enemy horde and die. Such heroes, though seen in books, are never traceable elsewhere."

It seems we should add here that the house that Nghiễm and his family lived in was not far from the Nguyễn Văn Trỗi Bridge on Công Lý Street during the anti-U.S. war, so one cannot neglect to mention the case of Lê Văn Tám who used gasoline to turn himself into a living torch in Thị Nghè in 1945 during the Resistance War against the French. Trần Huy Liệu, the head of the Information Bureau of the People's Democratic Republic of Vietnam determined that this man was a propagandistic creation who had never existed in reality.

Thirty-two years after 1975, at the instigation of the poet Nguyễn Quốc Thái (who was also the person who introduced Phạm Duy to the Phương Nam Company), the Phương Nam Company republished four short story collections of Dương Nghiễm Mậu: *A Pair of Eyes in Heaven* (*Đôi Mắt Trên Trời*), *I Must Be Resigned* (*Cũng Đành*), *Good Looks (Nhan Sắc)*, *The Sound of the Youngest Brother's Flute* (*Tiếng Sáo Người Em Út*), and the novel *Nguyệt in the Mango Grove* (*Nguyệt Đồng Xoài*) by Lê Xuyên. Immediately afterward, Vũ Hạnh, who was past eighty, like an old butcher who could not lay aside his cleaver, wrote an article in which he attacked Dương Nghiễm Mậu and Lê Xuyên, and poured blame on the Phương Nam Company.

Vũ Hạnh wrote, "The books of Dương Nghiễm Mậu are pervaded by a reactionary spirit that will push the young into opposition to the revolution, and resistance to the duty to liberate the country from the domination of the invading imperialists, and as for the books of Lê Xuyên, they are degenerate." Continuing, he wrote, "For this reason there is much indignation and rage among readers when they see that Phương Nam is printing and distributing the books of Dương Nghiễm Mậu… To take these poisonous weapons out, refresh them with new paint, and then hawk them in the market, is a serious offense to the honor of the country. And finally he added, "The authors Dương Nghiễm Mậu and Lê Xuyên are again living in the city and are being fairly treated; they have not met with any harassment at all."

It seems I should also record here that before 1975 many groups of writers, not devoid of compassion, had more than once signed petitions urging that Vũ Hạnh be pardoned. Vũ Hạnh was also shielded by the Vietnamese PEN Club, and when he was given a prison sentence, the priest Thanh Lãng himself, the chairman of the association, stepped forth to protect him. But Vũ Hạnh nevertheless continued to carry on his anti-government activities in public.

After 1975, many writers and journalists of the South died of mistreatment in prison, such as Hiếu Chân (Nguyễn Hoạt), Hoàng Vĩnh Lộc, Nguyễn Mạnh Côn, Phạm Văn Sơn, Trần Văn Tuyên, Trần Việt Sơn, Vũ Ngọc Các, Anh Tuấn (Nguyễn Tuấn Phát), and Dương Hùng Cường… or died soon after release from prison, like Hồ Hữu Tường and Vũ Hoàng Chương. The ones who survived all had to put aside their pens: Dương Nghiễm Mậu had to be a domestic lacquer worker and Lê Xuyên had to sit on the street selling cigarettes. Trần Lê Nguyễn, author of *The Storm of the Era* (*Bão Thời Đại*), had to stand selling newspapers to get through the days, Nguyễn Mộng Giác, author of *One Way Street* (*Đường Một Chiều*), had to work at a noodle factory as a food processing worker, and Trần Hoài Thư, author of *The Pensive Blade of Grass* (*Ngọn Cỏ Ngậm Ngùi*) had to turn into an *Itinerant Ice Cream Vender* (*Người Bán Cà Rem Dạo*.)

Nghiễm was a good-hearted person. If anyone mentioned the Vũ Hạnh incident to him, he would just laugh, and maintain a tolerant tone. He believed that the world had more good people than ones who were ill-disposed, and that the ones who were ill-disposed would come to see their own errors. Nghiễm was excessively optimistic. That he had been plunged in misery for more than forty years was due to the actions of such "ill-disposed" people – so now that he was "close to the earth and far from heaven," why had they not seen their error, what had they not repented? A person well acquainted with Vũ Hạnh observed that, "his fierceness was like a protective screen – a sort of *raison d'être*, a proof of the existence of Vũ Hạnh as a communist person."

An article, "Vũ Hạnh in the Old Days" ("Ngày Xưa Vũ Hạnh") says that, "though a concealed communist living in the region, he none the less lived elegantly and was treated with the respect due to a writer (Lý Đợi, Talawas, May 10, 2007). *Vũ Hạnh These Days* (*Vũ Hạnh Ngày Nay*, the name of a set of books by Huy Đức) lives among the victors and swaggers about obliviously and makes the fiercest noises in the Committee for the Evaluation of the Literature of the South in the National Library. His writing is a stream of clichés, of slogans thrown out with no thought: "the author is a puppet through and through, the content of his work shows him to be a reactionary, degenerate slave." Vũ Hạnh is just about as old as Võ Phiến and will soon step into his 90s, and still uses such expressions as "our party, the boat which, being oared along, carries the true doctrine," and he continues to pursue even the democratically-inclined younger writers. A typical example is the article he wrote criticising Nhã Thuyên and the group "Speak Out" (Nhóm Mở Miệng) with its well known spokesmen Lý Đợi and Bùi Chát ("What Can One See in a Master Dissertation With Fallacious Arguments" ["Thấy Gì Từ Một Luận Văn Sai Lạc," The Arts no. 29, 2013]).

Perhaps the tragedy of Vũ Hạnh is like that of the altered communists who stepped into the twenty-first century exemplifying bad faith–living with two faces. They keep on shouting slogans and beating war drums for things in which they have not the slightest remaining belief. Vũ Hạnh never stopped uttering harsh criticisms of the U.S., but he nevertheless sent his children there to study and then, when they grew up, they resided there. And Vũ Hạnh continued to go back and forth to the U.S. with no restraint whatsoever.

Left: Dương Nghiễm Mậu, (photo by Phan Nguyên, Saigon, 2011); right: Từ Hải and His Life Adventures, An Iron pen drawing by Nguyễn Trung converted to lacquer work by Dương Nghiễm Mậu. *(photo by Phí Từ Việt)*

To return to Nghiễm, many people still think that, aside from being imprisoned, and having to become a lacquer worker to make a living, Dương Nghiễm Mậu ceased writing.This is perhaps not correct. Nghiễm had no new books published within the country throughout a period of forty years after 1975. But, as far as I know, he continued writing, and among his writings is the "The Personal Account of Nguyễn Du," (Tự Truyện Nguyễn Du) which is evidently a large work. I believe he completed it, in every detail.

CALIFORNIA RAIN, SAIGON RAIN

California is still in drought, but perhaps there are downpours with enough drops to remind one of the rains in Saigon. I remember the day I went to visit a friend on one of those rainy afternoons, with many sections of flooded streets.

It is a happiness – distant, but still a happiness – to have a friend like Nghiễm, who, wherever he may be, and whatever upheavals may be occurring around him, is still the familiar Dương Nghiễm Mậu with that book *Good Looks* (*Nhan Sắc*), consistent and reliable as he has always been, and endowed with the courage to say "No." My impression of Nghiễm is that he lived in the mainstream of the literary life of the South, from very early in its history until 1975, and throughout the forty years that have since passed he has been right in his homeland, rising and descending with the fate of his country. He has been a quite reliable witness throughout that period, and everyone believes the things he writes.

CONCLUDING WORDS

My first intention was to write an article about my old and valued friend Dương Nghiễm Mậu, including his pilgrimage of forty years subsequent to the fall of the South. I had scarcely written seven thousand words when a series of recollections, like black and white movie clips, came unbidden into my mind, some of a public, and some of a very private nature, stirred into life by what I was writing.

So, forty years have elapsed between 1975 and 2015 – in the life of a human being, no more than a passing breeze, and only a blink in the eyes of history, but it has also been a long tortuous road filled with upheavals. In another eyeblink, the generation of people who authored books in the period 1954 to 1975 will disappear, as they all, without exception, return to dust. Some of them may evoke certain memories in me due to what they wrote, but they must also recount their lives of suffering, and the incessant deaths that occurred among them. As for the literature of the South we must not fail to produce a "white book, a *livre blanc," (sách trắng)* a repository of memories for future generations of Vietnamese.

With regard to restoring the legacy of the Literature of the South, we must not fail to mention one name: Trần Hoài Thư of the *Manuscripts in Thư's Library (Thư Quán Bản Thảo)*. He has had the courage and persistence through many years to devote himself to restoring works of that period that were hunted down and destroyed.

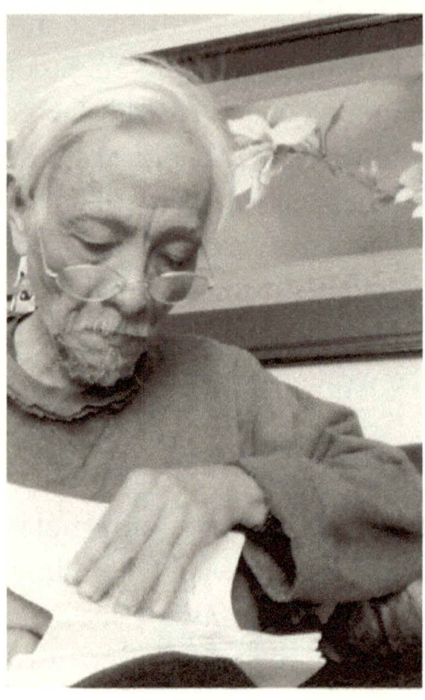

The writer Trần Hoài Thư sitting and stitching together legacies in the Bản Thảo Library.

(photo by THT from a video taken with an iPhone)

It is not too early to record the facts of an actual historical period, different from the fake versions that the communists have produced and are still producing, before history turns a page and we enter a new era.

DƯƠNG NGHIỄM MẬU HAS LEFT US

Nguyên Khai was the first person to announce the news: Dương Nghiễm Mậu suddenly passed away at 9:30 p.m. on Tuesday, Aug. 2, 2016 in Saigon, perhaps due to a heart attack. He was 80 when he died. I at once emailed a letter of condolence to his wife, Hồ Thị Ngọc Trang and his two children Phí Từ Việt and Phí Từ Việt Hà.

Situated abroad as I was, I responded to a request from Đinh Quang Anh Thái to represent the Dương Nghiễm Mậu's circle of friends by writing a few lines for publication in the newspaper *Người Việt*:

"The writer Dương Nghiễm Mậu suddenly passed away to the great regret of all his loving friends. He was not only a commanding figure in the world of Vietnamese literature, but also a person of great moral authority, as may be seen in the consistency of his work and actions in every situation of life faced him till the day of his death. 'What falls to earth is the earthly ghost; the brightness is what remains.' Farewell my friend."

A remaining matter that much concerned me was the legacy of Dương Nghiễm Mậu, which included *"The Personal Account of Nguyễn Du,"* a work that preoccupied him for a long time. I at once phoned Phí Ích Bành, a younger brother of Dương Nghiễm Mậu who is currently a journalist in southern California. He reassured me right away: "Don't worry, Vinh, the family is aware of this and is very concerned to do the right thing."

My hope, then, is that "The Personal Account of Nguyễn Du," a major work, and all the remaing parts of the legacy of Dương Nghiễm Mậu, shall one by one be published, first in southern California and then elsewhere. That is an important component of the literature of Vietnam in the present era.

Saigon 1975 – California 2015

NHẬT TIẾN AND *THE ABANDONED PORCH* STILL A SWIFT-SWALLOW ROVER SCOUT ON THE PATH OF LIFE

Nhật Tiến
(photo by Trần Cao Lĩnh)

"Wedded now to my profession"
(Đã mang lấy nghiệp vào thân) ~ Nguyễn Du

SCOUTING AT A YOUNG AGE

Bùi Nhật Tiến, pen name Nhật Tiến, was born on August 24, 1936 in Hanoi. In 1946, when he was ten years old, he had to relocate with his family to a series of other provinces, including Sơn Tây, Việt Trì, Hưng Hóa, and Phú Thọ. On returning to his old home in 1950, when he was 14, he had grown too big to live any more as a "cub scout," so he asked, rather late, to be admitted to the scouting movement as a member of the "Young Swallows Bình Than Troop." The Bình Than Troop belonged to the Đồng Nhân Scout District, which had an official anthem composed by Cung Thúc Tiến, a member of the Bạch Đằng Troop. This Cung Thúc Tiến was none other than the musician Cung Tiến, who would become well-known for his songs "Cherished Memory" ("Hoài Cảm") and "Golden Autumn" ("Thu Vàng")

The day he made his "oath of allegiance" to become a member of the Scouts of Vietnam, was a memorable event in the life of the writer and teacher Nhật Tiến. The oath-taking ceremony was organized in Láng Temple (Chùa Láng) five kilometers distant from Hanoi. In his memoirs, though written sixty years after the event, Nhật Tiến still feels the profound emotion he felt when, at the moment he uttered the oath, what he had dreamed about became a reality:

"I tremulously approached the flag of the troop. My companions were all silent and solemn, as they observed my actions. I stood erect before the flag. With my right hand I made a scouting-style salute. Lightly taking hold of a corner of the flag, I said in a clear, formal manner:

> *"Before the country's flag, which symbolizes the fatherland, and before the troop's flag, which symbolizes the Scouting spirit, I beg to swear upon my honor that:*
> *"First: I will be loyal to the Fatherland,*
> *"Second: I will seek to provide everyone with assistance,*
> *"And Third: I will obey all Scouting regulations.*

"After taking a Second-degree Scouting certificate (bằng Hạng Nhì), I was made the Leader of the Swallows Squad. In this squad, one of my young charges was Mr. Đỗ Tiến Đức, who later became a writer, and in 1969 won the National Literature and Art Prize for his work *Pink Cheeks* (*Má Hồng*) and became a cinematic director in The Cinema Department (Nha Điện Ảnh), and also the chief administrator of that organization. He is now the editor-in-chief of *The Times* (*Thời*

Luận) in Los Angeles. This was at first a printed publication, but has now gone online.

"I entered the Kha Đoàn (Venture Crew) when I was seventeen and was preparing to become a full scout at age 18. After emigrating to the South in 1954, I was active for many years in the Bạch Đằng Troop, which had four sub-troops: Chương Dương, Vân Đồn, Hàm Tử, and Tây Kết. I was given the responsibility of leading the Vân Đồn sub-group. This group included a person named Trương Trọng Trác who later rose to the position of Committee-member of the Scouts of Vietnam–and when he went overseas he became the editor-in-chief of the newspaper *These Days* (*Ngày Nay*) under the pen name Trọng Kim in Houston, Texas. He held this position until his death in 2009).

From this time on, I was entitled to sign my name as "Swift Swallow RS" (Én Nhanh nhẹn RS) in all my scouting communications. "RS" stood for "Rover Scout"

"In the summer of 1970, at a camp belonging to the Bạch Đằng Troop organized at Thủ Đức, I was presented with a walking stick that had on its head two horizontal stripes indicating the rank of "Rover Scout" (Tráng Sinh Lên Đường), a rank that young scouts wished ardently to achieve. From that moment on, I was able to sign my name as "Swift Swallow RS–"RS" was an abbreviation for "Rover Scout" in English and "Routier Scout" in French. It could also be interpreted as standing for "Rendre Service" or "providing assistance," which harmonized with the stated principles of scouting.

"The two words "Hướng Đạo" ("Scout," or "Scouting") were always sacred to me; they call up no end intense feelings, of indelible memories, and of comrades-in-arms who shared so much with each other, not just within the world of scouting, but out in the world as well."

Now, more than sixty-five years have flown by, Nhật Tiến still can sing the song of his troop and still in all circumstances lives according to the spirit of scouting, with its mottos of "being prepared," and "helping others." It seems to me that this spirit of scouting had a deep influence on Nhật Tiến's whole career as a teacher and writer. Listen to what he himself relates:

The White Shirt People (*Những Người Áo Trắng*) was written around 1955, when I was teaching at Bến Tre. It was full of recollections of my period of scouting in Hanoi. We would often go on charitable missions. In the winter, for example, we would push oxcarts through the streets in order to distribute clothing donated to help poor people. Or we would volunteer to stand by Sword Lake (Hồ Gươm) and sell works by the dramatist Văn Thuật to build up a fund to help compatriots whose homes had been flooded back then. We also often went to engage in activities in a camp for orphans on Hàng Đẫy Street. The image of all those orphans wearing white shirts back then, amid white walls, and older girls taking care of the juniors, have

Nhật Tiến (on the left) "Scouting Leaders".
(Photo taken in Orange County, 2014)

moved me a great deal. And I used those images from the orphans' camp to write my first work: *The White Shirt People*."

Thus, one can say pretty confidently that if Nhật Tiến had not had those years of activities in the scouting movement, we would not have *The White Shirt People*, not to speak of the works that came later on, such as *The Abandoned Porch* (*Thềm Hoang*).

THE PERIOD OF DREAMING TO BE A WRITER

Nhật Tiến began writing very early; from his early student days, he dreamed of being an author, and formed a literary group called "Sowing Life" (Gieo Sống). His first story was entitled "The Ring with the Jade Face" ("Chiếc Nhẫn Mặt Ngọc") and was published in the journal *Rivers and Mountains* (*Giang Sơn*). At that time, Nhật Tiến was fifteen.

On emigrating to the South in 1954, he lived at first in Đà Lạt. While there, he wrote a play for the Royal Musketeers Radio Station (Đài Tiếng Nói Ngự Lâm Quân; Đà Lạt at that time was still part of an imperial district). A short time after that, he moved with his family to Saigon. Though never a graduate of any school of pedagogy, he began working as a physics and chemistry teacher in various private schools, at first in the Mekong delta–Bến Tre and Mỹ Tho–and after three years, in Saigon. His first novel, *The White Shirt People*, was begun and completed when he was still teaching in the provinces.

The teaching profession provided a livelihood for the family, but a writing career was no doubt his only great dream. With robust creative invention, he wrote short stories and novels (including one in dramatic form) that appeared in various journals: *Culture in the Present Era* (*Văn Hóa Ngày Nay*), *New Wind* (*Tân Phong*), *The East* (*Đông Phương*), *Cyclopedia* (*Bách Khoa*), *Literature* (*Văn*), and *Literary Studies* (*Văn Học*). He was the chief of the Huyền Trân publishing house starting in 1959, and the editor-in-chief of the weekly *For Children* (*Thiếu Nhi*), published by Khai Trí from 1971 to 1975. In 1979 he managed to reach Thailand after a voyage full of deadly peril and then in 1980 settled in the U.S.

After reaching the U.S., Nhật Tiến could no longer support himself by teaching, so he trained himself in the field of computer hardware and after that worked fifteen years for a Japanese company before retiring. Nhật Tiến continued to write and publish while overseas. He also continued his scouting activities and was active in programs aimed at helping boat people. He resided in southern California.

PUBLISHED WORKS:

In Vietnam before 1975: *The White Shirt People* (*Những Người Áo Trắng*; a novel; Huyền Trân, 1959), *Lost Stars* (*Những Vì Sao Lạc*; a novel; Phượng Giang, 1960), *The Abandoned Porch* (*Thềm Hoang*, a novel, Đời Nay, 1961), *The Curtain Puller* (*Người Kéo Màn*, novel in dramatic form, Huyền Trân, 1962), *Clouds at Dusk* (*Mây Hoàng Hôn*, a novel, Phượng Giang, 1962), *Light in the Park* (*Ánh Sáng Công Viên*, a story collection, Ngày Nay, 1963), *Story of Little Phượng* (*Chuyện Bé Phượng*, a novel, Huyền Trân, 1964), *The Towering Rock Wall* (*Vách Đá Cheo Leo*; a novel; Đông Phương,

The covers of books by Nhật Tiến published in Vietnam before 1975 *(Nhật Tiến, personal archives)*

1965), *A Bird Chirping in Its Cage* (*Chim Hót Trong Lồng*, occasional essays, Huyền Trân, 1966), *Black Teardrops* (*Giọt Lệ Đen*, a story collection, Huyền Trân, 1968), *Hands of Jade (Tay Ngọc*, occasional essays, Huyền Trân, 1968), *Fitful Sleep* (*Giấc Ngủ Chập Chờn*; a novel Huyền Trân, 1969), *Cherished Homeland* (*Quê Nhà Yêu Dấu*, Huyền Trân, 1970), *Flying with the Wind* (*Theo Gió Ngàn Bay*, Huyền Trân), *Gifts of the River* (*Tặng Phẩm của Dòng Sông*, stories, Huyền Trân, 1972), *When I dreamed of Being a Writer* (*Thuở Mơ Làm Văn Sĩ*, Huyền Trân, 1973)… and a number of stories written for children, such as *The Testament* (*Lá Chúc Thư*), and *The Road up Thiên Mã Mountain* (*Đường Lên Núi Thiên Mã*)…

Published overseas after 1975: *Bugle Call* (*Tiếng Kèn*; 1981), *Sea Pirates in Thailand Bay* (*Hải Tặc Trong Vịnh Thái Lan*; written with Dương Phục and Vũ Thanh Thủy; 1981), *A Time Passing By* (*Một Thời Đang Qua*, 1985), *Sweat on the Rock* (*Mồ Hôi Của Đá*, 1988), *The Door* (*Cánh Cửa*, 1990), *My Homeland, Your Homeland* (*Quê Nhà, Quê Người*; written with Nhật Tuấn, published in-country, 1994), *The Unwanted* (*Thân Phận Dư Thừa*, translation of Nhật Tiến from *The Unwanted* by Kiên Nguyễn. 2002), *A Journey in the Written Word* (*Hành Trình Chữ Nghĩa*; 2012), *A Teacher in a Sleazy Time* (*Nhà Giáo Một Thời Nhếch Nhác*, 2012), *The Truth Cannot Be Buried* (*Sự Thật Không Thể Bị Chôn Vùi*, 2002), *A Time… Of That Sort* (*Một Thời… Như Thế*, 2012)

With more than twenty published works of many different types, the principal creations of Nhật Tiến are all related to the world of childhood. Nhật Tiến can be called “the writer of unfortunate childhood,” a writer with a socialist tendency. In an article on Nhật Tiến in his series of books on the literature of the South, Võ Phiến made the following observations: “At that time, everyone knew that there were many well-known writers who wrote about the world of childhood. Each treated the subject in his own way. The children in Duyên Anh’s stories were spirited and clever. The children in the stories of Lê Tất Điều were nearly all naughty. In the stories of Nhật Tiến they were unfortunate.”

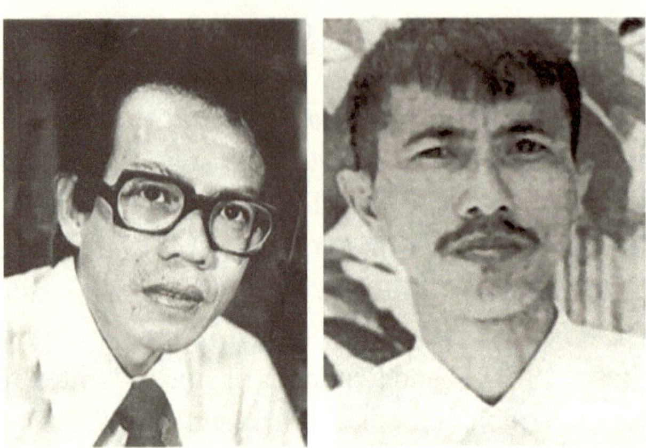

The writers Nhật Tiến (left) and Nguiễn Ngu Í (right)

THOUGHTS CONCERNING LITERARY CREATION

In 1961, Nhật Tiến had become well known due to three of his published works: *The White Shirt People* (*Những Người Áo Trắng*; 1959), *Lost Stars* (*Những Vì Sao Lạc*, 1960), and *The Abandoned Porch* (*Thềm Hoang*, 1961). In that year, he responded to a number of questions posed to him in an interview by Nguiễn Ngu Í of the journal *Cyclopedia* (*Bách Khoa*):

"What is the purpose of literary creation? Do you do it for yourself or for everybody?"

"In my opinion, there is a close connection between the writer and the society that surrounds him. From the moment the writer begins to work, he is ceaselessly preoccupied with its many scenes and situations. Each day has its detail; each place has its own feeling, regardless of all the things around him that have contributed to his feelings. Thus, when the work is completed, it will always to a greater or lesser extent bring benefit to both sides; the writer has a spiritual reward (I won't mention any material reward, because that is too small to be worth mentioning) and society gets the benefit of a cultural contribution.

"Does the creation of a work follow a defined path, or is it simply a matter of inspiration?"

"Perhaps "defined path" here has the meaning of "working method." If we take it in that sense, I can't say I have either tendency. Because if you speak of "method," that means that you have some system, that you follow some compulsory program, whereas if you speak of inspiration, then you must have much time, because inspiration comes only at particular moments. But because I follow a profession (author's note: teaching), there are times when I am exhausted for months and can't write a line. But when I meet circumstances that grant me free time, then I will write industriously regardless whether I have inspiration or not. Nevertheless, if I have inspiration, and also free time, then writing is easier."

"What happens between the time when a work first begins to form in your mind and the moment it is completed?"

"I begin with a character who lives amid circumstances that stir me to the utmost. Starting with that character, I write the first chapter. From that point on, I depend on elements that have appeared in the previous chapter (these elements come to me as I am writing) to write the next one. Usually, I start thinking about the conclusion only after I have written nine or ten chapters. In my opinion, this way of proceeding allows one to be more objective than adhering to a plot that has been set up from the beginning. Because if everything is decided in advance, the work will be constrained and many fresh new ideas will in consequence be lost."

"What experiences in life and literary creation have pleased you the most?"

"As for form, when I write, I like to hold to the idea that I am not engaged in literary composition, for to tell the truth, to describe scenes without falling into clichés is very difficult. To avoid that difficulty, I choose a quite simple style of writing. But choosing is one thing, while following that choice is another. That, I think, is a matter for the reader to judge. As for the content of a work, I must confess to you that I am in much perplexity about that, and don't dare to speak of "experiences" that might be placed in the pages of a journal. As for those of my works that have pleased me the most, it seems to me that the stories of mine that have appeared in print have not necessarily been noticed sufficiently so that everyone would know which ones I was referring to, so I must ask to be allowed not to respond to that question." Nhật Tiến

(excerpted from *Bách Khoa* 115, Oct. 15, 1961, pp, 103-104)

Nhật Tiến: a drawing by Tạ Ty. *(Source: Ten Faces in Today's Arts [Mười Khuôn Mặt Văn Nghệ Hôm Nay], Lá Bối, Saigon, 1971)*

In a short article limited to about seven thousand words that deals with an author of more than twenty works, it is hard to introduce Nhật Tiến in an adequate manner. On meeting with him personally, I asked him what works he would choose if he had to name only three to serve as an introduction. The ones he named were: *The Abandoned Porch*, *The Curtain Puller*, and *Fitful Sleep*. Those are also the choices I have made to introduce this very multifaceted writer.

The *Abandoned Porch* portrays various lives in "Grass Corner" ("Xóm Cỏ"), a residential pocket full of mud and stagnant water in the middle of Saigon where poor laborers live. Four mournful lines stand at the very beginning of the story.

Who impelled me to this place,
Dark by day and black by night?
Cradling a guitar, I pluck sad strains,
Evoking tunes to thrust away the days.

These four lines serve to introduce the main character Tốn, a blind performer who ekes out a living as a street singer. A fellow named Ích, without a father but shrewd beyond his years, serves Tốn as a pair of eyes. A prostitute called cô Huệ is well past her time of

The front cover of *The Abandoned Porch* (*Thềm Hoang*), by Nhật Tiến, Đời Nay, 1961; National Prize for Literature, 1961-1962

The front cover of the novel in dramatic form *The Curtain Puller* (*Người Kéo Màn*) by Nhật Tiến, Huyền Trân, Saigon, 1962

youth and beauty, but, due the imaginative descriptions of Ích, is still the object of Tốn's romantic dreams. A woman named U Tám, left a widow, while still young, grows infatuated with the honeyed words of a man, later known as Dượng Tám, a perfect ruffian who exploits his wife and is violent with his children. Another character, Lão Hói, pitifully immersed in alcohol and dependent for a living on acting as a deck-of-cards fortune teller, has a steadfast belief in Providence (Ông Trời.) As for Mr. Phó Ngữ, he has been left a widower, and has only a daughter whom he hopes will be able to find a kind and attentive husband, but this goal is never achieved. And then there is a soldier named Năm Trà who, having to go to a distant base, leaves his wife and children with his old mother. The wife, who is young and beautiful, cannot endure this lonely existence and decides to run away. Năm Trà's mother, because she has insufficient funds to take care of her three grandchildren, has to take them to an orphanage, and afterwards goes mad... The fates of these characters living together in "Grass Corner" add up to a dark and tragic portrait of poor people who have no means of escape. Wretchedness is the common denominator in the lives led by the residents of Grass Corner. The image of uncle Tốn, the blind street performer, and his companion Ích are always present in three hundred pages of the novel.

The climax of this social tragedy is signaled by the return of the soldier Năm Trà wearing faded and ragged fatigues. He meets his mother, who is now mad and does not recognize him. Faced with the tragedy of his destroyed family, Năm Trà goes mad as well, and to avenge himself burns down the neighborhood. The whole of "Grass Corner" is consumed in flame, along with the despairing cries of its inhabitants. Then a great rainfall descends on the heap of ashes as if intent on sweeping the place clean of the scattered remains of its abandoned porches. Upon reading the last page and closing the book, the reader may wonder if there will ever be a brighter day for the "Grass Corner" of the future? The content and style of this novel were such that it received the National Prize for Literature in 1961-1962.

Many people hold that Nhật Tiến's principal strength lay in writing short stories and novels on social themes, such as stories about unfortunate children. Actually, Nhật Tiến also wrote many plays, including works that were performed on the stage. As he writes, "In 1960, when a storm caused serious flooding in the Mekong delta, the Bạch Đằng Scout Troop and the Girl Scout Troop Thanh Quan participated in an effort to help the victims by putting on a show in Saigon's Thống Nhất ("Unification") Theater. For this show I made a three-act play entitled *Tempest* (*Cơn Giông*), in which the performers were all members of those two troops. One of the actors was the lawyer Trần Sơn Hà, who now lives in Orange County." (*A Scouting Life – Một Đời Hướng Đạo*, Nhật Tiến)

Nhật Tiến called *The Curtain Puller*, his fourth work, a "novel in the form of a play" (*tiểu thuyết kịch*). This was a very new concept to apply to "play," in the word's classic sense. Due to this, the work stirred up many reactions and disputes. Professor Nguyễn Văn Trung in his *Summary Investigation of Literary Studies* (*Lược Khảo Văn Học*), vol. 2, expressed disapproval of the new concept, saying: "A novel in the form of a play" leads simply to a confusion of two genres in which the particular possibilities of the genres thrown together are erased." The playwright Vi Huyền Đắc did not accept the idea that *The Curtain Puller* was a play. But Nhật Tiến himself, after half a century, is still pleased with *The Curtain Puller*. It was quite bold of him to combine the attributes of a novel, a play, and a film in order to write this work. Instead of having his characters appear on the stage only he gives them a variety of roles to play in the wider world. *The Curtain Puller* speaks of a set of relationships among members of an acting troupe, including the director, an old curtain puller, a clarinet-playing musician, an actress, a child, a fund-supplying Maecenas, and an author who writes plays. Every action unfolds amid deception, bribery, scheming, cheating, and conflict, generating tragic misconceptions right in their own lives. They show us the world of people active in the arts. Every character has roles, not only on the stage, but in the world behind it, in the make-up room and in the real world in which all the emotions seethe–delight, anger, love, and hatred–and with no lack of shameful fraud. This is a Nhật Tiến altogether different from the author who overflowed with love in *The White Shirt People* and *The Abandoned Porch*; now we have an author suspicious and pessimistic to the point of cruelty.

Fitful Sleep (Giấc Ngủ Chập Chờn) was written in the mid 1960s when the war in Vietnam promoted by Hanoi had spread to every province in the South. Nhật Tiến wrote about the hamlet of Vĩnh Hựu. It was agriculturally productive, and hence a region of both open and hidden conflict. By day it was controlled by the central government, but at night the authority lay with the other side. The families of the people who lived there were riven apart; some people followed this side and some the other, and they lost their lives due to this internecine conflict. They lived, assured neither of life nor death, amid a double wave of bullets and piled-up hatred and outrage that oppressed them night and day. The youths and even the little children of that village had originally all been closely attached to each other, but now that war had spread among them, neighbors and brothers killed each other, creating endless scenes of misery and pain. But the people of Vĩnh Hựu hamlet still remained indissolubly attached to the strip of earth where their umbilical cords were buried and never wished to leave it for another place. The elders often said to the younger folk:

"If you young folk want to kill each other somewhere, then do so; but you are forbidden to shoot each other in these lanes and walls. You all come from the same roots and tendrils. In one way or another, you are all connected to each other in family, in flesh, and in homeland. Killing each other on the land of your forebears is disgraceful." (*Fitful Sleep*, Huyền Trân, 1969, p. 63)

The book states a truth: that there was no popular uprising of people dissatisfied with the regime within what was called the "National Front for the Liberation of the South." Because of this implicit accusation, Hanoi judged the book to be reactionary in the extreme.

THE NATIONAL PRIZE FOR LITERATURE

The National Prize for Literature was established in 1957. The 21st issue of the journal *Văn Hữu*, published by the Department of Culture (Văn Hóa Vụ) in 1962, includes an article on this prize by the writer Hàn Phong: "A Brief History of the National Prize for Literature" It pertains to the period of the First Republic:

"A significant feature of the National Prize for Literature was that it placed no restrictions on the content or form of the works submitted for consideration. The works had to have been published during the year under review. In principle, the competition was to be held every year, but since published works were few, the prize was awarded in successive two-year periods.

First Period: 1955-57. The board of judges read 206 works published between 1954 and the end of 1956, submitted to them either by the authors or the publishers. These were of all types: books of scholarly research, fiction, poetry collections, and plays.

The board of judges included scholars, teachers, poets, novelists, and playwrights, such as Professor Nghiêm Toản, Nguyễn Thành

NGÀY TRAO TẶNG GIẢI VĂN CHƯƠNG TOÀN QUỐC 8-9-1962
Từ trái qua : VƯƠNG ĐỨC LỆ (*Giải Thơ*), NHẬT TIẾN (*Giải Tiểu Thuyết*)
ĐINH HÙNG (*Giải Thơ*), LÊ NGỌC TRỤ (*Giải Biên Khảo*), MAI TRUNG TĨNH (*Giải Thơ*)

The National Literary Award Ceremony of 1960-61 (from the left: Vương Đức Lệ, Nhật Tiến, Đinh Hùng, Lê Ngọc Trụ, Mai Trung Tĩnh.
(Nhật Tiến, personal archives)

Châu, Nguyễn Khắc Kham, Father [*linh mục*] Nguyễn Văn Thích, Trương Công Cừu, Hồ Biểu Chánh, Phú Đức, Bà Tùng Long, Vi Huyền Đắc, Đông Hồ, Trần Tuấn Khải, Vũ Hoàng Chương, and Vũ Khắc Khoan. The chairman of the board was the scholar Đoàn Quan Tấn. The award ceremony took place on August 25 in Independence Palace, and the prizes were presented by the president of the Republic of Vietnam.

The winning works, in the category of scholarship, were *Popular Literature* (*Văn Chương Bình Dân*) by Father Thanh Lãng, *Building Human Dignity* (*Xây Dựng Nhân Vị*) by Bùi Tuân and *The People of Former Times* (*Người Xưa*) by Trần Đình Khải.

The front cover of *Fitful Sleep* (*Giấc Ngủ Chập Chờn*), by Nhật Tiến, Huyền Trân, Saigon 1969;.

Issue 21 of the journal *Văn Hữu*, pub. by Văn Hóa Vụ, 1962 *(Thành Tôn, personal archives)*

The winning works in the fiction category were *Seeking a Road to Survival* (*Tìm Về Sinh Lộ*) by Kỳ Văn Nguyên, *Bringing Heart to the Writing of History* (*Đem Tâm Tình Viết Lịch Sử*) by Nguyễn Kiên Trung (that is, Nguyễn Mạnh Côn), and *The Homestead* (*Nếp Nhà*) by Bửu Kế.

In poetry, the winning works were *Bright Blossoms* (*Anh Hoa*) by Phạm Mạnh Viện, *The Dragon River Poetry Collection* (*Long Giang Thi Tập*) by Trần Hữu Thanh, the *Nam Trung Poetry Collection* (*Nam Trung Thi Tập*) by Nguyễn Văn Bình, and *The Fate of Fair Ones* (*Kiếp Hồng Nhan*) by Quang Hân.

The winning plays were: *Storm of the Era* (*Bão Thời Đại*) by Trần Lê Nguyễn, *A Bolshevik Love (Ái Tình Bôn-Sê-Vích)* by Thạch Bích and *A Two-Colored Shirt* (*Hai Màu Áo*) by Minh Đăng Khánh

Second Period: 1958-59. The National Prize for Literature in Period Two had a procedural change; this time the authors did not have to send in their works for consideration. The winning items were instead chosen by the board from all works published in the period from 1958 to the end of 1959. Because they did not conceive of this activity as a competition, the members of the board sought to read everything published in this period. And this time the board of judges changed their name to *The National Literary Award Council 1958-59* (author's note: previously it had been "the Board of Judges").

The National Literature Award Council 1958-59 was composed of many writers, artists, and professors, such as Hà Như Chi, Hà Thượng Nhân, Đái Đức Tuấn, Trần Hữu Thanh, Đỗ Đức Thu, Đông Hồ, and Vi Huyền Đắc. The chairman was Professor Trương Công Cừu, the president of Văn Khoa College.

In a five-month period, the members of this board read 54 scholarly works, 34 novels, and 3 plays, and in the end were awarded 7 prizes. The awards ceremony was organized in the Đô Thành Gallery and was presided over by Vice President Nguyễn Ngọc Thơ, representing the president.

In the category of scholarship, the winning works were *A New Investigation of the Book of Changes* (*Dịch Kinh Tân Khảo*) by Nguyễn Mạnh Bảo and *Vietnamese Literature: A Comprehensive Treatment* (*Việt Nam Văn Học Toàn Thư*) by Hoàng Trọng Miên.

The winning works of fiction were *The Boat Along the River* (*Đò Dọc*), by Bình Nguyên Lộc, *The Spirit of Turtle Tower* (*Thần Tháp Rùa*) by Vũ Khắc Khoan, *The Life of a Pilot* (*Đời Phi Công*) by Toàn Phong (author's note: Nguyễn Xuân Vinh) and *Night Rain at Year's End* (*Mưa Đêm Cuối Năm*) by Võ Phiến.

There was one prize for a book of poems: *Lanterns* (Hoa Đăng) by Vũ Hoàng Chương.

No prize was issued in the stage-play category.

Third Period: 1960-61. The Board of Judges for the National Prize for Literature changed direction in this period and adopted a different name; The Board for the Selection of Literary Prizes, 1960-61. This board was chaired by Thu Giang (Nguyễn Duy Cần) and included three subgroups. The subgroup for scholarly works was made up of Nguyễn Duy Cần, Nguyễn Đăng Thục, and Nguyễn Văn Trung. Another subgroup, for poetry, was made up of Vũ Hoàng Chương, Đông Hồ, and Thanh Tâm Tuyền. The third subgroup was for fiction and was made up of Vi Huyền Đắc, Vũ Khắc Khoan, Đỗ Đức Thu, and Bình Nguyên Lộc.

The selection board met three times, and examined 113 works: 37 scholarly books, 34 novels, 39 poetry collections, and 3 stage-plays, with the following results:

In the scholarly category there was one prize only: *A Dictionary of Vietnamese Orthography* (*Việt Ngữ Chánh Tả Tự Vị*) by Lê Ngọc Trụ.

In fiction, there were three prizes: *The Abandoned Porch* by Nhật Tiến, *Protect the Gold, Preserve the Jade* by Doãn Quốc Sỹ, and *The Old Stable*, by Linh Bảo.

In poetry, there were four prizes: *Path Into a Love Story* (*Đường Vào Tình Sử*) by Đinh Hùng, *Hope* (*Hy Vọng*) by Hoàng Bảo Việt, *Warm Nest* (*Tổ Ấm*) by Anh Tuyến, and *Forty Poems* (*40 Bài Thơ*) by Mai Trung Tĩnh and Vương Đức Lệ.

No prize was awarded in the stage-play category.
[end of quotation from Văn Hữu 21, pp. 76-81]

It seems worth recording here that there were continuous organizational improvements in each period of the National Prize for Literature, but one principle never changed: no requirement was ever placed on the content or form of the works under consideration. This is made clear in an article by the writer Nguiễn Ngu Í in *Bách Khoa* 138: "Thu Giang (Nguyễn Duy Cần), the chairman of the Selection Board in Period 3 of the prize stated that criteria of the board was summed up by the word 'literature,' meaning 'fine ideas and beautiful words,'" to which he added "the works chosen will be a reflection of a free culture, meaning that they will not be under the control of any system of thought and will not be required to follow any political or artistic tendency whatsoever."

After the prizes were issued, Lê Ngọc Trụ, representing all the writers who were awarded prizes, expressed his views on the matter. He said that it was to the greatest degree significant that the day of the award ceremony had fallen on the birth anniversary of Nguyễn Du, and suggested that he and all the prize winners should feel a holy responsibility toward the Vietnamese language and the future of Vietnamese culture. (Bách Khoa 138)

This was the third period of the prize and was also the last period that occurred under the First Republic. Due to a series of political upheavals, it was only in 1966 that the National Literary Prize was reinstituted.

It should also be recorded here that in the short nine-year span of the First Republic, culturally active figures established the first firm basis for literature and art in the South. The writers and poets who received prizes were all people who became major names in the twenty-year period of literature in the South, including the poets Đinh Hùng, Vũ Hoàng Chương, the writers Bình Nguyên Lộc, Nguyễn Mạnh Côn, Doãn Quốc Sỹ, Võ Phiến, Nhật Tiến, Linh Bảo…

NHẬT TIẾN AND THE LITERARY GREAT NHẤT LINH

At the end of 1955, through Trương Cam Vĩnh, the younger brother of the writer Trương Bảo Sơn, Nhất Linh received a draft copy of *The White Shirt People*, the first-completed work of Nhật Tiến. Nhật Linh saw Nhật Tiến's talent and at once sent the novel to Phượng Giang for publication. Nhất Linh introduced Nhật Tiến to the PEN Club (Văn Bút), then headed by him and at the same time invited Nhật Tiến to write for the journal Culture in the Present Era (*Văn Hóa Ngày Nay*). One must say that these two enjoyed a close friendship between 1955 and 1963.

In 1963, the political situation in the cities of the South was very turbulent, with demonstrations and self-immolations, while the smoke and fire of the war instigated by the North had spread to all the southern provinces. The death of the activist Nguyễn Tường Tam, also known as the writer Nhất Linh, was a sign of the tragedy of those times, and was part of the history of that era. The death of Nhất Linh, the leader of the Self-Reliance Literary Group was at that time a great shock to the young people of the South. I wish to record here a few personal reminiscences concerning the testament he left before his suicide.

It was possible that Nhất Linh made careful preparations for his own death for several weeks prior to killing himself. Pursued by secret agents, he thought it was possible that his farewell note might be seized by his pursuers. In 1963 there were as yet no xerox machines, scanners, or publication via the internet, such as now exist. Nhất Linh wrote a second copy of his farewell testament that was given to a group of students. At that time I was in the third year of my medical studies. On the first days of July 1963, Nguyễn Tường Quý drove his elder brother Nguyễn Tường Vũ (the son of Nguyễn Tường Thụy, the eldest brother in Nguyễn Tường's family) down to the Minh Mạng college campus (Đại Học xá Minh Mạng) and sought me out. Quý waited outside; only Nguyễn Tường Vũ came to see me. Without saying much, Vũ handed me a thin envelope, and let me know that it was one of two handwritten copies of Nhất Linh's farewell testament: *"We'll depend on you to keep this; you give it back*

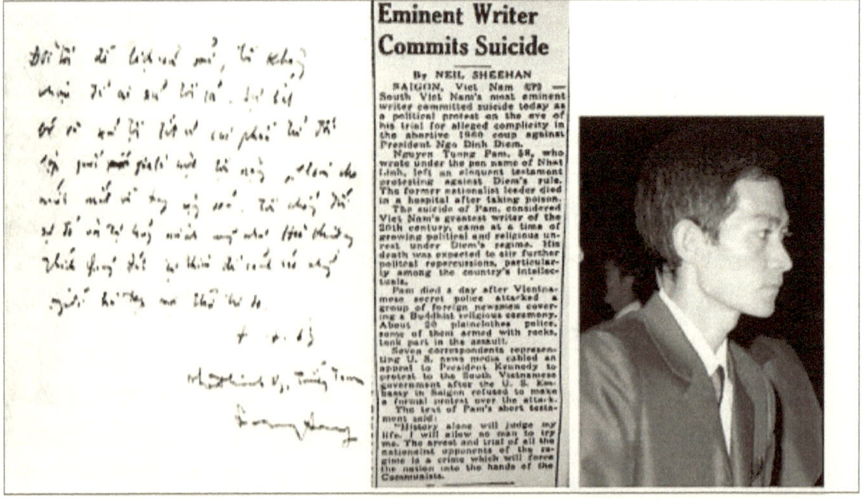

Eminent Writer Commits Suicide

By NEIL SHEEHAN

SAIGON, Viet Nam (UPI) — South Viet Nam's most eminent writer committed suicide today as a political protest on the eve of his trial for alleged complicity in the abortive 1960 coup against President Ngo Dinh Diem.

Nguyen Tuong Tam, 58, who wrote under the pen name of Nhat Linh, left an eloquent testament protesting against Diem's rule. The former nationalist leader died in a hospital after taking poison.

The suicide of Tam, considered Viet Nam's greatest writer of the 20th century, came at a time of growing political and religious unrest under Diem's regime. His death was expected to stir further political repercussions, particularly among the country's intellectuals.

Tam died a day after Vietnamese secret police attacked a group of foreign newsmen covering a Buddhist religious ceremony. About 20 plainclothes police, some of them armed with rocks, took part in the assault.

Seven correspondents representing U. S. news media cabled an appeal to President Kennedy to protest to the South Vietnamese government after the U. S. Embassy in Saigon refused to make a formal protest over the attack.

The text of Tam's short testament said:

"History alone will judge my life. I will allow no man to try me. The arrest and trial of all the nationalist opponents of the regime is a crime which will force the nation into the hands of the Communists.

Nhất Linh's testament (left), a UPI news notice (middle), and Nguyễn Tường Vũ in 1960 (right). *(Nguyễn Tường Quý and Nguyễn Tường Thiết, personal archives)*

when it is needed." When Nguyễn Tường Vũ went back, I quietly put this second copy of the testament, a piece of historical evidence, into a book cabinet between pages of Đào Duy Anh's hardcover thick dictionary published by Minh Tân in Paris.

The note, consisting of 71 words, was brief and succinct:

"Let history be my judge; I refuse to allow any individual to judge me. The arrest and conviction of all nationalist opponents of the regime is a great crime that will cause the country to fall into the hands of the communists. I am opposed to this and hereby destroy myself, like Abbot Thích Quảng Đức who set himself afire, so as to warn those who are trampling upon every liberty.

July 7, 1963
Nhất Linh – Nguyễn Tường Tam"

Nhất Linh sacrificed himself on July 7, 1963. Only one day later, a UPI news release written by Neil Sheehan, dated July 8, 1963, announced the event to all the world's newspapers:

"South Vietnam Eminent Writer Commits Suicide" by Neil Sheehan. "South Vietnam's most eminent writer committed suicide today as a political protest on the eve of his trial for alleged complicity in the abortive 1960 coup against President Ngo Dinh Diem. Nguyen Tương Tam [misspelled as "Pam" by Sheehan], 58, who wrote under the name of Nhat Linh, left an eloquent testament protesting against Diem's rule. The former nationalist leader died in a hospital after taking poison. The suicide of Tam, considered Vietnam's greatest writer of the 20th century, came at a time of growing political and religious unrest under Diem's regime. His death was expected to stir further political repercussions, particularly among the country's intellectuals… The text of Tam's short testament said, 'History alone will judge my life. I will allow no man to try me. The arrest and trial of all nationalist opponents of the regime is a crime that will force the nation into the hands of the communists.'" (UPI, July 8, 1963)

And thus, "copy one" of Nhất Linh's testament reached the hands of the international world. The copy I preserved no longer has the

The portrait of Nhất Linh by Nguyễn Gia Trí

crucial importance that it had when Vũ put it into my hands. Later, I learned from Lawyer Nguyễn Tường Bá that "copy one" had been delivered to the UPI news agency by Như Phong.

Nhất Linh's funeral took place on July 13, 1963. The greater part of those who paid their respects were college and middle school students. What chiefly moved them was that a distinguished writer had died, whereas those who shared his aims wished to represent Nhất Linh's death as a self-sacrifice for a political end. Ever since the 1930s Nhất Linh had been a public figure in two realms: literature and politics. The relative importance of these two aspects of his identity varied with the viewpoint of each individual. I still feel that it was his literary role that predominated on the day of his funeral. There was a photograph of the portrait of Nhất Linh done by the artist Nguyễn Gia Trí and a couplet by Vũ Hoàng Chương that made use of the titles of all his books:

"The weaver, the pair of friends, all in darkness, you must live; why end it all?

A life of rain and wind, of piercing cold, the white butterfly, golden evening not just autumn sunlight.

The death of a writer is always a tragedy in itself, if not a devastating misfortune. In some sense, every writer dies segment by segment with each work he writes. We must respect those deaths, and regard them as a common denominator of healing instead of division. There is no political regime that does not at length disappear, but writers live on their works.

The eulogy at the funeral was given by the young writer Nhật Tiến, then aged just 27, and surrounded by government security personnel. He expressed himself courageously as an independent writer, though at the time he was the vice chairman of the PEN Club (Văn Bút). Shedding deeply felt tears, he spoke thus of the death of the writer:

"This great literary spirit embodied the noble mission of the writer. This great man upheld the indomitable traditional spirit of a true writer."

A few days after Nhất Linh's funeral, when I met them again, I returned "copy two" of his testament to Nguyễn Tường Vũ and Nguyễn Tường Quý. Nguyễn Tường Vũ, very much an artist, and the man responsible for the layout of Nhất Linh's journal, *Culture in the Present Era*, died on May 19, 1991 while helping to carry out a United Nations charitable mission aimed at rescuing boat people at Palawan in the Philippines. Nguyễn Tường Quý still remembers how he drove Vũ to my Minh Mạng college campus so he could deliver into my hands the testament of "Uncle Tam" (Nhất Linh).

FROM SAIGON TO KOH KRA, THE ISLAND OF DEMONS

When Nhật Tiến was stuck in-country after 1975, the schools that employed him had not opened yet, his publishing house Huyền Trân had been forced to a halt, and he had to put aside his pen. Nhật Tiến and his whole family had to go out to the streets and run a café to survive.

A few days after April 30, 1975, Mai Thảo and Duyên Anh went to eat at this café on Duy Tân street. Next to the café on the same street was another café belonging to the creator of Loan Mắt Nhung (Nguyễn Thụy Long). Recalling this, Mai Thảo wrote:

"The spectacle that struck my eye then, of two cafés sitting side by side, both in front of a long low wall, was a scene of complete

The writer / boat person Nhật Tiến in 1980, sitting in a refugee camp in Songkhla, Thailand, writing an indictment of the tragedies in the Eastern Sea. *(Nhật Tiến, personal archives)*

contrast. Both were run by writers who had lost their livelihoods and had to manage cafés, facing new circumstances. The café of Nguyễn Thụy Long, with its disorderly array of wine glasses on the tables and the young customers, spoke clearly of the disorderly life that prevailed among them. The café of Nhật Tiến was totally different. It was healthier and had twice as much the air of a family-run enterprise, with neatly placed little dishes of water-spinach next to a smoking hot pan. Nhật Tiến's wife leaned pink-cheeked over a frying pan of deep yellow shrimp cakes, while the eldest daughter, her hair pulled tight and wearing a neatly pleated skirt, assisted her literary father in everything. I remember that the day we all ate there to support the "Abandoned Porch Café," (Thềm Hoang Quán) each of us had a plate of delicious shrimp cakes, and I jokingly said to Nhật Tiến, "You're skilled at washing bowls these days, right?" And Nhật Tiến laughed, it was a mild, ordinary laugh, the prematurely wise laugh, perhaps, of a teacher. Nhật Tiến always regarded himself, in all situations, as a teacher: "Skillful my eye! We all must do what we have to do!" ("Nhật Tiến Still Stands Outside Beneath the Sun," Literature no. 6; California, December 1982)

From the right: Nhật Tiến, Ngô Thế Vinh. *(photo by Đào Nhật Tiến, Dallas, Texas)*

Nhật Tiến too had to attend a one-month "political education" course along with many other writers and artists of the South, such as Hoài Bắc, Thái Thanh, Nguyễn Thị Vinh, Đỗ Phương Khanh, and Nguyễn Thụy Long… His teaching was in physics and chemistry, not literature, so after the one-month course he was able to resume teaching at his old private school. But in the end he was no longer able to be "a teacher in a sleazy time," so in November of 1979 he decided to "brave the ocean." Going with him on that venture was Từ Mẫn (Võ Thắng Tiết), originally the director of the publishing house *Lá Bối (Palm Leaves)*. Later, on U.S. soil, he became the director of the publishing house *Văn Nghệ ("The Arts")*.

The trip became devastating disaster when they encountered Thai pirates. They lived in hell for several weeks on the island of Koh Kra, afflicted by thirst and by violence. But they survived, were rescued, and were delivered to the refugee camp in Songkhla. There, the writer / boat person Nhật Tiến was one of the witnesses of the depredations of pirates in the Bay of Thailand. Together with the journalists Dương Phục and Vũ Thanh Thủy he wrote and immediately sent out for distribution accounts of the tragic disasters occurring in the Eastern Ocean, accounts which shook the conscience of the world and which were the first step in the formation of the Committee for the Rescue of Boat People, which continued to be active for many subsequent years.

NHẬT TIẾN, THE SWIFT ROVER SCOUT AT THE AGE OF 80

A week from now, on August 24, 2015, Nhật Tiến will have his 80th birthday. Here in America, that will also be the age at which Nhật Tiến will have to undergo tests to renew his driver's license. In preparation for that day, he has gone to an ophthalmologist to get laser treatment for the retina of his left eye. Before that he had already had cataract surgery. Now, with progressive lenses, he enjoys 20/20 vision. Now he is devoting all his time to getting ready for the written part of the DMV's exam. At whatever age he has always been enthusiastically attached to life in the full spirit of a devoted member of the scouting movement. Even at age 80 he is attentively studying lessons so that he can go, pen in hand, to take an examination! I think he will easily pass this test.

And so I send to him this hurriedly written seven thousand word essay. I must confess it is too short when compared with his full and varied life: a writer, a teacher, and a scout. Nhật Tiến is a direct and courageous man. Not everyone feels full sympathy with his actions and more than a few times, he had to suffer the penalty of being misunderstood or brutally suppressed. But one thing is not in doubt: whatever he says is the voice of his conscience.

Whatever the circumstances of his life, he has never ceased to be active. *He still "stands outside beneath the sun"*–the words of Mai Thảo. For me, Nhật Tiến will always be the "Swift Swallow Rover Scout on the Path of Life."

California, August 21, 2015

NGUYỄN ĐÌNH TOÀN FROM *THE GRASSY FIELD TO THE ROBE OF FADED DREAMS*

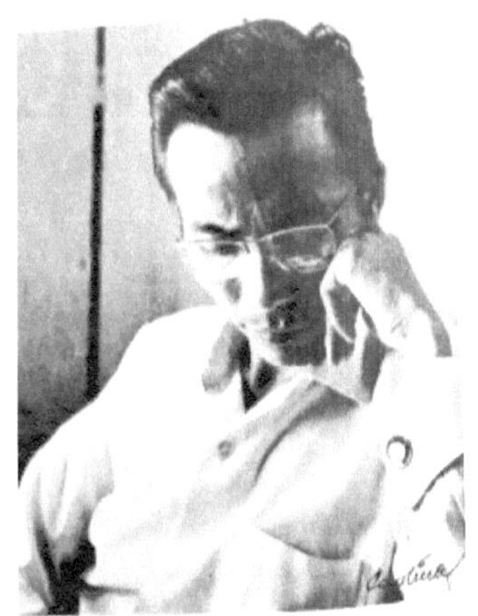

Nguyễn Đình Toàn.
(photo by Trần Cao Lĩnh)

"Who can know that joy lies wrapped in heaven's ills.
(Có biết đâu niềm vui đã nằm trong thiên tai)
Nguyễn Đình Toàn

BIOGRAPHICAL DATA

Nguyễn Đình Toàn initially used the pen name Tô Hà Vân, but became famous with his real name, which later turned into his official literary name. He was born on Sept. 6, 1936 in Gia Lâm District, next to the Red River, just outside of Hanoi. After emigrating to the South in 1954, he began to write prose and poetry, make plays, and compose music, working with the journals *Literature* (*Văn*) and *Literary Studies* (*Văn Học*) – for many years, he assisted Trần Phong Giao in selecting poems and stories for *Literature*. He also wrote serial pieces (feuilletons) for the publications *Freedom Daily* (*Tự Do*), *Political Discourse* (*Chính Luận*), *Building Up* (*Xây Dựng*) and *Front Line* (*Tiền Tuyến*), and worked as an editorial contributor for the Saigon Broadcasting Station, in which role he became particularly famous for his program "Themes in Music" ("Nhạc Chủ Đề") in the 1970s.

After 1975, he suffered the fate common to all writers and artists in the South. He was arrested twice and spent almost six years in labor reeducation camps, resettling in the U.S. toward the end of 1998, after which he and his wife Thu Hồng were responsible for the program "Reading Books" for VOA / Voice of America broadcasting station. Nguyễn Đình Toàn also wrote for the "Literature and Arts Section" of the weekly *Việt Tide*, run by the writer Nhật Tiến until his retirement. Nguyễn Đình Toàn currently lives with his family in southern California.

PUBLISHED WORKS

Prose: *The Hải Sisters* (*Chị Em Hải*; a novel, Tự Do, 1961), *Those Who Stand Aside* (*Những Kẻ Đứng Bên Lề*; a novel, Giao Điểm, 1964), *The Road* (*Con Đường; a novel, Giao Điểm 1965*), *The Days and Months* (*Ngày Tháng*, a novel; An Tiêm, 1968), *Outside* (*Phía Ngoài*, a short story collection; written with Huỳnh Phan Anh, Hồng Đức, 1969), *A Summer Night* (*Đêm Hè*, a novel; Hiện Đại, 1970), *Recess* (*Giờ Ra Chơi*, a novel, Khai Phóng, 1970), *A Forgotten Night* (*Đêm Lãng Quên*, Tân Văn, 1970), *No One* (*Không Một Ai*, a novel; Hiện Đại, 1971), *The City* (*Thành Phố*, a novel, Kẻ Sĩ, 1971), *The Fire* (*Đám Cháy*, short story collection, Tân Văn, 1971), *Ashes and Dust* (*Tro Than*, a novel, Đồng Nai 1972), *The Robe of Faded Dreams* (*Áo Mơ Phai*, a novel, Nguyễn Đình Vượng, 1972), *A Grassy Field* (*Đồng Cỏ*, a novel, Đồng Dao, Australia, 1994)

- Poetry: *Bitter Honey* (*Mật Đắng*, Huyền Trân, 1962)
- Drama: His plays were all for the radio, with the exception of *The Rainstorm* (*Cơn Mưa*), which Võ Phiến excerpted and had printed in his *Drama of South Vietnam*; his other manuscripts were lost.
- Music: *Yellow Daisies Porch* (*Hiên Cúc Vàng*, song collection, 1999), *I Wish to Say to You* (*Tôi Muốn Nói Với Em*, song collection, 2001), *Rain on the Orchid Plant* (*Mưa Trên Cây Hoàng Lan*, song collection, 2002).
- Memoirs: *A Rose in Gratitude*, vols. I and II (*Bông Hồng Tạ Ơn*, I & II, Đêm Trắng, 2006, 2012)

The Robe of Faded Dreams was awarded a National Literature and Art prize in 1973.

THE HẢI SISTERS

Nguyễn Đình Toàn no doubt began writing quite early; while still a youth in Hanoi he formed a literary group and chose his first pen name: Tô Hà Vân. On emigrating to the south, he lived at first with Nhật Tiến's family. He had no money to buy ordinary white paper, so his first literary drafts were written on the reverse sides of discarded news agency releases. When he began to publish things, he decided to use his real name as his pen name.

The Hải Sisters was Nguyễn Đình Toàn's earliest work; it is seldom referred to, but it has all the stylistic marks of "The Road" he was to follow throughout his subsequent career. The correspondent Lô Răng (Phan Lạc Phúc) relayed a draft copy of *The Hải Sisters* to the journalist Phạm Xuân Ninh, after which it reached the hands of the journalist Như Phong, author of *Smoke and Waves,* who was then the general secretary of the *Freedom Daily* (*Tự Do*). Như Phong saw immediately that this was a hidden gem and, recognizing the author's talent, arranged with *Freedom's* publisher to issue the novel at once, together with *Tested by Fire* (*Thử Lửa*) by Thao Trường (a pen name later changed to Thảo Trường). Both authors were born in 1936. With these two works, the earliest written by each, they became names to reckon with in the literature of the South.

The book-burning campaign after 1975, when Nguyễn Đình Toàn's books reduced to "dust and ashes."

THE ROBE OF FADED DREAMS

At the beginning of the 1960s, quite a few thick books were published that consisted of newspaper serial pieces, called "feuilletons." Along with those, there were translations of the Chinese swordsmanship and sorcery novels of Kim Dung and the romances of Quỳnh Dao to meet the needs of every sort of reader in that period. As for feuilletons, Nguyễn Thị Thụy Vũ characterised them as a means of writing *tiểu thuyết nhật trình* – "daily newspaper stories" – novels

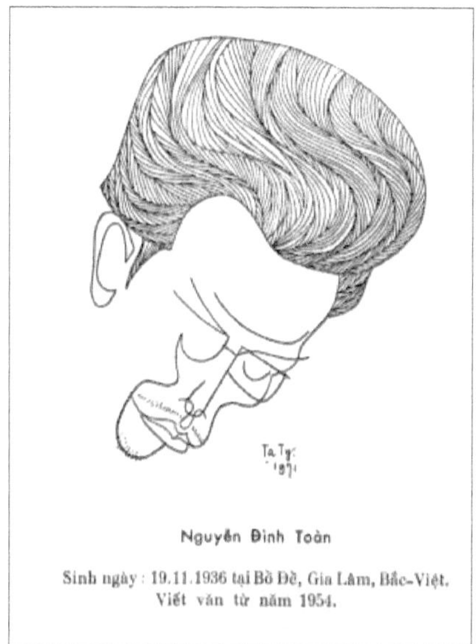

Two impressions of Nguyễn Đình Toàn by the artist Tạ Tỵ

and long stories that authors wrote every day and published in journals. A typical example of this was Mai Thảo, who would produce different works of fiction simultaneously for different publications. Sometimes he would go right to the offices of a journal and do his writing on the spot, handing each page to the typographer, as he completed them.

Nguyễn Đình Toàn, photo by Nguyễn Ngọc Dung, daughter of the photographer Nguyễn Cao Đàm.

And we must speak also of feuilleton-type novels written by many authors, of which a typical example is *A Million Piastres* (*Một Triệu Đồng*) by the journalist Như Phong, published in the pages of *Freedom Daily*. A popular story has it that when Như Phong came down with tuberculosis and had to discontinue his writing, the journal decided to continue the novel because it was popular with readers. In his memoir *I Am a Journalist* (*Tôi Làm Báo*) the writer and teacher Tạ Quang Khôi relates that "Mr. Nguyễn Hoạt requested each person to write a section until Mr. Như Phong could resume his work. And this novel of his continued to be written by the poet Đinh Hùng, the journalist Hiếu Chân (Nguyễn Hoạt) and after that by Tạ Quang Khôi until Như Phong returned to their editorial office.

As if it were a popular movement, writer after well-known writer began producing feuilleton-type novels in the manner of Mai Thảo. The list includes Thanh Tâm Tuyền, Nguyễn Đình Toàn, Thảo Trường, Bình Nguyên Lộc, Sơn Nam, Nhã Ca, Túy Hồng, and Nguyễn Thị Thụy Vũ… Many people have regarded those works as a variety of short-term escapist fiction suited to the needs of a consumer society.

MỘT SINH HOẠT CỦA VĂN BÚT TRƯỚC 1975:
BÁN TÁC PHẨM ĐỂ CỨU TRỢ NẠN NHÂN BÃO LỤT MIỀN TÂY
**Từ trái qua phải : PHẠM VIỆT TUYỀN-
NGUYỄN ĐÌNH TOÀN- NHẬT TIẾN-
MINH ĐỨC HOÀI TRINH- VŨ HOÀNG CHƯƠNG**

An activity of the Vietnamese PEN Club before 1975: Selling works to provide aid to flood victims in the Mekong Delta. From left to right: Phạm Việt Tuyền, Nguyễn Đình Toàn, Nhật Tiến, Minh Đức Hoài Trinh, and Vũ Hoàng Chương.

The writer Sơn Nam wrote feuilleton-novels, but he himself raised his voice in condemnation of the genre, saying that it was not true literature. To be fair, we must say that this feuilleton-fiction was not devoid of fine, even of very fine, works. The quality of the works concerned depended on the attitude, choices, and style of writing of the different authors.

Nguyễn Đình Toàn was himself no exception to this development. Aside from *The Hải Sisters*, written in its entirety before publication, almost all the rest of his productions were feuilleton novels printed as books only after appearing in parts. Examples of this were *The Road* (which had appeared in *Freedom Daily*), *The Grassy Field (Political Discourse Daily*), and *The Robe of Faded Dreams (Building Up Daily)* and others that Nguyễn Đình Toàn himself cannot recall. He had one remarkable strength: his drafts were all written once only and handed to the typesetting without change or correction. (Nguyễn Mộng Giác would later become the second author to proceed in this way; he wrote his drafts only once.) Nguyễn Đình Toàn maintained that he never sacrificed literary quality in choosing this mode of production.

If we take his works in chronological order, *The Robe of Faded Dreams* was the thirteenth of his feuilleton novels. It was also the work of his that was awarded the Literature and Art Prize (Giải Thưởng Văn Học Nghệ Thuật) in 1973.

In a review of *The Robe of Faded Dreams*, Huỳnh Phan Anh made the following observations: "We must acknowledge that the element called 'story' is excessively starved in this long 'story.' An ordinary reader may feel disappointed after reading *The Robe of Faded Dreams*. He may associate the book with a feeling of vague unease, and may have difficulty summarizing the events that the author has used more than three hundred pages to relate. It may be that the real 'story' in the book cannot be extracted from its pages, meaning that it cannot be summarized without loss of meaning. This is perhaps because the real story of *The Robe of Faded Dreams* is something that is incomplete, or something invisible, existing as a promise only."

Nguyễn Đình Toàn also discussed the methods he used in constructing the novel, which he regarded as a personal favorite, in the 1974 issue of *Literature*: "Every work, as it is written, is like a lit match; the author has the duty to create something, though the whole work may be nothing but the continuation of the first book. Many people have said to me that my way of writing is too long-breathed. But only a whole page with no punctuation marks is enough to convey all the aspects of the atmosphere of Hanoi. The chief character in the work is not one of its named personages, but is the city of Hanoi itself. Anyone living in that place must have the feeling of living in a dream, perhaps a dream that never fades like the mist of a slightly chilly drizzle in autumn... *The Robe of Faded Dreams* arose from that dream when I departed from Hanoi at the age of seventeen.

Thirty-two years later (Oct. 9, 2006), in a talk with Hoàng Khởi Phong on RFA, he said in response to a question about *The Robe of Faded Dreams*, "There are people who understand the times, people who see far and observe widely, who can foresee transformations in the situation of the world. Naturally, the things they foresee are in some cases mistaken. Only when the changes actually occur do they see whether they were correct or mistaken. I wrote that book based only on the presentiments of a person exposed to historical situations, just as a person is exposed to changes in the weather."

This response of Nguyễn Đình Toàn makes one think of the speech of Albert Camus in Stockholm 1957 when he received the Nobel Prize for literature. Camus observed that in today's world humanity is divided between a tiny minority who determine the course of history and the great majority who have to endure the consequences of historical upheavals. And Camus, the author of *The Plague*, held that the proper role of people in the fields of literature and art was to stand with all those whom history makes wretched. *("Le rôle de l'écrivain, du même coup, ne se sépare pas de devoirs difficiles. Par définition, il ne peut se mettre aujourd'hui au service de ceux qui font l'histoire: il est au service de ceux qui la subissent."* (Albert Camus, Discours de Suède, 1957)

The Robe of Faded Dreams consists of the presentiments of a man who feels that the city of Hanoi is about to be lost; *The Grassy Plain* is a work that foretells the imminent loss of Saigon. Nguyễn Đình Toàn responds sensitively to the changes in the weather just as he does to the upheavals of history. The foreboding or instinct of the author precedes the tragedy, shadows forth the shattering and separation that will occur, and has the character of prophecy.

Let us read Nguyễn Đình Toàn, so as to live in Hanoi in the days when it was about to be lost, but would never be lost, due to the three hundred pages of *The Robe of Faded Dreams*:

"July and then August [of 1954; author's note] went by rapidly, like the random spells of rain that poured down in the nights, and in the afternoons. The people of Hanoi abandoned their city, which in a short while the city was like a body deprived of blood. From many distant regions of the countryside, group after group of people, ragged and smeared with dirt came day after day burdened with goods on shoulder poles, leading each other back to Hanoi, where they lay everywhere in the parks, in the narrow alleys, on the sidewalks and filled the city hall, as they waited to be conducted to the airports and wharves to emigrate to the South.

"Each afternoon, Lan would sit on the balcony and gaze down at the city streets, at times empty and at times filled with jostling crowds of country people leading each other rapidly, as if running, by the lapels, and she looked at the forms of trees before the house; the closest ones had branches that spread out and touched the balcony like arms; while those further away, along the avenues, would in a single day, a single afternoon, turn yellow in great numbers, and then in another day, all their leaves would have the aspect of cloaks for the city, taking on still fainter shades, and would fall from their branches like dreams from a shallow forehead, like hair from the head of an invalid.

"Throughout many days, Lan had the feeling that the illness of the city, and of the rows of trees, was infecting her as well. Her limbs were heavy, unwilling to move. Breathing was difficult.

"As she awaited the day of final separation, she prayed that the departure would not come in a hurry, so that she could remain here longer, remain in Hanoi, share the pain of Hanoi, live with Hanoi, die with Hanoi, wilt and droop with Hanoi. It was plain that Hanoi was at the end of its strength; the drops on the branches, the drops on the leaves, were no different from the weeping of Hanoi." (*The Robe of Faded Dreams*, Chapter 9, Nguyễn Đình Vượng, 1972)

THE LITERATURE AND CULTURE PRIZE: A SECOND PRESENTATION

After 1975, nothing that could be burned survived. Nguyễn Đình Toàn said to me: "I don't have a single photo of the day the Literature and Art Prize was issued. But as for the medal itself, something very strange happened. A young friend of mine bought it on a Hanoi street, brought it here, and presented it to me as a gift. He said to me, 'Uncle, I'm presenting this to you a second time.' It happened that when he brought the medal to me, Cao Xuân Huy and his friend Trần Như Hùng from the Australian Broadcasting Station were with me as well. Cao Xuân Huy felt that this matter was just too marvelous; he wanted to turn it into a short story."

Toàn said to him "It would be like The Adventures of a Cricket" (a well known children's book by Tô Hoài). Holding in my hand the gilded copper medal discolored by time, I joked with Nguyễn Đình Toàn and his wife that it was lucky that the medal was not pure gold, otherwise it would have been melted down in some jewelry store in Hanoi.

The books of Nguyễn Đình Toàn were all put in the "degenerate culture" *(văn hóa đồi trụy)* category after 1975, so they were all confiscated and converted to "ashes and dust," – the fateful name of a work by Nguyễn Đình Toàn when the book-burning campaign spread throughout the South at that time.

The National Literature and Art Prize of 1972-73 consisted not just of a medal, but also of six hundred thousand piasters, which, according to the rates that prevailed at the time, was equivalent

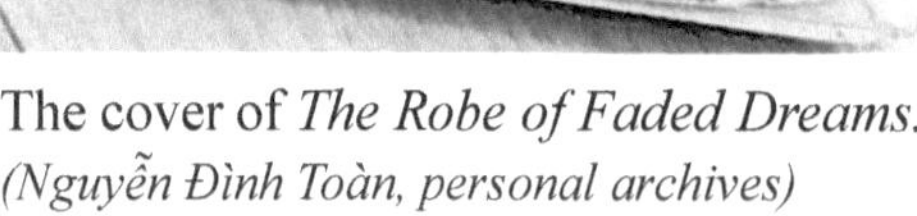
The cover of *The Robe of Faded Dreams.*
(Nguyễn Đình Toàn, personal archives)

The two faces of the medal presented to Nguyễn Đình Toàn in 1972-73 when he was awarded the National Literature and Art Prize (established by the president of Vietnam) for *The Robe of Faded Dreams.*

to forty taels of gold. It seems I should also mention here that the Literature and Art Prize of 1961 awarded to Nhật Tiến was worth forty thousand piasters, a sum that enabled him to purchase a Renault 4CV that ran well throughout the years that followed. Even though Nguyễn Vỹ complained that *"writers in An Nam were wretched as dogs,"* they were still highly valued in Vietnamese society.

THE "SLEEPLESS NIGHT" ("NUIT BLANCHE") GROUP

Throughout a period of twenty years beginning in 1954, literary movements unfolded one after another in complete freedom. The Self-Reliance Literary group was continued with the Culture in the Present Era group of Nhất Linh and the Creation group of Mai Thảo.

Thanh Tâm Tuyền rejected the literary styles of the pre-war period with efforts to renovate literature; The Viewpoint (Quan Điểm) group appeared, with Nghiêm Xuân Hồng, Vũ Khắc Khoan, and Mặc Đỗ, and these were followed by the "Sleepless Night" (Đêm Trắng) group, also called the "La Pagode" group, after the place where the members often gathered. This group was regarded as the "new novel" group of Saigon. With the exception of Nguyễn Đình Toàn and Nguyễn Quốc Trụ, the six members of this group were originally teachers: Huỳnh Phan Anh, Đặng Phùng Quân, Nguyễn Nhật Duật, and Nguyễn-Xuân Hoàng. The purpose of the group was to publish only works written by members. Though referred to as a "group," they were nevertheless independent writers with the common aim of renovating their work.

Most prominent in the group was Nguyễn Đình Toàn, with his new technique of writing stories that contained no stories, with pages consisting of long strings of words evoking feelings, like interior monologues. Nguyễn Đình Toàn succeeded in his effort to create a new kind of literature, but we should not for that reason suppose that he was imitating the French craze for the "nouveau roman" – "new novel." Thanh Tâm Tuyền and Dương Nghiễm Mậu are two other names associated with the leaning toward the "new novel" in Saigon of that time.

I should also mention here that Hoàng Ngọc Biên, though not a member of the Sleepless Night Group, was the first person to seriously investigate the *nouveau roman* movement in France, which in the mid 1950s was associated with the names Alain Robbe-Grillet, Nathalie Sarraute, Michel Butor, and Claude Simon. Hoàng Ngọc Biên translated some of Alain Robbe-Grillet's works and also exemplified some of the new French conceptions in his short-story collection *A Night of Sleep in the Province* (*Đêm Ngủ Ở Tỉnh*) published in Saigon by Cảo Thơm in 1970. But after Hoàng Ngọc Biên the "new novel" movement in Saigon was nothing but a name. Nothing that truly resembled the French movement came into being.

THEMES IN MUSIC

In the 1960s, three music programs existed that were greatly beloved by listeners: "Sounds of Silk and Bronze" (Tiếng Tơ Đồng), presented by the musician Hoàng Trọng, "Music of the Heart" (Tiếng Nhạc Tâm Tình), presented by Anh Ngọc and Mai Thảo, and "Themes in Music" (Nhạc Chủ Đề), presented by Nguyễn Đình Toàn. Each program had its own flavor, but "Themes of Music" perhaps inspired the most devotion. People would wait for it to come on the air each Thursday. The introductory words in the resonant voice of Nguyễn Đình Toàn entered into every listener's heart:

"A love song – the most earnest words uttered in a person's life– these words always begin in a place, a homeland, a city, a place where people have loved each other... everything about it– the season, the weather, the flowers and leaves, the grass and trees of such magical places combine to form a basis for happiness, and a basis for sorrowful tenderness"... (Nguyễn Đình Toàn, "Nhạc Chủ Đề 1970. Tình Ca Việt Nam, recorded before 1975, https://www.youtube. com/ watch?v=H3rrItsK5Z8)

It was not just women, but men as well, who were enthralled by the program. In Saigon the listeners were students, and on the battlefront the listeners were soldiers.

A soldier, later a handicapped veteran, the poet Phan Xuân Sinh, who now lives in Houston, Texas, recalled those times with emotion: "By now my old comrades and I are all around 60... I still remember those times on the battlefield with a transistor radio as small as a cigarette package with the tiny speaker pressed into my ear. For many minutes and seconds we were plunged into "Themes in Music" of Nguyễn Đình Toàn. He brought us many blessed moments of relaxation when we were dealing with life on the battlefield."

Professor Nguyễn Văn Tuấn from the Garvan Medical Research Institute in Australia has been a fan of "Themes in Music" before and after '75. He has written: "In my imagination it is like a miracle, making time run backwards. There I am, in some form, beneath a flickering light at night, sitting with my ear pressed to the radio, swallowing each introductory word of Nguyễn Đình Toàn, casting my soul into the entrancing melodies of love songs that never recede… And just recently, after listening again to Nguyễn Đình Toàn's CD *Love Songs of Vietnam 1970*, he had to exclaim, "each introduction to a song here is a piece of art in itself. Each expresses the literary and musical understanding of the one who selects them, Nguyễn Đình Toàn… And at last, those two friends with the surname Nguyễn came to understand each other as closely as Bá Nha (Mandarin: Bó Yá) and Tử Kỳ (Mandarin: Zhōng Zǐqí) when both were in other lands. They met, not in the "fearsome land of Vietnam" (the words of Nguyễn Đình Toàn in *The Grassy Field*), but on the vast free continent of America, where both of them were exiles.

The story of Nguyễn Đình Toàn is rich in images and the stuff of poetry – it can be read as if it were a prose poem. When he set words to a piece of music, the words were a poem in themselves. He wrote music, and became well known for some of his compositions–perhaps the melodies took flight from his initial poetic idea. The words of his "First Love Song" ("Tình Khúc Thứ Nhất") were a poem before they were combined with the music of Vũ Thành An.

"First Love Song"; sung by *Lệ Thu*
music composed by *Vũ Thành An*
lyrics by *Nguyễn Đình Toàn*

https://www.youtube.com.watch?v=T133AZzRTTY

First Love Song

Joy chases the drifting, windblown clouds,
Gloom rains heavily into life
Tears fall, fill up my youthful years
Those years far from people
A fairy-tale day arrives: you step atop your throne
Having heard the gold and lacquer droop,
I lose myself in gusts of incense
Hoping for some chance to join with you.

Who can know that joy lies wrapped in heaven's ills?
The wings of bats are blind in darkness.
Oh love, you speak no word to me;
What love does not conceal betrayal?
Please let us love like time creating drunken thunderstorms.
The leaves exclaim aloud the words of trees,
The winds impel the tracks of clouds
If we should love, then let our days be simple,
While still our eyes are not yet faded,
While still our hair remains unchanged,
When still our lips know how to make reply.
Love's joy gleams in moments only
We nourish gloom throughout our lives
So please preserve belief, though dreams don't come.
Though Heaven brings bitterness anew,
Please welcome it with calm,
For still I have a word of love for you.
In silence I illumine joy's path,
And spirits break the branch on this spring night
My steps astray, I descend to earth,
I become a lover in an empty sky,
I weep and dream of Heaven,
The day of going home is ever lost.
Having listened to seductive words,
I cause love to nourish wings,
But still some bits of joy on earth remain.

THE WATER OF THE MEKONG RIVER – THE EARTH'S BLOOD

Great masterpieces of literature often carry presentiments or even prophetic visions that can be connected to the events of one's life. *The Tale of Kiều* is an example. Any situation one faces may be connected to a line in that work.

I don't mean to say that Nguyễn Đình Toàn has created great masterworks, but I have been pleased to find in the pages of his books many presentiments that are worth quoting. Facing the prospect of a *The Nine Dragons Drained Dry, The East Sea in Turmoil*, he has compared the waters of the Mekong to "the blood of the earth."

"And then news came that a fisherman, Nguyễn Văn Chơn, and his wife in Lấp Vò District, Đồng Tháp Province were overjoyed when, ten days before Christmas, they caught a gigantic ray on the River Tiền between the hamlets of Tân Mỹ and Tân Khánh Trung. The ray was more than four meters long and two meters wide, and weighed about 270 kilograms. This type of ray, also called Selachian, bears the scientific name chondrichthyes, and is a cartilaginous fish living in salty waters. Beneath the excitement of catching such a huge ocean ray on a branch of the Tiền River, lay an omen of disaster: "Who can know that joy is concealed in heaven's ills?" as Nguyễn Đình Toàn's lines say, for the calamity of salt intrusion is moving ever deeper into the Mekong River Delta, a region originally overflowing with alluvial loam, rice, fruit trees, shrimp, and fish…" (*The Nine Dragons Drained Dry – The East Sea in Turmoil*, Chapter 14, Văn Nghệ, 2000)

THU HỒNG, "MADAME TÚ XƯƠNG"

The café La Pagode was generally the place where it was easy to meet Toàn and his artistic friends, who later evolved into the Sleepless Night group. Toàn came to this "pagoda" or Buddhist temple coffee shop just about every day to sit and write after putting in a day's work at the broadcasting station.

I got to meet Toàn's wife only when I went to visit him in his tiny house; it lay behind a row of acorn-bearing trees in an alley, also tiny, behind the Saigon Broadcasting Station. Thu Hồng was the name of his loyal partner of more than sixty years. She was six years younger than Nguyễn Đình Toàn and had the lissome physiognomy of a Modigliani model, but with a high forehead signifying the stubbornness with which she resisted the challenges of fate. She too was an announcer on one of the programs of the Saigon broadcasting station. Toàn was at that time quite ill with tuberculosis, and had to care for his first-born child. There were few medicines to treat tuberculosis then; they were more or less limited to two types: Rimifon and Streptomycin, which could make you deaf. Toàn often coughed blood, was physically feeble and, though only in his twenties, was continually obsessed with death. His poetry collection, *Bitter Honey*, was composed during this black and nearly despairing period of his life. When Võ Phiến wrote about this book of poems by Nguyễn Đình Toàn, he said that instead of the four Buddhist miseries, birth, illness, old age, and death, "*Bitter Honey* eliminates the word "old age (*lão*) and substitutes for it the word "love" (*ái*), which has a more terrible meaning still… "Birth, illness, love, and death," he says "sounds a little strange to the ear, but nevertheless may be found in every place, and every age." (*The Literature of South Vietnam, Poetry*, Văn Nghệ, 1999).

In the poem "Face Down *(Úp Mặt)*," Nguyễn Đình Toàn writes:

My hand caresses bony hollows;
My life concludes at twenty-four.

The ability to keep the fire alive in the cramped tiny dwelling of Nguyễn Đình Toàn and his wife at that time was perhaps due to the smile, always bright and patient, of Thu Hồng, Toàn's wife. For me, she is the very image of a "Madame Tú Xương."[1] At that time, and throughout the years that followed, she firmly held the family with its four children together and looked after her husband's well-being throughout his period of imprisonment.

"From olden times till now, the will of humans often triumph over that of Heaven." This "Madame Tú Xương" of the present era turned the prediction of *Bitter Honey* on its head, and Nguyễn Đình Toàn has now attained a great age. In September of this year, he will turn eighty.

And so Nguyễn Đình Toàn and his wife were able to come to the U.S., though they did so fairly late (1998). And through the years of the new millennium, after all the upheavals of their lives, Mrs. Thu

---

1 The reference here is to the wife of the poet Tú Xương (1870-1907). She is celebrated for the loyalty and resourcefulness with which she maintained a household for her feckless husband.

The writer Nguyễn Đình Toàn, and "Madame Tú Xương" Thu Hồng.
(photo by Đặng Tam Phong)

Hồng is still, as she always was, the image of "Madame Tú Xương," but she has begun to forget quite a few things, including things currently taking place in people's lives. But every time I phone Toàn and, finding him not at home, ask to speak with "Madame Tú Xương," then I hear lively laughter at the opposite end of the line–she knows at once who is speaking with her and remembers all the topics that concern us. One day not long ago I went to visit them, and spent half a morning with them in lively conversation. At the end of the visit, the two of them went down with me to the street to see me off. Toàn's wife said to me, quite spontaneously, "When are you going to pay us a visit, Vinh? Toàn reminded his wife that Vinh (me) had just come for a visit. She only laughed unconcernedly. I still thought that, had it not been for "Madame Tú Xương," Toàn perhaps could not have survived to his present age of eighty. Toàn did not dispute this, and wittily added, "and so now I must pay my debt to this lady." Toàn was speaking of the indispensable role he must now play every day in caring for his lifetime companion. The two now live like two birds with paired wings. Toàn cannot leave her alone in the house.

A PERSONAL NOTE

In her article *"Nguyễn Đình Toàn, the One Who Led Me into Music,"* the singer Quỳnh Giao observed that "Nguyễn Đình Toàn is a musician who needs no introduction." That statement is perhaps correct with regard to the generations who lived in the South in the period 1954 to 1975. But for the generations who were born and grew up after 1975, whether within the country or abroad, articles introducing this man talented in so many fields – literature, poetry, music, and drama – are very necessary. One can only be grateful that there have been many articles concerning him that explore every aspect of his life. In writing a new article, I ask myself what can remain to be discussed if not for a few entirely personal reminiscences of an old friend and literary colleague.

I am sending this article to "Madame Tú Xương" and Nguyễn Đình Toàn, author of *Bitter Honey*, just as he is miraculously on the verge of stepping into his eighties.

California, March 8, 2015

THE THIRD MONTH: THANH TÂM TUYỀN NO CHOICE BUT TO SHAKE OFF THE WITHERED MEMORIES

Thanh Tâm Tuyền
(Photo by Trần Cao Lĩnh)

"He cast away his memories and went on"
(Hắn rũ bỏ ký ức, và đi)
"Prelude To Departures, Returns"
("Prélude Cho Những Chuyến Đi, Về," 1982)

Cast away your memories – memories of people.
(Rũ bỏ ký ức – ký ức người)
"A Few Impromptu Words Presented to Intimate Friends"
("Vài Khúc Dạo Tặng Tri Âm," 1988)

Till the time that I must write as if nothing has occurred,
as if nothing has changed.
When will the time come when I can enjoy this?
So that I can resume writing?
(1993)

BIOGRAPHICAL DATA

Thanh Tâm Tuyền was born in March (March 13, 1936) and also died in March (March 22, 2006). This short article, published in March (March 22, 2015), was written to remember him on the ninth anniversary of his death:

Thanh Tâm Tuyền's real name was Dzư Văn Tâm. He was born in Vinh, Nghệ An. He lost his father very early. He started teaching at age sixteen, and published stories in the journal *Youth* (*Thanh Niên*). He was active in the Students' Association of Hanoi (Tổng hội Sinh Viên Hà Nội) along with Doãn Quốc Sỹ, Nguyễn Sỹ Tế, and Trần Thanh Hiệp, they found the magazine *Vietnamese Fire* (*Lửa Việt*). After emigrating to the South in 1954, he writes for the weeklies *Democracy* (*Dân Chủ*) and *The Vietnamese People* (*Người Việt*) and

A photo from 1960: TTT's close friends in the "Creation" group: From the left: Duy Thanh, Trần Lê Nguyễn, Thanh Tâm Tuyền, Ngọc Dũng.

(family of Thanh Tâm Tuyền, private archives)

A photo from 1964 on the occasion of TTT's marriage to Cao Thị Mai Hoa. From left: Trần Lê Nguyễn, Ngọc Dũng, Mai Thảo, Thanh Tâm Tuyền, Trần Thanh Hiệp, Nguyễn Sỹ Tế.
(family of Thanh Tâm Tuyền, private archives)

was one of the principal contributors to the journal *Creation* (Sáng *Tạo*) with Mai Thảo. He had a considerable influence on Vietnamese literature from 1956 to 1975, and during the years that followed.

Thanh Tâm Tuyền was recruited into the army in 1962, and rose eventually to the rank of captain. After 1975 he was imprisoned for seven years in various harshly-run camps in the far north of Vietnam, obtaining freedom finally in 1982. A fact that few people are aware of is that a few years after that, he lost his eldest son when the latter was attempting to make his escape from the country by ocean. From 1986 until the year of his death, he never ceased to pursue a hopeless quest for clues to his son's fate when he disappeared. He emigrated to the U.S. in 1990 and thereafter lived in seclusion. He passed away on 3/22/2006 when he had just turned seventy.

PUBLISHED WORKS

- Poetry: *I'm Not Lonely Anymore* (*Tôi Không Còn Cô Độc*, 1956), *Liên – Night, The Sun is Found (Liên – Đêm, Mặt Trời Tìm Thấy*, 1964, Saigon), *Poems from Somewhere Far* (*Thơ ở Đâu Xa,* 1990, U.S.)

- Fiction: *Fire in the Kitchen* (*Bếp Lửa*; 1957), *Visage* (*Khuôn Mặt*, 1964), *Along the Road* (*Dọc Đường*, 1967), *Muddy Sand* (*Cát Lầy*, 1966), *Ocean Mist* (*Mù Khơi*, 1970), *A Sound* (*Tiếng Động*, 1970)

Among his unpublished works is a novel, *Cancer* (*Ung Thư*) many parts of which were published in *Literature* (*Văn*) in Saigon. It was an important work written after *Fire in the Kitchen* that TTT referred to in a 1993 interview.

Nguyễn-Xuân Hoàng in an article on TTT that appeared in a special issue of *Literature* wrote: "Thanh Tâm Tuyền was like the first banner announcing the "free verse" of Vietnam, the person who remade our poetry. Đặng Tiến, in a retrospective appreciation of TTT, expressed some regret that no one had inherited his way of composing poetry. Then he went on to say, "Even Thanh Tâm Tuyền himself, in his later collection *Poems from Somewhere Far*, returned to traditional ways of writing poetry. But these were poems made with labor, in special conditions; they do not allow us to draw from them any theoretical conclusions."

THANH TÂM TUYỀN IN A LAND OF SNOW

Aside from the years and months when Thanh Tâm Tuyền suffered imprisonment, I occasionally had opportunities to meet him both before and after 1975. In his second home in the U.S., there were easy means of travel, but TTT moved about very little, and never went far. I usually communicated with him by letter, and once by telephone. Sometimes TTT would send me a book that pleased him. To allow you, reader, to understand TTT's life in the land of snow – a writer in exile from a land that he would much prefer not to have left behind – I will excerpt below a few letters he wrote me, so as to share with you a few small memories of a personal nature:

"St. Paul, December 31, 1992

"Dear brother Ngô Thế Vinh,

"We've been invaded here by a winter storm, and the temperature is much lower than it was the two previous years. Cold below zero in the Fahrenheit range is a usual thing. A cold wind blows that sometimes

Meeting again with friends in St. Paul, Minnesota. From left: Thanh Tâm Tuyền, Cung Tiến, Tô Thùy Yên, Cung Trầm Tưởng. *(family of Thanh Tâm Tuyền, private archives)*

brings the temperature down to forty or fifty degrees below zero. The streets are blanketed in white. Before, I always thought birds avoided the snow altogether, but having been here for three winters, I see with surprise that I was wrong. The birds still remain: crows, doves, sparrows… The doves and sparrows wait for the sun to come out and seek prey here and there in the public parks. Perhaps they are able to stay here in the winter because they have resting places under the roofs of houses from which a little warm air may come. There is in particular a kind of tree here, I don't know its name, the leaves of which wither and die in the wintertime, but still stick fast to the branches. Imagine, if you will, a whole valley-full of woods, with stark and withered trees standing in the white snow. I have asked many people and done some research, but I still don't know the name of the tree. When its leaves finally drop, that is when spring has arrived."

I received the above letter in 1992, and have been obsessed ever since by the thought of that tree of unknown name, the leaves of which all wither, but remain tightly attached to the branches. It seems an image of TTT himself, dead and withered, but with a heart that still clings to his homeland in Vietnam.

"St. Paul, December 14, 1993
"Dear brother Ngô Thế Vinh,

"I'm sending you a translation by Australia's Phan Lạc Phúc to read. The journal *Impressions du Sud* (*Impressions of the South*) has the original article, but I haven't received it. When I have it I'll copy it all out for you to read... Please convey my regards and good wishes to my two friends in poetry... now that it's the first of the year..."

The correspondent Lô-Răng (Phan Lạc Phúc) was originally the editor-in-chief of the daily *Front Line* (*Tiền Tuyến*) and was his literary friend both before 75 and during his many years of imprisonment in the labor camps of the North. Phan Lạc Phúc emigrated to Sydney, Australia in 1991. He was the author of two books, *Friends Near and Far* (*Bạn Bè Gần Xa*, Văn Nghệ publishing house, 2000) and *A Collection of Random Jottings* (*Tuyển Tập Tạp Ghi*, Văn Nghệ publishing house, 2002) that contain recollections of many tragic situations that he and his friends had passed through. Under the pen name Huy Quân, Phan Lạc Phúc had translated Thanh Tâm Tuyền: Poems Amid War and Amid Labor Camps, (*Thanh Tâm Tuyền: Thơ Trong Chiến Tranh và Trong Trại Cải Tạo*) with the addition of observations by the translator (author's note).

"St. Paul, November 12, 1994
"Dear brother Ngô Thế Vinh,

"Thank you for the audiobook you sent as a gift "to read on a distant road." Perhaps it is only when one must "run on distant roads" that one can see how useful books like these can be... This Saturday morning I plan to ride out to the lake near my house, so I can open and appreciate it...

"I'm sending you a gift in return: Henry Roth's first novel, *Call It Sleep*. It's been a very long time, several dozen years at least, that I have come across a novel that forces me to read it "all in one breath." I say "in one breath," but I nevertheless needed a week–reading it in the mornings, when I would wake up at 3:00 or 4:00, and in the afternoons and evenings. When I was still in Saigon, I read in the *Express* or

Nouvel Observateur about Henry Roth–and learned that his book had been republished after thirty years of being ignored. I remember from that time that he was making his living as a duck farmer, and as far as I knew was a writer who had shake off his pen and gone off to raise ducks. It was the early 1960's, Salinger had disappeared somewhere... I just hope you read it and find it interesting.

The novel *Call It Sleep* by Henry Roth was published in 1934; it relates the experiences of a boy growing up in a ghetto community of Jewish immigrants at the beginning of the twentieth century in New York. Sales were sluggish. It took the book 30 years to sell out. But when it was republished in 1964, it became a best seller with more than a million printed copies, and Time magazine in 2005 ranked it as one of the hundred best books written since 1923 (author's note).

This handwritten letter was fairly long, and reflected TTT's restlessness as he thought about the age thresholds faced by writers. In 1994, TTT was only 58 years old. He wrote:

"In the past, when knowing that Stendhal[1] had to be in his 50s to write Le Rouge et Le Noir, I was so impressed. Now, on seeing that Henry Roth at the age of seventy is only now returning to writing, my admiration is even greater, but to speak scientifically, the age of fifty in Stendhal's era was like the age of seventy these days, don't you think?"

Then TTT talks delightedly about the new book by Roth: "In the new book, interspersed in the narrative are bits of introspective monologue on the part of the narrator in the form of 'one-sided conversations' between the writer and his computer… I am still more obsessed with *Call It Sleep* than with the new book, perhaps because the subject is not different."

On coming to the States, TTT read and absorbed a great deal, and also, continuing to engage in "the glory of labor" (*lao động là vinh quang*: a slogan prevalent in communist labor camps), but being free

---

1 Stendhal: Marie-Henri Beÿle (1783 – 1844); French author known especially for his two novels Le Rouge et Le Noir (The Red and the Black) and La Chartreuse de Parme (The Charterhouse of Parma).

to follow his own wishes, he returned both to his studies and his work. He went on as follows in the letter: "At the end of the present month I'll quit my present job and work in an occupational (job-training) trade school near home. I won't have to worry as much about driving in the winter, and the atmosphere of a school will suit me better. I write this so you can feel glad for me."

"St. Paul, July 18, 1995
"Dear brother Ngô Thế Vinh,

"It's been a long time since I've heard from you. I'm sending the whole transcript of my replies to an interviewer in 1993… Yours, Tâm"

So 20 years ago (July 18, 1995), TTT sent me the full interview in French. TTT was good at foreign languages, including French and English. Through French, he very early became widely acquainted with the literature of the world, but this interview was perhaps conducted in Vietnamese with Lê Hữu Khóa at the Université de Provence (in Aix-en-Provence) and then translated into French. After that it was printed in the collection *La part d'exile: littérature vietnamienne / textes réunis et traduits par Lê Hữu Khóa*; Publication de l'Université de Provence, 1995.

Anh Ngô thế Vinh thân,
Lâu không được tin anh. Gửi anh toàn bài trả lời phỏng vấn năm 93 thay cho lời xin lỗi về mọi thất thố.
Lúc nào cũng cầu mong cho giấc mộng năm 2000 của anh trở thành hiện thực.
thân
St Paul 7/18/95
Tâm

A handwritten note from Thanh Tâm Tuyền to Ngô Thế Vinh.
(Ngô Thế Vinh, personal archives)

Not having the original in Vietnamese, I got in touch through the artist Đinh Cường with Lê Hữu Khóa, the author of the interview. But he had gone to teach at Université de Lille. In an email dated March 14, 2015, Lê Hữu Khóa let me know that he had gone on a trip at the behest of his university and was not in Europe; the Vietnamese copy of his interview with TTT was located in his library in Nice. He was very sorry that he was not in Nice.

While waiting to obtain the Vietnamese copy of the interview, I still want to write an article that can appear exactly on the ninth anniversary of his death, so I will include an excerpt from that interview below–but the text has followed a circular path: from the original in Vietnamese to a French translation, and then from French to Vietnamese. Though the style is not that of Thanh Tâm Tuyền, I hope that the content will convey the things that he really wished to express and perhaps help the reader to understand the circumstances that drove TTT to abandon the innovative free verse style of his work in the 1950s to the traditional forms he used at the end of his life.

POEMS WRITTEN DURING WAR AND IMPRISONMENT AN EXCERPT FROM THE INTERVIEW OF THANH TÂM TUYỀN WITH LÊ HỮU KHÓA

"Thanh Tâm Tuyền is a name that looms large in modern Vietnamese literature with two striking contributions to literary life subsequent to 1945. In poetry, he has done away with traditional forms involving rhyme and rhythm and now represents the free verse movement. His first two poetry collections, *I'm Not Lonely Anymore* and *Liên – Night, The Sun is Found* have opened up a new era in which poetry is no longer made according to the rules of verse.

"In prose, his first novel *Fire in the Kitchen* marked a new point of departure, if compared with classical methods of narrating stories. With Thanh Tâm Tuyền, a condensation of language contributes to an acceleration of rhythm and a mastery of esthetic effect.

"An author known to all, he was nevertheless given little steady attention by critics during the war years of 1954 to 1975, and even

Thanh Tâm Tuyền, 1993,
by Đinh Cường.
(Đinh Cường, personal archives)

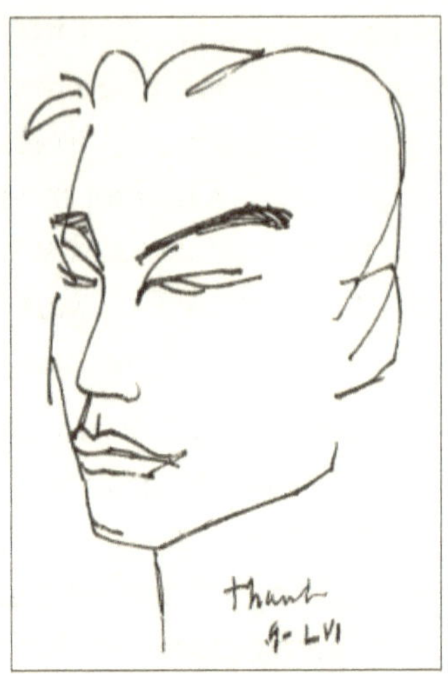

Thanh Tâm Tuyền,
sketch by Duy Thanh, 1956

LITTÉRATURE VIETNAMIENNE

LA PART D'EXIL

Textes réunis et traduits par Le Huu Khoa
Préface de Geneviève Moulaud-Fraisse
Postface de Trinh Van Thao

Groupe de recherche sur l'Extrême-Orient contemporain

1995

Publications de l'Université de Provence

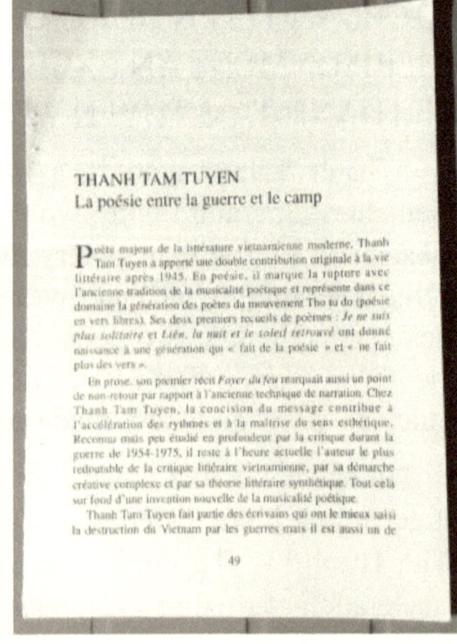

THANH TAM TUYEN
La poésie entre la guerre et le camp

Poète majeur de la littérature vietnamienne moderne, Thanh Tam Tuyen a apporté une double contribution originale à la vie littéraire après 1945. En poésie, il marque la rupture avec l'ancienne tradition de la musicalité poétique et représente dans ce domaine la génération des poètes du mouvement Tho tu do (poésie en vers libres). Ses deux premiers recueils de poèmes : *Je ne suis plus solitaire* et *Liên, la nuit et le soleil retrouvé* ont donné naissance à une génération qui « fait de la poésie » et « ne fait plus des vers ».

En prose, son premier récit *Foyer du feu* marquait aussi un point de non-retour par rapport à l'ancienne technique de narration. Chez Thanh Tam Tuyen, la concision du message contribue à l'accélération des rythmes et à la maîtrise du sens esthétique. Reconnu mais peu étudié en profondeur par la critique durant la guerre de 1954-1975, il reste à l'heure actuelle l'auteur le plus redoutable de la critique littéraire vietnamienne, par sa démarche créative complexe et par sa théorie littéraire synthétique. Tout cela sur fond d'une invention nouvelle de la musicalité poétique.

Thanh Tam Tuyen fait partie des écrivains qui ont le mieux saisi la destruction du Vietnam par les guerres mais il est aussi un de

49

Monograph, *La Part d'Exil* of the University of Provence (1995) containing the interview between Thanh Tâm Tuyền and Lê Hữu Khóa.

today he is a writer whom critics are chary of discussing due to his complex mode of creation and his synthetic approach to literary theory. All his work is based on a new foundation involving musicality in poetry.

The cover of the poetry collection *I'm Not Lonely Anymore*, Người Việt, Saigon, 1956. *(Đinh Cường, personal archives)*

"Thanh Tâm Tuyền is among the Vietnamese writers who possess a clear understanding of the war's destruction of Vietnam, and he was also personally exposed to the oppression of the current dictatorship. He was imprisoned for many years in labor reeducation camps under the oppressive rule of the new regime from 1975 to 1990." (Thanh Tâm Tuyền was imprisoned for seven years, being released in 1982; author's note)

LITERARY EXPERIENCE DURING THE WAR YEARS, 1954 – 1975

"Aside from poetry, I (Thanh Tâm Tuyền) have had two periods marked by works in prose. The first one was *Fire in the Kitchen* (1954), which described scenes in the life of Hanoi before 1954, when some people left for other places and some remained, both being constrained by unwilling choices, by separations, or by deaths. The book immediately aroused critical reactions among a number of "revolutionary" critics. In one review that appeared in *The Arts* (*Văn Nghệ*), one critic challenged me with a question: 'At a time when the people of the North are expending all their strength to build socialism, where does the character in *Fire in the Kitchen* take his stance?' I replied 'He is heading toward historical destruction,' every writer is a survivor.

"The second work, *Cancer* (1970), can be regarded as a continuation of *Fire in the Kitchen.* Cancer is a phenomenon that we accept amid the fickleness of fate and the cold indifference of death. That book never got published." (The novel *Cancer* appeared in parts in the journal *Writing*, beginning in 1964. It is the second important work of TTT, after *Fire in the Kitchen*; author's note.)

LITERARY EXPERIENCE DURING THE YEARS OF IMPRISONMENT IN LABOR REEDUCATION CAMPS, 1975 – 1982

"Faced with the disturbances and disorders that appeared in society in the period after 1975, I felt that I had lived my life – the time remaining to me would be a surplus, I don't bother thinking about it anymore. I was totally disillusioned. In 1975 the regime forced me and all my friends in the same situation to enter labor reeducation camps. We left the lowlands and went to the mountainous regions, calmly and without emotion. We were devoid of both hope and despair.

"I thought of 'disappearing' with no hope of return; I would be like the dregs of some substance washed away by the inundation of history. But I was wrong. They took us to the North, to stretches of old forest cut off from the world outside. They cast me without supervision into nature, free, with the mission of felling trees every day. I practiced climbing and descending mountains, awaiting an opportunity to escape. But there was never a day when I could see anything but the road that returned to the camp.

"Why do I say 'returned?' Is it "hopeless," or is it the disillusionment of the outcast, of the hopeless? At that time, I truly lived in the hope of a state of inexistence, in some inviolable region, a state of non-relation. But these things were not clear to me. Finally, I convinced myself that I had been resuscitated, meaning that poetry had returned to me. I felt fortunate and happy. But I was still as shy as a little child; I hid my first poems, not daring to show them to anyone.

"When, day after day, you live without feeling, without thinking at all of the future, without any nostalgia for the past and without any concern for the present, what remains to you? There remains that which has existed in you, and which still exists, whether you wish it or not.

"In order to live through the cheerless days, with the rain, with the burning hot summer days, with mist and frost, with the storms, with the changing seasons, I sought happiness in that personal thing, the thing within me, the sole thing I had brought along, that existed only within.

"What remained inside? Family, friends. Poems, ones, naturally, that I had read and internalized. A moment came when my memories started to operate fast, and began to read poems just for me. In such a place one starts to see strange lights. Times of ruin strengthen the power of poetry.

"Immersing oneself in a time with no history, or to speak more correctly, a time with no external history, one finds that the days and months of one's life have no direction, no goal, and exist simply in their inherent nakedness. Absolute nakedness. The nonexistence of life brings inner peace. This peaceful poetic state reigns over a still universe.

Since then, each poem is a closed time, separate from the movement of life. The time of anxiety suddenly becomes condensed time, there is no difference between (time) stagnation and passing.

"Making poetry in a labor reeducation camp is the same as returning to the poetry of popular tradition. The work routine in a camp is such that there are eight tense hours in each day, and no weekends. Each prisoner had his own universe; a mat to lie down on, fifty or sixty prisoners on two levels of bunk beds, about a hundred people in a shack under one roof. Writing was a luxury, a place to sit, time to write. With the pace imposed on the prisoners in the cold, hungry ... who could dare to think of literary creation? Even a genius, a supernatural ability cannot overcome such "inhibitions".

"Nevertheless, in the Vietnamese language people speak of *'making poetry,'* not of *'writing poetry'*; thus, people could make poetry anywhere, in any location, when walking, standing, lying, sitting, when awakening. Poetry comes to you without prior arrangement, with no appointed day or hour. People cannot seek it because they do not know where it is. There remains only a simple task: to greet it and converse with it. Poetry demands one just one thing: to preserve the purity of one's words – then that speech will decide the nature of its life.

"Poetry is usually reticent; it enters sometimes by the main door, and sometimes by some other small path; you have to listen attentively and pay attention. Poetry prefers to live in secrecy, to mask itself, so if your memory is not awake, you won't be able to recognize it.

"When you are 'engaging in labor for revolutionary goals', poetry will come to you. It will come unexpectedly, in the fields, in the tangled forests. When poetry comes, it forces you to pause. You begin to see the sky and forget the mechanical movement of your limbs. Poetry soon conducts you to a pure inner state, a state of auto-existence that brings pleasure. Because when poetry releases you, you return to the life that you had the hardihood to cast away. You see this life evolve into the rhythms of each line of verse. Working with your two hands only, your ears chase after the rhythms, the musicality of the verse. This adjustment brings about a necessary balance between the limitations of labor and the actions of accumulated memories.

"But actually, the business of making poetry in labor camps is attended by certain difficulties, as one cannot revise one's work, or indulge in any activity limited to the final stages of a composition, the joy of reading one's work aloud and sharing it with a group of friends. Poetry must be read and listened to. That is the ultimate fate of a poem. The fate of the voice and also the fate of many people's memories.

"When I regained my freedom, the first thing I did, while traveling home, was to withdraw myself and write down all the poems in my memory from my time of imprisonment. I was a person who had survived, but I no longer wished to be a writer, though that had always been a thing I longed for. As a line that I inscribed on my memory in labor camp says, *"The time has come for me to write as if nothing had happened, as if nothing had been modified."*

"And now I say to myself, 'When will such a time arrive, so that I can return to writing?'

This concludes the excerpt from Thanh Tâm Tuyền, "La Poésie entre la guerre et le camp," *Propos Recueillies et Traduit* par Lê Hữu Khóa.

READING THE POETRY OF THANH TÂM TUYỀN, 1956 – 1990

"Resurrection" ("Phục Sinh," 1956), is a famous free-verse poem from the early period of the journal *Creation* (*Sáng Tạo*):

Resurrection

About to weep as if swept with nausea,
I'm outside on the streets,
the sunlight crystalline
I call out my name to ease my memory
thanh tâm tuyền
why does the dying day shatter into tolling church bells
I seek some private, quiet place to kneel
for the little lad whose soul
is fearful of the fierce dog.
the dog is hungry, has no hue
I veer toward death as if desiring sleep
though standing upright on the bank.
the water, black and deep, is wide wake

I scream my name to calm my rage
thanh tâm tuyền
at night I stumble, fall, and whisper for a while my sins
the little child winds a bright red cloth about his head
and here's a wolf,
the kind of wolf that roams.
I want to kill myself,
An everlasting murderer.
I shout my name in grief,
thanh tâm tuyền
strangled, I fall over dead,
to have a resurrection.
each string of lives, connected all,
humans don't forgive the crime of murder
the executioners fall to their knees,
when resurrection comes,
the calling voice is reading sutras,
the centuries wait
I want to live; it's like a wish for death;
between breaths of prayer
my chest is lost in flame.
hesitant, I call,
dear one,
open my heart's door
my heart lives again, is like a child,
pure, like a wave of truth.

TTT 1956

Poem #7 in *Falling Down on Việt Hồng Mountain* (Ngã Trên Núi Việt Hồng) (1979) was made by Thanh Tâm Tuyền twenty-three years later, when he was imprisoned in a labor reeducation camp:

Falling Down on Việt Hồng Mountain In Yên Báy While Carrying Bamboo Loads

I tumble down the slope, the narrow path,
My body died from shock, long seconds pass.
Incessant drops of rain pelt down,
The day is growing faint amid the jungle
My limbs relax, my head on bamboo sheaves,
The sky I see is overcast with steady rain
I feel that someone's blowing on my body
My soul is in illusion, free from grievance,
The rain spreads out a dense white net.
In what direction lies the mountain village?
The numbing, chilly wind wraps tight my face,
Weak and yielding, I forget my smarting wounds,
Seek happiness alone in secrecy
My vision blurred by neverending drops,
I plumb the darkness seeking the way back
Rivers far, deep mountains, where is home?

Yên Báy 1979

In 1986, when he had left the labor camps of the Far North, but still had to live in the large prison that was Vietnam, Thanh Tâm Tuyền made the poem *Belated Tears for Snow Ox: Vũ Khắc Khoan* (Vũ Khắc Khoan had died on September 12, 1986).

In Memoriam Belated Tears for Snow Ox: Vũ Khắc Khoan

A region glowing dark, a field that stretches white,
In never-ending maple forests, rain descends.
The blossoms numb, in disarray, both day and night
The snow ox strives to still its trembling, fevered feet,
Eyes staring, gazing at the fatal, violent gusts

A thousand blows descend in flashes; flowers fly.
A wisp of life amid the ancient glacial ice,
The image of the beast forsakes the barren earth.

TTT 1986

Thanh Tâm Tuyền was very close to Vũ Khắc Khoan, and the two of them had one point in common; a style of writing made difficult by the great concentration and allusiveness of their language.

THE SNOWBIRD THANH TÂM TUYỀN: HIS GREAT DREAM

I cannot forget the haggard appearance of TTT in 1982, when he was newly released from incarceration. He appeared to have grown old, and his skin had the darkened cast of a person who had suffered chronic malaria. It is hard to imagine how a man with such a slim body, had survived seven years of imprisonment in which he suffered every day from cold and hunger in the thick forests and penetrating mists of the northern labor camps. Seven years of felling trees and stripping trunks in the mountains, of being stabbed through the thigh by bamboo, without the benefit of surgery or medicine, he still

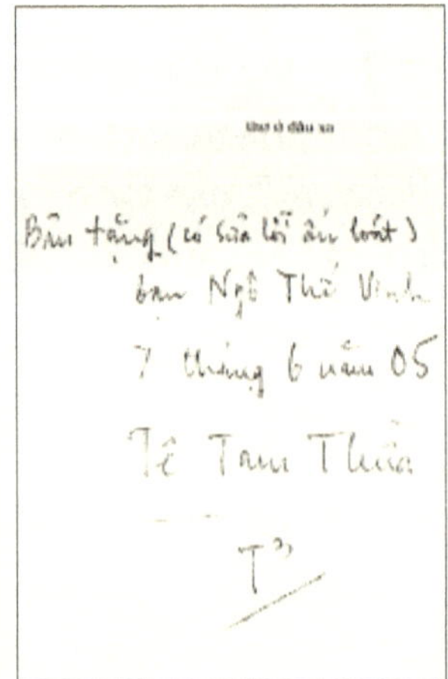

Poems from Somewhere Far (*Thơ ở Đâu Xa*), front cover by Duy Thanh, back cover by Ngọc Dũng. *(pub. by Trầm Phục Khắc, U.S., 1990)*

survived. While in prison he took up smoking water pipes to resist the cold, and, relying on his memory, made poems.

It is easy to see that in the years following 1975, he was living in the "25th hour" (*La vingt-cinquième heure*; the title of a work by C. V. Gheorghiu) of his country. The content of those experiences would have been sufficient to enable him to write the "Gulag Archipelago" of Vietnam. But he was utterly opposed to such a choice. He wanted to make a clean break; he wanted to erase that entire time from his memory. In 1982 after his release, right in Saigon, he wrote the following lines:

A Prelude to Trips Away, and to Trips of Return

He casts aside his memories and goes off,
In dark scenes, an empty, stupid silence.
Just now he coldly drops the savage war
He casts aside his memories and goes off.
In plumbless forests, trees stand bare of leaves,
The misty wind sweeps everywhere,
And now the tortuous twists of history
Sink storm by storm into a cheerless calm,
At daybreak or the depths of night, who knows,
The harsh time kills itself in silence
The woodland stream flows on without a sound
Between the banks it swells itself till full,
The tribulations, spasms of the past
Now circle round the time's events content.
He leads his steps where they cannot go back,
On ways unknown that lead one knows not where,
Each feeling hides and keeps its privacy,
Each matter wanders aimless, with no goal,
And thus he goes, no other way will do.

TTT 1982

In 1986, four years after his release, TTT continued his absolute refusal to acknowledge the past in another poem, also using the refrain "cast aside your memories":

A Few Impromptu Words to Intimate Friends

1.
Cast aside your memories–memories of people.
Dreaming, drown yourself.
Things can't be different.
Suppress your newborn words.
Piteous fate,
And cold uncertainty
Swallow your humiliation whole
The world is far away and near its end
The air is limitless, the waves in agony.
The clouds and fire are choked and still.
Just go. Be one who wavers back and forth.
Be insulted.
Cut off all binding oaths,
Break off all ties.
Secrete them somewhere,
Secrete them till they disappear.
Is there another way?
Let memories be cast aside beyond all records of the past.

2.
Heaven is a muddy, savage swamp,
Each night like all preceding nights encroaching,
Repose outside,
Dumb silence, buried.
It seems that trees are bare, deep in the woods,
The season's wind cuts in, blows everywhere
Cutting the chain of moments, blood veins burst;

The embryo breaks, the dream decays,
We vomit blood, it spurts in blackened spates

3.
Si cette nuit est une nuit de destin,
Bénédiction sur
Elle jusqu'à l'apparition de l'aurore
Chantent les chameliers tartares
Dans la nuit du désert.
(If this be a night of destiny,
Blessings be
Upon it till the coming of the dawn.
The Tartar camel drivers sing
In the night-time of the desert.)

4.
Like birds hovering here and there before the dawn,
Above the waste, at the end of the night of disaster
A hopeless call bursts forth in the silence,
Like a maddened stream in time of flood,
The whiteness of the tempest hides its source,
Falling on its wretched shores and banks.

TTT 1988

(Verse 3 may be found in *Le Temps du Mépris* by A. Malraux; author's note)[2]

In 1993, when TTT answered the questions put to him by Lê Hữu Khóa in his interview with him, he was still determined as ever to put

---

2 André Malraux (1901-1976), French author and statesman (minister of cultural affairs). His works include the novels *Les Conquérants* (*The Conquerors*, 1928), *La Voie Royale* (*The Royal Way*, 1930), *La Condition Humaine* (*Man's Fate*, 1933, winner of Goncourt Prize), and *Les Voix du Silence* (*The Voices of Silence*. 1951).

memory behind him: "Till the time that I must write as if nothing has occurred, as if nothing has changed."

The choice made by TTT – cast aside your memories, memories of people–cannot but make one think by association of ECT – electroconvulsive therapy. A medical treatment in which an electric current is introduced to the brain within the skull. This causes a change in the brain chemistry of the patient, such that memories are lost. The treatment is used in certain medical circumstances, as when the patient is in deep depression that cannot be alleviated by medication. It is a painful procedure that can only be applied when the patient has been made unconscious by anesthesia. It was typical of TTT that, depressed and stoic, he chose the road of memory abandonment without the aid of anesthesia.

... ECT – electroconvulsive therapy, a medical treatment, in which small electric currents are passed through the brain, causes changes in the brain chemistry to erase a patient's memories in certain medical conditions, often depression, when medical treatment is no longer effective. It is a painful process that must be performed under anesthesia.

A 1993 photograph of friends welcoming TTT to the U.S. at the Minneapolis – St. Paul airport in Minnesota. From the left: Cung Tiến, Thanh Tâm Tuyền, Tô Thùy Yên, and Cung Trầm Tưởng. *(family of TTT, private archives)*

TTT and his wife Cao Thị Mai Hoa on a visit to Washington D.C. The Washington monument is in the background.
(family of TTT, private archives)

Those who were close to Thanh Tâm Tuyền and understood him felt that the reason he preferred living a retired and secluded life, rejecting contact with others, lay in the fact that he wished to transform himself, and was quietly accumulating new experiences with that end in view. He was still reading a great deal, still seeking new things without cease, with the "great dream" of being a different person when he again entered the world. He would be an incarnated TTT, another TTT. He would be resurrected and would again be able to write. But, as if by predetermined fate, he ran out of time.

Twenty years after the death of Vũ Khắc Khoan (1986) and eight years after the death of Mai Thảo (1998), Thanh Tâm Tuyền of *I'm*

Not Lonely Anymore passed away at 11:30 a.m. on March 22, 2006 in St. Paul, Minnesota. Minnesota was also the place where Vũ Khắc Khoan of *The Spirit of Turtle Tower* had resettled. Among those of his friends who bore the coffin of the Snow Bird Thanh Tâm Tuyền to its resting place were Tô Thùy Yên, Cung Trầm Tưởng, Nguyễn Cao Đàm, and Cung Tiến.

"When in winter the leaf withers, dies, and leaves its branch, this also is when spring will come to Thanh Tâm Tuyền, but it will be in a different world."

I am sending this article to Thanh Tâm Tuyền's family as a commemoration of him on the occasion of his ninth death anniversary. And as I write this, I cannot avoid a twinge of concern when I wonder how much relation there might be, from a medical point of view, between his seven years of smoking water pipes and his death from lung cancer just as he was stepping into his seventies.

California, March 22, 2015

NGUYỄN-XUÂN HOÀNG ON THE SLOPE OF LIFE AND DEATH AND AUTUMN IN JAPAN

Nguyễn-Xuân Hoàng
(photo by Trần Cao Lĩnh)

If we maintain that living into one's seventies is a rare thing (*thất thập cổ lai hy*), then Nguyễn-Xuân Hoàng, who was born in 1937, has reached the age of 77 – a rare thing; but that concept of age belongs to the preceding generation. As we cross into the 21st century, with its advancements in medicine, living past 80 can't be considered rare.

I don't remember just how I first made Nguyễn-Xuân Hoàng's acquaintance, but he and I have been friends for a good many years. In the mid 1960s he helped lead the publishing house Sleepless Night

From the right: Nguyễn-Xuân Hoàng and Trịnh Công Sơn.
(Đinh Cường, personal archives)

(Đêm Trắng – Nuit Blanche), along with Huỳnh Phan Anh, Nguyễn Đình Toàn, Đặng Phùng Quân, Nguyễn Nhật Duật, and Nguyễn Quốc Trụ. They were all around thirty years old and full of creative juice, each in his own manner. They were regarded as exponents of the "nouveau roman" – "new novel," and the café La Pagode was the place where they regularly carried on their activities. And the people in this group all came to appear, more or less, as characters in Nguyễn-Xuân Hoàng's novels.

In those stormy years of warfare, I occasionally got to read the writings of this group's members and even make their acquaintance in various phases and surroundings, though our circumstances were very different, and though I was in Saigon only for short periods. After going overseas, the two people in that group with whom I maintained contact were Nguyễn-Xuân Hoàng and Nguyễn Đình Toàn.

These late and hurried lines are merely some fragmentary memories that I wish to send to my friend Nguyễn-Xuân Hoàng. After finishing high school in 1959, Hoàng at first thought of studying medicine, and became a student for one year in the PCB (Physics, Chemistry, and Biology) Faculty of Science, University of Saigon, but seeing that this line of study didn't suit him, he enrolled in the

Nguyễn-Xuân Hoàng with Võ Phiến in his Los Angeles house during the period when Hoàng was the editor in chief of the journal *21st Century* (*Thế Kỷ 21*)

(Viễn Phố, personal archives)

Philosophy Department of Đà Lạt University, where he was one year behind Hoàng Ngọc Biên. After his graduation in 1962, he taught philosophy for a year at Ngô Quyền High School in Biên Hòa, and then was transferred to Petrus Ký High School in Saigon, where he taught until 1975. But from 1970 on, he was better known as a writer and journalist than as a teacher. Starting in 1972, he was the editor-in-chief of the Saigon journal *Literature* (*Văn*), succeeding Trần Phong Giao, and was the author of two short-story collections, *Blind Mist* (Mù Sương), and *Birthday* (*Sinh Nhật*), an essay collection, *At Any Time, In Any Place* (*Bất Cứ Lúc Nào, Bất Cứ ở Đâu*), an essay collection, and two novels, *A Sector of Forest in Flames* (*Khu Rừng Hực Lửa*), and *The Heretic* (*Kẻ Tà Đạo*)...

In 1971, Nguyễn-Xuân Hoàng was still in Saigon working as a journalist and teacher, whereas I had gone with my unit to conduct operations in the Central Highlands, but each of us underwent an experience back then that seems worth recording. Due to the publication of the short story "The Battle of Saigon" ("Mặt Trận ở Sài Gòn"), in the journal *Presentations* (*Trình Bầy*) edited by

Thế Nguyên, I was summoned to court to face the charge of "using the press to interfere with public order and weaken the military discipline of the army – I was a part of it. On returning to Saigon to obey the court summons, I learned that Hoàng had also received a court summons because of his short story "Father and Elder Brother" ("Cha và Anh") in the journal *Issues* (*Vấn Đề*), run by Vũ Khắc Khoan, in which Hoàng had referred to the song "The Mother of Gio Linh" ("Bà Mẹ Gio Linh") by Phạm Duy. It turned out though that these events were just a storm in a teacup; there was "no interruption in the flow of life" – ran expression that I borrow here from Nguyễn-Xuân Hoàng.

Trapped in Vietnam after 1975, Hoàng, like most of his colleagues, endured many months and years of upheavals attendant on the changing fortunes of his country, but eventually, after ten years, he and his family were able to emigrate to the U.S. (1985). No longer a teacher, he worked full-time as a journalist and writer, first as the editor-in-chief of the newspaper *The Vietnamese People* (*Người Việt*), California (1989–1994) and the magazine *21st*

Literary activities in Little Saigon; from the right, Nguyễn-Xuân Hoàng, Thảo Trường, Trần Dạ Từ, and Nguyễn Mộng Giác. *(Viễn Phố personal archives)*

Visiters to Võ Phiến's house: from the left: Tạ Chí Đại Trường, Nguyễn-Xuân Hoàng, Võ Phiến, Nguyễn Huy Thiệp from Vietnam, and Peter Zinoman from Berkeley. *(Viễn Phố personal archives)*

Century (*Thế Kỷ 21)*, then as a member of the editorial board of *Literary Studies* (*Văn Học*) with Nguyễn Mộng Giác, and after that taking on the chief editorship of the journal *Literature* (*Văn*) when this position was transferred to him by Mai Thảo (1996). It seems worth recording as well that his responsibility for *Literature* caused Hoàng and his wife to incur a considerable debt to the printer of that journal, which took a long time to pay off. Four works by Nguyễn-Xuân Hoàng were published by Võ Thắng Tiết aka Từ Mẫn, the director of the Văn Nghệ publishing house: *Red Tiled House* (*Căn Nhà Ngói Đỏ*, short stories and essays), and the first two novels in a trilogy: *The One who Walks on Clouds* (*Người Đi Trên Mây*) and *Dust and Garbage* (*Bụi Và Rác*). The third novel in the trilogy, *Fire* (*Lửa*) has not yet been published.

In 1996, due to new work commitments, Hoàng and his wife relocated to the "golden flowers valley" (Silicon Valley) of San José, which became their last home. Hoàng continued to work as a full-time journalist, at first as the chief editor of *Việt Mercury*, which belonged to San José Mercury News, and after that became chief editor of the weekly *Việt Tribune*. This last activity was like a "family show,"

Nguyễn-Xuân Hoàng with some young friends in San José; from left: Hoàng Ngọc Nguyên, Bùi Văn Phú, Nguyễn-Xuân Hoàng, Hồ Quốc Đăng.

(Trương Gia Vy, personal archives)

shared between him and his wife Trương Gia Vy, which has lasted to the present time. They were close friends with Peter Zinoman and his wife Nguyệt Cầm, the translators of *Dumb Luck* (*Số Đỏ*) by Vũ Trọng Phụng. Hoàng was invited to be a lecturer in a Vietnamese literature course then being offered at U.C. Berkeley.

Nguyễn-Xuân Hoàng had a wide circle of acquaintances, though he always complained that he had few friends. It was due to this that his friends made up a new name for him: Nguyễn Đông Hoàng (substituting Đông, "winter" for Xuân, "spring"). And when they learned that he had fallen ill, many of his old students and friends came to visit him, and even wrote articles about him, a number of which were posted on the "Skin of Color" (Da Màu) website for many weeks, amounting in all to enough pages to make a book.

It has been close to twelve months since I got word from Trịnh Y Thư concerning Nguyễn-Xuân Hoàng's illness. All the news concerning Hoàng's state of health and his illness I have received either directly from Hoàng or from his friends Phùng Nguyễn and Trịnh Y Thư.

Nguyễn-Xuân Hoàng and Ngô Thế Vinh in the editorial office of the Việt Tribune, 2008. *(photo by Trương Gia Vy)*

For about three years before this happened, Nguyễn-Xuân Hoàng had often complained of back pain. In people over 70, this symptom is often attributed by family doctors to "spinal degeneration." Once, when his pain had grown greater, a doctor made X-rays of his entire spine and had made precisely this diagnosis. This time, however, X-rays revealed many little white spots around his spine, so the radiologist asked Hoàng if he had suffered shrapnel wounds in that area while in Vietnam. Hoàng assured him that nothing like this had happened.

When the time came that anti-inflammatory drugs and pain suppressants, including opiates, had no effect to speak of, Hoàng was taken to a hospital where he was given a series of tests, at the end of which a diagnosis was reached: he was suffering from a somewhat rare condition: sarcoma of the spine. "Sarcoma" refers to a type of cancer involving connective tissue, such as bones, cartilage, adipose tissue, muscles, and arteries…

This diagnosis was perhaps "not prompt," even if one hesitates to say "too late," and from that point on Hoàng was transferred to a Stanford University hospital specializing in oncology. I was not able to consult Hoàng's medical records, but I know that he passed

The front and back covers of The One Who Walks on Clouds, designed by Uyên Nguyên, republished by Người Việt.

through the stages of treatment known as chemotherapy and radiation therapy. It appeared that his illness had not been caught at an early enough stage to be treated through surgery. Nguyễn-Xuân Hoàng went courageously through all the "stages of the battle" until all forms of treatment were exhausted, treatments that of course involved highly unpleasant side effects.

Throughout this period of pain and limited mobility, and even now, having been transferred to a different unit for six weeks of rehabilitation, Nguyễn-Xuân Hoàng has not for a moment ceased pursuing his work with cell phone and laptop at hand. He has been concerned, not just with the newspaper *Việt Tribune*, which has continued to come out every week, but has continued to be active in journalism, which is both his profession and the source of his family's livelihood. In this period as well, he has been collaborating with Đinh Quang Anh Thái of the newspaper *Vietnamese People* (*Người Việt*) in the editing and layout of two books: *The One Who Walks on Clouds* (*Người Đi Trên Mây*), both of which had appeared in installments in the newspaper) and *Dust and Garbage* (*Bụi và Rác*) which has also been appearing in the paper and has reached installment No.100. Also while in the hospital, he was the person who chose the blurbs written by Nguyên Sa and Phạm Công Thiện on the back covers of those books.

When looking for an image of himself to out on the back cover, he chose a photo which showed him smoking a cigarette, perhaps on Phạm Ngũ Lão, the old "journalism street" around the year 1980. And

From the right: Nguyễn-Xuân Hoàng and Hoàng Ngọc Biên visiting Võ Phiến on March 1993. Now all three belong to the past.
(Viễn Phố, personal archives)

because of my "professional contrariness," I told him, jokingly, that that choice of his was politically incorrect; it would set a bad example for youngsters who, seeing the photo, would take up smoking so that they too could become famous authors.

Hoàng, however, didn't perceive this to be a joking matter, and solemnly informed me that of all the photos from his youth, he especially liked this one, and anyway, who in those days did not smoke? It was moreover very well-suited to the scenes portrayed in the book. Although he sent me an email saying he would trust me to make all decisions in his place, every matter was done in accordance with his wishes.

I reminded Đinh Quang Anh Thái that Nguyễn-Xuân Hoàng was still in full possession of his mental faculties; therefore he (Đinh Quang Anh Thái) should ask him directly about every matter that concerned the book; the patient should be encouraged to do anything that he was still able to do – this was actually a principle that I had absorbed in my study of rehabilitation medicine. The best form of occupational therapy for Hoàng was to keep him busy all the time. And even on his sickbed, this busyness kept him cheerful.

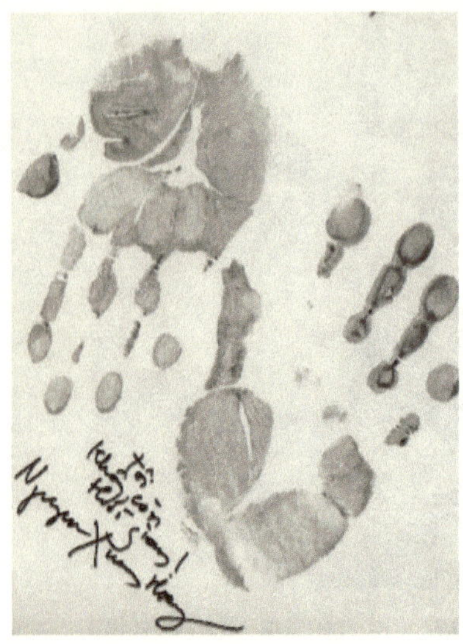

Nguyễn-Xuân Hoàng on Saigon's Phạm Ngũ Lão Street, where the journal *Literature* (*Văn*) was located. *(Nguyễn-Xuân Hoàng, personal archives)*

A handwritten note by Nguyễn-Xuân Hoàng: "I have no time left," together with an imprint of his hands. *(source: Phan Nguyên, Emprunt Empreinte)*

Hoàng also let it be known that when he was finished with publishing *Dust and Garbage*, he would write another novel to form a trilogy with the other two. The third book would have a simple, one-word title: *Fire* (*Lửa*), a name suggested to him by the conflagrations currently ravaging California. This work, like the previous ones, would be published in installments in *The Vietnamese People*.

Hoàng's friends, including me, could not conceal our pleasure when we saw that even while enduring the torture of his illness, he was still cherishing plans for the future.

For almost an entire year, Nguyễn-Xuân Hoàng moved in and out of Stanford University hospital on a virtually regular basis, sometimes for many days, and sometimes for shorter periods. The pain caused by cancer was his never-ending symptom.

On the morning of June 1, 2014 Nguyễn-Xuân Hoàng called me from his home and uttered just a few words in a very feeble voice: *"Vinh! I'm in too much pain! All I want is to die!"* At that point, a professional term came into my head: euthanasia or painless death, a procedure associated with Jack Kevorkian, by means of which a person with an incurable illness could die gently. Kevorkian was called "Dr. Death" in the press and was sentenced to eight years in prison on a charge of second-degree murder. "*Physician assisted suicide*" is to this day regarded as illegal. The choice of one's manner of death is up to the viewpoint and religion of every individual. But all I could do was to urge Hoàng to enter the Stanford hospital again, so that he could be treated with more pain suppressants. That same day, his wife Trương Gia Vy took him to the hospital. When I phoned to check on him, he said, that his pain had subsided somewhat, but that his sole wish now was to go home.

Then on the evening of the same day, I sent Hoàng a review by Dohamide of the book *The Nine Dragons Drained Dry, The East Sea in Turmoil*. I had for many years sent him things that I wished to see published in his journal *Việt Tribune*. Much to my surprise, he almost immediately sent a reply.

"Thank you, Ngô Thế Vinh," he wrote. "I shall ask your permission to print this in VOA and *Việt Tribune*. *Việt Tribune* is no problem, but VOA requires that the material they publish cannot appear anywhere else. Let me know beforehand when I send it to VOA, okay? – Nxh Sent from my iPhone." I replied at once that the article was "non-exclusive"; that it had already appeared in the Skin of Color (Da Màu) website and through Nguyên Giác (Phan Tấn Hải) had published it in *The Việt Journal* (*Việt Báo*.) His reply: "What a pity! Then we will only be able to publish it in *Việt Tribune*. –Nxh Sent from my iPhone."

These messages made me realize that for some time Hoàng had not only been in charge of the weekly issues of the *Việt Tribune*, but had also been maintaining a blog on VOA.

On the morning of June 7, 2014, Hoàng phoned and conveyed the news to me and Phùng Nguyễn that the doctors treating him at Stanford had met with his wife Vy and his children in order to tell them that they had given up – that there was nothing more they could do, and that they would release him from the hospital so he could return home. "I knew things would have to turn out this way," said

Hoàng, "but Vy wept piteously." How can you not weep, when you know that your lifelong companion is on a path leading to death and that his strength is getting less every day? And his circle of friends knew that Vy's health too had long been problematic. She had had ESRD – End-Stage Renal Disease for many years and had to perform peritoneal dialysis (filtering blood from the peritoneum lining in the abdomen) at home instead of going to a dialysis center three times a week for hemodialysis.

Thinking that I had not yet been informed of this, Phan Nhật Nam phoned me late that evening to tell me that Hoàng's illness had reached its final stage and that his Stanford doctors had decided to let him check out of the hospital. I understood that, rather than being delivered to a hospice care center, Hoàng had chosen to return home– living with his family would in all circumstances be more pleasant.

On the morning of June 10, 2014, I called Hoàng on his cell phone to check on him and learned that he was in a car with Vy and was going to the Stanford hospital. I was taken aback, and asked him if he decided to continue receiving treatment. He said no, he was just going in for a few rounds of "palliative radiation therapy" for people with incurable illnesses. Though a cure was not possible, there were some high-tech palliative measures that could help patients live out their few remaining days and months in a manner possessing some quality of life, with less pain and with more calm before the end.

On the morning of June 12, 2014, I phoned him again, and he let me know that he felt better after the radiation, had less pain, and had been able to sleep at night. As always, I did my best to avoid asking questions about his illness–that would just tire him out. So, the two friends just chatted haphazardly about literary topics. We talked about the Sleepless Night publishing house, and members of the "new novel" (Nouveau Roman) group, who in the 1950s were influenced by such French authors as Alain Robbe-Grillet, Nathalie Sarraute, Michel Butor and Claude Simon. According to Nguyễn-Xuân Hoàng, it was Huỳnh Phan Anh who first had the idea of founding the "Sleepless Night" group, so that they could publish everything written

Nguyễn-Xuân Hoàng paying a visit to Võ Phiến; from left: Từ Mẫn (Võ Thắng Tiết), Nguyễn-Xuân Hoàng, and Võ Phiến.
(Nguyễn-Xuân Hoàng, personal archives)

by the members. That group of 6 people mostly came from teaching backgrounds, except for Nguyễn Đình Toàn and Nguyễn Quốc Trụ.

Throughout the twenty-year period that began in 1954, literary movements in the South developed in entire freedom. The Self-Reliance Literary Group was succeeded by the Culture in the Present Era of Nhất Linh and the Creation group of Mai Thảo. Thanh Tâm Tuyền rejected pre-war styles and endeavored to remake literature. Then the "new novel" group came to the fore, but according to Nguyễn-Xuân Hoàng, it was Hoàng Ngọc Biên who, though he was not a member of the "Sleepless Night" group, actually inaugurated the work of researching the French "Nouveau Roman" movement, translated some works by Alain Robbe-Grillet, and himself exemplified this new style in a collection of short fiction entitled *A Night's Sleep in a Province* (*Đêm Ngủ ở Tỉnh*), published by Cảo Thơm in Saigon in 1970. According to Hoàng Ngọc Biên, aside from the title, in the years before 1975, there was really no "Nouveau Roman" (New Novel) movement in Saigon.

Techniques used in medicine may be said to have advanced considerably, but the underlying concept is not new; from the earliest times, new medical students have been taught at the outset to have a modest attitude toward their work: "to practice medicine is sometimes to cure, often to soothe, and always to comfort": *"La médecine c'est guérir parfois, soulager souvent, consoler toujours."* Ambroise Paré, a French surgeon of the sixteenth century, was the first person to enunciate this principle, but it probably originated in the practice of medicine in far more ancient times. I myself, the writer of these lines, have been practicing medicine in different environments both within and outside Vietnam for more than forty-five years but the death of a patient still makes me downcast, and makes me feel that life has been deprived of something.

That feeling of deprivation is even sharper when the departed happens to be one's own friend. I have had to witness Nghiêu Đề, a dear friend from my younger days, turn pale with suffering at the pain caused him by cancer of the pancreas; and I have seen Cao Xuân Huy of *My Gun Broke in March* (*Tháng Ba Gẫy Súng*) bold and manly as he was, writhe in pain under the torture of metastasized eye cancer. Now it was the turn of Nguyễn-Xuân Hoàng to endure the agony of this pain, so obstinate and so bizarre. It was easy to see the oceanic extent of the suffering that accompanies our basic condition: birth, age, illness, and death; and to see that what medicine can do to alleviate this can only go so far. This ocean is immense; one perceives no boundary to it. When I read the following lines by Vô Ngã (Phạm Khắc Hàm) I feel some consolation, though they are not by Nguyễn-Xuân Hoàng:

For ages we revere compassionate Guanyin,
As all created beings in dark error mourn.
A thousand years, the cereus glowing in the night,
Three thousand deep and distant regions feel its warmth.
...You like to fish for turtles, read the mystic chart.
Scoop up a little fish, perceive the basic truth.
We raise the pages, words set down for endless eons
Heaven and earth are trembling in the stygian dark,
...From that time on our ears are close-pressed to the wall,
The sutra's words irradiate the magic tower,
And love descends in steady drops upon the stones.

The cover of *The One Who Walks on Clouds*, designed by the artist Nguyễn Thị Hợp; right: Tanaka Aki, or "Autumn" of Japan, student of advanced studies in Vietnamese literature in the Tokyo Institute of Foreign Languages. *(photo by Ngô Thế Vinh)*

During lunch break that day, I met outside the hospital with some other doctors; one was Jewish, one was from the Middle East, and one was from India. The Indian doctor was vegetarian and we sat at the same table. It happened that a colleague of theirs had just died of cancer, and they were talking about the miseries he had undergone in his last days. Then they discussed what deaths they would choose themselves if a choice were possible.

The three likeliest conditions resulting in death these days are: a heart attack, which makes you die immediately, a stroke which can result in incapacitation, and a malignant cancer... And all three favored the heart attack as being the fastest of the three. And then, as if under the influence of that decision, they all ordered dishes with no lack of animal fat, and which of course were not in accordance with the nutritional guidelines set down by the American Heart Association.

But of course no one can choose an illness so as to die in a manner that suits them except for the very violent choice of suicide that may often be observed among writers: Ernest Hemingway (*The Old Man and the Sea*) by means of a gun (1961), Yukio Mishima (*The Temple of the Golden Pavilion*) by means of a sword (1970), Yasunari Kawabata (*Thousand Cranes*) by means of suffocation (1972), Nhất Linh (*A Decisive Break* – Đoạn Tuyệt) by means of cyanide (1963), and Tam Ích (*Art and Human Life* – Nghệ Thuật và Nhân Sinh) by means of hanging (1972).

Hoàng had lived, and was still living, a very full life, but I was aware that at any moment and in any place, my friend was ready to embark on the last mile of his perilous path to death. Mark Twain always regarded death in a light manner: "A man who lives fully is prepared to die at any time." And surely, at some time and in some place, Nguyễn-Xuân Hoàng would look back with a smile, and say like Mark Twain, "The report of my death was an exaggeration."

NGUYỄN XUÂN HOÀNG AND "AUTUMN IN JAPAN"

In July 2013, a conference on the journals *Customs* (Phong Hóa) and *These Days* (Ngày Nay) and *the Self-Reliance Literary Group* (Tự Lực Văn Đoàn) was organized in Little Saigon in south California. What was noteworthy about the conference was that a Japanese woman pursuing advanced studies in Vietnamese literature in the Tokyo University of Foreign Languages had been invited to present a paper there. And Nguyễn-Xuân Hoàng, who was then in San José, had been invited to come and preside over all the sessions. Though he had previously agreed to this, his worsening illness deprived him of the strength he needed to participate.

Tanaka Aki was the name of the Japanese invitee. "Aki" in Japanese means "autumn." She did not have the good fortune to meet Nguyễn-Xuân Hoàng, but she later came to have a deep admiration for him when she got to read *The One Who Walks on Clouds*, *Desert*, and *Dust and Garbage*. She was swept away at once with *The One Who Walks on Clouds* because of her concern with the environment and with the circumstances of life in Saigon before 1975. Aki had lived and worked in Vietnam for thirteen years, but that was in the post–'75 period. She wanted to translate *The One Who Walks on Clouds*, so she could share her appreciation of the novel with her Japanese compatriots.

Tanaka Aki had exchanged email messages with Nguyễn-Xuân Hoàng and imagined that she might be able to "see Mr. Hoàng lying on his sickbed assailed by pain, and might be able to share in the sadness and despair of his untreatable illness.

Ms. "Japanese Autumn" continued her reflections: "One day I opened my copy of *The One who Walks on Clouds*, and happened to see that Mr. Hoàng's signature was on the first page. I had paid no attention to this previously, so did not know about the signature. And I imagined to myself that in the middle of the night, when I was fast asleep, Mr Hoàng had flown from America to my house and left his signature in my book. After making the discovery, I wrote him an email with a photo of the signature attached, and asked him if it was indeed written by him. He assured me that it was. At that moment I decided that it was my fate to translate *The One Who Walks on Clouds*."

Then one day, she was looking at the website "Century Forum" (Diễn Đàn Thế Kỷ) and saw the article "Nguyễn-Xuân Hoàng on the Slope to Death" ("Nguyễn-Xuân Hoàng trên con dốc tử sinh") by Ngô Thế Vinh and hurriedly wrote an email to Nguyễn-Xuân Hoàng expressing her desire to translate *The One Walks on Clouds* into Japanese. "If you agree to have me translate it, I hope that whenever I finish a section I can send it for you to look at." Writing back, he said "I desire it very much." But then, before she could translate anything, she learned, while staying with her mother in Japan, that Hoàng had passed away, which filled her with regret.

Then, in 2016, when another September full of the atmosphere of Autumn in Japan had passed, I and Phạm Phú Minh met with Aki again in Huntington Beach. We learned then that she had not forgotten the promise she had made Nguyễn-Xuân Hoàng: "I don't know yet when I will be able to translate "The One Who Walks on Clouds," but

Several covers of books by Nguyễn-Xuân Hoàng.

I know that this goal will somehow be realized because it is a task that has been reserved for me by fate, just as my research in Vietnamese literature has been a part of my destiny." (Tanaka Aki – Nhà văn Nguyễn-Xuân Hoàng, Diễn Đàn Thế Kỷ, Sunday, Sept. 13, 2015)

BIOGRAPHICAL DATA

Born on July 7, 1937 in Nha Trang; former student of Võ Tánh, Nha Trang; former student of Pétrus Ký, Saigon; graduate of College of Pedagogy, Philosophy Department, Đà Lạt (1959–1962); responsible for philosophy program, Ngô Quyền School, Biên Hòa (1961– 962); then in Pétrus Ký School, Saigon (1962–1975).

Portrait of Nguyễn-Xuân Hoàng
(1937 – 2014)

Chief secretary of the journal *Literature* (*Văn*; 1972– 1974); chief secretary of the newspaper *The Vietnamese People* (*Người Việt*), California (1986–1997) and concurrently the chief secretary of the journal *21st Century* (*Thế Kỷ 21*), California, (1989–1994); director and editor-in-chief of the journal *Literature* (*Văn*) from September 1996, and concurrently the chief secretary of the weekly *Việt Mercury*, a subsidiary of the American daily paper *San José Mercury News* (from November 1998 to November 2005).

Auxiliary Lecturer in Vietnamese literature at UC-Berkeley (September 2001 to April 2003).

Last place of residence: San José in north California. Date of death: Sept. 13, 2014.

WORKS

Short Story Collections

Blind Mist (Mù Sương; 1966)
Birthday (Sinh Nhật; 1968)

Novels

Dust and Garbage (*Bụi và Rác*; 1996)
A Sector of Forest in Flame (*Khu Rừng Hực Lửa*; 1972);
The Heretic (*Kẻ Tà Đạo*; 1973)
The One Who Walks on Clouds (*Người Đi Trên Mây*; 1987)
Desert (*Sa Mạc*; 1989)

Other Genres

- *Thoughts While on Grass* (*Ý Nghĩ Trên Cỏ*; articles; 1971)
- *At Any Time, In Any Place* (*Bất Cứ Lúc Nào, Bất Cứ Ở Đâu*, occasional essays, 1974)
- *The Red-tiled House* (*Căn Nhà Ngói Đỏ*; miscellaneous impressions 1989)

Works Not Yet Published

- Fire (Lửa, a novel)
- Everyone Needs a Mother (Ai Cũng Cần Phải Có Một Bà Mẹ, occasional essays)
- Literary Notebook (Sổ Tay Văn Học)

NGUYỄN-XUÂN HOÀNG HAS PASSED AWAY

Nguyễn-Xuân Hoàng took leave of his family and friends at 10:50 a.m. on September 13, 2014, in San José, California, at the age of 77.

His burial service was carried out according to the rites of the Buddhist religion. His remains were cremated, and his ashes were delivered with a memorial plaque to the Liễu Quán temple.

Nguyễn-Xuân Hoàng chose to live and die as a writer. His wish was fulfilled.

Long Beach, June 2014

Huntington Beach, May 2016

HOÀNG NGỌC BIÊN
THE ROAD OF THE NEW NOVEL
AND THE RECOVERY OF TIME

Hoàng Ngọc Biên
(photo by Phan Bá Đương Saigon 1978)

The true paradises are the ones that are lost.
Les vrais paradis sont les paradis qu'on a perdu.
Marcel Proust, *Le Temps Retrouvé* (Time Regained)

BIOGRAPHICAL DATA

Hoàng Ngọc Biên (his real name was also his pen name) was born on Jan. 18, 1938 in Bích Khê village, Triệu Phong prefecture, Quảng Trị province, and went for elementary education to Thánh Mẫu (Holy Mother) Teresa School in Quảng Trị. In 1942, the entire

Hoàng Ngọc Biên (left) visiting Vũ Khắc Khoan (right) in his university faculty residence on Duy Tân Street, Saigon, 1968. *(Hoàng Ngọc Biên, personal archives)*

family moved to Huế. There, they lived in Vỹ Dạ (a suburb of Huế) for several years and then went with Biên's father to Đà Nẵng (Tourane) for a year, after which they returned to Quảng Trị. In 1950 he left home again to pursue further studies in Huế, and in 1952 returned to Quảng Trị.

In 1953 Biên went with his family to Saigon, studied at Kiến Thiết Private School and began to form a close relationship with one of his classmates there, Nguyễn Đăng Thường. He also began a long-lasting friendship there with Mark Frankland, an English journalist.[1]

In 1954 he met with Vũ Khắc Khoan for the first time, making the discovery that Khoan, who had just emigrated to Saigon from Hanoi, was closely related to the family as his mother's cousin.

---

1 Mark Frankland (1935-2012) was a former foreign correspondent of the Observer who had worked in the Soviet Union, Indochina, the United State and Eastern Europe. His memoir of the Cold War, "Child of my Time: An Englishman's Journey in A Divided World" (Chatto, 1999), won the PEN / Ackerley Prize in 2000.

(The dramatist Vũ Khắc Khoan was born on Feb. 27, 1917 in Hanoi. After emigrating to Saigon in 1954, he was a professor in a succession of schools: Chu Văn An, Faculty of Letters (Đại học Văn Khoa), and the National Drama School (Trường Quốc gia Kịch Nghệ) in Saigon. He was a member of the Viewpoint (Quan Điểm) group, one of the editors of the journal *Issues* (*Vấn Đề*), and the author of the dramas *The Spirit of Turtle Tower* (*Thần Tháp Rùa*) and *Genghis Khan* (Thành Cát Tư Hãn). He died in the U.S. in 1986, at the age of 69).

In 1958, Biên tested into Đà Lạt College of Pedagogy, where he studied French literature. During that period he made the acquaintance of the scholar Tam Ích, who was teaching French in Việt Anh High School. Biên still remembers the mountains of books in Tam Ích's house. Ích would also stop by to see Biên and borrow copies of the French journals *Le Figaro Littéraire* and *Arts et Spectacles* to which Biên had subscriptions.

(The scholar Tam Ích, real name Lê Nguyên Tiệp, was born in 1915 (in some places the year given is 1917) in Thanh Hóa, and moved in 1937 to the South, where he was a professor of literature and taught French in various high schools and in Vạn Hạnh University. He was the author of *Art and Human Life* (*Nghệ Thuật và Nhân Sinh*, Chân Trời Mới, 1941). In 1972 he committed suicide by hanging, when he was only 57).

At the college of pedagogy, he formed a close friendship with Professor Etiennette Poirson, a teacher whom he always revered, and later, in Saigon, she supplied Biên with a lot of material related to Proust, after which he became greatly enamored with the novel *In Search of Lost Time* (*À la Recherche Du Temps Perdu*).

In 1961, he graduated from the Đà Lạt College of Pedagogy and began teaching French in the Tống Phước Hiệp High School of Vĩnh Long, where one of his fellow students was Nguyễn Thu Hồng, who would become a graduate student specializing in French studies at Saigon College of Pedagogy. After another year this lady, who came from St. Paul's School, became Biên's lifetime partner, a relationship that has endured to the present day.

In 1964, he transferred to a high school in Tây Ninh, and then Tân An. There, he began the book *Written in the Midst of Summer* (*Viết Giữa Mùa Hè*). He sought out and then became close to the writer Võ Phiến, and often frequented his house on Trần Quang Diệu Lane during this period. The present writer also made Biên's acquaintance during this period.

Here is a "portrait in words" of Hoàng Ngọc Biên, as sketched by Võ Phiến: *"Biên had leftist leanings and was fond of Che Guevara; and he himself cultivated a moustache and let his hair grow down to the nape of his neck. He was just as infatuated with Proust as I was, but he organized his work in a thorough manner, not amateurishly, as I did; and he was good at painting and music. He and his wife were very compatible with me and my wife, and we often shared things in an atmosphere of intimacy. After April, 1975 Biên kept his moustache and long hair throughout the next sixteen years. When he left Saigon for the U.S. in October 1991, my sons [who were. still in Vietnam] felt that they had lost an uncle in the family. Throughout the previous sixteen years, whenever they had met with any big or little disturbance, Aunt and Uncle Biên had been there to find a solution for them. The two of them are now living in Salt Lake City, Utah."* (Selected Letters of Võ Phiến, Los Angeles, Dec. 4, 1991 [author's

From left: Mr. and Mrs. Võ Phiến and Mrs. and Mr. Hoàng Ngọc Biên. *(Hoàng Ngọc Biên, personal archives)*

From right: Hoàng Ngọc Biên and the artist Đinh Cường in San José, April, 2012.
(Đinh Cường, personal archives)

note: Võ Phiến and his wife came to the U.S. in April, 1975, but were only able to bring their daughter with them; his two sons Liên and Long, and their children, had no way to get out.]

In 1968, in the Learning Resource Center (Trung Tâm Học Liệu), Biên formed close relationships with Cao Thanh Tùng, Nguyễn Đồng, Nguyễn Thị Hợp, and Lê Thị Chí… Diễm Châu came from Indiana to Saigon and sought him out to discuss plans for establishing the journal *Presentations* (*Trình Bầy).* Biên went for nine weeks to Quang Trung to complete some military training. He also published a book: *Ten Contemporary French Authors: An Anthology* (*Tuyển Tập Mười Nhà Văn Pháp Hiện Đại*), brought out by Trình Bầy publishing house. This volume introduced the illustrious names of the new French novel movement, such as Michel Butor, Alain Robbe-Grillet, Nathalie Sarraute, and Claude Simon…

In 1970, the first issue of *Presentations / Trình Bầy* was published. Biên obtained a USAID scholarship for the study of book design and book production, and went to the U.S. to pursue this subject at McGraw-Hill, and was later transferred to a branch office of that company in Singapore. He also published a story collection, *A Night's*

Sleep in a Province (*Đêm Ngủ Ở Tỉnh*, published by Cảo Thơm); this work was an experiment in utilizing the techniques of the new novel.

In 1973 he taught French in Saigon's Bách Khoa University.

In 1975 and later on, he managed the cultural and social sections of the *Morning News Daily* (*Tin Sáng*), and after the departure of Nguyễn Đồng, who became a "boat person," he took on the technical section as well. The old associates whom he worked with in Saigon included Nguyễn Đồng, Nguyễn Thị Hợp, Cao Thanh Tùng, Đinh Cường, and Nguyễn-Xuân Hoàng as well.

In 1991, in October, he emigrated to the U.S., where, along with his two sons Hoàng Tân Nhân and Hoàng Tân Dân, enrolled in Salt Lake Community College, with the primary aim of becoming familiar with information technology. As he studied, Biên began to make computer drawings, using digital art techniques.

From July 1993 to 1998, he worked for the *Salt Lake City Weekly* as that publication's art director, and in 1999 switched to a new position as production coordinator.

In 2004 he began to participate in a project on the web forum <tienve.org> with *The Winter Journey*. This was a translation of *Le Voyage d'Hiver* by Georges Perec; Nguyễn Hưng Quốc had brought the book back from the home of Võ Phiến.

Suddenly, in that same year, his facial features suffered distortion on the left side, and speech became difficult for him. His friends were worried, because they thought he had had a stroke, but actually, the problem was merely Bell's palsy: the 7th cranial nerve, which controls facial movement and expression, was paralysed. Biên was treated with westerned medical techniques combined with acupuncture. Many cases of Bell's palsy clear up whether they are treated or not. He chose to retire the same year, at the age of 66, and moved with his wife to San José to live close to his son's family.

In 2011 he felt that his health was failing, and doctors found that he was suffering from last-stage cirrhosis and his name was put on the waiting list for liver transplant.

In 2012, on September 12, Biên underwent an organ transplant operation in Stanford University Hospital in Palo Alto. This was also the hospital where Nguyễn-Xuân Hoàng had been treated for sarcoma. Biên was a rare instance of a liver-transplant patient who underwent the procedure in his 70s – he was 74 at the time. Having been plucked from the jaws of death, Biên began slowly to recover. Later, he learned that his new liver had come from an American youth just over 30.

To Biên, wearing a Red Beret on Returning Home from a Liver Transplant

by Đinh Cường

He's on the list, he waits to change his liver,
At length it comes, and joyfully Hoàng Ngọc Biên
Is now at home. The face has grown more gaunt;
His spirit though is peaceful and alert;
His head is resting on a pillow with blue stripes;
And his beret is red (not as before dark gray)
The sparse beard by his mouth hides joking smiles
Rest on, oh Biên, regain your strength again
And you'll tell stories to your gathered friends
No thing can be more glad than this good news;
Our friend is out of care and back at home
His hand is still clutching mala prayer beads.
We chant: "Om mani padme hum hre-yih
The home of merciful Guanyin is like the moon,
With cool and soothing light extinguishing
The burning pains attendant on this life."
I always read in whispering tones
The sutra's verses in night's depths
My prayers were not of the beseeching kind;
But imbued instead with human love.
Our friend has had his life restored
This fall is one we shall remember.

Hoàng Ngọc Biên read a great deal, and mentally accumulated what he read. His activities were extremely varied. In addition to teaching, he wrote, composed poetry, translated books, painted pictures, and (what few people are aware of) composed music. As a member of the editorial board of *Presentations* (*Trình Bầy*,1961 –1975), he was in charge of artwork of all its publications in Vietnam (1975 – 1991) and after his emigration to the U.S. discharged the same responsibilities for the *Salt Lake City Weekly* (1993-2004).

Before 1975, exhibitions of his paintings were held at the University of Đà Lạt, the Goethe Institute, the Alliance Française, the Association of Young Vietnamese Artists (Hội Họa Sĩ Trẻ), the Saigon News and Information Room, La Dolce Vita (in the Continental Hotel), the Vũng Tàu Culture Center, and the drawing and painting division of McGraw-Hill, Singapore, 1972.

Published Before 1975

- *Ten Contemporary French Authors* (*p Hiện Đại*, Trình Bầy, 1969)
- *A Night's Sleep in a Province* (short story collection) (*Đêm Ngủ ở Tỉnh*, Cảo Thơm Saigon, 1970)
- *Marcel Proust: His Social Identity* (*Marcel Proust – Con Người Xã Hội*, Trình Bầy, 1974)

Published After 1975

- *Drinking Tea In the Early Morning,* poetry (*Uống Trà Sớm Mai*, Trình Bầy, USA, 1996)
- *The Person Who Bikes Into the City in the Morning*, short story collection (*Người Đạp Xe Vào Thành Phố Buổi Sáng*, Trình Bầy, USA, 1997)
- *A Car Trip,* a novel (*Chuyến Xe*, Trình Bầy, USA, 1997)
- *The Land, the People, and the Mythology of Vietnam*, poetry (*Đất và Người và Thần Thoại Việt Nam*, Trình Bầy, USA, 1997)
- *The Sea By Day and Night*, poetry (*Biển Ngày Đêm*, Trình Bầy, USA, 1999)

- *Homeland and Return*, two short essays written in response to a painting sticker by Nguyễn Đăng Thường (*Quê Hương, Người Về, Homeland, Returners,* Trình Bầy, USA, 2001)
- *By the Foot of Clouds at the End of Heaven*, poems (includes poetry by Đỗ Trung Quân and paintings by the artist Nguyễn Quỳnh) (*Chân Mây Cuối Trời*, Trình Bầy, USA, 2003)

Translations

- Andrei Sinyavsky, *The Poems of Pasternak: the Man and his Works* (*Thơ Pasternak, Con Người và Tác Phẩm*), Hồ Chí Minh City, 1988
- Joseph Brodsky, *Still Lives and Other Poems* (*Tĩnh Vật và Những Bài Thơ Khác*), Thuận Hóa, Huế, 1991
- Samuel Beckett, *First Love* (*Mối Tình Đầu*), a short narrative, Trình Bầy, USA, 1993
- *New Poems of Poland* (*Thơ Mới Ba Lan*), Trình Bầy, USA, 1993
- Samuel Beckett, *Marcel Proust*, a study (*Marcel Proust*), Trình Bầy, USA, 1993
- Jean Tardieu, *Hanoi Letters* (*Thư Hà Nội*), translated with Nguyễn Thu Hồng, Trình Bầy, USA, 2001
- Georges Perec, *The Winter Journey*, (novel) (*Chuyến Đi Mùa Đông*), Trình Bầy, USA, 2003
- Alain Robbe-Grillet, *DJINN* (novel), Trình Bầy, USA, 2003

HOÀNG NGỌC BIÊN AND THE PRESENTATIONS GROUP

Diễm Châu (Phạm Văn Rao) was born in Hải Phòng and emigrated to the South in 1954. He knew Thế Nguyên from his days in a migrant student camp in Phú Thọ. Diễm Châu graduated from a teachers' college with a degree in English and, after pursuing further studies in the U.S., returned to Saigon, sought out Hoàng Ngọc Biên, and persuaded him to join with him (Châu) in establishing the journal *Presentations* (*Trình Bầy*). Biên sat for many weeks with Diễm Châu in a café on the sidewalk of Sương Nguyệt Anh Street in Saigon and

Gathering in a concert at the Thanh Quan Student Dormitory; from left: Hoàng Ngọc Biên and his wife Thu Hồng, Trịnh Công Sơn, Trịnh Cung, Cao Thanh Tùng and his wife Kim Phượng. *(Hoàng Ngọc Biên, personal archives)*

composed an opinion piece for the journal's first issue: "The Road that Leads There" ("Con Đường Đi Tới"). Here is an excerpt:

"... The road that leads there is a road aimed at the establishment of a peaceful order, and in that enterprise, every Vietnamese person, without prejudice of ideology, will have a place to stand and enjoy the dignity of a person living in his homeland.

"... It is not possible to have peace with no conditions. A Vietnamese peace will absolutely be unable to accept the presence of any foreign power and will at the same time be unable to accept a mechanism, regime, or authority within the country that interferes with the liberation of Vietnamese people.

End of quotation.

Presentations was a left-leaning journal. Its outlook was anti-war in the midst of a storm of war between communist and national forces, with Diễm Châu as its editor-in-chief. Diễm Châu had the additional pen name Võ Hồng Ngự. Thế Nguyên was the journal's director. The journal enrolled many authors of that period with different outlooks. It was not just *Cyclopedia* (*Bách Khoa*), *Presentations* was in fact a "bean and sticky rice area" (meaning an area with both communist and national forces), with such writers as Nguyên Sa, Diễm Châu, Hoàng Ngọc Biên, Hoàng Ngọc Nguyên, Nguyễn Đăng Thường, Trùng Dương, Thảo Trường, Nguyễn Mộng Giác, Du Tử Lê, Mai Trung Tĩnh, Nguyễn Quốc Thái, Luân Hoán, Trần Hoài Thư, and Ngô Thế Vinh… Many of these people came from the army. There were also writers with communist leanings like Ngô Kha and Ngụy Ngữ… or communist agents such as Nguyễn Nguyên (Nguyễn Ngọc Lương), just as *Cyclopedia* had its Vũ Hạnh.

Presentations had an active existence for two years, from 1970 to 1972, producing 42 issues before they shut down. In any case, April 30, 1975 shattered the aspirations of the left-leaning intellectuals– who in the parlance of the time were referred to as the *third force* (*lực lượng thứ ba*); Diễm Châu and Hoàng Ngọc Biên belonged to it. Their aspirations were shattered because, after unification, not just the North, but the entire country had to live in a regime that strangled

Hoàng Ngọc Biên (1938 – 2019) and Diễm Châu (1937 – 2006), two intellectual colleagues in the *Presentations* group. Thế Nguyên was the director of the journal.

(Hoàng Ngọc Biên, personal archives)

all individual freedoms. Left-leaning intellectuals, if they were not thrown in prison, were suppressed and ill-treated–they were merely irrelevant bystanders. In the end they all became exiles, if not in other countries, then right in their own homeland. Diễm Châu relocated to France in 1983, and Hoàng Ngọc Biên emigrated to the U.S. in 1991. After going abroad, three people–Hoàng Ngọc Biên, Diễm Châu, and Nguyễn Đăng Thường–did their best to keep *Presentations* alive. For them, *Presentations*, as a publishing venue, was like the image of a broken dream. And, after undergoing a belated awakening, Diễm Châu became a political rightist until his death in 2006.

It seems worth noting here that even some renowned left-leaning intellectuals of the west experienced similar awakenings. When the tragedy of the boat people erupted in the East Sea, Jean-Paul Sartre, who had previously favored the communists, became an effective activist for "un bateau pour le Vietnam" ("a boat for Vietnam") to rescue the boat people. The experience with the Vietnamese communists has so far been a lesson for the entire world to absorb.

IN SEARCH OF LOST TIME WITH MARCEL PROUST

Beginning in 1959, and for many years thereafter, Biên took passionate delight in reading and translating the work of Marcel Proust and, some twelve years after this interest began, he published *Marcel Proust: His Social Identity* (*Marcel Proust: Con Người Xã Hội*) on the occasion of the hundredth anniversary of Proust's birth.

Proust was born on July 10, 1871 and died on November 18, 1922 at the age of 51. He left an enormous body of work comprising seven volumes and about a thousand pages, beginning with *À la Recherche du Temps Perdu* and ending with *Le Temps Retrouvé*. Proust turned into a revered literary monument, and his works have been the object of hundreds of theses and research projects from the time of his death to the present day.

The pages he wrote have enthralled all the generations that came after him. This is surely not simply because they are full of memories of a village, or a family, or a childhood of a little boy with a repressed

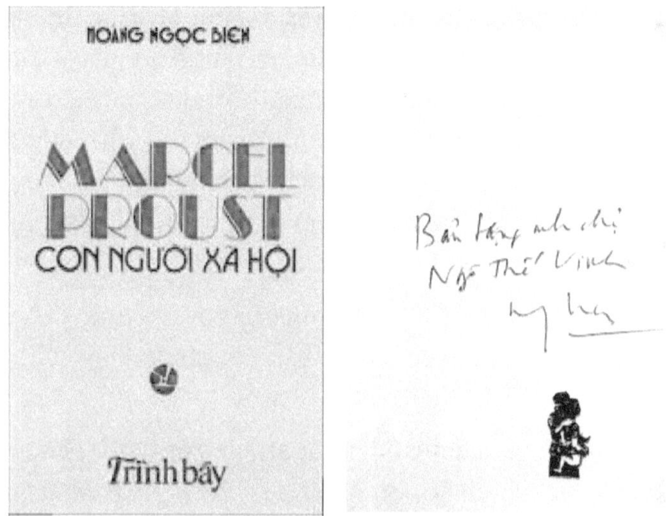

The cover of Hoàng Ngọc Biên's study *Marcel Proust: His Social Identity*, Trình Bầy, 1959 with the signature of the author.

The extremely artistic covers of *Presentations* were the creations of Hoàng Ngọc Biên. *(Hoàng Ngọc Biên, personal archives)*

and resentful spirit and with homosexual leanings. Proust once compared himself to Noah in the Bible, who, because of the flood, was locked in his boat for forty days and nights. He wrote: *"Jamais Noé ne put si bien voir le monde que de l'arche malgré qu'elle fait close et qu'il fit nuit sur la terre."* (Never was Noah able to see the world so well as on the ark, though it was locked and made all the world as dark as night."), Proust, *À la Recherche du Temps Perdu.*

Proust, with his ailing body, was immured in a tightly locked room and wrote mainly in the night. And in this enclosed space, he wrote about seemingly random scraps of experience, some sad or troublesome, some happy, some startling, some worth savoring… one would think these things too ordinary, too familiar – but the genius of the author was such that these things assume the form of an intellectual history imbued with character of poetry and music.

In *Le Temps Retrouvé* (*Time Regained*) Proust wrote, "The moment we perceive things and events they become something without form within us."

Cao Thanh Tùng, a cellist, has an article entitled "The Homeland of a Musician," in which he compares *À la Recherche du Temps Perdu* to "a huge symphony built upon the endless movement of time." It seems as if time has disappeared, but through the intellectual memory of Proust, it comes into view again and becomes deathless.

One can say that in his exploration of the new novel, Hoàng Ngọc Biên was influenced early and deeply by Proust, and did not have to wait for the "nouveau roman" movement with Michel Butor, Alain Robbe-Grillet, and Samuel Beckett that he read about in later years.

In 1967 in Saigon, Hoàng Ngọc Biên assisted Trần Phong Giao in bringing out two issues of *Literature* (*Văn*; nos 85 and 86) devoted to the works of Proust. Biên was at that time regarded as the chief specialist in that subject in the South.

THE "NEW NOVEL" MOVEMENT

Until 1954, Vietnamese novels more or less adhered to the classical pattern; they had plots, and their development was laid out in chronological order. Meanwhile, in the west, various writers broke with this tradition. These figures included Alain Robbe-Grillet, Michel Butor, Claude Simon, Claude Mauriac, and Nathalie Sarraute… Their works did not conform to the patterns that had prevailed for ages past. One can compare the changes taking place in the novel with the abandonment of strict forms in poetry and the appearance of free verse. The new novel was no longer laid out in chronological order, and its authors no longer used third-person pronouns and no longer stood outside the action. Events were conveyed through the eyes of many different characters, and plots were nearly done away with. As Michel Butor observed, "A novel is a groping search for something, and form is its most important element."

The new novel movement in France, though it made a lot of noise, was short-lived, and did not have a long-lasting influence. Its momentary dominance, however, did open up more expansive concepts with regard to the techniques of novel-construction.

In South Vietnam in the 1960s, a number of young authors sensitive to developments in the West embarked on the enterprise of experimenting with the techniques of the new novel. Among these authors, one must mention the members of the Nuit Blanche or Sleepless Night (Đêm Trắng) group which consisted of Huỳnh Phan Anh, Đặng Phùng Quân, Nguyễn Nhật Duật, Nguyễn-Xuân Hoàng, Nguyễn Đình Toàn, and Nguyễn Quốc Trụ. The idea of establishing the group originated with Huỳnh Phan Anh; the idea was to publish only works by members of the group. Except for Nguyễn Đình Toàn and Nguyễn Quốc Trụ, the members of the group were all teachers. They made no announcements and laid down no prescriptions; each did his writing independently with his own conceptions of expanded technique.

The cover of *Literature* (*Văn*), Issue 85, "Reading the Writings of Marcel Proust" ("Đọc Văn Marcel Proust") for which Hoàng Ngọc Biên was responsible. The cover was created by the artist Lê Thị Chí.

Dương Nghiễm Mậu did not read the French novels belonging to this movement, but Võ Phiến judged him to be the most successful in using the new techniques. "In *The Worm* (*Con Sâu*), a novel, for example, the pronoun "I" ("tôi") does not belong to one character; sometimes it is this individual and sometimes another. This shifting of perspective serves to emphasize the sudden shifts of attitudes toward different events. Mr. Dương also has the good point that, though he uses western techniques, he still retains the basic character of our people: When we read him, we do not detect any trace of influence from outside; the reader feels comfortable at every level and feels that the atmosphere is familiar." (*A General View of Literature in South Vietnam*, pp. 260-262).

But according to Nguyễn-Xuân Hoàng and Nguyễn Đình Toàn, it was Hoàng Ngọc Biên himself who was actually the first person to study the French "new novel" movement. He translated a number of works by Alain Robbe-Grillet, wrote articles concerning ten contemporary French authors, and also exemplified their innovations in his story collection *A Night's Sleep in a Province*. His close friends jokingly bestowed a hyphenated name on him in those days: "Biên-Butor." Michel Butor was at that time one of the principal leaders of the French "new novel" movement.

Among the stories in this collection, there is nothing of Hoàng Ngọc Biên himself; there is only the cold, dispassionate gaze of someone gazing from the outside at the events described. No thoughts or feelings of the author appear. Here is an excerpt from a short story in *A Night's Sleep in a Province*:

> *His head bent, he walked unsteadily with short and long steps along Highway 4, which led him into the provincial seat. He was walking in a sudden summer rainstorm beneath a sky that, also suddenly, had turned gray and black, crept low, and then by gradual degrees became less dense. The tiny raindrops flew in the direction of the wind that blew from the iron bridge and slapped violently and with freezing cold against his face – he carefully avoided the puddles that had grown deep after several days of rain and the long streams of water coursing along the crisscrossing ruts made by vehicles that still often*

Left: the cover of *Ten Contemporary French Authors*, Trình Bầy, 1969. Right: the cover of *A Night's Sleep in a Province*, short story collection, Cảo Thơm, Saigon 1970.

veered onto the road shoulders, their wheels turning up the yellow earth. He passed a drink stand on the right, and then another drink stand, with low, drooping roofs not higher than a hand could reach. He went past an army base on the left with rusted iron gates that stood immovable, incapable of being fastened. He went past a group of churches set in back of a spacious field, shaded with leafy trees, but the leaves had taken on a layer of the yellow dust that rose from the highway, with its trucks and troop vehicles speeding past continuously with each passing second–And now some refreshing glimpses of blue began to appear here and there.

He passed an elementary school built at the side of a church, a school that was now devoid of the chanting voices of children mingled with the high preemptory voices of sisters beating their rulers on the tables. He went past an area of ground prepared just a year ago as a landing field for combat helicopters, cranes, machinery and piles of grey rocks were there, and long metal girders lying atop each other, as if in preparation for the construction of a larger airfield.

The provincial seat began to become visible, as a temple peeked out behind some ornamental trees that could be seen beyond two sparse hedges, with two lines of gold painted Chinese characters with a red background on two large pillars which, washed clean by the rain, showed forth clearly. He walked past some low, sloping thatched roofs, sopping wet, and some bright red tiled roofs, their redness more bright after the rain, that were partially visible features of two Cao Đài temples, one new and one old, with engraved figures, like arabesques, twisting this way and that. He walked by an inspection station–the old railway station reminded him of the many trains that had gone there in the past.

Throughout the forty pages of *A Night's Sleep in a Province*, this level, impassive tone is maintained, flowing smoothly, with the effect of a stream-of-consciousness, with rich images and touches of poetry The reader follows the steps of the protagonist who remains unnamed, unconnected to any region, and possessing no specified reason for his journey. The things in the scenes he walks through are described as faithfully as if reflected in a mirror, but any feelings connected with these scenes must be supplied by the reader; the author divulges nothing of this sort.

Though very close to Hoàng Ngọc Biên and with a great respect for his talent, Võ Phiến was sometimes a bit bewildered by him, as may be seen in some words he wrote in a letter to the essayist Nguyễn Hưng Quốc.

"Is the writing of Hoàng Ngọc Biên seeking to escape from the pre-theoretical period of Vietnamese literature? Do you suppose he has managed to find a new theoretical direction?"

As for Hoàng Ngọc Biên himself, he has continued, in all the works he has published since, to patiently adhere to his self-chosen "new novel" style. The stories of Hoàng Ngọc Biên do not appeal to every taste; he is not a "writer for the many," so his name is not as well known as some others.

READING HOÀNG NGỌC BIÊN'S POETRY

Biên wrote a great many poems. Looking at a poem selected from his verse collection *The Sea by Day and Night*, Trình Bầy, USA, 1999, I see that it begins with a quotation:

When a man dies,
His portraits change.
Anna Akhmatova

A Place To Rest One's Back

A bit of sun,
A bit of rain,
A bit of gentle light at end of day,
A bit of Buddha spirit,
A bit of God,
A bit of storm at night,
A bit of cloud,
A bit of wind,
A bit of hell,
I stop by for fun,
A bit of heaven,
And stretch out at ease, supine.

The front covers of *"The Sea by Day and Night"*

HOÀNG NGỌC BIÊN IN THE REALM OF PAINTING

Hoàng Ngọc Biên never acknowledged that he was one of the figures who established the Association of Young Vietnamese Artists (Hội Họa Sĩ Trẻ), but he had paintings that were included in that group's exhibitions and, according to Trịnh Cung, his name was on the official list of members, starting in the 1970s.

An exhibition of the Association of Young Vietnamese Artists, Alliance Française: from left: Đinh Cường, Mai Chửng, Dương Nghiễm Mậu, Hoàng Ngọc Biên, Nguyên Khai, Nguyễn Trung, Hồ Thành Đức, Nguyễn Đồng.

(Association of Young Vietnamese Artists, archives)

HỘI HỌA SĨ TRẺ V.N

TRIỂN LÃM HỘI HỌA
VÀ ĐIÊU KHẮC

HOÀNG NGỌC BIÊN
MAI CHỬNG ĐINH CƯỜNG
TRỊNH CUNG CÙ NGUYỄN
NGUYỄN ĐỒNG
NGUYÊN KHAI NGHIÊU ĐỀ
HỒ THÀNH ĐỨC
NGUYỄN TRUNG

GOETHE INSTITUT bảo trợ

Left: catalogue for an exhibition of the Association of Young Artists held at the Goethe Institute in 1969; right: "Feu Rouges" / "Red Light ," by Hoàng Ngọc Biên, acrylic, 1972. ***(source: Nghệ Thuật Tạo Hình VN Hiện Đại, Huỳnh Hữu Ủy, VAALA, 2008)***

A piece of digital art: "Saigon, April 30," a work that made Hoàng Ngọc Biên shed tears. *(Hoàng Ngọc Biên, personal archives)*

Four digital artworks; top left: "Deep Sea," 2014; top right: "By the Foot of the Mountain," 2015; bottom left: "Cold Moon," 2006; bottom right: "Hands," 2001. *(Hoàng Ngọc Biên, personal archives)*

It is true that Nguyên Khai in 1994 boldly expanded the outlook of artists by opening to them the world of modern computer technology. He created oil paintings full of characteristic masterstrokes, but also used computer chips as a new medium in his painting. Hoàng Ngọc Biên, however, had begun at the very beginning of the 1990s to use digital techniques, and created many graphics in which the strokes were pure and simple, but which were special from the standpoint of composition and color.

Biên got to study abroad in Singapore when he attended the McGraw-Hill School of Book Design and Book Production, and later he studied in Japan as well. His talents were exemplified as well in the book covers he designed which were at once classical and personally characteristic.

Several book covers designed by Hoàng Ngọc Biên.
(Hoàng Ngọc Biên, personal archives)

As early as 1977, Hoàng Ngọc Biên laid out his views with regard to painting or art in general: "I like to gaze at the creations of painters, whatever their stage of completion. They are like experiments, or one might also say experimental games. In this regard, the plastic arts are like the other arts: music, dancing, literature, architecture, sculpture, even films… and including even translations, every result may be viewed as a suggestion, or something in the nature of a suggestion. When a work of art is put before the public, it should never be regarded as a perfected thing. And this attitude does not lessen the value of artistic projects; it heightens both our judgement and the nature of the work itself." "Notes on Artistic Work" *("Ghi Chép Về Công Việc Nghệ Thuật")*, Saigon, 1977.

PORTRAITS OF HOÀNG NGỌC BIÊN

Phái Street (Phố Phái)

for bùi xuân phái

Streaks of blue and pink
Corners lonely and deserted
The colors gray.
A square attic,
Ashes of former times,
Black brush strokes carry on the memory:

Sketches of Hoàng Ngọc Biên by Bùi Xuân Phái, Oct. 25, 1979
(Hoàng Ngọc Biên, personal archives)

Portraits of Hoàng Ngọc Biên by the hands of (from left:) Nguyễn Quỳnh, Đinh Cường, Đỗ Trung Quân, and a sketch by Nguyễn Đăng Thường.

This sadness
Of Phái Street,
A thousand years

Autumn Lake, a Song Composed by Hoàng Ngọc Biên

Biên recalls that when he was little, his Quảng Trị village had a children's singing group with five voices. In that group were two of his siblings, together with two friends who were about the same age, and his cousin Nguyễn Văn Dziệp–later known as the singer Duy Khánh. Biên began to study music and became sworn brothers with Cao Cự Phúc–the musician Hoàng Nguyên, who at that time was 20 years old and had just returned from a war zone, and guided Biên in his musical studies. Biên was chosen to be the lead vocalist by brother Phúc. The sole song that Biên still remembers is "Song of the River Thao" ("Khúc Hát Sông Thao") by Đỗ Nhuận.

In 1955, after moving to Saigon, Biên continued his musical studies with Võ Đức Tuyết, the younger brother of the pianist and composer Võ Đức Thu. Biên wrote his first song, "Autumn Lake,"

Discussing about Art; from left: Huỳnh Hữu Ủy and Hoàng Ngọc Biên.
(Source: Huỳnh Hữu Ủy, Nghệ Thuật Tạo Hình VN Hiện Đại)

("Hồ Thu") when he was 17, during a stay in the dreamy and poetic surroundings of Đà Lạt (1955). Biên composed music early, before he began to produce literature and make poems. "Autumn Lake" is a lightly melancholy song with clear, limpid lyrics. Biên recalls that the song was performed by the singer Tâm Vấn on Saigon's National Broadcasting Station.

Lyrics of "Autumn Lake"

The wind is on the rise, as if recalling seasons past,
The sound of autumn lightly nears, leaves fall beside the lake.
Sadness drifts along the lake of olden times, familiar spots,
The fragrance is already far, why yearn for days gone by?
The sails are dreaming on the water's silent surface,
Amid returning steps one listens to the shore-bound waves,
And dusk descends indifferent on the lake's reflection.
The one of old treads worn-out paths in search of autumn,
The season's fragrance is no more, I listen, lost in gloom.

From left: Hoàng Ngọc Biên, Võ Phiến, and Nghiêm Xuân Hồng in Võ Phiến's Los Angeles home. *(Viễn Phố, personal archives)*

Hoàng Ngọc Biên and Ngô Thế Vinh standing in his “book garage,” San José, May 2, 2008. *(photo by Nguyễn-Xuân Hoàng)*

A meeting in the “Paired Dragons” (Song Long) Restaurant in Little Saigon from left, sitting: Hoàng Ngọc Biên, Nguyễn Đồng; from left, standing: Ngô Thế Vinh, Thành Tôn. *(Ngô Thế Vinh, personal archives)*

The autumn lake takes on the air of former years,
The leaves and flowers fade and wither with the golden clouds,
I hear the rustling sounds of autumn, bringing pain,
The autumn wind returning seems to speak of bygone seasons,
The golden leaves of autumn lightly carpet all the lake.
The sky and clouds recall in sorrow this land's thousand years,
And autumn's scent returns and trembles sadly in the stems.

In 1961, a "Guitar and Song Recital" was organized on the campus of Đà Lạt University, in which a female trio performed "Autumn Lake." Biên provided additional vocal lines in the accompaniment for that occasion.

The singer Ngọc Mai, digital images produced by Hoàng Ngọc Biên.

Even Biên's close friends are not aware that he composes music. The song *"Autumn Lake"* has been little promoted, but it was recently performed by the young singer Ngọc Mai. Ngọc Mai was also born in Quảng Trị, and graduated from the Saigon Music Conservatory in 2010 and has won many prizes. She currently teaches instrumental music in the Saigon Music Conservatory.

California, February 07, 2016

ENTERING THE REALM OF CREATED IMAGES ĐINH CƯỜNG, THE AWAKENED

Đinh Cường, *photo by Phan Bá Dương*, Saigon 1978.
(Source: Modern Vietnamese Visual Arts / Nghệ Thuật Tạo Hình Việt Nam Hiện Đại, by Huỳnh Hữu Uỷ, VAALA 2008)

BIOGRAPHICAL DATA

Real name: Đinh Văn Cường. He was born July 5, 1939 in Thủ Dầu Một, Bình Dương province, an area rich in pottery and lacquerware, and home of the Thủ Dầu Một Fine Arts School, founded by the French in 1901. (Thủ Dầu Một was also the place where the French put Nguyễn Gia Trí under house arrest after he was released from the Sơn La prison camp.)

- 1951 – 1957 attended the Pétrus Ký High School in Saigon
- 1963 graduated from the Advanced Studies Art Institute at Huế

- 1964 graduated from the National Advanced Studies College of Pedagogy and Art Institute in Saigon
- 1962 Silver Prize awarded for the painting "Mythology" ("Thần Thoại") in the Spring Fine Arts Exhibition in Saigon.
- 1962 prize awarded for the painting "Church" ("Nhà Thờ") in the First International Fine Arts Exhibition at the Embassy of the Republic of China (Taiwan) in Saigon
- 1963 Second Silver Prize awarded for the painting "Evidence" (Chứng Tích), Spring Fine Arts Exhibition, Saigon
- 1969 – 1971 member of the board of directors of the Association of Young Vietnamese Artists
- 1963 – 1967 Fine Arts Professor at the Đồng Khánh Female High School in Huế.
- 1967 – 1975 Professor in the Advanced Studies Art Institute at Huế.

In his younger days, Đinh Cường lived at various times in Huế, Đà Lạt, and Saigon, and then wandered through a number of different locations in the world before settling down in Burke, Virginia.

Đinh Cường had more than twenty exhibitions in Vietnam (including venues in Đà Lạt, Huế, Saigon, Đà Nẵng, Nha Trang, and Pleiku) and abroad, including venues in France, Japan, the U.S., Brazil, Tunisia, India, and Singapore.

According to an exhibition brochure, by 2005, Đinh Cường had had twenty-four solo exhibitions and twenty-one additional exhibitions with other artists.

Published Books

- *Raking Leaves Outside by Night*, poems (*Cào Lá Ngoài Sân Đêm*), Thư Ấn Quán, U.S., 2014
- *I Come Back and Stand Bewildered*; poems (*Tôi Về Đứng Ngẩn Ngơ*), Quán Văn, Saigon, 2014
- *Entering the Realm of Created Images I*, essays on art (*Đi Vào Cõi Tạo Hình I*), Văn Mới, California, 2015.

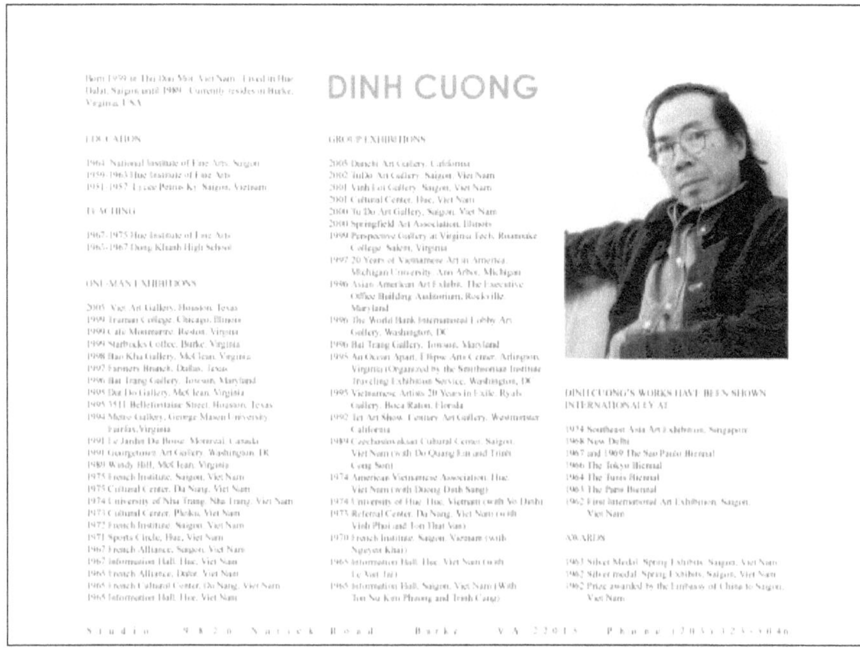

DINH CUONG

A professional brochure listing Đinh Cường's artistic activities and accomplishments, Burke, Virginia period.

ENTERING THE REALM OF CREATED IMAGES

This is in two volumes. Volume I deals with the Fine Arts Academy of Indochina established by the French, dwelling on the period from the 1930s to the transitional year of 1954, when the Geneva Accords took force and divided the country. Volume II deals with artists during the period 1957 – 1966, the years when the Association of Young Vietnamese Artists was formed.

This is in two volumes. Volume I deals with the Indochina College of Fine Arts established by the French

Entering the Realm of Created Images, Volume I deals with sixteen artists of reputation. Following the order in which they are presented, these are: Lê Phổ, Lê Văn Đệ, Mai Thứ, Nguyễn Gia Trí, Tôn Thất Đào, Nguyễn Đỗ Cung, Điềm Phùng Thị, Trương Thị Thịnh, Tạ Tỵ, Văn Đen, Lê Văn Phương, Võ Đình, Bùi Xuân Phái, Thái Tuấn, Duy Thanh, and Ngọc Dũng. It does not have the character of

The front covers of *Raking Leaves Outside by Night* (left) and *I Come Back and Stand Bewildered* (right).

The cover of *Entering the Realm of Created Images* and, on the right, the author's inscription.

a scholarly work, consisting instead of a series of occasional essays. Đinh Cường creates lively portraits of every artist whom he had an opportunity to meet and interact with, to which he adds rich and often very personal materials that he perhaps kept in his possession. The paintings selected for inclusion in the book reflect the fine judgement of the author in choosings works that illustrate the personalities and abilities of each artist.

Đinh Cường and Doãn Quốc Sỹ. *(Đinh Cường, personal archives)*

Đinh Cường and Võ Phiến. *(Đinh Cường, personal archives)*

For me, the book *Entering the Realm of Created Images*, vol 1, has personal associations; it carries me, like a flashback, to such personalities of a former era as Tôn Thất Đào, Mai Thứ, and Tạ Tỵ. It makes me recall the years when I studied drawing under the artist Tôn Thất Đào when I was a middle-school student in Huế.

THE ARTIST MAI THỨ

The name of the artist Mai Trung Thứ, especially, draws me into even more distant recollections. In the years when I had not yet begun to exist–before the 1940s–my revered father was a French professor at the Khải Định High School during the same period in which Mai Trung Thứ was a professor of painting. The two gentlemen were acquainted with each other during that period. In 1952, after my family returned from Thanh Hóa to live in Hanoi, the artist Mai Thứ was living in France. He and my father kept in touch with each other. I was eleven at the time, and knew of Mai Thứ's appearance only through a few photographs that he sent as gifts. They are no longer in my possession, except for two that can still be seen in our family album, that show him in his Paris studio.

Just as Đinh Cường observed, "to see again the world of little children in the paintings of Mai Thứ is a joy, a source of happiness." And this has been a joy, not just to those looking at his paintings; Mai Thứ has greatly increased the joy and happiness of countless unfortunate children on all five continents through those of his paintings of children that have appeared on UNICEF postcards of the United Nations International Children's Emergency Fund, which supports its successor, the United Nations Children's Fund.

Artist Mai Thứ in his studio, Paris 1952 *(Ngô Thế Vinh, personal archives)*

Top: "A Mother Giving Embroidery Lessons"; bottom: "Calligraphy" images on UNICEF postcards, used to help support the United Nations International Children's Emergency Fund (UNICEF).

(source: Mai Lan Phương, daughter of the artist Mai Thứ)

THE ARTIST TẠ TỴ

Beginning in the pre-1975 era, I had opportunities to look at Tạ Tỵ's paintings, read his poetry, and even look at his books containing literary observations, *Ten Faces of People in the Arts* (*Mười Khuôn Mặt Văn Nghệ*, Nam Chi Tùng Thư, Saigon, 1970) and *Ten Faces of People in Today's Art World* (*Mười Khuôn Mặt Văn Nghệ Hôm Nay*, Lá Bối, Saigon, 1972), and I remember feeling that each author in these volumes was depicted in a sharply individualized manner. Tạ Tỵ was a graduate of the Indochinese Academy of Fine Arts / l'école des Beaux-Arts de l'Indochine / Cao Đẳng Mỹ Thuật Đông Dương, but he didn't confine himself to the procedures and styles in which he had been trained at that school, but instead ceaselessly pursued what was new and was regarded as an avant-garde artist in Cubism painting very early in Vietnam since the 1950s and Abstract painting in later years.

Tạ Tỵ was a graduate of the Indochina College of Fine Arts was regarded as an avant-garde artist in Cubism painting very early in Vietnam since the 1950s and Abstract painting in later years.

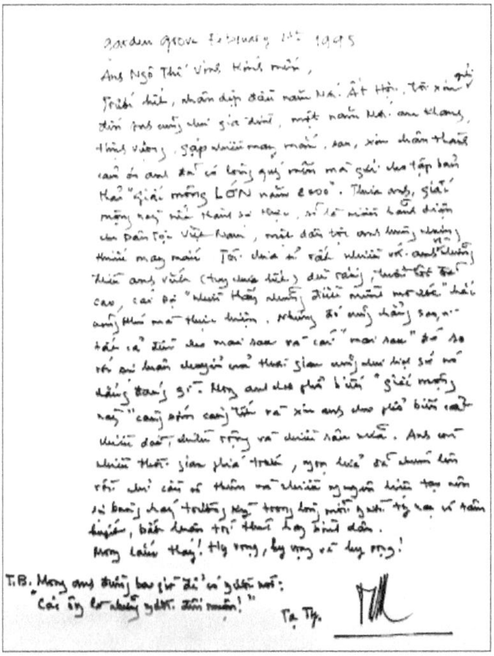

Tạ Tỵ's handwriting, January 2, 1995.

It was actually only since the 1990s on American soil, when we both shared the unwelcome fate of exile that I made his acquaintance. Tạ Tỵ belonged to the same generation as Vũ Khắc Khoan, Mặc Đỗ, and Nghiêm Xuân Hồng; he was a generation older than me. He had read "A Small Dream for the Year 2000" ("Giấc Mộng Con năm 2000"), and with great warmth shared with me a plan of his for a cultural

Paintings by Tạ Tỵ; left: "Remembering Hanoi", 1947; right: "Fragments of Life in Exile," oil, 2000; *(Đinh Cường, personal archives)*

park abroad, that he wished to name "The Great Dream." In a personal letter that he sent to me from Garden Grove on Feb. 1, 1995, he wrote: "I share a great deal in the things you have written, though I have grown old in years, and the things I dream of will certainly be difficult to realize, but that scarcely matters, because it all belongs to the future, and that future, compared with the evolution of time as well as its past, isn't worth anything. The flame has already been lit, and all we need is more fuel to make it burst into a long lasting conflagration in the soul of every loyal refugee, whether he be an intellectual or a commoner. How I wish for it! I hope, and hope, and hope! I hope you never allow people to say, 'You gentlemen all arrived too late!"

And, on a purely personal occasion, he confided to me that he was ready to contribute a number of his larger, more significant works to this Cultural Park whenever it could be brought into being. But then, quite unexpectedly, he let me know in another personal letter written from San Diego on July 27, 2000, that he had decided to return to Vietnam to live: "though I can't know in advance what will happen in my life, I nevertheless wish to seek repose in Vietnam, the place where I was born and lived for more than sixty years. After returning there, I will wash my hands forever of everything concerned with the brush, and wait for my entrance into the realm of nothingness. I miss you all very much." Tạ Tỵ.

Then, with no fanfare whatsoever, he returned to Saigon, and lived his final years in the company of his youngest daughter. He died on August 24, 2004 at the age of 83. He fulfilled his wish to pass his days of retirement in his homeland. His body, after cremation, returned to dust, but his name and works live on in the stream of our people's culture.

THE ASSOCIATION OF YOUNG VIETNAMESE ARTISTS

During the 1960s, a new generation of artists came to prominence, including such figures as Đinh Cường, Nguyễn Trung, Nghiêu Đề, Cù Nguyễn, Lâm Triết, Trịnh Cung, and Nguyên Khai… they were not

A meeting on Sept. 11, 1983 to celebrate the birthday of Thái Tuấn; back row, from left: Trần Lê Nguyễn, Đinh Cường, and Thanh Tâm Tuyền; front row, from left: Thái Tuấn, Quang Dũng, and Doãn Quốc Sỹ. (Quang Dũng, author of the poem "Western Advance," ["Tây Tiến"] was a childhood classmate of Thái Tuấn)

Đinh Cường, and Kiều Chinh. *(Đinh Cường, personal archives)*

From left: Nguyễn Mộng Giác, Đinh Cường, Khánh Trường, and Nguyễn-Xuân Hoàng. *(Đinh Cường, personal archives)*

only young in years, but were all characterised by a desire to engage in a ceaseless search for ways to rejuvenate the art of Vietnam. The Association of Young Vietnamese Artists was formally established in 1966, with following statement of purpose:

We, a number of young artists, unafraid of any spiritual or material difficulties that we may face, are hereby establishing an organizationto be called The Association Young Vietnamese Artists, and in doing so hope to create opportunities to meet and exchange experience, and based on these exchanges create new and original modes of expression in a pure and open atmosphere.

But one does not have to wait until 1966, the year this group was established, to see remarkable developments in art. Throughout the twenty years from 1954 to 1975, painting and sculpture in the South underwent bold, enthusiastic, and robust development along with all the other branches of art in a fortunate historical confluence arising from the benign conditions that prevailed there. The artists involved were in their twenties and thirties, regardless whether they were association members or not. Some, like Đinh Cường, Lâm Triết, Nguyễn Trung, Trịnh Cung, Nguyễn Phước, and Nguyên Khai had graduated from the College of Fine Arts; some, like Nghiêu Đề had left before graduating, and some, like Cù Nguyễn didn't come from an academy, but they were all like seams of jade in ore, people who had the opportunity to develop their talents to the utmost and create paintings of value in the free atmosphere of South Vietnam.

Through my old and close friend Nghiêu Đề, I had the opportunity to establish acquaintance and interact with his friends who were among that era's young artists, among whom were Lâm Triết, Cù Nguyễn, Nguyễn Trung, Nguyên Khai, Trịnh Cung, Đinh Cường, and then, after a few years, Nguyễn Lâm and Hồ Hữu Thủ.

LOOKING AT ĐINH CƯỜNG'S PAINTINGS

In the course of observations on the art of painting, Đinh Cường once said, "I drew in all surroundings in every location. I never knew why. Sometimes I was close to despair and every now and then I felt as though I had been rescued. And I would continue to draw, continue to meditate."

Đinh Cường became well-known before he graduated from the College of Fine Arts in 1963, having won a silver medal in the Spring Exhibition of 1962 with the painting "Mythology" (Thần Thoại.)

Beginning with his period of figurative painting, Đinh Cường attained fame at once for his paintings of a romantic period in which,

Left: "Passing over the La Vang Sandy Hill" (Qua Đồi Cát La Vang), oil; collection of General Ngô Quang Trưởng. Right: "Garden of Boulders" ("Vườn Đá Tảng"; oil; 1994)

with delicate lines he showed a Đà Lạt with poetic, misty, mountain roads in deserted surroundings in which a lonely bird could be seen perched on the tip of a church's bell tower.

A person viewing the paintings of Đinh Cường cannot but be led by association to a memory of a church steeple in a black-and-white French film, *Les Dimanches de Ville d'Avray* (*Sundays and Cybèle*), that everyone was familiar with back in 1962. It was about an aviator who, in the course of attacking a group of enemy vehicles, grows convinced that he has killed a young girl by mistake. His plane is shot down and, though he survives, he suffers a total loss of memory. Later he meets a ten-year-old orphan girl named Cybèle who has been left in an orphanage to be cared for by nuns. He is sure that she is the girl who died in the bombing, and from that point on, an innocent and pure attachment forms between the aviator and the girl. But this beautiful, chaste attachment becomes an object of suspicion and then a scandal in the town of Avray, and the story ends in tragedy. Đinh Cường on one occasion related that once, when he went to France, he paid a visit to Avray Village, and sought out the spire atop the bell tower that had appeared in the film, with a rooster perched on its tip.

After more than half a century of continuous creation, Đinh Cường has been the subject of many articles that attempt to assess and criticise his paintings. Almost all of these articles speak of their poetic or romantic quality.

Trịnh Công Sơn wrote: "In painting, Đinh Cường is the poet of nostalgia." (Tuổi Trẻ, September 1986).

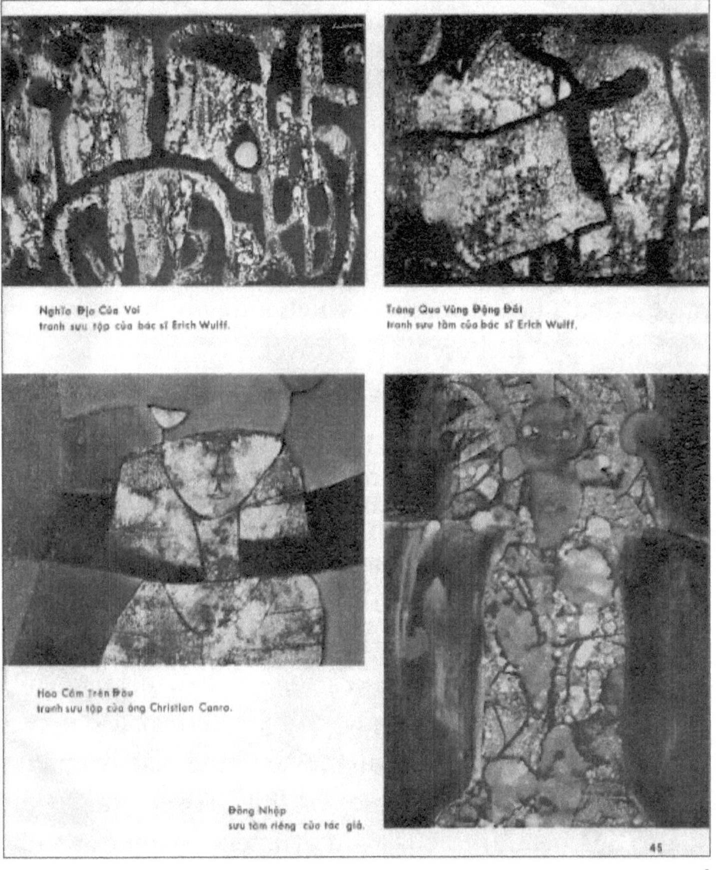

Paintings of Đinh Cường from the pages of *Free World* (Thế Giới Tự Do), Volume XIV; No. 8, 1967, Saigon.

Đặng Tiến, in a French-language article entitled "Đinh Cường, La Source Résurgente / A Soul With No Limits" (Tấm Lòng Vô Hạn), that served to introduce an exhibition of his works at the Galerie d'Annam 2010, wrote "The paintings of Đinh Cường in their essence are perhaps the recollections of a rose whose color and fragrance have been offered up to the human world. And art is nostalgia for a scent, isn't it?" (Orléans, October 2010).

Đinh Cường and Huỳnh Hữu Ủy.

Huỳnh Hữu Ủy had the following to say: "Đinh Cường established a universe suffused with poetry, a fusion of feeling with brushwork expressing a uniquely personal train of thought. In these works, the harmony of the colors and the design of the strokes are the means of expressing a mode of thought that includes many depths and reflects many images of our life and time.

Bùi Giáng spoke of the poetic substance of Đinh Cường's paintings in a French-language poem that he presented to Đinh Cường in 1972:

Le Poème de la Peinture / The Poem on the Painting

Il s'en va comme le Poisson d'eau douce
Sa Peinture rêveuse s'en va comme le Demeurer du Demeurant
Qui déploie son ordre et se refuse
Sur le mode de la Double Réserve

He comes along, a fish in gentle water
His dreamy painting like a remnant of a remnant
Imposing his own order, self-effacing
in a mode of double-layered reserve.

Je n'ai rien à lui dire sinon peut-être
Que le Poème de la Peinture
S'entend à merveille avec la Peinture du Poème
Comme la Reine des Almées
S'appelle aussi bien l'Almées des Reines
Que le Retour de la convalescente qui chante sa joie
A réjoui immensément l'Enfant des Riveraines
Au bord de l'Abîme des Abîmes

I've nothing to observe to him, except perhaps
That the Poem on the Painting
Sounds perfectly like a Painting on a Poem
Just as the Queen of supplicants
Is called as well the alms-receiving queen,
That the return of the recovered one who sings his joy
Gives joy as well to the Child of the Riverbanks
Upon the edge of the Abyss of the Abysses.

Vous n'avez rien à lui dire sinon peut-être
Que l'Éclaircie de l'Être lui est favorable
Comme l'Éraflure du Temps lui est favorisante
Lorsque la Terre advient à l'émergence
Tandis qu'un Monde s'ouvre

You'll have no words, except perhaps
To say the glory of existence favors him,
The glory of the times, too, favors him
When earth comes up to its emergence
And the world opens up.

Bùi Giáng, 1972

Le Poème de la Peinture
(tặng Đinh Cường)

rêveuse

Il s'en va comme le Poisson d'eau douce
Sa Peinture s'en va comme le Demeurer du
Demeurant
Qui déploie son ordre et se refuse
Sur le mode de la Double Réserve

Je n'ai rien à lui dire sinon peut-être
Que le Poème de la Peinture
S'entend à merveille avec la Peinture du Poème
Comme la Reine des Almées
S'appelle aussi bien l'Almée des Reines
Que le Retour de la Convalescente qui chante sa
joie
A réjoui immensément l'Enfant des Riveraines
Au bord de l'Abîme des Abîmes

Vous n'avez rien à lui dire sinon peut-être
Que l'Éclaircie de l'Être lui est favorable
Comme l'Éraflure du Temps lui est favorisante
Lorsque la Terre advient à l'émergence
Tandis qu'un Monde s'ouvre

Top: the handwriting of Bùi Giáng, "Poem on Painting" ("Bài Thơ Hội Họa"), presented to Đinh Cường in 1972. Bottom: a Vietnamese interpretation of Bùi Giáng's French poem by Ngô Văn Tao (Ngô Văn Quế, mathematics professor at Montréal College; friend of Bùi Giáng) *(source: DNSG, Spring 2009)*

Le Poème De La Peinture

(Thơ tiếng Pháp Bùi Giáng viết tặng họa sĩ Đinh Cường Sài Gòn 1972, lần đầu công bố)

Họa thi

Như cá lượn theo dòng
Anh vẽ như mơ mòng
Cho người đi kẻ ở
An nhiên và tự tại
Khước từ
trong quá đỗi đoan trang

Tôi sẽ nói gì cùng anh
Khi trong thơ đã có họa
Anh vẽ rồi một bài thơ
Cho Nữ hoàng Thánh mẫu
Cho Thánh mẫu Nữ hoàng
Và người bệnh phục hồi
Trong tiếng trẻ hát bên sông
Bên vực sâu của Tiền Đường

Ai sẽ nói gì cùng anh
Khi tồn sinh là tia sáng
Thời gian trong một thoáng không đi
Mặt đất cội nghiêng mình
Vũ trụ - vì anh - đã lên hương

Chúng tôi sẽ nói gì cùng anh
Trăn trở biến thiên xứ sở này
Trong đêm thao thức đợi ngày mai
Bình minh của kỷ nguyên mới
Chiếu sáng lối anh đi
Cho anh - Người tài của hội họa
Khi ở vườn khuya Hư Cực
Chúng tôi là trái trên cây
Muộn màng chín muộn
Trong những ngày quá muộn màng

Như cá lượn theo giòng
Anh vẽ chiêm bao và mộng mị
Vỗ cánh theo đàn chim muộn
- tới rồi thời của Vũ Tướng -
Lìa bỏ bến đất này
Bay tìm bến nước xa...

Ngô Văn Tao phỏng dịch, 1994

Đinh Cường and Bùi Giáng, Saigon, 1987.

In a personal setting, Đinh Cường once told me that he was most pleased by an article on his work by Đỗ Long Vân, a fine arts critic and a friend who had shared a studio with him on Hoa Hồng ("Rose") Street for two years in Đà Lạt. The article, in French, was later translated into Vietnamese in an inspired manner by Bửu Ý. The original and the translation are given below:

"Nul éclat. Aucune dissonance. Une pâte sombre et dense, légère malgré cela, et qui chante comme de l'or. C'est un or nocturne dont toute la lumière est tournée vers l'intérieur. Cela ennuie tout d'abord, et puis l'on finit par aimer cette pudeur obstinée, qui, pour sembler sans audace, n'en est pas moins durement conquise. Il suffit d'ailleurs de regarder Cường au travail et l'on voit que le charme simple et lisse qui séduit lentement en ses toiles, jamais Cường ne l'a atteint du premier coup, mais qu'il est l'aboutissement de longs essais ou se conjuguent le hasard et l'on ne sait quelle fatalité. Ses toiles débutent toujours dans l'éclat. Cela commence comme une explosion de fleurs et, presque toujours, cela devient un océan et nuit bleue et noire, non la veille nuit sanglante qui obsède la mémoire de son souvenir, mais la jeunesse du monde dont tous les trésors enfouis s'éveillent pour illuminer de leur éclat fragile cette première nuit qui s'appellerait aussi bien l'aurore. Car voilà que du fond de la terre des lueurs nous viennent, que l'espace s'entrouvre dans un envol d'acier, que des cristaux scintillent tandis qu'au-dessus de l' abîme, des villes en dérive tentent d'aller ensemble…"

No splendor, no dissonance. An impasto dense and somber, but still light, calls out like gold. It is a gold ingot in the night that directs all its light inward. This at first is boring, but in the end makes one grow fond of its obstinate reticence, which though devoid of audacity, is not for that reason less adamant in its conquest. As for how he achieves this, it is only necessary to look at him as he works, and one can see that the simple, smooth charm that slowly seduces the viewer of his canvases is never achieved all at once, but is always the outcome of a long process of exploration in which chance is conjoined with some unguessable kind of predetermined necessity. His canvases always begin with a burst of light. It is like an explosion of flowers, and almost always this turns into an ocean, a blue and black night, not the ancient bloody night that haunts the memory, but the youth of the world, in which buried treasures wait to be illumined by the fragile beams that will be the dawn of this first day. For at the bottom of this land of lights, space enters into a flight of steel, which with crystalline gleams emerges from the abyss, encouraging villages to fly up together…"

After Đà Lạt, Đinh Cường lived for a long time in Huế. There he created paintings with the "sad and subdued colors" (the words of Huỳnh Hữu Ủy) of the Inner City, and of the ancient capital of Huế, at once majestic and shabby, half hidden beneath layers of moss.

Đinh Cường met with early success but he continued to seek new paths. There was a six-year period (1969 – 1975) in which he entered the realm of abstract painting.

Responding to an interviewer in *Free World* (*Thế Giới Tự Do*), Volume XIV; No. 8; 1967, Saigon, Đinh Cường expressed himself as follows: "I gradually stripped away all thoughts of objects; or to use more philosophical language, I abandoned the forms of things so as to concentrate solely on the matter of the paint itself." But in the end he returned to the creation of images in paintings so characteristic of him, that they scarcely required a signature for the spectator to know who the artist was. In terms of quantity, he created perhaps close to a thousand paintings. He resettled in the U.S. in 1989, and by the year 2000, a space of ten years, he had five exhibitions, not counting various exhibitions that took place within Vietnam.

According to Đỗ Hồng Ngọc (the poet Đỗ Nghê) and Thân Trọng Minh (the writer and poet Lữ Kiều), two of this writer's colleagues, Đinh Cường, though he found out he was ill in 2011, still went back to Vietnam that year for a joint exhibition with Thân Trọng Minh. By 2013 he had become feeble, but he still went back to Vietnam to meet friends and participate in a second exhibition. In 2015 he made preparations to return for another painting exhibition, an important one, in Đà Nẵng, at the Museum of Chàm Sculpture (Viện Bảo Tàng Điêu Khắc Chàm), but this had to be postponed because the artist had embarked on a course of chemotherapy.

Aside from his artistic paintings, most of which were oils, and which formed the major part of his output, mention must also be made of the many sketches he created of his colleagues in the arts, as well as some he made of himself. This is also an aspect of his genius.

Đinh Cường had occasion at times to admire the power of persistence of Khánh Trường, especially after the latter fell prey to illnesses: two strokes, cancer of the vocal cords, stomach bleeding, and kidney failure, which compelled him to undergo peritoneal dialysis every night. In spite of all this, Khánh Trường still created the work "Sun at Dusk" ("Tịch Dương"), accepted commissions to create book covers, made many paintings on Zen themes, and had three exhibitions of his work. Commenting on this, Đinh Cường wrote, "… a person whom I imagined had died, but who lived again, lived gloriously so as to Cross to the Shore, the Shore of tranquil existence. ("Khánh Trường, the Power of Silence," Virginia, Jan. 8, 2012)

But then Đinh Cường himself had to endure many ups and downs in his health that at times subjected him to suffering, but his power to do work continued undisturbed through all the phases of his illness.

Top: Đinh Cường's studio on Hòa Bình ("Peace") Street, Huế, Inner City; bottom: "Huế Nostalgia," oil, by Đinh Cường. *(Đinh Cường, personal archives)*

Top left: Đinh Cường's studio on Rose Street in Đà Lạt, 1963; top right: Đỗ Long Vân and Đinh Cường, Đà Lạt, 1963. Bottom: "Đà Lạt Nostalgia," oil, by Đinh Cường *(Đinh Cường, personal archives)*

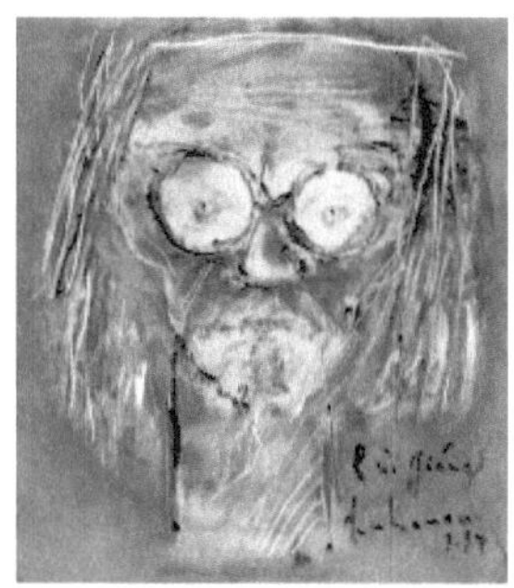
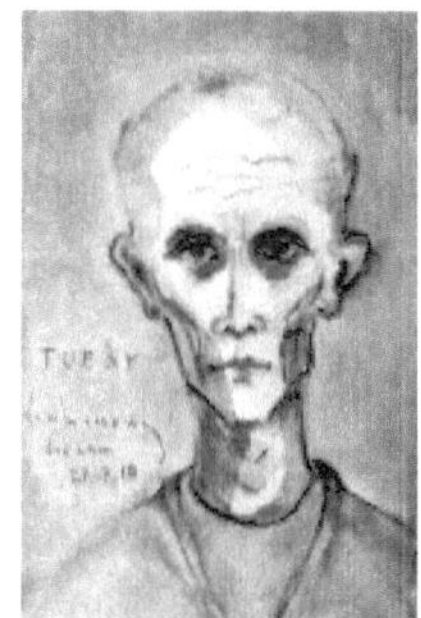

Sketches of artistic figures by Đinh Cường; top, from left: Bùi Giáng, Tuệ Sỹ, and Nguyễn Đức Sơn. Bottom, from left: Doãn Quốc Sỹ, Võ Phiến, Thanh Tâm Tuyền, and Nguyễn Đình Toàn

READING ĐINH CƯỜNG'S POEMS

Sweeping Leaves in the Yard at Night

Dedicated to Bửu Ý

As dusk grows deep the twigs are bare
I grope; all things are lost in mist
Amid a thousand layered shadows, I feel cold
The falling leaves rustle at year's end,
Throughout the day I hear the sound of crows
Beside the moss-green porch they call
At times pretending to sleep late,
My dreams are full of solitude.
Near dusk I go out to an unknown river pier,
And on the other side streetlights flicker on,

And only then I see that winter days
Are calling to some nameless sun:
A friend of old who hails a friend
The wings of geese convey the call;
I stand alone, all cold,
And sweep the yard of leaves by night.

Virginia, Nov., 1997

LOOKING AT ĐINH CƯỜNG'S NEWER PAINTINGS

The Friday Poems

Birth, old age, illness, and death are the four miseries of corporeal existence from which no living thing escapes. I myself, the writer of this book, have spent forty-six years practicing medicine and have myself been a seriously ill patient during the years following my release from prison (re-education camp), and it was only then that I fully grasped the meaning of the saying "there are no illnesses, only people who suffer from illnesses." In a book entitled *When Doctors Are Patients* by Max Pinner and Benjamin F. Miller (W.W. Norton and Co., New York, 1952), a true record may be found of the experiences that doctors themselves must undergo when they face serious or untreatable illnesses. Max Pinner, himself a doctor, reaches this conclusion: "An ill person doesn't simply face an illness, but must deal with a total collapse."

I had those endless thoughts after speaking with Đinh Cường on the telephone. The voice of my friend was warm and calm, just as it had always been. I was aware, though, of reports concerning his health after he had crossed the threshold of 70 –and a traumatic brain injury and a bald head after starting a round of chemo made his friends very anxious. Three years earlier, he was in a traffic accident which, though minor, caused a blood clot to form in his cranium. According to my colleague Nguyễn Tường Giang, an old friend who was very close to Đinh Cường, he returned to entire normalcy after a trepanation to remove the clot, retaining only a concave scar produced by the procedure.

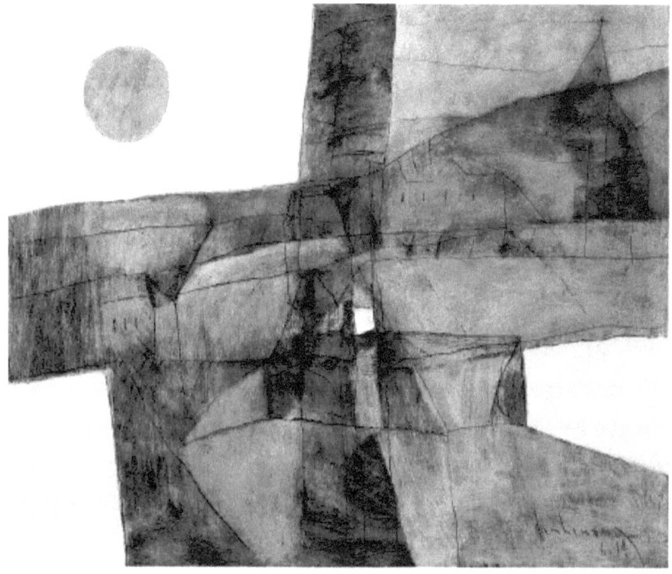

Composition in Gray I, Oil on canvas, 30 x 40 inches, Đinh Cường 2014.

Composition in Gray II, Oil on canvas, 30 x 30 inches, Đinh Cường 2014.

But a bit more than four years ago, in 2011, Đinh Cường was diagnosed with a different illness: prostate cancer. Prostate cancer, like breast cancer in women, is a fairly common disease. With the advances that have taken place in medicine, both types of cancer can in many circumstances be cured if they are detected early and treated appropriately. There is no lack of people who have had prostate cancer for more than thirty years and have remained healthy and strong into their nineties. If such people reach that age, they often die of other causes

I'm not sure whether Đinh Cường's illness was diagnosed early or not but, perhaps because he was more than seventy years old, his doctors chose hormonotherapy rather than surgery as the best way to deal with his illness. His condition subsided for a while, but then the chemo had to be resumed, with all the side effects that entailed. He endured it all courageously.

He would sit in a chemo chair, excessively familiar to him, gazing at the drops of medication as they descended their plastic tubes, but that was just a physical detail; Đinh Cường would still make poems or small paintings, and then the next day his friends would come to take him to breakfast or brunch. Sometimes it would be Nguyễn Mạnh

Đinh Cường and Ngô Thế Vinh in the artist's garage studio in Burke, Virginia, 1993. *(photo by Như Phong Lê Văn Tiến)*

Hùng and / or Nguyễn Tường Giang, sometimes Phùng Nguyễn and Như Hạnh, sometimes Nguyễn Thế Toàn (known as Toàn Bò), sometimes Nguyễn Minh Nữu, sometimes Phạm Cao Hoàng, and in addition to these, all his friends from distant places would come to visit him. Đinh Cường was very sociable, and would sally forth from his house almost every day, surrounded always by an affectionate group of friends.

I would phone my friend from afar: 9:00 in the morning in California is the same as noon in the east, and I would be cheered by the voice of Đinh Cường, as deep and strong as ever, and then he would turn the phone over to someone else, sometimes with Phùng Nguyễn of *The Tower of Memory* (*Tháp Ký Ức*) of the website "Skin of Color," at Starbucks, and sometimes to Nguyễn Tường Giang of *Drifting Smoke Above the Lake* (*Khói Hồ Bay*) from the Café Montmartre or Le Chat Noir, and he would refer to his old friend Nguyễn Tường Vũ, and to Thế Uyên of *Gray Attitude* (*Thái Độ Xám*), and then to Duy Lam of *My Family* (*Gia Đình Tôi*) with a report of his declining health, and then the phone would be turned over to Nguyễn Mạnh Hùng of George Mason University, who had just returned from Beijing and Nanning, with impressions of the just established "think tanks" of China, the members of which were relatively young – around forty – not aged and decrepit like their counterparts in Vietnam – a Vietnam that was still conscientiously trying to follow the example of China but was almost always twenty years behind, leading one to think of something said by Lê Khả Phiêu, the general secretary of the communist party of Vietnam, that had caused many Vietnamese to wrinkle their brows: "If the Chinese succeed in their

"Autoportrait" by Đinh Cường; made in a Starbucks café, April 17, 2015.

renovation, then we too will succeed; if they fail in their renovation, then we too will fail." (FEER, June 22, 2000)

Though I was thousands of miles away from him, cell phones and email messages made me feel that we were as close as if we lived in the same small village.

Sent to Ngô Thế Vinh:

Beside the chemo chair in yonder room,
The nylon tubes hang loosely down.
Two IV bags filled with fluid clear as tears:
I raise my gaze, the drops fall one by one
The drops drip down, and I recall Văn Cao:
From heaven blue
There drop
Some Cham tower drops;
Quy Nhơn. The day you came there, the early months of 1985:
Three Quy Nhơn poems: Quy Nhơn I, Quy Nhơn II, Quy Nhơn III
You wrote them down: three cello pieces, beautiful as ancient myths.
The sea escorts some groups of swallows back,
The sun dries out the just-formed buds of coconuts,
... around Quy Nhơn,
I was like a child who dotes on myth.[1]
Drip, drip, drip: I raise my eyes again;
To see it drawing near the final drop,
Two hours, eyes half closed, two hours, drawing breath, chemo, chemo…
And then it seems I hear a lively dance tune, leaping Africans
And then I see to hear the urgent words of Đỗ Hồng Ngọc:
You have to live–and live quite differently–live content–
Who can do another's breathing? Who can do another's meditation?

Virginia, July 10, 2015

---

1 Văn Cao – *Lá (Leaves)* – Poetry, published by Tác Phẩm Mới, 1988

A ĐINH CƯỜNG AWAKENED

I recall now an interview of Đinh Cường conducted by Nguyễn Nam Anh (this was one of the pen names of Nguyễn-Xuân Hoàng) almost a quarter of a century ago. On that occasion Đinh Cường said, "It is a fact that our life down here is in concrete terms cruel and bitter. The more cruel and bitter it is, the more calm and quiet I become. As a result of this, I have come to recognize a principle: Do everything you can for some good piece of work. This will at times bring you fulfillment. My paintings have kept me alive–I cannot abandon drawing. (Tạp Chí Thế Kỷ 21, No. 23: March, 1991)

"The more cruel and bitter life becomes, the more calm and quiet I become." Twenty-four years after talking with Nguyễn-Xuân Hoàng, Đinh Cường in fact adhered strictly to this principle, even in the cruel and extreme circumstances to which his failing health exposed him. Nguyễn-Xuân Hoàng himself had been dead for a year – his death occurred on Sept. 12, 2014. Đinh Cường was still breathing; he lived on, intact, second by second and day by day. He still painted and made poems. And in the year 2015 he completed two books of art criticism: Entering the Realm of Created Images, vols. I and II. As Đinh Cường said to himself: "I must live, and live quite differently; I must live content." He was a Đinh Cường who had experienced an awakening, though perched unsteadily on the road to death.

The front cover of Đinh Cường's collection, "Leaving Reveals One's Depth of Feeling." Published by Hội Nhà Văn, Huế, 2016

On Friday, August 28, 2015, a chemo day for Đinh Cường, he was picked up at the hospital by Nguyễn Thế Toàn. I chatted with him on the phone as he went back–he was still a Đinh Cường with a warm and composed voice. He and his friend chatted as unconcernedly as if they were returning from a picnic. The next day, a Saturday morning, Đinh Cường took Nguyễn Đình Thuần to Washington D.C. to see the paintings in the National Gallery of Art, and then went with him to a gathering of friends that lasted till the small hours. Đinh Cường remained with them throughout, which was a joy to all his friends in distant places who wanted to hear about his health.

THE PASSING OF ĐINH CƯỜNG

Đinh Cường died on January 7, 2016 in Virginia, USA, in the place where he had settled in 1990. A collection of items by and about Đinh Cường consisting of more than 700 pages was completed by his friends and published in Huế on January 7, 2017, his first death anniversary: *Leaving Reveals One's Depth of Feeling (Ra Đi Mới Biết Lòng Vô Hạn)*. It was in four sections; "Traces Left By Đinh Cường," "Đinh Cường Viewed From Many Viewpoints," "The Creative World of Đinh Cường," and "Materials and Images," the last section including rare and precious items kept by his family and friends.

And so, we bid a last farewell to Đinh Cường. Two lines of verse that he himself wrote will serve to evoke his endlessly creative life:

To leave reveals one's feelings' depths;
Mist deepens on the River Hương.

Long Beach, September 6, 2015
Long Beach 2017

REMEMBERING A DEAR FRIEND NGHIÊU ĐỀ (1939 – 1998) BIRD TRACKS LEFT IN THE SAND

Portrait of Nghiêu Đề
(Nghiêu Đề, Việt Art Society, 1998)

This essay consists solely of personal thoughts and cherished recollections concerning my dear friend Nghiêu Đề, with whom I had a friendship lasting forty years. The author of this article does not belong to the art world so it is not easy for me to do justice to the work of a talented artist who, though his work was not great in quantity, nevertheless left a lasting mark on the history of art in Vietnam through the creative work he did in the period 1960 – 1970 in the Association of Young Vietnamese Artists, of which he was a strikingly distinctive member.

Ngô Thế Vinh

NGHIÊU ĐỀ, BIOGRAPHICAL DATA

Nghiêu Đề's real name was Nguyễn Tiếp, but "Trai" was the name by which he was called at home. He was born in 1939 in Quảng Ngãi. He was the eldest son in a family with six sons and daughters. He studied at the Gia Định College of Fine Arts, but left of his own volition before graduation. He was a member of the Association of Young Vietnamese Artists. He was the recipient of the Silver Medal for Fine Arts in Spring, 1961, and was a participant in exhibitions held in many countries. Aside from painting, he also wrote stories and composed poetry, but he later came to regard these two activities as "missteps," and felt that he should not strive to enter the world of writers. A published work of his was *The Hundred-Year Hairdo* (*Ngọn Tóc Trăm Năm*), Saigon, 1965. He moved to the U.S. with his family in 1985, and died on November 9, 1998 in San Diego, California before attaining his 60th birthday.

In August 2014, when Trịnh Cung was still in the U.S., I suggested to him that he should write an article about his old associate Nghiêu Đề. Trịnh Cung (who also had been a member of the Association of Young Vietnamese Artists) agreed to write an article by November, in time for Nghiêu Đề's sixteenth death anniversary. But when November came, I saw only two short lines introducing the artist on the website "Skin of Color" (Da Màu) together with two paintings selected from the book *Nghiêu Đề* put out by the Việt Art Society. Trịnh Cung let me know that he had been unable to find enough material, and had had to "give-the-matter-up.com." ("botay.com").

I wasn't surprised that Trịnh Cung came up with a blank when searching for information on Nghiêu Đề, a person who throughout his life never appeared to desire to possess anything. His career, it would

Nghiêu Đề with his wife and three children, Little Búp (Bé Búp), little Bi (Bé Bi), and little Sài Gòn (Bé Saigon), when they had just arrived in San Diego in 1985. *(from Nghiêu Đề's family photo album)*

Nghiêu Đề at the age of 16 in front of the Tax Commerce Building; people and scenes that no longer exist; top right: Nguiễn Ngu Í; bottom right: Nghiêu Đề. *(Nghiêu Đề family, personal archives)*

seem, consisted of bird-tracks left in the sand – traces that would soon be erased by the waves of time. He did not have the character of a man who takes care to collect his creations and make durable defenses for them. A perfect example of a person who *did* possess such qualities was his friend, the artist Đinh Cường, who kept an entire storehouse of personal memorabilia that few others could equal.

With this article, I am merely, to borrow the words of the artist Khánh Trường, acting as "a lover of bygone things" attempting to scoop up and assemble some sand and stones, so as to rediscover times that have disappeared along with my dear friend Nghiêu Đề.

NGHIÊU ĐỀ AND HIS FRIENDS

When I began my first year as a medical student, instead of virtuously concentrating on the curriculum as my classmates did, I fell at once into a love for writing, journalism and participation in the many amusements of the circle of artists who surrounded Nghiêu Đề. We differed a good deal from each other, so I don't know how we became so close.

Nghiêu Đề led a wandering life, and had many close friends from early childhood, when he lived in a small neighborhood named Bùi Viện near an International Crossroads (Ngã Tư Quốc Tế) in Saigon. It was an area full of adventures much frequented by us. Many of the youths in that group had undiscovered talent–they were like "jade hidden in stone" (ngọc ẩn thạch). In the world of artists, these people included Nguyễn Trung, Cù Nguyễn, Lâm Triết, and Nguyên Khai. Among poets and writers, they included Trần Dạ Từ, Nguyễn Đức Sơn / Sao Trên Rừng, Trần Tuấn Kiệt, Trần Đức Uyển / Tú Kếu, Nguyễn Nghiệp Nhượng, and Nguyễn Thụy Long. Each person had his own style, coupled with a burning desire for achievement – their common characteristic. Their creative abilities were strong, so they quickly created many works, and became well-known. Nghiêu Đề also had many intergenerational friends, now deceased, whom I knew from the days when they worked for the journal *Cyclopedia* (*Bách Khoa*), such as Lê Ngộ Châu, Nguiễn Ngu Í, Võ Phiến, and Vũ Hạnh…

THE CHIRPING OF THE NGUYỆT BIRD

In response to a question asked him by Nguiễn Ngu Í in an interview recorded in *Cyclopedia* 137, Sept. 15, 1962, Nghiêu Đề replied as if he were a person walking on clouds:

"In the place I come from, there is a strange type of bird, all white, and with a delicate wraith-like body. It usually flies about alone in the nighttime. People say it flies high, and sometimes alights on the surface of the moon, from which it never returns. Its name is 'Nguyệt' [Sino-Vietnamese for "moon"] and the sound of its chirping is deeply attractive. I have no idea why I love it so much. I know only that each time it flies past making its distinctive call, I feel moved. It seems to me now that the art I yearn for is something utterly natural like the calling of the Nguyệt Bird."

When I inquired about this with the poet Luân Hoán and other friends from Nghiêu Đề's homeland, I found that none of them had ever seen or heard the chirping of the Nguyệt bird. But that scarcely matters. The Nguyệt bird, with its white plumage, wraith-like body, that flies alone to the moon at night, surely exists, just as young Cuội surely sits at the foot of a banyan tree on the moon. The Nguyệt bird still flies high and alights on the moon, never returning. Could it be that it is itself the realm of transcendence as well as the lifelong dream of Nghiêu Đề?

THE TRƯỜNG SƠN PRINTING HOUSE

Prior to the 1960s, the principal name in the printing technology of the South was Typo. The pages of books and journals in that era were compiled, letter by letter, from groups of lead fonts. The Typo workers were generally Chinese from the Chợ Lớn sector of Saigon. They weren't fluent in Vietnamese, but the speed with which they set type was remarkable. Offset technology back then was rare. A privately run establishment was Cliché Dầu, a place that Nghiêu Đề and I often went to so as to order metal offset printing plates for journal covers or art replicas. Phạm Ngũ Lão was still regarded as Saigon's "journal street," but the Trường Sơn Printing House of the

Some covers of the student journal *Medicine and Compassion* (*Y Khoa Tình Thương*) designed by Nghiêu Đề.
[manuscript archives in Thư Quán Bản Thảo]

writer Nguyễn Thị Vinh was situated on Nguyễn An Ninh Street. It included a large-scale Typo machine for journals as well as a number of smaller, pedal-operated machines. The student journal *Medicine and Compassion* (*Y Khoa Tình Thương*) of the School of Medicine, *The Living Earth* (*Đất Sống*) of the School of Pharmacy, and *Literary Studies* (*Văn Học*) of Dương Kiền were all printed there. Nghiêu Đề and I often met each other there, especially when we wished to present covers, designed by him, for the spring issues.

NGHIÊU ĐỀ AND THE ART OF CREATING COVERS

The writer Võ Phiến held Nghiêu Đề in special regard. Here is an anecdote involving his book *Farewell* (*Giã Từ*): Võ Phiến relied on Nghiêu Đề to design covers for his book. In those days, attractive

A pair of cross-generational friends: from right: Nghiêu Đề and Võ Phiến, Dec. 1987. *(Viễn Phố, personal archives)*

fonts suitable for use on covers were very scarce. Sometimes one had to search for them on the covers of American magazines sold in kiosks on Lê Lợi Street and cut out what you wanted, letter by letter, paste them into your design and add diacritics. Due to his determination to create a beautiful cover, Nghiêu Đề decided against "adding whiskers" to these letters; that is, he didn't add diacritical marks to the title. Another purpose of his was by this means to provide the reader with an opportunity to consider all the various possibilities: Gia Tư ("personal family"), Giả Tu ("false self-cultivation"), Giả Tù ("pretended imprisonment"), Giã

The cover of Võ Phiến's Farewell (Giã Từ) with no diacritics over the letters in the title, leaving the reader to guess its meaning. *(Phan Nguyên, Emprunt Empreinte, archives)*

Tự ("threshing characters")... The book was published by Thời Mới. Soon after the book appeared, Nghiêu Đề received a gift copy from Võ Phiến with some solemn words of dedication: "*This is the volume with the designs that satisfy me the most.*"

Whoever had a book about to be published wanted Nghiêu Đề to design the cover. He never said no to anybody–but whether the cover would appear by a given date was an entirely different matter. Concerning this, the poet Luân Hoán wrote: "He was totally devoted to his friends and did not often turn down art-related jobs. But it was not an easy matter to get him to complete a cover promptly. He had a relaxed attitude toward his commitments, preferring to work only when inspired. He didn't want to be confined or nagged." The spring-issue covers he designed for Lê Ngộ Châu's *Cyclopedia* and for the medical students' *Medicine and Compassion* all involved much waiting, and in one or two cases were never completed.

In particular, four books of mine, *Storm Clouds* (*Mây Bão*) 1963; *Night Shadows* (*Bóng Đêm*), 1964; *Seasonal Wind* (*Gió Mùa*); and *The Green Belt* (*Vòng Đai Xanh*) had covers handcrafted by Nghiêu Đề.

There was a brief period, quite rare in his career, when Nghiêu Đề did a great deal of work. Aside from painting, he was responsible for all the covers and illustrations for the more elegant books put out by Cảo Thơm, including *Echoes of an Era* (*Vang Bóng Một Thời*) by Nguyễn Tuân, and after 1975, when the author came from the North to visit Saigon, he was very pleased and honored to be able hold in his hands the very artistic edition of his own work that had been published in the South.

THE MINH MẠNG UNIVERSITY DORMITORY AND THE ARTIST NGHIÊU ĐỀ

Before 1975 era, Nghiêu Đề's paintings were oils, the dimensions of which were fairly large. When they were newly completed, and the paint was still wet, if they weren't put face down into old, dusty frames, they were often carried away by friends. Sometimes a need arose to make a painting, but there was no money to purchase a canvas. In such cases, Nghiêu Đề would sometimes take an old painting and create a new one on the old surface. Room 3/7 in my university dormitory was a place with a painting by Nghiêu Đề on the wall ("Moon"; see reproduction below). A short while later Nghiêu Đề sold this painting; I don't know who the present owner of this memory-laden painting may be. It is one of three reproductions that my friend, the engineer Nguyễn Công Thuần took photos of from my novel *A Seasonal Wind*, preserved in the library of Cornell University.

Some covers designed by Nghiêu Đề: *Storm Clouds* (*Mây Bão*) 1963 and 1993; *Night Shadows* (*Bóng Đêm*), 1964; and *The Nine Dragons Drained Dry – The East Sea in Turmoil* (*Cửu Long Cạn Dòng, Biển Đông Dậy Sóng*), art by Nghiêu Đề, designed by Khánh Trường, 2000. *(Ngô Thế Vinh, personal archives)*

"Moon" (Trăng) oil painting, first reproduction in the novel *A Seasonal Wind* (*Gió Mùa*), 1965. (source: Cornell University Library; Call no.: Wason PL 4389, N473, G4)

Foreign travelers or Vietnamese tourists who have lived long in distant places often cherish Nghiêu Đề's paintings and wish to purchase some when they visit Vietnam. Since it was never feasible to produce enough paintings to fulfill orders on demand, Nghiêu Đề's "gallery" consisted of works scattered among his friends. Nghiêu Đề painted little, and did not have enough paintings to sell, and the prices for his paintings were usually very high. Every time he sold a painting, he would turn into a new person for a few days. He no longer relied only on his old Mobylette, which rarely had a full tank of gas. He would seek out his friends and entertain them royally until he had spent his last sou.

Nghiêu Đề spoke of this himself in an interview with the journalist Nguiễn Ngu Í recorded in *Cyclopedia* magazine, Sept. 15, 1962: "I don't like my paintings when more than an hour has passed after their completion. I usually place them backward in some dusty corner… I'm grateful to my friends, who often come and take them somewhere else–I feel easier that way. Every time I sell a painting, it seems to me that the money has rained down on me from heaven. So I cast it all to the winds without the slightest regret. Oftentimes it seems to me that the money is excessive, that I don't deserve it! It's as if I got it by cheating someone. I am grateful for the generosity of all those who love my painting–their generosity knows no bounds!

"Young Woman" (Thiếu Nữ) reproductions 2 and 3 in the novel A Seasonal Wind (Gió Mùa), Sông Mã, 1965 (source: Cornell University Library; Call no., Wason PL 4389, N473, G4)

THE "MATIÈRE" OF NGHIÊU ĐỀ'S PAINTINGS

The expression "image creation" (*tạo hình*), perhaps fails to correspond perfectly with Nghiêu Đề's conception of art, though image creation is an important phase in each of Nghiêu Đề's oil paintings. According to him, the talent of an artist consists of the beauty of the "stuff" (*chất liệu*) on the empty space or background of a painting. I have sat for hours, silently following the brush strokes made by Nghiêu Đề, so as to see how the initial rough layers of paint were transformed into a gentle, light-filled blue background, though in the whole process gleaming shafts of light were never lacking. The "stuff" was meltingly soft and the composition sure but light, in a way very characteristic of the artist.

Nghiêu Đề, when discussing each painting, often referred to the word "matière." I have never found a Vietnamese term used among artists suitable to represent the French word. Nguyên Khai referred to it as the "gamme màu," and Huỳnh Hữu Ủy called it simply the "stuff" (*chất*), as in the "stuff" of the paintings of Nguyễn Trung, Cù Nguyễn, or Lâm Triết... To return to the subject of the brush strokes involved in image creation, according to Nghiêu Đề, these were not things that could be copied from life: *"an artist is one who seeks the correct line between two mistaken one's offered by reality."*

Recently, when discussing the beauty of a painting, Trịnh Cung distinguished five elements: thought, composition, line, color or light, and attractiveness of the "stuff" or matière. One can say that the fifth element, attraction of the "stuff" is the one that creates a feeling of transcendence, and is also a feature of Nghiêu Đề's style.

After 1975, there was a period when Nghiêu Đề, shifted to lacquer painting along with Nguyễn Lâm and Hồ Hữu Thủ, but later on, he himself acknowledged that this form of art was too dependant on technique, and said that after he had applied several layers of paint to achieve the lacquer effect, the "stuff" of a painting would suddenly elude his artistic control. When Nghiêu Đề moved to the U.S. in 1984, he brought along a number of very fine lacquer paintings, but even though they were a financial success, he decided to bid farewell to lacquer painting and returned to the extremely artistic style of the paintings he produced in the period 1960 – 1970, such as: "Night" ("Đêm"), "Confiding One's Feelings" ("Tỏ Tình"), "The Realm of Transcendance" ("Vùng Thanh Thoát"), and most representatively "Portrait" ("Chân Dung"), which won the Silver Prize in the 1961 Spring Fine Arts Exhibition.

NGHIÊU ĐỀ AND *THE HUNDRED-YEAR HAIRDO*

The story of Nghiêu Đề is like a series of prose poems. Just as with his paintings, Nghiêu Đề never expressed satisfaction with any of his creations. But in spite of everything, he had a collection of stories: *The Hundred-Year Hairdo* (*Ngọn Tóc Trăm Năm*) was published by Sông Mã in 1965. It was a beautifully attractive book, even though it was put together in a hand-made manner by the tiny printing house Nguyễn Trọng, hidden in an alley behind Lăng Ông in Gia Định. It was printed, two pages at a time, on a rotating panel of a pedal-operated machine, with a set of worn fonts. The owner, also the worker, of this printing shop held Nghiêu Đề in very high esteem, so he charged him only a moderate price for the paper and printing, but it took a long time to print the book with its 122 pages including reproductions, and the work could only be done in intervals between other jobs. Usually the author and I would come down to the shop each weekend, holding some printed pages of the book still smelling of ink and fresh paper. Only a small number of books were printed, so perhaps few people knew of it or retained copies. I should record another detail here: When I met Nghiêu Đề on American soil in 1985, I learned for the first time that the owner of the Nguyễn Trọng printing shop in those days was a high-ranking Việt Cộng cadre living incognito in the region. The chief business of his printing shop was perhaps the printing of propaganda sheets and secret Communist Front documents.

I was very moved to see a special printed copy of *The Hundred-Year Hairdo*, perhaps the only one printed on croquis paper, in the book cabinet of Bé Búp, Nghiêu Đề's daughter in San Diego. It was a leather-bound hardcover book, and the name Nguyễn Toản was visible in gold letters on the spine. This was the name of Nghiêu Đề's father, whom he loved with all his heart. His father died rather early, when Nghiêu Đề's family was still living in a multi-story apartment building on Duy Tân Street. The family later moved to a different location: 19B on Lý Trần Quán Street in Saigon. This was also the place that Nghiêu Đề and I chose for the Sông Mã publishing house. *The Hundred-Year Hairdo*, with its four short stories and four artistic reproductions was like an opportunity for friends to get together.

Nguyễn-Xuân Hoàng, knowing that Nghiêu Đề was the author of *The Hundred-Year Hairdo*, asked Nghiêu Đề on a couple of occasions to submit a story to the journal *Literature* (*Văn*), but Nghiêu Đề just laughed. Nguyễn-Xuân Hoàng said, "Sometimes Nghiêu Đề would submit a poem to *Lierature*, but I was never given a single new short story. I asked him about this many times, and he would say, 'Colors are already sufficient. Poetry is a step too far, and a short story would be another such misstep…" (Some Reminiscences of Nghiêu Đề ["Một Chút Kỷ Niệm với Nghiêu Đề"], Nguyễn-Xuân Hoàng, San José, November 16, 1998)

• Here is the data concerning this book:
The Hundred-Year Hairdo (*Ngọn Tóc Trăm Năm*), stories by nghiêu đề
cover: designed by nguyễn trung
artistic reproductions: lâm triết, cù nguyễn, nguyễn trung, and nghiêu đề
layout: trần dạ từ, Sông Mã, Saigon, 1965
Table of Contents:
page 7: "Deer" (Nai), oil painting, lâm triết
page 9: "An Expanse of Green Grass" ("Vùng Cỏ Xanh")
page 37: "Grass and Flowers" (Thảo và Hoa), oil painting, cù nguyễn
page 39: "Brothers of the Earth" ("Người Anh Em Của Đất")
page 67: "The Realm of Transcendence" ("Vùng Thanh Thoát"), oil painting, nghiêu đề
page 69: "The Hundred-Year Hairdo" ("Ngọn Tóc Trăm Năm")
page 93: "Portrait" ("Chân Dung"), oil painting, Nguyễn Trung
page 95: "Shade of the Sea" ("Khoảng Rợp Của Biển)

The Hundred-Year Hairdo (*Ngọn Tóc Trăm Năm*), short stories by Nghiêu Đề; cover design by Nguyễn Trung, Sông Mã, 1965, Saigon. *(Nghiêu Đề family, personal archives)*

When Nghiêu Đề fell prey to a serious illness, his wife Giang and his children joined with the Việt Art Society in preparing a book about Nghiêu Đề. I wasn't surprised to learn that, aside from their friend's paintings, this group didn't want to introduce the content of *The Hundred-Year Hairdo* into the volume as a summation of his career. Though Nghiêu Đề himself repudiated the volume, its pages nevertheless have a distinct value as being part of the culture of the South before 1975.

A GLIMPSE OF NGHIÊU ĐỀ IN *THE GREEN BELT*

Triết, the main character in *The Green Belt*, was a literary creation, who, after becoming a war correspondent in the novel, was based partly on Nghiêu Đề and partly on elements that I found within myself.

"... Routinely, each morning, when the paper had been readied for printing, I left the editorial office and walked downstairs to chat with the girl who was the secretary or went to the beginning of the alley and ordered a cup of thick, bitter coffee and sat down to shoot the breeze with anyone who happened to be there–often a group of printing shop workers or typesetters. Peace and quietude filled the rest of the day. As I moved up the dimly lit spiral staircase to my office, the air seemed condensed with cold, frozen and abandoned. Black typewriters lay dormant on tables. The chairs added dark vertical shapes to the scene.

The novel Green Belt by Ngô Thế Vinh, cover design by Nghiêu Đề, Thái Độ Publisher, 1970 *(source: Cornell University Library; Call no.: Wason PL 4389 N473, V9)*

Sometimes the familiar was tinted with the strangeness that had marked the first few days following my arrival. Had I still been painting, perhaps I could have worked with such first impressions. Having cast aside my canvases, I could not avoid having longing thoughts about them.

After a fire had destroyed most of my work, I ceased to attach any value to painting and had no idea how long this attitude might last. But even so, I took part in a recent exhibition by contributing of four large paintings, works that still remained in the possession of my group of friends. That my name should be added to the list of participants was nothing to protest or comment about. The surprising thing was that, right on the first day of the exhibition, I was the first person to sell many paintings – I sold three of the four I exhibited. The painting "Black Cat on a Pink Carpet" was requested for purchase by a lady named Như Nguyện ("Full Satisfaction"), and two other paintings were purchased by an American whom I later learned was a journalist named Davis. My paintings were of the sort that did not readily please viewers, so they were priced high, so as to make up for their low sales. Due to the sale, I was able to repay some sizable debts, and supply myself with a typewriter and an excellent camera. Like a farmer enjoying an unseasonable harvest, I was able to say farewell to painting while receiving a belated favor from it. (The Green Belt [Vòng Đai Xanh], Chapter 1, Thái Độ Publisher, 1970)

A DIFFERENT NGHIÊU ĐỀ

Since he refused to be tied to the ordinary laws and routines of life, it would be easy to regard Nghiêu Đề as a person adrift, a floating person with no regard for life. He got along readily with everyone, but at the same time maintained a certain haughtiness that he applied, not to others, but to himself. As a friend he was generous and supportive, and never a bit inclined to evil, but at the same time, he was cynical – he said that dogs and humans were the same species. To adopt an expression of Oscar Wilde's, he was a person who "knows the price of everything and the value of nothing."

Surrounded as he was by a cruel and terrible war, he was close friends with many writers and poets in the front lines. He did not criticize them, but chose himself to stand aside from the conflict. He lived among colors, in a tranquil and peaceful realm. He himself was the very image of the "Nguyệt bird," and lived in the world as a dreamer of fantasies, emitting ravishingly attractive calls, and visiting the moon at night. He made me think of the character Sơn Ca ("Mountain Song") in Vũ Khắc Khoan's play *Genghis Khan*.

Once, as I was looking through the pages of *A Hundred-Year Hairdo*, a photo dropped from the book by pure coincidence. Though it was old and darkened by time, I still could recognize the two young wanderers in the photo – they were Nghiêu Đề and Lâm Triết, squatting together on a dusty road, back in the days when they rented an attic together to paint and gather with their friends–a place where the owner also kept pigs and chickens. The air there was hard to breathe, both night and day, but they remained there a good many years nourishing their great dreams. Then Nghiêu Đề won the Silver Prize for his painting "Portrait" in the Spring Exhibition of 1961, and then Lâm Triết won the Gold Prize with his painting "Horse" in the Spring Exhibition of 1962. Nghiêu Đề is now dead, and Lâm Triết has ceased to "contend with the wild wind" – he has bade farewell to Saigon and is living quietly in the green surroundings of his home area in Bình Định.

Two wanderers on dusty roads with roll-up mats and shoulder bags; from left: Nghiêu Đề and Lâm Triết.
(Nghiêu Đề family, personal archives)

THREE PAINTINGS BY NGHIÊU ĐỀ MADE IN THE U.S. NEAR THE END OF HIS LIFE

1986: "Lotus Blossom Composition" ("Bố cục Sen"). This shows an elegant young woman rising from a group of lotus blossoms. It was completed only after Nghiêu Đề had moved to the U.S. with his family. The money he got for it enabled him to purchase a piano for his children. The journey this painting made has something of the marvelous about it. From San Diego it followed the purchaser back to Vietnam, and after a period passed into the hands of a different owner. Then it passed into the ownership of a third person, and has by now

"Lotus Blossom Composition," oil painting by Nghiêu Đề, 1986 *(from the collection of Nguyễn Văn Hưng)*

returned to the U.S. The image presented here is that of a photo taken by the author of this book in a house near Huntington Beach.

1988: "Banana Grove": Here a young girl nestled in a banana grove colored a tender green. Unlike the ripely developed young women beloved by Nghiêu Đề before 1975, here we have only young girls with the naïve aspect of the artist's own daughters. In contrast to his pre-75 paintings, the oils that Nghiêu Đề made in the U.S., while retaining the blue shades of his earlier painting, have traces of gold and red, bearing witness, apparently, to moments of happiness. This painting was purchased by someone who came down to San Diego from Los Angeles for that purpose – I don't remember who now owns the painting.

"Banana Grove" ("Vườn Chuối"), oil painting, Nghiêu Đề, 1988
(album, Nghiêu Đề family)

"Bé Saigon," portrait of Nghiêu Đề's youngest daughter (1998). Still unfinished, this is perhaps his last oil painting; he was at work on it a few months before his death.
(Nghiêu Đề family collection)

1998: "Bé Saigon": When Nghiêu Đề knew that he had fallen ill, he very quickly lost the bloom of health, but amid fits of pain that made him pale, he still strove to make a portrait of this, his youngest daughter, "Little Saigon," who was then nineteen years old. This was perhaps his last oil painting, still unfinished, made a few months before he died. This rare and meaningful painting still hangs in the San Diego home of Nguyễn Nghiêu Ngung (Cu Bi), a son of Nghiêu Đề.

Sketch by Chóe (the artist Nguyễn Hải Chí, made in 1993 upon meeting Nghiêu Đề again after 18 years *(Nghiêu Đề family, personal archives)*

The front and back covers of *The Selected Works of Nghiêu Đề*, Viet Art Society 1998. *(Ngô Thế Vinh, personal archives)*

Võ Phiến speaking at the publication ceremony of The Selected Works of Nghiêu Đề, May 1999. (*Photo by Phan Diên; Viễn Phố, personal archives)*

After Nghiêu Đề died on November 9, 1998 in San Diego, California, the Việt Art Society with great promptitude brought out a set of books entitled *The Selected Works of Nghiêu Đề*. It appeared the same year and included: The interview conducted by Nguiễn Ngu Í concerning his views on art (*Cyclopedia Magazine No.* 137, Sept. 15, 1962), memorials written about him by several of his friends, such as Thái Tuấn, Huỳnh Hữu Ủy, Trần Dạ Từ, Đỗ Quý Toàn, Du Tử Lê, and English adaptation by Lê Thọ Giáo; and, of greatest value, a number of rare paintings of his that his family was able to collect. Many of Nghiêu Đề's friends attended the publication event.

This belated article is written to commemorate my dear friend, and also to serve as a gift to his wife Giang and his children Cu Bi, Bé Búp and Bé Sài Gòn on the occasion of his nineteenth death anniversary.

Sài Gòn 1958
California 2014 – 2017

BETWEEN TWO CENTURIES
FIFTY-FIVE YEARS OF NGUYÊN KHAI'S ART
STILL AS POETIC AS EVER

Portrait of Nguyên Khai

NGUYÊN KHAI, BIOGRAPHICAL DATA

Real name: Nguyễn Phước Bửu Khải. He was born in Huế on Sept. 1, 1940. He studied two years (1960-61) at the Huế College of Fine Arts (Trường Cao Đẳng Mỹ Thuật Huế) and then transferred to the Gia Định College of Fine Arts (Trường Cao Đẳng Mỹ Thuật Gia Định) where he completed his third and fourth years of training (1962-63). In the year of his graduation from art school, 1963, he won a bronze prize in that year's Spring Art Exhibition in Saigon. He was one of a number of youths in the Administrative Council (Hội

Đồng Quản Trị) and from 1966 on played a distinctive role in the Association of Young Vietnamese Artists (Hội Họa Sĩ Trẻ Việt Nam). Nguyên Khai participated in just about every exhibition organized by that group (1966 –1975) as well as those that took place under the auspices of the Alliance Français (24 Gia Long Street, Saigon at the Centre Culturel Français on Đồn Đất Street) and the Goethe Institute (Phan Đình Phùng Street; 1968 – 1975).

The French art critic Marc Planchon, a person very focused on the members of the Association of Young Vietnamese Artists, wrote about Nguyên Khai in the October 1, 1964 issue of the Journal d'Extrême Orient:

"Il a tout juste vingt-quatre ans, et, d'apparence, cette maigreur famélique, et ce regard brûlant dans un visage émacié qui font songer à ces écoliers moyenâgeux, des temps scholastiques, plus nourris d'idées effervescentes que de bonne chair, dans leur effort vers la connaissance, plus heureux de constructions logiques sur des prémisses imaginaires, que de considérer simplement le fait matériel dans sa plate réalité."

(He is just twenty-four years old, and, in appearance, has the starving thinness, the burning look in an emaciated face reminiscent of the

Nguyên Khai as a scrawny student at the Spring 1965 Art Exhibition in Saigon.

NNEE — N. 4.766

JEUDI 1er OCTOBRE 1

LE JOURNAL D'EXTRÊME-ORIENT

AU HALL DE L'INFORMATION

ŒUVRES DE NGUYEN KHAI
Peintures ? ou poèmes peints ?

L'inauguration de l'exposi-
on, dimanche dernier, et le
mbre impressionnant de ré-
mpenses attribuées au pein-
au cours des dernières
nées, ont déjà été rapportés
r le J.E.O. Nous épargnerons
nc au lecteur une redite...
entrons directement dans le
du sujet.

Nguyên Khai, soutenu en
tte occasion par l'Association

par Marc PLANCHON

après un passage aux Beaux
Arts de Huê. Il a tout juste
vingt-quatre ans et, d'appa-
rence, cette maigreur famé-
lique et ce regard brûlant dans
un visage émacié qui font son-
ger à ces escholiers moyenna-
geux, des temps de la scho-
lastique, plus nourris d'idées

L'artiste, de nos jours,
plus qu'il ne voit. Sensibl
trouble profond du monde
derne, en pleine évolution
ciale, politique et économ
— et instable —, il est do
par une obscure poussé
terne, critique d'un état
mal équilibré entre des
et des insuffisances. L'ar
réagit et s'analyse. La na
extérieure en sa réalité d
rait ; elle n'est plus qu'un

Article by the art critic Marc Planchon in *Journal d'Extrême Orient*, October 1, 1964 on the Art Exhibition held in the Saigon News and Information Department with the title: "The Works of Nguyên Khai: Paintings? Or Painted Poems?"

medieval schoolboys, of scholastic times, who fed more on effervescent ideas than on good flesh, and in their effort towards knowledge, were happier with logical constructions on imaginary premises, than in simply occupying their minds material fact in its flat reality.)

If Marc Planchon could now meet Nguyên Khai again, more than half a century later, he would see a person still as scrawny as he was long ago, with the sole addition of the many marks made on his visage by the passage of time.

Nguyên Khai was stuck in Vietnam with his family for six years after 1975, and finally left as a boat person in 1981, settling in south California. There, he continued to paint and take part in exhibitions.

The year 2003 can be regarded as a turning point in the creative career of Nguyên Khai. He took part that year in an exhibition held in the meeting hall of the newspaper Viễn Đông ("Far East") in Little Saigon. That exhibition included works of his in which he had the audacity to create images out of chips removed from discarded computers. Though this was an example of "mixed media," these works nevertheless retained the beauty, harmoniousness, and dreamy poetic suggestiveness of his other productions. One can say that this was a pioneering step in his work, a fusion of the world of humankind with that of computers.

But at some point earlier than that, in 2000, Nguyên Khai had a successful exhibition at Artcore in Los Angeles. The art critic Collette Chattopadhyay wrote a review of the exhibition that included the following: "The works of Nguyên Khai conduct the gaze of the viewer in a delicate and complicated manner from the art of the royal courts of Asia and the perfect natural images of the sun, the moon, and the four seasons to contemporary images of machinery and computer parts and time-indicating watches. As if sending us signs of the new millennium about to arrive, these works cast a gaze at our cultural and social values at the end of the twentieth century together with the weighty accomplishments of the past, but at the same time step into the scientific and technical realm of the present age."

The works of Nguyên Khai employ many techniques: oil painting, mixed media, lacquery, monoprints, bas-relief, and ceramics, and are rich in style and content, encompassing both expressionism and abstraction. His work does not fall clearly into periods, but he continues to work steadily and to seek new paths, though he is now stepping into old age. His color combinations are more sure and practiced than ever.

His most recent exhibition was in Little Saigon in June 2016; it marked his fifty-fifth year of painting (1961 – 2016). That is more than half a lifetime, but perhaps age means nothing in the life of an artist whose creative fires still burn fiercely.

EXHIBITIONS

2016 Viet Bao Gallery, Westminster, California
2015 Viet Bao Gallery, Westminster, California
2012 Viet Art Gallery, Houston, Texas
2007 Palette Art Gallery, Houston, Texas
2006 Viet Bao Kinh Te Gallery, Garden Grove, California
2005 Viet Art Gallery, Houston, Texas
2004 Hoa Mai Gallery, Paris, France
2003 "Forty Years of Artistry", Vien Dong Gallery, California
2002 Vinh Loi Gallery, Saigon, Vietnam
2001 Old Courthouse Museum, California
2000 Artcore L.A. Gallery, California
1998 Cuttress Gallery, Pomona, California
1997 "Salt and Pepper," Inst. of Contemporary Art Gallery, San José, California
1996 Pacific Asia Museum, Pasadena, California
1995 Smithsonian Institution Traveling Exhibition
1995 Gallery at Boca Raton, Florida
1994 "East and West," Wignall Museum, California
1987 UCLA Art Gallery, Burbank, California
1982 UC Irvine Gallery of Art, California
1969 The Sao Paulo Biennial, Brazil

Two images of the artist's wife Lan Phương, a woman as devoted and resourceful as the wife of the poet Tú Xương, and also the inspiration for his poetic paintings.

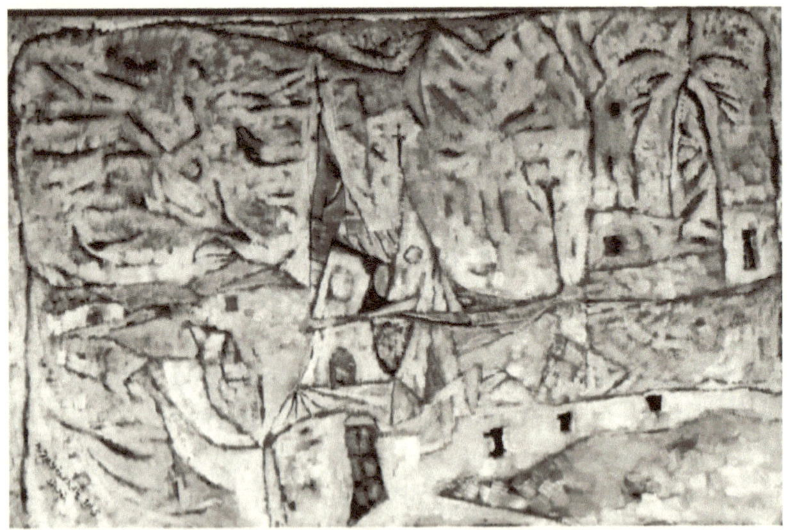

The painting "Church" ("Nhà Thờ"), 1965, made in a period of his life when, to avoid military service, Nguyên Khai lived in hiding, as if in an oasis.

1968 The New Delhi Biennial, India
1967 The Tokyo Biennial, Japan
1965 The Paris Biennial, France

ASSESSMENTS OF NGUYÊN KHAI

Though they include many types, the works of Nguyên Khai are comprised most significantly of oil paintings, both figurative and abstract, belonging to many different phases of his career. Regardless of their type, the reigning element in all these shining and poetic works is the beautiful, pure quality of the *stuff* – the matière – of the painting: the half-hidden and half-visible interplay of hues, which he managed with utter fluency.

Nguyên Khai pretending to drink manna from heaven during a moment of great happiness.

The art critic Huỳnh Hữu Uỷ in his *Modern Vietnamese Visual Arts* (Nghệ *Thuật Tạo Hình Việt Nam Hiện Đại*), 2008, had the following to say: "The paintings of Nguyên Khai are poems created by means of colors on canvases. They portray a limitlessly noble and poetic world that seems to have existed from the very beginning. His art is to make that preexisting world visible.

Let us see what Hoàng Ngọc Biên, the pioneering artist of the "new novel"in the South, who lived in the same neighborhood as Nguyên Khai, had to say about his friend: "Nguyên Khai has always been a quiet, deeply reflective person – both in his life and in his work. When he lived in the Tân Định district of Saigon, he lived alone and painted in almost complete solitude in a fairly spacious room, seldom communicating with any outsiders. Khai had a lot of friends, but he seemed to

CHRISTINE COTTER

Asian Families.

in U.S.

omen from North
st vulnerable, Ri-
e is no indication
, urbanized or pre-
ized women have

n a violent home at
hildren is battered
sometimes by a
epression, distrac-
oesn't realize what

endous amount of
their legal rights.
understand what
band abuse them
ontribute to their
by their inability
husband's right to
aid. "They're very
d out what their

CHRISTINE COTTER

Tran Lan Phuong and her husband Buu Khai are pictured in their home in Anaheim with their three children, Cong Huyen Bich Dao, 9, left, 7-month-old Cong Huyen Bao Quyen and Vinh Thang, 8.

other states to escape again—this time from the closeness of the communities and reprisals from their husbands.

sea, will not consider remarriage, Vo said.

Refugee women also worry that they will be blamed if their children

A newspaper article introducing Nguyên Khai and his family, *Los Angeles Times* May 30, 1998

lose little time socializing with them; it appeared that he reserved almost all his time seeking what was new in art. Saigon in those days was alive with enthusiasm for the works of Modigliani and Chagall. Nguyên Khai was perhaps not immune to the stimulation afforded by the works of those artists, but his own conversations with the moon, the stars, the heavens, and with people never came to an end. The paintings of Nguyên Khai, even when he adopted some new technique, always had a distinctive composition, and an unusual light. But the very quietude with which he pursued his aims enabled him to reflect the noisy concerns of his age. He was a thoroughgoing person.

The prose-writer and poet Nguyễn Đình Toàn made some insightful observations when he saw some paintings by Nguyên Khai: "the poetic and dreamy psychology of the artist always pervades everything lying beneath the colors and lines. It is as if he wants to conceal or diminish these qualities rather than openly display them."

The artist Đinh Cường, also a member of the Association of Young Vietnamese Artists, had this to say: "Nguyên Khai is an artist with a fully formed character, which may be seen in his poetic and dreamy paintings steeped in the scents and sounds of Huế, the place where he lived with his family in a roomy, old-fashioned dwelling in Gia Hội. The young women in his paintings have an aristocratic air, particularly in the double portraits, unique to him."

Adding his voice to the others, Trịnh Cung had these observations: "Throughout his more than half a century of artistic activity, Nguyên Khai, for me, has been like a honeybee, living unchanged in absolute quiet, and flying everywhere in search of rare flowers to obtain nectar for himself and others. Let us gaze at the paintings Nguyên Khai has created from his childhood to the present day. Whether oils or multimedia creations, their present beauty still pours forth sweetness; their endless poetic softness makes us feel that we have been lifted clear of the dark and cruel toils of mundane reality."

The poet Trịnh Y Thư once asked him to explain the relationship between art and reality. In answer, Nguyên Khai said, "Art does not turn its back on reality, but also does not illustrate reality. Art gives us another means of viewing things; a means of viewing things that are not realistic, so that the true nature of goodness and beauty can be expressed.

It seems that all artists of genius have a point of common agreement concerning the nature of art. When speaking of his own conception on this point, Nghiêu Đề also maintained that art is not something created by copying life, and used a witty metaphor: "The artist," he said, "is one who seeks the correct line between two mistaken lines offered by reality."

MATTERS ASSOCIATED WITH THE STATUE "TIME"

The sculpture "Time" ("Thời Gian") 1981, is the only work that Nguyên Khai created on the Galang Island in Indonesia. It was originally a piece of coral raised from the sea, and a milling knife was the only tool used by the artist to carve it.

Vĩnh Thăng, the artist's son, was just seven years old when he and his father came to the island. Later, having grown up in the U.S., he recorded the following recollections concerning this work:

"This piece of sculpture at first had no significance for me, but with the passage of time. I came to see that marvelous meanings lay concealed in it. Before, I thought that this work was an embodiment of a dream that had been gradually dying in my father's soul, but later I realized I was wrong. My father and I have different ways of looking at success. My father adheres to the Eastern concept. According to my father, success does not consist of riches or fame, but consists instead of inner growth and existence. I grew up in the U.S., so I have a more western way of thinking. But when I think of the time my father has lost, it is not obvious to me that he has lost anything. My father devoted all the time given to him to creation, to the art that he adored.

"My father made this piece of sculpture on Galang Island when our family had just managed to escape from Vietnam. It was the sole possession that my family brought into the U.S. It wasn't easy to bring it with us. I still clearly remember what took place that day. As we entered customs, they examined all our luggage. I can still see the expression of alarm in my father's eyes when the warning buzzer went off as my father's sculpture passed through the metal detector. My father's voice trembled as he spoke a few English words: "Art mine, I keep, O.K.?" It is our great good fortune that we have been

The sculpture "Time"
("Thời Gian"), 1981, the only work
created by Nguyên Khai on Galang
Island, made from a piece of coral
raised from the ocean and carved
only with a milling knife.

Nguyên Khai with his wife and children on Galang Island.

able to keep that work with us till the present day. We placed it in the living room, facing south."

"The work is attractive to look at, but held no meaning for me at the time. Bearing the colors of sea and sand, it is a portrait of an Asian girl with a well-bred, aristocratic appearance. My father once told me that the work stood not just for his own hope and desire, but much more. He was an artist whose freedom had been taken away when the communists had occupied the South by force. Our family escaped that place with the dream of seeking a free existence. My father's dream was not just for us but for himself as well. His whole dream was that he would be able to create freely and develop spiritually.

"I was mistaken at first when I thought that my father's dream was to become a famous and wealthy artist. I came to realize that it would be difficult for my father to become famous on American soil and that he would have to start from the beginning again. The U.S. was a new country, very different from our own; we had ahead of us only roads leading into the future, and the work entitled 'Time.'" (Excerpted from "The Time," by Vĩnh Thăng, The Writers Post, July 1999)

REACHING THE DREAM HOUSE

When I came to Nguyên Khai's house, I usually went together with Đổ Hoàng and his wife. Đổ Hoàng was my colleague in medicine, but Đường Thiện Đồng had been the playmate of Bửu Khải (ie Nguyên Khai) when they were still both toddlers in the Gia Hội elementary school. Đổ Hoàng's house had quite a few paintings by Nguyên Khai on display, so I was in the habit of referring to it jokingly as the "Nguyên Khai mini-museum." I made Nguyên Khai's acquaintance in the 60s, perhaps around the same time as I got to know my close friend Nghiêu Đề.

The living room where Lan Phương Nguyên Khai's wife (a "Madame Tú Xương of our era like the wife of Nguyễn Đình Toàn; see Chapter Eight) received guests was in the upper part of the house. But each time I went there, I liked to descend to his studio. I say "studio," but it was actually just a small, poorly lit garage – it was

Nostalgia in the Paintings of Nguyên Khai "In New York Also, The Cathedral of the Holy Mother" (Cũng Có Nhà Thờ Đức Bà ở New York), 2009.

sometimes necessary to use a few lamps there to do work, even in the daytime.

Among other people, Nguyễn Đình Toàn was amazed at this and wrote, "Any person of normal judgement must wonder how anyone can make paintings in such conditions."

The paintings of Nguyên Khai were not only beautiful, but at times imbued with dreamy nostalgia. Even when he wandered among the skyscrapers of New York, the outlines of Saigon's Cathedral of the Holy Mother might reappear to him in imagination from some day in the distant past (painting: "In New York Also, the Cathedral of the Holy Mother," 2009)

The upper level of his house may have been neatly arranged, but down in his studio, canvasses were stacked on each other every which-way, tubes of paint and stubbly brushes, sometimes still wet, sometimes dry and stiff, still smeared with color, creating a jumble that seemed to leave no room for a person to walk. Paintings, some familiar, some new, were piled on top of each other, and there would be an unfinished work still on the easel.

Nguyên Khai was always pleasantly animated when talking about paintings in progress. How would the meaning of the painting turn out in the end? This was sometimes a surprise to the artist himself–something he could not foresee in advance. Unforeseen shifts of this sort often occur both in painting and literature.

Behind this garage full of paintings was a small spot reserved for a garden, a peaceful spot that I was fond of lingering in. The area was very small. Aside from a few bonsai trees that Nguyên Khai shaped and trimmed himself, the space had fruit trees of the four seasons–guavas, crispy persimmons, oranges, limes, and grapefruit, a row of red pomegranates, and rarest of all, a starfruit tree that had not yet begun to bear fruit. One could see from this that Nguyên Khai knew how to tend trees. Even if a tree came from a different spot and had

Painting no. 24 (Tranh Số 24) by Nguyên Khai, 1967 (recently found in the collection of an Arizona Gallery).

An unfinished painting resting on an easel in Nguyên Khai's garage studio.

Bird and Lunar Eclipse (Chim và Nguyệt Thực), lacquer painting, Nguyên Khai

Imperial City (Hoàng Thành), lacquer painting, Nguyên Khai, 1987

Painting of a Horse (Tranh Ngựa), Nguyên Khai, 1993

Tea, Early and Late
(Trà Sớm Trà Muộn),
still life, Nguyên Khai, 2001

With My Mother's Tea Set,
in Remembrance of the Day
She Died (Với Bộ Đồ Trà của Mẹ,
Tưởng Nhớ Ngày Mẹ Mất), still life,
Nguyên Khai, 2001

Conductive Circuit (Mạch Dẫn), mixed media, Nguyên Khai, 1995

The Smile of the Buddha
(Nụ Cười Đức Phật), bas relief,
Nguyên Khai *(collection of Đổ Hoàng, Newport Beach)*

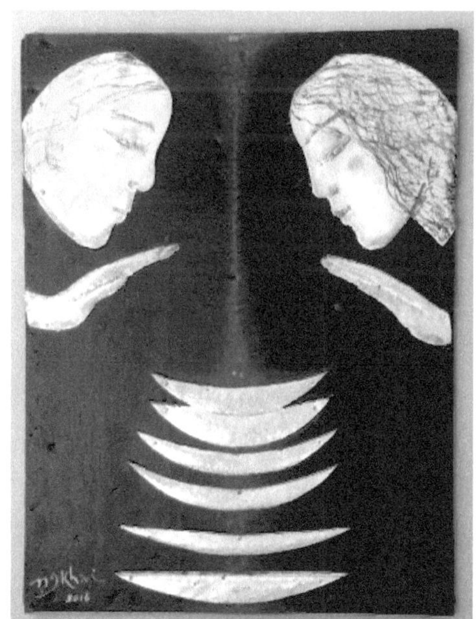

Lunar Eclipse (Nguyệt Thực), Nguyên Khai, 2016;
in the Exhibition "Fifty-five Years of the Art of Nguyên Khai"
(55 Năm Hội Họa Nguyên Khai) 1961– 2016

From Saigon 1975 to Houston 2005, seven members of the Association of Young Vietnamese Artists meeting each other again after thirty years: from left: Đinh Cường, Nguyễn Phước, Nguyên Khai, Nguyễn Lâm, Nguyễn Trung, Hồ Hữu Thủ, and Trịnh Cung.

not fruited for years, it would bear fruit copiously a year after being moved to this spot.

Gazing at the paintings, the bonsai trees and the colors of the fruits in the garden provided me with moments of delightful relaxation. When night overspread the sky, and I would step inside, there was always a delicious meal on the table, and on leaving the house, I was never empty-handed – I would always have a sack of hand-picked fruit, or a package of *xôi vò* or sticky rice – a purely Northern delicacy, not something provided by "Mệ Bửu Khải" [childhood name of Nguyên Khai] to show off the culinary skills of his wife."

LITTLE SAIGON: A CULTURAL SKETCH

Nguyên Khai lived contentedly with his family for many years in a little house in Tustin, Orange County, not far from Little Saigon. The first time I went there, Trịnh Cung, who was with me, exclaimed, "This is a house one can dream of!"

The Exhibition "Paintings of Nguyên Khai, 2016"; from right: Nguyên Khai and Ngô Thế Vinh.

The Exhibition "Paintings of Nguyên Khai, 2016"; from left: Nguyên Khai and his wife Lan Phương; Ngô Thế Vinh and Trịnh Cung.

As I mentioned earlier in my portrait of Mai Thảo (Chapter Five,) I was distressed to find, after the death of that writer, that his "desk-in-exile" (bàn-viết-lữ-thứ), one of the sole items in his meagerly furnished room, had disappeared – my hope had been to preserve it as part of a memorial to his life and work in Little Saigon.

We must hope that a "Nguyên Khai Gallery" will appear in virtual space, perhaps with an address such as "nguyenkhaiart.com," and that the "dreamed-of house" (to borrow Trịnh Cung's expression) in Tustin, Orange County, together with a number of paintings will be included in it, so as to add a distinctive color to the culture of the first generation of Vietnamese to live in the "refugee capital" of the nation.

Tustin, California, June 10, 2016

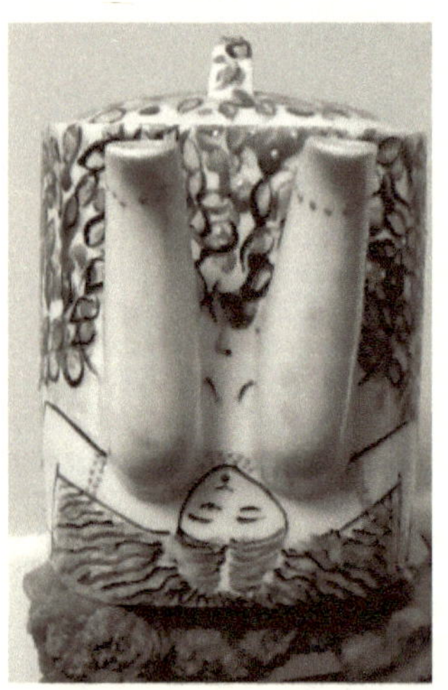

A drawing on an enamel tea vase

Nguyên Khai's bonsai art

The red pomegranates, persimmons, starfruits, and grapefruits: fruits of the four seasons next to Nguyên Khai's backyard garden wall

MY GUN BROKE IN MARCH CAO XUÂN HUY DUELS WITH THE GOD OF DEATH

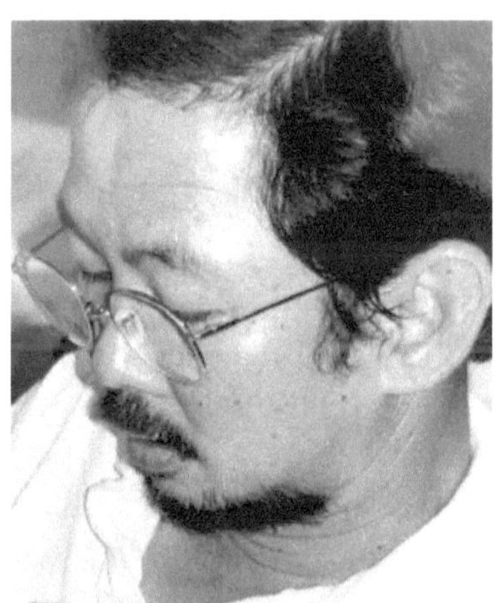

Cao Xuân Huy in everyday life
(Trịnh Y Thư, personal archives)

The writer Cao Xuân Huy died on November 12, 2010–so six years have passed since then. What appears below is an article written jointly by Ngô Thế Vinh, Nguyễn-Xuân Hoàng, and Trịnh Y Thư to remember the author of *My Gun Broke in March* on the occasion of his sixth death anniversary.

CAO XUÂN HUY, BIOGRAPHICAL DATA

Born in September, 1947; father's family from Bắc Ninh, mother's from Hà Nam in North Vietnam.

October 1954: emigrated to the South with his mother.
February 1968: enlisted in the Marine Corps of the Republic of Vietnam.
March 1975: arrested and imprisoned.
September 1979: released from prison.
December 1982: escaped from Vietnam by sea.
October 1983: came to the U.S. .
1984: settled in South California
2005: became the editor of the journal *Literary Studies* (*Văn Học*), remaining in that position until April, 2008.
November 12, 2010: died in Lake Forest, South California

WORKS:

My Gun Broke in March (Tháng Ba Gãy Súng), 1985
A Few Small Matters (Vài Mẩu Chuyện), 2010

PERSONAL ELEMENTS IN CAO XUÂN HUY'S *MY GUN BROKE IN MARCH*

I'm not a writer, just a soldier, a combat soldier, in the literal meaning of that expression, and the things I write about in this book are simply events, events that are a hundred per cent true, recounted in words. I write about the things that we soldiers have directly taken part in, but which no one has written about, while things that *many* people have written about, no one has experienced.

Among people about the same as me – people who were less than ten when they emigrated from the North to the South – except for a few who had close family members who had been killed by the Việt Cộng – almost no one really hated the Việt Cộng, because who, among the youngsters my age and younger, had the slightest idea who the Việt Cộng were? A similar observation can be made with regard to people who were less than ten when they emigrated with their parents to the U.S. after 1975 and now live here. They hate the Việt Cộng to be sure, but it is merely a hatred passed down in the family: Their mothers and fathers hate the Việt Cộng, so they do the same, but there is nothing intense about their feeling.

So, when I grew older, and had some ability to judge things on my own, there was a disadvantage I could not get over: The Southern Republic's system of propaganda had more the effect of "anti-propaganda" than of propaganda proper. So, when I entered the armed services, I volunteered to enter a unit that engaged in actual combat, not so much because I hated the enemy, but more because my surging, youthful blood was stimulated by battlefield situations.

Nevertheless, because I was in a unit that regularly engaged in combat, I shared in its dangers, and in its common experience of life and death. I felt bound to my comrades-in-arms, as if we were all blood brothers. I loved my unit, and I loved the colors of my cap and shirt. I loved my superiors and I loved our unit commanders. I calmly accepted all the bad habits of my superiors and commanders, and I myself had a great many bad habits.

But when my two commanders were a colonel in charge of a brigade and a lieutenant colonel in charge of a sub-brigade including four combat battalions plus supporting units, amounting in all to about four thousand men, ran to save themselves when their troops were hard-pressed, I was overcome with rage. I killed the Việt Cộng without the slightest hesitation, but not because I hated them. I did so because there was a clear line between us and the Việt Cộng, we were on opposite sides of a war front, when the two met, we had to use every means in our power to kill each other. But when one's leaders turned into deserters, one had to lose belief in them and be overcome with shame, because these were people whom one had respected and whose orders one had striven to obey absolutely.

The captain of a ship must live and die with his ship; the commander of a unit must live and die with his unit. What I wish to speak of is a commander's spirit of responsibility. A person who possesses power but is devoid of a sense of responsibility, is no different from a traitor. We lost, not because the enemy was strong, but because there were too many traitors and cowards. It is due to my hatred of the cowardice and irresponsibility of of our commanders that the images of the final days before the brigade dispersed and was captured, due to terror inspired by a company of guerilla soldiers in the last half of 1975 are like a film clip lying in my memory – all I must do is press a button, and the scenes unfold with complete clarity accompanied by all the thoughts and feelings I was subject to at the time.

I have carried all these pain-filled, shameful memories for a dozen years now, throughout my years of imprisonment, and my passage through refugee camps. And now, in the U.S., I read in a newspaper a statement made by a former Vietnamese general, that was more or less as follows: "Losing the country was everybody's fault; those in high positions must be considered greatly at fault, while those in lesser positions, to be slightly at fault." It occurred to me immediately that those who stabbed the warriors in the back and those warriors who offered their backs to be stabbed by their chiefs were equally at fault. This was the button that set the film in motion and impelled me to relate this story.

What I want to say in this book is that there is no one who does not turn to look at the place where he has just tumbled down, and also there is no one who does not turn to look at the shit he has just excreted. To take a spill is one's own fault, and if one's shit stinks, the shit is still one's own – so why, for the past dozen years, has no one turned to look at the fault that caused him to fall into his own pile of shit, but has only given vent to curses and tirades against others– the unusually courageous ones admit only to a generally shared offense: "those in high positions are greatly at fault, while those in minor positions are slightly at fault," in the manner of the saying that "the nation's survival or destruction is the responsibility even of the lowliest commoner." If the lowliest commoner is at fault, then who is without fault? Thus, I too must admit to being at fault."

I forget who it was who said the following: "The rulers and officers of a former dynasty need have no shame for anything whatsoever, because when they had a lord and held power in their hands, they were unable to accomplish even the slightest deed, so now that there remains to them only a shelf for their robes and a bag of rice, how can they accomplish anything aside from the clothes-shelf and the rice bag?

My Gun Broke in March (Tháng Ba Gãy Súng), first published by Văn Khoa, 1986; republished by Văn Học (*Literary Studies*) in 2004. This is the most frequently republished war Memoir in overseas Vietnamese communities.

Our land is not a chessboard which, once a game has been lost, can be swept clean in order to set up pieces for a new game in which the generals are still generals, and the troops are still troops. It is not as if all the slaughtered chariots, horses, and pawns can be set up again in readiness for a new battle.

That those who lost their intellect and were devoid of courage as well, and were capable of nothing but the contemptible ability to use the courage of others, so that they at length had no recourse but to flee the country, deceiving everyone so that the millions who had the courage to fight had to enter prison camps–that such people should still be so shameless as to appear before the public as "fathers and mothers of the people"–is simply too much to be borne. Though their contemporaries may be able to overlook their stinking and cowardly past, history will be incapable of absolving them. Even the words "anti-communist" once borne by the high-ranking ones are no longer appropriate; the expression must be saved for a generation that will replace them. Only those adopting a new stance will be worthy of the term. Only when names are correct and language is fitting can the Việt Cộng be vanquished and the nation recovered. Only the mute and lowly pawns who were sent here and there with bowed heads, and the new leaders of today are qualified to assume such roles.

This volume is not a novel but a memoir. This is because I have never been a writer, and because I have no expertise with regard to arranging events in a narrative structure. As for the word "March," everyone will know what that means. As for "my gun broke," I wish to speak of a matter painful to any soldier: a gun with no ammunition has no more value than a piece of rotten wood–I myself have led assault companies to their objectives with nothing to fire with but my mouth. Could our guns have been broken if ammunition had still been supplied to us? This is what I wish to express with the words "my gun broke."

And I call *My Gun Broke in March* a memoir because I accept full responsibility for everything recorded in it, for all the place names, for all the names of individuals, and for all the names of military units. All the accounts of what happened are true, one hundred per cent true. I have not introduced even the smallest fictional detail. I have no doubt forgotten a great deal, and because of the lowness of my rank and responsibilities, there were no doubt many factors that I was not aware of. I have included everything that I saw with my eyes and heard with my ears, as well as all the orders that I was given, and all the orders that I carried out.

If *My Gun Broke in March* were a novel, I would have to place a disclaimer at the beginning, saying: The characters and events in this book are all the imaginary creations of the author;

any resemblance they may have to real persons or occurrences are purely coincidental… While the fact of the matter is that the only thing contrary to my wishes is that I may have insufficient skill to write all the things I must write. *Cao Xuân Huy.*

NGUYỄN-XUÂN HOÀNG READS CAO XUÂN HUY

"My Gun Broke in March." What initially attracted me to the book was its title. It was a simple title. A gun breaking in March was a simple and attractive idea. March was the month the Central Region met with disaster, when the red tornado from the north whirled southward. Some more time had to pass before the horde could pour into beloved Saigon on the miserable and fearsome occasion known as "Black April." Cao Xuân Huy raises the question: "Who wrecked the guns of our army, the guns of our courageous soldiers, so full of experience and strategic skill? Who tied their hands, when they still had guns, but had nothing in their ammunition bags?"

The author allows us to see that in the lower ranks the people and the things they did reflected a loss of faith in a number of people in positions of command, "elder brothers worthy of respect" who when hard-pressed deserted their troops and ran away to save their skins, without concerning themselves about whether those they left behind lived or died!

My Gun Broke portrays a gigantic flood that took place in a pitiless war, and submerged the destiny of an entire people. On the sandy banks next to the upheaval, people heard the sounds of skulls cracking beneath the tracks of tanks.

It is a book with very few smiles, but with great quantities of blood and tears. The element of happiness is slight and dry, whereas that of pain and misery is richly abundant; cruelty and hatred are commonplace, while mildness and correct behavior are distant things.

The writing style of *My Gun Broke in March* is simple, natural, and luminously clear. But the reader knows full well that to be able to produce all those words that appear so natural, Cao Xuân Huy had to pay a rather high price; he had to duel with the God of Death in hairs-breadth situations in order to maintain his human dignity. One can say that *My Gun Broke in March* was written in passion before being polished by a practised literary pen. This fact does nothing to diminish the vitality of this work.

Anyone fond of reading books knows that world-famous authors, such as Flaubert, Hemingway, Dickens, and Tolstoy all employed a simple and natural style when they wrote.

Once when I met the author, I asked him why he characterized *My Gun Broke in March* as a memoir rather than as a story (*truyện kể*) or a historical narrative (*truyện ký*). He replied, "Because I refrained from putting the slightest fictional detail into it. Everything I wrote in the book were things that my eyes saw and my ears heard. I regret only that my abilities are not sufficient to write everything I needed to write."

It is true enough that fiction is essential to literature, but reality is itself so huge and deep that a modest imagination is sometimes poor and shallow by comparison. Or, putting it another way, we can say that though fiction is necessary to art, reality must always provide the basis required for fiction to assume a firm and stable form.

It is this element of reality that has endowed the pen of Cao Xuân Huy with such special color, and has filled *My Gun Broke in March* with a fiery freshness that no work of fiction could hope to achieve.

And the art of Cao Xuân Huy lies in his ability to endow his work with a persuasiveness stronger than that of reality itself.

What most appeals to me in *My Gun Broke in March* are its bits of dialogue. They are unedited, but neither superfluous nor commonplace. They have not passed through the filtration system of "literary theory." They are alive and sharp. And they are very close to us, the readers.

In answer to someone who asked him what motives impelled him to write the book, he said "There is no one who does not turn to look at the place where he has just tumbled down, and also there is no one who does not turn to look at the shit he has just excreted. To take a spill is one's own fault, and if one's shit stinks, the shit is still one's own–so why, for the past dozen years, has no one turned to look at the fault that caused him to fall into his own pile of shit, but has only given vent to curses and tirades against others."?

This statement naturally has aspects that need to be discussed and further explored, but here, in the context of *My Gun Broke in March*, this statement has its own way of being understood.

Before taking up his pen and writing of the days and months in the history of a battle of which he himself is one of the witnesses, Cao Xuân Huy was a warrior in a branch of service heard of by all; the Marines.

In terms of lived experience Cao Xuân Huy has all that it takes to convey the realities of the battlefield in his pages of fiery prose.

As Cao Xuân Huy observes, "Our land is not a chessboard which, once a game has been lost, can be swept clean in order to set up pieces for a new game in which the generals are still generals, and troops are still troops. It is not as if all the slaughtered chariots, horses, and pawns can be set up again in readiness for a new battle."

But this thought of his is not a place where he wishes to come to a halt. It is offered rather as a thought that can make us wish to reflect further.

After turning over the final page of *My Gun Broke in March*, the reader feels that there is something still unfinished. The final period in the story of our nation's destiny can only appear on the page of a subsequent volume.

But in any case, the cruel and horrifying images and the feelings of anxiety and fear remain in us like a sediment.

And in that sediment there also remain place names, local scenes, familiar venues in withered regions of the rural countryside, including the weather conditions in those regions which our own bodies have withstood, and above all, there remain in us the images of people–including ourselves–enshrouded in the bleak and lonely destinies brought upon us by violent historical upheavals.

All these people and events seem to have appeared only yesterday as we read this book, and seem to be still moving and evolving somewhere around us.

In *My Gun Broke in March*, Cao Xuân Huy has pages of prose that describe human beings in an honest and simple way, a thing that Ernest Hemingway said was "the most difficult to achieve in the world."

Nguyễn-Xuân Hoàng
Santa Anna, April 1986
(Source: Talawas http://talawas.org/talaDB/show/File.)

We are informed also that *My Gun Broke in March* has been reprinted 14 times, and that there are copies of the book in all the libraries of the world. There is perhaps no other book in overseas communities that has been reprinted so many times or which has been sought by so many people. The book has also been introduced in its entirety in the novel *A Season When the Ocean Stirred* (*Mùa Biển Động*) by Nguyễn Mộng Giác."

The book *A Few Small Matters* (*Vài Mẩu Chuyện*), a short story collection, pub. by Văn Học (*Literary Studies*) in 2010

Cao Xuân Huy was full of gaiety and laughter throughout a signing session in a meeting room in the offices of the *Việt Herald* in Little Saigon on July 10, 2010

A DIFFERENT CAO XUÂN HUY

Based on my friendship of many years with Huy, and with the agreement of his wife and his two daughters, Chúc Dung and Xuân Dung, this article will now turn to medical matters and speak of a different Cao Xuân Huy, a man afflicted with illness perched vertiginously on a path leading to death who fought with all his strength against his illness until the final seconds and minutes, and departed this life with all his dignity intact.

Melanoma is a type of cancer that develops from melanocytes – cells that produce the pigment melanin – the element that determines the skin colors of the various races. Usually, melanoma is a type of skin cancer, but the eye also may be the place where this type of cancer develops, though this is somewhat rare. Eye melanoma is not as easy to identify as skin melanoma. When discovered, it is often too late. That was Cao Xuân Huy's situation. He suddenly found one day that when he closed one eye, he saw nothing with the other. He informed me of this right away.

When one suddenly loses vision in one eye, one thinks at first of other urgent factors that might have this result (such as retinal detachment, stroke, migraine, or glaucoma) instead of eye cancer. A Vietnamese eye doctor who was the first to examine Huy and make a clinical diagnosis said that this might be the result of a rare mushroom-like growth on the retina. But a few days later, before much time had passed, UCLA provided Huy with an accurate diagnosis: ocular melanoma. From this point on I shall refer to his condition simply as eye-melanoma.

For unknown reasons, there are greater numbers of people who suffer from eye-melanoma among those who, unlike Huy, are white-skinned and have blue eyes. But perhaps another explanation can be considered: the oncogenic (cancer-causing) effect of prolonged over-exposure to sunlight–Huy might be considered "over-qualified" for this, due to his long years as a soldier in all four military districts (bốn vùng chiến thuật), and after that, his years of heavy labor in Vietnam's tropical prisons. We might further postulate that his condition may have been due to a "mutated gene" that issued a random order for all his melanin cells to keep multiplying instead of successively growing old and dying, as normal cells do. Medical science has identified molecular markers found in chromosomes that may be used to identify metastases.

Eye-melanoma is a rare and insidious type of cancer that, when discovered, has produced metastases in more than fifty per cent of cases, so the life expectancy of the patients concerned is very short: from two to seven months. Only about fifteen per cent of such patients live longer than twelve months. The reason for this is that eye-melanoma with liver-metastases resists every sort of treatment.

Eye-melanoma may at first present no symptoms whatsoever, and when symptoms do appear there may be nothing unusual about them–they may consist simply of flashing lights, blurred vision, aching in the eye from glaucoma-caused pressure, or, as in Huy's case, loss of vision; and its clinical progression is very uncertain prior to the appearance of metastatic symptoms in the liver, lungs, brain, or bones.

Investigative and diagnostic methods for this illness include: blood tests to determine liver function, ultrasonic tests to discover growths within the eye, ocular blood-flow tests with contrast agents, and possibly biopsies to see if any growths in the eye are cancerous. These tests must then be repeated at intervals, and followed up by further blood tests, lung X-rays, and CT and MRI scans so as to catch any metastases at an early stage. UCLA applied nearly all of these standard procedures to Cao Xuân Huy.

But the decisive factor is still time. Tests sometimes show that liver function is still normal even after the illness has invaded that organ in the form of micrometastases, or very small groups of cancerous cells.

Skin-melanoma and eye-melanoma have a shared designation, but they are actually two different "beasts." Chemotherapy can be an effective treatment for skin-melanoma, but it has almost no effect on the other illness. Little data has been gathered on the treatment of metastases coming from eye-melanoma. Treatment of metastases is considered effective if the tumors concerned shrink by fifty per cent or more. Shrinkage of fifteen per cent or less is no different from what might occur with a placebo, and in such cases, chemo treatments are generally discontinued, since they serve no purpose and would only increase the physical misery of the patient in the short time still remaining to him.

Cao Xuân Huy was not a candidate for surgery. He was given radiation therapy from the start in the afflicted eye in the form of brachytherapy, or the implantation of radioactive seeds.

After receiving this treatment, Cao Xuân Huy continued to be closely followed by UCLA. Because he could only see with one eye, his depth perception was significantly affected, but he calmly continued to live as usual, driving every day the fairly long distance from his home in Lake Forest to his place of work in Little Saigon. He found that it was more difficult to drive when he returned home after dark.

Chemotherapy is used to treat melanoma both of the skin and of the eyes. The chemicals are fed into the veins and carried by the

Cao Xuân Huy's smile

blood to the cancerous areas, where they quickly kill the "enemy" cells. An unavoidable side result, however, is that healthy cells are killed as well. And so there are endless side effects that compel quite a few patients to terminate their treatment. These effects may include depression, fatigue, nausea, weight loss, and a reduction in the quantity of white blood cells, leading to a reduced ability to fight off illnesses that may themselves cause death. Advances in treatment have led to the introduction of new medicines that can reduce the severity of these side effects. Only about twenty per cent of skin-melanoma patients respond to these treatments. We do not yet have any type of chemotherapy effective in treating metastases resulting from eye-melanoma, as in the case of Cao Xuân Huy.

The metastatic tumors resulting from this type of melanoma are of more than one kind, and since many of them appear throughout the liver, surgical resection is not an option in these cases.

To sum up, some types of cancer can be cured, but one can only say that eye-melanoma with metastates is not yet on that list; it is among the most malignant of cancers, and remains a challenge to be addressed by medicine in the twenty-first century.

Just as in his writing, in which Cao Xuân Huy calmly set down all that was good and bad in his experiences, he now spoke with same calm of his eye cancer, while those who listened to him could not escape feelings of sharp concern and alarm. After meeting with Huy, a close friend of his said, "his illness is a desperate one, but he acts in such a way that he is a source of comfort to others!"

As I followed the developments in Huy's condition, I came to realize that he might be termed "a model patient." He gave up alcohol with ease, and acted with strict personal discipline in all phases of his treatment. He received the most advanced care available, as was his due. And in return, he supplied to medicine a perfect "case study" to use in the effort to conquer this savage type of eye cancer.

Huy courageously bore everything, rising serenely above the miseries resulting from treatments that held little promise of victory. He was warned in advance that if he accepted treatment, the quality of the days and months he had left might be affected, and might even be reduced in number.

Huy and I continued to communicate with each other on a weekly basis by cell phone. This would usually take place on Thursdays after his return from an appointment at UCLA. I was usually the one who made the phone call, but on one occasion Huy called me first to inform me that a CT scan at UCLA had revealed the presence of a small tumor in his liver. With eye-melanoma, this can often be the result of a metastasis, but it also could have been a "primary tumor"–the incidence of hepatitis B among Vietnamese and other Asians is quite high. In any case, his condition was very hard to treat.

Cao Xuân Huy with his wife and two daughters,
Chúc Dung and Xuân Dung. *(Cao Xuân Huy family archives)*

The soldier Cao Xuân Huy
with his aged mother in 2007
(TQLC, Australia, archives)

Cao Xuân Huy
and his wife in 2007.
(Cao Xuân Huy family archives)

The following week, Huy's daughter took her father into UCLA to get a biopsy, and didn't hear her father make the slightest complaint during this painful procedure. The biopsy confirmed that the tumor was a metastatic growth caused by Huy's eye-melanoma. This could not be treated with surgery, but radiation and chemotherapy were of no use in treating this kind of metastasis. The battle that lay ahead for Huy was fiercer still. He was thoroughly aware that the prognosis was dim, but he nevertheless accepted a round of chemotherapy, the first, that would involve receiving a dose each Wednesday for six weeks. Huy endured the first round with ease, though he of course experienced various side-effects from the chemicals. During this period, he continued to drive to work and meet with his friends on weekends. The evaluation after this first round showed that the metastatic tumor had stabilized; it had not grown or spread. It was like a bit of light at the end of the tunnel, but it still cannot be said that the treatment was successful. In this very unequal battle, the first victory was not one of elimination, but one in which the enemy is made to "halt in his tracks." Huy accepted a second round of chemotherapy that would also involve weekly visits to the hospital for six weeks.

The losses suffered by the enemy in this second round cannot be known, but it was plain that Huy began to pay a heavy price. After his first treatment, Huy let the people with him know that, aside from the familiar side-effects, he felt pain in his whole body this time, as if his "flesh was being torn apart"–his own words. Huy had never been accustomed to cry out in response to pain–it appeared that his "pain threshold was quite high. Even pain on the order of 10/10 did not tempt him to give up the battle. When the second week came Huy insisted on continuing the treatment, even though the staff was hesitant. Again, he felt that his flesh was being torn apart, but this time the pain was greater and lasted for several days, so that he needed to take pain suppressants. This marked an important turning point in his treatment. It was a decision reached by the staff treating him, not by Huy. His hardihood and strength of spirit was out of all proportion to his physical condition. He needed a period of respite before another course of treatment could begin.

Then the third round of treatment began. Huy was informed that the metastatic tumor was bigger, and that there were now more such tumors in his liver. Huy himself felt that the region around his liver was bigger and harder than before, and that eating and drinking was difficult. From that point on, Huy lost color and weight, and became rapidly weaker, though his spirit was still resilient. He was calm as always, and did not appear to regret anything.

Once when I met Huy, he was already too weak to stand steadily on his feet – he was close to collapsing on the floor, but he still was unwilling to grasp the hands of people next to him.

There was thus nothing UCLA could do anymore, and they sent Huy back home with his family doctor. Rather than entering a hospice, Huy continued to live at home, cared for lovingly by his wife and two daughters.

Sunday, November 7, 2010 was the engagement ceremony of Huy's second daughter (Xuân Dung). It was organized earlier by the family so that Huy would be able to share in his daughter's happiness. I later became aware that though Cao Xuân Huy was a bold and manly

The green beret Cao Xuân Huy (left) meeting with his RVN marine comrades. (Marines of the Republic of Vietnam, archives)

fellow, he was not devoid of fear – he was very fearful of his second daughter. He was sometimes able to ignore bits of advice that I gave him, but anything that Xuân Dung requested of him he received like an order – I knew for sure that he would do it.

After that day, Huy's waves of pain would make him curl up like a fetus, but he still didn't want to take many pain suppressants. He finally needed morphine in quantities that were increased every two hours every day, but this only partly suppressed the savage assaults of his pain. Huy still bore up against it stoically, never groaning or complaining, and still at moments smiled and laughed when close friends or associates who revered him came to visit.

Five days later, on a Saturday afternoon at 4:53 p.m. on November 12, 2010, Huy died peacefully and with fulfilled wishes, still in the loving care of his wife and daughters, as well as two other people who were close friends; one of them, Dr. Nguyễn Đức, had just arrived from Florida; he had been close to Huy since childhood. The other, Trần Như Hùng, was a friend from their days in the armed forces of the Republic of Vietnam; he had just arrived, barely in time, from Australia.

Cao Xuân Huy with friends; from the right: Hoàng Khởi Phong, Hoàng Chính Nghĩa, Cao Xuân Huy and Ngô Thế Vinh *(photo by Phạm Bích Hoan, 2006)*

From the right: Cao Xuân Huy, Hoàng Khởi Phong, Hoàng Chính Nghĩa, Khánh Trường, Phan Nhật Nam.
(Khánh Trường, personal archives)

Traversing the vertiginous road that leads to death, pitted against an enemy much stronger than himself, Cao Xuân Huy behaved always like a model patient, fought his final battle with spirit, and departed this world with all his dignity intact.

A POEM IN MARCH, TRỊNH Y THƯ

I received Trịnh Y Thư's email message on Nov. 12, 2016, the sixth death anniversary of Cao Xuân Huy. It included a poem he wrote on the night of the day that CXH breathed his last. The photo attached to the message was one that Trịnh Y Thư took at the moment when CXH's ashes were released at Laguna Beach a hundred days later.

Surrender To The Waves In March

In March the heights of heaven are the shade of blood,
And vultures strike the knell, a spreading pall of death.
In March the corpses of the young and old
Lie cold and still together listening to the whistling wind.
Along the reedy bank of Cửa Việt, the waves emit a roar;

The city's unfamiliar; the advancing waves are homeless;
Names and deeds are lost like wisps of hair;
Night descends, and rains pour down as in a dream;
The wine is red, the blood adheres, there's nothing to be done;
A haggard yellow orchid waits my coming by the gate.
The bitter bullets of the past still swell our wounded flesh.
March returns to red and sandy shores,
March drifts off like mountain mist,
The soil strange, the resting place all strange
Beyond the peaks one hears the caves still roaring
Dull and dark at night beneath the moon,
He sees approach the day his flesh will change to ash
He lies in realms all strange and sees the former sea,
the sand all white, the houses browned with coconuts,
Oh carry him away in March.

(Trịnh Y Thư, November 11, 2010)

California, Nov. 12, 2010

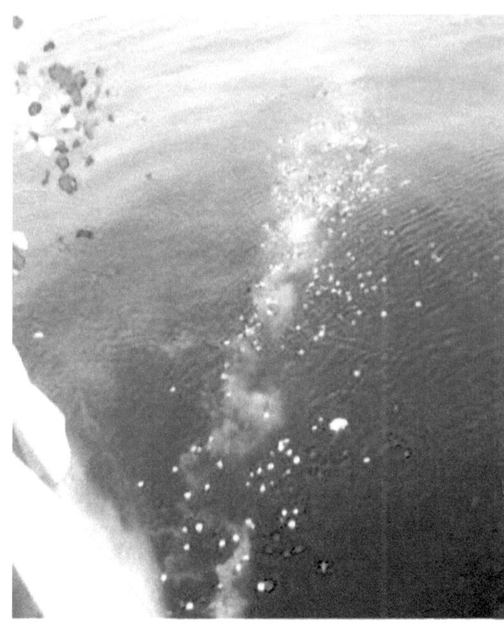

The scattering of
Cao Xuân Huy's ashes
in the sea
by Laguna Beach,
100 days after his death

PHÙNG NGUYỄN
AS IF WE NEVER BADE HIM FAREWELL

Phùng Nguyễn, California, May 2015
(photo by Ngô Thế Vinh)

"The only certainty in this life is uncertainty"
Sent to all friends of Phùng Nguyễn

PHÙNG NGUYỄN, BIOGRAPHICAL DATA

The writer Phùng Nguyễn, real name Nguyễn Đức Phùng, was born in 1950 in Quảng Nam. He was the eldest brother in a family with many siblings. He finished elementary school in a rural village. In 1961 the young lad passed the entrance exam to the sixth grade at the Trần Quý Cáp Middle School in Hội An. Three years later, in 1964, he went with his family to Saigon.

There was an important phase in his life that Phùng Nguyễn omitted in his autobiographical notes: he entered the armed services in 1968 when he was just 18 and became a wounded veteran released from service before 1975. My belief is that the days and months when he wore a uniform, though not long in duration, had a deep influence subsequently on his development as a writer.

The notes that Phùng Nguyễn put together himself for official distribution record only events that occurred from 1984 on, after he set foot on American soil:

Place of birth: Quảng Nam, Vietnam
Relocated to the United States in May, 1984.

Completed a Bachelor's Degree summa cum laude in business administration and information science in 1990 and a Master's Degree in business administration (MBA) in 1992 at California State University (Bakersfield, California)

Worked in the field of information science from 1990 on. Most recent position held: Director of Information Systems, Jaco Oil Company, California.

Published many articles and other writings in periodicals such as *Literature* (*Văn*, USA), *Literary Studies* (*Văn Học*, USA), *Confluence* (*Hợp Lưu*, USA), *Viet* (*Việt*, Australia), and *21st Century* (*Thế Kỷ 21*, USA), and online journals such as talawas.org, tienve.org, and damau.org.

Published, designed, built up, and preserved online articles for the publications *Literary Studies* (*Văn Học*), *Literature* (*Văn*), *Confluence* (*Hợp Lưu*), and *Viet* (*Việt*) from 1997 to 2002.

Acted as editor-in-chief for the literary journal *Confluence* (*Hợp Lưu*, California, USA) from June 2002 to April 2003.

Founded the online literary journal *Skin of Color* (*Da Màu*, July, 2006) together with the writer Đặng Thơ Thơ and the poet Đỗ Lê Anh Đào.

Editor and technical director for the journal *Skin of Color* from 2006 to 2015.

Founded and built up the online library "eBook Bookshelf" ("Kệ Sách eBook": kesach.org). Brought this resource into activity in May, 2008, and has by now published and distributed more than 150 Vietnamese works free of charge in the ebook formats Scribd.com and Smashwords.com.

Editor of the blog "Forest and Trees" ("Rừng và Cây") on the Vietnamese Voice of America station (VOA).

Published books:

- *Tower of Memory* (*Tháp Ký Ức*), short stories; Văn, 1988, California, USA
- *Oakland Night and Other Stories* (*Đêm Oakland và Những Truyện Khác*), short stories, Văn, 2001, California, USA

Books to be published in 2015:

- a short story collection
- Phùng Nguyễn essays
  (end of excerpt)

Phùng Nguyễn's blog "Forest and Trees" on Voice of America (VOA) was devoted to the analysis of notable cultural developments in Vietnam and at the same time was a meeting place for authors close to him within the country and abroad. The first article on the blog was by Phùng Nguyễn: "The Independent Vietnamese Writers' Association: Fact or Footnote?" ("Văn đoàn Độc lập Việt Nam: Sự kiện hay Cước chú?"). It was posted on July 16, 2015, and the last article "Heaven's Fate" ("Mệnh Trời"), also by Phùng Nguyễn, was posted on November 20, 2015 as a kind of last testament, for he had passed away three days earlier. VOA preceded the article with a moving tribute:

"Sunday, November 22 will be the day that the funeral ceremony for the writer Phùng Nguyễn will take place. On this occasion the Vietnamese VOA would like to present to our readers this posthumous article by the departed author as a final farewell from him to his readers, his friends, and all who revered him. This is his last blog, but we believe that his humane ideals and values and those of his literary friends encouraged and protected by the blog that he led will never be obliterated, whatever Heaven's Fate may hold in store for us."

In view of the sudden passing of the writer Phùng Nguyễn, VOA also posted an obituary, coupled with words of condolence, as follows:

A photographic portrait of Phùng Nguyễn on the blog "Forest and Trees" on VOA.

The writer Phùng Nguyễn, the editor and principal contributor to the blog "Forest and Trees," on Vietnamese Voice of America, passed away suddenly on November 17, 2015, in Maryland. Though the period of his work with VOA was not long in duration, his rigorous, original, and distinctive articles and those of his poetic and literary friends whom he invited to write on matters relating to culture, have attracted the attention of many Vietnamese readers both inside and outside the country and have been highly valued by them. His premature departure from the world will be a loss difficult to compensate for, not only among writers, but among the readers who loved his blog "Forest and Trees." We, the Vietnamese VOA staff, beg to express our sincere condolences to all who were close to him for this great loss. His precious contributions will always be regarded with the greatest respect by the Vietnamese Voice of America."

If we take stock of the data, we can see that the blog "Forest and Trees" was active only for a period of four months, with a total of thirty-five articles, of which sixteen were by Phùng Nguyễn. He had written many insightful articles before then that had appeared in such periodicals as *Literature* (*Văn*), *Literary Studies* (*Văn Học*), *Confluence* (*Hợp Lưu*), *Viet* (*Việt*), and *Twenty-first Century* (*Thế Kỷ 21*), and online journals such as talawas.org, tienve.org, and damau.org…

A PORTRAIT OF PHÙNG NGUYỄN THE SOLDIER

In a valedictory essay about Phùng Nguyễn, the writer Trần Hoài Thư made a sketch of his activities: "From the "Bridge of the Milky Way" (Ô Thước)[1] to Talawas to "Skin of Color" ("Da Màu"), and other Vietnamese forums of discussion, one could always discern the presence of Phùng Nguyễn. In former times Phùng Nguyễn carried a gun, whereas now he carries a laptop wherever he goes. I have followed this traveler throughout his journies and have limitless admiration for him."

Trần Hoài Thư went on: "Though Phùng Nguyễn and I met only one or two times, it nevertheless seems that we were closely allied in our common quests, in our writing activities, and even in our lives. In the first place, we were both IT (information technology) people. Secondly, we both wore uniforms prior to 1975. Thirdly, we both engaged in authorship out of a common love for literature and writing.

On Saturday evening, November 21, 2015 when Phùng Nguyễn's last rites were being performed, I sent an email message to Trần Hoài Thư as follows:

Phùng Nguyễn almost never discussed the period when he was in our armed forces, but according to what I know, he enlisted after 1968 (Tết Mậu Thân) and then, being wounded, had to remain for many months in the Republic's General Hospital (Tổng Y viện Cộng Hoà) until he withdrew from the service. Do you know any more details about the period when he served and when he was in the hospital? I'm writing an article about Phùng Nguyễn.

Trần Hoài Thư replied the same night: "My dear Ngô Thế Vinh – I know nothing. All I did was read his autobiographical notes. Try your best to learn more about this matter. Phùng Nguyễn enlisted when he was 18, and still in high school."

---

1 Ô Thước: The bridge across the heavenly river (the Milky Way) formed by crows and magpies on the seventh day of the seventh lunar month so the heavenly cowherd and the heavenly weaver girl can be reunited.

When I met Phùng Nguyễn not long ago, he seemed as healthy as a young man, and looked younger than his age. His skin was tanned, his face square, and his forehead high, and he spoke and laughed with normal vigor. On one occasion I was walking shoulder to shoulder with him across a stretch of seashore at Huntington Beach. While we walked, he got a phone call from Đinh Cường, so I lagged behind. Phùng Nguyễn wanted to keep on walking as he waited and, as he walked, I suddenly noticed that he was leaning a little to the right. Considering the possibilities, I thought that perhaps he had had a light case of polio as a child–that illness was not uncommon in Vietnam. Though I had the thought, I asked no questions. On another occasion we were walking across another stretch of seashore in Laguna Beach. The weather was sunny and warm, and Phùng Nguyễn was wearing shorts. I noticed that his right leg, though not crooked or atrophied, had many small scars. I asked Phùng Nguyễn about it, and he gave me a brief account, detailing how, when he was operating with his unit in a swampy area, one of his comrades stepped on a mine. A few men died as a result, whereas Phùng Nguyễn was merely wounded; two of his leg bones were broken. He had to be taken to the Republic's General Hospital to undergo reconstructive surgery and have a cast put on. Unfortunately, his wounds got infected, and resisted antibiotic treatments. He had to undergo several operations involving bone and skin grafts. He had to lie many months in the hospital, enduring severe pain. On one occasion his pain and discomfort were so severe that he begged to have his leg amputated, but his doctor refused to do it. Phùng still recalled that this doctor was cold and impassive when confronting his pain, that his name was "Thái," and that it was he who was responsible for saving his leg, so he would not become a cripple – but he was never able in later years to meet his benefactor again.

Wishing to obtain further information on Phùng Nguyễn the soldier, I sent an email message inquiring about this to Khánh Trường, the "Street Artist of New York," as Mai Thảo called him, and the person who founded the journal *Confluence* (*Hợp Lưu*) and served as its editor-in-chief until he transferred that responsibility to

Phùng Nguyễn in 2002. Khánh Trường, who was born in 1948, can be considered a member of the same generation as Phùng Nguyễn, who was born in 1950, and moreover had the same place of origin: Quảng Nam. Khánh Trường's military history included a service as a paratrooper, and he was wounded more than once prior to his discharge. Khánh Trường would surely know something about Phùng Nguyễn's days as a soldier. But in fact he knew nothing. He replied at once: "I never heard Phùng Nguyễn talk about his soldiering days. He apparently was in the service and suffered a leg wound and now has something a little wrong with his walking – that was a total surprise to me. One day after I returned from a visit to Võ Phiến, he stopped by for a visit. Everything seemed normal. That's all I can say!

At the suggestion of the poet Thành Tôn, I communicated with Trần Trung Đạo in Boston – he was the author of the poem "A Mother's Laugh that Transformed Eternity" ("Đổi Cả Thiên Thu Tiếng Mẹ Cười") and was also a former student of Trần Quý Cáp. This was his response: "Phùng Nguyễn talked very little about his years in Saigon. When he was with Trần Quý Cáp, he wrote a fairly clear account and published it in *Tower of Memory* (*Tháp Ký Ức*). Let me try asking the friends of Trần Quý Cáp to see if they know anything. I'll let you know what I hear.

Unwilling to stop at that stage, I relied on the help of Diệu Chi, the wife of Nguyễn Mộng Giác, to communicate with another friend of Phùng Nguyễn, Huy Văn (Trương Văn Hùng), who had gone with Phùng Nguyễn to visit Tạ Chí Đại Trường on the day when the funeral of the writer Võ Phiến took place. Huy Văn took a photo of Tạ Chí Đại Trường and Phùng Nguyễn with Phùng's iPhone. I hoped it could still be recovered. Huy Văn was able to corroborate some information I had regarding Phùng Nguyễn, but there was still a twenty-year empty spot from 1964 to 1984, the period Phùng Nguyễn lived in Saigon.

Knowing that Huy Văn was an IT expert who belonged to the same generation as Phùng Nguyễn, also wrote articles for the journal *Literary Studies* (*Văn Học*) and was very close with Phùng Nguyễn's family, I called him up and arranged to go with him to visit Phùng

Nguyễn's mother two days after Thanksgiving. I had no address, but by following some directions given me by Hồ Như, I managed to find the house of a younger sister of Phùng Nguyễn in a Huntington Beach neighborhood where the streets all bore names of fish, such as Bluefish, Stingray, and Carp. This was also the area where Phùng Nguyễn's mother often came to visit her daughter.

A few days later, through the phone number given by Đặng Thơ Thơ, I was able to learn some facts recounted to me by the grief-stricken voice of Phùng Nguyễn's younger sister, and all at once the twenty-year gap was to some degree filled up.

In 1964, unable to live any more in the Central region, an area made very insecure by the ongoing civil war, (it was a so-called "beans and sticky rice area"), now half destroyed by floods, Phùng's mother decided to take her children to the South to seek a living. As the eldest son in the family, Phùng had to go out in the world at the age of fourteen to help his mother take care of his younger siblings. During the day he worked as a mason or as an employee of a woodworking shop, while at night he went with books under his arm to a private school.

In 1968, before he completed high school, he was recruited at the age of eighteen into the Quang Trung Military Training Camp, and upon graduation served as a communications soldier. After being wounded by a mine in 1971, he had to remain for a long time in the Republic's General Hospital until he was able to return on crutches to his family, at which time he was discharged.

After 1975, he was unable to get away from the country for nine years. As a wounded "puppet" soldier, he worked at a variety of laborious jobs to support his family until in 1984, they were able to emigrate to the U.S., helped by the sponsorship of one of his younger sisters. For several years after this emigration, Phùng Nguyễn had to work in various menial capacities in order to survive, such as harvesting onions in farmers' fields and washing trays in pizza shops; only at night could he attend schools and study.

The literary critic Nguyễn Vy Khanh wrote fourteen years ago about the element of "autofiction" in the two published works of Phùng Nguyễn. From the semi-autobiographical passages he refers to, one can learn more about the experiences of Phùng Nguyễn as a soldier and as a wounded veteran.

"He was still very young. At that time, he was lying in the Cộng Hòa General military hospital receiving treatment. People were trying to treat his injured leg, which had been broken to pieces, by torturing him in every conceivable way, and he was in such pain that he would beseech them each time to cut the leg off and throw it away, but they wouldn't listen to him! He lay suffering on his iron bed, a hard, stiff plaster cast on his leg, his hands grasping huge needles with dangling plastic tubes. Powerless and despairing, he would lie waiting for the agonies of pain that would assail him twice a day, once in the morning and once in the afternoon, when the nurses would come and change his bandages. There was nothing to do but lie there and curse his waves of pain.

If Phan Nhật Nam wrote battlefield reports filled with blood, sweat, and tears, then one can say that Phùng Nguyễn wrote about the mine fragments and bits of bullets scattered over those areas. Phùng Nguyễn also wrote about the wounded comrades who surrounded him. Here is an excerpt:

"You have nothing to do but kill time and play a game of chess. You have a lot of opponents whose looks and character stimulate revulsion. There is a character who goes by the name of "One-eyed Stork Spirit" with a black complexion and only one eye. The thing that disturbs you the most is not the barrages of artillery he brings out on the chessboard, but his habit of plucking out his false left eye – a stone object – from time to time, polishing and admiring it like a precious family heirloom. The red and bruised cavity remaining on the left gazes mockingly at you–a sickening sight. And there were many other monstrous nicknamed people among his chess-playing companions, young soldiers with missing arms and broken frames, gathered here after being cut down on some battlefield–how could one remember

them all! But the most repulsive of all was "Loner Who Seeks Defeat" (Độc Cô Cầu Bại 獨孤求敗), a sergeant of mature years who had no legs! He sat calmly on a wheelchair beside his bed with a horse-shit colored blanket spread over his stumps, lost in deliberation as he attacked you with deep and deadly schemes. Losing, his expression was glum until he had a rare opportunity to be victorious. But you would regretfully let those moments pass by when you saw the drops of sweat emerging at the base of his hair and his rough fingers wandering uncertainly on the hospital blanket and the tiny streaks of red in his yellowed eyes with their pitifully nervous expression. He would raise a piece and make a move... smugly. "Loner Who Seeks Defeat" beat you that time, but he never had another opportunity to do that." Oakland Night and Other Matters (*Đêm Oakland và Những Chuyện Khác*), "Burning Up to the Grass-Tips" ("Cháy Lên Những Ngọn Cỏ"), pp. 31-32.

What was Phùng Nguyễn's view of the war after he left the country? Here is another excerpt:

"He [i.e. Đức, a young friend of Phùng Nguyễn's] who lived alone and had no real responsibilities toward anyone. He went out often, and went nwhenever he pleased. That fact alone often made me jealous in the extreme. ["I" refers to another young friend of Phùng Nguyễn's.] I was older than Đức–old enough to kill people and be killed by others in a perfectly legal manner, before Đức had had the opportunity to participate in the big game that people call war. Aside from that, it was just that I was born and grew up in a poverty-stricken village marked all over with vestiges of bombs that would have been sufficient to make him turn pale. Within high walls surrounding a luxurious villa cut off from all the dangers outside, people have the right to cultivate spiritual needs that are endlessly exorbitant, for example having complex personal thoughts about the nature of war... Either people live with it, or they have thoughts about it." (*Oakland Nights*), "Questions" (Câu Hỏi, p. 13)

"*If I have to describe my relation to the war that has passed, I often think of a chap who has lost everything in a final round of chess, who is at a loss as to what he should do next. The winner will never consent to sweeping the board clean for another game. Just standing there and complaining will do no good at all. So one must just cast the matter aside, consoling oneself with the thought that at least you completed the game, though in an utterly unskillful manner."*

Few people know that when they participated in that board game called war, part of it consisted of the bones and blood of the young communications soldier Phùng Nguyễn.

STEPPING INTO THE MAINSTREAM

Because he came to the U.S. as an immigrant, he couldn't enjoy the assistance that was given to people who came as refugees, so Phùng and his family had to throw themselves into the search for work right away – in general, minimum-wage work.

Empty-handed at the age of thirty-four, and having just come to a new continent, Phùng Nguyễn embarked for the first time in his life on a career as a book-toting student. As a village youngster in Vietnam, he had never completed high school and he was now a disabled ex-soldier as well, but he proved at once that he was an outstanding student. With firm and steady steps, he entered the mainstream, gaining a full complement of academic degrees in just six years. In 1990 he gained a bachelor's degree in information science and business administration, and in 1992 obtained an MBA: Master's in Business Administration.

From 1990 on he worked in the field of business administration, and after twenty years rose to the position of Computer Science Director for the Jaco Oil Company in California.

Having attained the age when one "listens with comprehension" (the age of sixty), and having reached a fully satisfactory stage of intellectual and financial development, Phùng Nguyễn found himself faced with a choice: should he continue working in his principal field, or should he concentrate on cultivating domestic happiness with his new family? As a man of resolution and deep feeling, he chose, to use his words, the "second commitment."

He ended his relationship with Jaco in Bakersfield, a company with which he had had a close connection for twenty years, and from which he had enjoyed many benefits, in order to go back to the east to live. In doing so, Phùng Nguyễn gained domestic happiness with his family and a warm circle of close friends, but this was achieved at some personal cost: the emptiness left in the soul of a professional expert when he steps away from his main occupation, exposure to bitterly cold weather conditions that did not suit his health, and some unwelcome experiences with a new heart doctor in whom he had little trust. Phùng Nguyễn confided to me that it was not possible to enjoy both choices, and that he never had second thoughts about his decision.

PHÙNG NGUYỄN THE WRITER

In his preface to *The Tower of Memory*, the first of Phùng Nguyễn's books, Nguyễn-Xuân Hoàng wrote: "*The Tower of Memory* is a collection of incidents related to the destiny of a human being, but they are conveyed through scraps of ordinary existence, some centered on love, some on youth and inexperience, and some on home and homeland. They reflect the past and present of a group of people who were just getting into their twenties when they went out from Saigon. Phùng Nguyễn's stories are light, and suffused with the breath of a simple, but unsettled life, and are written in an easy but attractive style. His pages are filled with a highly literary sort of beauty."

In an epilogue to the same book, Nguyễn Mộng Giác added the following observations: "Phùng Nguyễn's first short stories, rise above those of writers of the generation before him and those of his own generation who left the South of Vietnam as refugees, the sort of stories that form the principal substance of overseas Vietnamese literature. Phùng Nguyễn dwells on past events, treating them as memories to be cherished, but he doesn't stop there. He turns these past images into thoughts about human life."

The Tower of Memory, Phùng Nguyễn's first short story, was chosen by Nguyễn Mộng Giác, the editor-in-chief, and Thạch Hãn (Lê Thọ Giáo), the general secretary of the journal *Literary Studies*

The Tower of Memory (*Tháp Ký Ức*), Văn, 1998, with fifteen stories, and a preface by Nguyễn-Xuân Hoàng and an epilogue by Nguyễn Mộng Giác.

Oakland Nights and Other Stories (*Đêm Oakland và Những Truyện Khác*), Văn, 2001 no preface or epilogue, consists of sixteen stories.

(*Văn Học*) for inclusion in their Tết 1995 issue. The story attracted attention and stirred up controversies. *The Tower of Memory* can be regarded as the personal narrative of Phùng Nguyễn with a character, evidently the author, who refers to himself as "tôi" (I, me). What is most worthy of attention is the question posed at the beginning of his life by the narrator, then a boy who had just turned eleven, to his teacher, Tố Quyên, when she says to him, "I hope you will always look to the future." "But," the boy said, "we still stubbornly hold to the belief that hope has two directions; it does not go in just one direction as you have affirmed. If hope can only consist of looking to the future, then this life is just too sad." That was what caused Phùng Nguyễn wish, many years later, to meet that teacher again, so as to ask once again, "Can hope be directed only to the future? "Or can it go both forward and backward?"

In a party that was of course held in the office of *Literary Studies*, in the home of Nguyễn Mộng Giác, the writers Võ Phiến, Nghiêm Xuân Hồng, Nguyễn-Xuân Hoàng, and other literary friends questioned the author about Tố Quyên, the teacher in *The Tower of Memory*.

That question is something that Phùng Nguyễn carried with him throughout his life, due simply to his wish by to find a way to leap past the terrible abyss that lies between the reality of the past and all the things that are still to come.

With regard to those of his compatriots in their twenties and thirties living abroad, he wrote: "Regardless of the great differences in our ages and in our war experiences, I believe that Đức and I belong to that group of people standing unsteadily on planks going in opposite directions, a struggling to maintain our balance, so as not to fall into the black abyss that lies beneath. Actually, when the flimsy plank I stand on carries me back to the past, I have more opportunities to succeed. There are matters lying there that will follow me to the end of my life. For many years I have been drawn backward more than I have been pushed forward." (*Oakland Nights*, "A Question" ["Câu Hỏi"])

"The Bird Calls by the Garden" ("Chim Gáy Sau Vườn") transcends the mode of personal narration and is instead a strikingly original short story filled with the author's humane outlook, in which the most horrible wounds of the war just past are recalled – an endlessly cruel war undertaken in the name of various foreign ideologies that plunged an entire people into the tragedy of civil conflict.

In the midst of the devastating destruction depicted in "The Bird Calls," there is still a place where an obstinate love can grow between a girl named Xuyến and her older and younger brothers, among whom are Thuận and Tấn, who were pushed into opposing sides and were thus forced to kill each other. A trench behind the garden conceals a trap to kill Tấn when, one day, he returns to observe the death anniversary of his mother. But the tragedy of the story lies in the death of Xuyến, Tấn's younger sister, and the person Thuận loves – an example of the fate of so many innocent people caught between the two sides of the war. (*Oakland Nights*, p. 51)

The writer Thảo Trường once made the following observation: "I have an urgent desire to thrust the entire war into a single short story, to put an entire era that I personally lived through into that story. I still desire that, without cease." When I read "The Bird Calls by the Garden," I cannot but recall that observation by Thảo Trường, though I know full well that when he wrote "The Bird Calls by the Garden," Phùng Nguyễn had no such desire.

Why write? That is a question that confronts every writer. Phùng Nguyễn wrote: "Later I recognized that the very necessity that I had to share with others was the motive that pushed toward writing rather than toward other activities. Could it be because I was unable to overcome a fear generated by the gap between things that have happened and things that are still to happen? I am endlessly confused as I wait for an answer."

Phùng Nguyễn placed great hope on literature: "And amid the desolate ruins, who knows whether a phoenix, shining and splendid, will step forth, a phoenix with wings long enough to soar over the huge blank space that exists between what has happened and something that has yet to happen."

PHÙNG NGUYỄN THE LITERARY CRITIC

The Tower of Memory in Nguyễn Mộng Giác's journal *Literary Studies* (*Văn Học*) was the first short story by Phùng Nguyễn that I read, and was the work with which I began to make the acquaintance of this new author.

"The Fitful Reflections of Lữ Phương"[2] on the Talawas website was my introduction to the insightful literary criticism of Phùng Nguyễn.

---

2 Lữ Phương, real name: Lê Văn Phương, born in 1938 in North Vietnam. In 1954, he emigrated to the South, worked as a teacher, activist, journalist, contributor to Literary News (Tin Văn). In 1968, he left the city, went into jungle, joined the Liberation Front of the South, became a communist party member, and was assigned the position of Deputy Minister of Culture in this temporary government. After 1975, Lữ Phương went back to Saigon disgraced, but still played an important role to tracing down and destroying books classified as decadent Southern literature.

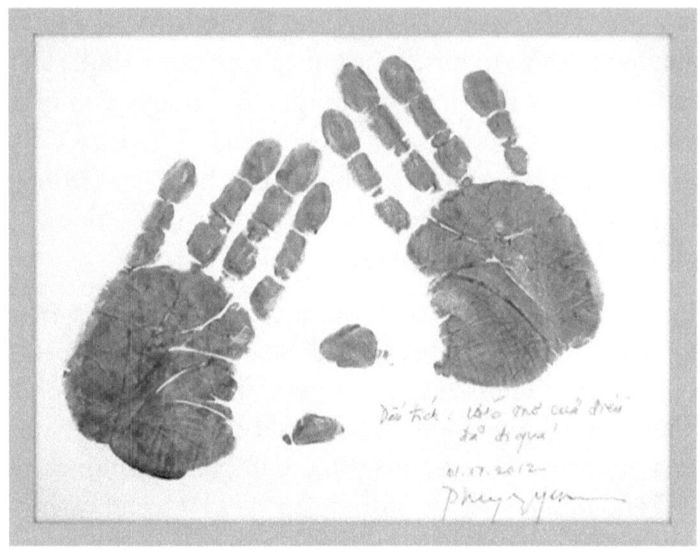

Phùng Nguyễn's hand imprints, with the notation:
"Hoping that this matter is now passed!; Jan 17, 2012
(source: Emprunt Empreinte)

Both the literary and the critical output of Phùng Nguyễn made a deep impression on me.

Not long ago, I read an article to be posted on the blog "Forest and Trees" on VOA that touched on the obedience to Beijing of Prime Minister Hun Sen and compared it to the loyalty to China of the Vietnamese Communist Party. In this article Phùng Nguyễn wrote:

"Thus, from now on, seeing how utterly loyal he is to the heaven-ordained dynasty, it would appear that the Vietnamese Communist Party now has a fearsome enemy."

I excerpted that sentence and put into an email message with the subject line "Quote of the day" as a kind of lament that would at the same time let Phùng know that I had read his new article. This was perhaps the last email message I exchanged with Phùng, but it received no answer. On the morning of the same day, November 17, I called Phùng on my cell phone, but only got his voicemail. I thought that since Maryland's fall season had arrived, Phùng was no doubt taking a lakeshore walk; it didn't occur to me that he might be in the hospital.

Phùng Nguyễn: a Man of Character

Having a friend like Phùng Nguyễn was a great happiness. At our first meeting, I felt his directness and reliability at once. His character was expressed in everything he did; he was gallant and devoted with all his associates.

Phùng Nguyễn and Tạ Chí Đại Trường got to know each other in the period when they worked for the journal *Literary Studies* (*Văn Học*). On the morning of October 3, 2015, Phùng Nguyễn had arranged to meet me at the memorial service for the writer Võ Phiến, but a few hours before that was to occur, Diệu Chi, the wife of Nguyễn Mộng Giác, informed him that Tạ Chí Đại Trường had just visited her to make a last farewell and was about to fly back to Saigon. Trường was in the final phase of liver cancer, and had chosen to die in Vietnam. Hearing this, Phùng Nguyễn let it be known that he intended, by

The last photo of Phùng Nguyễn with Tạ Chí Đại Trường, Garden Grove, south California, Saturday, Oct. 3, 2015
(Phùng Nguyễn family archives)

Phùng Nguyễn and Huy Văn, as two young writers whose articles were appearing in Nguyễn Mộng Giác's journal *Literary Studies*, Saturday, Oct. 3, 2015 *(Huy Văn, personal archives)*

From left: Lê Thánh Thư, Trần Thị NgH, Phùng Nguyễn, Dương Nghiễm Mậu, Sài Gòn 2014 *(Phan Nguyên, personal archives)*

whatever means necessary, to meet Đại Trường a last time. Though he knew that Đại Trường could not eat or drink anything, he and his friend Huy Văn nevertheless bought some Brodard spring rolls that Đại Trường particularly liked.

On the evening of that day, Tạ Chí Đại Trường boarded the plane that brought him home to Vietnam. I learned also that Đại Trường had put several articles into Phùng Nguyễn's keeping, with instructions that they should be published only after his death. I hope that Ms. Quỳnh Loan, Phùng Nguyễn's wife, will be able to retrieve those manuscripts, and that they will not be lost.

At the end of May 2015, when Phùng Nguyễn had flown to California to visit his mother, I met Phùng and he let me know that he was about to take charge of a blog called "Forest and Trees" ("Rừng và Cây"), and invited me to play a role on that platform, saying, as an inducement, that VOA articles had a very wide distribution within the territory of Vietnam. I thought that with Phùng Nguyễn's reputation for reliability and his wide circle of acquaintances he would be able to gain the participation of many literary friends.

A gathering with Đinh Cường, in the Saigon Café, Maryland, June 16, 2015. From the right: Phùng Nguyễn, Lữ Quỳnh, Phạm Cao Hoàng, Nguyễn Quang Chơn, Đinh Cường, Duyên, Tùng, Lãm Thúy, Nguyễn Minh Nữu.
(Source: blog of Phạm Cao Hoàng)

Phùng Nguyễn was very suave and uninhibited when arguing with others, but he was also very firmly attached to his principles. But when people agreed with him, it was because his powers of persuasion were so great, not because he showed any inclination to force others to adopt his point of view. In meetings with all sorts of different opinions, some entirely opposed to his own, he had the ability to bring people into harmony and create a lively and democratic atmosphere and he often managed to have the last word. This could be characterized as "leadership ability," an attribute he had developed in his years of belonging to a mainstream profession.

Trịnh Cung, who worked with him on the blog "Skin of Color" ("Da Màu") had this to say of him: "For me, Phùng Nguyễn was a model of free thought, of democracy, and of opposition to discrimination. I only got to know Phùng a few years ago, but felt very close to him in all matters relating to literature and politics in which he always inclined to freedom and the cultivation of civilized values. Phùng particularly respected the right of others to choose their own political points of view, but he was also very fair in distinguishing between evil and humanity, which he took to be a more important factor than literary ability in judging the worth of a writer."

Phùng Nguyễn's articles discussing the various internal problems of Vietnam induced commentators in "Vietnam Forum" ("Việt Nam Diễn Đàn") to observe that he had "a degree of understanding rare among those who live overseas."

A SMALL PERSONAL INTRUSION

When writing these portraits of artistic figures, I always feel that turning the spotlight on myself is something to be strictly avoided. But I feel I must introduce a bit of personal information here, because it is related in a way to my literary friend Phùng Nguyễn.

About four months ago, Phùng Nguyễn sent me three questions to respond to, and just a few days ago he reminded me of this: "You still owe me responses to those three questions, Vinh." I shall record the three questions here as a kind of final testament of his, and I feel sad when I reflect that I will never have an opportunity to give him my responses:

The three questions of Phùng Nguyễn for Ngô Thế Vinh were related to three of my projects:

- The Mekong River, a great love.
- Being Summoned to Court due to "The Battle of Saigon."
- Portraits of writers and artists.

Dear Phùng Nguyễn: I never imagined that I would be writing an article about you so soon. It was a short while ago that I met you, and a short while ago that you passed away–and seeking information about you was very difficult, especially that which concerned the period of your life that you never wished to discuss. You died, and the world of literature and criticism lost a mighty general. Your utterly unexpected departure makes me think of a saying that I saw somewhere, though I no longer remember the source: "The only certainty in this life is uncertainty."

A PHÙNG NGUYỄN ENAMORED OF THE SEA

I'm not sure when it began, but Phùng Nguyễn adored the sea. During the years he lived in Bakersfield, a place relatively far from the ocean, he would spend one to two hours driving to the places along the coast whose beauty he most enjoyed. During the short days from the East Coast to California to visit his mother, he would drive out to the ocean shore very early and walk four or five miles, sometimes by himself, and sometimes with his two younger sisters. Phùng liked to do his walking early, because at that time the air was pure and few people were about. His heart must have been in good shape to allow him to walk so far while maintaining his swift pace. As for me there were only two days on the weekend when I was able to go walking with Phùng. Our meeting spot was the Huntington Beach Pier, which I jokingly called "the bridge to the frontier."

Just last October, we sat and had breakfast together at the Café Heidelberg, a German restaurant on the Pacific Coast Highway where one could gaze out on a stretch of ocean. The two of us promised each other that we would return there, and take seats on a "Rooftop Lounge," from which high vantage point one could gaze out at a wide expanse of ocean – it was said to be very beautiful in the evening – and on the other side of the view would be our homeland. But this time, Phùng Nguyễn did not keep his promise, though he had always been a person who did so.

On Saturday, one week later, Huy Văn and I went together to visit Phùng's aged mother – she was more than ninety years old. She belonged to the Phan lineage, to which Phan Khôi also belonged, and was from the same area in Điện Bàn Quảng Nam as he. She recounted stories from the hardscrabble days of Phùng's early childhood with the copious tears of a mother who has just lost a son. A box containing his ashes rested at the head of her beda. She read Buddhist prayers over them every evening. Her daughter let me know that at such times she would also talk softly with Phùng. She burst into tears when she mentioned something Phùng had said to her the last time they were together: "Do you know, mother, that I love you very much?" During the week that followed, the ashes were taken back to the East. His younger sister told me that Phùng's last wish was that his ashes be scattered over the ocean, but that it be the Pacific Ocean, with his homeland on the other side.

I am very moved as I write this article; it is like a farewell that I share with all the close friends of Phùng Nguyễn, with their huge shared burden of grief.

MY RESPONSES TO PHÙNG NGUYỄN'S THREE QUESTIONS

Phùng Nguyễn died on November 17, 2015. Dazed by his sudden death at an age when his intellect and creativity should have been at their height, I wrote an article devoted to his memory entitled, "Phùng Nguyễn, As If We Never Bade Him Farewell."[3] Stirred to memories of him by this, I reread some of his writings, and this made me realize

---

3 Diễn Đàn Thế Ky http//www.diendantheiy.net/2016/12/ngo-vinh–hung-nguyen-nhu-vhua-he-gia.html#more

Phùng Nguyễn standing in front of the Huntington Beach Mural, Oct 4, 2015

Phùng Nguyễn and Ngô Thế Vinh on the oceanshore at Laguna Beach, Oct 11, 2015

Phùng Nguyễn and Ngô Thế Vinh, Huntington Beach Pier, Oct 4, 2015

that for the past two years I had owed him responses to his three questions–so now I must give what I owe him, and this will serve also as an incense offering to his spirit.

I. PHÙNG NGUYỄN, THE MEKONG RIVER: A GREAT LOVE

"It would not be too far from the truth to say that everybody has some great love. The writer Ngô Thế Vinh is no exception to this. The object of his infatuation comes from a remote region on the Tibetan plateau five thousand meters above sea-level. She begins with tentative steps in the province of Qinghai, then goes hesitantly through the province of Yunnan in south central China, before crossing the borders of Myanmar, Laos, Thailand, and Cambodia, and at last Vietnam, the place where she concludes a journey of more than four thousand eight hundred kilometers and blends into the Eastern Sea in such places as the Tiền and Hậu river mouths. She goes by many names: Dza Chu, Lan Thương, Mae Nam Khong, Tonle Thom, Cửu Long… but she is known in the majority of places by the name Mekong.

"Mekong River was the inspiration for the documentary novel *The Nine Dragons Drained Dry – The East Sea in Turmoil* and the documentary monograph *Mekong – The Occluding River*, as well as dozens of valuable studies and research reports on the changes in the ecology of the Mekong in recent decades by the writer Ngô Thế Vinh. This inspiration has, over the months and years, made Ngô

Thế Vinh a notable expert on this river of unsurpassed importance to Southeast Asia.

"Due to its economic value and to the serious nature of the changes wrought upon the ecology of the river all along its passage to the sea, the foreign relations of the countries involved have grown more complex, especially since the erection of many big and small hydroelectric dams along its course. Vietnam has met with more economic and diplomatic difficulties than any other country in the region with regard to the nagging problems arising from the disadvantageous changes to the ecology of the Mekong and, concurrently, Beijing's schemes for expansion in the region of the Southeastern Sea.

"So to the writer Ngô Thế Vinh, I address this question: What is it about the river Mekong that caused you to grow obsessed with it? From the standpoint of one who thorough understands the situation, can you share with our readers your insights with regard to the ecological changes to the Mekong and their possible future consequences?"

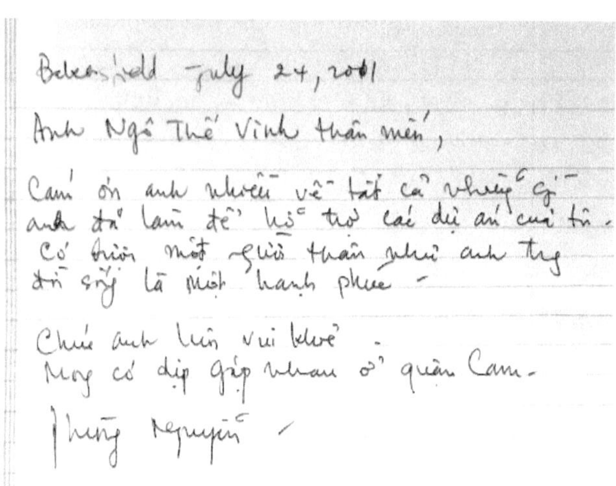

Bakersfield July 24, 2011

Anh Ngô Thế Vinh thân mến,

Cám ơn anh nhiều về tất cả những gì anh đã làm để hỗ trợ các dự án của tôi. Có được một người thân như anh trong đời sống là một hạnh phúc.

Chúc anh luôn vui khỏe.
Mong có dịp gặp nhau ở quán Cam.

Phùng Nguyễn

In this age of emails, a handwritten note is a rare thing. Here is one of Phùng Nguyễn's from his time in Bakersfield, California in 2011 *(Ngô Thế Vinh, personal archives)*

I. Ngô Thế Vinh Replies

I have an unforgettable memory of a day in 1995 when I met with the journalist Như Phong (Lê Văn Tiến) in Little Saigon, the "Vietnamese refugee capital." It was a fine, sunny Saturday morning in southern California. Như Phong had invited me that day to meet a group of young friends in the group "Friends of the Mekong" (Nhóm Bạn Cửu Long). I had never previously heard of it, because they were having their first discussion meeting in the activity room of the paper *The Vietnamese People* (*Người Việt*). Present at the panel that day were the engineer Phạm Phan Long, the PhD Phạm Văn Hải, and the journalist Đỗ Quý Toàn. One can say that the engineer Phạm Phan Long was the first person in the overseas community to raise the alarm about the danger to which the Mekong would soon be exposed due to the plans being made in China to build a series of dams starting at the entrance to Yunnan Province, though at that time only one dam had been completed: the one at Manwan (1993) on the river Lancang – the Chinese name for the Mekong.

That was indeed a day when "my destiny began," for that was the first time I came face to face with a new disaster facing the country: the ever-progressing stages of unsustainable development being inflicted on the Mekong River, at the end of which lay the country of Vietnam. From that day on, I had a new group of friends, including the engineer Phạm Phan Long, the engineer Ngô Minh Triết, the engineer Nguyễn Hữu Chung, as well as other individuals belonging to the Mekong Forum, the forerunner of the Việt Ecology Foundation, which arose later.

And then I must mention an article that appeared the in-country journal *Youth* (*Tuổi Trẻ*) on Nov. 3, 1996: "Exploiting the Mekong River: A Vietnamese Point of View" ("Khai thác sông Mekong: nhìn từ góc độ Việt Nam"). The name Phạm Phan Long was given as the author, but it was actually written by four specialists in different overseas countries: Dr. Phạm Văn Hải (U.S.), the engineer Nguyễn Hữu Chung (Canada), Dr. Bình An Sơn (Australia,) and the engineer Phạm Phan Long (U.S.). The content of the article was absolutely topical and up-to-date. And as for me, the article made me aware that this was a grave problem carrying long-term consequences for the river and all the countries along its length, which in its entirety constituted the rice basket of the entire country.

In 1999, the Mekong Association expanded due to a conference organized by the Mekong Forum and the Vietnamese-American Science and Technology Society in south California under the title "Conference on the Danger Faced by the River Basin, Countries, and Peoples Along the Mekong River Due to Development Projects." Participating in the conference were representatives of the related Tiền Giang and Hậu Giang areas, and Aviva Imhof belonging to the International Rivers Network, and Dr. Sin Meng Srun of the Cambodian Association in the U.S. The result of this conference was an announcement entitled "The 1999 Mekong River Declaration," which was sent to the MRC/ Mekong River Commission and other related organizations.

The journalist Như Phong was active with us in the "Friends of the Mekong" until the day of his death and by his participation contributed his geopolitical understanding of the relation of the Mekong problem with the fate of the country.

In the same period as well, I undertook field trips to observe the situation from Yunnan Province in China, down to Laos, Thailand, Cambodia, and the Mekong Delta region in Vietnam. In the course of these journeys, another purpose was to observe and document the deterioration of the river, resulting from the series of exploitative and destructive projects that had resulted in ecological damage, diminishing people's resources and creating pollution... all these degenerative developments were happening more swiftly than many people had foreseen.

And so, throughout the next twenty-two years, until 2017, I remained an enduring and active associate of the "Friends of the Mekong," warning of the dangers inherent in the Mekong development projects, along with the other "storm-foretelling birds" living in countries along the upper reaches of the river, the chief one of which remains mighty China.

I have seen enough to know that the nearly twenty million people who live in the Mekong delta are still "blind to information," and have not realized that they have the right to raise their voices in calling for the defense of the mighty river which provides their life blood, even if one does not accuse them of ignoring the matter and letting it drop.

According to the Strategic Environmental Assessment put out by the International Center for Environmental Management / ICEM (Australia), aside from the initial dams put up in Yunnan Province, dams built further downstream have created a series of major problems, as follows: (1) changes in the course of the river; (2) danger to fisheries and sources of food; (3) a multi-faceted threat to the water ecology of the region; (4) changes in the ecology of the entire river; (5) a decrease in alluvial soil, resulting in the loss of evenness in the flow of water and the erosion of banks along the river and in regions close to the ocean; (6) a decrease in agricultural production, especially in the Tonle Sap and Vietnamese delta regions; (7) damage to the traditional life and culture of inhabitants of the Mekong regions that will persist for decades to come.

It is not just a question of the damage caused by the dams themselves; one must take account as well of plans to divert water from the Mekong in Thailand, and China's plans to carry out a rapids-blasting project on the upper Mekong for mines along Mekong waterfalls in China and Thailand so as to widen commercial navigation improvement.

One may mention some results already currently observable. In recent years the Tonle Sap area has not had enough water, even in the rainy season, to supply water to the ocean-like lake in that area–this immense lake is like the heart of Cambodia, and it has gradually been drying up; in the recent year of 2016, the catchment area there had no Rising Water Season, and was subject to a severe drought. The fact that Nguyễn Tấn Dũng, the prime minister of Vietnam, had to appeal to China to release water from the dam reservoir at Jinhong to relieve the drought in the Mekong Delta was an extremely ominous sign.

What is now the most worrisome factor in all this? Vietnam has clearly failed to be vigilant and has made no preparations to deal with this "ecological war without a battlefront" perpetrated by China. By rights, the leadership should have been concerned about this danger a number of years ago. By now, Laos plans to build nine more dams along the Mekong in Laos and two more in Cambodia will make efforts to confront the danger far more complicated, and Vietnam does not yet have a strategy.

Looking at the region from a geopolitical point of view, we must bear witness to the fact that the Mekong River is draining dry and the East Sea is in turmoil, as well as the artery that supplies the people's life-blood in that region is being occupied and squeezed dry by a China that has a violent and rampaging ambition to expand.

In the course of his research on Vietnam, SarDesai concluded that the two factors most decisive in destroying and building up our society have been: the need to confront a strong enemy to the north, and the need to withstand severe climatic conditions and, in most recent times, climate change. Vietnam is a country caught in the two halves of a pincer.

When Vietnam lost the Hoàng Sa Islands, Professor Hoàng Xuân Hãn wrote the following in the journal Historical Geography (Sử Địa) in 1974: "One of the obvious lessons of history is that every time a country grows weak due to internal divisions, a nearby power will invade and occupy some part of its territory. The present occupation of Hoàng Sa [and fourteen years later the occupation of Trường Sa; author's note] is a symptom of our people's civil conflict… Though there have been many past and present comments on the matter, those within and without the country all say that those islands are part of Vietnamese territory." And this shows as well that another cause of weakness and division within the country is that the Vietnamese Communist Party is extremely obedient to China.

Only the democratization of the country can bring about an opportunity to restore the unity and strength of the Vietnamese people; this is essential to our survival.

II. PHÙNG NGUYỄN: GOING TO COURT DUE TO "THE BATTLE OF SAIGON" 1972

"In 1972 the Saigon journal *Cyclopedia* [*Bách Khoa*] published an interview with the writer Ngô Thế Vinh, author of "The Battle of Saigon," with regard to his being summoned to court. *Cyclopedia* introduced the author and his situation as follows:

"The writer Ngô Thế Vinh, author of the novel *The Green Belt* (*Vòng Đai Xanh*), who, before Tết of this year was awarded the 1971 national prize for literature, was summoned to court after Tết on the charge that his article "The Battle of Saigon" ("Mặt Trận ở Sài Gòn") that appeared in *Presentations* (Trình Bầy), had "done damage to public order and weakened the discipline and fighting spirit of the army." If the prize given for *The Green Belt* had stirred less excitement than the one given for poetry, the court case of Ngô Thế Vinh became a topic taken by a great many authors writing for both civil and military magazines, and public opinion was united in its support of a writer who was in the army and, on the day he received his prize, was busy participating in operations in the highlands. We therefore have had a conversation with this author in order to enable the readers of *Cyclopedia* to have a clear grasp of how *The Green Belt* came into being and what its author thinks concerning his current court case.

"We beg also to record the following: Ngô Thế Vinh was born in 1941 in Thanh Hóa. He was the editor-in-chief of the journal *Medicine and Compassion* (*Tình Thương*), run by a group of medical students who sought to promote civil culture in the period 1963-1967. After graduating from medical school in 1968, he became a Special Forces army medic with the rank of Chief Medical Officer of the 81st Airborne Ranger Group. His publications include the novels *Storm Clouds* (*Mây Bão*; 1963), *Night Shadows* (*Bóng Đêm*; 1964), *Seasonal Winds* (*Gió Mùa*; 1965), and *The Green Belt* (*Vòng Đai Xanh*; 1970).

"In the aforementioned interview, the writer Ngô Thế Vinh discusses a series of social problems in the South that must be dealt with in the opening years of the 1970s, from the demands for self-government being made by our highland brethren in Tây Nguyên to the censorship system being imposed on journals and literary works. To obtain a clearer view of the different aspects touched upon by Ngô Thế Vinh, you are invited to read the entire *Cyclopedia* interview here.

"My dear Ngô Thế Vinh: The court case involving the "The Battle of Saigon" shows that the censorship system in the South in the period when the court case ran its course was not a bit less strict than that of the communist government in Hanoi. Under that system also, items were confiscated, portions of text were cut out, people were punished and even taken to court to face trials. As a person who was directly involved in this, what observations do you have concerning the censorship systems in the North and the South? Is it fair to say that the Southern system was "better" or more "considerate" than the Northern one?"

II. Ngô Thế Vinh Replies

Before entering into details, I can reply at once to Phùng by saying that the "basic nature" of the Northern and Southern political systems was utterly different, so when you speak of "censorship systems," no comparison you make can avoid being unstable and forced, because the two regimes had no common system of values.

The essential nature of the communist regime consisted of the enforcement of government decisions; there was no freedom of thought and no possibility of independent research. The merciless cruelty of the regime toward intellectuals and artists in the North was a matter of consistent policy consisting of crude coercion; they were forced to surrender their freedom and become unthinking tools of the regime. If they failed to do this, they naturally became "enemies of the party," but carried the additional designation of "enemies of the people." They were destroyed through imprisonment and hard labor, without ever being given a public trial, or, if not that, then they would be isolated, threatened with hunger and thirst, and deprived of influence until the day they died, not to speak of the things suffered by those close to them, who were also punished for being co-conspirators.

In official terms, the North did not have a "system of censorship," but instead something that worked even more perfectly: an apparatus of fear-inducing oppression that caused "censorship" to lie within the head of every writer and journalist until it became an unconscious, automatic response. This was a far more poisonous and ruthless policy, because it destroyed the humanity of those concerned and took away their ability to create. The *Humanities* (*Nhân Văn*) and *Belles Lettres* (*Giai Phẩm*) affair is a typical example of this, but one easily see that this was merely the "tip of the iceberg" in the seventy-year history of the communist party in Vietnam.

To return to the literature of the South in the period 54-75, we must acknowledge right away that there was not a single creative artist of that period who did not have an adverse reaction when the problem of censorship was raised. With no intention of defending it, we must nevertheless place ourselves in the circumstances of the country at that time, with a savage military conflict going on, and concealed communist agents everywhere. These agents would pretend to be striving for democratic freedoms, while their actual goal was to create a secret war front that would destabilize society and weaken the young republic of the South just emerging from an era of feudalism, and that was why there was some remnant of censorship: the objective was to stop communist infiltration.

Then we must also take note of the importance of a movement to oppose the "degradation of culture" originating in portions of the Chinese community of Chợ Lớn. These consisted of highly immoral publications with fake insignia of government approval that were illegally printed and distributed to purveyors of pornographic novels and magazines aimed at poisoning the country's children and young people.

I cannot but recall the tenor of life in the rear areas of the South in those times, the most typical being those that prevailed in the two largest cities: Saigon and Huế. At a time when all the battlefields of the nation were in turmoil, the cities themselves never enjoyed peace, but instead were the scenes of a different war. To take Saigon first, I wish to mention the assassinations of students, professors, and journalists organized by members of communist units. At that time, I myself was a student, and was a member of the editorial board, and then the editor-in-chief, of the monthly journal [*Tình Thương*] put out by Saigon medical students (1964 – 1966) and may be regarded as a witness to those events:

"I must also record a few events that have become part of history: in the Medical School alone, two professors were assassinated (Professor Trần Anh, Anatomy, and Professor Lê Minh Trí, Otorhinolaryngology), and then it became the turn of the second-year medical student Trần Quốc Chương (son of the Judge Trần Thúc Linh) – he had spent a period as a communist guerilla in the maquis, and then returned to school. He was gagged, had his arms bound, and then was hurled to the ground from the third floor of a building right within the grounds of the medical school on Hồng Bàng Street, a particularly atrocious death. The law student Lê Khắc Sinh Nhật was also shot dead. Two other students – they were in the Faculty of Letters – were shot and severely wounded, but fortunately survived; these were Ngô Vương Toại and Bùi Hồng Sĩ; these two subsequently emigrated to the United States (Ngô Vương Toại died in the U.S. on April 3, 2014).

As for me, aside from being a student in the medical school, I was on the school's board of representatives and was the editor-in-chief of the student journal *Medicine and Compassion*, and like all my classmates fought for the autonomy of the university, while at the same time striving to stop communist infiltration, so my name was entered into the "black notebook" of the communist "Dare-to-Die" commandos along with seventeen students in other branches of study.

There was clearly a price to be paid for engaging in journalism, even in student publications, during this period. [Concerning journalistic activities in the South in the period 1954 – 1975, one cannot fail to mention the sacrifices of such journalists as Từ Chung of the daily *Political Discourse* (*Chính Luận*) in 1965. Another well-known figure who was attacked but survived was Chu Tử, the editor of the journal *Life* (*Sống*).]

After graduation, I volunteered to join the Special Forces, and served in the 81st Airborne Rangers' Group, operating mainly in the highland region. I continued to write while serving; *The Green Belt* (*Vòng Đai Xanh*; 1970) and *The Battle of Saigon* (*Mặt Trận ở Sài Gòn*; 1972) were finished in this period of military service. Looking back on that period, I must say that the censorship system in the South was rather fragmented–a situation arising from a lack of personnel in that department. This led to a number of works of value being banned–but the authors concerned later had opportunities to discuss their cases with the Coordinating Office of the Cultural Branch of the Information Board.

And when I worked for the student journal *Medicine and Compassion*, though I had some run-ins with the army security chief Nguyễn Ngọc Loan, I was not subsequently pursued or harassed by army police or security personnel because the journal espoused positions contrary to those of the army or dealt with prohibited works. It seems I should also mention here that in the period 54-75, there were a number of authors known to be communists in concealment, such as Vũ Hạnh and Nguyễn Ngọc Lương, who were allowed to be active as writers and even to publish journals.

I also wish to record here a personal experience as a writer in the South during that period: My first novel, *Storm Clouds* (*Mây Bão*; 1963) was not granted a seal of approval by the censorship committee. I went to the Ministry of Information to protest this. I was then a 22-year-old medical student. I was received by Phạm Xuân Thái, the Information minister, a very suave and intelligent man. He said that he had not yet read the book, but that, according to the report of the committee, the book's content reflected too many negative aspects of society at that time. He talked with me about the professional attitude of a writer: of the need to reflect the positive sides of society instead of only portraying its reverse sides. Then, in response to a request of mine, he agreed to have a different member of the censorship board read *Storm Clouds*. This second reader was Nguyễn Thanh Đàm, who was none other than the poet Song Hồ. He liked the book a great deal, and said to me that it had the marks of a work that would become important in the future. The book was issued a permission certificate and Song Hồ in subsequent years became a literary friend of mine until his death in the U.S. in 2009.

And then came *The Green Belt* (*Vòng Đai Xanh*), a documentary novel about a war going on at that time which was forgotten in the midst of the Vietnam war. In it, the various indigenous peoples of the highlands belonging to FULRO, "Front Unifié de Lutte des Races Opprimées" (Unified Front in the Struggle of the Oppressed Races") rose up to demand self-rule for the Tây Nguyên region. *The Green Belt* was also at first prohibited, but the army writer Thế Uyên argued strenuously on its behalf with the Ministry of Information, with the result that the book was published, and after that won a prize.

The phenomenon of "confiscation, excision, punishment, and being called to court" that Phùng refers to was in my opinion simply a transitory reaction to circumstances, and was also the result of differing degrees of intellectual development among members of the censorship committee. The measures used that were apparently so severe, including court summons, were actually just a game played in a democratic society, and the people involved returned afterwards to their usual activities almost as if nothing had happened, so the whole thing could be seen as "a storm in a teacup."

Here is another example: in 1972 the writer Nguyễn-Xuân Hoàng was in Saigon working as a journalist and a teacher, whereas I was with my unit operating in Tây Nguyên, but we both went through an experience worth recording here. Because of my short story "The Battle of Saigon," I received a court summons to answer to the charge of "using the media to disturb the social order and to diminish the discipline and fighting spirit of the army," though I myself was a member of the armed forces. When I went to Saigon to answer the summons, Nguyễn-Xuân Hoàng told me that he too had received a court summons due to his short story "My Father and Elder Brother" ("Cha Và Anh") which had

From the right: Phùng Nguyễn and Ngô Thế Vinh at Duke's Huntington Beach in May, 2015

appeared in the journal *Issues* (*Vấn Đề*) of Vũ Khắc Khoan. His offense was apparently that he had referred in the story to "The Mother of Gio Linh" (Bà Mẹ Gio Linh) a song by Phạm Duy.

Hoàng and I both went to court, and we both had lawyer-friends who volunteered to defend us. The final court statements in the two cases had a merely symbolic character. Nguyễn-Xuân Hoàng returned to journalism and teaching, and I returned to engage in operations with my unit, and not long after that was able to pursue further studies in San Francisco in Rehabilitation Medicine. Hoàng and I continued to publish books. And, to use Hoàng's expression, our lives "didn't stop running along." This is something beyond the comprehension of creative artists who lived under the communist regime of the North and then in the South after 1975.

In a world in which the warfront was full of blood and fire, and in which the rear areas had no lack of disturbances and partisanship, the writers and artists of the South still had a certain degree of freedom to create as they wished. The proof of this is the huge and varied quantity of work produced in the period 54-75.

As a writer, I have never raised my voice to defend the existence of a censorship system, but now that I have the space and leisure to look back on that period, I can regard such censorship as existed in the South as a sort of "collateral damage" in a communist – republican war in which culture and journalism were engaged in a further war.

III. PHÙNG NGUYỄN: PORTRAITS OF WRITERS AND ARTISTS

In November of 2010, the web-journal *Skin of Color* presented the article "A Different Cao Xuân Huy" by Ngô Thế Vinh in order to commemorate in a highly unusual manner the author of *My Gun Broke in March*. The article began with a section introducing and explaining *Melanoma*, a rare type of cancer that the writer Cao Xuân

Phùng Nguyễn's elderly mother with Ngô Thế Vinh
(photo by Huy Văn, Dec. 5, 2015)

Huy had the misfortune to suffer, and that compelled him to depart from this mortal realm in a hasty manner. In June of 2014, also in the web-journal "Skin of Color," Ngô Thế Vinh sent his readers another article entitled "Nguyễn-Xuân Hoàng on the Road between Life and Death." Unlike the article about Cao Xuân Huy, this one offered a relatively balanced and dispassionate view of this author's character, writings and the illness from which he suffered. According to him, this around the period when Ngô Thế Vinh the writer began to join forces with Ngô Thế Vinh the doctor, the former medic in the 81st Airborne Ranger Group, in his quest to (re-)create portraits of the writers, poets and artists who were close to him. After his articles concerning Cao Xuân Huy and Nguyễn-Xuân Hoàng, came additional ones on Nghiêu Đề, Dương Nghiễm Mậu, Thanh Tâm Tuyền. And then articles on Võ Phiến, Mặc Đỗ, Linh Bảo, Nguyễn Đình Toàn, Nhật Tiến, and recently, one on Đinh Cường.

"An observation shared by many is the following: Though the writers and artists that Ngô Thế Vinh chose for his portraits exhibit the greatest possible variety, the articles have one thing in common: His subjects have all either died, or are caught in the mortal toils of "Birth, Age, Illness, and Death" and are in the twilight of their years. This makes readers wonder: could the physical distress of his subjects be one of determining factors in Ngô Thế Vinh's choice of people to write about?

"Passing through the mortal gates and bearing portraits,
He totes a bag filled half with doctor's, half with writer's tools."

"And so, my dear Ngô Thế Vinh, what proportion in each portrait is devoted to medicine, and what proportion to literature?"

III. Ngô Thế Vinh Replies

My series of portraits of writers and artists came to me as by chance. It began with an article entitled "Remembering my Dear Friend Nghiêu Đề." The artist Nghiêu Đề was my friend from times when we were both very young. After writing it, I got feedback from several old friends of his, among whom was Đinh Cường, who was very pleased with the article and said, "It would be impossible to write of Nghiêu Đề more successfully than you have." He suggested that the article be included in a book he was about to publish: *Entering the Realm of the Created Image, Vol. II* (*Đi Vào Cõi Tạo Hình II*), which was about all the artists of his generation who in the years 1957 to 1966 were active in the Association of Young Vietnamese Artists. This suggestion gave me great pleasure. And then there were the words of encouragement that came from Phạm Phú Minh of "Century Forum" ("Diễn Đàn Thế Kỷ), Phùng Nguyễn the editor-in-chief of "Skin of Color" (Da Màu), and the poet Thành Tôn every time they read one of my new cultural portraits.

Dr. Hà Ngọc Thuần, a colleague of mine who now lives in Australia and who was once a journalism student with me during my years of involvement with Medicine and Compassion in 1964-66 and who was regarded as one of the more learned writers among the Saigon medical students at that time, sent me an email message in which he said: "Having seen the articles of Ngô Thế Vinh that you have posted on the web, I can say that you have definitely succeeded in the genre of the biographical essay. With their incisive comments, deft blended strokes, bits of personal narrative, they enable the reader to become acquainted with the artists at once, and stimulate a desire to learn more about them. With the "web-essay" of our technically accomplished age, we have articles that are more concise, have more images, and often with vivid stretches of video, with speech and music. So in the article about Nguyễn Đình Toàn, for example, we can hear sounds from his program "Themes in Music," from more than half a century ago, and in the article on Hoàng Ngọc Biên, we can hear the song "Autumn Lake" performed by the singer Ngọc Mai–who could have known that Hoàng Ngọc Biên wrote music as well? And in the articles about artists, we can appreciate their works in full color with a vividness very difficult to achieve in a printed book."

Mr. Phạm Phú Minh, the author of *Hanoi in My Eyes* (*Hà Nội Trong Mắt Tôi*) editor-in-chief of "Century Forum" ("Diễn Đàn Thế Kỷ"), said to me abruptly one day, "Vinh, I now have a new way of looking at you." The remark surprised me a little. He explained: "Up to now, I have always regarded you as a person who conducts research on the Mekong River. Now I see that you are the author of portraits of overseas people who are active in the cultural sphere."

It was also Phạm Phú Minh who, responding on a different occasion to my article "Years of Disillusionment of Professor Phạm Hoàng Hộ and the book *Trees and Plants of Vietnam* (*Cây Cỏ Việt Nam*)," wrote: "If I say that the article that Vinh has written about Phạm Hoàng Hộ is very fine, then it will seem that I have said nothing whatsoever. The constantly used word "fine" ["hay"] is too general; and says nothing about the character of the things this author has written. One must say that this article is of a scholarly and broadly inclusive nature: the profound insights of a literary man, the specialized concerns of a scientist, the threat posed by the future of a river… each topic is discussed by him in all the aspects necessary to be developed."

Studying the Mekong River was a planned intention that I had cherished for more than twenty years, but writing portraits of people in the arts had never been an intention of mine. I must say though that each time I had an occasion to write about an artistic colleague or a figure in the arts, recording parts of the paths they traveled and the stretches of the lives we had lived, it was a great joy to do so.

As for the question posed by Phùng Nguyễn – what factors induced me to choose the personages that I introduced into my series of portraits – it was all very accidental. It was not because, as he suggested, that they had all either died, or entered into the twilight of their lives, or because they were wrestling with the problems of Birth, Age, Illness, and Death"–the important factor was that I had a close personal relationship with each of these people, and due to this, it was easy for me to access materials concerning them and to call up personal memories of our interactions.

Once, before I had written anything about him, I had a conversation with Nguyễn Đình Toàn in which I emphasized a personal principle: that in my writings, including the series of cultural portraits, an article could be missing concrete materials, but the ones included in the article must be accurate and not mistaken. That being the case, the question remains: in each portrait, how much is concerned with medicine, and how much to portraiture?

It is not the case that every portrait includes a section devoted to medical matters; medical topics emerge in special circumstances, as in the cases of Cao Xuân Huy, Nguyễn-Xuân Hoàng, and Đinh Cường. How could I not be concerned with medicine when my own friends had fallen ill and were precariously perched between life and death? And when not every sick person can easily accept the reality of his own illness? And it was also not easy for me to go deeply into medical matters when the pains suffered by my friends were suffered by me as well.

A further aspect of this lies in the realm of medical ethics. That is the right to privacy of the ill person, which doctors must respect. Due to this, I did not feel that I enjoyed the freedom to write whatever I wished about the illnesses suffered by my subjects. I had the greatest respect for their right to privacy. So, for example, when Cao Xuân Huy, my close friend for many years, died, I was able to write about the details of his illness only because his wife and two adult daughters gave me permission to do so.

If these friends of mine were still alive, and could read these articles concerning them, they would have an absolute right to accept or reject the presence of these medical details. Nguyễn-Xuân Hoàng accepted the inclusion of details concerning the sarcoma from which he suffered when he read my draft. Nguyễn Đình Toàn said, "Vinh, I read your article this morning, and feel very strange about it, as if it were about some other person. It's a good thing that all those true facts have now turned into falsehoods [i.e. passed by], so one need not fear them"

The portrait of Đinh Cường was a special case. At first he accepted my draft, but later on let me know that it made him apprehensive. He requested me to reduce the medical details as much as possible and replace them with the "autoportrait" of April 2015 that he sent me after undergoing a chemo treatment. He felt that this would lighten the tone of the article. I, of course, treated this last request of my friend with absolute respect.

Upon completion of eighteen of these portraits of cultural figures, I received many suggestions that I should publish them as a collection. If there should be a book of this sort, "recreating the images of writers, poets, and artists," then this will be a book page dedicated to Phùng Nguyễn.

BY WAY OF A CONCLUSION

The three questions of yours, Phùng Nguyễn, (that you sent to Nhã Thuyên, Trần Mộng Tú, and Hoàng Hưng)… are in themselves sufficient to demonstrate that you read everything sent you by your correspondents with care, and that you brought all your faculties to bear upon them. With each question you asked, and with the answers I provided, I can see the faint sprouting of a plan for a large-scale literary project of yours and cannot imagine what name you might have attached to it. Perhaps this is one of the uncompleted projects that was broken off along with your life that was "interrupted in mid-journey."

It would be a great injustice to you if I replied in an offhand manner to your questions. For me, each of your questions, Phùng Nguyễn, has the character of a challenge, and seems to outline a topic for a dissertation. Though you are no longer with us, I must still, with the utmost respect, complete answers to each one, and at the same time send them to members of the younger generation, born after the end of the Vietnam war in 1975, as a step toward recovering a time that has passed away.

California 03/2015 – 03/2017

FEELING FOR THE HOMELAND IN THE MUSIC OF PHẠM DUY AND HIS VARIOUS PORTRAITS

"This photo was taken when he was preparing to celebrate his 90th birthday. On Thống Nhất Boulevard, clinging to the wall surrounding The School of Pharmacy is a large and beautiful banyan tree. I chose that place with the thought that Phạm Duy is like a great and ancient tree in the music of Vietnam". *(Words and photo by Nguyễn Phong Quang)*

PREFACE:

I thank all my near and distant friends who love the music of Phạm Duy and the man as well who, reposing trust in me, have given me permission to use many precious materials, including personal correspondence extending over a period of close to thirty years with no motive other than to help the writer have a sufficiency of documents.

They in fact have given me enough to serve as the basis of a book–but that will be a project for the future. This is merely a short essay, in which I hope to be able to sketch a few features of a great artist: Phạm Duy, the idol of many people through many generations, with a life both inspiring and complicated. Phạm Duy lived in two successive centuries, "weeping and laughing with the developing fortunes of his country, experiencing the prolonged tragedy of modern Vietnamese history, at once heroic and endlessly sad."

PHẠM DUY AND HIS DISTANCES

Phạm Duy was born in 1921, so he is separated from me by a generation in all aspects of his activities and environment. In the 1940s, when the anti-French Resistance War broke out, and I went with my family to seek refuge in a countryside spot in Thanh Hóa in Interzone IV, I too, together with my little companions, would sing and hum the song "A Countryside Child" ("Em Bé Quê") and other Resistance songs by Phạm Duy. My memories of the war in that period consist simply of the image of a beautiful capital in Thanh Hóa that was leveled to the ground due to the scorched-earth policies of the Việt Minh. Interzone IV was still regarded as a relatively secure area; no western legionnaires came there to conduct sweeps, and if there were bombs, they were dropped from on a great height from French "B vingt-neufs" (B-29s) that flew along the length of the Mã River, roaring and moaning in the sky, and then at intervals releasing cascades of booming shells that would sink passenger's boats. There were no infantry units, just people on the river going here and there to sell merchandise. The greatest instance of mass death that I witnessed was the bombing by two French planes of Rừng Thông (Pine Forest) Market – the scene was full of blood and dead bodies.

In 1951, when I returned to Hanoi to attend to a family matter, I learned that Phạm Duy, the composer of "A Countryside Child," had for a time worked as a radio repairman for an uncle of mine on Hàng Gai Street. Having heard this detail, I soon forgot it, but now, seventy years later, reading volume one of The Memoirs of Phạm Duy, I have learned for the first time about his childhood:

> "I was expelled from the Industrial Training School before I had completed my first year there because my violations of school regulations were a bit frequent: getting into fights, sneaking away from the school when I was supposed to be confined to the premises, and so forth. My worst offense occurred one day when I had made some mistake or other, but wouldn't put up with having my ears boxed by Besançon – so I traded insults with the "factory chief," and raised my hammer to strike him as well. I was expelled immediately afterward. Not daring to return home for fear of facing "Mr. Elder Brother," I boarded a bus for Trạm Chôi and went to stay with the family of my wet nurse.
>
> "After a few weeks in hiding, I crept back home and was immediately banished to quarters in the garage. And thus, after long being looked upon as a stubborn, incorrigible child, I became, after my expulsion from the school, the object of the disparagement both of my elder brother and my elder brother-in-law. On a particular night during a meal, one of those two, I don't remember which, said something that went too far, and I left, slamming the door. True to the sarcastic words of my brother-in-law, who often remarked that I was a "sans foutiste" (total screw-up), I was totally through with the need for the loving attention or the protection or support of any adult whatsoever!
>
> "I stayed for a few weeks with a family I knew and then obtained a job at the Nguyễn Đình Thụ radio repair shop on Hàng Gai street."

[Author's note: The engineer Nguyễn Đình Thụ was my mother's elder brother and a friend of Phạm Duy's elder brother, the agrégé Phạm Duy Khiêm, from the days when they were both students in France.]

Phạm Duy continues:

> "Though I was only a little into my sixteenth year, I had some understanding of radio technology and had assembled a small radio myself to which one could listen by means of a crystal, so

> I found much to interest and delight me in this new job. Radios in the formative era of electronics still used vacuum tubes and electric circuits of the *hétérodyne* type. If one were to compare this to the electronic "chips" now in use, one could say that I entered electronics in the era of its actual genesis. The Nguyễn Đình Thụ radio repair shop was right at the entrance to Hàng Gai Street, so I had the opportunity to witness how the young people of Hanoi lived in the last years of the 1930s."

I take note of these matters here, because they serve to explain Phạm Duy's superb technical abilities when he subsequently entered the high-tech realm of digital technology. When this occurred in the 1980s, he became the earliest Vietnamese musician to be able to use computers to write and distribute music and to write his memoirs.

PHẠM DUY AND HIS MULTIMEDIA CD ROM OF 1995

During the months and years when he lived in the U.S., a land of science and technology, Phạm Duy very swiftly found ways to study and adapt to this technology. He was very proud to be the first in the overseas Vietnamese community to create a multimedia CD ROM. Near the end of Volume 4 of his Memoirs, he wrote:

> "I was the most fortunate of people, because I was able to make the acquaintance of the computer from the very dawn of this invention. My son Duy Cường and I began to use computers toward the end of the 1980s. At first, we used them simply as a substitute for typewriters, but back then no one had as yet been able to put Vietnamese fonts into computers. We had to search and search before we found an engineer, Mr. Nguyễn Văn Tâm, working for the NASA Space Agency, who had made a set of Vietnamese fonts – he was the first person to do this."

Author's Note: Up to the present moment I have known only two Vietnamese engineers in the U.S. who created sets of Vietnamese-language software. The earliest was Nguyễn Việt. He was born in Hanoi and grew up in Đà Lạt. From 1969 to 1975 he served as an officer in the navy of the Republic of Vietnam. He emigrated to the

U.S. in 1975, gained a bachelor's degree in 1979, and a master's degree in 1985. He founded the company Diplomat, formerly located in Newport Beach. He created a set of Vietnamese fonts bearing the imprimatur "VN Labs" and gained an honorary certificate recognizing this creation in 1985.

The second person was the engineer Hồ Thành Việt. Born in Nha Trang, he was six years younger than Nguyễn Việt, and also emigrated to the U.S. in 1975. After gaining a bachelor's degree in engineering in 1985, he worked for Diplomat, and after that established his own place of business in Westminster, where, in 1988, he produced his own set of Vietnamese fonts, called VNI. Though the set produced by Nguyễn Việt of VN labs already existed. Hồ Thành Việt had

BUSINESS

1992 Was a Year of Stunning Losses for Many Insurers

Year of Disasters

Two rival Orange County businessmen with similar backgrounds aspire to someday help modernize Vietnam and improve its literacy rate with their native language software.

Parallel Paths

Vietnamese Immigrants Share Heritage, High-Tech Hopes

CERTIFICATE OF COPYRIGHT REGISTRATION

FORM TX

TXu 182-791

JAN - 7 1985

ACTING REGISTER OF COPYRIGHTS
United States of America

1 TITLE OF THIS WORK: VIETNAMESE CHARACTERS GENERATION FOR THE IBM PERSONAL COMPUTER

2 a NAME OF AUTHOR: VIET NGUYEN — 1949 — U.S.A. — ENTIRE TEXT

4 VIET NGUYEN

424524 JAN 7 85

Left: A page from the Los Angeles Times, February 21, 1993, by the journalist Dean Takahashi. It concerns the two Vietnamese-American computer engineers who were the first to create Vietnamese fonts: the engineer Nguyễn Việt with his VN Labs set, and the engineer Hồ Thành Việt with his VNI set. Right: A document showing that Nguyễn Việt received a diploma in 1985 recognizing his creation of the VN Labs fonts, and stating that he was the person who went to Phạm Duy's house on Hunter Lane in Midway City to help him install the VN Labs set on Phạm Duy's IBM PC computer *(Ngô Thế Vinh, personal archives)*

better marketing skills, so his fonts came to be more widely used in traditional and overseas Vietnamese communities.

Because Phạm Duy referred twice to "the NASA engineer Nguyễn Văn Tâm" as "the first person who made a set of digital Vietnamese fonts, the present author got in touch with Dr. Trương Hồng Sơn, that is, the writer and artist Trương Vũ, who emigrated to the U.S. in 1976 and worked for NASA until his retirement, to make a respectful inquiry concerning this person. I received the following email response from Dr. Trương Hồng Sơn: "My dear Ngô Thế Vinh, I really have no idea! It's rather strange. I know of no engineer working for NASA named Nguyễn Văn Tâm. NASA has many centers. Aside from former colleagues of mine, NASA had many contractors, the names of whom are not necessarily known to me. Nevertheless, my impressions regarding the first people to create Vietnamese fonts are the same as yours.

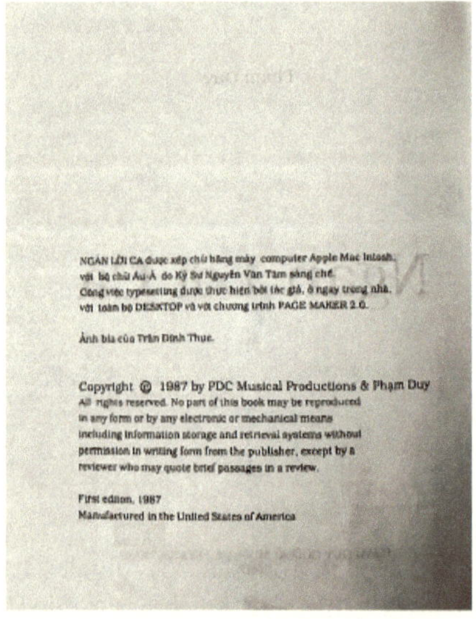

NGÀN LỜI CA được xếp chữ bằng máy computer Apple Mac Intosh, với bộ chữ Âu-Á do Kỹ Sư Nguyễn Văn Tâm sáng chế. Công việc typesetting được thực hiện bởi tác giả, ở ngay trong nhà, với toàn bộ DESKTOP và với chương trình PAGE MAKER 2.0.

Ảnh bìa của Trần Đình Thục.

Copyright © 1987 by PDC Musical Productions & Phạm Duy
All rights reserved. No part of this book may be reproduced in any form or by any electronic or mechanical means including information storage and retrieval systems without permission in writing form from the publisher, except by a reviewer who may quote brief passages in a review.

First edition, 1987
Manufactured in the United States of America

The book *Phạm Duy: Thousand Sets of Lyrics* (*Phạm Duy Ngàn Lời Ca*) was first published in 1987. One of its pages has the following notation: *Thousand Sets of Lyrics* was laid out on an Apple-Macintosh computer with Vietnamese fonts created by the engineer Nguyễn Văn Tâm. The typesetting was done at home by the author using the programs Desktop and Pagemaker 2.0.

(Đỗ Việt Anh, personal archives)

In 1985, the only existing Vietnamese fonts were those of VN Labs. In 1988 VNI fonts became available as well, but these two sets of fonts could be used only with IBM PCs. It is thus possible that there was an engineer named Nguyễn Văn Tâm who was the first to create a set of fonts for the Apple Macintosh used by Phạm Duy.

I, the present author, have reached no conclusion on this matter– and can only hope that after this article is made generally available, the engineer Nguyễn Văn Tâm will read it and make himself known to me, so that "what belongs to Caesar may be rendered unto Caesar."

Phạm Duy continues as follows:

> "And so, the two of us installed Vietnamese fonts on the machine and began using computers to write articles, write my Memoirs, and write books on music, and especially to preserve the contents of my many messy files" – the words of Phạm Duy – "and it took a long time for us to find musical software to produce scores and arrangements, and to purchase artistic software so as to create images and graphic designs – until at last, thanks to the computer, we gained the ability to create CD ROMs.
>
> "Just as we had been the first people to produce audio CDs, now, with the cooperation of a young engineer in San José, Bùi Minh Cương, we produced the first Vietnamese CD ROM." [author's note: the engineer Bùi Minh Cương was the maternal nephew of the journalist Bùi Bảo Trúc.]
>
> "This was a very beautiful marriage of technology with art. We created this earliest Vietnamese CD-ROM, "A Journey through the Motherland (Hành Trình Trên Đất Mẹ), in the hope that we could bring a bit of the cultural heritage of our country to present as a gift to the coming generation, which, perhaps because its members had been born and raised overseas, had been cut off from the spiritual life of our people."
>
> *(The Memoirs of Phạm Duy, Vol. 4)*

Views of a CD ROM given by Phạm Duy to Ngô Thế Vinh. This was the first Vietnamese CD ROM created overseas in 1987. An American Jewish doctor who worked in the same hospital with me was quite surprised at the high proportion of Vietnamese who came here to pursue careers, and when he held in his hands the audio CD of the song cycle entitled *The National Road* (*Con Đường Cái Quan*) by Phạm Duy, and then another that had performances of Chopin by the pianist Đặng Thái Sơn, he observed to me that, "You overseas Vietnamese have advanced further here in twenty years than other peoples have in a hundred. I never supposed that you all would be able to enter so early into the world of high-tech." *(Ngô Thế Vinh, personal archives)*

TWENTY YEARS OF SPLENDOR IN SOUTH VIETNAM

To return to the period 1954 – 1975: after the Geneva Agreement divided the country in two, more than a million people who had experienced life under communist rule, abandoned their homes, lands, and belongings in the North and emigrated to the South.

Phạm Duy had abandoned the Resistance War and returned to Hanoi, and then moved to the South in 1951. From the South to the North, he and his family grew famous through the Thăng Long Performance Group (Ban Hợp Ca Thăng Long), the members of which were Phạm Duy, Hoài Bắc, Hoài Trung, Thái Hằng, Thái Thanh, and Khánh Ngọc.

In the 1960s, when I had entered the Saigon School of Medicine and was active as a journalist through my connection with the periodical *Tình Thương / Medicine and Compassion*, I became acquainted with Lê Ngộ Châu, and through him met Phạm Duy a couple of times in the editorial office of the journal *Bách Khoa / Cyclopedia*. He was not one of the writers who worked for that publication, but he was very close to Lê Ngộ Châu–the two of them had been friends in Military District IV during the Resistance War. Bách Khoa published a number of studies of Phạm Duy and his

The Thăng Long Performance Group, featured in "Pink Nights of Saigon"; front row, from left: Thái Hằng, Khánh Ngọc, Thái Thanh; back row from left: Phạm Duy, Hoài Bắc (Phạm Đình Chương), Hoài Trung (Phạm Đình Viêm) *(Phạm Duy, personal archives)*

music written by George E. Gauthier, a musicologist from Canada [*Cyclopedia* 332 (Nov. 1, 1970), 334, 335, 337/338 (Xuân Tân Hợi), 339, 340, 342, 345, 346, 347, 350, 353, 354, 355, 363, 367, 372, and 375 (Aug. 15, 1972)], and also an interview with him conducted by the journalist Lê Phương Chi (*Cyclopedia* 241-242, 243)] (Phạm Lệ Hương, personal archives)

Through some stories told me by Lê Ngộ Châu, I got to know a few other aspects of Phạm Duy, including the circumstances surrounding the creation of the song "A Little Something for a Keepsake" ("Còn Chút Gì Để Nhớ"), a setting of a poem by Vũ Hữu Định.

Anecdote 1: Lê Ngộ Châu and Trí Đăng (1970)

Around the year 1970, the editorial office of *Bách Khoa/Cyclopedia* received a poem entitled "A Little Something for a Keepsake" by Vũ Hữu Định, a person virtually unknown to Lê Ngộ Châu, but because he thought the poem was particularly fine, with its graceful images of the mountainous neighborhoods of Pleiku, he had Trí Đăng (the head of the Trí Đăng printing house that published *Cyclopedia*,) ride on a motorcycle to the home of Phạm Duy in the Chu Mạnh Trinh residential quarter, a crossroads in Phú Nhuận (a sector of Saigon), a place where many famous performers and writers (including Năm Châu, Nguyễn Mạnh Côn, Duyên Anh, Minh Trang, and Kim Tước) lived with their families. Lê Ngộ Châu suggested to Phạm Duy that he set Vũ Hữu Định's poem to music – though he didn't yet know who that author was. In only two days, Phạm Duy gave wings to the poem by writing a song of the same title that was aired on the Saigon Broadcasting Station with the ageless voice of Thái Thanh. Setting poems to music was one of Phạm Duy's special gifts.

Anecdote 2: A Recollection of Trương Điện Thắng, with an Account by Phạm Duy

According to an in-country journalist, Trương Điện Thắng, the song "A Little Something for a Keepsake" was in 1971-1972 among the most requested songs on the program "Music by Request" on the Saigon Broadcasting Station. The author of the poem, Vũ Hữu Định,

Cover of the first edition of "*A Little Something for a Keepsake*," lyrics by Vũ Hữu Định, music by Phạm Duy, 1970.

was at that time just over thirty… he was in Saigon dodging the draft, drifting here and there between Lâm Đồng, Bảo Lộc, Pleiku. He lived in the shade with many pen names, such as Hàn Giang Tử and Vũ Hữu Định… he was a young fellow whose place of origin was An Cựu, but he spoke with a Quảng Nam accent. He never expected that the gifted songwriter Phạm Duy would pay him any attention. Using the pen name Vũ Hữu Định, he began to appear in Lê Ngộ Châu's journal *Cyclopedia* and the weekly arts magazine *Khởi Hành* managed by Viên Linh. The poem "A Little Something for a Keepsake" appeared in *Khởi Hành* and was copied into a notebook by the author Võ Phiến. Later on, when we met Phạm Duy in Nha Trang for a *Duyên Dáng Việt Nam* program No. 16 (12/2006), Phạm Duy told us at dinner that he once went to pay a visit to Võ Phiến, but found that he had gone elsewhere. Seeing Võ Phiến's notebook as he waited in the study for the writer's return, he turned over a few pages and happened upon the poem. "At the time I didn't know who Vũ Hữu Định was, but the language and rhythm of the poem made me decide to set it to music."

(Còn Chút Gì Để Nhớ, or the Fate of Each Creation, Trương Điện Thắng@T.Van 2017)

Anecdote 3: Phạm Duy, Late in Life, Recollects an Event

In his *Echoes of a Former Era* (*Vang Vọng Một Thời*; Phương Nam Books, 2015) Phạm Duy offers yet another account of the song's origin:

> Saigon 1972: I went to Pleiku to investigate the music of the Western Highlands (Tây Nguyên). During the week that I spent there, I got to meet a young poet who had been stationed there with his military unit to that border region. Back then, the provincial capital of Pleiku was very small. The young poet Vũ Hữu Định described, in an adorable little poem, the little city, "where he had gone for a moment or two to revisit some

9.

Còn Chút Gì Để Nhớ

Saigon 1972. Tôi đi Pleiku để nghiên cứu nhạc Tây Nguyên. Trong một tuần lễ ở đó, tôi được gặp vài nhà thơ trẻ bị động viên đang đóng quân tại miền biên giới này. Lúc đó tỉnh lỵ Pleiku còn nhỏ hẹp lắm. Một nhà thơ trẻ, Vũ Hữu Định, đã mô tả cái thành phố *đi dăm phút đã về chốn cũ*... trong một bài thơ rất dễ thương. Tôi phổ nhạc ngay lập tức, không thêm thắt hay sửa đổi một chữ nào trong bài thơ. Cũng vì tôi đang nghiên cứu nhạc Thượng nên tôi dùng ngay ngũ cung cơ bản - cung (do mi fa sol si do) trong phần giai điệu.

Còn Chút Gì Để Nhớ

(Theo thơ Vũ Hữu Định - Phạm Duy phổ nhạc)

Phố núi cao, phố núi đầy sương
Phố núi cây xanh trời thấp thật buồn
Anh khách lạ đi lên đi xuống
May mà có em đời còn dễ thương.
Em Pleiku má đỏ môi hồng
Ở đây buổi chiều quanh năm mùa Đông
Nên tóc em ướt và mắt em ướt
Nên em mềm như mây chiều buồng.

The book *Echoes of a Former Era*, in which Phạm Duy provides an account of his musical setting of the poem "A Little Something for a Keepsake" by Vũ Hữu Định. *(Phạm Phú Minh, personal archives)*

old haunts." I set it to music at once, making no alteration in the words. Since I was just then studying the music of the highlands, I gave it a pentatonic (do mi fa sol si do) melody.

(Echoes of a Former Era by Phạm Duy, Phương Nam, 2015)

What is beyond doubt is that Phạm Duy set music to the poem "A Little Something for a Keepsake" by Vũ Hữu Định, but there are three anecdotes that purport to tell how this occurred, and there may be others as well, so it seems I should record what I can in this location, so that the reader may decide for himself "which of these truths is true."

...

I perhaps met Phạm Duy on a few other occasions in the restaurant La Pagode, where my literary friend Nguyễn Đình Toàn came almost every day to sit and write. He related to me, as a diverting anecdote, that Phạm Duy was desperately afflicted with stinginess. He could never conduct his hand out of his pocket after it had come into contact with his wallet. Though Toàn was fifteen years younger than the songwriter, the two of them nevertheless used the casual pronouns "mày" and "tao" with each other in conversation – that was like Mai Thảo and Vũ Hoàng Chương, who did the same, though Chương was almost a dozen years older than Mai Thảo. In that period too, I got to read a couple of books about Phạm Duy: *Phạm Duy Still Sits There Dejected* (Phạm Duy Còn Đó Nỗi Buồn) by Tạ Tỵ, and *The Death Process of Phạm Duy* (Phạm Duy Đã Chết Như Thế Nào?) by Nguyễn Trọng Văn.

After 1975, when I was still in labor reeducation camp, my friends and I heard a number of strange rumors – one was that General (and former Vice President) Nguyễn Cao Kỳ had returned to the Catholic settlement of Tân Sa Châu, where he was heading a resistance organization dedicated to retaking the country; stranger still was a story that Phạm Duy had vomited blood and died on the stage with a guitar in his arms while singing his song-cycle *A Flock of Birds Who Forsook Their Land* (*Bầy Chim Bỏ Xứ*). "The National Road" Goes Out to the Spratly and Paracel Islands.

I crossed to the U.S. eight years later and met Phạm Duy in southern California in a totally altered set of circumstances. I'm not too clear about when my connection with the Mekong / Cửu Long River started, but the song "Dusk Falls Again Upon the River" ("Chiều Về Trên Sông") by Phạm Duy had more than a little to do with my strengthening attachment to that river turned deep red by its alluvial soils.

In the 1990s, when I was writing the final chapters of my book *The Nine Dragons Drained Dry – The East Sea in Turmoil* (*Cửu Long Cạn Dòng Biển Đông Dậy Sóng*), I was confronted with the grim prospect of a Vietnam hemmed in by China, not only by that country's actions along the Mekong River pouring south from its plateau origins, but also in the East Sea, where China had seized and occupied Vietnam's Paracel Islands (1974) and the submerged Gạc Ma reefs that form part of the Spratly archipelago (1988).

The appearance of Phạm Duy's song-cycle *The National Road* (*Con Đường Cái Quan*), referring to the long highway in the united Vietnam that runs all the way from the Nam Quan Pass down to the southernmost province of Cà Mau, had a unifying influence on people's hearts. But if we take a more comprehensive view, "the National Road" does not stop there, because deep in the hearts of every Vietnamese person, the road has a further section stretching across the ocean, so as to join Vietnam to her islands, the Spratlys and Paracels. That is what impelled Phạm Duy and I to meet twenty-seven years ago. He surely remembered the conversation we had one day at his home on Hunter Street in Midway City, for from that time on he regularly sent me materials concerning all his activities.

In 2006, I sent him another discussion of the Spratly – Paracel matter in the form of a chapter in my book *Mekong – the Occluding River*, that peered three hundred years into the future, and that expressed confidence that those islands would one day be returned to their rightful owner.

THE MEMOIRS OF PHẠM DUY

Phạm Duy's four volumes of memoirs with more than one thousand five hundred pages, record quite faithfully all the spectacular ups and downs of his private life and of his country over a span of two

The front covers of the first three volumes of *The Memoirs of Phạm Duy*, published by Phạm Duy and Phạm Duy Cường. Volume 4, "The Period of Residence in the U.S." ("Thời Di Cư Qua Mỹ") was distributed on the internet in the form of a pdf. The cover design for these books was by Trần Đình Thục.
(Nguyễn Công Thuần, personal archives)

centuries, and all of this in a lively, straight-forward style. A positive quality of the work is that, throughout its four volumes, he speaks ill of no one, and also does not hide many details of a very personal nature concerning himself. He is not only a musician of immense talent – some call him a genius – but in this set of memoirs, so full of life and feeling, he shows himself to be a true writer as well, just as he shows himself to be a true poet in *Thousand Sets of Lyrics*.

An American scholar, Dr. Eric Henry, has expressed the view that this set of memoirs is not only attractive, but can help scholars understand the nature of Vietnamese society both when convulsed by war and when enjoying times of peace. He has completed an English translation of the entire work that has been accepted for publication by Cornell University Press. The two-stage project of 1) completing the translation and 2) securing a reliable U.S. publisher was a thing that Phạm Duy desired with all his heart when he was still alive. But after his passing, his children withheld agreement for this to be done, so publication of The Memoirs of Phạm Duy is still prohibited.

Phạm Duy and Dr. Eric Henry, the translator of *The Memoirs of Phạm Duy* met each other in a Saigon café on July 30, 2009. This set of photos with humorous subtitles by the photographer Nguyễn Phong Quang, a friend of Eric, are here arranged in clockwise order from the photo in the upper left: a) "Recounting Stories to Each Other"; b) "Arguing"; c) bottom right: "Convincing Each Other Isn't Easy"; and d) "We finally Reach Agreement." *(photos and captions by Nguyễn Phong Quang, materials sent to Ngô Thế Vinh by Eric Henry)*

Here Phạm Duy was displaying a copy of his four-volume Memoirs, translated by Dr. Eric Henry, to two journalists working for Phố BolsaTV. According to the translator Eric Henry, a lack of agreement among the surviving children of Phạm Duy has made it impossible to gain permission for the publication of this work. *(materials from the archives of BolsaTV, Jan. 26, 2012)*

ANTI-COMMUNISM AND SUPPORTING A FAMILY

Though Phạm Duy is "celebrated" for his many love affairs, all who are acquainted with him know that that this father was enormously devoted to his children. Though he was a songwriter of great stature whose songs are performed all over the five continents, and though the fees paid to singers who performed his songs were perhaps high, but there is no adequate compensation for a composer of such remarkable gifts. One can say that, during the two decades following 1975, the life-in-exile of Phạm Duy and his family was fairly arduous; but Phạm Duy remained optimistic, and didn't shrink from any activity that might help improve the life of his wife Thái Hằng and his eight children. During the first two years, when he lived in Florida, he not only went on a number of small performance tours, but wrote a self-study book for guitar beginners, and produced by hand copies of some old cassette tapes that he had managed to bring with him[1] that he sold and distributed by means of the U.S. postal system… thus, he "was able to support his family, the half that was in the U.S., and the half that was in Saigon."

Phạm Duy saved all the money he could earn to help support his four eldest sons, who were stuck in Vietnam, and then remitted additional sums to them, so they could successfully escape by boat and be reunited with their parents. Phạm Duy was economical to such a degree that he would sometimes not grant his children's requests for small sums to buy toys, and the children would refer to him among themselves as "stingy dad."

This "stinginess" in him was in fact a virtue, but many people referred to it in order to make fun of him. His wife Thái Hằng was kind, gentle, and devoted, and was regarded by many as a saint. She sacrificed her career as a singer very early after bearing her last child, Thái Hạnh, and devoted all her time to caring for her eight

---

1 In the Memoirs, Vol. 1V, Chapter 1, he says: "As we were hurrying to leave, the two of us managed to take two small suitcases with us to Guam; we lost the one that contained our clothes, but luckily held on to the other one, which had priceless items such as old photos and cassettes.

children. But she was not a Madame Tú Xương, who, as the verse says, "throughout the year sold goods along the river, so that five children and one husband might be fed."

Unlike the poet Tú Xương (that admirable woman's feckless husband), Phạm Duy with one wife and eight children, took upon himself the entire responsibility of supporting his family. He was not only an artist richly endowed with creative power, but traveled everywhere performing, concerning which the poet Nguyên Sa remarked that he was a "formidable athlete," and, more humorously, that he presented the spectacle of "a youth of twenty aged a thousand years." (excerpted from *Vietnamese Artists Abroad* (*Nghệ sĩ Việt Nam ở Hải ngoại*). Not only that, he was a very responsible father who loved his children. As he once confided to a friend, "If I were not like this, who would take care of my children?" This can only cause us to admire him more.

From Florida he moved to California, which has a large expatriate Vietnamese community. There, he still had to work with energy to support a crowded family with twelve people: Phạm Duy, his wife, and eight children plus two grandchildren in a three-bedroom house in Midway City, a place that Phạm Duy named "Thị Trấn Giữa Đàng".

A thing that not everyone knows about Phạm Duy is that for a time he considered opening a restaurant or becoming a real estate agent, and that he even consented to act as a driver transporting patients on a daily basis to and from doctors' offices in Orange County. At the same time, he reserved all his remaining time for his chief passion: music.

In Volume IV of his Memoirs, he recorded the following:

> "During the period when I "met" Nguyễn Chí Thiện, Dr. Trần Ngọc Ninh, a friend of mine, moved down from Denver, Colorado and opened an office in Santa Ana. I had just bought a new house right next to my old one to "save the lives" of the twelve people in my family who, because they had been living communally for a long time in a house with only three bedrooms and a single bathroom, had to "murder" each

other (just kidding) every morning if they wished to relieve themselves, brush their teeth, wash their faces, or bathe! After spending a bit more money to put additional bedrooms and bathrooms in each house, my family lived from then on in a state of gentle amity worthy of the scenes described in the *National Language Education Textbook* (*Quốc Văn Giáo Khoa Thư*). I was then surrounded with sufficient tranquility to complete two jobs I had just begun: putting together a lecture on "Fifty years of *Tân Nhạc*" and setting poems by Nguyễn Chí Thiện to music, so as to complete my cycle of twenty *Songs of Imprisonment* (Ngục Ca).

"Having solved the problem of quotidian existence for my entire family, I had lots of free time on my hands; and since my friend Ninh and his wife needed someone to take patients to and from his office (old people and newly arrived people who didn't yet have cars), I had no hesitation in taking on this work. During my youth, I had been a steelworker, an electric plant worker, a farmer, and a teacher. When I came to America, it seemed quite likely that I would have to resume doing work of a physical nature, but since I was resourceful, I found ways of making a living with my mind instead.

The crowded family of Phạm Duy, with twelve people gathered in a three-bedroom house in Midway City *(from the Memoirs of Phạm Duy, Vol. 4)*

"But now I had the means (a car), the health, and the time–and at this juncture, I was not yet receiving invitations to come and sing from as many places as I would in subsequent years–so why shouldn't I do this to earn some money? Even if it was only petty cash–just a little bit more than what I had to spend on gasoline! But this very leisurely kind of work didn't last long, because a number of doctors were taken to court for defrauding the medicare system. When I agreed to take on this work to help both patients and doctors, I was totally naive and straightforward; I knew nothing of the abuses that were occurring, for the simple reason that my friend Ninh never did such things. But now I saw that I had to distance myself from this milieu in which such a big scandal was occurring, so I stopped helping patients get to their doctor's appointments. I had moreover started getting more invitations to sing, once my twenty *Songs of Imprisonment* were completed.

"In any case, I wish to express my gratitude for the days when I practiced the distinguished profession of chauffeuring (just like the White Russian Princes who were communist refugees in Paris), because this work gave me an opportunity to enjoy contact with ordinary people, some of whom had been here since 1975, and some of whom had only recently escaped from Vietnam by sea.

"I got to know by this means the thoughts and feelings of the refugees and to know more about the concealed joys and sorrows of refugee communities. This intimate contact with the people was no different in nature from my experiences in the days when I went to sing by train, bus, and boat, or when I traveled everywhere on foot during the Resistance. Wherever I went, I learned a lot from the people.

"And aside from this, whenever I took a patient to the doctor's office, I had to wait a long time before I could take the patient back home, so I had a lot of time to compose. So while Dr. Ninh was having his patient stick out his tongue for him to look at, or asking his patient to roll up the sleeve to measure tension, I would sit in his office biting a pencil while writing an "imprisonment" song next to bottles of antibiotic fluid. No wonder those songs are imbued with a hospital atmosphere, as well as the prison atmosphere of the poems. In moments of leisure, we would sit and exchange artistic gossip in the examining room, or over lunch at a nearby restaurant. One could say that Dr. Trần Ngọc Ninh was the earliest auditor of the "imprisonment" songs.

A NEW YEAR LETTER FROM 1995, THE YEAR "ẤT HỢI"
Spring Festival Congratulations, 31 January, 1995

Today, the first day of the lunar year, I'm taking up my pen (actually, opening up my computer) to announce a few joyous pieces of news:

The musician Phạm Duy with Dr. Trần Ngọc Ninh in the 1980s. Dr. Trần Ngọc Ninh was among the earliest "boat people"; he arrived in Malaysia in 1977, then took refuge in the U.S. After gaining a new medical degree in his new country, he moved from Denver, Colorado to Santa Ana, where he established an office.
Phạm Duy wrote, "As Mr. and Mrs. Ninh needed someone to take patients back and forth to his office (old people, or newly arrived people who didn't yet have a car), I didn't disdain doing this sort of work and entered into it right away."

1- My family just enjoyed the addition of a maternal grandchild, the daughter of Thái Thảo and Tuấn Ngọc.[2]
She came into the world on the last day of the old year, just as her maternal grandma did sixty-five years ago.

2- The Phạm Duy Foundation, an organization I have thought of establishing for years, has now officially come into being. The founder is Ms. Phan Tú Khanh of Los Altos, CA, USA. There is now a copy of the by-laws to send to those whom I have invited to serve on the Board of Trustees. Naturally I wish to respectfully invite you to be a member or supporter of this foundation. It is possible that the foundation will officially announce its existence or hold its first meeting in April 1995, to mark my twentieth year abroad. And one of its first tasks will be to organize a symposium on the music of Phạm Duy or the position of that composer in the history of Vietnam's "new music."

3- Though it has not yet come into formal operation, the foundation supports in principle the creation of a CD ROM on the music of Phạm Duy. I and the engineer Bùi Minh Cương (the person in charge of technology) have agreed to put the work *The National Road* into this CD in such a way that people will be able to sing its melodies in Karaoke style–and perhaps have their grandchildren sing along as well, so they will not forget the Vietnamese language.

Because it will be an audio-visual product with a multimedia character, this CD ROM, aside from music, which shall be its chief component, will possess the following features:

a. section that will explain, in Vietnamese and English, the people and events in the work that have mythological or historical significance.

b. a section explaining how the song-cycle came into being and how it was promoted.

c. a section analyzing the music and lyrics in the song-cycle.

---

2 Tuấn Ngọc, a singer, was Thái Thảo's husband.

d. all the articles written about the song-cycle in Vietnamese journals and newspapers will be included.

e. many images of scenes in the homeland will be included as well.

These glad tidings came to me before I stepped into the new year, a year in which I think it will not be necessary for me to say or do anything further. I never dreamed that, before closing my eyes, I would see that of all the appreciation that has been expressed to me, the most precious has not come from the government in the home country, or from some international learned organization, but from people who love music, of whom Ms. Phan Tú Khanh is the most outstanding representative. No less precious to me has been the appreciation of the engineer Bùi Minh Cương, who has helped me promote my music through the medium of the CD ROM. In the near future, with the help of all my friends, I will easily be able to add to this all my literary work, comprising *Thousand Sets of Lyrics* and my four volumes of Memoirs, together with about a thousand songs, all of which can be put into CD ROMs as well.

I think that, on this first day of the new year, the most beautiful thing of all for me is to ask to share my joy with all my friends. I am not as bashful about this as I might have been in my first years of exile. Twenty years have passed, and I have been able to continue my career as a wandering singer, and above all I have been able to live in the most technologically advanced nation in the world, and have been able to bring that technology into my own work, with the most positive possible results. It has been thoroughly worthwhile! Hurrah for life!

I wish, my friend, that you will be able to step into the new year with a joy that equals mine! With much affection, etc.

1- The first page is attached to this message. Please look at the Purpose of the Organization in Article 2: Purposes

2- I hereby solemnly invite my friends Đỗ Văn (England), Thụy

Khuê (France), Mộng Thường (Australia), Đỗ Quý Toàn (Canada), Steve Addiss, Nguyễn Ngọc Bích, Đỗ Ngọc Yến, and Phạm Văn Kỳ Thanh (U.S.)

3- Who among you can help with French?

PS: Lê Hữu Khóa has a Symposium project. Attached.

RETURN TO VIETNAM; EXPLORATORY JOURNEYS

Many people think that it was only after the death of his wife Thái Hằng in 1999 that Phạm Duy began to think of returning to Vietnam to live, but this is not altogether the case.

Quite early before 1994, through letters sent back to Vietnam, and to friends, Phạm Duy expressed his desire to return to live in Vietnam, with the hope of reclaiming the three houses in Phú Nhuận that he owned and left behind when he hastily left the country in 1975.

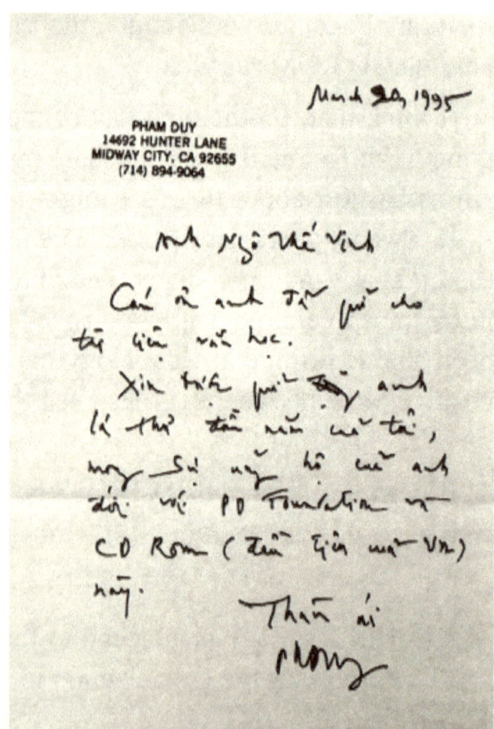

PHAM DUY
14692 HUNTER LANE
MIDWAY CITY, CA 92655
(714) 894-9064

A handwritten letter from Phạm Duy to Ngô Thế Vinh. Below: Lunar New Year's greeting from Phạm Duy to his friends. *(Ngô Thế Vinh, personal archives)*

Mùng Một Tết Ất Hợi
31 February 1995

Hôm nay, ngày đầu năm, tôi khai bút (đúng ra là khai máy vi tính) để báo cáo anh chị vài tin mừng:

1) Gia đình tôi vừa có thêm cháu ngoại, con gái của Thái Thảo/Tuấn Ngọc, ra đời vào đúng ngày cuối năm, giống như bà ngoại cháu 65 năm về trước.

2) Tổ chức **Pham Duy Foundation** dự tính thành lập từ lâu, nay đã chính thức ra đời. Người sáng lập là chị Phan Tú Khanh ở Los Altos, CA-USA. Hiện nay, đã có bản **điều lệ (by-law)** (1) để gửi tới những người mà tôi mời vào **Hội Đồng Quản Trị (Board Of Trustees)** (2). Lẽ tất nhiên, tôi kính mời bạn làm hội viên hoặc bảo trợ viên của foundation này. Có thể foundation sẽ chính thức công bố (hay mở kỳ họp đầu tiên) vào tháng 4-1995 để đánh dấu 20 năm hải ngoại. Và một trong những công tác đầu tiên là tổ chức một cuộc **hội thảo (symposium)** về **Nhạc PD** hay **chỗ đứng của PD trong lịch sử tân nhạc**.

3) Dù chưa chính thức hoạt động, foundation đang bảo trợ tinh thần việc thực hiện một CD ROM về Nhạc PD. Tôi và Kỹ Sư Bùi Cường (là người nắm phần kỹ thuật) đã đồng ý đưa nhạc phẩm CON ĐƯỜNG CÁI QUAN vào CD ROM đầu tiên này. Bản nhạc không lời sẽ có những giòng lời Anh, Việt ngữ (3) để dẫn hiện ra để trước hết, người mua CD ROM này có thể hát phần Việt ngữ theo kiểu karaoke. Hoặc cho con cháu hát theo để không quên tiếng Việt.

Vì là đĩa audio-visual có tính chất **multimedia**, ngoài trọng tâm là âm nhạc ra, CD ROM này có thêm những mục như:

a) mục giải thích (bằng Anh, Việt ngữ) những nhân vật hay sự việc mang tính chất huyền sử, lịch sử trong trường ca

b) mục viết về trường ca ra đời trong hoàn cảnh nào, phổ biến ra sao v.v...

c) mục giải thích nhạc ngữ, lời ca của trường ca

d) tất cả những bài báo viết về trường ca này trong mấy chục năm qua đều được cho vào CD ROM

e) rất nhiều hình ảnh quê hương cùng hiện diện trong CD ROM

Những tin vui này đã đến với tôi trước khi chúng ta bước vào năm mới, một năm mà tôi tưởng rằng sẽ chẳng còn gì để nói, để làm nữa. Tôi không ngờ rằng trước khi nhắm mắt lại được thấy phần thưởng cao quý nhất đến với tôi, không phải đến từ chính quyền trong nước hay một hàn lâm viện quốc tế... mà hoàn toàn đến từ những người yêu nhạc mà chị Phan Tú Khanh là đại diện tích cực nhất. Phần thưởng không kém phần quý báu là kỹ sư Bùi Cường đã giúp tôi phổ biến tác phẩm qua hình thức CD ROM. Trong tương lai rất gần, với sự giúp đỡ của bè bạn, tôi có thể dễ dàng cho phần văn chương gồm cuốn NGÀN LỜI CA và 4 cuốn hồi ký, về phần âm nhạc với một số hoặc tất cả trên dưới 1000 nhạc phẩm của tôi vào CD ROM.

Tôi nghĩ rằng, vào ngày đầu của một năm mới, điều đẹp nhất đối với tôi là xin được chia vui cùng bạn. Không tiêu cực như vào lúc đầu của kiếp lưu vong, hai mươi năm đã trôi qua, được tiếp tục hành nghề hát rong và nhất là được sống ở một nước với nền kỹ thuật cao nhất và biết đem kỹ thuật này vào nghề mọn của mình, với kết quả tích cực nhất... thật là đáng sống! Hoan hô cuộc đời.

Chúc bạn, bước vào năm mới, cũng vui như tôi. Rất thân ái!

(1) Trang đầu đính kèm vào thư này. Xin coi mục đích của tổ chức nơi **Article 2 : Purposes**.
(2) Tôi trân trọng mời các quý bạn Đỗ Văn (Anh Quốc), Thụy Khuê (Pháp Quốc), Mộng Thường (Úc), Đỗ Quý Toàn (Gia Nã Đại), Steve Addiss, Nguyễn Ngọc Bích, Đỗ Ngọc Yến, Phạm Văn Kỳ Thanh (Mỹ)
(3) Ai là người có thể giúp tôi Pháp Ngữ?

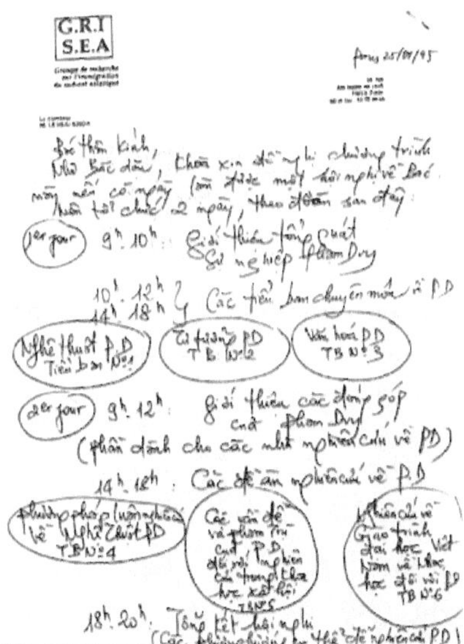

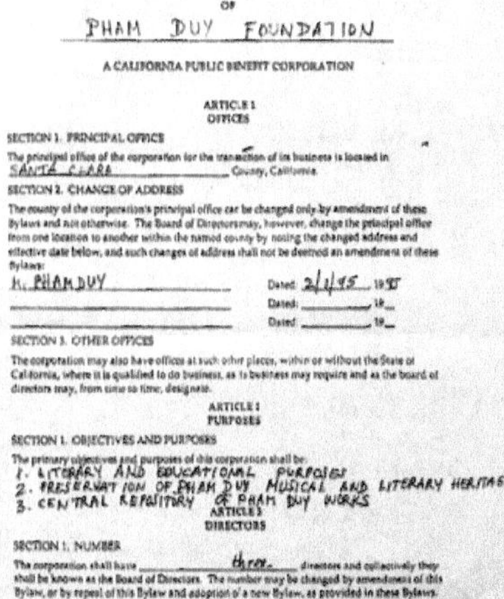

BYLAWS

OF

PHAM DUY FOUNDATION

A CALIFORNIA PUBLIC BENEFIT CORPORATION

ARTICLE 1
OFFICES

SECTION 1. PRINCIPAL OFFICE

The principal office of the corporation for the transaction of its business is located in SANTA CLARA County, California.

SECTION 2. CHANGE OF ADDRESS

The county of the corporation's principal office can be changed only by amendment of these Bylaws and not otherwise. The Board of Directors may, however, change the principal office from one location to another within the named county by noting the changed address and effective date below, and such changes of address shall not be deemed an amendment of these Bylaws:

K. PHAM DUY Dated: 2/1/95, 19__
Dated: ______, 19__
Dated: ______, 19__

SECTION 3. OTHER OFFICES

The corporation may also have offices at such other places, within or without the State of California, where it is qualified to do business, as its business may require and as the board of directors may, from time to time, designate.

ARTICLE 2
PURPOSES

SECTION 1. OBJECTIVES AND PURPOSES

The primary objectives and purposes of this corporation shall be:
1. LITERARY AND EDUCATIONAL PURPOSES
2. PRESERVATION OF PHAM DUY MUSICAL AND LITERARY HERITAGE
3. CENTRAL REPOSITORY OF PHAM DUY WORKS

ARTICLE 3
DIRECTORS

SECTION 1. NUMBER

The corporation shall have three directors and collectively they shall be known as the Board of Directors. The number may be changed by amendment of this Bylaw, or by repeal of this Bylaw and adoption of a new Bylaw, as provided in these Bylaws.

Left: Sketch of a plan for a conference on "research into the musical output of Phạm Duy" by Lê Hữu Khóa, Director the Southeast Asian Immigration Research Group (Groupe de Recherche sur l'Immigration du sud-est asiatique or GRISEA), from Paris; and right: A copy of the bylaws of the Phạm Duy Foundation *(Ngô Thế Vinh, personal archives)*

In a personal letter, written on August 16, 1994, sent to a young friend of his working in Singapore, Võ Tá Hân (an MIT graduate and an expert in banking economy, the director of Singapore Finance, a skilled classical guitar player, a devotee of Phạm Duy's music and a paternal nephew of the writer Linh Bảo), Phạm Duy wrote: *"Anh Hân, you know full well how much I am loved by the people in the overseas community. If I now return to a still-communist Vietnam, they will at once boycott me entirely."*

In the same letter Phạm Duy continued as follows: "You should remember that starting in 1988, with the ten-song cycle *Wanderer's Songs* (*Rong Ca*), I stopped creating the sort of music referred to as "anti-communist." With that song-cycle I cast aside the twentieth century so as to welcome a new mode of life. What, then, are the Zen Songs (*Thiền Ca*)? They are: "round, like bullets of black bronze, on which the marks of blood have dried, and which have forgotten war. Bullets are created to kill people, so if even they can forget the war, how much more must that be the case with people. (The regime, too, has forgotten "the American bastards" who bombed us, don't you see?) And if you listen to *The Flock of Birds Who Forsook their Homeland* (*Bầy Chim Bỏ Xứ*) you will see that I advocate the idea that the peaceful birds and the fierce birds can all coexist with each other. Near the end of the cycle, the lyrics say, "Let the hawks, however fierce, live near the border..." meaning that we stand much in need of the communists to guard against China, which is always eager, surely, to invade our land.

"Anyway, I am immensely pleased when I see that I am understood by some young people, such as Đỗ Trung Quân and Lưu Trọng Văn [the son of the poet Lưu Trọng Lư.] When I met Trần Tiến in France, I heard that [the songwriter] Dương Thụ always speaks on my behalf. That's enough for me! There's no need for me to meet with one or two officials who will take pity on me as if welcoming a prodigal son! I hear that Trần Văn Khê has said that in the executive council there are only a couple of people who remain opposed to me." *(Phạm Duy, Letter, Aug.16, 1994)*

Phạm Duy
14693 Hunter Lane
MIDWAY CITY
CA 92655 U.S.A.
Phone: (714) 894 9064
FAX: (714) 895 9722

19 tháng 6, 1994

Anh Hoàng Thượng Khanh
Tổ 12 22 Phường Trung Liệt
Đống Đa Hà Nội

Bao nhiêu năm qua, không được tin tức gì về anh; trong cuốn Hồi Ký phát hành năm 90, tôi vẫn nhớ tới anh và nhắc tên anh trong đoạn viết về Bình-Trị-Thiên; hôm nay bỗng được tin anh qua anh bạn P.L. Tiếp, tôi vội vàng viết vội vài hàng chữ, trước khi viết nhiều thư dài, nối tiếp tình bạn thắm thiết đã trong những ngày gian khổ. Mong anh giữ gìn sức khoẻ để có ngày mình gặp lại nhau trên quê hương yêu quý.

Anh nên gặp chị Văn Phương Thanh ở số phone 252-130 để biết nhiều về tôi.

Rất thân mến./

New Releases
sách HỒI KÝ PHẠM DUY - CD& Cassette Người Tình Già Trên Đầu Non; Bầy Chim Bỏ Xứ

This is the first letter that Phạm Duy wrote to Hoàng Thượng Khanh on June 19, 1994, sent via Võ Tá Hân's fax machine in Singapore, so as to be forwarded to Hanoi.
(Võ Tá Hân, personal archives)

HOÀNG THƯỢNG KHANH AND SONGS IN THE STYLE OF THE CENTRAL REGION.

Phạm Duy was overjoyed when, through the writer Phan Lạc Tiếp in San Diego, he found the means to contact an old friend from his Resistance War days half a century hence, who was now living in Hanoi. This was Hoàng Thượng Khanh. And in the days that followed he wrote a series of emotion-filled letters to him.

Letter Number Two:

July 4, 1994

"My dear Hoàng Thượng Khanh,

"Two weeks ago, when Phan Lạc Tiếp let me know in a phone call that he had met Hoàng Thượng Khanh in Hanoi, and, after writing a few hurried lines to Khanh, I received Khanh's letter. The letter was still that of the "super-sensible" person whom I knew in Huế in 1944 when I was a singer in the Đức Huy Troupe, and in 1946 when I sang at Quán Nghệ Sĩ, the person who later in 1948 when you shared the sweet *chia ngọt sẻ bùi* with me during a fairly long period in the military district near Ba Lòng, Quảng Trị.

"After the half century that C.V. Gheorghiu and Günter Grass called "the era devoid of decency" and Camus called "the plague era," and Marquez called "the era of vomit and diarrhea," because the machinery of the world's governments turned the world into a vast killing field (and Vietnam was the victim of those mighty powers), and especially after nearly half a century of mutual separation, the two of us have survived, so that we may meet again today by means of letters, and some day not far away by means of a warm embrace, laughing amid tears and weeping amid laughter–ah me, what happiness!

I remember most the days when the two of us sat by some river in the military district, rubbing and washing all the deep red sores on our feet – our lives then were wretched in the extreme, so why were our hearts so blithe? Why, eating only moldy rice with shrimp paste and enduring a terrible storm (do you remember that storm?) and living in danger and difficulty in the midst of the enemy stationed at Đại Lược… why was I still able to compose such fine songs as "Returning to the Central Region" ("Về Miền Trung"), "The Mother of Gio Linh" ("Bà Mẹ Gio Linh"), and "Twelve Lullabies" ("Mười Hai Lời Ru")? The answer is quite simple: at that time we were still very young, we intensely loved our land, and I in particular was able to enjoy a friendship bestowed on me by you. In your letter you wrote, "I have not even for a moment forgotten Duy." And in this letter I beg to imitate that sentence: "I have not even for a moment forgotten Khanh." And I ask to add: "If it were not for Khanh, it is by no means certain that I could have written "Returning to the Central Region."

With this letter, I hope you will recall cherished memories from the three occasions when we met, write them down on paper, or record them into a cassette, and send them to me so that I may keep them as living testimony for a museum devoted to my work (a sure thing) that will come into being in the future. Here, overseas, I have organized a few “Phạm Duy conferences,” so that music lovers will be able to do the work of collecting materials and promoting the music of Phạm Duy. My music, as you will see, Khanh, does not consist of songs celebrating martial valor or mourning tragic events in a sad and glorious past, or songs concentrating on the human condition (especially the condition of those who know their homeland), or laments concerning the condition of the land… this music also bears the imprint of a witness to our era – the *Wanderer's Songs* (*Rong Ca*), for example contain the inner feelings of a man who has lived through the twentieth century, and is now singing for the 2000s, but without the severity of C.V. Gheorghiu and Günter Grass, who called it “the era devoid of decency,” or Camus, who called it “the plague era, or Marquez, who called it the era of vomit and diarrhea, as I mentioned above.

A critic who wrote about me said, “he sings of the century, sings of open spatial dimensions and long stretches of time, and never sings of constricted emotions entangled with particular circumstances. One must have enough strength to fly with the mighty Roc bird–only then can one and have a more all-encompassing vision. My *Songs of the Dao* (*Đạo Ca*) and *Zen Songs* (*Thiền Ca*) also are not just the productions of the fellow wandering through villages beating a wooden clapper to summon the faithful; they rather reflect the voice of an old fellow who has witnessed the times he has lived in. To have this type of singing, it seems to me, satisfies our needs: *“round, like bullets of black bronze, on which the marks of blood have dried and have forgotten battlefields.”*

Naturally, Khanh, you will let me know how you have lived in a land afflicted with more injustices than can be resolved in a year, a month, or a day. We shall avoid talking about politics. We shall exchange only the confidences that lie close to the hearts of two old friends. Just as you have said, “The time that remains is short!” And I too have sung the line, “when one day remains, give way to that day's joy!” So, write a long letter, okay? And let my friend Ms. Văn Dương

Thành – whom I'm sure you've met – send it in order to avoid the expense of stamps.

Finally, since I have the honor to know Tố Uyên, the friend of Băng Thanh [author's note: the younger sister of the writer Linh Bảo] please send my affectionate greetings to the Huế damsel surnamed Võ, the girl who with her younger sister and I – in a certain past life – strolled along a Vỹ Dạ street – how gentle the summer sun was, and the sultry breeze!

With all my affection,

Phạm Duy

Enclosed with this was another, handwritten, letter dated three days later, July 7, 1994, to Võ Tá Hân *(The letter on page 467.)*

On Aug. 15, 1994, Phạm Duy, still in his Midway City home, faxed Võ Tá Hân a third letter for Hoàng Thượng Khanh, his old friend living in Hanoi . In this letter he wished to express everything that lay in his heart:

"Hân: I have just received a letter from Hoàng Thượng Khanh. I wrote a reply, which I make haste to fax to you (see below) so as to ask you to do me the favor of forwarding it to him. Thank you very much."

The third letter, August 15, 1994:

"Dear Hoàng Thượng Khanh:

"Today Mrs Nguyễn returned to the U.S., bearing your letter and the photo that you had her take. In it, you look more calm than in the photo that Võ Tá Hân took of you last month. Bravo!

"Since you wish to know about my family circumstances, I'll make a report:

"As of October of this year, I will have reached the age of 75. Though I had more love-partners than anyone else in the arts during the romantic period of 1945, I am nevertheless the most obedient of husbands, and still revere Madame Thái Hằng with whom I was married due to the good offices of General Nguyễn Sơn, who was also the matchmaker and chief celebrant on that occasion (say, if

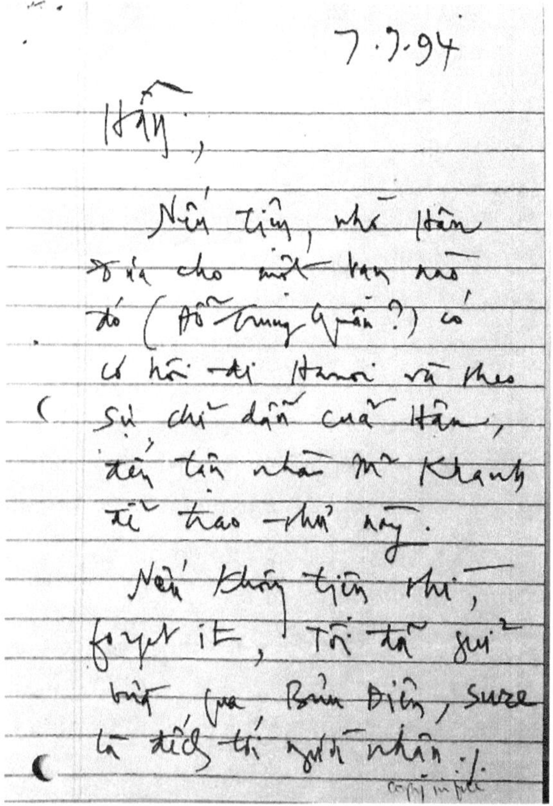

7.7.94

Hằng,

Nếu tiện, nhờ Hằng đưa cho một bạn nào đó (Đỗ Trung Quân?) có cơ hội đi Hanoi và theo sự chỉ dẫn của Hằng, đến tận nhà Mẹ Khanh để trao thư này.

Nếu không tiện thì, forget it, Tôi đã gửi thư qua Bưu Điện, sure là tới tay người nhận ./.

Another handwritten, letter dated three days later, July 7, 1994.

you should happen to meet Mrs. Nguyễn Sơn, could you ask her if she still has a photo of the Duy-Hằng marriage ceremony?). This married couple have been together for almost half a century–we have eight children (five boys, three girls, and six paternal and maternal grandchildren). Almost all of them have husbands and wives, but they still live with us in three houses on the same street. We've been in the U.S. for twenty years, and have paid taxes throughout our working lives, so since the day of my retirement [Phạm Duy retired in 1985 when he was 64] I have received enough pension money to live on and have not had to rely on my children. Speaking broadly, from the time we left the North and settled in the South (1951), we always had enough to eat in my family, and before I went to the U.S. I had three houses in Phú Nhuận. On arriving in the U.S., I had twenty dollars in my pocket, but I was able to build my life up again and now have three houses as I did before.

In recent years, my situation has changed. It has begun to seem to me that I can sell my house and live the years that still remain to me in my homeland. But as it happened, my wife and one of my sons went back to Vietnam in April 1994, and when they returned, I saw that my return would not be at all convenient – so I had to resign myself to remaining in this "temporary perch" abroad. To be quite frank, I have become excessively accustomed to life in the U.S. As one ages, health concerns assume supreme importance. The science of medicine over here is very advanced, which I find reassuring (I've had two operations, one on my lungs and one on my bladder).

"Voilà! You asked, so I had no choice but to lay out these details – I hadn't the slightest intention of bragging.

"Your evocation of the Hàng Vôi school on 16 Carreau Street in Hưng Yên moved me very much–but if some day I should return to my old haunts, will they still have traces of their old charm?

One individual* wrote about me as follows: Phạm Duy, perceiving a huge turning point in the life of our people, wrote "Feeling for the Homeland" ("Tình Hoài Hương") as a kind of summation, a recognition that from now on we would be far from the homeland not only in space, but in time – an immensely extended time – forming a nostalgia that was like a witness to the period. After 1945, Vietnam stepped into a new era, a new world, that forever erased the concept of "the old homeland," as it had been understood before. So Duy portrays the homeland with all the alluring traits of a former time – the fields, the bamboo fences, the waves of smoke, the rivers, the banyan trees, the water buffalo, the aged mothers – but without a single word that suggests the dream of return. What is there now to return to! He does not entertain fantasies of going back to the past, as in the early days of the Resistance; he perceives the blow of fate that has descended on Vietnam, which shall force her to enter a totally new era. From 'feeling for the homeland,' he has sensed signs heralding a new sensibility.

The slanting rays tilt differently,
I live in joy on ten thousand paths;
Love lodges in a thousand places
Let our love be like a mighty sea!

"In this era, he can only sing notes giving voice to a premonition: the people of Vietnam must now step out of the warm cradle of the countryside that has belonged to them for thousands of years, this outward step entered people's consciousnesses and began to be realized from the days of the Tonkin Free School (Đông Kinh Nghĩa Thục) and the 'Eastward Bound Movement,' (Đông Du) but never came fully into existence. Writing further about this period, he said, "It was pain-filled, because I was far from my native land and had no hope of returning. After nine years of warfare the dream of Hoàng Giác–

"Go back to the ancient homeland and relive the gentle dream;
Go back to the ancient homeland and seek the bygone days –"

...clearly could never again become a reality; the image of bygone days had flown quite away. Phạm Duy gazed at the changing rays of preceding dusk and saw nothing that required him to gaze back without cease at the homeland, and instead exchanged the warm clouds of smoke for love lodging in a thousand places, and exchanged his love of country for a wide and mighty road of love. He became a human being embarking on adventures, not a person attached to one slender strip of territory. The adventures are those of a man whose homeland has disappeared."

[*The individual referred to was Phạm Xuân Đài, the author of the article "On Homeland Dreams" ('Giấc Hương Quan") in his book of occasional essays "Hanoi in my Eyes" (Hà Nội Trong Mắt Tôi, pub. 1994) that Phạm Duy quotes from in this letter. Phạm Xuân Đài also wrote an article entitled "Death in the Songs of Phạm Duy" (Cái Chết Trong Ca Khúc Phạm Duy), which appeared in the journal Twenty-first Century (Thế Kỷ 21). That article inspired Phạm Duy to make a series of videos introducing and explaining those of his works that deal with this theme. https://www.youtube.com/watch?v=8uzseMiSGOo.

[Phạm Xuân Đài is a person who has long admired and revered Phạm Duy. When he heard that I was writing a portrait of Phạm Duy, he supplied me with relevant materials and photos. He also urged me to write only of the larger aspects of his work and avoid petty details concerning his everyday existence. – author's note]

"I borrow the above words of Khanh because they concern a topic that can easily give rise to tender feelings: the homeland! The homeland is more than just a cluster of sweet star fruits [*chùm khế ngọt*]. The homeland is above all the people one has known–the friends, the love-partners… Who are Vietnamese people of today? Of my friends, who of them are still around? If I hadn't by chance come upon you, Khanh, then perhaps Văn Cao would be the only friend I have left. As for lovers (meaning those who love my music), what freedom do they have to listen to music? In view of this, if I should never return at all to Vietnam (for whatever reason), then I will have chosen long ago to become a person of a thousand places.

Time to end, eh? This has been a long letter. I promise to write another and shall hope for one from you. I send my greetings to Tố Uyên and Băng Thanh and hope that all goes well for them.

Phạm Duy

These three letters sent by Phạm Duy to Hoàng Thượng Khanh, his friend from the Resistance – both now departed from the world – are not only literary works but also a very truthful record of the very complex developments taking place in his feelings of this man who loved his country.

Through these letters we can see that Phạm Duy, though writing with some abandon, was at the same time patiently seeking a way "to transcend all barriers" and find a way to return to Vietnam. Only in 2000 did he obtain permission to return, so that he could personally observe the new aspect of the land. And when he returned, he gave me, as a souvenir of that trip, a photo of himself pouring alcoholic spirits on the grave of Văn Cao, a dear companion of his in the long ago days of the Resistance:

With great seriousness and, naturally, with great savoir faire – an inborn quality of his – Phạm Duy continued his exploratory visits throughout the following five years and, after Resolution 36, and especially after getting to sign a twenty-year contract (2005 – 2025) with Phạm Thị Lệ, the director of the Phương Nam Book Company, Phạm Duy saw that he would be able to return to Vietnam to live, a request that he had formally submitted to the regime in 2000. The response of the government was that he must wait until 2005. And now that time had arrived for Phạm Duy and his family.

Phạm Duy visiting the grave of Văn Cao in the spring of 2000 with a belated bottle of wine. In the photo Phạm Duy was pouring wine on the grave in the course of his first return trip to Vietnam *(Ngô Thế Vinh, personal archives)*

SEEING OFF PHẠM DUY ON HIS RETURN JOURNEY TO THE HOMELAND

At 84, after living in the U.S. for thirty years, with many thorough preparations for this final decision of his life, Phạm Duy left to spend the rest of his life in Vietnam. Before his day of departure, the journalist Đỗ Việt Anh, a person who adored the sentiment-filled music of the composer – and who at that time was the editor-in-chief of the newspaper *Người Việt* – got together with friends and organized a warm going-away party for him.

PHẠM DUY, "THE DAY OF RETURN"

One can say that in his early days, Phạm Duy led the swashbuckling life of a youth who, throwing himself into patriotic activities, left his footprints throughout the land, from north to south. Then, during his thirty years in the U.S., he had opportunities to perform all over the five continents. At 84, having earned the right to enjoy "Le Repos du Guerrier," he made a drastic choice, not devoid of inner difficulty and turmoil. Phạm Duy abandoned an overseas Vietnamese community that loved him and chose to live the last years of his life in Vietnam.

Having settled peacefully in his homeland in 2005, Phạm Duy enjoyed recalling that in the days following 1975, a colossal photo of him – his words – was exhibited in the "Exhibition House of U.S. and Puppet Crimes" at 28 Trần Quý Cáp Street, which was also the location of the Saigon School of Medicine in former days. The new regime at that time regarded him as a fellow who had betrayed the Resistance and as a symbol of the poison of Western-Puppet culture.

[author's note: my novel *Vòng Đai Xanh / The Green Belt* about the Highland minority peoples was also exhibited there as a piece of cultural trash left over from the U.S. puppet regime.]

But, very luckily, in the last days of April 1975, Phạm Duy's name was included in a list of names that the CIA operative Ed Jones was charged with rescuing, and he got to the U.S. before it was too late.

Thái Thanh, the singer whose voice gave wings to Phạm Duy's music, bearing a bouquet of flowers, said some words of farewell to Phạm Duy.

(Photo by Huỳnh Tuấn Kiệt; Đỗ Việt Anh, personal archives)

A quartet of singers, Thái Thanh, Quỳnh Giao, Lệ Thu, and Mai Hương singing a farewell to Phạm Duy. All four have now joined the ranks of the departed.

(Photo by Huỳnh Tuấn Kiệt; Đỗ Việt Anh, personal archives)

Phạm Duy knew perfectly well that if he had remained, and been lured into the "reeducation camps" like countless other artists of the South, he would have gone straight to perdition (đi đoong) – his words – and most likely would never have had an opportunity to "return to the homeland," as he had now done.

Let me quote here some paragraphs from *Volume 4 of Phạm Duy's Memoirs*, which will read here like a flashback:

> "That was also the day when Saigon was "liberated," as it were, by the forces of the North. A man lying next to me was tuning into the Saigon broadcasting station with a tiny radio. Everyone in the room drifted over to listen. When I heard announcements concerning the victory of the Northern troops and the defeat of the Republic, I was overwhelmed with sadness. It seemed pointless to keep on lying there with my hands over my ears, so I descended the staircase and went out from the barracks.
>
> "Only at this point did I become conscious of the fact that Guam was an island. I stood before the vast ocean, silent and indifferent. I noticed that I wasn't the slightest bit stirred by the sight of the ocean's endless expanse, as I had always been previously. I was no longer "me." Turning away from the ocean, I wal\ked listlessly back toward the barracks.
>
> "On passing by the camp's communication office, I suddenly heard the voice of a news announcer coming from all the loudspeakers:
>
> *"President Dương Văn Minh*[3] *is calling upon Republican*

---

3 Dương Văn Minh (1916–2001), often referred to as "Minh Lớn" or "Big Minh" because of his large physical stature, was the last president of South Vietnam, a position that he held for three days, from April 28 to April 30, 1975. In 1940, after graduating from the Non-commissioned Officer's Academy at Thủ Dầu Một, he joined the French army with the rank of "aspirant" (*chuẩn úy*). In 1955 after helping Ngô Đình Diệm by leading "Operation Hoàng Diệu" in which he destroyed the Bình Xuyên forces in the Mekong delta, he was made a brigadier general. He then helped put down the Hòa Hảo forces led by Ba Cụt. He soon lost favor with Ngô Đình Diệm, however, because the later doubted his loyalty. Later,

soldiers to lay down their arms and surrender.

"Feeling sadder still, I hastened back to the barracks and plopped down on the wooden floor. Everyone was still huddled around the radio to hear news concerning the day when Northern troops entered Saigon. Suddenly the voice of Trịnh Công Sơn[4] came from the radio singing the song "Joining Arms in a Great Embrace" *(Nối Vòng Tay Lớn)*. The voice was out of tune and the guitar accompaniment was full of mistakes. With a painful twinge, I thought about what my fate might have been had I been unable to get away. Would I have had to do something like that? The owner of the radio cursed and switched it off before the song was finished, upon which the listeners dispersed in sorrow."

More From *Volume 4 of Phạm Duy's Memoirs - Chapter Twenty*:

"For ages, "people" have used every means they could think of to create a rift between me and Trịnh Công Sơn. But no one was ever able to do anything that hindered our mutual collegial affection, even though we sometimes held different points of view. In 1988, I happened to run into Trịnh Công Sơn in Paris. Together with Đặng Tiến, we strolled from place to place on the sidewalks or sat in cafés shooting the breeze. We didn't spend a second discussing politics or art… but when I asked to entrust the "young lover" with the task of bringing the *Ten Wanderer's Songs* back to Vietnam, Sơn's reply was immediate: "Okay." Due to this, the confessions of "the old lover" got to circulate within the country. In the

---

when Minh, a Buddhist, observed the repressive measures taken against Buddhists by Ngô Đình Diệm, he began to be opposed to the regime, and in 1963 became the leader of the coalition that overthrew Diệm. In 1971 he briefly challenged Nguyễn Văn Thiệu in a presidential election, but then withdrew, saying that the elective process was rigged. In 1983 the Vietnamese socialist government gave him permission to resettle wherever he liked. He went first to France, but then joined the family of his daughter and son-in-law in California.

4 Trịnh Công Sơn: a celebrated singer-songwriter.

In 1988, Phạm Duy had an unlooked - for meeting with Trịnh Công Sơn in Paris. From left: Trịnh Công Sơn, Phạm Duy, Đặng Tiến.
(Phạm Duy, personal archives)

> summer of 2001, when I had business that took me back to Saigon, I persuaded Trần Văn Khê,[5] a few days after Sơn's public funeral observances, to go with me to burn some incense before his altar. As we did so, I made a particular point of bowing in recognition of the favor he did me in bringing the *Wanderer's Songs* back to the homeland on my behalf."
>
> *(end of quotation, Phạm Duy Memoirs, Volume 4)*

Today the "Exhibition House of U.S. and Puppet Crimes" has had its name changed; it is now the "War Remnants Museum," but still maintains its exhibits, with cannons, bombs, and ammunition, including seven-ton bombs, CBUs, tanks, and helicopters that the imperialist Americans left behind, plus the "tiger cages" with barbed wire symbolizing the atrocities visited upon imprisoned revolutionary soldiers by the American puppet government, which were brought there from the Côn Đảo and Phú Quốc islands. This place has become a hotspot of tourism and propaganda attracting hundreds of thousands of visitors every year.

---

5 Trần Văn Khê: a celebrated Vietnamese musicologist who during much of his career lived and taught in Paris

PHẠM DUY: THINGS HE WROTE AND SAID

In interviews he gave after arriving in Vietnam, on being asked what impelled him to return, he gave very eloquent and convincing answers. He emphasized that he was after all a Vietnamese, so his return was like "a leaf falling to the tree's base" or like "a fish returning to the river's source." He had brought along his *Thousand Sets of Lyrics* and was living with people who had long loved his music.

At first he would say, with a touch of reserve that, having returned, his choice would be to "remain quiet," and that if he made some noises, this would be only for commercial reasons–he would comply with the demands of the Phương Nam Company to help promote the sale of his CDs and books.

But later on, he ceased to "remain quiet," but made bold observations about a number of things. I shall here quote a few things he said in the course of two interviews that he gave in January, 2012, words showing that he was very consistent in his opinions and didn't choose to qualify them in any way.

1) Interview with P.D. conducted by Dr. Nguyễn Nhã on Jan. 12, 2012
2) Interview with P.D. conducted by two journalists, Eccetera and Vũ Hoàng Lân for PhoBolsaTV.com on January 28, 2013.

Here are the links:

https://www.youtube.com/watch?v=9mS22Qu71EI
https://www.youtube.com/watch?v=TBaGpXMqihQ
https://www.youtube.com/watch?v=0gMKBykyp8Y

[*Author's note:* these interviews with Phạm Duy are both more than two hours long–so to merely excerpt a couple of his remarks from them may not do justice to the context in which they occurred; I, therefore, suggest to the reader that he take the time to use the links provided here to listen to the interviews in their entirety. The English title of these interviews is "Phạm Duy in his own words."]

A portrait of Phạm Duy at 91 in an interview with Nguyễn Nhã on Jan. 12, 2012. Phạm Duy prepared carefully for this interview and read a number of notations that he had written out beforehand. *(Phạm Duy, personal archives)*

Phạm Duy at 91 in an interview conducted by the journalists Eccetera and Vũ Hoàng Lân on Jan. 28, 2013. Phạm Duy praised their station, PhoBolsaTV, and said that he had watched it regularly since his return to Vietnam. *(Phạm Duy, personal archives)*

A COUPLE OF EXCERPTS

1. Comments on Vietnamese Refugees Living Abroad

When Phạm Duy spoke of the Vietnamese abroad, and the rifts among the refugee community, he was talking about a community he had lived with for thirty years. And now, in the three-story house on Lê Đại Hành Street in Saigon's Eleventh District that the Phương Nam Company had supplied for him, he spoke of the refugees as follows: "One has to say that before accomplishing a thing they threatened their neighborhoods, and then they went to the U.S. without a single sou in their pockets and depended on handouts, while demanding that people somehow oppose the communists, and they organized a few associations for this purpose with three, or at most four members."

As for people who still harbored hatred for the communists in their hearts, he said, as if offering counsel: "We must know enough to give thanks, know enough to beg for pardon, and know enough to forget!" And as for the former prime minister Nguyễn Cao Kỳ, who had some relation to his family, he had words of praise: "Mr. Kỳ is courageous; though he was once vice president of the land, he was able to humble himself and return to Vietnam!" He went on and said if in the future there should be a reconciliation between the people on the two sides of the war, "Mr. Kỳ would be able to represent the people abroad to the Vietnamese government." [sic].

On reading Volume 4 of his Memoirs, we can see that throughout the first twenty years of his sojourn abroad, he participated energetically in anti-communist movements with the Vietnamese abroad. He set the satirical poems of Cao Tần (Lê Tất Điều) to music, created the twenty "Prison Songs" of the famous "Prison Gentleman" (Ngục Sĩ) Nguyễn Chí Thiện, and, in the course of his performance tours all over the world, expressed his agreement with the "reconquest" movement of Hoàng Cơ Minh.

Comments on Resolution 36 and the Reconciliation Policy of Hanoi

Mentioning Resolution 36, he expressed satisfaction with the statement of Nguyễn Thanh Sơn, the Assistant Minister of Foreign Affairs, with regard to the policy of reconciliation and said that that statement was the factor that caused him to make the decision to ask permission to return to Vietnam. He asked to be instated as a citizen, and was proud of his new certificate of residency that was issued to him a year later and his happiness was renewed every time the government granted permission for one of his songs to be performed.

On going to Hanoi, he praised the present modernity of life in the city, and the impressive scale of the residents' dwelling places – that, he said, was a source of great joy to him. And he made similar comments with regard to the development of Saigon, as evidenced in such places as the Phú Mỹ Hưng urban development area, with houses more beautiful even than those in the U.S. He praised Vietnam as a place where people could eat and spend money even more freely than in the U.S. [sic]. And people knew that one of his birthday celebrations had been organized in the home of Lê Thành Ân, an American of Vietnamese origin who had been the Consul General for the U.S. in Saigon City. His style of life in Saigon no longer resembled the one he had experienced in the days of "A Countryside Mother" and "A Countryside Child," but had turned into an existence with the elite.

Comments on the Threat from China and the Calamitous Developments in the Eastern Ocean

Phạm Duy praised the "wise foreign policy" of Communist Vietnam, which had to exist "beneath the armpit" of China. According to him, there was no real danger that Vietnam might turn into a Chinese protectorate state after losing the Spratly and Paracel Islands in armed conflicts. He placed his reliance on the possibility of negotiations between the countries involved. Any hurried protest against the situation might harm the chances of reaching a peaceful solution. In this connection he mentioned the heated protest against the annexation that had been made by Cù Huy Hà Vũ, the son of his one-time friend, the poet Huy Cận.

[author's note: in 2011, Cù Huy Hà Vũ made a public protest against the nine-slash line "shaped like an ox's tongue" that China had drawn in the Eastern Sea, indicating a claim to a vast area that included the Spratly and Paracel Islands]

Phạm Duy and his family became American citizens in 1984. When he returned to Vietnam in 2005, he asked to resume his citizenship there, and the poet Nguyễn Quốc Thái, who held him in very high regard, helped him a year later to obtain certificates of citizenship and residency. But Phạm Duy still kept his "passport"–his proof of U.S. citizenship. And he remarked jokingly to Dr. Nguyễn Nhã, the man who interviewed him on Jan. 12, 2012, that if the Chinese should attack Vietnam and get all the way to Nha Trang, he would still be able to seek refuge in the American Consulate in Saigon, because he was a U.S. citizen [sic]. *(sources: Phạm Duy Memoirs, Volume 4, and, Nguyễn Quốc Thái, personal archives)*

Then, in a scornful tone, he reiterated to Dr. Nguyễn Nhã the idea that he could take refuge in the U.S. consulate in Saigon if China attacked and got as far as Nha Trang.

Comments 42 Years Later on his Firm Friend and Supporter Tạ Tỵ

In the autumn of 1970, when he learned that Tạ Tỵ had written a book devoted to him, he sent Tạ Tỵ a two-page handwritten letter to express his gratitude. I quote:

"Sent to my dear friend Tạ Tỵ:

"I was truly moved and at the same time truly embarrassed when I learned you had devoted such a capacious book about me after having written about ten other people active in the arts in our land.

"Moved, because in the turbulence of these times, it is rare for anyone to want to shine a light on my person and my career, and especially when the person in question is Tạ Tỵ, who from the time preceding the Resistance War, the time of the Resistance itself, and throughout the post Resistance up to the time of the imminent dissolution of this war, you have always been close to me, and have always understood what is in me, both the good and the bad..." (*Phạm Duy Still Sits There Dejected [Phạm Duy Còn Đó Nỗi Buồn]*, pub. 1971 by Nguyễn Nhã's Văn Sử Học).

But forty-two years after the publication of *Phạm Duy Still Sits There Dejected* and seven years after he went back to live in Saigon – at the age of ninety-one – he spoke very differently about Tạ Tỵ., who for ages had been among the closest of his friends. When Dr. Nguyễn Nhã held the book in his hands, the book that Tạ Tỵ had written about him – Phạm Duy, playing with an idiom used in the title, referred to it as "the Desire to Laugh" and "the Desire to Vomit," and remarked that it was "miserably written," but that he could not criticize it, because the author had been in the psychological warfare division, and so could not do any better."

In his talk with Nguyễn Nhã, he also uttered the following words: "Tạ Tỵ didn't tell the truth in the book he wrote about his days in

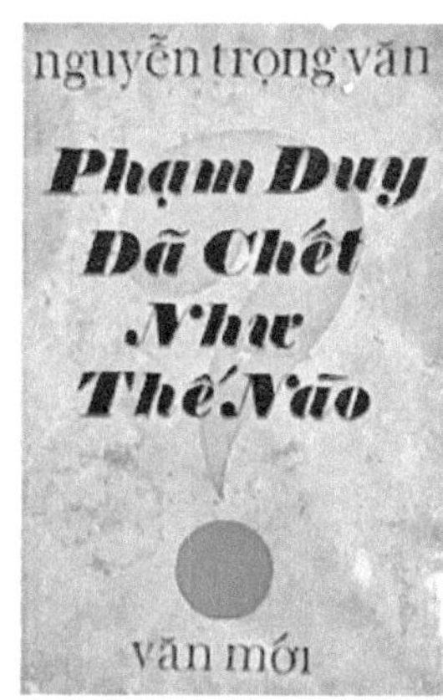

Left: the cover of the book *Phạm Duy Still Sits There Dejected* by Tạ Tỵ (Văn Sử Học, 1971); middle: Tạ Tỵ's self-portrait; right: the cover of the book The Death Process of Phạm Duy by Nguyễn Trọng Văn (Văn Mới, 1971)

[Thành Tôn, personal archives]

From left: another line-portrait of Phạm Duy by Tạ Tỵ, 1970; Phạm Duy's two-page handwritten letter to Tạ Tỵ, thanking him for having written the book *Phạm Duy Still Sits There Dejected.*

labor camp." [Phạm Duy did not at the time remember the name of the book, but everyone knows that he was talking about Tạ Tỵ's memoir *The Depths of Hell* (*Đáy Địa Ngục*, Thằng Mõ, 1985).

After the fall of the South in 1975, Tạ Tỵ did not enjoy the good fortune of Phạm Duy. Unlike him, he was not conducted out of the country by the CIA. Instead, he was arrested and imprisoned in labor reform camps for six years. *The Depths of Hell* records his experiences in those years of imprisonment and heavy labor, with "food insufficient to make one full and hunger insufficient to result in death." When he emerged from the camps in 1981, and met again with Lê Ngộ Châu in the former editorial office of *Cyclopedia*, Tạ Tỵ was a mere shadow of his former self, with white hair and loose teeth. After that, Tạ Tỵ made two brave attempts to cross the ocean. The second time, he managed to reach the island of Pulau Bidong in Malaysia, and began at once to write his memoir of imprisonment. (*Cultural Portraits*, Volume 2, Ngô Thế Vinh, Việt Ecology Press, 2022)

The modern history of Vietnam has, as one of its products, a "white book" on the archipelago of Vietnamese prisons stretching from the South to the North, that emerged after 1975, a place where a great many southern writers, journalists, artists among whom there was no lack of friends of Phạm Duy, some even of his own generation, who died of neglect in prison, like Hiếu Chân Nguyễn Hoạt, Nguyễn Mạnh

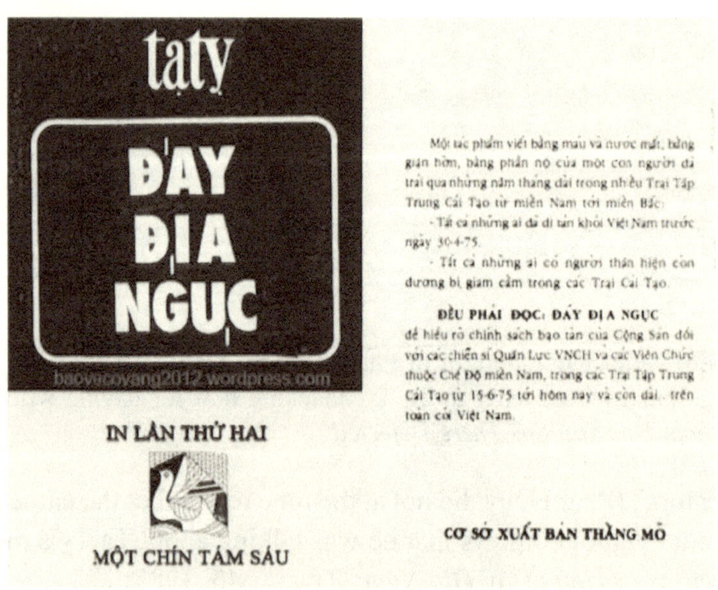

The cover of the book *Depths of Hell* (*Đáy Địa Ngục*, Thằng Mõ, 1986, U.S.), a memoir of the six years that the author spent as a prisoner in labor reform camps. It is not clear whether Phạm Duy ever read the book. Tạ Tỵ, an old friend of Phạm Duy's, had died seven years before the date of the interview, in 2004.

Côn, Hoàng Vĩnh Lộc, Phạm Văn Sơn, Trần Văn Tuyên, Trần Việt Sơn, Vũ Ngọc Các, Anh Tuấn Trần Tuấn Phát, Dương Hùng Cường… or who died soon after leaving prison, like Vũ Hoàng Chương and Hồ Hữu Tường.

And now, in the Vietnamese press, one sees images of Phạm Duy and his children as returnees, able once again to walk upon the National Road of former days. And one sees, as well, on brightly lit stages from Saigon to Hanoi, an utterly changed Phạm Duy, who, still with his head of white hair, holds scripts from which he reads to the audience, his arms holding multi-colored bouquets amid the avid applause of his audiences.

PHẠM DUY: HIS HUGE ACCOMPLISHMENT AND HIS MORAL STATURE

After thirty years of living in the U.S. amid the love and regard of the overseas Vietnamese community, Phạm Duy chose to go back to Vietnam and end his days there. He had every right to make such a decision; it must viewed by all with respect. And in accordance with this desire, he lived and died in Vietnam.

Phạm Duy's huge musical endowment may be seen especially in "Feeling for the Homeland," ("Tình Quê Hương"), a song that has entered deeply into the hearts of many generations. Phạm Duy is in himself a gigantic, awe-inspiring monument in the modern history of music in Vietnam. The present generation, and the ones that are to come, will continue to sing a number of his songs.

Young people seek to draw near him as if he were a sublime spirit; they not only revere his great genius, but yearn to see in him a person of great moral stature. But then they see that he was not equally great in both realms.

Like many other artistic people, Phạm Duy abandoned the Resistance War very early and returned to the cities, for the perfectly justifiable reason that he could not accept participation in a "command culture" directed by communists, and was determined to protect his personal creative freedom.

Suffused with inspiration, and living in a free environment, he created songs in which both notes and lyrics were of deathless value. But as time passed, and as era yielded to era, those who loved his music could not avoid surprise when they observed that he "censored himself"; he revised the original lyrics of songs he had written during the Resistance to make them accord better with changed times and circumstances. Whoever followed all the steps in his career could not fail to be disappointed when they too lost their bearings in this pursuit.

Phạm Duy's great longevity allowed him to experience two centuries, to live every phase as he "wept and laughed with the changing fortunes of his country."

No one can suppose that Phạm Duy did not understand the communists; they can only imagine that in the last years of his life, his powers of judgement were no longer sharp. That being the case, we can see only a person exemplifying the ordinary run of humanity, meaning a person afflicted with all the usual moral ills of human beings. I don't wish to say a thing about his very complicated romantic adventures with women–that was an aspect of his private life and must be treated with respect. I wish to speak only of his relations with people in general and of matters related to his professional career.

In writing a portrait of Phạm Duy, it is easy to see that he himself created many self-portraits in the successive phases of his career. Phạm Duy always emphasized that he was simply a Vietnamese musician, and was completely unconcerned with politics. But in a manner totally contradictory, he chose at the end of his life, after building up a huge legacy of music, to live in a country that was not yet free, that was still a land with a "command culture"–he chose to resign himself to the life of a caged bird. No one forced him to do it, but often, on his own volition, he made public statements that had political overtones, or that seemed to express conformity with the tendencies promoted by the regime, so that even those who loved and defended him had to frown with disapproval.

After the passing of Phạm Duy, more than a few of Phạm Duy's songs were still prohibited. The song "Vietnam, Vietnam" which the composer himself was very pleased with, and which he referred to in 2012, was never approved, though he had requested several times that approval be given to it. The hidden reason why the "winning side" was never willing to agree to this was that many people had suggested that this song could be selected as the national anthem of a future, democratic, Vietnam.

When Phạm Duy died, the new, "public" Phạm Duy, a creation of Resolution 36, died with him. Though there was no official pronouncement on the matter, it seemed there was a directive coming from high in the power structure, that Phạm's reputation could no longer be noisily celebrated or promoted. Books by Phạm Duy, including his four-volume set of memoirs and books written about him could no longer gain easy approval.

A PHOTO BOOK: PHẠM DUY, THE DAY OF RETURN (2005-2013)

A typical example of this is a book of images compiled by the photographer Nguyễn Phong Quang, entitled *The Day of Return* (*Ngày Trở Về*). It had previously been accepted by the publishing house Trẻ (Youth) with the intention of bringing it out on Phạm Duy's death anniversary (Jan. 28, 2014), but it has not yet, as of 2022, been approved for publication, though eight years have passed since that date. The regime has given no reason whatsoever for this.

Though Nguyễn Phong Quang is an amateur photographer, he creates beautiful photographic images due to his reverence for Phạm Duy and his passionate devotion to his music; so as soon as Phạm Duy began returning to Vietnam, he followed the songwriter's every step. Thus, it can be said that Nguyễn Phong Quang is the only person in possession of a complete photographic record of the last thirteen years of Phạm Duy's life, from the time of his first return to Vietnam until the day of his death on a hospital sickbed.

People with a thorough understanding of the state of affairs within the country have come to the following conclusion: In the days following Phạm Duy's death, an unwritten directive came into being that no permission was to be given for the publication of any materials having to do with Phạm Duy! It appears that they had made sufficient use of Phạm Duy during the period when "openness" was an announced policy. The regime now had no further need of him! Another factor involved was that of professional jealousy–a number of leaders in the cultural life of the cities who did not want Phạm Duy's productions to stand beside their own and did not want others to celebrate his accomplishments more than their own.

PHẠM DUY AND HIS PORTRAITS

To draw a portrait of someone as full of life as Phạm Duy is not an easy matter. One can't confine one's observations to a single point of view; one must look at him from many points of view in order to see his many different faces. If one were to combine all his different layers, one could create a portrait animated by his spirit. To borrow an expression of Tạ Tỵ's, it would be a "four-dimensional" portrait, or, to borrow a technical term used in the plastic arts, it would be a "cubist" portrait. What this means is that there can be no single portrait of Phạm Duy; he was always changing in form and color as time went on.

A man who lived in two centuries, Phạm Duy did work replete with the turbulence and power of the four-thousand-year-long tragedy of the country – and the tragedy of a Vietnamese man who was both great and petty, both beautiful and ugly.

Phạm Duy died at the age of 92 – as poet Nguyễn Du put it, *"The body falls away; the essence brightly stays"* ("Thác là thể phách, còn là tinh anh"). The essence is the huge musical legacy he created. Once this legacy has been subjected to the winnowing process of time, of three hundred or more years, what remains will be deathless melodies filled with the fragrance of the homeland, and carrying some portion of the people's soul. I wish him eternal rest in the embrace of the soil of the motherland that bears the sacred name of Vietnam – or, as people say, the homeland.

A bronze bust of Phạm Duy
by the sculptor Nguyễn Văn Anh,
created on the basis of a photo by the
photographer Nguyễn Phong Quang
and under the direction of Duy Cường,
Phạm Duy's son.

BY WAY OF CONCLUSION

On the day of Phạm Duy's death – Jan. 27, 2013 – the poet Trần Mộng Tú, looking back on his life with emotion, wrote *"A Thankful Tribute to Phạm Duy,"* a composition splendid as a poem, that looks back on the totality of his career. Having been granted the author's permission, I beg to quote this prose poem here as a conclusion to this portrait of the musician.

From left to right: A bronze bust of Phạm Duy, Phạm Duy's tomb, the tomb of his wife Thái Hằng, and the tomb of his eldest son Duy Quang.

(Photo by Nguyễn Phong Quang)

A quotation written out by Phạm Duy, and engraved on stone from the song "Love of Country" ("Tình Ca"): "I've loved the language of my land from when I first came into life, oh people." ("Tôi yêu tiếng nước tôi, từ khi mới ra đời, người ơi.")

(Photo by Nguyễn Phong Quang)

A Thankful Tribute to Phạm Duy
by Trần Mộng Tú

From his ten fingers there poured down a thousand, thousand glistening, multi-colored tears, and there sprang up songs of victory filled with laughter for the people of Vietnam;

You wrote the history of our people by means of music, shooting notes instead of bullets throughout the long perspective of a war brought on us by invaders;

You made live on all our lips the achievements of our forebears, the heroes of our people;

You wept and laughed in notes and verses, gifts to love, to humankind, to our homeland, to our people;

You bound up the wounds of war, lit fires in pursuit of peace;

You swung your arm, and the clouds on high resembled silk, the seas became like broken crystal; you engraved the image of our Father Lạc Long Quân upon the mountains, then no longer made of stone, you cast the love of Mother Âu Cơ down among the seas, then longer oceans.

The words in all your songs were limpid, full of feeling, tender, expansive as the feelings of our people, lovely as pieces of white jade, clear as drops of rain;

You went up to the forests, and the forests changed their leaves; you went down to pure springs, and the springs burst into tears; by means of music, and the feelings of our people, you went from the Ải Nam Quan (Youyi Pass) to the promontory of Cà Mau throughout your life that knew no rest;

The love of country in your lyrics made both those who sang, and those who heard your songs shed tears;

The coursing blood running through your wounds turned into honey, your clouds were the breathing of people's dwellings, your little children were water buffalo, your torn blouses and kitchen hearths were our mothers, your manioc tubers and bowls of tea were our children;

Beneath your hands our Việt speech became the sacred language of our land, the language of our people, you conferred the essence of our language on our people as a gift;

Your music is suffused with feeling for our native kind, our native land;

In the love of couples among our kind, you made immortal maidens fall to earth, and pink grass sprout on mountainsides, never afterward to fade; you shuddered with joy amid your melodies!

You were pure, you were vulgar, you were holy, you broke apart the world with music;

You drank, you ate, you breathed amid your melodies and lyrics.

You lived your life, all aspects of your life, by means of music, never letting a single second of it go to waste;

You bequeathed to your compatriots and to the treasury of the music of our people a legacy that no other land can take away.

You are a precious gift that the god of how many generations of our forebears nurtured into being and conferred upon our people in the present age.

You came to life and lay to rest within our homeland, this land of Vietnam.

And for this I beg to present to you a Solemn Word of Thanks.

[Trần Mộng Tú, Jan. 27, 2013]

Little Saigon, July 4, 2022

VIETNAM – HOMECOMINGS OF THE FORMER SOLDIER ERIC HENRY

This image is taken from the jacket of
Garden of Eloquence / Shuō Yuàn by Liú Xiàng,
translated and introduced by Eric Henry,
University of Washington Press, 2021.
(Photo by Nguyễn Phong Quang)

**

Prefatory Remark:

It was my original intention to combine this portrait with my portrait of Phạm Duy. But then my Phạm Duy portrait came to be almost fifty pages long, so I had to separate my portrait of Eric Henry and turn it into a separate article, while retaining the hope that readers would regard these two portraits as mutually supplementary, for both form part of a process of seeking to understand tân nhạc, the "new music" of Vietnam, together with the difficulties surrounding the publication of the translated Memoirs of Phạm Duy, a manuscript slated to be brought out by Cornell University Press. It seems I should mention as well that the library of Cornell University is the place with the most comprehensive collection of the literature of South Vietnam in the period 1954 – 1975, a collection that the book-burning fire of the communist Vietnamese has been powerless to reach and destroy.

ERIC HENRY AND ME

The first time I met Dr. Eric Henry was five years ago (2017), and I was surprised on that occasion when I saw that he had little of the air of a soldier, though he had formerly been stationed in Vietnam as a military man in the U.S. Army. As he entered his twenties – the age of military service – he made a simple decision: he would enlist in the army and fulfill his civic duties, and then return to his studies. From the time he entered the service Eric continued to be very fond of study, and had some understanding of Eastern cultures, including those of China and Vietnam in particular. Eric has a gift for languages, and speaks Vietnamese in a fairly fluent and precise manner, without any trace of the vulgarities picked up by GIs in bars during their tours of duty in Vietnam. Having come to a land at war with many religions like Vietnam, he learned how to respond in a witty and satisfactory manner to questions that can easily cause divisions among people, such as: "What religion do you follow?" – "I follow the religion of wife-worship." And that religion was implicitly recognized as a widely-spread phenomenon among male soldiers of that time – though when he came to Vietnam, Eric was still a bachelor.

Left: Eric Henry at age 27. After completing a twelve-month intensive Vietnamese language course at the Defense Language Institute at Fort Bliss, next to El Paso, Texas, Eric was sent to Vietnam to serve in the Intelligence Branch of the 25th Infantry Division at Củ Chi. The photo dates from 1970. Eric says, "At that time, I could speak Vietnamese, but had not yet begun to study Chinese." *Right:* Ngô Thế Vinh at age 28 in a photo from 1969, after completing training with the Special Forces Airborne Unit at Động Ba Thìn and entering the Green Berets, later 81st Airborne Ranger Group.

Forty-two years after the Vietnam War, the former American soldier Eric Henry, now a scholar, and the former soldier of the Republic of Vietnam, Ngô Thế Vinh, now a doctor in a VA hospital, having become septuagenarians, met each other in Huntington Beach, California, when Eric had come to meet with members of the Phạm Duy family – to discuss a contract with Cornell University Press that would lead to the publication, in English, of The Memoirs of Phạm Duy – a project dear to the heart of Phạm Duy when he was still alive, but which had still not been accomplished at the time of his death (Jan. 27, 2013). *[photo by Phạm Lệ Hương, from personal archives of Ngô Thế Vinh]*

Only after I learned of his awareness that I too was a writer, did I come to realize that Eric had read the novel *The Green Belt*, from a Vietnamese edition [*Vòng Đai Xanh*] published in California in 1987 by the Văn Nghệ publishing house. Eric let me know that he still kept the book on his shelves and that he too was concerned with the minority peoples living in the Western Highlands. Due to this literary connection, it was easier for us to converse.

Eric Henry let me know that he was a devotee of the music of Phạm Duy, that he had read the Memoirs of Phạm Duy with delight, and that in a bit over a year he had made a translation of that 1,500-page-long work. This translation was accepted for publication by Cornell University Press as long ago as 2009, four years before Phạm Duy's death, but to this day, thirteen years later (2009 – 2022), it has remained in manuscript form.

ERIC HENRY FIVE YEARS LATER

Just now, in the year 2022, when I looked in the catalogue of Cornell University Press for the English edition of The Memoirs of Phạm Duy, so I could give it to an American friend with a strong interest in Vietnamese culture, and failed to find it, I got in touch with Eric and learned that the book had not yet been published, the reason being that when Phạm Duy died he left no will giving the right of inheritance to any of his children, and as a result his seven surviving children have been unable to come to an agreement to give permission for the book to be published.

After that, Eric and I exchanged a long series of email messages through which I learned of the many arduous steps he has taken in his negotiations with the family, and in which I promised to do everything I could to see that The Memoirs of Phạm Duy were published at the earliest possible date.

Reception for Eric Henry in the home of Phạm Lệ Hương, Huntington Beach, California. From left: Ngô Thế Vinh, Nguyễn Duy Chính, Phạm Phú Minh, Eric Henry, Bùi Bích Hà, Trần Huy Bích.

(Photo by Phạm Lệ Hương)

Eric Henry appreciated the painting "Mother and Child" by the artist Lemur.

(Photo by Ngô Thế Vinh)

ERIC HENRY AND THE NEW MUSIC [TÂN NHẠC] OF VIETNAM

That was in July of 2005, only two months after "Phạm Duy's Day of Return," when, in response to one of Quỳnh Lệ's questions, "How would you characterize and evaluate the music of Vietnam," Eric Henry came out with some rather surprising and interesting observations:

"...Vietnamese music is in general pervaded by a sense of melancholy. Most of the songs in this tradition belong to three main themes: remembrance of a now distant homeland, nostalgia for a long departed romantic relationship, or yearning to return to a cherished time far in the past – often the singer-speaker's childhood. All three of these themes are accompanied by a mood of pain and sorrow. This is totally different from the nature of Chinese music, which is mostly strong and joyous, and made up of regular, symmetrical eight-measure phrases. Western music also is usually laid out in eight- or sixteen-measure phrases. The music of Vietnam is relatively rich in

A photograph of the composer Phạm Duy and the PhD Eric Henry in the café Nirvana / Niết Bàn, 29 Phùng Khắc Khoan Street, Đa Kao Ward, District 1, Saigon, with the following note from Eric: "On the morning of July 9, 2005, I went to Nirvana to meet Ms. Quỳnh Lệ, a journalist who worked for the magazine *People in Far-away Lands / Người Viễn Xứ*, and who said that she wished to interview me. When Phạm Duy learned that I was going there for that purpose, he volunteered at once to accompany me there to help me respond to Ms. Lệ's inquiries.

(Photo by Quỳnh Lệ, personal archives of Eric Henry)

phrases that do not fit this mold. Listening to these "irregular" phrases is like venturing into a new land.

Trịnh Y Thư is an intergenerational friend of mine, a poet, a writer, a fine classical guitarist, and a celebrated translator of many classic works. He became well known right away with his *Đời Nhẹ Khôn Kham / The Unbearable Lightness of Being* by the Czech-French writer Milan Kundera published in the magazine *Literary Studies / Văn Học* in 2002 – and he is also the person who wrote the preface to *Literary and Cultural Portraits, Volume Two* of the present author (2022). Trịnh Y Thư was very pleased with the observations of Eric Henry concerning the New Music of Vietnam. This is what he wrote:

"My dear Ngô Thế Vinh: The observations of Professor Henry are extremely accurate. Vietnamese music is in general full of nostalgia, and perhaps this is a general trait of Vietnamese people, always turning with fond yearning to the past – a past sometimes simplified, as if seen through a lens – and due to this, the music is laden with tender emotion, and is divorced from reality, because it must depend to a great extent on imagination. The music says little about reality, about the actual experiences of people in the world, or about the relations of people with others, or with the natural world, or with their surroundings. Though created in a time of merciless warfare, the music says little about warfare. There are only a few anti-war songs by Trịnh Công Sơn and some poems set to music by Phạm Duy, nothing else.

"And with regard to techniques of composition, Professor Henry's observations are also very correct. Most Vietnamese musicians created melodies in direct response to feeling; few made music based on classical principles. The music followed the lyrics, and sometimes served only as a means of giving expression to the words. There were a few exceptions to this, such as Cung Tiến and Vũ Thành… The principal thing to note is that Vietnamese music emphasized melody above all; any song that had a fine melody, mellifluous and romantic, was popular with listeners. That is the reason Vietnamese music is very poor in harmonic content. A song usually contains only three or four modulations.

"…Nevertheless, according to the viewpoint of Professor Henry, the traits I have mentioned above are all strong points in Vietnamese music, because they depart from what is standard, they are free from conventional restraints, which are sometimes very hackneyed… Trịnh Y Thư"

…After reading the opinions of Trịnh Y Thư, Eric had a further observation: "The way Mr. Trịnh Y Thư evaluates Vietnamese music is different from mine."

"…Thank you, Mr. Vinh, for letting me see the observations on Vietnamese music of Mr. Trịnh Y Thư. My response is: "Though he feels that I was not mistaken in setting forth traits of Vietnamese music in my discussion with Ms. Quỳnh Lệ, I still feel that his evaluation of this music is not close to mine – because he feels that these traits are shortcomings, whereas I feel that they are strong points! I have devoted quite a bit of study to the popular song traditions of various Asian countries. China, Korea, Japan, Taiwan, and the Philippines naturally all have a number of supremely beautiful songs – but they still don't have as many as Vietnam – and the degree of depth in those traditions also does not equal that of Vietnam! I sometimes say to people that the Vietnamese are the Italians of the Far East!

And when Eric Henry speaks of the music of Phạm Duy, he has the same enthusiasm:

"The songs of Phạm Duy are rich in content. They can be divided into many periods: the period of the Resistance, the period of his residence in the South and his period of exile abroad. Just the music he wrote in exile can be divided into many phases. Phạm Duy's music is not as a whole characterized by the sorrow and pain that one notices in the work of most other Vietnamese songwriters. His songs sometimes express pain, but they are nevertheless not steeped in misery. He often creates songs that tell stories. His themes are diverse and have a limitless variety of shades and textures. For example each of his songs that deal with mothers has some quality unique to itself, such as "The Mother of Gio Linh," ("Bà Mẹ Gio Linh") and "A Countryside Mother" ("Bà Mẹ Quê")

Through the attention I have paid to such works, I have learned that the music of Vietnam is a field of study and that, within that field, the music of Phạm Duy is a further field of study. When one speaks of the quantity, variety, and quality of this music, the work of Phạm Duy alone accounts for about half of this tradition. Therefore if the music of Phạm Duy ceased to be promoted, then Vietnamese music as a whole would suffer a considerable setback. I believe that Phạm Duy needs to be numbered among those who loved their country. But most Vietnamese living outside the country also have this love. And, looking back in history, it seems to me that those who belonged to the Nationalist Party also loved their country, not just the Việt Minh. In recent years Vietnam has adopted more relaxed policies with regard to Vietnamese living abroad. I would guess that the Vietnamese government will grant permission for the fine songs of Phạm Duy to be performed.

In light of current realities, it is easy to see that Eric Henry is both too optimistic and too early in his optimism when he says that the Vietnamese government will grant permission for the fine songs of Phạm Duy to be performed. Through this article, I wish to announce to Mr. Eric Henry that: only when Vietnam enters into a period of democracy and has a system that allows for freedom in the arts, will the music of Phạm Duy be able to take flight and flourish.

THE DIFFICULTIES ENCOUNTERED BY ERIC HENRY WITH THE MEMOIRS OF PHẠM DUY

"The history of the efforts I have made to publish the Memoirs of Phạm Duy is like the history of the Cold War between the United States and the Soviet Union. It has been an endlessly protracted and complex history. Where should I begin in order to give you a clear account?" (excerpted from an email sent to the author by Dr. Eric Henry on May 4, 2022)

How did Eric Henry Come to Meet the Composer Phạm Duy?

Eric Henry gives the following account:

"Near the end of summer in 2003, when I was visiting Little Saigon, I met and conversed with the journalist Đỗ Ngọc Yến. It was

In 1975, Phạm Duy, in his first days as a refugee, met Đỗ Ngọc Yến in the U.S. From left: Đỗ Ngọc Yến, Thái Hằng, Đỗ Quý Toàn, Phạm Duy, and Lê Tất Điều.

(personal archives of Phạm Duy)

In 2002, Đỗ Ngọc Yến, the founder of the newspaper Người Việt (The Vietnamese People), welcomed Phạm Duy to a meeting of the Committee on the music of Phạm Duy. As Eric Henry relates, it was Đỗ Ngọc Yến (left) who enabled him to make the acquaintance of the Phạm Duy family.

(Ngô Thế Vinh, personal archives)

he who gave me the means of becoming acquainted with the Phạm Duy family.

"At that time, Phạm Duy had still not returned from a trip to Vietnam so I didn't get to meet him, but I nevertheless made the acquaintance of Mr. Phạm Duy Hùng, the third son of the composer. When we met in his father's house in Midway City, we talked about two hours about his father's music and, as we talked, I also learned that Duy Hùng was a fine guitarist. He invited me to name any song sung by the Beatles, promising that he could perform it on the guitar. So I mentioned the song "Across the Universe" by John Lennon, and Hùng, without a moment's hesitation, played and sang the song for me in an utterly perfect manner – not a note was out of place.

Five months later, in January of 2004, when I came again to California, I met Phạm Duy for the first time. I met him again two months later, and after two additional months, I suggested to him in a letter sent through the postal system, that I make an English translation of his *Memoirs*. The content of the letter was as follows:

To the musician Phạm Duy:

Enclosed with this are the first three chapters of your Memoirs in English translation. Please take a glance at them. I feel that the four volumes of your Memoirs will be of the utmost value to anyone seeking to gain a better understanding of Vietnam in the century just passed.

If you feel that my translation of these few chapters is acceptable, then I will go on with the job, and will seek a publisher for it later on – I feel that your agreement to this will help me negotiate with publishers – but if you don't want me to do this – perhaps you already have a translator, for example – then I shall stop at once.

I feel that translating what you write is full of interest and not very difficult – if I set aside an hour every evening for this work, I can finish a chapter in three to five days, and whenever I encounter a difficulty, I can consult with a number of people who live close by. Let me mention incidentally that this summer I will be in Vietnam with ten students from June 13 to August 12 – the location will be the Phạm Ngọc Thạch Guest House – and that after that I will be in Orange County from August 12 to 17. I hope that the composition of your "Homeland Fragrance" song cycle is proceeding apace. Echoes of the melodies are still in my ears."

Phạm Duy: "Because I am Tarzan"

"Every time I sent an email message to Phạm Duy to ask a few questions about places in the Memoirs, he would reply very promptly – I usually had to wait only one or two hours. In one of my messages to him, I raised a few questions as usual, but said that I knew he was very busy just then organizing a show, so there was no need for him to reply quickly. It would give me no trouble to wait. Then, as usual, his reply came in one or two hours. In this reply, he said: "Just as you say, I am currently very busy, but I can still answer your questions quickly, because I am... Tarzan!" After that, in a different message that he sent me, he said, "Do you see? Tarzan is still swinging from branch to branch in the jungle!"

Phạm Duy: "...so that I can jump in after you"

"When I first made Phạm Duy's acquaintance, I – Eric Henry – promised him that I would complete two tasks; I would first of all complete the translation of his four volumes of memoirs, and then would find a publisher for the work in the United States.

"I finished the translation a year later and after four more years found a publisher: Southeast Asia Publications of Cornell University, which later became part of Cornell University Press. Then I returned to Vietnam to create a set of 1,500 footnotes concerning the people and places mentioned in the Memoirs and in order to sign a contract with Phạm Duy and Cornell University.

"When we were about to sign the contract, Phạm Duy suddenly remembered that he had signed a different contract a few years earlier with the Phương Nam Culture Company, which stated that the company held exclusive rights to all the works of Phạm Duy – but the

Memoirs were not a song – surely he (Phạm Duy) would be able to sign the contract with Cornell.

"But when Phạm Duy inquired about this with Phương Nam, he found that the word "works" included not just his music, but his books as well. This meant that he had no right to sign a different contract with Cornell.

"This, to me – Eric Henry– was a calamitous disappointment, and I wrote a message to Phạm Duy saying half-jokingly and half-seriously that if no way could be found in the future to publish the *Memoirs* in English, then I would have no choice but to commit suicide by jumping into a river.

"In his reply to this, Phạm Duy said that I need not be too concerned about this. There would surely be a way to publish the *Memoirs* at some point in the future. And he suggested a few approaches I might use to reach this goal.

And at the end of the message, he added a postscript: "Whenever you decide to jump into the river, let me know, okay – so I can jump in after you!" This detail is an illustration of the humor and optimism of the man.

AN AUTOBIOGRAPHICAL ACCOUNT BY ERIC HENRY

Since I had the intention of writing a "Portrait of Eric Henry" along with my "Portrait of Phạm Duy," I asked him to supply me with an autobiography, and he responded with the following message (Sunday, May 8, 2022):

"I reread the biographical notice I produced for the BBC, which I will supply to you here, with a few corrections and additions: "I was born in 1943 (March 15). My parents were both professional musicians. When I was a child, I studied the piano and due to my parents' influence came to love and understand western classical music. From around the year 1960, I began to play and teach piano for a living. I knew nothing whatsoever about Vietnam at that time, not to speak of Vietnamese music. In 1968, I enlisted in the U.S. Army and took a twelve-month intensive course in Vietnamese.

"In 1970, I was stationed in Vietnam (Củ Chi, Xuân Lộc, and then Quảng Trị) with the army. Along with serving as a translator, I interviewed a fair number of North Vietnamese prisoners. I was acquainted at the time *The Tale of Kiều* (a celebrated narrative poem from the early nineteenth century) and a number of novels by Khái Hưng, Nhất Linh, and Duyên Anh, but I still knew little about Vietnamese popular music. Once, listening to the singing of one of my language teachers, I wrote out the notes of the song "I Take You Over the River" ("Tôi Đưa Em Sang Sông" by Nhật Ngân). I had also heard a bit about the musical reputations of Phạm Duy and Trịnh Công Sơn.

"Then I left Vietnam in the summer of 1971. After that I became a graduate student in Chinese Literature at Yale University. In 1980, I began to teach Chinese, first at Dartmouth College, and then, from 1982 on, at the University of North Carolina. In 1995, I began to offer courses in Vietnamese at Carolina, and, starting in 1999, began watching *Paris By Night* videos, hoping thereby to be able to have better conversations with my second-generation Vietnamese students, whom I knew saw such videos in their parents' homes. I was very astonished to see that, of the songs performed on these videos, about forty per cent had artistic value, and that the singing of the performers was in many cases attractive and skillful.

"From the year 2000 on, I used every means in my power to deepen my understanding of Vietnamese music. And in more recent years, I have also sought to gain some understanding of the song cultures of Japan, Korea, China, Taiwan, and the Philippines. In 2002 or thereabouts, while visiting a Vietnamese bookstore in Falls Church, Virginia, I saw, purchased, and took home Volume I of the Phạm Duy *Memoirs*, and saw at once that it possessed great value for anyone seeking to understand Vietnam's recent history.

As for the scholarly activities of Eric Henry, I would like to present here some excerpts from: "Eric Henry Curriculum Vitæ, University of North Carolina":

Degrees Conferred:

- Ph.D, 1979, Chinese Literature, Yale University, Department of East Asian Languages and Literatures. Dissertation Title: "Chinese Amusement: An Introduction to the Plays of Li Yü"
- M.Ph, 1976, Chinese Literature, Yale University, Department of East Asian Languages and Literatures. Research Paper Title: "On the Nature, Structure, and Evolution of the *Chin Yun Ch'iao chuan,* a Popular Novel of the Early Ch'ing"
- B.A. 1972, English Literature, Amherst College, summa cum laude. Senior thesis title: *"On Đoạn Trường Tân Thanh*, the National Poem of the Vietnamese"

Other education:

- 1977-78: One-year intensive language study at the International University Program for Chinese Language Studies at the Stanford Center in Taipei
- 1968-69: One-year intensive language training in Vietnamese at the Defense Language Institute Support Command, Fort Bliss, Texas

PUBLISHED WORKS:

Books:

Chinese Amusement: The Lively Plays of Li Yü 李漁: Henry, Eric. Hamden, CT: Shoestring Press (Archon Books), 1980, xvi, 288 pp.

Translations:

Garden of Eloquence; a translation of *Shuō Yuàn* 說苑 in bilingual format with textual notes; commissioned by the editorial board of The Culture and Civilization of China (a joint program of the American Council of Learned Societies and Washington University Press). *Shuō Yuàn* is a collection of 718 items, of which most are historical narratives, compiled by Liú Xiàng 劉向 and presented to the throne in 17 BCE. Seattle: University of Washington Press, 2022, 1,242 pages

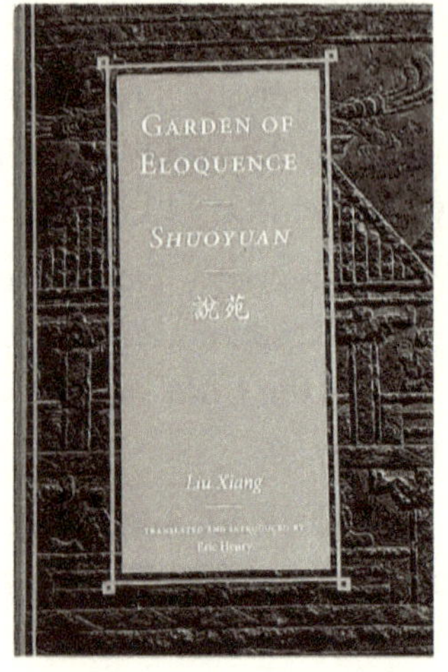

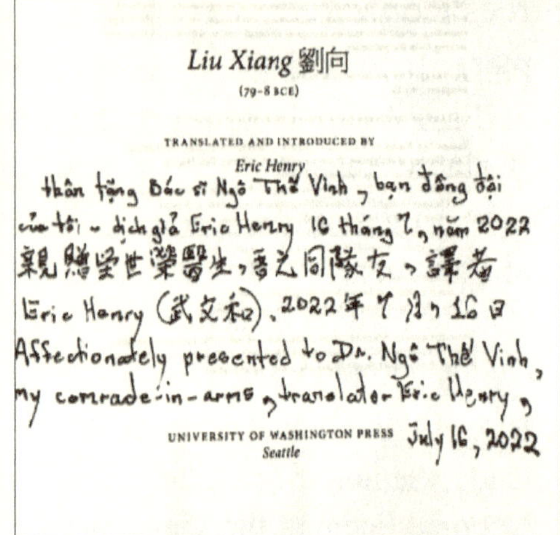
Liu Xiang 劉向

(79–8 BCE)

TRANSLATED AND INTRODUCED BY

Eric Henry

thân tặng Bác sĩ Ngô Thế Vinh, bạn đồng đội của tôi - dịch giả Eric Henry 16 tháng 7, năm 2022

親贈吳世榮醫生，吾之同隊友，譯者 Eric Henry (武文和), 2022年7月16日

Affectionately presented to Dr. Ngô Thế Vinh, my comrade-in-arms, translator Eric Henry, July 16, 2022

UNIVERSITY OF WASHINGTON PRESS

Seattle

Left: The front cover of the book *Garden of Eloquence* (Shuō Yuàn 說怨) by Liú Xiàng, a 1,232-page book translated and introduced by Eric Henry, published by University of Washington Press, Seattle in 2021; right: page with a written dedication in three languages: Vietnamese, Chinese, and English. Professor Henry's use of the name Wǔ Wénhé 武文和 to refer to himself is explained below. *(Ngô Thế Vinh, personal archives)*

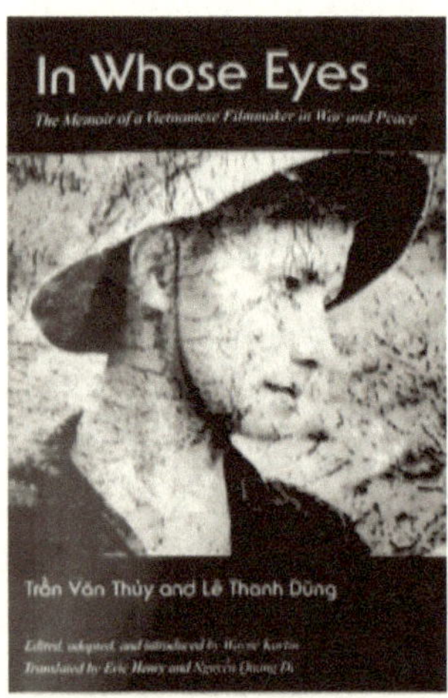

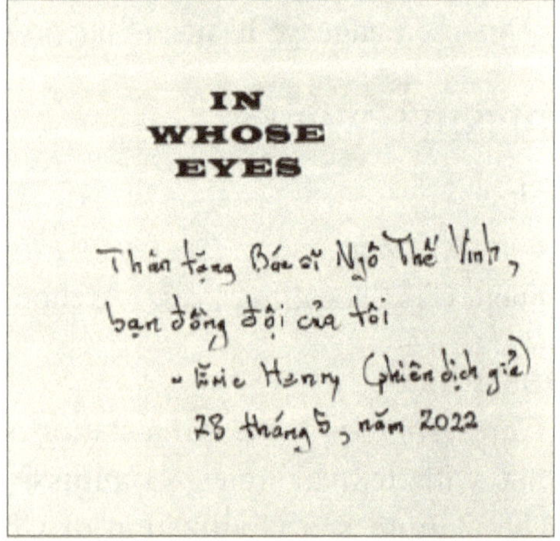
IN WHOSE EYES

Thân tặng Bác sĩ Ngô Thế Vinh, bạn đồng đội của tôi - Eric Henry (phiên dịch giả) 28 tháng 5, năm 2022

Left: front cover of the book *In Whose Eyes*, published by the University of Massachusetts Press, 2016. This is an English translation of the memoirs of the filmmaker Trần Văn Thủy: *Chuyện Nghề của Thủy* (2014). Right: words of dedication written in the book by the translator: "Presented in friendship to my comrade-in-arms Dr. Ngô Thế Vinh, Eric Henry, May 28, 2022.

(Ngô Thế Vinh, personal archives)

In Whose Eyes; a translation, with Nguyễn Quang Dy and Wayne Karlin, of *Chuyện Nghề Của Thủy* by Trần Văn Thủy and Lê Thanh Dũng (2013), Amherst: University of Massachusetts Press, 2016, xv, 219 pp.

Book Chapters and Scholarly Articles

- "Running Amok in Early China"; in *Behaving Badly in Ancient China* edited by Norman Rothschild and Leslie Wallace; Honolulu: University of Hawaii Press, 2017, pp. 171-188
- "Some East Asian Popular Song Lyrics" *Southeastern Review of Asian Studies* 33 (Jan. 2012)
- "Evidence for a Usurpation in Sòng" *Warring States Papers* 1 (2010), pp. 227-230
- "A Note on *Chūnqiū Shìyǔ* 春秋事語, Item 5" *Warring States Papers* 1 (2010), pp. 55-58.
- "The Submerged History of Yuè" Sino-Platonic Papers, pub. by Victor Mair, Univ. of Pennsylvania, no. 176 (June, 2007)
- "Bước Đường Lữ Thứ," ("Footsteps of a Wayfarer") *Carolina Việt Bá*o (22, Oct. 2006), pp. 79 – 84 (in Vietnamese; consists of cross-cultural observations prompted by travel in China and Vietnam)
- "Phạm Duy và lịch sử Việt Nam hiện đại" (a translation by Phổ Tịnh of the article below); posted on the website TALAWAS (2005)
- "Phạm Duy and Modern Vietnamese History," *Southeastern Review of Asian Studies* 27 (2005), pp. 89 – 105
- *Tân Nhạc*: Notes Toward a Social History of Vietnamese Music in the 20th Century *Michigan Quarterly*; 44.1 (winter, 2005), pp. 135-147
- Anachronisms in *Lüshì Chunqiu* 呂氏春秋 and *Shuōyuàn* 說苑*; Early Medieval China*, vol 9 (2003), pp. 127-138
- "Chinese and Indigenous Influences in Vietnamese Verse Romances of the 19th Century" *Crossroads* 15.2 (2001); pp. 1 – 40

- "The Social Significance of Nudity in Early China," *Fashion Theory* 3.4 (Dec., 1999), pp. 1-12
- "*Junzi yue* 君子曰 Versus *Zhongni yue* 仲尼 in *Zuo zhuan*"; *Harvard Journal of Asiatic Studies* 58.1 (June, 1999), pp. 125-161
- "Chu-ko Liang 諸葛亮 in the Eyes of His Contemporaries," *Harvard Journal of Asiatic Studies* 52.2 (Dec., 1992), pp. 589-612
- "The Motif of Recognition in Early China," *Harvard Journal of Asiatic Studies* 47.1 (June, 1987), pp. 5-30
- "On the Nature of the Kieu Story," *Vietnam Forum* (Yale University Council on Southeast Asian Studies) 3 (Winter-Spring 1984), pp. 61-98

Book Reviews

- *Poetic Transformations: Eighteenth-Century Cultural Projects on the Mekong Plains*, Claudine Ang; Harvard University Asia Center, 2019, in *China Review International,* 25.1 (2020)
- *The Commentarial Transformation of the Spring and Autumn,* Newell Ann Van Auken; Albany; SUNY Press, 2016, in *Dao: A Journal of Comparative Philosophy,* Fall 2018
- *The Kim Vân Kiều of Nguyễn Du (1765 – 1820),* translated by Vladislav Zhukov; Canberra; Pandanus Books, 2004, in *Journal of Vietnamese Studies* 3:1 (Winter 2008), pp. 240-245
- *Persons, Roles, and Minds: Identity in Peony Pavilion and Peach Blossom Fan*, Tina Lu, Stanford University Press, 2001; 2001; in *CLEAR* [summer, 2002]
- *Guanzi: Political, Economic, and Philosophical Essays from Early China; A Study and Translation. Volume II.* By W. Allyn Rickett. Princeton: Princeton University Press, 1998; in *Journal of Asian Studies* [1999]

Not Yet Published:

Books:

- "Historical Narrative in Early China" (a study of genre and content among the narratives collected in *Zuo zhuàn* 左傳, *Guó yu* 國語, *Zhànguócè* 戰國策, and *Shijì* 史記; 336 pp.)
- "Readings in Chinese Historical Legend" (course textbook; 543 pages)
- "*Xīn xù Summaries*" (detailed summaries of the 176 narratives of the extant *Xīn xù* 新序 , with notes on sources and allusions; a research tool; a collaboration with Professor Anne Kinney)
- "Chinese Phrase Lexicon." Approx. 10,000 phrases, proverbs, and short classical passages cross-referenced by lexical item; computer document in process of expansion.
- "Vietnamese Proverb Lexicon." Similar in scope and concept to the above, but more focused on proverbs; computer document in process of expansion.

Translations:

- 1. From classical Chinese:

  "Tales from the Principalities" (a bilingual edition of *Guóyŭ* 國語, with introduction and notes; approx. 1,000 pp. *Guóyŭ* 國語 is a collection dating from c. 300 BCE consisting of 243 historical narratives)

  "Chronicle of the States of the Eastern Chou, Vol. I" (a translation, Chinese to English, of the first forty chapters of *Dong Zhou liè guó zhì*; 東周列國志; 762 pp.

- 2. From Vietnamese:

  Memoirs (*Hồi Ký*) by Phạm Duy, four volumes (approximately 1,200 pages); *Volume One: Coming of Age in the North; Volume Two: The Resistance; Volume Three: The Period of Division; Volume Four: My Sojourn Abroad*. More than 1,500 detailed footnotes on persons, places, and events, to be published by Cornell University Press.

"Half a century ago, when I began studying Vietnamese at the Defense Language Institute in Fort Bliss, Texas, I encouraged the people around me to call me "anh Hòa," because at that time I often made use of a dictionary by a scholar of that name: Nguyễn Đình Hòa. A few months later, when I realized that I needed a more complete name, I chose "Văn" as the middle element, as it seemed that the use of this syllable in names for males was a habit common to many Vietnamese families – and after that, I chose Võ or Vũ as a surname, because it seemed that the name "Vũ Văn Hòa" was... agreeable to the ear. After returning to Vietnam and starting to associate with Vietnamese people, I gradually ceased to use the name "Hòa," because it seemed to me that the Vietnamese had no problem whatsoever with the name "Eric." But whenever I was engaged socially with Chinese people, I continued to use my "Eastern-style" name, because I saw that they liked to call me "Mr. Wǔ (Wǔ Xiānshēng 武先生) and didn't very readily use the word "Eric."

Upon reading the titles of all the things that Eric Henry had written, I was astonished, and asked Eric what his secret was for finding time to write so many things. Eric replied at once:

"My dear Mr. Vinh,

"I feel that you are the "prolific author" and, in contrast to me, you have a profession that you follow in parallel to the writing profession: you are a doctor! But, if you are interested in asking me if I have any secret for being a productive author, I would reply as follows:

"I am essentially a lazy person. But at the same time, I am a person with a strong preference for adherence to routine. If you want to complete a written work, you have to establish a set of habits – like writing one page every day, for example. If you maintain this habit for a year, then at the end of the year, you will have 365 pages – enough for an entire book!

"Nevertheless, among all the animals in the natural world, my greatest admiration and appreciation is reserved for the sloth of Central and South America. If only I could hang continuously from a branch like that inimitable animal! With appreciation and respect, Eric Henry"

ERIC AND THE MEMOIRS OF PHẠM DUY

And here begins a long series of email messages that Eric and I sent to each other concerning the arduous thirteen-year history of the English Memoirs of Phạm Duy, which still, even today cannot be published:

Email 1 (May 4, 2022): My dear Dr. Ngô Thế Vinh:

"Thank you very much for your concern with the matter of publishing the translated Memoirs of Phạm Duy. The history of my efforts, and those of my "allies" to publish this book resembles the history of the U.S. – Soviet cold war – it is an endlessly long and complex stretch of history – where can I begin, if I am to give a clear account of all that happened?

"Once, in 2009, Phạm Duy and I were about to sign a contract with Cornell Southeast Asia Publications to publish the book – but a company called Phương Nam refused to permit this, because a few years earlier Phạm Duy had signed a contract with that company giving them the exclusive right to publish and promote all the works of Phạm Duy, including his literary works (such as, for example, his Memoirs).

"Later, in the year 2012, a few months before he died, Phạm Duy made a change in this contract, according to which this exclusive right of the Phương Nam Company would be be effective only within the territory of Vietnam, and would not be effective anywhere else. This measure solved the problem with Phương Nam, but it did not solve the problem with the children of Phạm Duy, and in particular with Duy Đức, the youngest son of Phạm Duy.

"Sorry, I'll have to stop writing this for now – I'll explain further tomorrow afternoon. Respectfully, Eric"

Email 2 (May 5, 2022): Dear Dr. Vinh:

"Aside from Duy Đức, another person involved in this matter is Tina Phạm, the family lawyer for Phạm Duy and his family. I have exchanged messages with Tina ever since 2009. According to

Tina, Duy Đức needs to demand that the Cornell Press promise to indemnify Phạm Duy's family in the event that they are sued by the Phương Nam Company. But Sarah Grossman, Cornell's managing editor, says that Cornell's press cannot issue a document that makes such a promise. Instead, she supplied me with a different document stating categorically that Cornell University Press will not seek to sell this book anywhere in the territory of Vietnam. But Tina and Duy Đức were still not satisfied with this guarantee."

After that, Eric Henry communicated with the Phương Nam company. By this time, Phương Nam had a new director and assistant director. Eric received the following reply from Trịnh Hải Phương, the vice-director of the company:

"My respectful greetings to Mr. Eric Henry:

"I am Trịnh Hải Phương, the vice-director of company TNHH MTV Phương Nam Books. We have received your letter, Mr. Henry, in which you suggest that we grant permission for the publication in the United States of the English translation of The Memoirs of Phạm Duy. After reexamining the content of the contract giving us the exclusive right to publish and promote the works of Phạm Duy, we saw that the Phương Nam Company has this right only within the territory of Vietnam. Therefore, we do not have this right in territories of countries other than Vietnam.

"As for your suggestion, this is a matter that resides entirely in the discretion of the family of Phạm Duy, that is, his heirs. This being the case, you can communicate with the family of the musician Phạm Duy in order to discuss this matter. Respectfully, Trịnh Hải Phương"

Having received this letter, I responded to it as follows:

"Dear Mr. Trịnh Hải Phương:

"Thank you very much for your reply. Your letter is extremely clear and helpful. I shall let Cornell and the family of Phạm Duy know about your letter right away. I feel that all parties to this discussion will feel reassured (and in the English translation of the Memoirs, I will speak of the important role played by the Phương Nam Company played in Phạm Duy's return to Vietnam. I feel that if it had not been for Phương Nam, he would not have been able to carry out this return). Once again please accept my sincere thanks to you and your colleagues. I wish you the best, Eric Henry"

And Mr. Trịnh Hải Phương replied as follows:

"Respectful greetings to Mr. Eric Henry:

"Thank you for your reply. The Phương Nam Company made only a small contribution to the promotion of Phạm Duy's fine artistic productions among the people of Vietnam.

"I am personally very impressed with the work you have done for Phạm Duy and hope that your translation of his Memoirs will soon take place. Sincerely, Trịnh Hải Phương"

"Thus, the Phương Nam Company not only does not object to this matter, but hopes that the publication of the English Memoirs will soon take place."

Email 3 (May 7, 2022): Dear Dr. Vinh:

Thanks for sending me the lunar new year card from 1996 and the letter from 1995, both of which have on them the handwriting of the late musician. I will continue supplying you with details concerning my efforts to publish the Memoirs of Phạm Duy. Yours, Eric

"Thank you for communicating with Duy Minh, Duy Cường, and Duy Đức. I feel that, just like me, Duy Cường is very eager for Cornell to publish the Memoirs. Yours, Eric"

Email 4 (May 10, 2022): Dear Dr. Vinh:

"Today or tomorrow, I will write you a bit more about my efforts to publish the Memoirs. Ah, I almost forgot: the three publishing contracts I sent you are not the slightest bit 'classified.' Please quote whatever you like from them! I wish you comfort and peace of mind, Eric"

The new three-story house in the Lê Đại Hành neighborhood in Ward 13 of District 11, Saigon. In the image on the left, Duy Minh, Phạm Duy, and the architect were standing before it. Having moved into his new home, "the great athlete Phạm Duy" (to quote an expression used by the poet Nguyên Sa) continued to work hard and devotedly in front of his Macintosh equipment, though he was by then close to ninety years old. *(Photo by Nguyễn Phong Quang)*

This was the place where Phạm Duy lived the last eight years of his life. If nothing happened to alter the arrangement, this house would become the possession of the Phạm Duy family after twenty years (2005 – 2025).

(Photo by Nguyễn Phong Quang)

THREE LETTERS OF NGÔ THẾ VINH SENT TO THE SONS OF PHẠM DUY

I talked on the phone with Phạm Duy Minh, the second son of the composer Phạm Duy, who is still living in his father's old house in Midway City. I spoke to him of the immense significance that the publication of a translation of his father's memoirs by a prestigious university press would have for his father's musical legacy. This was a thing that Phạm Duy greatly wished for when he was alive.

But then I learned from Duy Minh – now the eldest of Phạm Duy's seven surviving children after the death of Duy Quang – that all seven

A photo taken in August 2006 in Phạm Duy's house in the Lê Đại Hành residential quarter. From the left, the people are: Eric Henry, the translator of the Memoirs of Phạm Duy, Phạm Duy himself, who was by then eighty-five years old, and Harry Diakoff, a lifelong friend of Eric's who is also deeply attracted to Phạm Duy's music. Harry had made videos of two young women, friends of his, doing interpretive dances to two of Phạm Duy's songs: "The Day of Return" ("Ngày Trở Về") and "Lullaby" ("Ru Con"). On seeing those two videos, Phạm Duy expressed enthusiastic interest in them.

(personal archives, with explanatory words, of Eric Henry)

have an equal right of inheritance. Unless all of them, *seven out of seven*, are in agreement, there cannot be a publishing contract with Cornell University. And then Duy Minh gave me the email addresses of three people – Duy Minh, Duy Cường, and Duy Đức – so that I could get in touch with them and discuss the matter.

And so, below are three letters I wrote to the composer's offspring with the sole purpose of finding a way of overcoming obstacles to the prompt publication of the Memoirs.

Letter 1:

To: Duy Minh, Duy Cường, Duy Đức and other members of the family of the composer Phạm Duy.

Subject: The Memoirs of Phạm Duy (to be published by Cornell University Press)

"I, Vinh, am aware that when he was alive, and especially during his final years, your father Phạm Duy viewed the publication in the U.S. of the English translation of his memoirs with the greatest concern and hope. In 2012, one year before he passed away, he referred proudly to this translation [photo]. By now, in the year 2022, ten years have passed since then, and this English translation remains in the offices of Cornell in the form of a draft manuscript. And the person who made this translation, is Eric Henry, a PhD. Eric is a good friend of mine. This year he is seventy-nine years old (he was born in 1943). As a doctor, a matter that greatly concerns me is that he is in his late seventies, a perilous age that few people manage to reach. If he should have a sudden physical crisis, then all his labors on this work, and those of Phạm Duy will be in danger of falling into oblivion! That would be most regrettable!

"I have come to know that what most concerns you all about this publication is that it might violate the terms of a contract that your father signed with the Phương Nam Company, but that possibility does not exist – because, before he died, your father ensured that the contract would say that its provisions were effective solely within the territory of Vietnam!

"I am sending you two Word documents as attachments that contain four letters exchanged between Dr. Henry and the board of directors of the Phương Nam Company in which it is confirmed that the publication of the Memoirs in the U.S. will not violate the contract with Phương Nam.

"And so the ultimate decision with regard to this matter lies with the seven of you: the children and heirs of the legacy of Phạm Duy.

"In view of this, I suggest to you, Duy Minh, Duy Cường, Duy Đức, and all your brothers and sisters within the family discuss this matter with each other, so that you can reach a just decision with regard to the legacy of your father. Because the time available to us, for biological reasons, is not without limit.

"With warm regards, Ngô Thế Vinh, MD"
Việt Ecology Press

Letter 2:

To: Duy Minh, Duy Cường, Duy Đức and other members of the family of the composer Phạm Duy.

Subject: The Memoirs of Phạm Duy (to be published by Cornell University Press)

"After the letter I sent yesterday, I now wish to send you (Duy Minh, Duy Cường, Duy Đức and all your brothers and sisters) the attached document drawn up by Sarah Grossman of Cornell University guaranteeing that the press will make no attempt whatsoever to sell The Memoirs of Phạm Duy within the territory of Vietnam.

"After you all have had a thorough discussion of this and have reached a common decision, let me ask you Duy Minh, as the oldest in the family, to remember to give me a prompt reply, so I can know your decision.

"Warm regards, Ngô Thế Vinh, MD"
Việt Ecology Press

Letter 3:

To: Duy Minh, Duy Cường, Duy Đức and other members of the family of the composer Phạm Duy.

Subject: The Memoirs of Phạm Duy (to be published by Cornell University Press)

"This is my third email message to you all (Duy Minh, Duy Cường, Duy Đức and all your brothers and sisters). I have had my own personal experience with U.S. publishing houses in the mainstream industry, and I know that they conduct their businesses in a highly principled fashion.

"Though your father agreed from the very beginning to work closely with Dr. Eric Henry in creating the compendious English version of the Memoirs of Phạm Duy, the press, now that he has passed away, still needs a statement of permission from his heirs in order to publish the work. I am sending a draft of such a statement as an attachment to this message. This a simple, but important formality that must be observed so as to bring this matter to a conclusion:"

Statement of Permission; Draft Copy

To: Eric Henry
Cc: Cornell University Press

I, Phạm Duy Minh, the son of the Vietnamese song composer and author Phạm Duy, am the copyright proprietor (representing both myself and my six brothers and sisters), of the musical and literary works of my father, including his four-volume set of Vietnamese-language memoirs, Hồi Ký Phạm Duy. I, Phạm Duy Minh, hereby grant you permission to promote your annotated English translation of this autobiographical work, which I have seen and approved.

With this letter I certify as well that I grant you permission to publish this work with Cornell University Press.

Signed,
Phạm Duy Minh

"January 27, 2023 will be the tenth death anniversary of the composer Phạm Duy. This fast approaching anniversary will have much more meaning if, instead of the usual flowers, fruit, and incense on the table before his portrait, there is a copy of the book *The Memoirs of Phạm Duy*, a thing that I know for sure he ardently wished for when alive.

"A book published by a university as famous as Cornell will surely be added to the collections of all the great libraries of the world. It will form the basis of many research projects. This will be a great honor, not only for Phạm Duy himself, but for the second and third generations of his family. Please do not abandon this great project in mid-journey – this can lead only to futile regret later on.

"By whatever means, Duy Minh, Duy Cường, Duy Đức, and all your brothers and sisters need to make every effort to make it possible for your father's dream to be realized, so that there will be no need for you all later to utter the words "I'm sorry."

"I am myself very busy, but due to the great esteem I have for the music and contributions to culture of the composer Phạm Duy, I have not hesitated to share my inmost feelings on this matter with you all.

"Let me repeat a request once more: after you all have discussed this and reached a conclusion that you all agree on, please, Duy Minh, as the eldest brother in the family, let me know the result right away, so as to end my suspense.

"Last but not least – think big, okay friends?"

"With warmest regards, Ngô Thế Vinh"

Việt Ecology Press

Letter 3, continuation:

Before sending the above, I had sent Eric a version that had an additional concluding paragraph, as follows:

"In the 1970s, when I was attending a meeting of the Asian Students Association in Japan, I saw many colorful billboards advertising the film Love Story, based on a novel of the same name by Erich Segal. A catchphrase from that work was: 'Love means never having to say you're sorry.' This now makes me think of the love of the sons and daughters of Phạm Duy for their father. You must use every possible means to make the realization of your father's dream possible. So you will not have to say "We're sorry" later on.

"These are my most ardent, inmost wishes and concerns, and I write to share them with you all.

"With warmest regards, Ngô Thế Vinh"

Việt Ecology Press

Eric let me know that he was most pleased with the letter I sent before. He wrote:

"Dear Mr. Vinh: Actually, I was very pleased by the draft email [3] that you sent for me to read yesterday. I felt it was eloquent enough to convulse the heavens and shake the earth, and had sufficient power to make ghosts and spirits shed tears. Nevertheless, if you feel that the newest version will be more effective, then I beg to second your decision. I trust your judgement."

The third message was sent and received, but the only result was further silence on the part of the sons and daughters of Phạm Duy.

I do not know what tomorrow will bring for the Memoirs of Phạm Duy. Que sera sera. But in the meantime, Eric's trust in me was great enough that he sent me a complete digital copy of his draft of the Memoirs, as *"an avowal of faith so that there may be a memento of this occasion" / "Của tin gọi một chút này làm ghi"* (Nguyễn Du)

PHẠM DUY – ERIC HENRY AND HUẾ

In an article entitled "Phạm Duy and Huế," intended as a congratulation to Phạm Duy on attaining the great age of ninety (in 2011), Đặng Tiến wrote:

"The musician Phạm Duy had no early, intimate connection with the land or people of Huế, but this region, so full of magic, left in his music many lasting images and echoes, especially after he drew close Huế on four occasions: in 1944 when he went there to sing, in 1946 when, after the August revolution, he visited the city on his way back to the North from the southern war zone, in 1948 when he went there as a Resistance soldier, and in 1953, when he left the resistance to return to the occupied regions.

And it was not just on those four occasions that he visited Huế – he returned there many times after the decade of the 1960s when the Vietnamese War reached its most ferocious stage, and during which he wrote his ten "Heart Songs," *(Tâm Ca)* of which number five, "Bequeathed to My Sweetheart," *(Để Lại Cho Em)* a setting of a poem by Nguyễn Đắc Xuân, made a particularly strong impression in that era:

Heart Song Number Five: "Bequeathed to My Sweetheart"

(Music: Phạm Duy; lyrics: Nguyễn Đắc Xuân)

I leave you, dear, our streams and mountains,
I leave you, dear, a lovely land,
A land of towering courage,
Of which a holy echo only still remains,
I leave you, dear, my cowardice,
I leave you, dear, a life exhausted,
I leave you, dear, our land's bedraggled soul,
The road of life contracted, no way forward left,
The hearts of people are enraged,
I leave you, dear, the wrongs I've done…

A reflection of my later encounter with Phạm Duy and Nguyễn Đắc Xuân in a house on the shore of the River Hương is contained in Chapter Seventeen of my novel *The Green Belt* (*Vòng Đai Xanh*) with the fictional character Vy, a "battling" Buddhist student modeled on Nguyễn Đắc Xuân and a well-known folk song writer who in fact is Phạm Duy.

On a couple of occasions when he came to Saigon, Nguyễn Đắc Xuân visited the office of my journal *Medicine and Compassion* (Y Khoa Tình Thương) with a poem or two of his own that he wished the journal to publish.

Around the month of April in 1965, when I was the editor-in-chief of *Medicine and Compassion*, Nguyễn Đắc Xuân paid a visit to the monks in the Già Lam Pagoda in the course of which he came as well to our office at 103 Nguyễn Bỉnh Khiêm Street near Saigon Radio Station, with an article entitled *"The Âu ca Song of Phạm Duy,"* after which the article appeared in issue number 17, which came out in May, 1965. Nguyễn Đắc Xuân was very enamored with the music of Phạm Duy, and especially with his song lyrics.

A year later, in 1966, I met Nguyễn Đắc Xuân in Huế when I was participating in the Journey to the Từ Đàm Pagoda and, together with

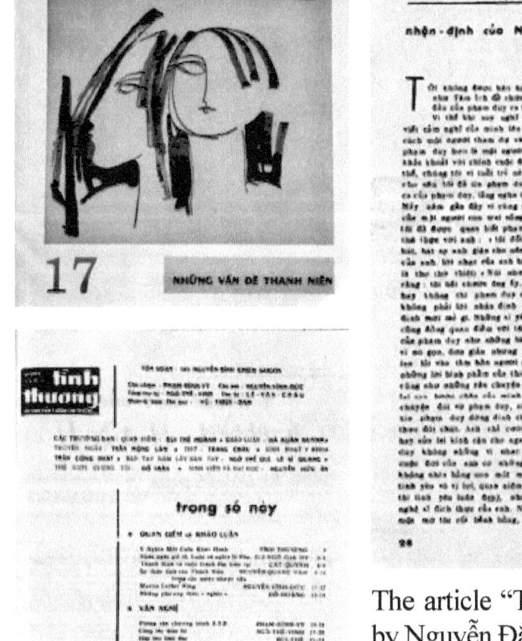

tình thương

17

NHỮNG VẤN ĐỀ THANH NIÊN

tình thương

trong số này

17

THÁNG 5-1965

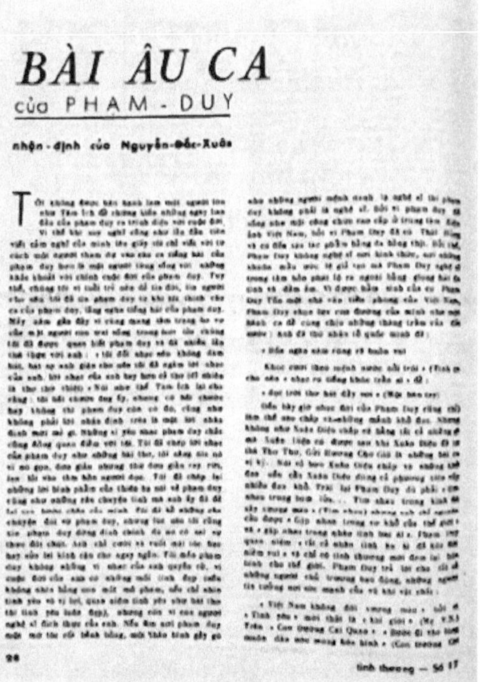

BÀI ÂU CA

của PHẠM - DUY

nhận-định của Nguyễn-Đắc-Xuân

tình thương — Số 17

The article "The Âu Ca song of Phạm Duy" by Nguyễn Đắc Xuân was printed in *Medicine and Compassion* Number 17 in May 1965. In the same year Phạm Duy composed music for Nguyễn Đắc Xuân's poem "Bequeathed to My Sweetheart."

(Ngô Thế Vinh, personal archives)

the Publisher of *Medicine and Compassion*, Phạm Đình Vy, carried out a 96-minute interview with The Venerable Thích Trí Quang.

At that time, Nguyễn Đắc Xuân was a student in the graduating class of the Huế Vietnamese-Chinese Teacher's College and was the leader of the Huế "Determined-to-Die" – Quyết Tử – students, a group regarded as one of the principal components of the urban struggle movement promulgated by disguised communist agents in the region. The group hid beneath the protective religious disguise of Buddhism. Later, when they were exposed and pursued, Xuân fled, lived in various pagodas, and then later, toward the end of 1966, escaped to the communist-controlled area.

When Tết of 1968 came, Nguyễn Đắc Xuân came down from the mountains, revealed his identity as a communist cadre, and was present in Huế throughout the protracted period of the Tết 1968 massacre, during which more than three thousand of the city's citizens were murdered were buried in mass graves.

After 1975, his record of service to the communist cause was sufficient for the party member Nguyễn Đắc Xuân to be given a position as officer of information and propaganda for Huế. He was also admitted to the Vietnamese Writers Association, was made the general secretary of the Huế branch of the Writers Association and was given many additional positions as well.

And from 1966 until the present day – the year 2022 – I have never again had occasion to meet the "determined-to-die" student of those distant days. Now Xuân has acquired the further reputation of being "a writer on the city of Huế" – there are even people willing to consider him a "historian." At the age of 85 (he was born in 1937) Nguyễn Đắc Xuân is no longer the impoverished student of former times. In an interview with Phan Anh that appeared in the People's Police newspaper, he said, with an air of pride, "That I built a house was possible because I write books; that I sent my children to study abroad was possible because I write books; and that I live a healthy life is possible because I write books." (People's Police Newspaper, "Interview with the Researcher Nguyễn Đắc Xuân," March 25, 2019)

Nguyễn Đắc Xuân – regarded as an expert in Huế history – has said the following about this ancient capital: "There is nowhere else that can be as peaceful as the surface of the river Hương, but which can also be enveloped in such fierce waves. When visitors come from a distance to visit the place, they see only the slow, easy-going pace of life in the city, and don't understand that Huế can experience upheavals not comparable to any others within our country."

And the "upheaval that can't be compared to any other within our country" was of course the Huế massacre of 1968. It lasted 26 days or, to speak more accurately, for 624 hours – and every hour was a "twenty-fifth hour" for the people who survived – and in the "eye of the storm that transpired there, the reputable Nguyễn Đắc Xuân is always referred to, both as a participant and as a "living witness."

THE "RED" NGUYỄN ĐẮC XUÂN AND "YELLOW MUSIC"

In the summer of 2017, four years after the death of Phạm Duy, Dr. Eric Henry was invited to give a talk at the Huế conservatory of music, the title of which was at first given as *"The Music of East Asia – The Music of Phạm Duy"* ("Nhạc Á Đông – Nhạc Phạm Duy") which later had to be changed to "The History of Popular Music in Vietnam and in Neighboring Countries" ("Lịch sử Nhạc Phổ thông Việt Nam và các Nước Láng giềng"). The name Phạm Duy could not be allowed to appear on a poster for a cultural event of that sort. In an email message, Eric Henry let me know everything that happened in the course of that trip to Huế:

"When I spoke with the audience, I wanted to let them hear a short conversational exchange that I once had with Phạm Duy. The composer once posed this question to me: "What do you think of yellow music (*nhạc vàng*)? My answer was, "I feel that yellow music is truthful music." [On hearing this, Phạm Duy made no reply – he looked as if he half agreed and half disagreed with me.]

"When I discussed this matter with Nguyễn Đắc Xuân, he gave me a "warning." In a public setting like the Huế Music Conservatory, I

Above: Dr. Eric Henry on the stage of the Huế Music Conservatory giving his June 7, 2017 lecture, originally to be entitled *"The Music of East Asia – The Music of Phạm Duy"* and then renamed "The History of Popular Music in Vietnam and in Neighboring Countries." Below: Eric Henry giving a piano performance of Phạm Duy's *"A Boat Bound for a Distant Place"* ("Thuyền Viễn Xứ"). As for Phạm Duy's two narrative songs, "A Faintly Scented Hair Clasp" ("Chiếc Kẹp Tóc Thơm Tho") and "A Tragic Tale of Love" ("Tình Sầu"), I played excerpts only, to help the audience understand their structure. *(Eric Henry, personal archives)*

could not say that yellow music was "truthful," for if I said that, every one of my listeners would see that if "truthful music" existed, there must also be a kind of music that was "untruthful" – and everyone would at once understand what that "untruthful music" must be: "red music (*nhạc đỏ*)."

"So I had to follow the advice of Nguyễn Đắc Xuân and censor myself. When speaking with the audience, I had to pretend that my answer to Phạm Duy had been, "Yellow music is a kind of music that expresses the sincere thoughts about the life of ordinary people." ("Nhạc vàng là một loại nhạc mà biểu tỏ cảm tưởng chân thành về đời sống của người bình thường.") I detested that sentence. It was so dishonest, so untrue!"

In his talk, Dr. Eric Henry talked about the fundamental traits of "new music" in Southeast Asia and also in Korea and China. When speaking of the music of Vietnam, he stressed that in this musical tradition, the figure most worthy of attention was Phạm Duy, whose productions were as varied as the paintings of Picasso.

"In my talk at the conservatory, I also recounted a parable, "Two Children" ("Hai đứa bé") to illustrate the basic difference between the music of Phạm Duy and that of Trịnh Công Sơn. This was perhaps the only part of my talk that was a bit humorous in tone. This is what I said:

"Once, when I went to visit the composer at his home in Midway City in California, I was sitting next to him on a sofa, and we began conversing about the differences between his music and that of Trịnh Công Sơn. I remarked to Phạm Duy then that this topic always made me think of a humorous story that I begged permission to recount to him. I was a little fearful that the story might give him some offense, but I was not too fearful, because I knew that, in addition to being brilliantly intelligent, Phạm Duy had a lively sense of humor, so I thought he would be able to appreciate the tale. Here it is:

> *Two Children: One day a married couple came to see a psychiatrist. They were extremely worried because each of*

their two children had a serious psychological problem – one child was totally, excessively, and unreasonably optimistic. The other child suffered from the opposite condition – he was totally, excessively, and unreasonably pessimistic.

After listening to all that the parents had to say, the psychiatrist said, "Okay, I have a way of dealing with these problems. The treatment I have in mind will require three days to administer. Please return here tomorrow with your two children."

When the parents returned the next day with their children, the psychiatrist had prepared two rooms, each with its own character. One room was filled with toys. The toys were of every conceivable variety and were made with fine attention to detail and alluring colors. The toys were bright and beautiful. The second room was full of horseshit. It held horseshit only; nothing else was in the room.

And the doctor led the pessimistic child into the room filled with toys. He was to remain there for three days. Then he led the optimistic child into the room filled with horseshit. He too was to remain in the room for three days. When the specified time had passed, the adults entered the room filled with toys, and saw that the pessimistic child was weeping continuously with big tears rolling down his cheeks."
Concerned, the psychiatrist asked,
"What's the matter? Don't you like the toys?"
In answer, the child said:

"These toys are truly beautiful. They are exquisitely made, and worthy of being cherished with all one's soul. And that is precisely why I am so deeply grieved. For I know that they cannot last for an eternity. The day will come when all of these beautiful toys will have fallen to pieces." And having said this the child burst into tears and wept more grievously than before.

Then the adults stepped into the room full of horseshit. They found that the optimistic child was full was bubbling with happiness and enthusiasm. He was whooping with joy and jumping all over the room, from one corner to another.

The psychiatrist asked:
"Why are you in such a good mood? Aren't you disgusted by all this horseshit?"
And the child exclaimed:
"With all this shit around, there must be a real horse somewhere!" And he continued jumping around and whooping with joy.

...

"Then I said to the audience, 'Now please allow me to ask you all, how you feel about this story – Which child is Phạm Duy and which is Trịnh Công Sơn?'" (When I told the story to Phạm Duy, I could see that the detail he liked the best was the horseshit in the second room, but he expressed no opinion with regard to the implied comparison I wished to make concerning his music and Trịnh Công Sơn's.)"

"After recounting the story about the two children, I discussed two narrative songs by Phạm Duy, "A Faintly Scented Hair Clasp" and "A Tragic Tale of Love" (numbers 9 and 4 of the *Homeland Fragrance Songs*, or *Hương Ca*)."

(Here, Dr. Henry made a detailed analysis of the themes, lyrics, structure, and melodies of these two songs, both from the set of ten "homeland" songs that Phạm Duy composed in the last two years before he chose to return to Vietnam to live.)

As for the students at the Huế conservatory, they made no response whatsoever, the reason being that they were sitting together with hundreds of their fellow students, among whom were members of the "cultural police" who always kept an eye on such public events. How could they have had sufficient courage to ask questions or express viewpoints? It is much to be regretted that there was no opportunity for Dr. Henry to meet privately with a few students – if that had been possible, the results would surely have been different.

A SMALL PERSONAL EXCHANGE

Having received some gifts of books from Eric Henry, I decided to return the favor by sending him my books of cultural portraits through Amazon. Only three days later, I received this response:

"Bravo! Amazon kept its promise! I have just received Literary, Artistic, and Cultural Portraits, Volumes 1 and 2. On looking through Volume 2, I was pleased and especially interested to see that you had paid attention to the plastic arts in your portraits of the artist Tạ Tỵ and the sculptors Lê Ngọc Huệ and Mai Chửng. I am also very eager to see what you have written about John Steinbeck. For many years I have been deeply in love with the beautiful literary language that Steinbeck created in his novel (an early one, almost his first) Tortilla Flat. With these two books of yours, I now have an opportunity to educate myself about many aspects of Vietnamese culture. This is a great joy!

Then in a message that came later, he wrote:

"I have looked again at your first volume of portraits, and see that aside from the articles about Hoàng Ngọc Biên, Đinh Cường, and Nghiêu Đề, you also have one about Nguyên Khai. I am very eager to know more about people who have offered up their whole lives in the service of this art!

"Like you, I have been lucky enough over the years to grow quite close to many "out-of-the-ordinary" people. How regrettable it is that they are all gradually "entering the eternal realm." I should try to follow your example and write a book of "portraits" to do proper honor to them."

And without doubt, it was surely from this moment that a new relationship between us developed – Dr. Henry now intends to make an English translation of the one thousand-plus pages of my two volumes of cultural portraits. I of course clearly understand that Eric is also very busy with a multitude of other yet-to-be-completed projects.

"To begin a thing is the most difficult of tasks" ("vạn sự khởi đầu nan"), as we are accustomed to say. I also reminded him of a saying: "The arduousness of the journey arises, not from the rivers and mountains that impede our way, but from our fear of mountains, our avoidance of rivers" (*"Đường đi khó, không khó vì ngăn sông cách núi, mà khó vì lòng người ngại núi e sông."*) And the following day, I received another message from Eric:

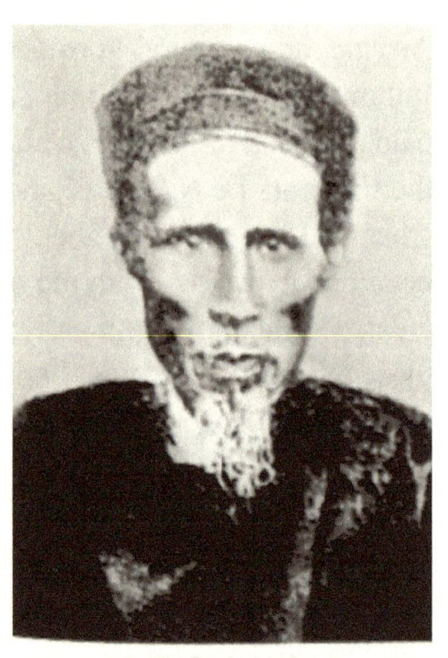

Nguyễn Bá Học

"Dear Mr. Vinh, below this is a photo of old Mr. Nguyễn Bá Học (1857-1921), the author of the deathless maxim "The arduousness of the journey arises, not from the rivers and mountains that impede our way, but from our fear of mountains, our avoidance of rivers." I have silently repeated that sentence to myself over and over for the past fifty years or so; it is a fundamental aspect of Eric Henry's life. This maxim appears to be a variant of a couple of lines in the poetry of Bó Juyì 白居易 (772-846): "The arduousness of the journey arises, not from rivers and not from mountains, but from the inconstancy of human feelings" 路難不在水不在山，只在人情反覆間. The meaning is a little different, but still profound. Nevertheless, it lacks something of the grandeur of Nguyễn Bá Học's maxim.

Not long after that I received "A Portrait of Mặc Đỗ," the first translation of a chapter in the book, which he plans to entitle The Creative World of South Vietnam, 1954 – 1975. And then in the weeks that followed, I began to receive, every two weeks or ten days, a new translated chapter. Today the chapter happened to be number six, the one about Dương Nghiễm Mậu: "Forty Years of Dương Nghiễm Mậu and the Autobiography of Nguyễn Du. It arrived together with a message that I would like to share with the reader as a means of concluding this article:

"Dear Mr. Vinh: You are in truth a "journalist of journalists" (Eric was here borrowing an expression I used in my Portrait of Như Phong). The world apparently has no means of concealing any secrets from you – I fear that before long your understanding of the past of Eric Henry will surpass that of Eric Henry himself!

"I am currently thinking of a letter describing your work that I can send to a publisher. I'm thinking of calling your first book of portraits "The Creative World of South Vietnam, Volume 1: Eighteen Literary, Artistic, and Cultural Portraits." I have made a list of the items in volume 1, so that editors can see what it contains – and I shall make a corresponding list for volume 2. I'm beginning to think about ways of communicating with publishers. Eric."

Eric Henry burning incense before the unfinished grave of the composer Phạm Duy. Eric wrote that the photo was taken on November 13, 2013. On that day he went with Nguyễn Phong Quang, Duy Cường, and a female friend of Cường's from Saigon to the cemetery in Bình Dương Province to visit the grave of Phạm Duy. The grave at that time had not yet been completed, and did not as yet have a sculptured image of the composer.

(Photo by Nguyễn Phong Quang)

To complete a one-thousand-plus page translation and then find a reputable American University Press to publish it will be a long and exhausting journey of the sort evoked in a line of verse by poet Tản Đà:

"With heavy shoulder-load, I see the endless road unfold ahead." And so we wish each other "sturdy legs and flesh not withered."

And the two of us are not forgetting for an instant that everything possible must be done to ensure the early publication of the English *Memoirs of Phạm Duy*, a dream dear to the heart of the musician that is still not realized.

Little Saigon, August 8, 2022

References:

1. "Phạm Duy and Modern Vietnamese History," Eric Henry, *Southeastern Review of Asian Studies 27 (2005*), pp. 89 – 105.
2. *Memoirs of Phạm Duy.* Translated from the Vietnamese by Eric Henry. To be published by Cornell University Press.
3. "The Curious Memoirs of the Vietnamese Composer Phạm Duy," John C. Schafer. *Journal of Southeast Asia Studies. Feb 2012. The National University of Singapore, 2012.*
4. *Phạm Duy Studies / Tìm hiểu Nhạc Phạm Duy*, many authors; internally distributed. [source: Phạm Duy, January 2007]
5. "An Interview with the Linguistics Professor Dr. Eric Henry" (Phỏng Vấn GS ngôn ngữ học Tiến sĩ Eric Henry), Quỳnh Lệ, *People in Far-away Lands* (*Người Viễn Xứ*) 17/07/2005.

IN SEARCH OF TIME GONE BY REMEMBERING AN ILLUSTRIOUS PROFESSOR, DOCTOR PHẠM BIỂU TÂM, PROFESSOR OF MEDICINE

Professor Phạm Biểu Tâm in the Bình Dân Hospital, 1960.
Every morning, he would go with the residents and students to visit the clinic before going to the operating room.
(family of Professor Phạm Biểu Tâm, personal archives)

This is a supplemented version of an article that at first was a collection of personal reminiscences that I contributed to an occasion celebrating the one hundredth anniversary of the birth of Professor Phạm Biểu Tâm, an illustrious professor who in the century just past left indelible marks on the profession of medicine in Vietnam.

SOME BIOGRAPHICAL DETAILS

Professor Phạm Biểu Tâm was born on Dec. 13, 1913 in the city of Huế in Thừa Thiên Province and died at the age of 86 on Dec. 11, 1999 in the U.S.

Toward the end of his life, he let it be known that though he was born and raised in the Central Region of Vietnam, his family roots were in the South. Excerpted below is a passage from a letter written by Phạm Hữu Nhơn, a younger brother of Professor Phạm Biểu Tâm. Nhơn was originally a general among the chiefs of staff in the army of the Republic of Vietnam, and the letter was sent to Bông, which was the household name of Phạm Biểu Trung, Professor Tâm's eldest son.

"My dear Bông: Your father was born on Dec. 13, 1913. His home was the village of Nam Trung, in Phú Vang District, Thừa Thiên Province, and his forebears were people of scholarly achievement. His great-grandfather Commandant Phạm Tấn, a southerner whose place of origin the village of Long Phú (Bến Lức, Gò Công) in Gia Định Province. He was summoned by the Gia Long emperor to assume an official position up in Bắc Hà (Ninh Bình and Nam Định). His grandfather was Phạm Năng Tuần, who held the court title of "Officer of the Academy" (Hàn Lâm Viên Đại Phu.) He was the one who opened and established the village of Nam Trung, Thừa Thiên Province so as to provide a place to live for officials with southern origins. Tâm's father was Phạm Hữu Văn, who attained the *tiến sĩ* or doctoral degree in 1913, the Quý Sửu year. He held a series of official positions, the last of which was governor (Bố Chánh) of Thanh Hóa Province and was given the title of "Senior Minister" (Thượng Thư Trị Sứ) upon his retirement."

"Professor Phạm Biểu Tâm attended elementary school in Huế, middle school in Vinh, the capital of Nghệ An, and then the Quốc Học School in Huế, followed by the Bưởi High School in Hanoi."

"Throughout his childhood and youth, Professor Phạm Biểu Tâm was a member of the Boy Scouts, and was very active in that organization during the fiery years of Vietnam's initial independence.

The professor and his wife in their home on Ngô Thời Nhiệm Street (1970)

He was a registered member of the Lam Sơn troop led by Hoàng Đạo Thúy, and during the 1930s participated in training activities in Bạch Mã, Huế. It can be said that he remained close to the Vietnamese scouting movement throughout his life, and remained always a bold young man who undertook missions. Not only was he the longest-serving intern at the Phủ Doãn Hospital, but according to Professor Trần Ngọc Ninh, "Tâm was the chairman of the Association of Students in 1942, was a member of the Students' Basketball Team, and held a position of special honor in the Vietnamese Sailboating Association."

In 1932, Professor Tâm commenced studies at the Hanoi Medical School, one year later than Dr. Tôn Thất Tùng. After graduation, he voluntarily continued working as an intern and then as a resident in the hospital staff there for eight years. It was only in 1947 that he presented his medical dissertation, the subject of which had a cultural dimension: "Introduction de la Médecine Occidentale en Extrême Orient" (The Introduction of Western Medicine in the Far East).

As for his personal life, Professor Tâm was married to Madam Công Tằng Tôn Nữ Tuyết Lê in 1944. She had been a student in the Đồng Khánh Female High School in Huế, and was very advanced in her thinking. The two of them had five children, three boys and two girls. Their names, in order, were Phạm Biểu Trung, Phạm Biểu Chí, Phạm Biểu Kim Hoàn, Phạm Biểu Kim Liên, and Phạm Biểu Tình, but at home they were all called names based on objects that can be found in an operating room: Bông (Cotton), Gạc (Gauze), Băng (Bandage), Kim (Needle), and Chỉ (Thread). They also had an adopted daughter named Trần Thị Hồng.

In 1948, Professor Tâm was awarded an agrégation degree in medicine (Professeur Agrégé des Universités) in Paris, and at the same time, together with Professor Trần Quang Đệ, became a famous professor of surgery at the place that later became known as the Chợ Rẫy Hospital. After returning to Vietnam, Professor Tâm continued to teach at Hanoi Medical School while also serving as the director

Professor Phạm Biểu Tâm and his wife, and five children, who at home bore the names Bông, Gạc, Băng, Kim, and Chỉ. *(Phạm Biểu Tâm family archives)*

Professor Phạm Biểu Tâm and Doctor and Nguyễn Xuân Chữ, a cancer specialist, during their participation in "Cancer Week" (Semaine Du Cancer; 1950). Behind them was a poster in Vietnamese with the slogan: "The more cancer is ignored, the less hope there is for recovery. Come for an examination at the Anti-Cancer Center at Yersin Hospital, Hanoi."

(Professor Phạm Biểu Tâm family archives)

of the Yersin Hospital (also called the Phủ Doãn Hospital) until the signing of the Geneva Accords in 1954, dividing the country into North and South.

In 1950, the National Army of Vietnam was established, with the result that in 1951 the branch of military medicine came into being, and Professor Tâm for a time became the deputy director of the military school of medicine with the rank of Lieutenant Colonel (trung tá).

In 1954 Professor Tâm emigrated with his family to the South, where he was appointed the director of the Bình Dân Hospital, which had been newly constructed on Phan Thanh Giản Street in Saigon. He was at the same time the chief of the department of surgery there. Most of the medical personnel of the Phủ Doãn Hospital emigrated to the South and took up positions in the Bình Dân Hospital. This was also a teaching hospital affiliated with the only University of Medicine, Dentistry and Pharmacy in South Vietnam at that time.

When the Franco-Vietnamese School of Medicine was turned over to the Vietnamese by the French (on May 11, 1955), Professor Tâm was made the dean there, and was also the first dean for the mixed Medicine and Pharmacy Program in Saigon (Faculté Mixte de Médecine et Pharmacie).

In 1962, the American Medical Association (AMA) donated a large sum of money to enable Vietnam to build a Medical Education Center with up-to-date modern equipment on Hồng Bàng Street in Chợ Lớn including a School of Medicine (Phase One) and a Teaching Hospital (Phase Two). The first installation ceremony was presided over by President Ngô Đình Diệm.

After the upheaval of 1963, Professor Tâm remained with the School of Medicine until March 1967, when General Nguyễn Cao Kỳ, who was then the Chairman of the Central Executive Committee, unilaterally signed an order directing that Professor Tâm's position as Dean of Faculty of Medicine be abolished and replaced by a five-person committee. This was also the first time in the South Vietnam that politics intervened in the university autonomy. Professor Tâm stepped down with stoic silence from his position as dean and continued his work as Professor of Surgery, lecturing and treating patients in Surgery, Section B in Bình Dân Hospital.

At the time that the AMA project was unfolding, Professor Tâm saw to it that coordination took place with the Saigon Medical School so that improvements could take place in all the basic clinical disciplines, such as internal medicine, obstetrics, pediatrics, surgery, anesthesiology, and radiology… with the plan that after completing their training on site, the instructors would go to schools in the U.S. for further training. In this period, Professor Tâm exerted himself to the utmost to develop medical training programs for instructors in the Surgery Department of the Medical School.

The Curriculum Committee, with a number of professors in the Saigon School of Medicine; from left: Prof. Trần Ngọc Ninh, Prof. Trịnh Văn Tuất, Prof. Trần Vỹ, Prof. Caubet, Prof. Phạm Biểu Tâm, Prof. Huard, Prof. Trần Đình Đệ, Prof. Nguyễn Đình Cát, Prof Nguyễn Hữu, and Prof. Ngô Gia Hy.

(Professor Phạm Biểu Tâm family archives)

Professor Phạm Biểu Tâm, Dean at the Saigon School of Medicine, and Father Cao Văn Luận, Rector (from 1957) of Huế University, taking part in an International Conference on Education.

(Professor Phạm Biểu Tâm family archives)

The dissertation defense of Dr. Nguyễn Tấn Hồng the Hanoi School of Medicine (1952) with Professor Phạm Biểu Tâm in the certification committee.

(Professor Phạm Biểu Tâm family archives)

Photo taken after a dissertation defense of two candidates: Nguyễn Khắc Minh and Đào Hữu Anh at the Saigon Medical School, (1960) members of the certification committee were in the front row; from left: Professor Nguyễn Hữu, Professor Phạm Biểu Tâm, Professor Trần Đình Đệ, and Professor Trịnh Văn Tuất. (Doctors Nguyễn Khắc Minh and Đào Hữu Anh both later became professors at the Medical School)

(Professor Phạm Biểu Tâm family archives)

Laying the foundation stone (1962) for the Medical Education Center on Hồng Bàng Street in Chợ Lớn. From left: Professor Phạm Biểu Tâm, Dean at the Saigon School of Medicine, President Ngô Đình Diệm, Professor Nguyễn Quang Trình, and Professor Lê Văn Thới. Standing in the rear was U.S. Ambassador Frederick E. Nolting, Jr.

Front row, from left: Professor Phạm Biểu Tâm, President Ngô Đình Diệm, Architect Ngô Viết Thụ, Professor Nguyễn Quang Trình, Rector of the University of Saigon. The Medical Education Center on Hồng Bàng Street was completed three years later in 1966 *(Professor Phạm Biểu Tâm family archives)*

The collaboration between Henry T. Bahnson, an eminent professor from Pittsburgh College, and Professor Phạm Biểu Tâm at Bình Dân Hospital was viewed as the most successful of the programs supported by the AMA.

It seems I should also record here that a student there, Dr. Nghiêm Đạo Đại, later became a famous professor of surgery who specialized in liver, pancreas, and kidney transplants at the Hahnemann / Drexel University in Pittsburgh. Despite his eminence, he never forgot his debt to Professor Tâm: "I deeply internalized all the lessons taught at the Bình Dân 'incubator.' It is a fact that after being on the faculty of Iowa University for seven years, and on the faculty of Hahnemann / Drexel University College of Medicine in Pittsburgh, Pennsylvania for more than twenty years, I feel that I enjoyed great good fortune in having been able to absorb the things taught so meticulously by the instructors at the Bình Dân Hospital. Those teachers equipped me with skills that I have been able to use throughout my life as an instructor."

After the upheaval of 1975, Professor Tâm had to live in extremely difficult circumstances–he had to coexist with the victors, who worshiped ideology alone and placed no weight on specialized skills, with the slogan "loyalty to the party is worth more than professional competence." Nevertheless, he continued to serve the medical profession with his whole soul, reverencing and caring for his patients without regard to their degree of wealth, their ethnic identity, or their political loyalties. He continued his work as a teacher and trained many generations of medical students and doctors. As always, he was reserved and professionally dedicated, doing much and saying little. Amid adverse circumstances, he never gave way to anger; he stayed in the background but always worked in a thorough and knowledgeable manner and his simple advice was always repeated among his students: "Do your best, and regard the care of patients as the immediate responsibility of the doctor."

In spite of their relatively great experience, people with advanced training who remained in Hanoi after 1954, having lived under the previous regime were never more than passively tolerated–their roles were never emphasized, and they were never trusted by the regime. This was the experience, too, of Professor Phạm Hoàng Hộ in Saigon after 1975. It was a difficult period that he referred to as "the years of vain dreams."

In 1984, Professor Phạm Biểu Tâm had no choice but to retire at the age of 71, after a stroke paralyzed the left side of his body. Having

The medical center on Hồng Bàng Street, Chợ Lớn three years after its completion (Phase 1). The construction of a teaching hospital (Phase 2) had to stop due to political upheavals, a situation that persisted up to 1975.

Prof. Phạm Biểu Tâm visiting a medical center in Minnesota in the 1960s. This was an initial step in the blending of the Vietnamese medical system with those of France and the U.S. *(Professor Phạm Biểu Tâm family archives)*

A reception in Professor Tâm's home for a conference of medical postgraduates in 1972. From left: Dr. Steven Reeder, Prof. Phạm Biểu Tâm, Văn Kỳ Chương, Nguyễn Hữu Chí, Phan Văn Tường, Prof. Anatolio Cruz, Prof. Norman Hoover, Prof. Đào Đức Hoành, Prof. Phan Ngọc Dương, Văn Kỳ Nam, Lê Quang Dũng, Nguyễn Khắc Lân, Nguyễn Tiến Dy, Văn Tần, and Nguyễn Đỗ Duy *(Professor Phạm Biểu Tâm family archives)*

no opportunity to recover from this blow, in 1989 he had to abandon the homeland that he cherished, the place where he had offered up nearly the whole of his life in service to his patients and to the art of medicine, so as to join his children in the U.S.

SOME PERSONAL RECOLLECTIONS

The words that follow were written four years ago for a gathering commemorating the one hundredth anniversary of the birth of Professor Phạm Biểu Tâm. They consist only of very personal recollections of the man–they do not involve lecture halls or hospitals, but have to do with Professor Tâm as a participant in everyday life. Throughout my years of medical training, I was never his student, but nevertheless feel that I was very close to him, both during my years of training and during the later years when I had left medical school far behind. He served as dean of a medical school for only twelve years (1955 – 1967), but the marks of his influence on generations of medical students lasted much longer, and affected even people who never studied with him or met him face to face.

In only two more days it will be the hundredth anniversary of the birth of Professor Phạm Biểu Tâm (Dec. 13, 1913). Today, Dec. 11, 2013, is the death anniversary of the professor; thus, fourteen years have passed since he was alive (he died on Dec. 11, 1999), and when I went to convey my condolences to his widow, she reminded me that I might perhaps write an article about the professor. But before I could fulfill her request, she herself passed away.

The biography of Professor Phạm Biểu Tâm has received a fairly clear and complete treatment from my colleague Hà Ngọc Thuần in Australia. It seems I should mention here that Hà Ngọc Thuần and Nghiêm Sỹ Tuấn were the two main contributors to the journal *Medicine and Compassion* and were also the co-translator into Vietnamese of a valuable monograph entitled *The Story of Medicine* of Kenneth Walker that they used under the pseudonym Hà Hợp Nghiêm. This appeared in installments in *Medicine and Compassion* until the journal was discontinued in 1966.

In complete contrast to the weighty and solemn manner of Professor Trần Quang Đệ, who was also a famous Vietnamese surgeon, and who, like him, had obtained an agrégation degree in medicine in Paris in 1948, Professor Tâm always appeared small and unobtrusive, like a bookish young scholar, with the quick reactions of a bold young man. His facial features were not attractive, but expressed intelligence, and could be described – using the words of my colleague Đường Thiện Đồng – as those of a valued general.

Before stepping into the Medical School, I had heard of the ability and upright behavior of Professor Phạm Biểu Tâm and heard many anecdotes concerning his activities in everyday life. He was one of a number of bold young men from the ranks of the scout movement of the 1930s. who were emblematic of a new ethos of active social service. Though he was not a game-playing athlete, he was a soccer enthusiast. My friends in the Minh Mạng University dormitory related that he always could be seen in the bleachers when there was a soccer

Prof. Phạm Biểu Tâm talking with medical students in an auditorium at 28 Trần Quý Cáp Street, Saigon after his arrest during the upheaval of 1963. *(Source: Life Magazine, 1963)*

match in the Tao Đàn playing field, and would shout and throw his hat in the air along with the others to show his support for the home team.

On occasions when I met him, I saw that he was a very simple, uncomplicated man, who quickly established a close bond and a feeling of trust in those he dealt with, but would also maintain a certain reserve, so as to maintain mutual respect. My memories of encounters with him are like bits of broken movie film.

The period from 1963 to 1967 was very disturbed in South Vietnam, with never-ending street demonstrations and strikes by students. The most disturbed school of all was that of Medicine, which at that time still had its headquarters at 28 Trần Quý Cáp Street, Saigon. The directorship of the School of Medicine at that time was

The cover of the first issue of the journal *Medicine and Compassion* (*Y Khoa Tình Thương*), which appeared in Jan. 1964 and was published until its discontinuance in 1966, comprising 30 issues in all.
(archives of the manuscript library of Trần Hoài Thư)

Mến tặng
anh Ngô Viết Thụ

Nghệ-sĩ như anh khó kiếm ra
Kỳ-công La-Mã đã tài ba
Còn kiêm điêu-khắc cùng hội-họa
Vui thú tinh-thần khá thiết-tha.

Phạm Biểu Tâm
Tết Dương-lịch 1975
(19-11- Giáp-Dần)

A poem by Professor Phạm Biểu Tâm in his own handwriting, sent in 1975 to the architect Ngô Viết Thụ, the designer of Independence Palace, and the Medical Education Center (1962).

a truly difficult position. Professor Tâm had to maintain the usual daily activities and the hospitals while at the same time honoring the principle that universities should be autonomous, or self-governing. He was always open to discussion and, out of respect for him, the various groups of protesting students behaved in a responsible manner, with exception of a few undercover communist agents who blindly carried out the directives of their leaders. The ups and downs of the Medical School in this political whirlwind, which included spilled blood and assassinations, continued until April 1975.

When the first issue of *Medicine and Compassion* came out in 1964, Professor Phạm Biểu Tâm, as Dean of the Medical School, expressed satisfaction with the journal's appearance and said that its aims were entirely consistent with the mission of those who "wore White Coats." He also wrote an editorial introducing the publication that was included in the first issue. Though he was not markedly demonstrative, we all understood that our journal enjoyed the steady spiritual support of the Medical School Dean. *Medicine and Compassion* was not only the journal of student authors, but also regularly included articles written by medical professors, such as Trần Ngọc Ninh, Trần Văn Bảng, Nguyễn Đình Cát, Ngô Gia Hy, and Vũ Thị Thoa…

Upon completing their programs, the medical students, whether destined for civil or military careers, all served in the armed services in branches chosen by themselves or to which they were directed. They were doctors in the midst of a war, so a number of my fellow students at various points lost their lives, such as Đoàn Mạnh Hoạch, Trương Bá Hân, Đỗ Vinh, Trần Ngọc Minh, Phạm Bá Lương, Nguyễn Văn Nhứt, Trần Thái, Lê Hữu Sanh, Nghiêm Sỹ Tuấn, Phạm Đình Bách… without counting all those who died in the labor reform camps in the South and North, or who died at sea when attempting to escape from the country later.

Among those who died or disappeared after escaping from the camps, there were at least two whom I knew: Dr. Nguyễn Hữu Ân (Strategic Technical Direction; Nha Kỹ Thuật) who used to live in the dormitory of Minh Mạng University, together with Dr. Vũ Văn Quynh (paratroopers), the elder brother of Dr. Vũ Văn Dzi who now lives in Oklahoma.

Since it is of particular personal significance to me, I cannot refrain from mentioning Trần Ngọc Minh. He lived unobtrusively for a number of years in the Minh Mạng University dormitory, not only in Section 7 like me, but next to the room I was in for years. After graduating, he joined the marines, and lost his life in a fierce battle that took place at Việt An Valley, Quảng Tín in 1965. A few years later, a new military hospital that was established on Nguyễn Tri Phương Street right next to the Military Medical School was named after him.

What moves me the most is the death of Nghiêm Sỹ Tuấn, with whom I worked closely in the editorial office of *Medicine and Compassion.* Upon graduation, his decision to join the paratroopers, according to his close friend Đặng Vũ Vương, was in response to what he regarded as a "personal challenge." He was wounded more than once, but still volunteered to return to the battlefront, until he at last lost his life in the battle of Khe Sanh in 1968 while rescuing a comrade.

Due to my concern for the various Highlands peoples, which had begun when I was still a journalist for *Medicine and Compassion*, I chose upon graduation to serve in a Special Forces unit, the principal operating area of which was in the western highlands (Tây Nguyên). It was also in this period that I obtained more "living data" that enabled me to complete *The Green Belt*. Every time I had a chance to go to Saigon, I would seek out an opportunity to visit Professor Phạm Biểu Tâm. The Medical School had now moved to a new location on Hồng Bàng street called the Center for Medical Education. One can easily see that, even though he was in Saigon, Professor Tâm always maintained a pretty clear idea of the ongoing military activities of his students.

After 1975, except for a few individuals who managed to escape beforehand, the great majority of the doctors who remained were put into labor reform camps. Though the precise circumstances varied a

The old Medical School, at 28 Trần Quý Cáp Street, a place where a generation of doctors received their training. After 1975, it became a place devoted to exhibitions concerning "The Crimes of the American Puppets" (Tội Ác Mỹ Ngụy) *(source: internet)*

bit from case to case, there was an overall similarity: they were all imprisoned in conditions of hunger and thirst, made to endure heavy labor, and forced into modes of study that amounted to brainwashing. It was during this period that sacks of rotten rice bearing the characters "Đại Mễ" 大米 ("big rice-grains") arriving from the People's Republic of China were imported into the labor-reform camps to feed the detainees. There was no difference between that situation and what Solzhenitsyn describes in The Gulag Archipelago; but this archipelago was "Made in Vietnam," with many fine, cruel measures imported from China.

It was ironic indeed that my first labor camp was in Suối Máu ("Blood Stream"), a place that had been a training center for the 81st Airborne Rangers Group, a unit that I had served. As if it was an unvarying policy of theirs, they never kept a prisoner locked in the same place for long. After serving a period of time, the prisoners were always split off and sent to some different camp. After Suối Máu, I was transferred, in succession, to Trảng Lớn in Tây Ninh, to Đồng

Ban in Phước Long and finally to Bù Gia Mập in Bình Phước. A number of others were taken to the North, where they discovered that conditions there were much more harsh.

When I got out of prison after more than three years, I returned to a Saigon that had taken on an entirely different aspect. The school at 28 Trần Quý Cáp Street, which used to be filled with shade provided by green trees, had now become an exhibit hall: "The Crimes of the American Puppets." Exhibited were not only weapons, ammunition, tiger cages,[1] and instruments of torture, but "poisonous" books and magazines: products of the "new colonialism." Among those books was my novel, *The Green Belt*.

One day, I happened across Professor Tâm strolling along a stretch of Trương Minh Giảng Street near the Saigon Archbishop Building on a corner of Phan Đình Phùng Street. I stopped riding my rattletrap of a bike, and ran up to greet him. The two of us spoke little, but I could read the emotions inspired by recent events in his eyes. When we parted, he made two brief comments: I must get a chest X-ray made of my lungs, and now that I was out of the labor camps, I must try to eat a little more meat. These two bits of advice showed that the professor had no illusions about the conditions faced by his students in the labor reform camps.

Around the beginning of 1981, near the time of the Tết celebrations of the year of the Rooster (Tân Dậu), the two of us were still in Saigon, and we both attended an end-of-the-year party that included former medical students from many classes in which the most crowded being class of 1968. Professor Hoàng Tiến Bảo and Phạm Biểu Tâm both took part. The feelings of the participants had an aspect of forced gaiety. Professor Tâm was not a drinker, but he brought wine with him to contribute to the festivities. He raised the wine bottles high so the students could see them, and said something like the following: "This time, you can all rest easy–this is not counterfeit wine, because the bottles were given to me by a priest." It was always Professor Tâm's

1 These were barbed-wire cages used by the Vietnamese to confine prisoners during the Vietnam war.

habit to speak in an indirect manner, suggesting, rather than stating, what his meaning was. And no one then misunderstood what he was hinting at on that occasion: the South had entered an impossible-to-avoid era of lies.

After the 1975 upheaval, Professor Tâm continued to enjoy some respect and deference from the new regime due to his special character and abilities. He went on with his activities like a farmer aware that the weather is not propitious, but who still bends to his tasks of diking and soil preparation so that his planting and cultivation can continue. He never in his life kept an office; his existence had a spartan simplicity. Every day he would go to the Bình Dân Hospital to make diagnoses, carry out operations, and devote himself to care of his patients and the instruction of the younger doctors. The regime had need of the professor due to his established standing, but they never reposed any trust in him. The evidence for this is that his home on Ngô Thời Nhiệm Street was at least twice invaded and searched by the security police. And each time this happened, the secretary of the Hồ Chí Minh City Party Committee formally apologized, saying that the search was occasioned by an error made by his inferiors. Such explanations were in reality simply expressions of the double-faced nature of the regime.

In 1984, when he was more than seventy, after more than forty years of wielding the scalpel, and of devotion to his patients and to new generations of doctors, Professor Tâm had to retire suddenly because of a stroke. At that time, I had already gone to the U.S., where I was reunited with my family after a separation of eight years. I was at the same time treating myself for tuberculosis and preparing to go back to school. In accordance with a fine tradition that exists among the extended family of doctors, colleagues who had gone to the U.S. earlier brought me cases of books, including textbooks. Those friends had all passed their examinations; some had done so three or four years earlier, but were still waiting for acceptance into a residency program that would allow them to obtain their doctor's licenses.

I made the mistake back then of taking the FLEX/ECFMG exams after only a hurried period of study. I passed the exam, but with a score that was not high; this meant that during that time of "shut doors," I had very little hope of being accepted into a residency program in any hospital. The road back to my profession seemed long indeed. A professor at UCLA introduced me to an MPH (Master of Public Health) program. This seemed to offer a new door; I hoped that with a degree in Public Health, I would be able to work for WHO (World Health Organization), a subsidiary of the United Nations, in Southeast Asian and African countries.

In that period, I also remade the acquaintance of Professor Hoàng Tiến Bảo, who always encouraged me to return to the medical profession. Professor Bảo would always go by bus to a church to attend mass before going to USC (the University of Southern California). Every day the two of us would enter Norris Medical Library on Zonal Street and sit studying in expectation of retaking our examinations. Together with him I acted as an unpaid clinical fellow in the Department of Medicine / Hypertension Service with Professors DeQuattro and Barndt – that was the only means by which we could get letters of recommendation from American professors, and it also allowed us to become familiar with the hospital environment there. This was in spite of the fact that Professor Bảo had studied orthopedics in the U.S. before 1975 and that I also had spent time in the U.S. working in Rehab in San Francisco.

The U.S. medical system treated foreign doctors who came to the U.S. as immigrants, and wished to practice in this country, with cool and ruthless indifference. The treatment accorded them was very different from that extended to foreign doctors who came to the U.S. for post-doctoral training with the intention of returning to their country. But according to the opinion of some, this is actually a very fair selection process that exists only in the U.S. Professor Bảo and I were not exceptions to this rule; we had to start all over again from step one, though everyone knew that Professor Bảo was worthy to be engaged as a distinguished professor of orthopedic surgery at any medical school.

Later, working at various hospitals in New York, I had occasion to observe the situation of a highly reputable OB-GYN professor from

Poland who had to work as an EKG technician and a Russian surgeon who had to work as a respiratory therapist. They were the first in their families to come to the U.S. and, because of their age, were not in a position to start their education all over again, so they endured their sacrifices so as to pave the way for the upcoming generation.

Professor Bảo was more concerned for the welfare of his students than for his own. He once took a bus to the home of a student to urge him to continue with his studies and not give up the struggle; and when he himself was faced with medical examinations, he led a delegation of students to the California Medical Board in Sacramento to demand that those of his students who graduated in Vietnam after 1975 be given the right to take the ECFMG exams (they lasted two days) to enter programs of graduate medical education in the United States to get a license to return to the practice of medicine.

And his efforts at last paid off. Professor Bảo passed his examinations with ease, completed a year of internship, and obtained a licence to practice medicine in California. As for me, I had to toil quite a bit to pass the FMGEMS examinations with a score better than eighty per cent in order to be accepted into a residency program. In March 1988, through the National Resident Matching Program (NRMP) I was accepted into the internal medicine programs of some teaching hospitals in New York. It was Professor Bảo, also, who shared with me the happy news that his students, too, would be able to embark on this challenging three-year process. Professor Hoàng Tiến Bảo has now passed away (Jan. 20, 2008). I and his many other students will never forget the fine example he set for us with his expansive spirit and generous humanity.

I MEET MY FORMER PROFESSOR AGAIN IN HIS OLD AGE

After my belated return to being a hospital resident at the age of forty-seven, I learned in New York from my old classmate Đường Thiện Đồng that Professor Phạm Biểu Tâm had just, in 1989, come with his family to be reunited with his children – that was five years

Professor Hoàng Tiến Bảo (right) paying a visit to Professor Phạm Biểu Tâm in Tustin, Orange County, South California.
(archives of TSYS, Canada)

after his stroke. I had his address in Santa Ana, so I wrote him a letter asking how he was, and received in the mail a reply written by hand. The handwriting was very attractive. I recalled that he was right-handed and guessed that the stroke had affected only his left side:

"Santa Ana, August 25, 1989. I've received the postal letter that you sent me and my family. As I looked at your handwriting, I recalled the way you looked back in the days when you were still in Saigon. Later on I had occasion to return to the place where you used to work – surely you never suspected that – it was the Orthopedic Center at the corner of Bà Huyện Thanh Quan and Hiền Vương Streets, because at that point I was undergoing physical therapy for my new illness. The young ladies who helped with my routines there all asked, "Do you know Dr. Vinh?" to which I would reply. "You bet I do!" And I remember the set of books you sent me to look at when you were still in the army…"

Back in the period 1972-1973, I had had the good fortune to study Rehabilitation Medicine at the Letterman General Hospital in Presidio San Francisco, so afterwards, having gained training in that specialty,

I taught and worked for a period in the Center for Rehabilitation Medicine at 70 Bà Huyện Thanh Quan Street in Saigon. A number of the physiotherapists who worked there had been trained by me in the courses that I gave there. And then – who on earth could have predicted that in the ordinary course of their professional duties, those young women who had been my students would have the honor of caring for an eminent professor who was "the teacher of their own teacher!"

It seems that Professors Phạm Biểu Tâm and Nguyễn Hữu both got to visit the U.S. at a very early period. On receiving a postcard that I sent him from New York, Professor Tâm wrote: "You're making me remember the first time I set foot in New York City in 1951 nearly half a century ago! That was the time when I went to gaze at the Empire State Building and the Rockefeller Center. Those sights made me raise my head and strive to count all the stories in the buildings – before I could count them all I felt that I was being swooped up in an elevator to some dizzying height. Now, my desire to return is not so strong – every period in one's life has the pleasures proper to that period."

After a year of hospital residency in New York State, with its cold winters steeped in snow yielding to excessively hot and humid summers, I was able to return to sunny, warm California and visit Professor Tâm. It was with feelings of mingled joy and sorrow that I met him again in a place more than half a world away from our home. Clasping his soft and warm hand, an instinct left over from earlier scouting days impelled me to gently squeezed his left hand, and, at a loss to say anything else, murmur, "Who knows, professor, how many peoples' lives have been saved by these two hands of yours…" "It was nothing really to speak of, Vinh." Moved, he strove to say a few more words, but I could not understand what they were. I understood that after undergoing a stroke, people are subject to changes in many areas other than that caused by the event itself, and that these include changes in emotion, sentiment, and psychology. I observed that such changes had in fact taken place in the professor. Originally a quiet, reserved person, he had become a person easily moved.

AN INCOMPLETE MEDICAL PROJECT

Professor Tâm continued to be mentally alert. His memory of events was nearly perfect when he recalled his days in the Hanoi Phủ Doãn Hospital and, later the Bình Dân Hospital in Saigon. If his memories of those places could be recorded, they would be of priceless, even unique, value if they could form part of a General History of the School of Medicine in Hanoi and Saigon.

I took the liberty of suggesting to him that I bring a miniature tape recorder, so that he could record all his memories of those places. I promised that I would subsequently make a transcript of everything he said. But Professor Tâm dissuaded me at once: "Vinh, don't worry about this – that job will be undertaken by Nguyễn Đức Nguyên, and he will make sure that it is done well." That allayed my worry, because I remembered that Nguyên had already completed a very thorough set of books entitled *Bibliographie des Thèses de Médecine (Tome I: Hanoi 1935-1954; Saigon 1947-1970; Tome II: Saigon 1971-1972; Tome III: Huế 1967-1972*)

When I returned to New York, Professor Tâm also sent me a letter with the information I needed to communicate with Nguyễn Đức Nguyên, who was then living in Maryland:

"Santa Ana, Aug. 12, 1990: "Vinh, thanks for reserving time to pay me a visit, which has also allowed me to visit you. I beg to first do what I promised and copy down Nguyên's current address:

N. D. NGUYÊN c/o Kathy Nguyên
11616 Stewart Lane Apt. 302
Silver Spring, Maryland 20904

This way we won't forget. I hope you will soon meet again with this person, who can do just what you desire. Since he too has had this desire, he will be reassured when you meet him. With affection, Yours, Phạm Biểu Tâm."

I bade farewell to New York after three years of "volunteer self-reform" – an expression used by Vũ Văn Dzi, a colleague of mine who worked in an Oklahoma VA hospital and went to the U.S. from 1979.

I returned to California in 1991 and worked in a VA hospital in Long Beach where most of the patients were former American GIs who had returned from Vietnam. During this period I continued to communicate regularly with Dr. Nguyễn Đức Nguyên and was able, step by step, to follow the progress he was making on his project:

Professor Phạm Biểu Tâm and his student Ngô Thế Vinh in the professor's home in Tustin, Santa Ana, 1990.
(photo by Đường Thiện Đồng)

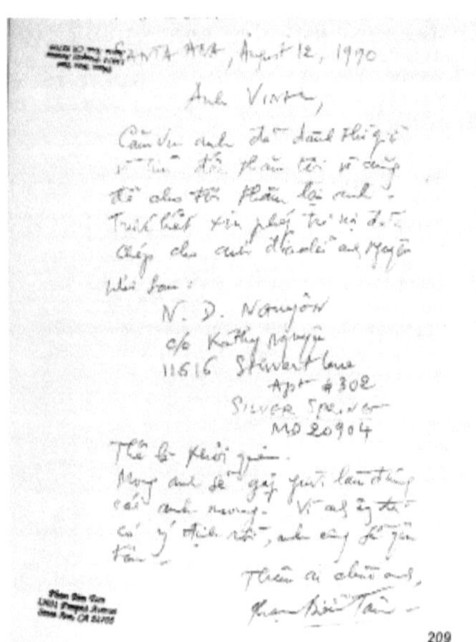

Santa Ana, August 12, 1990

Anh Vinh,

[illegible]

N. D. Nguyên
c/o Kathy Nguyễn
11616 Stewart Lane
Apt #302
Silver Spring
MD 20904

[illegible]

209

A handwritten letter from Professor Tâm sent from Santa Ana, Aug. 12, 1990.
(Ngô Thế Vinh, personal archives)

"Silver Spring, Feb. 11, 1994. Dear Vinh: That you mention *The History of The Hanoi-Saigon School of Medicine* on the dedication page [of the book you sent] pleases me no end; I still remember that you urged me to compile this book a long time ago. It can be said that the first part, which goes to 1945, can be regarded as complete. As for the part dealing with the Medical School from the time it came to us until 1954 and then from the time of its removal to Saigon to the time when the U.S. government began helping the Ngô Đình Diệm government overhaul the education system – and in particular medical education – some needful materials are still lacking. I am relying on an American woman who used to work for the USOM in Saigon to look for them on my behalf; I have also written letters to several American doctors who previously had dealings with the Medical Center Program, in order to obtain materials and photographs. The State Department archives are enormous – only specialists can hope to find anything there. After the AMA signed a contract for it in 1966-67, the book *Saigon Medical School: An Experiment in International Medical Education* by Messrs. Ruhe, Singer, and Hoover appeared; this was fairly complete. Probably you've read it already? The reason I'm taking so long is because I'm waiting for materials and photos to supplement what I've done; this will make the book more attractive. If it consists of nothing but words, few people will want to read it..."

IN A DIFFERENT LETTER, NGUYÊN WROTE THE FOLLOWING:

"Silver Spring, Dec. 28, 1995. Thanks for asking about my *History of the Medical School.* The material I've collected is sufficient for Part One (Hanoi – 1954). As for Part Two (Saigon – 1975), I am seeking more materials in the U.S. State Department to have an adequate basis for writing about the period that started when we began to receive U.S. assistance. Since I have your ear, I'd like to ask you about matters concerning book publication over here. Do publishers take charge of the whole process from beginning to end, and what sort of copyright will I enjoy? If I give it to them in the form of a computer document, and all they need to do is print it, how will they calculate the expense? I'm thinking of making a trip to California some time before Tết. If I can manage the trip, I'll let you know beforehand – perhaps we can meet somewhere and have a long conversation about books. Yours, Nguyễn Đức Nguyên."

When Nguyên asked me about publishing things in the U.S., I optimistically imagined that his work had reached the stage of completion. Nguyên was a perfectionist; he wanted his work to satisfy him in every respect before bringing it out. But my concern was different. Nguyên had already reached an age rarely attained by anyone – and anything could happen. I remembered that I had already expressed the view to him that one could never know when a work

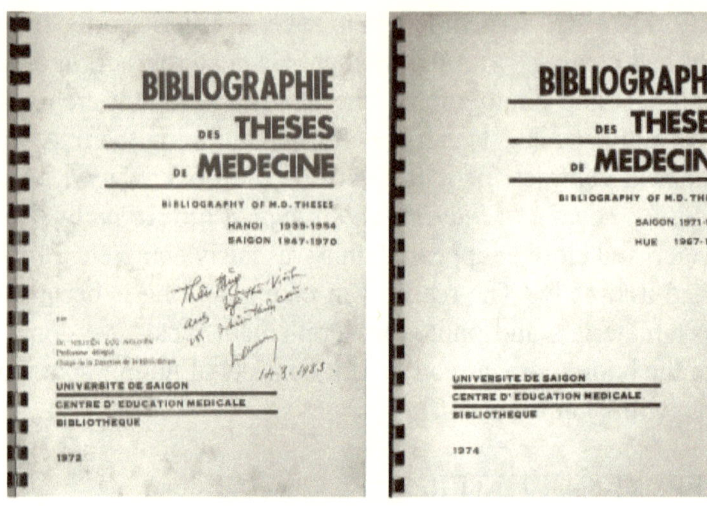

Bibliography of Medical Theses;
Vol. 1: Hanoi 1935-1954, Saigon 1947-1970;
Vol 2: Saigon 1971-1972, Hue 1967-1972.
(Ngô Thế Vinh, personal archives)

would reach perfection, and suggested that he published whatever he had completed. He would still have time to adjust it later.

But then, most regrettably, I lost contact with Nguyễn Đức Nguyên; he changed his address, his phone number, and his email address. I had learned that he was comparable in age to Professor Trần Ngọc Ninh (born 1923) and, like him, had entered his nineties. I pray that his project will not be lost, and that it will appear in accordance with the belief and hope of Professor Phạm Biểu Tâm during the decades at the close of the previous century.

COMPASSION THAT LIVES ON FOR A HUNDRED YEARS

On Dec. 13, 2013, the one-hundred-year anniversary of the birth Professor Phạm Biểu Tâm (1913-2013), the generations that came afterward look back upon him as a person who made huge contributions to building a School of Medicine endowed with a tradition of excellence together with an able training staff and a student body chosen fairly but strictly. Though he did this in a time of war, this school had the potential to develop into a world-class Medical Center. After 1975, however, this splendid foundation for the future was ruined by the communist regime.

Remembering the years when I was close to Professor Tâm, he seemed to me a living embodiment of the Oath of Hippocrates, a bright example for all the generations of physicians, not only with regard to excellence, but also with regard to professional ethics. He will always exemplify the spirit of a bold, committed young scout of the Bạch Mã troop.

Professor Phạm Biểu Tâm passed away on Dec. 11, 1999 amid the love and sorrow of his family, his students, and the entire Vietnamese medical community abroad and even within the country, sorrow for an esteemed teacher who, beginning in the previous century, left a lasting mark on Vietnamese medicine.

To commemorate Professor Phạm Biểu Tâm, I shall read a contemplative zen poem of his own composition, that may bring some consolation to us all:

Trăm năm trước thì ta chưa có
Trăm năm sau có cũng như không
Cuộc đời sắc sắc không không
Trăm năm còn lại tấm lòng từ bi...

(A hundred years ago, no me as yet existed;
A further hundred years, and no me will remain
Life is filled with images, that is: with emptiness;
The hundred years, once over, leave compassion only.)

California, July 20, 2017

YEARS OF DREAMING IN VAIN PROFESSOR PHẠM HOÀNG HỘ AND THE FLORA OF VIETNAM

Portrait of Professor Phạm Hoàng Hộ
(from the back cover of his book)

Peter Shaw Ashton, the Charles Bullard Professor of Forestry at Harvard University, had the following to say about Phạm Hoàng Hộ:

"With its notes in English, together with its finely executed line drawings of more than 10,500 species, *The Illustrated Flora of Vietnam* by Professor Phạm Hoàng Hộ has for the first time supplied English readers with an up-to-date body of research on a topic that few of us have known anything about. This work will stand as a monument to the determination, self-sacrifice, and encyclopedic knowledge, as well as the courage of the author. Professor Phạm Hoàng Hộ with virtually no assistance brought this vast project, a scientific exposition of plant biology, to fruition at the University of Saigon in a period of months and years when he was beset with every conceivable difficulty. In these challenging circumstances, he collected the materials he needed for this outstanding work, and undertook journeys to collect specimens on which to base his illustrations. And now that this work has been published, it will serve as an inspiration for young botanists, both in Vietnam and in other countries.

"*The Flora of Vietnam* has data, perhaps, on as many as 12,000 different plant species. Because the region described lies next to the tropical Asian shores of the Pacific Ocean, it is a corridor for the periodic, endlessly rich, north-south migration of vegetation from South China and for the even richer migration of vegetation from equatorial Malaysia. On mountain spurs there still remain conifers and flowering plants – angiosperm taxa – of incomparable importance, while on level plains traces remain as well that link these regions with the islands of the Philippines, and Indonesian Borneo. This richness is now on the verge of disappearing. The work of Professor Phạm Hoàng Hộ, which is like a database of all surviving plants, will act as a support to the efforts of the Vietnamese government in its campaign to replant, restore, and preserve the botanical heritage of the land."

SOME BIOGRAPHICAL DETAILS

The official papers of Professor Phạm Hoàng Hộ state that he was born on Aug. 3 1931 in An Bình, Cần Thơ. But according to an obituary recently supplied by his family, he was born in 1929 (the Kỷ Tỵ year) and died on Jan. 29, 2017 in Montréal, Canada at the age of 89. His son Phạm Hoàng Dũng confirmed this: *"My father was born in the year Kỷ Tỵ, 1929, but in accordance with an old custom, no official record was made of this until much later, in 1931."*

Academic Degrees:

- 1955 Bachelor of Science; valedictorian in botany, Paris
- 1955 Post-graduate in Natural Science, Paris
- 1956 Agrégé* in the Natural Sciences
- 1962 PhD in Science / Natural Sciences, Paris

Positions held:

- 1957 – 1984 Head of the Botanical Department, Faculty of Science, Saigon
- 1965 – 1984 Professor of Botany, Faculty of Science, Saigon
- 1962 – 1966 Director of the Institute of Oceanology, Nha Trang
- 1963 – 1963, Dean, Saigon University of Pedagogy
- 1963 Minister of Education
- 1966 – 1970 founding president of the University of Cần Thơ
- 1978 – 1984 Editor of the weekly magazine Popular Science (Khoa học Phổ thông) , Saigon
- 1984 – 1989 Research Professor in the National Museum of Natural Science, Paris

Memberships in Scientific Organizations:

- 1956 Member of the Botanical Society, France
- 1963 Member of the International Phycological Society
- 1964 Founding Member of the Biological Society, Vietnam
- 1965 Vice President of the Terminological Commission, Vietnam
- 1967 Member of the International Society of University Presidents
- 1969 Founding Member of the University of Cần Thơ Yearbook Committee
- 1971 Member of the Committee for Assessing the Results of Agent Orange Contamination in Vietnam, National Academy of Science, U.S.
- 1973 Ecological Advisor for the International Mekong River Commission

Printed Items:

- 1956 *The Flora of South Vietnam* (*Cây Cỏ Miền Nam Việt Nam*); *Floré Illustré du Sud Vietnam*), Vietnamese Ministry of Education, One vol., 803 pp., 275 plates
- 1964 *The Biology of Plants* (Sinh Học Thực Vật), Vietnamese Ministry of Education, One Vol., 861 pp., many illustrations
- 1968 *Angiosperms* (*Hiển Hoa Bí Tử),* Center for Pedagogical Materials, Vietnamese Ministry of Education, 506 pp., 264 plates.
- 1969 *Seaweeds of Vietnam* (*Rong Biển Việt Nam*), Center for Pedagogical Materials, Vietnamese Ministry of Education, 558 pp., 493 figs.
- 1970 *The Flora of South Vietnam*, Vol. 1, 2nd printing, Center for Pedagogical Materials, Vietnamese Ministry of Education, 1115 pp., figs. 2787
- 1972 *The Flora South Vietnam*, Vol. 2, 2nd printing, Center for Pedagogical Materials, Vietnamese Ministry of Education, 1139 pp., figs. 5272

An Illustrated Flora of Vietnam (Cây Cỏ Việt Nam):

- 1991 Collection 1, Vol. 1: Missing Plants; Lõa Tử. Omitted Flowers to Tiliaceae.
- 1992 Collection 1, Vol. 2: Omitted Flowers from Elaegnaceae to Apiaceae
- 1993 Collection 1, Vol. 3: From Smilacaceae… Cyperaceae… Poaceae… to Orchidaceae
- 1991 Collection 2, Vol. 1: Omitted Flowers to Sterculiaceae to Fabaceae
- 1993 Collection 2, Vol. 2: From Daphniphyllum… Fagaceae… Apocynaceae… to Scrophulariaceae
- 1993 Collection 2, Vol. 3: From Smilacaceae… Cyperaceae… Poaceae… to Orchidaceae
- 1998 *Medicinal Flora in Vietnam*, Youth Publishers (nxb Trẻ), Ho Chi Minh City; 860 pp.; describes 2149 medicinal plants that grow in Vietnam.

Also, in his "Summary of Scientific Activities," Professor Phạm Hoàng Hộ tells us the following: "Perhaps because, when I was little, I lived among gardens and green fields in the lush area nourished by the Mekong River, I formed an attachment to trees and plants from an early age, I will never be able to forget such images as that of water lilies in fields or lakes, glistening beneath the sun's rays in the early morning, or the image of Longan blossoms sunning themselves at the edges of fields. So, botany and tropical biology attracted me until it became time to go abroad to study. And while studying at the Institute of Science in Paris, I began to seek an understanding of the flora of Southeast Asia. My first scientific contact with plant life took place in the National Museum of Natural History in Paris. When I was just beginning to study Natural Science, I entered the greenhouse of the museum to see if there were any of our plants there. And so, it was there that I made some of my first drawings! I remember a few types of orchids that I drew right in that greenhouse in 1950. Those are the most "ancient" of the drawings in my book on Vietnamese flora. And later, when I did my thesis, also at that institute, I had my first opportunity to pay attention to their Botany Collection, and saw a number of images, especially those pertaining to the species Ficus, that were difficult, because not many types had as yet been drawn, and I was reluctant to face the challenge. Later, after returning home, I found that this type of plant was difficult to find. Actually, at that time, my ambitions were modest. Later, when I learned about the types of Ficus to be found in Vietnam, I was overjoyed.

After I passed the examination for the Agrégation,* in which I came out sixth, ahead of three hundred other candidates, and among only thirty who passed, I returned home.

(Author's Note: This degree must be distinguished from the "thạc sĩ" or master's degree current in Vietnam. To obtain the Agrégé degree in France you had to pass a very rigorous examination and were then entitled to be a titular professor at a lycée (middle school) or at any institution of higher learning in such fields as Science, Medicine, or Law.)

Professor Hộ added the following: "At that time my ambition was simply to return and teach at a middle school, and use my leisure hours to seek to understand the flora of the Six Southern Provinces (Lục tỉnh) only, but the College of Saigon and the Nha Trang Institute of Oceanography "yanked" me forth to teach and lecture and look after the Oceanography Institute. While working in Nha Trang I took an academic interest in ocean seaweed, regarding this as a duty. After a few more years of research under the direction of Professor J. Feldmann, I completed my PhD thesis and submitted it to the university in Paris in 1961. This project was recorded in the Yearbook of the Faculty of Science, Saigon and in the volume *The Seaweeds of Vietnam* (*Rong Biển Việt Nam*) as well as a few articles in scientific journals.

In Saigon, my main duty was teaching Botany and Botanical Biology (replacing the French Professor Roger, a specialist in mushrooms that cause diseases in plants) for students in general and specialized curricula. It was because I wished to teach well, and in a manner well adapted to the tropical conditions prevailing in Vietnam, that the objects of my research were all things that belonged to my life work, and would later be included in The Flora of South Vietnam. (Excerpted from materials in the family archives of Professor Phạm Hoàng Hộ: "Academic Degrees and Scientific Career of Phạm Hoàng Hộ, Professor of Botany")

In the years 1959-60, the author of this book, then merely a pre-med student in the PCB (Physique Chimie Biologie), division at the Faculty of Science, Saigon, got to study under Professor Hộ, who had just returned from France after obtaining an Agrégé degree and was teaching a course in plant biology. Though I only got to study under him for a year, he left an indelible impression on me, as well as all his other students. After entering the School of Medicine, I could no longer study under him, but I still held him in deep regard, followed the steps in his career, and collected the books containing the results of his research.

In the early 1990s, the scientific community both within and outside the country were overjoyed when Professor Hộ's *Flora of*

The two volumes of *The Flora of South Vietnam*, Center for Pedagogical Materials, Ministry of Education, Republic of Vietnam, 1970 *(source: Internet: Sách Xưa)*

Vietnam began to be published in stages. According to Professor Thái Công Tụng, now settled in Montréal, the books of Professor Hộ are all collected in the Bibliothèque du Jardin Botanique Montréal, Canada, and of course may be found in many large libraries throughout the world.

The Flora of Vietnam consists in its entirety of two sections, each of which is in three volumes, amounting in all to 3,600 pages, not counting the glossaries listing all the Vietnamese names and all the Latin names of the species dealt with, lists that he began in the years and months of his sojourn in France and continued conscientiously to expand subsequently.

I myself came into early possession of the six volumes of The Flora of Vietnam when my elder colleague, Dr. Phạm Văn Hoàng, a younger brother of Professor Hộ's who was formerly the director of the Cần Thơ Center for Rehabilitation Medicine, sent the work to me as a gift.

It seems I should also mention here that before 1975, Professor Hộ served as environmental advisor to the Mekong River Committee and that, around the year 1974, he and Professor Thái Công Tụng published a book detailing the results of a joint research project in this area: *The Mekong Delta: Its Environment, Its Problems* (published by the Ministry of Agriculture, Republic of Vietnam in 1974). When I sought to track down and obtain this historically meaningful material, Professor Thái Công Tụng informed me with sadness that it had been utterly destroyed after the war.

Why were the scientific works of Professor Hộ published in Vietnamese, though the language he relied on throughout his research and teaching career was French?

In the preface to his book *Seaweeds of Vietnam*, published in 1969, he wrote: "This book started out as a work in French, when I was working at the Institute and Museum of Oceanology in Nha Trang, because I cherished the hope that, if published in that language, the results of our research would be displayed to all the world – I had silently promised this to myself when I submitted my dissertation.

"But now I have changed my mind and published it in Vietnamese. This is to demonstrate that any language, if used with exactitude, can be used to convey information at any level. I know many people hold the view that publishing something in a language that is not international is a waste of time – how can other researchers know what it contains? But I believe that this scruple is unnecessary. It is of more value for the book to be known and used by a few million Vietnamese than for the book to be appreciated by a few thousand specialists. I have discarded the vainglorious ambition to compete with foreigners so that I may gain a name for myself and shed reflected glory on the people of Vietnam. I believe that such a vainglorious ambition is impractical – the existence of one skilled Vietnamese is not as desirable as the existence of many Vietnamese of more moderate attainments. To hold a torch to illuminate the streets of foreigners does not meet the needs of the time when one's own land is still in darkness. The vainglory alluded to above is actually just a way of evading responsibility; it

Phạm-hoàng Hộ, sanh năm 1931 tại Anbinh, Cầntho, Thạcsĩ Vạnvậthọc, Tiếnsĩ Khoahọc (Paris), Giáosư thậtthụ tại trường Đạihọc Khoahọc Sàigòn, Việntrưởng sánglậpviên Đạihọc Cầnthơ, cựu Tổngtrưởng Quốcgia Giáodục Việtnam Cộnghòa, nguyên Giáosư khảocứu tại Viện Bảotàng Thiênnhiên Quốcgia Paris, hộiviên nhiều Hội Khoahọc Quốctế. Là tácgiả của nhiều ấnphẩm về thựcvậthọc Việtnam: Rong biển Việtnam (1969), Tảohọc (1972) Sinhhọc Thựcvật (in kỳ tư 1973), Hiểnhoa Bìtử (in kỳ nhì 1975)...

"By providing annotations on each species in English, as well as the fine line drawings for every one of the c. 10,500 species, the Illustrated Flora of Vietnam provides the English speaking reader with the first, as well as a fully up to date and comprehensive reference for a flora hitherto little known to us. This work will stand as a monument to the determination, dedication, scholarship and even courage of its author. Professor Pham hoang Ho almost single-handedly upheld standards of academic excellence in biology at the University of Saigon during its most difficult years. Under extraordinarily difficult circumstances, Professor Ho was able to gather the materials for this remarkable series and even to visit the field to gather fresh material for illustration. It is symptomatic of our times that he is now publishing this work, which will be such a stimulus to young biologists in Vietnam, privately overseas.

"The flora of Vietnam may finally contain more than 12,000 phanerogams. This is because the country, pressed against the Pacific edge of the Asian tropics, has been a corridor for the periodic north-south migration of the very rich subtropical flora of South China and even richer equatorial flora of Malaysia. Her mountains still harbor conifer and angiosperm taxa of exceptional importance, while the lowlands bear evidence of past connections with the Philippines and Borneo. All this wealth is now perilously close to extinction. The valient efforts of the current government of the Republic of Vietnam to plan and implement a comprehensive conservation strategy will be critically assisted by this manual, which will also stand as a record of the flora as it now exists.

Peter Shaw Ashton
Charles Bullard Professor of Forestry
Harvard university

An autobiographical account by Professor Phạm Hoàng Hộ with the Foreword by Peter Shaw Ashton and Professor Charles Bullard, a forestologist at Harvard, that appeared on the back cover of his book *The Flora of Vietnam* (Second Section, Vol. 2), published 1993 in Montréal".

is to cast aside, in an unforgivable manner, one's duty to the rising generations.

"Creating a scientific culture that we can call our own is an endlessly immense task. Many scholars, feeling that the task is simply too big, are inclined to accept the easiest solution: to study directly from the scientific literature in foreign languages, a literature that is endlessly rich, and teeming with content. This mode of study would produce many skillful people, but we must not forget that the current basis of our civilization is the culture of our people as a whole, not that of a few people of unusual accomplishment within this whole. We must not allow the richness of foreign cultures to crush our own culture. Did not the Japanese, a century ago, remain undismayed by the overwhelming strength of the scientific accomplishments of foreign countries? And now have they not created a scientific culture of their own that in the near future shall be superior that of those very countries?

Above all, I hear resounding in my ears at all times something said by Nguyễn Văn Vĩnh: whether Vietnam, this land of ours, turns out well or ill will depend entirely on our adoption of the national script (chữ quốc ngữ). In the world that is to come, cultural subservience, especially in the realm of science, will be the principal form taken by subservience. (from the preface to *The Seaweeds of Vietnam*, Educational Materials Center, Ministry of Education, published 1969).

The covers of some volumes in the vast work, *The Flora of Vietnam*, comprising two divisions and six volumes, published overseas. *(Source: Ngô Thế Vinh)*

A DIFFICULT PHASE

The image of Professor Phạm Hoàng Hộ in the years following 1975 is emblematic of the bitter experiences of a whole generation of Southern intellectuals, of whom he was a typical example.

According to Professor Phạm Hoàng Hộ, *The Flora of Vietnam* came into being in four phases:

– First phase of research: With collaborative input from Professor Nguyễn Văn Dương on those parts of the work that involved pharmaceutical plants, The Flora of South Vietnam, published by the Ministry of Education in 1960, described 1,650 species commonly found in the South. "That was the groping, exploratory phase, comprising studies of plant specimens not yet familiar to a student who had just returned to his native land after graduating from a program of study in a remote place."

– Second phase of research: When *The Flora of South Vietnam* was published again in 1970, the number of species described had grown to 5,328. "That phase I regard as a golden era for a botanist working in our land of Vietnam. Compared with conditions that now prevail, it was a time when I could work peacefully and when I enjoyed many conveniences, some personal and some supplied by the country, and above all I enjoyed the encouragement from all sides, both from friends and from the government."

– Third phase of research: "Continuing my endeavors beyond the year 1975, I introduced 2,500 more species descriptions and expanded the scope of the work to include the entire territory of Vietnam.

After the upheaval of 1975, Professor Phạm Hoàng Hộ, like his friend and scientific colleague Professor Nguyễn Duy Xuân, chose to remain behind, so as to build up the country after years of warfare had culminated in unification, but this came at a very heavy price, as he wrote later, "*In those years I lived in the vain fantasy that I would see the country improve. It was the phase of traveling by bicycle, eating moldy rice, and imagining that flowers would bloom by the roads in my native land.*"

Though Professor Phạm Hoàng Hộ still held the title "Vice Department Chair" (phó khoa trưởng) at the Institute of Science, the regime used left-over intellectuals, of which he was one, for purposes of display alone; he was given no educational role that matched his title. Because he was not a party member, he could never participate in the meetings of those who were. Whenever a problem arose, the party members would meet to resolve the issue; he was never informed as to what took place at these meetings. In 1977, after experiencing a few days of political study in what was to be an eighteen-month course in "scientific socialism," reserved for Southern intellectuals in Hồ Chí Minh City, Professor Hộ protested right away to the introduction into the curriculum of so many hours of political study, warning his superiors that "if political studies are enforced too strongly, scientists will no longer be equipped with the basics." (Huy Đức, *The Victorious Side* [*Bên Thắng Cuộc*])

And then we must note as well a certain minority of intellectuals who, adapting to the times, began at once to collaborate with the new regime and, paying no regard to personal honor, were prepared to offer up "scientific" programs in order to help celebrate such national holidays such as February 3 or May 19 and promulgated such sayings as "eating a few kilos of potatoes is as fortifying as eating a kilo of beef," or "cassava root is even more nutritious than rice…" Such specimens of pseudoscience rapidly became the stuff of satirical anecdotes that spread throughout the labor reform camps, where prisoners from the South all suffered from hunger and malnutrition, subsisting as they did on such rations as moldy "đại mễ" rice from China, or bo bo and cassava tubers (called "khoai mì" in the South and "sắn" in the North).

Professor Hộ, like a number of other principled Southern scientists who had remained behind, saw that he could not continue to live in such a dishonest and corrupt society and that he would be unable to avoid putting an end to his years of living in a "vain fantasy." And then the opportunity he needed arrived. When the government of France invited him in 1984 to come and teach in that country, he resolved to live there as an exile.

– Fourth phase of research: This was the phase that Professor Hộ characterized as "the most precious and the most pain-filled." Writing further about this period, he said, "It was pain-filled because I was far from my native land and had no hope of returning. It was pain-filled because I was far from my dear family and because I had bade a final farewell to my kind mother, who had dedicated her whole life to her children. It was pain-filled because I saw that my dear country was in an unutterably sad, miserable, and hopeless situation."

But then he gallantly rose above that pain, patiently immersing himself in the Paris Museum of Natural History where he worked with ceaseless energy for six years. The National Museum of Natural History (Musée National d'Histoire Naturelle; MNHN), belonging to the Sorbonne University system and situated on the left bank of the Seine was established around the time of the French Revolution in the eighteenth century.

The French Museum of Natural History in Paris, the place where Professor Phạm Hoàng Hộ worked continuously for six years to complete *The Flora of Vietnam*. *(Source: internet)*

Professor Hộ once observed, "There has rarely been a botanist, especially one from Vietnam, who after collecting specimens in his own country, got to continue his research in France's National Museum of Natural History, which has the richest collection in the world, comprising eight million to ten million specimens. For Vietnam particularly, this is an irreplaceable treasure, because it includes more than ten thousand plants collected in our country. During the six years that I spent working there, no day ever passed, whether cold and humid or dry and hot, when, upon my return, I would not shout "What a great day this has been!" because I had learned at least one thing rare, or strange, or new about Vietnam." In this last phase, he added about three thousand more specimens to The Botany of Vietnam, raising the total to about ten thousand five hundred.

In France, when he met a former student, now a member of the faculty of the Institute of Science in Saigon, who was also working in the National Museum of Natural History (in the Ichthyology Laboratory) Professor Hộ made the following comments to him:

I do my best to get better all the time as I work. The collections in France are rich and managed with full scientific rigor. Because their specimens were collected twenty to forty years ago, many of them have aged, so we cannot work hurriedly, for fear that our efforts might go to waste… Many Chinese from the mainland, Taiwan, and Singapore also come here to study collections made in Southeast Asia by France. I don't know what their principal aims are. One must know what natural resources one's own country has. If you yourself don't know, and others do, then those others will use all their knowledge for their own people. This is true no matter what area of research is involved. If the activities of others go unchecked, then they will be in control–they will sit on a throne, while you will grovel in the dust. This is called "independence," but it is actually a form of subservience worse than that which existed in the French colonial period!"

Upon completing *The Flora of Vietnam*, Professor Hộ acknowledged the great debt he owed to The National Museum of Natural History and to his French colleagues. With utter sincerity, he said, "I have completed things that I could not have imagined in my maddest dreams when I was little–a slave in a colonized land, a pupil in an ordinary elementary school in a small province–how could I ever have dreamed that I would author a book, however insignificant? I may have adored the plants and trees around me, but how could I have dreamed that I would seek to become familiar with the flora of the entire country!"

And so the "suffering intellectual" Phạm Hoàng Hộ raised himself up and completed the "mad dream" that had once seemed impossible, and became the pillar of botanical science in Vietnam and one of the main pillars of that science in the world.

A LITTLE SCHOLARLY ANECDOTE

In his book *A Rose Presented in Gratitude*, the writer Nguyễn Đình Toàn recorded the following memories of Professor Phạm Hoàng Hộ: "In the years prior to 1975, Professor Hộ's work was still entitled *The Flora of South Vietnam*. The division of the country limited the scope of his book. Nevertheless, this work by Professor Hộ was valued not only by botanical specialists but, as the writer Võ Phiến recounts in his *Literature of the South*, written after 75, many writers (including Nguyễn Đình Toàn, the undersigned) sought out *The Flora of South Vietnam* to learn more about the vegetation surrounding them, so that they could introduce this information into their own work when needed. It is possible that even Professor Hộ never knew anything of this observation.

ESTABLISHING THE UNIVERSITY OF CẦN THƠ

Due to the advocacy of a number of Cần Thơ intellectuals in the 1960s, chief among whom were Professor Phạm Hoàng Hộ and Doctor Lê Văn Thuấn, permission was given on March 31, 1966 for University of Cần Thơ to be established. This was the first university to be founded in the Mekong River Delta area. Professor Hộ was its first rector, serving in that capacity from 1966 to 1970.

Due to the wide and deep respect he inspired, due both to his research and to his personal character, Professor Hộ was able to attract "gray matter" of the highest quality then existing in the South; in the realm of agriculture alone, he obtained the services of such famed scholars as Professor Tôn Thất Trình, Professor Thái Công Tụng, Dr. Nguyễn Viết Trương, Dr. Trần Đăng Hồng, due to whose contributions high yield rice began to be introduced to the delta region for the first time.

And then one must take note of the faculty as a whole, which was so full of ability that the University of Cần Thơ swiftly became a highly reputable center of research and education in the midst of a vast region rich in natural resources that had not yet been exploited. To appreciate the results of the first phase of this institution in its founding years, one has only to look at the activities of its first students who graduated from there four years later.

Professor Đỗ Bá Khê, a member of Professor Hộ's "think tank" was one such student – his graduation date was 47 years ago. In his college graduation speech, he gave expression to a comprehensive view of the role of the college in the future of the delta region:

"Today (December 19, 1970), in this age of science and technology, the provinces of the Mekong River Delta are hopefully awaiting a light that will illuminate the way shone by the University of Cần Thơ, and are dreaming of the appearance of a new horizon adorned with drooping yellow rice plants, gardens, and orchards full of trees, in which people will exist at ease, in a prosperous community and a just society.

HIS FRIEND AND COLLEAGUE PROFESSOR NGUYỄN DUY XUÂN

In 1970 the first stage in the establishment of the University of Cần Thơ was complete. In that year, in order to be able to return to Saigon and continue his research and teaching activities, Professor Phạm Hoàng Hộ extended a formal invitation to Professor Nguyễn Duy Xuân to take his place and become the second president of the University of Cần Thơ.

Professor Nguyễn Duy Xuân was also from Cần Thơ. He was four years older than Professor Phạm Hoàng Hộ, having been born in 1925. He obtained a PhD in economics at Vanderbilt University in the U.S. and returned to Vietnam in 1963 as a law professor. Having received the presidency from Professor Hộ, Professor Xuân energetically developed all aspects of the University of Cần Thơ from programs of instruction to faculty training, built new lecture halls and laboratories, and established new dormitories, so as to welcome students from all regions of the Western Region. He was a pioneer in setting up a system of credit-hours (instead of the previous certificate system) such as were used in U.S. colleges. He also sent a group of faculty members to study abroad. An outstanding member of this group was Trần Phước Đường, who obtained a PhD from the University of Michigan and afterwards returned to Cần Thơ University as a member of the biology department. Professor Đường later, from 1989 to 1997, became president of the university.

In 1972 he also extended a personal invitation to Võ Tòng Xuân, then a young student in agricultural studies working on assignment at the International Rice Horticulture Institute at Los Banos Philippines, to come and teach at Cần Thơ University. Võ Tòng Xuân later recounted that when he received the letter of invitation from Professor Nguyễn Duy Xuân, he said in the letter that "the Mekong River Delta was the rice-basket of the region, so there was a great need there for agricultural scientists. That was among the reasons that caused me to return to Cần Thơ University. Doctor Võ Tòng Xuân later became a famous professor of agricultural science, known as "Doctor Rice." His name came to be attached to the development of high-yield rice rice, and he later became the president of the University of An Giang, the second largest university in the region after Cần Thơ University.

In the space of only nine years (1966 – 1975), under the energetic direction of its first two presidents, Professor Phạm Hoàng Hộ and Professor Nguyễn Duy Xuân, the university of Cần Thơ became a beacon of scholarship in the Western Region, becoming a center of scientific training and research, and was important especially for developing the two areas of pedagogy and agriculture. It came to be entirely comparable to the older universities that had existed in the South and contributed greatly to the improvement of conditions in the Mekong River Delta.

FROM VAIN FANTASY TO TRAGEDY

Only a few days prior to the upheaval of April 30, 1975, Professor Nguyễn Duy Xuân, a committed intellectual like Professor Phạm Hoàng Hộ, decided to remain in the deadly circumstances that surrounded him. He also courageously agreed to become the Minister of Culture and Education, becoming the last holder of that position under the Southern Republic. Before a week more had passed, the government of the South collapsed, and President Dương Văn Minh surrendered to the conquerors.

Professor Nguyễn Duy Xuân was put into a labor reform camp and after that was conducted to the North and imprisoned in the Hà Nam Ninh labor camp with no prospect of return. Võ Tòng Xuân recounts that in the course of a trip he made to attend a conference in Hanoi in 1983, he went to the Ba Sao ("three stars") reeducation camp in Hà Nam Ninh to visit the man who had been the president when he attended Cần Thơ University. Professor Nguyễn Duy Xuân was delighted to meet his colleague and, though suffering the privations of a prisoner, questioned him eagerly about the state of affairs at Cần Thơ University, the place that he and Professor Hộ had founded and built up.

I, the author of this piece, cannot refrain from asking myself: if it had not been for the cruel and useless eleven-year imprisonment imposed by the communist victors – if Professor Nguyễn Duy Xuân. a talented and patriotic man with a doctorate in economics, had remained where he was and continued to build up Cần Thơ University to the same degree that he and his predecessor had done in the years 1966 to 1975, how far might that university have advanced?

1983 was the first year that the two professors surnamed Xuân got to meet each other, and that meeting also proved to be their last. Professor Nguyễn Duy Xuân continued to be imprisoned there for another three years, making a total of eleven, and he at length died there on November 10, 1986 in circumstances of hunger and disease for which there was no medicine. He was buried in a shallow grave in the camp cemetery in a mountainous area behind the camp.

It was only in 2015, almost twenty years later, when Professor Nguyễn Duy Xuân's remains were recovered by his daughter, Nguyễn Thị Nguyệt Nga, who came from France for the purpose, and moved his remains to a permanent site in Thiên Hưng Temple, in Bình Thạnh District, Saigon. Aside from members of his family, the people who attended the Buddhist rites accompanying the reburial included former faculty members at the university, and people who had graduated there before 1975, like Professor Võ Tòng Xuân, Doctor Nguyễn Tăng Tôn, Dr. Nguyễn Văn Mận, K.S. Minh, and Mr. Hòa (a former administrator at the university).

CẦN THƠ UNIVERSITY AFTER 1975

The replacement for Professor Nguyễn Duy Xuân as president of the university was Mr. Phạm Sơn Khai, a Southerner who had joined the party. His academic specialty was "the history of the party." He was raised to the presidency and led Cần Thơ University for thirteen years from 1976 to 1989.

The Ba Sao labor reform camp in Hà Nam Ninh. The line of mountains behind the camp is the burial place of many prisoners from the South after 1975

From the left: Professor Võ Tòng Xuân, Ms. Nguyễn Thị Nguyệt Nga, the daughter of Nguyễn Duy Xuân holding a container with her father's remains, her boyfriend Alan, and a close friend.

(Võ Tòng Xuân, personal archives)

From 1975 on, the new government advocated an educational system in which "being a communist" was more important than having specialized skills, so the curriculum of Cần Thơ University, like those of all the universities in the South had a new and compulsory course: "Marx-Leninism and the thought of Hồ Chí Minh," a course that "teachers were unwilling to teach and students were unwilling to study," but which nevertheless was preserved up to the present day. For forty-two years–almost half a century–there was not a single privately established university in the whole territory of Vietnam. It is too early to talk about "the democratization of Vietnam" when all of the universities and "think tanks" remain under the direction of Communist Party branch organizations

In an email message to me, Võ Tòng Xuân wrote as follows: "I shall always remember that when Professor Hộ travelled there, he was particularly careful with regard to food and drink–he would always bring his own food and thermoses containing his own water."

In March 1981, Professor Võ Tòng Xuân invited Professor Phạm Hoàng Hộ to participate in a Cần Thơ University research expedition to Đồng Tháp Mười. From left: Doctor Trần Thượng Tuấn, Doctor Nguyễn Thị Thu Cúc (half-hidden), Mr. Đỗ Thanh Ren, Professor Võ Tòng Xuân, Professor Trần Phước Đường, a staff member of the Quy Hoạch Branch-University, Professor Phạm Hoàng Hộ, and a staff-member of the Đồng Tháp government. *(Võ Tòng Xuân, personal archives).*

The presidents of Cần Thơ University from the time of its founding until 2023: Professor Phạm Hoàng Hộ (1966-1970), Professor Nguyễn Duy Xuân (1970-1975), Mr. Phạm Sơn Khai (1975-1989), Professor Trần Phước Đường (1989-1997), Doctor Trần Thượng Tuấn, (1997-2002), Doctor Lê Quang Minh (2002-2006), Professor Nguyễn Anh Tuấn (2006-2012), Doctor Hà Thanh Toàn (2012-2023). *(Lê Anh Tuấn, personal archives)*

Professor Phạm Hoàng Hộ next to a portrait-bust created by the Canadian sculptor Dr. Megerditch Tarakdjian on the occasion of his 80th birthday celebration organized by a group of his students in Montréal, Canada.

THE 80TH BIRTHDAY OF PROFESSOR PHẠM HOÀNG HỘ

In July of 2009, in Montréal, a number of his students organized a celebration of the eightieth birthday of Professor Phạm Hoàng Hộ, where they presented him with a portrait-bust accompanied by a heart-felt inscription: "This bust is not only the image of an eminent professor of botany, but is also an emblem of an intellectual of the South, who offered up his whole life to science, a man whose modesty greatly exceeds his talent, and who loves his homeland with all his heart.

An event, also full of meaning on that occasion, was the reading, by Dr. Tăng Quang Kiệt, of some words of tribute written by Professor Phùng Trung Ngân, then resident in California, the man who founded and served as the chair of the Department of Ecology and who was also the Dean at the Saigon Institute of Science in 1973-1975, a colleague and contemporary of Professor Hộ:

"My dear friend Hộ, I sincerely thank your friends and family for allowing me to contribute some words to this solemn occasion. Having attained the age of eighty, you have made an immense contribution to the study of the flora of Vietnam and at the same time have served as a guide to all the students who love the plant life and the natural world of Vietnam. As a person who worked closely with you in the enterprise of providing botanical education to the younger generation in Vietnam, I observed your total dedication to your field and the passion with which you pursued your research. The result was your immense work, *The Flora of Vietnam* and, above all, the manner in which you supplemented our knowledge of the flora of the entire country with descriptions of all the precious specimens that had been placed unto the Botanical Museum of Paris only to be forgotten. Before 1975, you and I often led students to participate in on-site training in the Lâm Đồng– Đà Lạt area, when we would have them go to the top of Lâm Viên, one of the mountains more than 2000 meters high in the South. At such times we often shared the hope that, after the return of peace, we could go together to the North and conduct research on the flora of the Fansipan peak in the Hoàng Liên mountain range, more than 3000 meters high. I am very sorry, at this late date, that this cherished hope of ours will probably never be realized. Nevertheless, on your own initiative, you communicated with those in the environs of Fansipan through the specimens in the Paris Museum that you described and added to *The Flora of Vietnam* for the advancement of science. I am very lucky to have been your close professional associate for many years and to have been able to benefit by observing the care with which you pursued your work, your devotion to teaching and the passion with which you carried out your researches."

HIS LAST WILL AND TESTAMENT: KEEP THE MOTHERLAND GREEN

In the last volume of *The Flora of Vietnam* (Section 2, volume 3), published in Montréal in 1993, on the two pages headed by the words "By way of a Preface," Professor Phạm Hoàng Hộ left some words that can be regarded as his "Last Will and Testament for Vietnam:

"The plant species of Vietnam are perhaps about 12,000 in number. This accounts only for those species that have nutritive veins; in other words, it does not include seaweed, moss, and mushrooms.

"That is among the richest collections of botanical specimens in the world. This richness is a blessing for Vietnam. As I wrote in 1968, the natural world is a benefactor beyond compare for all of humanity. The natural world gives us our daily food. The natural world supplies us, and especially supplies Vietnam, with a place where we can peacefully exist. How many are the beautiful relationships that have begun with a few betel nuts, with a mouthful of areca leaves? How many of us have come into life without the assistance of a piece of bamboo to cut the umbilical cord that connects us to our mothers? In moments full of life and leisure, it is the natural world that supplies humanity with the delicious and healthy fluids that allows us to share in the drunken satisfaction of the universe. In moments of illness, it is also the natural world that supplies us with efficacious herbal medicines.

These observations apply even more to us Vietnamese, we who live in a culture that in countless respects is based upon vegetation.

But this great benefactor of ours is being secretly undermined, for the health of our mountains and waterways has subsided to a dangerous degree; the fertility of our soils has been depleted over a vast area, and areas subject to desertification are spreading rapidly. Things have reached the point where we can sing the lines "Do you hear, oh spirits? The mountains and rivers are in crisis. What deep forests still exist? They day by day recede. Where now are the thousand trees that have served us as a refuge? [author's note: These lines are from the song "The Diên Hồng Assembly" ("Hội Nghị Diên Hồng), music by Lưu Hữu Phước, lyrics by Huỳnh Văn Tiểng]

It is our duty to preserve this botanical treasure. The need to preserve and restore the natural world in our country is extremely urgent. It can be accomplished, because every one of us, whether big or little, can contribute to this preservation. Small actions performed every day, can be as significant as great actions.

To refrain from casting aside matches and cigarette stubs is to contribute to the effort to avoid forest fires. To refrain from felling trees for no reason is to protect our natural world. Growing trees is a responsibility of the government and of companies that exploit forests. But around our own homes we can grow trees that are unusual, special, seldom seen in our own area, or which are native to Vietnam alone.

Our people love to grow ornamental trees, but ordinary people can also grow unusual or special trees; this is an activity no less delightful and beautiful. Every small town should have a park or a botanical garden, if not large, then at least a little one, so as to display some of the local trees–they need not be especially useful or beautiful. What is unusual about a *dó* tree? But that is a tree that provides shade to people resting by the road. All our villages, districts, and provinces should form the habit of growing such attractive trees. We need not wait for forestry institutes or nature conservancies to protect our precious resources for future generations; we can contribute to this protection ourselves. Growing unusual and special trees can be an important means of attracting visiting tourists. Our *tiên hưởng* water orchid (*dendrobium amabile*) can be found only in a foreign botanical garden, and creators of that garden are so pleased with it that they have had it recorded in a *Book of Famous World Sites*."

We can bestow honors each year on people who have grown fine or unusual trees. Of course, those who grow trees only to receive honors cannot be compared with those who brought in rhizobium [nitrogen-fixing soil bacteria] to increase our production of soybeans, those who grew *dó* trees to produce agarwood, or those who imported high-yield rice or grapes. But if as many as a thousand people, or a million people make their own small contributions, the sum total of those actions will surely be significant.

I feel that great contributions are difficult to bring about. People of heroic resolve, it seems to me, are not limited to those who accomplish great deeds. Small daily contributions are also deeds proper to people of heroic resolve, though they may be nameless. Nameless heroes are no less splendid than those known to all. If you can make such small contributions, you surely will have no need to feel sorrowful or ashamed at having failed your ancestral land, your native hills and streams." [excerpted from "By Way of a Preface," in *The Flora of Vietnam*, Section 2, volume 3, Montréal 1993.,"

With this "Last Will and Testament" of Professor Phạm Hoàng Hộ, we can see that Plant Biology is not just an academic discipline, but something that must enter our lives. "Keeping the motherland green" must be regarded as a guiding principle behind every level of education and in popular education as well; it is an overriding value that must pervade all forms of government and that must be observed by the entire world: "Keep this planet green."

BY WAY OF CONCLUSION

Professor Phạm Hoàng Hộ regarded *The Flora of Vietnam* as his lifetime project, and dedicated the work as follows:

"To all those who survive or who have died in prisons because they decided in April, 1975 to remain behind and continue serving their country.

"To the memory of Professor Nguyễn Duy Xuân, the president of Cần Thơ University, who died on November 10, 1986 at the labor reform camp at Hà Nam Ninh.

"To the still-fragrant souls of all those who drowned in the Eastern Sea".

I beg to send these words to the fragrant spirit of Professor Phạm Hoàng Hộ, a great scientist, a monument of integrity, and man of heroic resolve, whose spirit is emblematic of a whole class of intellectuals who endured every misery throughout their lives to serve their society in an endlessly dismal period. This short and hurried article, written in sorrowful remembrance, is like a stick of incense offered by a student who remembers his teacher with the words of the poet Nguyễn Du: ***"The soul is gone, the bright essence remains" (Thác là thể phách còn là tinh anh).***

And I do this with the wish that one day "flowers will bloom by the homeland waysides" and that there will be a statue of the professor on Mount Fansipan, towering more than three thousand feet in the Hoàng Liên mountain range, so that generations of students may continue to be guided by him in conducting research on the Flora of Vietnam.

California 05/02/2017

EPILOGUE

Creative World of South Vietnam 1954-1975 and Overseas to the Present (2025)

by Trịnh Y Thư

1.

This book, entitled *Creative World of South Vietnam 1954-1975 and Overseas to the Present* (2025), originally known as *Literary, Artistic, and Cultural Portraits*, by the eminent author Ngô Thế Vinh with English translation by the American scholar Eric Henry is a unique book, in the sense that it presents to the general readers fresh images of many personalities including writers, novelists, poets, journalists, painters, musicians and other cultural figures, who, by all accounts, have been among the most respected and influential intellectuals in Vietnam.

Endowed throughout with the author's warm, story-telling style, Ngô Thế Vinh's book is a rich compilation of documents, a rare collection of portraits of literary and cultural figures of an era considered the most turbulent in the nation from the second half of the 20th century until now. Ngô Thế Vinh does not pretend to be a critic. He does not stand on a podium to criticize the works or careers of the figures he writes about. One reason for this is that they are not strangers to him but friends in art, talented figures who in the most difficult conditions devoted almost their entire lives to the creation of a humane and artistically significant body of literature, art, and music for the nation. From the depth of his memories, the author penetrates every corner of his and their souls, sometimes from under the thick layer of the dust of time, trying to find just the right tones with which to create his beautiful, nostalgic pages, filled with the warmth of friendship, and with all manner of humanity. The studies in this book all have the character of sketches that convey the living environment, the creative circumstances, of his subjects who, like him, were artists and intellectuals. Interwoven with his narratives are spaces and times filled with memories, with each memory being cherished and treasured like a precious object. However, if we read attentively, we can detect another element in these accounts: beneath the relatively gentle, soft layer of color on the narrative surface, there is a firm conviction, a resolute view, plus a bit of pride, concerning a body literature, art and science that developed freely in Vietnam in the period from 1954 to 1975 and which, to some extent, continues to exist overseas, whose breakthroughs in terms of ideology, art, and human life seem never to have been surpassed.

2.

Of the many people portrayed, only two people from the post-1975 generation of writers are mentioned, Cao Xuân Huy and Phùng Nguyễn. However, whether earlier or later, all of them experienced the violent, stormy, unstable conditions that prevailed in the nation in the second half of the 20th century. Therefore, whether we like it or not, history exists everywhere and sticks to everyone's life. The existence of humans is tied and linked to the surrounding world just as closely as a snail adhering to its shell. The world is an inseparable dimension of humanity; as the world changes, injustice and misery also change. The world we exist in has a historical dimension. The life process of us all unfolds in time marked by milestones (such as, for example, April 30, 1975). This book by Ngô Thế Vinh does not deviate from that basic aspect of the human condition, but it rejects historical prejudice and focuses only on episodes that are important, that are anthropologically significant, whether forgotten or remembered, with no special weight given to the views of historians or politicians.

History is manifested in the handwritten note that accompanied Nhất Linh's last will and testament, given by one student to another in front of a university dormitory. History appeared in the touching farewell in the midst of the 25th-hour chaos between journalist Như Phong Lê Văn Tiến and Đỗ Thúc Vịnh's family on Tự Đức Street. History darted from the darkness when: "*... after the surrender order was issued, one could see from several high floors a shower of confetti, all white, the color of the personal papers of the military and government officials that needed to be torn up before the communists completely controlled Saigon.*" History appeared as "*the shoes and caps of military uniforms were hastily shed and thrown in tatters on the street.*" History appeared when writer Lê Tất Điều saw the writer Võ Phiến weeping on the ship anchored offshore during their flight from the country, leaving the homeland with no prospect of return. History appeared when writer Phạm Việt Châu committed suicide at his home after the Communists took complete control over the South. History appeared in the immeasurable pain of the poet Thanh Tâm Tuyền when his son went missing while crossing the sea. History appeared when writer Nhật Tiến and two journalists Dương Phục-Vũ Thanh Thủy "*sent news to the world about the tragedy in the East Sea, which shook the conscience of the world and which also led to the initial step in forming the Committee to Rescue Refugees that would operate for many years to come.*" The list goes on.

That history, in the drunkenness of victory by the winning side, became so turbulent that it led to an act of extreme barbarism: the book-burning campaign.

As a writer having to witness such barbaric counter-cultural acts, Ngô Thế Vinh must have felt extreme pain. He mentions it many times in his book. Let's listen to him describe the book burning scene in tones that express his indignation:

> *"... They trampled on books, set fire to stacks of books, and even entire book warehouses. Books that most of them had never read, including a whole bookshelf of a series entitled "Learning to Be Morally Mature." Books by so-called "literary commandos" were also displayed in the exhibition building of "American and Puppet Crimes," along with weapons of war and tiger cages, and of course there were books by Dương Nghiễm Mậu, including this writer's own work Green Belt."*

Or in another passage, less indignant but no less painful, commenting on the writer Nguyễn Đình Toàn, he says:

> *"Nguyễn Đình Toàn's books were classified as decadent culture after 1975; so all of them were confiscated and turned into "Ashes," the name of a prophetic work by Nguyen Dinh Toan himself in the book burning campaign that spread throughout the South at that time."*

"*We need a history in its entirety, not to fall back into it, but in order to escape it,*" the Spanish philosopher José Ortega Y Gasset once said. Our human history over the past hundred years has had too many holes, each one as big as the one that Ngô Thế Vinh presents. How can we have a history in its entirety when instead of patching up the holes to make them whole, we tear them apart even more? If Mr. Ortega Y Gasset were still alive, he would probably shake his head in dismay at us. And Ngô Thế Vinh, faced with that upheaval, cannot contain his anger. With a steely voice, he says:

> *"Not only did this unjust imprisonment destroy bodies, it also killed the creativity of artists during their most productive years. It was an attempt to destroy an entire culture to its roots: before the tribunal of history, who must take responsibility for these eternal crimes?"*

To ask is to answer. But when will that tribunal be established to judge the guilty? Half a century has passed in oblivion, and perhaps the "eternal crime" that Ngô Thế Vinh reminds us of will quietly drift into eternity.

3.

Ngô Thế Vinh does not follow any particular formula in this series of articles. He writes his "portraits" spontaneously, in accordance with his own feelings and personal relationships. Thanks to that, we are not faced here with a series of matter-of-fact biographical accounts. On the contrary, each portrait has unique aspects. Each portrait is a story with different levels of emotion, sometimes passionate, sometimes melancholy, sometimes bitter, sometimes angry, sometimes smiling, but also at times tearful. Through Ngô Thế Vinh's flexible but honest pen, the subjects of these portraits become suddenly "brighter", closer to the reader, and we are given the means to gain a better understanding of their work.

He tells us much about the life and literary career of the writer Mặc Đỗ, and does not hide his admiration and respect for the senior writer in the famous *Quan Điểm* ("Viewpoint") group of South Vietnam. Each short story of Mặc Đỗ is considered by him to be a "*pearl in a pearl necklace*" and he writes that "*his language is rich in imagery but concise and refined.*"

He also loves the novels and short stories of the writer Linh Bảo such as "*North Wind*", "*Rainy Nights*" and "*The Old Horse Stable*." According to Ngô Thế Vinh, "*Linh Bảo's pen is intelligent and sharp, mockingly revealing the negative aspects of life. Her style is cruelly mischievous, even at times bitter*." The women in Linh Bảo's works, though tough and enduring, are always "unfortunate victims of circumstance." He goes further when he comments that through her works, Linh Bảo was fighting for women's rights, a noteworthy datum for those who wish to research Feminism in the literary works of female writers in South Vietnam during the period 54-75.

Restless Sleep, a novel by Nhật Tiến about the devastation wrought in a remote village due to the circumstance that it was Nationalist by day and Viet Cong by night, is also mentioned by him with nostalgia and sorrow:

> "*... the villagers lived half-dead between two lines of bullets with hatred surrounding them day and night. The young men*

and children in that village were close to each other, but when the war broke out, neighbors and even brothers killed each other, causing many tragic and painful scenes."

Ngô Thế Vinh mentioned as well that this book by Nhật Tiến "*stated truthfully that there was no mass uprising of people protesting the Republican regime, as the so-called National Liberation Front claimed in their propaganda,"* and that is why the book and its author were condemned by the Hanoi Communist leadership as extremely reactionary, a *one-size-fits-all charge* for anyone who disagreed with their political line.

Ngô Thế Vinh is by nature a social writer sensitive to the periods in which he lives. His works throughout his career demonstrate this, and it is not surprising that he sympathizes with works such as *Restless Sleep* by the writer Nhật Tiến or the novels of another writer, Nguyễn Đình Toàn. He writes about Nguyễn Đình Toàn as follows:

> "Faded Dream *is a premonition of a Hanoi that is about to be lost, and Field of Grass, another work, depicts a Saigon that is about to fall. Nguyễn Đình Toàn, he writes, is sensitive to changes in weather as well as to historical changes. The writer's premonition or intuition before the tragedy, before the separations, is prophetic."*

Ngô Thế Vinh has a special admiration for the series of books entitled *Twenty Years of Literature in South Vietnam* compiled by by Võ Phiến. Võ Phiến devoted great effort to this monumental work. When it was released to the overseas public, it was criticized by a minority of readers as biased (failure to mention some important authors), narrow in its view of poetry (failure to mention innovative poets), and lacking in serious criticism (because the style was sometimes mocking and satirical), etc. However, the majority, writers as well as readers, enthusiastically welcomed the book as a valuable and worthy work that lay beyond the capability of most others. Ngô Thế Vinh was in the majority. He expresses his opinion on that controversy in these terms:

"Võ Phiến's research work needs to be evaluated in a way that takes account of the circumstances of its birth: it emerged in the first decade right after 1975, when within the country there was a comprehensive strategy of destruction aimed at wiping out twenty years of South Vietnamese literature. This effort at rescue and collection should be considered a worthy beginning. Everyone should understand that Võ Phiến's "unprofessional" effort will never be the only or the last book of Vietnamese literary criticism: it is rather a facilitating step, a roadmap leading to quantities of reference material, it is like a launching pad for the more comprehensive works to come. This will be the responsibility of professional critics. They will need to have the courage to inaugurate a serious evaluation of the literature of 1954-75. They will need to create praiseworthy works of criticism themselves, instead of just focusing on the "half-empty part" of Võ Phiến's series of studies. A question therefore arises: Who among us can seriously start such a research work? And a further question: Who will inherit the rich collection of documents that Võ Phiến had before it falls into oblivion?"

The answer to both questions asked by Ngô Thế Vinh can only be a single "Not yet." No one has been able to do it, even though 30 years have passed since Võ Phiến completed the last book in the series.

(It should also be added that though the Communist regime tried in every conceivable way to wipe out the twenty-year literature of the South, the truth is that it still exists today and is preserved and loved by later generations, both overseas and within the country. More importantly, the streams of thought that originated from it, most importantly the idea of freedom, have remained with us forever. You can burn many books, even the books of the most brilliant minds, but the ideas in those books have flowed through millions of rivers and will continue to flow forever. No brutal force can bury the most basic and beautiful human qualities.)

With respectable figures who devoted their whole lives to fighting or contributing their talents and knowledge to the country, such as journalist Như Phong Lê Văn Tiến, Doctor Phạm Biểu Tâm, scientist Phạm Hoàng Hộ, etc., Ngô Thế Vinh always emphasizes his respect. But with his personal associates, like the painter Nghiêu Đề, whom he refers to as his *close friend,* it is different. Here, we encounter a kind-hearted Ngô Thế Vinh, who loves and cares for his friends, and sees even his friends' trivial faults as something engaging, nothing to be bothered about.

An interesting aspect of the "portraits" in this book is that Ngô Thế Vinh often tells us about the "health status" of his subjects. A substantial number of his words, including many medical terms, concern the serious illnesses that took the lives of his literary friends. Cao Xuân Huy stubbornly gritted his teeth as he endured his "*melanoma of the eye with liver metastasis";* Nguyễn Xuân Hoàng struggled on the slope of life and death with "*sarcoma of the spine.*" Ngô Thế Vinh sometimes, in fact, sees his friends with the eyes of a doctor. This is easy to understand, for in real life he *is* a medical doctor, and for his literary and artistic friends, he often bore the nurturing, motherly image of a caring physician.

Where does Dr. Vinh's kindness come from? From his innate nature? From the education he received at home and in school? From the years spent beside the sick, suffering from the pain of life? From the influence of shining examples such as Dr. Phạm Biểu Tâm? Perhaps it is all of the above. That kindness is reflected in the picture he draws of Mai Thảo when he ponders, with a hint of sadness and bitterness, that author's writing desk in exile:

> *"Mai Thảo's living quarters were also the editorial office of his journal Literature. Every time I visited him, I would notice his desk next to the low frame of a window that gave a clear view of the scene outside. On his bookshelf, few of his books were visible, just a few French volumes, a few issues of Literature, and a couple of new books his literary friends sent him."*

Or, at Dương Nghiễm Mậu's house, during a family meal after the cataclysm that befell the country, his own fate, his friends' fate, and the country's fate seem to be intertwined:

"If it wasn't a day when I had to work late, I would stop by the market to buy something to add to the family meal. Adding meat and protein would make that day a feast for the two kids. Every time we met, Nghiễm and I were quiet. It seems Nghiễm wrote somewhere that there are things that don't need to be said because people already understand each other."

Yes, the book has pages that are heartfelt and heartbreakingly beautiful. Friendship, especially friendship in literature and art, does not come about overnight. From the convergence point, it needs to be distilled and refined over many years with a sincere and earnest heart. That convergence point is the passion for literature and art that Ngô Thế Vinh and his friends have in abundance.

That passion, it seems, flowed very early in the veins of writer Ngô Thế Vinh and his friends.

4.

According to Ngô Thế Vinh, there were several important literary groups that existed in South Vietnam before 1975: 1) *Tự Lực Văn Đoàn* (the Self-Reliance Literary Group) continued as *Văn Hóa Ngày Nay* (The Culture in the Present Era) headed by Nhất Linh; 2) *Sáng Tạo* (Creation) with Mai Thảo and Thanh Tâm Tuyền, who rejected pre-war forms and tried to invent new genres; 3) *Quan Điểm* (Viewpoint) with Nghiêm Xuân Hồng, Vũ Khắc Khoan, and Mặc Đỗ; 4) *Đêm Trắng* (*All Night*; also known as the *La Pagode group* after the name of the restaurant where they gathered and discussed literature) was thought to be the *New Novel group* of Saigon.

Ngô Thế Vinh does not say which group he belonged to; perhaps he was an outsider, but through some of his thoughts, we can guess that he had special feelings for the *Đêm Trắng* group, which included writers and poets, most of whom were teachers, such as: Huỳnh Phan Anh, Đặng Phùng Quân, Nguyễn Nhật Duật, Nguyễn Xuân Hoàng, Nguyễn Đình Toàn and Nguyễn Quốc Trụ. The writer he praises most in the group is Nguyễn Đình Toàn:

> *"Standing out in this group is Nguyễn Đình Toàn with his new writing technique, writing "stories without stories," the pages are a series of emotional images with long internal monologues. Nguyễn Đình Toàn succeeded in his effort to renew literature, but that does not mean he was influenced by, or followed, the French new novel movement."*

He talks also about the literary innovations of this period:

> *"Thanh Tâm Tuyền and Dương Nghiễm Mậu are two other names that are also mentioned when talking about the new-novel trend in Saigon at that time. I should also mention here that Hoàng Ngọc Biên was not in the Đêm Trắng group, but he was the first person to really research the Nouveau Roman movement in France, in the mid-1950s with names such as Alain Roble-Grillet, Nathalie Sarraute, Michel Butor, Claude Simon... Hoàng Ngọc Biên translated some works of Alain Roble-Grillet. Also, according to Hoàng Ngọc Biên, the term "new novel" though it indeed was a term used in the twenty years of Southern Literature, no comparable movement actually existed in Saigon "in the fashionable sense" of the New Novel movement originating from the West."*

The period lasted only twenty years, but there was never a period before or after in Vietnamese literature that flourished as this one did, and there was never a period with more talent. Yet it was called decadent and reactionary and then mercilessly crushed. An entire, beautiful humanistic culture of the nation was hunted down and extirpated to its roots. And we understand Ngô Thế Vinh's sadness and rage as he recounts this story.

5.

Only three talented painters of the *South Vietnamese Fine Arts* movement in the 60's – Đinh Cường, Nguyên Khai, Nghiêu Đề – are mentioned in the book. They are painters with whom Ngô Thế Vinh had a sincere and long-lasting friendship, but through them he also mentions other famous painters such as Mai Trung Thứ, Tạ Tỵ, etc., and especially the development of a high level of achievement in the *Fine Arts of South Vietnam* in the 60's. Here is another highlight from the pages of Ngô Thế Vinh:

"They were in their 20s and 30s, whether in the Vietnamese Young Artists Association or not. Some graduated from the Fine Arts School like Đinh Cường, Lâm Triết, Nguyễn Trung, Trịnh Cung, Nguyễn Phước, Nguyên Khai, or dropped out like Nghiêu Đề, or did not come from the Fine Arts School at all, like Cù Nguyễn, but they were all "hidden gems," talented figures who had the opportunity to bring their creativity to the highest level in the free atmosphere of the South."

Once again we see the element of "freedom" mentioned by Ngô Thế Vinh as a necessary and sufficient condition for any kind of artistic creation. The painter Trịnh Cung talks about the *Young Artists Association* in his two books published overseas – *Issues Concerning the Fine Arts in Vietnam* and *Comments and Questions on the Fine Arts* – with some pride. According to Trịnh Cung, the world of Fine Arts in South Vietnam did not have to wait for the Young Artists Association to form in the mid-60's in order to flourish. Since the establishment of the First Republic, Saigon had had remarkable achievements in Fine Arts, for which the unforgettable milestone was the first international exhibition held in 1962 at *Tao Đàn* Central Park with the participation of the world's leading painting schools of such countries as Italy, the Netherlands, France, and Spain... Paintings by Vietnamese artists from this time on were sought after by many foreign collectors.

In fact, Vietnam has a rich tradition of Fine Arts, the main launching pad of which was the Indochina School of Fine Arts founded by the French in 1924 in Hanoi. Before the August Revolution, there was a team of talented painters that included Bùi Xuân Phái, Nguyễn Tư Nghiêm, Dương Bích Liên among others. However, that promising initiative was blocked by the dialectical dogma of Socialist Realism.

Stalin imposed that ideology as the main creative method for all literary and artistic disciplines in Soviet society, and it was gradually "exported" to other Communist countries, including North Vietnam.

The results are so clear that there is no need to go into detail on this point.

Meanwhile, after the Geneva Agreement of 1954, a number of Northern painters emigrated to the South, among whom were Thái Tuấn, Duy Thanh, and Ngọc Dũng, Tạ Tỵ, along with a number of others who studied abroad in Europe returned to Saigon, bringing with them concepts of artistic Modernism. All of them contributed to creating a fresh wind for the development of Southern culture in general, and Vietnamese modern art in particular, with the center being the capital Saigon at that time. Having access to Western art books and magazines, participating in international exhibitions (in Vietnam or abroad), having almost total creative freedom, Southern artists freely approached and quickly absorbed schools of Modernism such as Symbolism, Surrealism, Abstraction, Expres-sionism, Abstract Expressionism, Fauvism, Cubism, and so on. Thanks to that, the Saigon visual arts scene from its infancy developed with steady strides, capable of speaking the same common world language of painting.

After the milestone of the first international exhibition in 1962 was the second milestone, the establishment of the Young Artists Association in 1966 with the participation of most of the talented artists, still young, in their twenties or early thirties, but quite famous at that time like Nguyễn Trung, Trịnh Cung, Nguyễn Lâm, Nguyên Khai, Đinh Cường, Ngy Cao Nguyên, Hồ Hữu Thủ, Rừng, La Hon, Đỗ Quang Em, Hồ Thành Đức, Nguyễn Phước, Hoàng Ngọc Biên... The echoes of the Young Artists Association still exist today, proving that its influence was not small. Another noteworthy point is that, along with the efforts of innovation with clear Western influence, the stream of traditional aesthetic paintings still flowed on, with noteworthy paintings by artists such as Tú Duyên, Nguyễn Siên, Trần Văn Thọ... Nguyễn Gia Trí especially was considered a pioneer in the field of lacquer painting, conquering connoisseurs with his profound emotion, and his blending of Renaissance styles with Modernism; or Lê Văn Đệ's silk paintings, the characteristic style of which radiated a simple, gentle, and profound fragrance and color.

In this way, the growth of South Vietnamese Fine Arts in the period 54-75, as presented by Ngô Thế Vinh in this book, was an inevitable response to the favorable conditions that existed in the academic, ideological, and political environment of that time. Along with literature, it can be seen as a golden age of Vietnamese Fine Arts, never seen before or after.

6.

If one were to choose only one musician to portray, it would perhaps be hard to know who to choose other than Phạm Duy. And Ngô Thế Vinh chose Phạm Duy for this series of "portraits." A bigger-than-life, awe-inspiring figure, Phạm Duy had a musical career that spanned two centuries, from the time of the Resistance War against the French to his 30 years of living abroad. He has always been admired, respected, even worshipped by multiple generations of Vietnamese. He is a prolific and tireless composer and song-writer, whose work falls into many genres, from songs like nursery rhymes to pieces influenced by Western classical music, from short songs of a few bars to long, richly variegated suites. But his most successful creations are songs with the melodies imbued with homeland sentiment. His music has entered the hearts of the nation, and almost all of us remember and occasionally hum one of his songs. Therefore, it is not too much to call Phạm Duy the greatest songwriter and composer of modern Vietnam. Ngô Thế Vinh, like us, has a heart full of respect and admiration for Phạm Duy. However, he does not delve into the musical depth of that famous musician, but allows readers to see him through the lens of everyday details, and especially the story of his return to Vietnam to live the last years of his life. With a rich selection of documents and images, the author of the book paints a true portrait of Phạm Duy in his twilight years, grieved due to his life in exile, still deeply attached to his homeland, and missing his old friends, feelings that motivated him to find a way to return, though that return brought not only joy, but unnecessary sorrow. However, that is Phạm Duy in the eyes of those who understand him, and one of those people is Ngô Thế Vinh.

He writes: "*... After thirty years of living in the U.S. amid the love and regard of the overseas Vietnamese community, Phạm Duy chose to go back to Vietnam and ended his days there. He had every right to make such a decision; it must be viewed by all with respect. And in accordance with this desire, he lived and died in Vietnam.*"

Phạm Duy, after all, is a complex and controversial character. That's precisely the reason why Ngô Thế Vinh found many paradoxical traits in the man.

> *"Phạm Duy always emphasized that he was simply a Vietnamese musician, and completely unconcerned with politics. But in a manner totally contradictory, he chose at the end of his life, after building up a huge legacy of music, to live in a country that was not yet free, that was still a land with a "command culture." He chose to resign himself to the life of a caged bird. No one forced him to do it, but often, on his own volition, he made public statements that had political overtones, or that seemed to express conformity with the tendencies promoted by the regime, so that even those who loved and defended him had to frown with disapproval."*

7.

This collection of *Literary, Artistic, and Cultural Portraits* by writer Ngô Thế Vinh is not a *Who's Who* of Vietnamese artists and cultural figures. It does not have the ambition to paint a panoramic picture or do in-depth research on any artist. It is rather a personal account. It also does not expand on secondary points outside of literary and artistic life. After reading the book, we still do not know in what circumstances the writer Nhật Tiến wrote the novel *Thềm Hoang (The Abandoned Porch)* or who the female character in the novel *Một Chủ Nhật Khác (A Different Sunday)* by Thanh Tâm Tuyền was in real life, etc. These things seem not very relevant to the Vietnamese literary research community. But Ngô Thế Vinh has given us a multi-dimensional overview of a literary period that was – according to writer Võ Phiến – unlucky (due to a lack of criticism) and unfortunate (due to destruction). The book is also a valuable source of information, an extremely useful resource for those who want to learn more about Vietnamese literature and arts.

For his literary friends, for the figures whom Ngô Thế Vinh always admired and respected, and for us, the readers, he has absolutely fulfilled what he wanted to do, which was, "*Let this little token of trust be set down faithfully. (Của tin gọi một chút này làm ghi.)*

TRỊNH Y THƯ

Photo by Nguyễn Bá Khanh

Born in 1952 in Hanoi. Writer, poet, translator. Former editor-in-chief of Văn Học magazine (California). Currently in charge of the Văn Học Press publishing house; Editor-in-chief of Việt Báo Weekly; Editor of Văn Việt forum.

Published translations: Đời nhẹ khôn kham (The Unbearable Lightness of Being - Milan Kundera); Căn phòng riêng — Virginia Woolf; Jane Eyre — Charlotte Brontë; Gặp gỡ với định mệnh - nhiều tác giả; Tập sách cái cười & sự lãng quên (The Book of Laughter and Forgetting – Milan Kundera).

Published works: Người đàn bà khác (The Other Woman – short story collection); Chỉ là đồ chơi (Just a Toy – essay); Phế tích của ảo ảnh (Ruins of Illusion – poetry); Theo dấu thư hương (Following the Fragrant Letters – essay), Đường về thủy phủ (The Road to the Water Palace – novel). Currently residing in California, USA.

INDEX

A

B

C

D

Đ

E

F

G

H

I

M

N

Nh

O

P

Ph

Q

R

S

T

Th

Tr

U

V

W

X

Y

Z

www.ingramcontent.com/pod-product-compliance
Lightning Source LLC
Chambersburg PA
CBHW020636120726
47906CB00001B/4

9781088177860